Also by JONATHAN D. SPENCE

Also by JANET CHEN

Photo by Mark Czjakowski, courtesy of Princeton University

JANET Y. CHEN is Professor of History and East Asian Studies at Princeton University, where she has taught courses on modern China and East Asia since 2006. She is the author of *Guilty of Indigence: The Urban Poor in China, 1900–1953*, a study of the destitute homeless during a time of war and revolution, and *The Sounds of Mandarin: Learning to Speak a National Language in China and Taiwan, 1913–1960*, a social history of how people learned to speak Mandarin.

Photo by Janet Chen

JONATHAN D. SPENCE was the Sterling Professor of History Emeritus at Yale University, where he taught for over forty years. Born in England in 1936, he was educated at Winchester College and Cambridge University. He commenced graduate work at Yale in 1959 and earned a PhD in history in 1965. Recognized as a leading authority in the field of modern Chinese history, Spence was a prolific author and essayist, having written a dozen books and numerous articles and reviews. His famous course on modern China at Yale was consistently one of the most popular on campus. *The Search for Modern China*, which grew out of that course, won the Lionel Gelber Award and the Kiriyama Book Prize. Among other honors, he received MacArthur and Guggenheim fellowships and honorary degrees from Columbia University, Oxford University, and the Chinese University of Hong Kong. Spence was appointed in 2010 by the National Endowment for the Humanities to deliver the annual Jefferson Lecture at the Library of Congress, the highest honor offered by the American government for achievement in the humanities. Spence passed away in 2021, at the age of 85.

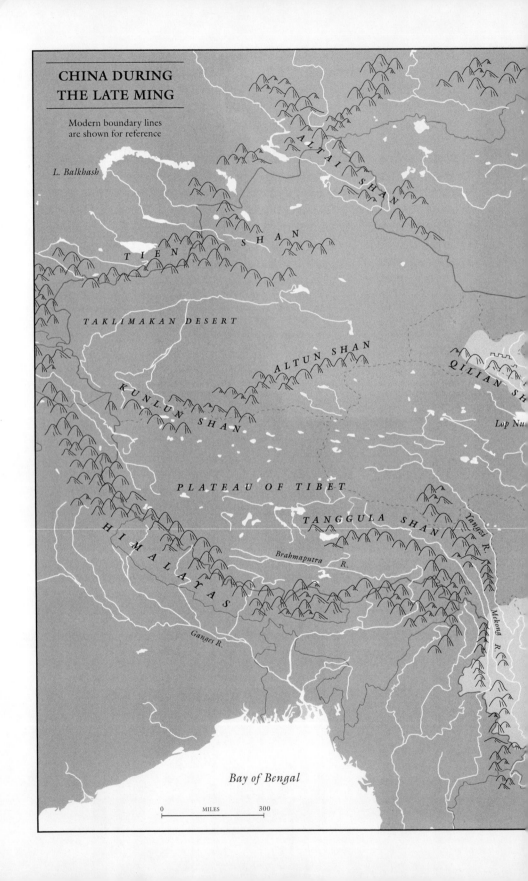

CHINA DURING
THE LATE MING

Modern boundary lines
are shown for reference

L. Balkhash

A L T A I   S H A N

T I E N   S H A N

TAKLIMAKAN DESERT

ALTUN SHAN

QILIAN SH

Lop Nu

K U N L U N   S H A N

PLATEAU OF TIBET

TANGGULA SHAN

Yangzi R.

Brahmaputra   R.

H I M A L A Y A S

Ganges R.

Mekong   R.

Bay of Bengal

0   MILES   300

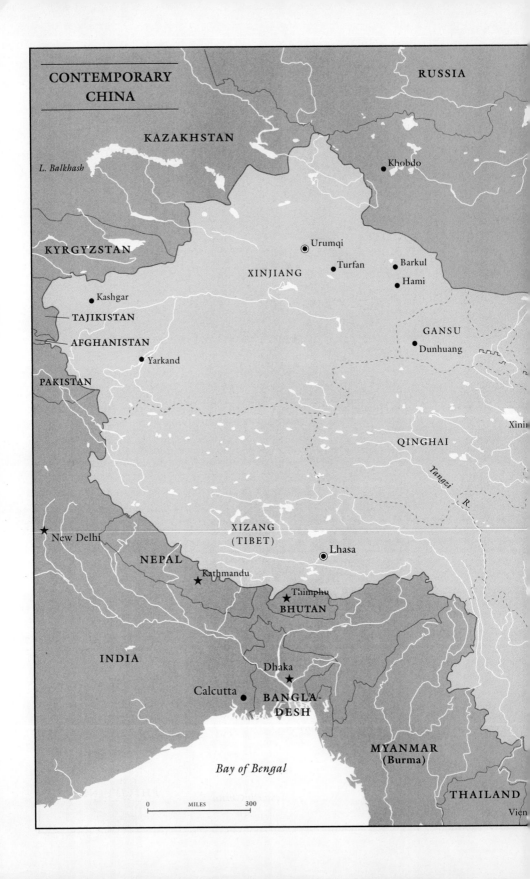

CONTEMPORARY CHINA

RUSSIA

KAZAKHSTAN

L. Balkhash

Khobdo

KYRGYZSTAN

⊙ Urumqi

XINJIANG

Turfan

Barkul

Hami

Kashgar

TAJIKISTAN

AFGHANISTAN

Yarkand

GANSU

Dunhuang

PAKISTAN

QINGHAI

Xini

Yangzi

R.

New Delhi

XIZANG
(TIBET)

Lhasa ⊙

NEPAL

Kathmandu

Thimphu

BHUTAN

INDIA

Dhaka

Calcutta

BANGLA-
DESH

MYANMAR
(Burma)

Bay of Bengal

THAILAND

Vien

0   MILES   300

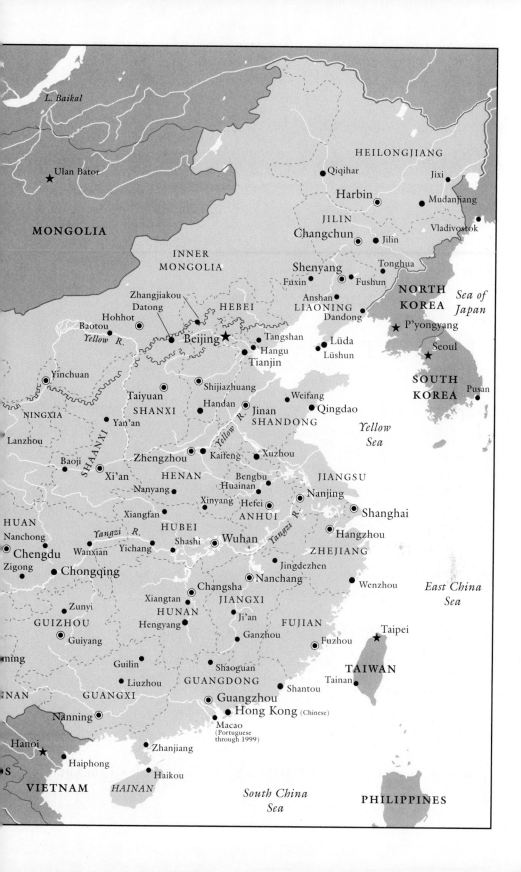

JONATHAN D. SPENCE
JANET Y. CHEN

W • W • NORTON & COMPANY | New York • London

THE SEARCH FOR
MODERN
CHINA

FOURTH EDITION

Editor in Chief, Social Sciences: Justin Cahill
Editor: Steve Forman
Assistant Editor: Clara Drimmer
Project Editor: Elizabeth Coletti
Managing Editor: Kim Yi
Production Managers: Allison Gudenau, Rich Bretan
Media Editor: Carson Russell
Media Editorial Assistant: Katherine Kopp
Photo Editor: Amla Sanghvi
Permissions Associate: Patricia Wong
Book Design: Anne-Michelle Gallero
Composition: Westchester Book Group
Manufacturing: Sheridan

ISBN: 978-1-324-07002-3

W. W. Norton & Company, Inc., 500 Fifth Avenue, New York, NY 10110
wwnorton.com

W. W. Norton & Company Ltd., 15 Carlisle Street, London W1D 3BS
1 2 3 4 5 6 7 8 9 0

In Memory of Jonathan Spence (1936–2021),
Historian and Teacher to all

Contents

Maps

Tables

Preface to the Fourth Edition

When Norton first approached me about undertaking a fourth edition of *The Search for Modern China*, I thought the idea was preposterous. The book is one of the best history textbooks ever written and a genre-defying bestseller. Who would tamper with a masterpiece? It was an honor to be tapped for this project, which I approached as an intellectual challenge. With the passing of Jonathan Spence in December 2021, it also became a way to pay tribute to his legacy.

In the revision process, my primary guiding principle was to preserve Jonathan's signature style and narrative voice. I kept the organizational structure of the previous editions, with new material blended in and cuts made as unobtrusively as possible. The goal was to add key findings from new research, while bringing the text closer to 600 pages through selective editing.

The revisions introduced in this edition reflect the enormous research output of the past thirty years on modern Chinese history. Thanks to the opening of archives in the People's Republic of China (PRC) and the easing of political constraints on academic research there, as well as a proliferation of international scholarly exchanges, the early years of the twenty-first century were an exciting time to be a young scholar in the field. I first started in the PhD program at Yale in 1999, and in every subsequent year conditions for research improved. Looking back, we enjoyed a golden age with unparalleled opportunities to consult records held in Chinese institutional archives, to conduct oral history interviews with those who had experienced the major transformations of the previous century, and to collaborate with Chinese colleagues. In those heady days, we investigated questions previously considered impossible to answer and grappled with new interpretations that overturned old certitudes.

So much has changed. As of this writing in 2024, to the collective lament of researchers, we have been confronting a discernible reversal, including curtailed archival access, greater restrictions on academic research imposed by the PRC government, and wariness about collaboration. But we can also count our blessings, as every subfield of Chinese history, energized during that golden age, produced voluminous new scholarship.

The revisions draw from this bounty and incorporate new findings into the narrative. To complement the previous edition's emphasis on political developments and intellectual life, I turned to themes from social history and added new details about the education of women in the high Qing, the suffrage movement of the early Republic, the plight of refugees during World War II, and the effects of the Marriage Laws of 1950 and 1980.

For the Qing dynasty, the imperial conquest and reconquest of Xinjiang, the vast territory in the northwest, receive more detailed attention. In the explanation of the vexing problems of foreign relations, trade, and law, the emphasis shifts from Qing weakness and obstinance to a more explicit discussion of European predatory behavior. Following the arc of new scholarship, the evaluation of late Qing reforms features an integrated discussion of the New Policies, now framed as an ambitious attempt by the ruling dynasty to redefine the state and its relationship to society.

For the Republican period, the narrative incorporates the emphasis of new scholarship on the Nationalist regime's state-building aspirations and successes. The proliferation of studies on the War of Resistance against Japan have provided illuminating perspectives on life in the temporary capitals of Wuhan and Chongqing, as well as Wang Jingwei's collaboration with the Japanese.

One of the chief benefits of the relatively open archival policies and political climate of the early twenty-first century was the blossoming of PRC history as a vibrant subfield of research. The chapters on the early 1950s draw on new insights about the process of regime consolidation, management of the economy, land reform, the *hukou* system of household registration, and the ethnic classification project. For the high tide of the revolution, from the late 1950s to the early 1970s, a discussion of the famine that followed the Great Leap Forward has been added, along with new details about the Sino-Soviet split and the rustication movement that sent millions of urban youths to the countryside during the Cultural Revolution. To conclude, the epilogue reflects on the transition to Xi Jinping's new authoritarianism and how China's past matters in its present.

Acknowledgments

In the years it took to cross the finish line on this project, I benefited from the kindness and support of many people.

To Jonathan Spence, I owe a lifetime of intellectual and personal debts. For twenty-five years, Annping Chin has cheered me on—thank you for your faith in me.

I am grateful for the support of Angela Creager and Anna Shields, two incomparable department chairs who performed their thankless jobs with grace and generosity. A sabbatical year funded by Princeton University and the Department of History provided the time to write. Many thanks to He Bian for permitting me to attend her lecture course on early modern China and for answering many questions.

Several Princeton graduate students helped with crucial research tasks that moved this project along. Xiao Sun, Yanlin Lu, and Greg Martin contributed their expertise on the 1950s and Sino-Soviet relations. Charlie Argon shared his deep knowledge of Qing history and critical reflections on every chapter of the third edition.

The team at Norton deserves much credit for shepherding this book through the lengthy production process. There were many, many words to copyedit and proofread. As editor, Justin Cahill patiently tolerated the countless delays. He also coaxed Steve Forman out of retirement to wrangle the manuscript to the finish line. Steve read the draft chapters with great care and offered dozens of insightful suggestions. Angie Merila, Clara Drimmer, Amla Sanghvi, and Elizabeth Coletti were superbly helpful and efficient in coordinating the details.

My family has watched all of this with bemusement and exasperation. Thank you for always interrupting and nudging me to live in the present, rather than dwelling endlessly on the past.

The Use of Pinyin

The pinyin system for romanizing Chinese has its origins in a system of romanization developed in Soviet East Asia in the early 1930s and employed later that decade in parts of China. With some modifications, pinyin itself was introduced by the Chinese in the 1950s. It is now the official romanization system in the People's Republic of China, has been adopted by the United Nations and other world agencies, and has become the system most commonly used in scholarship and journalism, largely supplanting the older Wade-Giles system. The pinyin system is pronounced as it looks, in most cases, the most important exceptions being the pinyin "c," pronounced like "ts," and the "q," which is pronounced like "ch." In some cases where the consonant break is unclear, an apostrophe is used to aid in pronunciation: hence the cities of Xi'an and Yan'an (to distinguish them from xian or yanan) or the name Hong Ren'gan (not reng-an).

The Search for Modern China uses pinyin romanization throughout, with some exceptions for place names and personal names that are long familiar in the West or difficult to recognize in pinyin. Thus Chiang Kai-shek is used rather than Jiang Jieshi.

There follows a table of conversions between pinyin and Wade-Giles romanizations.

PINYIN TO WADE-GILES*

Pinyin	Wade-Giles	Pinyin	Wade-Giles	Pinyin	Wade-Giles	Pinyin	Wade-Giles
a	a	cong	ts'ung	gong	kung	kei	k'ei
ai	ai	cou	ts'ou	gou	kou	ken	k'en
an	an	cu	ts'u	gu	ku	keng	k'eng
ang	ang	cuan	ts'uan	gua	kua	kong	k'ung
ao	ao	cui	ts'ui	guai	kuai	kou	k'ou
		cun	ts'un	guan	kuan	ku	k'u
ba	pa	cuo	ts'o	guang	kuang	kua	k'ua
bai	pai			gui	kuei	kuai	k'uai
ban	pan	da	ta	gun	kun	kuan	k'uan
bang	pang	dai	tai	guo	kuo	kuang	k'uang
bao	pao	dan	tan			kui	k'uei
bei	pei	dang	tang	ha	ha	kun	k'un
ben	pen	dao	tao	hai	hai	kuo	k'uo
beng	peng	de	te	han	han		
bi	pi	deng	teng	hang	hang	la	la
bian	pien	di	ti	hao	hao	lai	lai
biao	piao	dian	tien	he	ho	lan	lan
bie	pieh	diao	tiao	hei	hei	lang	lang
bin	pin	die	tieh	hen	hen	lao	lao
bing	ping	ding	ting	heng	heng	le	le
bo	po	diu	tiu	hong	hung	lei	lei
bou	pou	dong	tung	hou	hou	leng	leng
bu	pu	dou	tou	hu	hu	li	li
		du	tu	hua	hua	lia	lia
ca	ts'a	duan	tuan	huai	huai	lian	lien
cai	ts'ai	dui	tui	huan	huan	liang	liang
can	ts'an	dun	tun	huang	huang	liao	liao
cang	ts'ang	duo	to	hui	hui	lie	lieh
cao	ts'ao			hun	hun	lin	lin
ce	ts'e	e	o	huo	huo	ling	ling
cen	ts'en	en	en			liu	liu
ceng	ts'eng	er	erh	ji	chi	long	lung
cha	ch'a			jia	chia	lou	lou
chai	ch'ai	fa	fa	jian	chien	lu	lu
chan	ch'an	fan	fan	jiang	chiang	lü	lü
chang	ch'ang	fang	fang	jiao	chiao	luan	luan
chao	ch'ao	fei	fei	jie	chieh	lüan	lüan
che	ch'e	fen	fen	jin	chin	lüe	lüeh
chen	ch'en	feng	feng	jing	ching	lun	lun
cheng	ch'eng	fo	fo	jiong	chiung	luo	lo
chi	ch'ih	fou	fou	jiu	chiu		
chong	ch'ung	fu	fu	ju	chü	ma	ma
chou	ch'ou			juan	chüan	mai	mai
chu	ch'u	ga	ka	jue	chüeh	man	man
chua	ch'ua	gai	kai	jun	chün	mang	mang
chuai	ch'uai	gan	kan			mao	mao
chuan	ch'uan	gang	kang	ka	k'a	mei	mei
chuang	ch'uang	gao	kao	kai	k'ai	men	men
chui	ch'ui	ge	ko	kan	k'an	meng	meng
chun	ch'un	gei	kei	kang	k'ang	mi	mi
chuo	ch'o	gen	ken	kao	k'ao	mian	mien
ci	tz'u	geng	keng	ke	k'o	miao	miao

*From *People's Republic of China: Administrative Atlas* (Washington, D.C.: Central Intelligence Agency, 1975), 46–47.

PINYIN TO WADE-GILES

Pinyin	Wade-Giles	Pinyin	Wade-Giles	Pinyin	Wade-Giles	Pinyin	Wade-Giles
mie	mieh	qian	ch'ien	si	ssu	ya	ya
min	min	qiang	ch'iang	song	sung	yai	yai
ming	ming	qiao	ch'iao	sou	sou	yan	yen
miu	miu	qie	ch'ieh	su	su	yang	yang
mo	mo	qin	ch'in	suan	suan	yao	yao
mou	mou	qing	ch'ing	sui	sui	ye	yeh
mu	mu	qiong	ch'iung	sun	sun	yi	i
		qiu	ch'iu	suo	so	yin	yin
na	na	qu	ch'ü			ying	ying
nai	nai	quan	ch'üan	ta	t'a	yong	yung
nan	nan	que	ch'üeh	tai	t'ai	you	yu
nang	nang	qun	ch'ün	tan	t'an	yu	yü
nao	nao			tang	t'ang	yuan	yüan
nei	nei	ran	jan	tao	t'ao	yue	yüeh
nen	nen	rang	jang	te	t'e	yun	yün
neng	neng	rao	jao	teng	t'eng		
ni	ni	re	je	ti	t'i	za	tsa
nian	nien	ren	jen	tian	t'ien	zai	tsai
niang	niang	reng	jeng	tiao	t'iao	zan	tsan
niao	niao	ri	jih	tie	t'ieh	zang	tsang
nie	nieh	rong	jung	ting	t'ing	zao	tsao
nin	nin	rou	jou	tong	t'ung	ze	tse
ning	ning	ru	ju	tou	t'ou	zei	tsei
niu	niu	ruan	juan	tu	t'u	zen	tsen
nong	nung	rui	jui	tuan	t'uan	zeng	tseng
nou	nou	run	jun	tui	t'ui	zha	cha
nu	nu	ruo	jo	tun	t'un	zhai	chai
nü	nü			tuo	t'o	zhan	chan
nuan	nuan	sa	sa			zhang	chang
nüe	nüeh	sai	sai	wa	wa	zhao	chao
nuo	no	san	san	wai	wai	zhe	che
		sang	sang	wan	wan	zhen	chen
ou	ou	sao	sao	wang	wang	zheng	cheng
		se	se	wei	wei	zhi	chih
pa	p'a	sen	sen	wen	wen	zhong	chung
pai	p'ai	seng	seng	weng	weng	zhou	chou
pan	p'an	sha	sha	wo	wo	zhu	chu
pang	p'ang	shai	shai	wu	wu	zhua	chua
pao	p'ao	shan	shan			zhuai	chuai
pei	p'ei	shang	shang	xi	hsi	zhuan	chuan
pen	p'en	shao	shao	xia	hsia	zhuang	chuang
peng	p'eng	she	she	xian	hsien	zhui	chui
pi	p'i	shen	shen	xiang	hsiang	zhun	chun
pian	p'ien	sheng	sheng	xiao	hsiao	zhuo	cho
piao	p'iao	shi	shih	xie	hsieh	zi	tzu
pie	p'ieh	shou	shou	xin	hsin	zong	tsung
pin	p'in	shu	shu	xing	hsing	zou	tsou
ping	p'ing	shua	shua	xiong	hsiung	zu	tsu
po	p'o	shuai	shuai	xiu	hsiu	zuan	tsuan
pou	p'ou	shuan	shuan	xu	hsü	zui	tsui
pu	p'u	shuang	shuang	xuan	hsüan	zun	tsun
		shui	shui	xue	hsüeh	zuo	tso
qi	ch'i	shun	shun	xun	hsün		
qia	ch'ia	shuo	shuo				

CHAPTER 1

The Late Ming

THE GLORY OF THE MING

In the year 1600 C.E., China appeared to be the largest and most sophisticated of all the unified realms on Earth. The extent of its territory was unparalleled at a time when Russia was only just beginning to coalesce as a country, the Ottomans were overstretched in their variegated domains, India was fragmented between Mughal and Hindu rulers, and a grim combination of infectious disease and Spanish conquerors had decimated the once great empires of Mexico and Peru. In contrast, China's population of some 120 million was far larger than that of all the European countries combined.

There was certainly pomp and stately ritual in capitals from Kyoto to Prague, from Delhi to Paris, but none of these cities could boast of a palace complex like that in Beijing, where, nestled behind immense walls, the gleaming yellow roofs and spacious marble courts of the Forbidden City symbolized the majesty of the Chinese emperor. Laid out in a meticulous geometrical order, the grand stairways and mighty doors of each successive palace building and throne hall were precisely aligned with the arches leading out of Beijing to the south, speaking to all comers of the connectedness of things personified in this man the Chinese termed the Son of Heaven.

Rulers in Europe, India, Japan, Russia, and the Ottoman Empire were all struggling to develop systematic bureaucracies that would expand their tax base and manage their swelling territories effectively, as well as draw to new royal power centers the resources of agriculture and trade. But China's bureaucracy was already firmly in place, bonded by an immense body of statutory laws and provisions that, in theory at least, could offer pertinent advice on any problem that might arise in the daily life of the people.

One segment of this bureaucracy lived in Beijing, serving the emperor in an elaborate hierarchy that divided the country's business among six ministries dealing, respectively, with finance, personnel, rituals, laws, military affairs, and public works. Also in the capital were the senior scholars and academicians who advised the emperor on ritual matters and wrote the official histories. This concourse of official functionaries worked in uneasy proximity with the enormous palace staff who attended to the emperor's personal needs: the court women and their eunuch watchmen, the imperial children and their nurses, the elite bodyguards, the kitchen staff, the grooms, the sweepers, and the water carriers.

The other segment of the bureaucracy consisted of those assigned to posts in the fifteen major provinces into which China was divided during the Ming dynasty. These posts also were arranged hierarchically, from the provincial governor at the top, down through the prefects in major cities, to the magistrates in the counties. Below the magistrates were the police, couriers, militiamen, and tax gatherers, who extracted a regular flow of revenue from the agrarian population. A group of officials known as censors kept watch over the integrity of the bureaucracy, both in Beijing and in the provinces.

With hindsight we can see that the Ming dynasty, whose emperors had ruled China since 1368, was past its political peak by the early seventeenth century; yet in the years around 1600, China's cultural life was in an ebullient condition that few, if any, other countries could match. If one points to the figures of exceptional brilliance or insight in late sixteenth-century European society, one will easily find their equivalents in genius and imagination working away in China at just the same time. There may have been no Chinese dramatist with quite the range of Shakespeare, but in the 1590s Tang Xianzu was writing plays of thwarted, youthful love, of family drama and social dissonance, that were every bit as rich and complex as *A Midsummer Night's Dream* and *Romeo and Juliet*. And if there was no precise equal to Miguel de Cervantes's *Don Quixote*, it was in the 1590s that the beloved novel of religious quest and picaresque adventure, *The Journey to the West*, was published. This novel's central hero, a mischievous monkey with human traits who accompanies the monk-hero on his action-filled travels to India in search of Buddhist scriptures, has remained a central part of Chinese folk culture to this day. Without pushing further for near parallels, within this same period, essayists, philosophers, poets, landscape painters, religious theorists, historians, and medical scholars all produced a profusion of significant works, many of which are now regarded as classics.

Perhaps in all this outpouring, it was the works of the short-story writers and the popular novelists that made the most important commentary about the vitality of Ming society, for they pointed to a new readership in the towns, to new levels of literacy, and to a new focus on the details of daily life. In a society that was largely male-dominated, they also indicated a growing audience of literate women. The larger implications of expanding female literacy were suggested in the writings of late Ming social theorists, who argued that educating women would enhance the general life of society by bringing improvements in morals, child rearing, and household management. Other critics countered that too much independence for women was harmful and threatened to corrode the good order of society and the family.

Novels, paintings, and plays, along with the imperial compendia on court life and bureaucratic practice, all suggest the splendors—for the wealthy—of life in the late Ming. Living mainly in the larger commercial towns, the wealthy were bonded together in clan or lineage organizations based on family descent through the male line. These lineages often held large amounts of land that provided income for support of their own schools, charity to those fallen on hard times, and the maintenance of ancestral halls in which family members offered sacrifices to the dead. The spacious compounds of the rich, protected by massive gates and high walls, often contained large and elaborate gardens, which not only served decorative and recreational functions, but also produced fruit, food, and flowers for the owners and their families. The homes of the wealthy were filled with the products of artisans, who were sometimes employed in state-directed manufactories but more often grouped in small, guild-controlled workshops. Embroidered silks that brought luster to the female form were always in demand by the rich, along with the exquisite blue and white porcelain that graced lavish dinner parties. Glimmering lacquer, ornamental jade, feathery latticework, delicate ivory, cloisonné, and shining rosewood furniture made the homes of the rich places of beauty. And the elegantly carved brush holders of wood or stone, the luxurious paper, even the ink sticks and the stones on which they were rubbed and mixed with water to produce the best ink, all combined to make of every scholar's desk a ritual and an aesthetic world. In the late years of the Ming, an elaborate system of connoisseurship had grown around such objects, and the newly rich sought out prestigious art dealers to help them stock their homes in a fitting manner.

Complementing the domestic decor, the food and drink of the wealthy were a constant delight: pungent shrimp and bean curd, crisp duck and water chestnuts, sweetmeats, clear teas, smooth alcohol of grain or grape, fresh and preserved fruits and juices—all of these followed in stately sequence at parties during which literature, religion, and poetry were discussed over the courses. After the meal, as wine continued to flow, prize scroll paintings might be produced from the family collection, and new works of art, seeking to capture the essence of some old master, would be created by the skimming brushes of the inebriated guests.

At its upper social and economic levels, this was a highly educated society, held together intellectually by a common group of texts that reached back before the time of Confucius to the early days of the unification of a northern Chinese state in the second millennium B.C.E. While theorists debated its merits for women, education was rigorous and protracted for the boys of wealthy families, introducing them to the rhythms of classical Chinese around the age of six. They then kept at their studies in school or with private tutors, memorizing, translating, drilling until, in their late twenties or early thirties, they might be ready to tackle the state examinations. Success in these examinations, which rose in a hierarchy of difficulty from those held locally to those conducted in the capital, allegedly under the supervision of the emperor himself, brought access to lucrative bureaucratic office and immense social prestige. Women were barred by law from taking the state examinations, but those of elite background often learned to write classical poetry from their parents or brothers. Elite women could also choose private female tutors and engage in a varied intellectual life with other women through correspondence, the exchange of poems, and social visits. Book printing with wooden blocks, developed in China since the tenth century, made feasible the wide distribution of works of philosophy, poetry, history, and moral exhortation and the maintenance of extensive private libraries.

Though frowned on by some purists, the dissemination of popular works of entertainment was also accelerating in the late sixteenth century, making for a rich and elaborate cultural mix. City dwellers could call on new images of tamed nature to contrast with their own noise and bustle, and find a sense of order in works of art that interpreted the world for them. The possibilities for this sense of contentment were caught to perfection in 1598 by the dramatist Tang Xianzu in his play

The Peony Pavilion
In this scene from the play by the Ming dramatist Tang Xianzu, the heroine paints her self-portrait while her maid looks on.

The Peony Pavilion. Tang puts his words into the mouth of a scholar and provincial bureaucrat named Du Bao. One side of Du Bao's happiness comes from the fact that administrative business is running smoothly:

> The mountains are at their loveliest
> and court cases dwindle,
> "The birds I saw off at dawn,
> at dusk I watch return,"
> petals from the vase cover my seal box,
> the curtains hang undisturbed.

This sense of peace and order, in turn, prompts a more direct response to nature, when official duties can be put aside altogether, and nature and the simple pleasures enjoyed on their own terms:

> Pink of almond fully open,
> iris blades unsheathed,
> fields of spring warming to season's life.
> Over thatched hut by bamboo fence juts a tavern flag,
> rain clears, and the smoke spirals from kitchen stoves.[1]

It was a fine vision, and for many these were indeed glorious days. As long as the country's borders remained quiet, as long as the bureaucracy worked smoothly, as long as the farmers who did the hard work in the fields and the artisans who made all the beautiful objects remained content with their lot—then perhaps the splendors of the Ming would endure.

TOWN AND FARM

The towns and cities of Ming China, especially in the more densely populated eastern part of the country, had a bustling and thriving air. There were many Buddhist and Daoist temples, ancestral meeting halls, and shrines to Confucius, and a scattering of mosques and synagogues. Some cities were busy bureaucratic centers, where local officials had their offices and carried out their tax collection and administrative tasks. Others were commercial centers, where trade and local markets dictated the patterns of daily life. Most were walled, closed their gates at night, and imposed some form of curfew.

As with towns and cities elsewhere in the world, those in China could be distinguished by their services and their levels of specialization. Local market towns, for instance, were the bases for coffin makers, ironworkers, tailors, and noodle makers. Their retail shops offered for sale such semispecialized goods as tools, wine, and religious supplies, including incense, candles, and paper money to burn at sacrifices. Larger market towns, which drew on a flow of traders and wealthy purchasers from a wider region, could support cloth-dyeing establishments, shoemakers, iron foundries, and sellers of bamboo, fine cloth, and teas. Rising up the hierarchy to the local cities that coordinated the trade of several regional market towns, there were shops selling expensive stationery, leather goods, ornamental lanterns, altar carvings, flour, and the services of tinsmiths and seal cutters. Here, too, visitors could find pawnshops and local "banks" to handle money exchanges, rent a sedan chair, and visit a comfortably appointed brothel.[2] As the cities grew larger and their clientele richer, one found ever more specialized luxury goods and services, along with the kinds of ambience in which wealth edged—sometimes dramatically, sometimes unobtrusively—into the realms of decadence, snobbery, and exploitation.

At the base of the urban hierarchy, below the market towns, were small local townships where the population was too poor and scattered to support many shops and artisans, and where most goods were sold only by traveling peddlers at periodic markets. Such townships housed neither the wealthy nor any government officials; as a result, the simplest of teahouses, or perhaps a roadside stall, or an occasional temple fair would be the sole focus for relaxation. Nevertheless, such smaller townships performed an array of important functions, for they served as the bases for news and gossip, matchmaking, simple schooling, local religious festivals, traveling theater groups, tax collection, and the distribution of famine relief in times of emergency.

Just as the towns and cities of Ming China represented a spectrum of goods and services, architecture, sophistication, and administrative staffing, making any simple generalization about them risky, so, too, was the countryside endless in its variety. Indeed the distinction between town and country was blurred, for suburban areas of intensive farming lay just outside and sometimes even within the city walls, and artisans might work on farms in peak periods, or farmers work temporarily in towns during times of dearth.

South of the Huai River, which cuts across China between the Yellow River and the Yangzi, the country was most prosperous, for here climate and soil combined to make intensive rice cultivation possible. The region was crisscrossed by myriad rivers, canals, and irrigation streams that fed lush paddies in which the young rice shoots grew, or flowed into lakes and ponds where fish and ducks were raised. Here the seasonal flooding of the paddy fields returned needed nutrients to the soil. In the regions just south of the Yangzi River, farmers cultivated mulberry trees for leaves to feed silkworms, as well as tea bushes and a host of other products that created extra resources and allowed for a richly diversified rural economy. Farther to the south, sugarcane and citrus were added to the basic crops; in the mountainous southwest, forests of bamboo and valuable hardwood lumber brought in extra revenue. Water transport was fast and cheap in south China. Its villages boasted strong lineage organizations that helped to bond communities together.

Although there were many prosperous farming villages north of the Huai River, life there was harsher. The cold in winter was extreme, as icy winds blew in from Mongolia, eroding the land and filling the rivers with silt. The main crops were wheat and millet, grown with much toil on overworked land, which the scattered farming communities painstakingly fertilized with every scrap of human and animal waste they could recycle. Fruit trees such as apple and pear grew well, as did soybeans and cotton. But by the end of the sixteenth century, much of the land was deforested, and the Yellow River was an unpredictable force as its silt-laden waters meandered across the wide plains to the sea. Unhindered by the dikes, paddies, and canals of the south, bandit armies could move men and equipment easily across the northern countryside, while cavalry forces could race ahead and to the flanks, returning to warn the foot soldiers of danger from opposing forces. Lineage organizations were weaker here, villages more isolated, and social life often more fragmented. The owner-cultivator, living not far above subsistence level, was more common than either the prosperous landlord or the tenant farmer. Millions of farmers, who owned a little more land than they needed for subsistence, might hire occasional seasonal laborers. Others, owning less, might rent an extra fraction of an acre or hire themselves out as casual labor in the busy season. And most rural homes supplemented income through handicraft production that connected the household economy to a commercial network.

The urban and rural diversity of Ming society reflected an economy growing more commercialized and increasingly monetized. The tax system, however, was designed for an agrarian society and had not adapted to this new economic landscape. In the early sixteenth century, local jurisdictions experimented with converting taxes due in grain and labor service into monetary equivalents paid in silver. Formalized and implemented on a national basis in the 1570s, this consolidation into a single tax in silver—known as the "single whip" reform—enabled more efficient national and local fiscal management and eased payment transfers between jurisdictions. It also fatefully linked the economy and agrarian livelihoods to global markets in silver.

The new economic conditions of the late Ming brought prosperity to many, but for others it meant greater volatility and precarity. In times of crisis, when natural calamities destroyed the harvest and brought extreme deprivation, there were various forms of mutual aid, loans, or relief grain supplies that could help to tide families over. Perhaps some sort of part-time labor could be secured; children could be indentured, on short- or long-term contracts, for domestic service with the rich. But if, on top of all the other hardships, the fabric of law and order within the society began to unravel, then the situation could become dangerous. If the market towns closed their gates, if bands of desperate men began to roam the countryside, seizing the few stores that the rural families had laid in against the coming winter, or stealing the last seed grain saved for the next spring's planting, then the poor farmers may have no choice but to abandon the fields and to swell the armies of the hungry and the homeless.

In the early 1600s, despite the apparent prosperity of the wealthier elite, there were signs that this dangerous unraveling might be at hand. Without state-sponsored work or relief for their own needy inhabitants, the very towns that barred their gates to the rural poor might erupt from within. Driven to desperation by high taxes and uncertain labor prospects, thousands of silk weavers in the Yangzi delta city of Suzhou went on strike in 1601, burning down houses and killing hated local tyrants. That same year, in the porcelain-manufacturing city of Jingdezhen in Jiangxi province, thousands of workers rioted over low wages and the Ming court's demand that they meet heightened production quotas of the exquisite "dragon bowls" made for palace use. One potter threw himself into a blazing kiln and perished to underline his fellows' plight. Many other cities and towns saw some kind of social and economic protest in the same period.

Instability in the urban world was matched by unrest in the countryside. There were incidents of rural protest in the late Ming, as in earlier periods, that can be seen as having elements of class conflict. These incidents, often accompanied by violence, were of two main kinds: protests by indentured laborers or "bondservants" against their masters in attempts to regain their free status as farmers, and strikes by tenants who refused to pay what they regarded as unjust rents.

Even if they were not common, there were enough such incidents to offer a serious warning to the wealthier Chinese. In the same play, *The Peony Pavilion*, in which he speaks glowingly of the joys of the official's life, Tang Xianzu gently mocks rustic yokels, putting into deliberately inelegant verse the rough-and-ready labor of their days:

> Slippery mud,
> sloppery thud,
> short rake, long plough, clutch 'em as they slide.
> After rainy night sow rice and hemp,
> when sky clears fetch out the muck,
> then a stink like long-pickled fish
> floats on the breeze.[3]

The verses sounded amusing. But Tang's audience had not yet begun to think through the implications of what might happen when those who labored under such conditions sought to overthrow their masters.

CORRUPTION AND HARDSHIP

In the midst of the rich cultural and economic life of the late Ming, therefore, there were hints of weakness in the social structure. Part of the trouble sprang from the very center of the state. The emperor Wanli, who reigned from 1572 to 1620, had started out as a conscientious young ruler, guided by intelligent and experienced advisers. But from the 1580s onward, Emperor Wanli spent more and more time behind the innermost walls of the Forbidden City. He had grown aggravated by quarrels with bureaucrats about which of his sons should be named heir apparent to the throne, frustrated by overprotective courtiers, and disgusted by the constant bickering among his own senior advisers. For years on end he held no court audiences, refused to read state papers, and even stopped filling the vacancies that occurred in the upper levels of officialdom.

The result was that considerable power accrued to the court eunuchs—the castrated male attendants whose job was to supervise the management of day-to-day business in the palace. The practice of using eunuchs in the imperial court had existed for more than 2,000 years, but Ming rulers employed many more than their predecessors, and by Wanli's time there were over 10,000 in the capital. Since the emperor would not come out from the inner recesses of the Forbidden City—an area closed to all except the imperial family and their personal attendants—the eunuchs became crucial intermediaries between the outer bureaucratic world and the inner imperial one. Any senior official with business that demanded the emperor's attention had to persuade a eunuch to carry the message for him; the eunuchs, in turn, asked for fees for such service, and soon the more powerful ones were flattered and bribed by ambitious officials. In the 1590s, the eunuchs, many of whom were identified with certain court factions, began to play a central role in the political life of the country. Their influence grew as Emperor Wanli assigned them to collect revenues in the provinces.

Although it was always dangerous to criticize the emperor and his favorites, certain officials and prominent scholars were deeply disturbed by the situation. As scholars will, they sought a theoretical cause for the trouble: many of them concluded that the corruption sprang from a breakdown of the general ethical standards, from flaws in the educational system, and from the growth of an unbridled individualism. The villain, to many of these critics, was the earlier Ming philosopher Wang Yangming, who had argued in his writings that the keys to ethical understanding lay in our own moral nature; any person had the power, through innate knowledge, to understand the meaning of existence. Wang expressed this in a letter to a friend:

> Innate knowledge is identical with the Way. That it is present in the mind is true not only in the cases of the sages and worthies, but even in that of ordinary people. When one is free from the driving force and observations of material desires, and just follows innate knowledge and leaves it to continue to function and operate, everything will be in accord with the Way.[4]

"To learn," Wang added, "simply means to learn to follow innate knowledge." But he also advocated a creative blending of knowledge with action, and, in the teachings and practice of some of his more extreme followers, Wang's doctrine led to the rejection of normative forms of education and the call for a new egalitarianism.

To combat these trends, certain late-sixteenth-century scholars who held a rigorously moral view of Confucian thought began to gather in philosophical societies. Here they prepared for the state examinations and heard lectures on ethics; from ethics, their debates spread to politics; and political debate, in turn, began to generate a desire for political reform. By 1611, the most famous of these societies—founded in 1604 and known as the Donglin Society from the name of a willow grove in which a group of scholars used to meet—had become a major force in politics. Donglin partisans used their influence to have corrupt officials removed from their posts. The status of the Donglin faction rose further after Emperor Wanli's death in 1620, when many of them were called to serve in the bureaucracy under Wanli's son. But the mysterious death of the young monarch only one month after his enthronement poisoned the atmosphere at court. The illiterate eunuch Wei Zhongxian, favorite of the new Emperor Tianqi, became the power behind the throne. At the peak of his influence, Wei dictated edicts on behalf of the emperor, manipulated senior personnel appointments, and built an imperial-style tomb for himself. Shrines and temples in his honor were erected across the country. He became the archnemesis of the Donglin faction, one of whom wrote a scathing memorial enumerating Wei's twenty-four crimes, which included allegations of multiple murders and the usurpation of imperial authority.

With Emperor Tianqi's acquiescence, between 1624 and 1627 Wei and a group of court officials led a concerted campaign of terror against the Donglin members, many of whom were tortured, killed, or driven to suicide. Although Wei himself was eventually condemned and took his own life in 1627, the damage to the state's prestige had been severe, and was perhaps irreparable. As one of the Donglin leaders—having heard that he was about to be arrested, and knowing that this could only mean his death—wrote in a farewell letter to his friends, "I formerly was a great minister, and when a great minister accepts disgrace the state is also disgraced."[5]

The political crisis and partisan violence in the imperial center exacerbated an already dangerous situation in the fields of foreign policy and the economy. The Ming dynasty had faced a number of threats during the sixteenth century, most prominently from the nomadic tribes of Mongols who raised their horses and sheep on the steppes to the north and northwest of Beijing, and from pirates on the southeast coast. Mongol forces, which earlier had interacted with the Ming dynasty through trade and diplomacy, now raided regularly. On one occasion they captured a Ming emperor campaigning against them, and on another they rode almost to the gates of the capital. By the late sixteenth century, despite attempts to strengthen the Great Wall and its military garrisons, the Ming managed to hold the Mongol raiders in check only by paying them regular subsidies. On the southeast coast, cities were ravaged by pirate groups, sometimes numbering in the hundreds and including a great many Japanese, Chinese fugitives, and Black slaves who had escaped from the Portuguese outpost at Macao. These pirate groups looted almost at will, seizing men and women for ransom.

Although the worst of these pirate attacks had been stopped by the 1570s, Japanese military power grew stronger, and in the 1590s an army led by Toyotomi Hideyoshi invaded Korea. Fighting was heavy, and since the Ming regarded Korea as a loyal and dependent ally, troops were sent in force to help the hard-pressed Koreans. The war might have continued, at terrible cost to all three countries, had not domestic turmoil in Japan, coupled with effective disruption of Japanese supply lines by the Korean navy, led to the recall of Japanese troops from Korea in 1598.

Macao also represented a different kind of problem. The Portuguese had occupied this town, on the tip of a peninsula to the southwest of Guangzhou (Canton), with the tacit consent of the Ming dynasty in the 1550s. By the 1600s, following the emperor's ban of direct trade by Chinese merchants with Japan, the Portuguese had moved into the resulting commercial vacuum as middlemen. They made fortunes by buying up Chinese silk in local markets and shipping it to Japan, where they traded it for silver from Japanese mines. With this silver, which was valued more highly in China than in Japan, the Portuguese returned and bought larger stocks of Chinese silk. The steady flow of silver brought by the Portuguese into China was itself just one element in the larger pattern of silver shipments that brought major economic effects to all parts of the world in the sixteenth century.

At the heart of this global network lay the fantastic silver riches of the mines in Mexico and Peru, which were being exploited under royal license by the Spanish conquerors of those territories. Silver from the Americas began to reach China in the 1570s, when Spain established a new base at Manila in the Philippines. Eager to profit from this new silver supply, thousands of Chinese traders began to congregate in Manila, selling cloth and silk in bulk and speeding the flow of specie back to their homeland. As silver circulated more widely, commercial activity spread, more and more Westerners joined in the profitable trade with China, and silver-bullion deposits grew impressively. At the same time, the massive influx of silver brought not only new wealth to Chinese merchants but also a range of problems that included a dependence on foreign silver, unpredictable periods of inflation, and erratic economic growth in certain cities. Late Ming attempts at currency stabilization were not successful.

Thus, before Wanli's reign ended with his death in 1620, a complicated economic slide was in process. The thriving world of the Ming merchants, which had led to the efficient distribution of luxury goods on a countrywide basis and had spawned an effective proto-banking system based on notes of exchange, suffered from the military troubles of the times. The government proved unable to capture revenue from the expansion of commerce and suffered from underfunding. The uneven effects of the "single whip" tax reform benefitted the more commercialized economies of the Yangzi delta and the southeast coast, at the expense of interior provinces. Inefficiencies in flood control and famine relief led to further local crises, which, in turn, reduced the amount of land that could be taxed effectively.

During the last years of Emperor Wanli's reign and under his successors, the situation grew critical. Famines became common, especially in north China, worsened by unusually cold and dry weather that shortened the growing season for crops by as much as two weeks. (Sometimes termed the "little ice age" of the seventeenth century, similar effects were felt in farming areas around the world during this period.) In China, seven consecutive years of drought, in combination with natural disasters, produced extreme social dislocations and an acute subsistence crisis.[6] When such devastating conditions are set alongside the constant strains of military recruitment and desertions, a declining relief system for the indigent, and the abandonment of virtually all major irrigation and flood-control projects, the pressures on the country and the tensions they began to engender can be well imagined. And as rapidly became apparent, neither the court nor the bureaucracy in Beijing or the countryside seemed to have the ability, the resources, or the will to do very much about it.

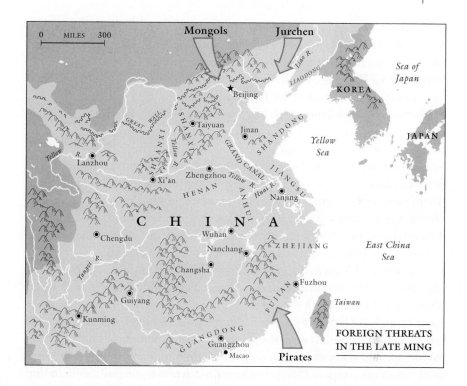

FOREIGN THREATS
IN THE LATE MING

THE MING COLLAPSE

In the early decades of the seventeenth century, the Ming court slowly lost control of its rural bureaucracy and, as a result, of its tax structure. Pressed at the same time for more money to pay and supply the troops needed to counter the attacks of the Jurchen tribesmen who were growing in power and seizing great areas of land in Manchuria, the court both increased extra levies on those populated areas that it still controlled and laid off many employees in the northwest, where the danger to the state seemed less pressing. One of those laid off in this economy move was a post-station attendant from a rural family named Li Zicheng.

Li had worked previously in a wine shop and as an ironworker's apprentice, and was typical of a number of rootless, violent men who lived in Shaanxi at the time. A barren province of northwest China, Shaanxi covered the area within the great bend of the Yellow River and ran through bleak mountain countryside up to the Great Wall. About as far from Beijing as Chicago is from Washington, D.C., but ringed by mountains and difficult to access, Shaanxi province had in the past proved a natural bastion where groups of rebels had built up their forces prior to breaking out and attacking the richer and more populated lands to the east and the south.

In 1630 Li Zicheng enrolled in a military unit in western Shaanxi, but once again the government let him down. Deprived of promised supplies, Li and other soldiers mutinied, and over the next few years Li emerged as a leader among a group of uprooted men that numbered in the thousands, proving himself a skillful tactician. In 1634 Li was captured near the southern Shaanxi border by a capable Ming general, who bottled up the rebel forces in a mountain gorge. Li was released after promising that he would take his troops back to the northern part of the province, but the agreement fell apart after a magistrate executed thirty-six of the surrendered rebels. Li and his men retaliated by killing local officials and taking once more to the hills.

During the 1630s, some of the most powerful rebel leaders assigned different regions of north China to their armies and tried to coordinate an attack on Beijing. But synchronized military activity proved difficult with such motley and undisciplined forces. By the end of the year the informal alliance was breaking apart, though not before the rebels had captured and looted some of the imperial Ming burial grounds outside the capital. The emperor now on the throne, Wanli's grandson Chongzhen, responded by donning mourning, apologizing to his ancestors in special temple ceremonies, arresting several commanding officers, and executing the eunuch guardian of the royal tombs. For his part, in a bitter quarrel that showed how easily the rebel alliance could fragment, Li Zicheng demanded of his fellow rebels that he be given the captured eunuch musicians whose job had been to play ritual music at the tombs. The rebel leader who held the musicians, Zhang Xianzhong, reluctantly complied, but smashed all their instruments first. Li then killed the unfortunate musicians.

Over the next few years, the armies of these two leaders, Li and Zhang, roamed over much of northern and central China, occasionally cooperating with each other but more often feuding as they competed with both the Ming and other rebel bands for territory and followers. By the early 1640s, each had seized a base area for himself: Zhang Xianzhong, who like Li had once served in the Ming forces in Shaanxi before deserting, was in the city of Chengdu in the prosperous heartland of Sichuan province, deep inland along the Yangzi River; Li was established in Hubei, but his jurisdiction included most of Shaanxi and Henan provinces as well.

The ravages caused by the armies of Li and Zhang were augmented by epidemics that struck at this same time. Some estimates, noted by Chinese observers, suggest that these epidemics caused many communities to suffer losses of half or more of their inhabitants. One scholar wrote of Zhejiang province in 1642 that "the symptoms of pestilence arose again on a large

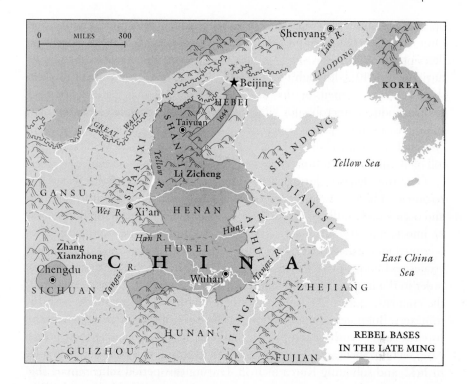

0 MILES 300

Shenyang
Liao R.
LIAODONG
★ Beijing
HEBEI 1644
KOREA
GREAT WALL
SHANXI
Taiyuan
Yellow R.
SHANDONG
Yellow Sea
Li Zicheng
GANSU
JIANGSU
Wei R. Xi'an
HENAN
Han R.
Huai R.
Zhang
Xianzhong
HUBEI
ANHUI
Yangzi R.
East China
Sea
Chengdu
R.
C H I N A
Yangzi
Wuhan
SICHUAN Yangzi
ZHEJIANG
HUNAN
JIANGXI
REBEL BASES
IN THE LATE MING
GUIZHOU
FUJIAN

scale, affecting eight or nine out of every ten households. It even reached the point where in a household of ten or twenty people a single uninfected person could not be found, or where in such a household there was not one saved. Therefore at first the bodies were buried in coffins, and next in grasses, but finally they were left on the beds." An observer in Henan province noted that in one city there in the summer of 1643 "there were few signs of human life in the streets and all that was heard was the buzzing of flies."[7]

So serious was the loss of life that it prompted a rethinking of traditional Chinese theories of medicine, and although no solutions were found, medical books of the time began to develop a new theory of epidemics. One doctor, living near the Yangzi delta area, wrote in 1642 that China was obviously being affected not just by variants in weather or temperature but by a change in the balance of heaven and earth caused by "deviant *qi*," *qi* being the normally neutral forces within nature. Such deviant *qi*, he wrote, "appear mainly in years of war and famine." Unseen and unheard, they struck apparently at will: "If the people clash against them, they produce the various diseases, each according to its nature. As for the diseases produced, sometimes everyone has swollen neck glands and sometimes everyone's face and head swell up. . . . Sometimes everyone suffers from diarrhoea and intermittent fever. Or it might be cramps, or pustules, or a rash, or itching scabs, or boils."[8] The description and analysis suggest that China suffered some form of plague during the 1640s, although its exact nature cannot be determined. Possibly the Jurchen tribesmen, by this time known as "Manchus," in their earlier raids introduced microbes for which the Chinese had no natural antibodies, leading to a catastrophic loss of life. Between 1630 and 1644, the cumulative effects of war, natural disasters, and epidemics produced a devastating death toll of 40 million, an estimated 20 percent of the total population.[9]

The Ming dynasty, during these closing years, was not completely without resources. There were loyal generals who led their troops against the rebels and occasionally inflicted defeats on them—or at least forced them to retreat or into temporary surrender. And in many areas the wealthy local elites recruited and armed their own militia forces so that they could defend their estates and hometowns. Emperor Chongzhen himself did try to bring some order to the imperial government; he sought to repress the worst excesses of the eunuchs, and unlike his grandfather, Wanli, he met regularly with his ministers. But much of his attention was focused on the northeast, where the Jurchen leader Nurhaci and his son had been steadily widening their power base, seizing Shenyang (Mukden) in 1625, taking much of Inner Mongolia in 1632, and subduing Korea in 1638. During this period some remarkable Chinese generals fought bravely in Manchuria, especially in the mid-1620s, and recaptured several cities. But factional fighting in Beijing and a constant shortage of funds hampered the Ming cause.

Foremost among the Ming generals was Yuan Chonghuan, whose career may be seen as exemplifying some of these late Ming tensions. A classically educated scholar from south China, Yuan entered the Beijing bureaucracy as a young man. In 1622 he went on an inspection tour of southern Manchuria and grew convinced that he could defend the crucial passes that led to Beijing. As a staff member in the ministry of war, with a good knowledge of European firearms apparently garnered from his cook, who knew some Westerners, Yuan was able to hold the Liao River against Nurhaci. In 1628 he was named field marshal of all northeastern forces, but for reasons of jealousy he executed one of his most talented subordinates the following year. When, in 1630, Manchu raiding parties appeared near Beijing, Yuan was falsely accused of colluding with them and was tried on a trumped-up charge of treason. With hostile courtiers, friends of the man he had killed, and groups of eunuchs all arrayed against him, Yuan had no chance of clearing himself. Instead he was condemned to death by way of the most publicly humiliating and painful punishment that the Ming penal code allowed for: being cut to pieces in the marketplace of Beijing. Later scholars mourned him as one of China's greatest generals. No one of his talents came forward to succeed him; on the contrary, though some northern generals remained loyal to the Ming cause after his death, many others began to surrender to the Manchus, taking their troops over to the enemy with them.

Finally it was not the Manchus, but the rebel Li Zicheng who brought down the Ming dynasty. In 1644 Li mounted a huge attack on Beijing, moving across north China with hundreds of thousands of troops, sacking the towns that resisted him, and incorporating into his own army the forces of those that surrendered. He waged a skillful propaganda war, pointing to the excesses and cruelties of the Ming regime and promising a new era of peace and prosperity to the people. In April 1644 his armies entered the capital without a fight, the city gates having been treacherously opened at his coming. It is recorded that Emperor Chongzhen, after hearing that the rebels had entered the city, rang a bell to summon his ministers in order to get their advice or assistance. When none of them appeared, the emperor walked to the imperial garden just outside the walls of the Forbidden City. In this garden was a hill, from the crest of which the emperor and his consorts used to look out over the panorama of the imperial city. This time the emperor did not mount the hill, but attached a cord to a tree at its foot, and there hanged himself. So died the last ruler of the dynasty that had ruled China since 1368.

CHAPTER 2

The Manchu Conquest

THE RISE OF THE QING

While the Ming dynasty was sliding into a final decline, its eventual successor was rising in the northeast. The people later known as the Manchus were Jurchen tribes, who claimed descent from the Jin dynasty that ruled north China from 1122 to 1234. After their defeat, they had retreated northward to the Sungari River region. By the fifteenth century, there were three main Jurchen groups, whose territory (the present-day Heilongjiang and Jilin provinces) the Ming dynasty claimed as part of its frontier defensive system. The Jurchen nominally accepted the political authority of the Ming and in return received honorific titles and trading privileges. In this ecologically diverse region, some Jurchen had stayed near the Sungari River and lived mainly by fishing and hunting. Others established a base in the vicinity of the Changbai mountains near the Korean border, where they developed a mixed agricultural and hunting economy. Yet others moved to more fertile, open land east of the Liao River, where they mingled with Mongol tribes and Chinese emigrants, and practiced settled agriculture or thrived as traders of furs, horses, and ginseng.

In the late sixteenth century, a chieftain of the Aisin Gioro clan named Nurhaci rose to leadership, out of the shifting alliances and rivalries among the Jurchen groups. As a young man Nurhaci had traveled to Beijing on tribute missions, which were lucrative opportunities to present the Ming court with horses in exchange for "rewards": silk, silver, and trading licenses. Through skillful domination of the ginseng trade, his clan accumulated a near-monopoly on exporting the highly valued medicinal root to the Ming. The accumulated profits from this commercializing economy, in the form of a steady inflow of Ming silver, would provide the resources to fund the conquest.[1]

A Korean diplomatic envoy who visited Nurhaci's base camp around this time noted the rude simplicity of the Jurchen weapons and defensive stockades, Nurhaci's own bluff manner and tough physique, and the distinctive hairstyle, clothing, and massive silver earrings worn by some of his attendant generals. But if initially Nurhaci seemed uncouth to such a visitor, he soon showed his abilities. Between 1610 and 1620 Nurhaci steadily increased his power at the expense of neighboring Jurchen and Mongol tribes, either dominating them by warfare or allying with them through marriage. He instituted the Eight Banners system, which organized his troops and their families into eight different groups of "banners," which were distinguished according to color (yellow, red, blue, and white, four plain and four bordered). The banners served as identification devices in battle, and membership was used as the basis for population registration in daily life. Nurhaci also assembled large numbers of craftsmen to manufacture weapons and armor, and appointed a group of scholars to develop a writing system for the Jurchen language, based on Mongolian script. In 1616 he took the important symbolic step of declaring himself the "khan" (ruler) of a second Jin dynasty, thus evoking the past glory of the Jurchen people, claiming the mantle of Mongol political legitimacy, and issuing a provocative challenge to the Ming state. Two years later Nurhaci openly declared the end of his allegiance to the Ming. In an announcement of his intentions, he enumerated a list of seven grievances against the Ming, including responsibility for the murders of his grandfather and father. He then launched a series of shattering military blows at mixed Chinese and Jurchen settlements east of the Liao River, in the region known as Liaodong.*

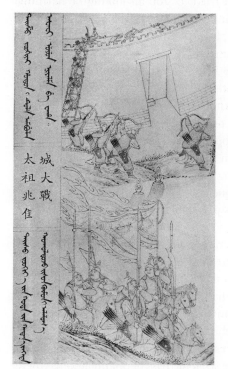

Nurhaci defeats forty men
Jurchen chieftain Nurhaci organized Mongol and Jurchen tribes in a united front against the Ming. In the image, Nurhaci is shown on horseback with a sword raised in his hand. He was described as single-handedly finishing off forty Chinese soldiers.

*Dong is Chinese for "east."

The Ming rulers had regarded Liaodong as part of their domain and maintained garrisons and outposts there. Nurhaci used a mixture of threats and blandishments to induce the Ming commanders to surrender, sending them elaborate messages written out for him by Chinese advisers in his employ. To one officer he wrote, "Even if you fight, you certainly will not win. . . . If you do not fight, but surrender, I shall let you keep your former office and shall care benevolently for you. But if you fight, how can our arrows know who you are?"[2] Nurhaci also tried to undermine Ming influence in Liaodong by posing as a reformist ruler who had come to bring a better life to the Chinese, and he urged those who lived west of the Liao River to join him in his new kingdom. "Do not think that the land and houses will not be yours, that they will belong to a master," he wrote in another message that was distributed in the countryside. "All will equally be the Khan's subjects and will live and work the fields on an equal basis."[3] On other occasions, Nurhaci claimed he would take over the benevolent functions of the ideal ruler that had so obviously been neglected by Wanli in his waning years, saying that he would never let "the rich accumulate their grain and have it rot away," but would "nourish the begging poor."

Nurhaci disciplined his troops and tried to stop all looting or harming of the civilian population, publicly punishing guilty soldiers. To those Chinese with education who surrendered, he offered a chance of serving in the growing Jurchen bureaucracy, and senior Chinese officials who came over to his side were offered marriage into his family, honorific titles, and high office. Shenyang and Liaoyang fell to his troops in 1621, and in 1625 he made Shenyang his capital. Soon all the territory east of the Liao River and some land west of the river were under his control.

Initially Nurhaci faced little overt opposition, despite the order that men who surrendered must follow Jurchen practice to shave the fronts of their foreheads and wear their hair in a long braid or "queue." But in some areas the reception was mixed: some conquered Chinese settlers welcomed the Jurchen with flutes and drums; others poisoned the wells in attempts to kill Nurhaci's troops. Nor is there any easy way to categorize the fates of those who were now in Nurhaci's power. Some were rewarded as promised, others were moved from their city homes to work for the Jurchen on the land. Some were enslaved, others—most notably those with some knowledge of artillery—were registered in new military formations known as "Chinese martial" banner units. Although still in an embryonic state, these units were later to play a critical role in the Manchu victories.

As early as 1622, Nurhaci had expressed his intention of attacking China by sending an army down through the strategic pass of Shanhaiguan, where the Great Wall ends at the North China Sea. He might well have done so the following year had not a serious rebellion against his rule broken out among the Chinese in Liaodong. What prompted the uprising is not known, but there were many possible causes. With the arrival of large numbers of Jurchen troops, there was intense pressure on the available farmland. Shortages of grain and salt grew to crisis proportions, and famine was reported in some areas. Compulsory grain rationing was introduced, and Chinese under Jurchen control had to spend a portion of their time working designated parcels of land without compensation. In many areas of Liaodong, partly as a control measure and partly because there was a housing shortage, the Jurchen moved into Chinese homes to live and eat as co-occupants. The Chinese responded by setting fires, poisoning wells once again, killing Jurchen women and children, hiding their grain, or fleeing into the mountains. Some Chinese killed border guards and tried to escape to the south; those caught were killed in turn by the Jurchen. The Ming court did not take advantage of the uprising, however, and it was soon suppressed by Nurhaci's troops. A second revolt of the Chinese took place in 1625 and was even more ruthlessly repressed.

The Ming generals had failed to respond to either of these uprisings, but late in 1625 these generals began a series of vigorous counterattacks and won their first serious victories over Nurhaci in 1626. Later that same year, Nurhaci died. In accordance with Jurchen custom—a custom derived from the Mongols of Central Asia—he had not left his dominions and the title of khan to one successor, but instead had ordered them divided among his most able sons and nephews.

Not surprisingly, there followed a protracted struggle for power. The victor was Nurhaci's eighth son, Hong Taiji, who had been the general commanding the plain yellow and bordered yellow banners. This son was helped to power by Chinese advisers, and he responded by taking a more favorable view of the Chinese and their institutions than his father had. Six ministries, in imitation of those at the Ming court, were established, and Chinese were employed throughout this new bureaucracy. Nominally, the senior ministers were all Jurchen notables, but they were often absent on military or other business, leaving the practical running of affairs to their Chinese subordinates.

On the grounds that it was punitive to the Chinese, Hong Taiji abolished the registration system instituted by Nurhaci; he also held competitive examinations for the civil service in Liaodong, following the Ming model. He ordered reforms to standardize the Manchu written language and make it more serviceable in a new era of record keeping, census taking, and tax

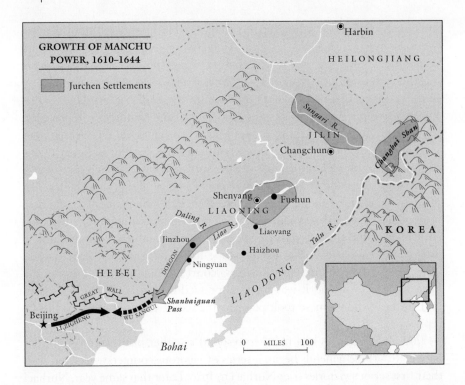

gathering. A literary institute established in 1629 and the expansion of literacy education for young males in the banner system indicated the growing importance of written Manchu in a multi-lingual environment.[4] Hong Taiji continued his father's strategy of forming alliances with Mongol tribes: twelve of his daughters married their chieftains. A swelling number of Chinese defectors from the Ming cause, many of them officers who brought their own troops along with them, sought service with the new khan, who responded generously—too generously, thought some of his advisers, who protested that Chinese "boors without character" were filling the court.

Boors or not, the defection of the senior Chinese generals assigned to defend the area near the mouth of the Yalu River, and the northern areas of Shandong province, brought new power to Hong Taiji. In 1637 he established two full Chinese banners on the lines of Nurhaci's earlier system, increasing the number to four in 1639 and to eight in 1642. There was already a parallel structure of eight Mongol banners, formed in 1635, from those who had pledged themselves to Hong Taiji's service. Other Mongol companies were divided and absorbed into existing Manchu banners. So by the early 1640s, the Jurchen leader had constructed a multiethnic military and administrative structure, which was used to provide soldiers for active combat on a rotating system, to register and protect their wives and children, and to supervise work on the land.

Even before this, in 1636, Hong Taiji had taken a symbolic step that went beyond that taken by Nurhaci in establishing the Jin dynasty in 1616: Hong Taiji decided to abolish his fledgling state's connection with the tribal past that was associated with the Jurchen name and the memories it evoked of servitude to the Ming dynasty. He declared the formation of a new dynasty called the Qing, claiming greater power and a wider mandate than the former Jin. Meaning "pure" or "clear" in Chinese, *Qing* (pronounced "Ching") had a dramatically different connotation in the Manchu language, meaning "martial" or "warrior." From 1636 until the final abdication of the Manchus in 1912, Qing was the dynastic name for the successive Manchu rulers and for the empire over which they ruled. Instead of Jurchen, Hong Taiji's people were in the future to be known as Manchus, unless they were otherwise identified as being from Mongol or "Chinese martial" roots. "Manchu" seems to have been a self-selected marker of identity, chosen by the ruler himself.[5]

Hong Taiji now seemed poised for wider conquests. In the 1630s he had extended his influence into territory controlled by various Mongol aristocratic lineages (in present-day Inner Mongolia), through diplomatic and marital alliances. He had conquered Korea in 1638, forcing the king to renounce his loyalty to the Ming and to give his sons to the Manchus as hostages. Inside China, the Ming failures were evident everywhere, with the rebels Li Zicheng and Zhang Xianzhong in control of much of the western and northern parts of the country. Manchu raiding parties had crossed the Great Wall north of Beijing and looted the area near the capital, along with wide swathes of land in Shandong province. They seized women and children, draft animals, silk, and silver, and left burnt-out, devastated cities in their wake.

In 1642, the strategic Ming city of Jinzhou, south of the Daling River, finally fell after a sporadic ten-year siege in which the Manchus had been repulsed again and again by the Ming garrison troops. Two of the last few talented Ming generals surrendered after the battle and were suitably rewarded. But the mainland route to Beijing through the pass at Shanhaiguan was still guarded by the redoubtable Ming general Wu Sangui, and in 1643 Hong Taiji suddenly died, leaving his younger brother Dorgon as a regent for the compromise choice as heir, Hong Taiji's ninth son, a five-year-old boy.

At this juncture the prospect for further Manchu expansion looked doubtful. Li Zicheng and his rebel army controlled Beijing, which they had seized in April 1644. But Li then led his forces out of the capital and advanced across the plains to attack General Wu Sangui, whom Li saw as the last major defender of the Ming cause. General Wu turned from the Shanhai-guan pass and marched westward to confront Li. Seizing the incredible opportunity, the regent Dorgon rallied and led the armies of the Manchu, Mongol, and Chinese banners swiftly down the coast, crossing the border into China unopposed in May. Nurhaci's dream had become a reality.

CONQUERING THE MING

With the Qing armies to his east and Li Zicheng's forces to his west, General Wu Sangui was in a desperate situation. His only hope to survive was by allying with one of his opponents. Among arguments for joining Li were the fact that he was Chinese, that he promised to end the abuses that had mounted in the late Ming state, and that he held Wu's father as a hostage. Otherwise, Li was an unknown quantity, violent and uneducated. After seiz-ing Beijing, Li had allowed his troops to loot and ravage the city, attacking and pillaging the homes of senior officials, seizing their relatives for ransom, or demanding enormous payoffs in "protection money." Even though Li had declared the formal founding of a new dynasty, he was unable to control his own generals, and Wu might well have wondered how effective Li would be in unifying the country.

As for allying with the Manchus, there was the disadvantage that they were ethnically non-Chinese, and their Jurchen background included them in a history of frontier people whom the Chinese had traditionally despised. Furthermore, they had terrorized parts of north China in their earlier raids and had virtually wiped out some of the cities they had occupied. Yet in their favor was the development of their embryonic regime, the Qing, which offered a promise of order: the six ministries, the examination system, the formation of the Chinese banners, the large numbers of Chinese advisers in senior positions—all were encouraging signs to Wu.

For a combination of these reasons and, according to popular tales, because Li had seized one of Wu's favorite concubines, General Wu Sangui threw in his lot with the Manchus, fought off the army that Li sent against him, and invited Dorgon to join him in recapturing Beijing. Li retaliated by executing Wu's father and displaying his head on the city wall. But the morale of Li's troops was fading fast, and not even his formal assumption of imperial rank on June 3, 1644, could shore him up. The next day he and his troops, weighed down by booty, fled to the west. On the sixth of June, the forces of Dorgon and Wu entered the capital, and the boy emperor was

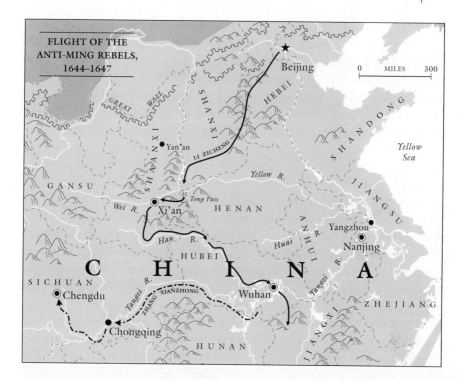

FLIGHT OF THE
ANTI-MING REBELS,
1644–1647

enthroned in the Forbidden City with the reign title of Shunzhi, meaning
"obedience in rule." The adopting of a traditional Chinese title by the young
emperor showed that the Manchus now formally claimed the Mandate of
Heaven to rule China.

Although the reigning Ming emperor had hanged himself in April, and a
new Qing emperor now sat on the throne, this did not mean the Ming cause
was dead. Many members of the imperial family had fled the capital at Li's
coming, and hundreds of princes of various collateral branches of the family
were living on their estates throughout China. The sanctity of their dynastic name, which had endured since 1368, was not to be lightly dismissed.
For hundreds of thousands of Chinese scholars and officials, the Ming name
remained worth fighting and dying for.

It would take the Manchus seventeen years to hunt down the last Ming
pretenders, but since they claimed to have entered Beijing as the righteous
avengers of the martyred Ming emperor, they also had to hunt down and destroy
the leading anti-Ming rebels. Li Zicheng was their first target, as he fled southwest with his army to the Shaanxi city of Xi'an, where his career as a military rebel had commenced some twenty years earlier. After consolidating

their hold on neighboring Shanxi* province, Qing forces, in the spring of 1645, closed in on Li with a skillfully executed pincer movement. Forced out of Xi'an, Li fled with a dwindling number of followers to the city of Wuchang, crossed the Yangzi, and was finally cornered in the mountains on the northern border of Jiangxi province. In the summer of 1645, he died there—either by suicide, according to one source, or beaten to death by farmers from whom he was trying to steal food, according to another.

While this campaign was underway, the second major rebel leader, Zhang Xianzhong, had moved away from his base in central China and traveled westward up the Yangzi River, through its steep gorges, and into Sichuan province. After briefly seizing the river town of Chongqing, he made his capital in the well-protected city of Chengdu. It was there, in December 1644, that he declared the formation of a new "Great Western Kingdom." Initially Zhang established a civilian bureaucracy staffed by scholars (many of whom were coerced into service), held examinations, and minted coinage. But in the ensuing years, Zhang seems to have gradually drifted into a world of megalomania and cruelty. He laid long-range "plans" to conquer not only southern and eastern China, but also Mongolia, Korea, the Philippines, and Annam (present-day Vietnam). He inflicted terrible punishments on those he believed were trying to betray him, even decimating whole regiments of his own armies. He finally abandoned Chengdu in late 1646, burning much of it to the ground, and conducted a scorched-earth campaign of appalling thoroughness as he marched eastward. In January 1647, he was killed by Qing troops.

The elimination of Li and Zhang was essential to the success of Manchu conquest plans, but most of the energies of the Manchus had to be spent on suppressing those members of the Ming ruling house who might be able to rally a viable national resistance. Considering the sense of loyalty that Chinese scholars were taught to feel toward their dynasty, and their strong inclination to protect their ancestral homes from aggressors, a skillful survivor of the Ming ruling house should have been able to assemble millions of supporters. The first who tried to rally support for the Ming cause was one of Emperor Wanli's grandsons, the prince of Fu. From his base in Nanjing the prince tried to make a deal with the regent Dorgon, offering the Manchus valuable presents and an annual subsidy if they would return beyond the Great Wall to Liaodong. Dorgon responded by saying he would allow the prince to maintain a small independent kingdom if he abandoned his imperial claims, an offer the prince rejected.

---

* Note the similarity of *Shanxi* and *Shaanxi*—highly confusing in English. The Chinese characters for the first syllable are quite different, though in both names *-xi* stands for "west."

Over the next few months, when the prince of Fu should have been preparing Nanjing's defenses, his court was torn by the bitter quarrels and recriminations that had plagued Emperor Wanli, including internecine struggles for power between pro- and anti-eunuch factions that echoed the previous battles between the Donglin partisans and Wei Zhongxian. While the Ming generals and senior officials bickered, a Qing army advanced south down the line of the great man-made inland waterway, the Grand Canal, and besieged the wealthy commercial city of Yangzhou in May 1645. The Ming troops, who had prepared batteries of cannon to defend the city walls, held out there for one week. But they were finally defeated by the superior cannon power of the Qing, and the city was sacked for ten terrible days as a warning to others who might resist. The defenders of Nanjing put up almost no resistance and surrendered in early June. The prince of Fu was captured and sent to Beijing, where he died the following year. But elsewhere, Ming loyalists in Jiangyin (about 100 miles downstream from Nanjing on the Yangzi River) refused an offer of amnesty and rallied local defense to keep Qing forces at bay for eighty-three days. In October, when two dozen siege cannon brought from Nanjing finally shattered the city walls, leaders of the resistance immolated their families and died by suicide rather than surrender. Qing soldiers followed the order from Beijing to "fill the city with corpses before you sheathe your swords." Of a population of nearly 100,000, fewer than 100 were left alive.[6]

With the prince of Fu's death, the situation grew more complicated as new claimants to the Ming throne appeared. Two brothers, descendants of the founding Ming emperor, attempted successively to lead resistance against the Manchus on the eastern coast, first in Fuzhou (across from the island of Taiwan) and then in the southern trading entrepôt of Guangzhou. The Fuzhou prince was caught and executed in late 1646; his younger brother was executed in 1647, when Guangzhou fell. Another descendant of the Ming founder led a series of unsuccessful attempts to rally resistance against the Qing up and down the east coast, basing his court for a time at Xiamen (Amoy), as well as on Zhoushan Island, and even for a short period on a boat. He abandoned his title in 1653, and thereafter resistance to the Qing on the east coast rested with supporters of the last Ming claimant, the prince of Gui.

The final hope of the Ming imperial cause, the prince of Gui was the last known surviving grandson of Wanli. When Beijing fell, he was a pampered twenty-one-year-old with no experience in governmental or military affairs. Forced to flee from his ancestral estates in Hunan when the rebel Zhang Xianzhong attacked the area, he moved south to Zhaoqing, west of Guangzhou. Over the objections of his mother, who warned that he was too young and delicate for the role, a group of fugitive officials named him emperor there in late 1646. Driven out of Guangdong province, the prince of Gui and

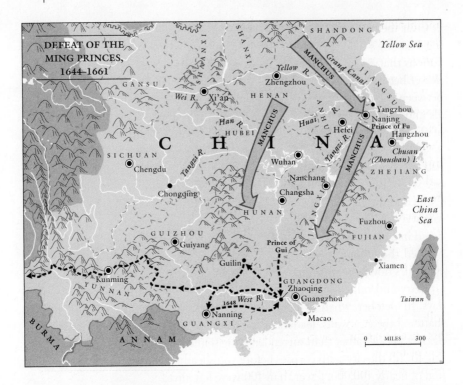

his court spent the next year and a half roaming across Guangxi province as Qing armies pursued him.

Despite the remarkable feats of the Qing armies, their conquest of this vast area was inevitably partial, and Chinese who bitterly resented the Manchu invasion and the Ming humiliation had time to collect their forces. In 1648 a number of former Ming officials who collaborated with the Manchus threw off their allegiance to the Qing and declared themselves dedicated to the cause of Ming restoration. The prince of Gui suddenly found himself welcomed back to Zhaoqing by numerous and enthusiastic supporters, while Qing troops in Guangzhou were massacred. As had earlier fugitive regimes, this "emperor" sought to reassemble a working bureaucracy, to hold examinations, to set up a viable military command, and to construct some kind of provincial administration that could control the countryside and collect taxes. But his court, like the others, was torn by factional strife and failed to lead a concerted opposition to the Manchus.

By early 1650 Qing forces had rallied and suppressed the key areas of declared support for the prince of Gui's regime, and had launched a two-pronged counterattack on his southern base. In December 1650, the prince and his followers fled from Guangdong province into Guangxi. For the next decade, no longer a court in any meaningful sense but simply a band of fugitives, they retreated steadily westward—from Guangxi into Guizhou province, then to Yunnan, before crossing the border into Burma.

The king of Burma, who initially offered sanctuary but changed his mind, massacred most of the prince of Gui's followers, and thereafter held the "emperor" and his family virtual prisoners. It was General Wu Sangui, once the Ming guardian of the Shanhaiguan passes, who in 1661 spearheaded a final attack by the Qing armies into Burma. The Burmese handed over the sad remnants of the Ming court to Wu, who had them transported back into Yunnan. There, in early in 1662, the last "emperor" of the Ming and his only son were executed by strangulation.

ADAPTING TO CHINA

The Qing had seized Beijing in 1644 with startling ease, and by 1662 had killed the last Ming claimants, but the succession of military victories did not mean that they had solved the problem of how to rule China. Dorgon, as regent for the child emperor Shunzhi, inherited a hybrid system of government, in which a tentative version of the Ming dynasty's six ministries was combined with the military and administrative Eight-Banners organization of the Manchus. He now had to adapt these institutions to the task of controlling a continent-sized country.

On one issue at least—that of Manchu dress and hairstyle—Dorgon was determined to make the Chinese adapt, rather than the reverse. Only a day after entering Beijing, he issued a decree stating that, henceforth, all Chinese men must shave their foreheads and have their hair braided in back in the Manchu-style queue, just as Nurhaci had ordered in Liaodong. A storm of protest led Dorgon to cancel the decree, but the following June another order was issued that Chinese *military* men must adopt the queue; this was to make it easier for the Manchus to identify their enemies in battle and assure them that those who had surrendered would remain loyal in the future. But Dorgon's senior advisers felt that this did not go far enough. In July 1645, Dorgon reissued the order that every Chinese man must shave his forehead and begin to grow the queue within ten days or face execution. The Chinese faced a stark choice: "Keep your hair and lose your head," as this order was summarized in popular parlance, "or lose your hair and keep your head."[7]

Ming Chinese men had prized long and elaborately dressed hair as a sign of masculinity and elegance, and they bitterly resented Dorgon's decree. In many areas the order led them to take up arms against the Qing even when they had already surrendered, but this time Dorgon stayed firm. Further decrees ordered the Chinese to adopt the Manchu style of dress—high collar and tight jacket fastened at the right shoulder—rather than wear the loosely hanging robes of the Ming. In another departure, Manchu women were forbidden to bind their feet to make them smaller, as Chinese girls and women had been doing for centuries. Despite the pain caused by this practice, the "three-inch golden lotuses" had become the measure of feminine beauty and a marker of elite status. Female labor that depended on skillful hands, such as spinning and weaving, kept women in the household; natural feet denoted the lower status of outdoor physical labor, such as agriculture. In refusing to go along with the custom, the Manchus both asserted their cultural independence and created an effective barrier to the intermarriage of Manchus and Chinese. It became almost unheard of for Manchu bannerwomen to marry Chinese civilian men, though it was comparatively common for Manchu bannermen to take Chinese women as their secondary consorts or concubines. The offspring of such marriages were considered to be Manchu.[8]

At the imperial court, the Manchus reduced the number of eunuchs serving the palace, mindful of the harm they had caused the previous regime. Though eunuchs remained as supervisors in the imperial women's quarters, other court duties and financial tasks were assigned to Chinese bondservants who had been captured and indentured in Liaodong in the 1620s and 1630s. An elite corps of bannermen assumed duties as palace guards.

Each of the eight banners was settled in a territorial zone outside the Beijing palace walls so that the emperor and his family lived surrounded by their most loyal troops. The Chinese inhabitants of Beijing were forcibly relocated to the southern part of the city; although this initially caused much hardship, the southern area swiftly became a thriving commercial and residential quarter. In addition, the Manchus confiscated hundreds of thousands of acres of fertile farmland in northern China—much of which had belonged to the Ming imperial family—to provide food and rewards for the garrison armies. In all, some 40,000 Manchu bannermen received approximately six acres each, with much larger estates being granted to senior Manchu officers.

In a further attempt to segregate the Chinese from the Manchus, Dorgon ordered the removal of many Chinese farmers in this north China area. Shrewd Chinese landlords, realizing the possibilities of exploiting this period of dynastic transition, seized unclaimed or abandoned land for themselves. The result was widespread chaos and devastation. Thousands of former farmers became vagabonds or bandits, or fled the area altogether. Many Manchus, however, were incapable of farming the land themselves, and they soon leased their plots to Chinese tenants on various types of contracts. Some of these contracts reduced the Chinese to an almost serflike dependency. Within twenty-five years of the conquest, about 5 million acres of land in a 150-mile radius around Beijing had been taken over by the Manchus. Still, neither a full-fledged feudal system nor any form of enslaved labor ever grew ensconced, and Chinese patterns of agricultural work, tenancy, and independent ownership slowly revived.

In most areas of governmental and intellectual organization, the Manchus were content to follow Chinese precedents. The six ministries (of personnel, finance, rituals, war, justice, and public works) were retained intact, although the leadership of each ministry was placed in the hands of two presidents, one a Manchu and one a Chinese bannerman or a civilian Chinese. A similar multiethnic dyarchy of four men (two Manchus and two Chinese) held the title of vice-president in each ministry. As liaison between the ministries and the emperor's immediate circle, the senior positions known as "grand secretaries" were also perpetuated. There were seven grand secretaries serving together in the early years of Shunzhi's reign: two were Manchu, two were Chinese bannermen, and three were former senior Ming officials who had recently surrendered.

Accomplished Chinese scholars who offered their loyalty to the Manchus were appointed to staff positions in the various ministries and in the Grand Secretariat. To bring new men into the bureaucracy, the national examinations on the classical literary tradition were reinstituted in 1646, when 373 degrees were awarded, mainly to candidates in the capital region or the bordering provinces of Shanxi and Shandong. To broaden the geographical spread another 298 degrees were given in 1647, mainly to candidates from the reconquered provinces of Jiangsu and Anhui.

The Qing could consolidate their administration in the provinces only after destroying the Ming opposition, but slowly they installed their own officials on a system similar to that of the Ming. They initially subdivided the fifteen main provinces that had existed under the Ming into twenty-two units, but eventually they cut back that number and simply divided in two each of the three largest provinces to make them easier to administer. Each of these eighteen provinces was under a governor, and in the early Qing most of these governors were Chinese bannermen. Dorgon clearly believed these men had proven their loyalty to his regime, and the fact that they were ethnically Chinese and spoke the Chinese language would make them more acceptable to their compatriots across the country. Under each governor were two officials who supervised, respectively, the economy and the practice of justice in the province, and a number of supervisory censors and intendants. Then came the prefects, based in the larger cities, who supervised the local county magistrates in charge of day-to-day administration and tax collection in the towns and countryside.

Candidates for scholarly degrees anxiously awaiting their examination results, Ming dynasty
It was critical for the early Qing emperors to inspire scholars to confer on the new dynasty the loyalty they had given the Ming.

Manchu power was spread very thinly over China's vast territory, and though the Qing established military garrisons in most of the key provincial cities, the new dynasty survived by maintaining a tenuous balance of power among three components of its state. First were the Manchus themselves, who had their own language and their own aristocratic rankings based on earlier Jurchen connections or on descent from Nurhaci. The Manchus tried to maintain their martial superiority through such practices as hunting and mounted archery; and they emphasized their cultural distinctness by using the Manchu spoken and written language. Though for practical reasons they had to let Chinese officials use Chinese for administrative documents, important documents were written in or translated into Manchu. The Manchus also kept to their own private religious practices, which were conducted by shamanic priests and priestesses in temple compounds to which the Chinese were denied access.

Second came the other bannermen, both Mongol and Chinese, most of whom were from families that had surrendered well before the conquest of 1644. With the Mongol bannermen posted mainly on the north and northwestern border regions, it was the Chinese bannermen who played the greater part in governing the inner provinces. They had their own hierarchies, based partly on noble titles granted by Nurhaci or Hong Taiji and partly by the date on which they had surrendered—those who had surrendered earliest often had the highest status. Many of these bannermen spoke both Manchu and Chinese, and had absorbed the martial culture of the former while retaining the social mores of the latter. Both Mongol and Chinese bannermen were invaluable to the Manchus; without their support, there would probably have been no conquest and certainly no consolidation.

Third came the ethnic Chinese—usually known as Han Chinese. These Chinese could be either active or passive collaborators, or they could choose to be resisters, again either actively or passively. Some of them, like Wu Sangui, were active collaborators with the Manchus (though never enrolled as bannermen); some defied the Manchus and died fighting them; some, as we will see, chose passive resistance. But most, seeing the way the wind was blowing, acquiesced to the new order.

Those Han Chinese from wealthy backgrounds tried to make sure that they could hold onto their ancestral lands and, if successful, proceeded to enroll their sons in the state examinations and to apply for bureaucratic office under the new regime. But the Qing had reason to be cautious about the loyalty of this group, as they had learned in 1648 when thousands of surrendered Chinese had risen to defend the Ming cause in the Guangzhou area. Millions more in the rich farmland south of the Yangzi cast off their allegiance when the warrior general Zheng Chenggong (in English called Koxinga, using a romanized form of his honorific name) launched an attack on the city of Nanjing in the late 1650s. Though their resistance was rapidly suppressed by Qing troops, it had been a dangerous moment. In the south, the Qing initially made no attempt to establish a strong presence. Instead, once the Ming claimants were dead, they let Wu Sangui and two other Chinese generals who had long before defected to the Manchus administer the huge territories as virtually independent fiefdoms.

The Manchu rulers were conscious that the Ming dynasty had fallen in part because of factional battles and court intrigues, but they were not immune to the same weaknesses. For instance, both of the nobly born generals who had been pivotal in the suppression of the rebel regimes of Zhang Xianzhong and Li Zicheng were later arrested on trumped-up charges of treachery and died mysteriously in prison. The regent Dorgon himself behaved extravagantly and outrageously, arrogating to himself nearly imperial powers, seizing control of several banners and ousting their generals, marrying the widow of one of his dead rivals, demanding concubines from Korea, and planning to build a palace fortress in Rehe (Jehol), north of Beijing.

When Dorgon died in 1650, the Manchu nobles fell to fighting over his inheritance, and the Qing regime was in danger of fragmenting.

By clever maneuvering, however, the young emperor Shunzhi, now aged thirteen, was able to consolidate his hold on the throne. Though raised as a Manchu, Shunzhi seems to have been far more adaptable to Chinese ways than most of the senior Manchus around him. Astute enough to avoid being dominated by the magnates who succeeded Dorgon, and militarily shrewd enough to push the attacks on the last Ming supporters through to a successful conclusion, he also studied the Chinese language carefully and was deeply influenced by a number of devout Chinese Buddhist monks with whom he studied. For the last year of his life, Shunzhi grew passionately enamored of one of his junior consorts and neglected the reigning empress. At the same time he returned considerable power to the palace eunuchs and revived several eunuch bureaus that had been disbanded at the time of the Qing conquest. The reasons for this are not clear, but possibly Shunzhi wanted to make the inner court more privately his own, without Manchu bodyguards and bondservants to report his movements back to his relatives.

In another unusual development, Shunzhi became close friends with a Catholic Jesuit missionary, Father Johann Adam Schall von Bell. Jesuits from Europe had been seeking converts in China since the late Ming. Some Jesuits had been captured by Zhang Xianzhong and marched with his armies in Sichuan; others had accompanied the fleeing troops of the southern Ming pretenders. Schall von Bell was one of a small group that had been in Beijing in 1644 and had decided to risk staying there. Because he had a high level of scientific skill, Dorgon appointed him to direct the Imperial Bureau of Astronomy. Since the imperial court was expected to determine the calendar for the entire country, it would greatly reinforce Shunzhi's claim to be Son of Heaven if the calculations were as precise as

Jesuit missionary Johann Adam Schall von Bell Schall von Bell wears the badge of office of a senior Chinese official in a Western engraving.

possible. Schall von Bell's favored status may also have been another way for Emperor Shunzhi to express his independence, or to seek a father figure in place of the one he had lost so young. Shunzhi called the sixty-year-old Schall von Bell "Grandpa," summoned him regularly for conferences on religion and politics, and allowed him to build a church in Beijing.

Shunzhi died suddenly in 1661, probably from smallpox, not long after his beloved consort. But far from mourning his passing, the four senior Manchus who took over as regents for Shunzhi's young son almost immediately vilified his memory. Claiming that they had Shunzhi's last will and testament in their possession, they publicized this document to the country at large. According to the regents, Shunzhi blamed himself for betraying the martial norms of his Manchu ancestors, for favoring the eunuchs, and for valuing Chinese advisers more than Manchus. "One reason that the Ming lost the empire," said the document, "was that they made the error of relying on eunuchs. I was clearly aware of their corruption, but I was unable to heed this warning. . . . I have caused the Manchu statesmen to have no desire to serve and their zeal has been dissipated."[9]

The four regents—among whom Oboi, a veteran general, rapidly became the most powerful—moved decisively to change the policies of Shunzhi. They executed the leading eunuch and abolished the eunuch offices, establishing in their place an imperial-household system supervised by Manchus. They insisted on much tougher tax-collection policies throughout the countryside. In one famous case in Jiangsu, they ordered the investigation of over 13,000 wealthy Chinese declared delinquent in their tax payments; at least eighteen were publicly executed and thousands more deprived of their scholarly degrees.

In other developments, Father Schall von Bell was arrested and thrown into prison, Manchus were promoted to high positions, and senior Chinese scholars were humiliated. In an attempt to starve out the last anti-Manchu rebels on the island of Taiwan by depriving them of all support from allies living along the eastern coast, the regents ordered the relocation of the Chinese coastal population twenty miles inland, despite all the suffering such an order caused. By the end of the 1660s, it looked as though the policy of peaceful adaptation that in various ways had been developed by Nurhaci, Hong Taiji, Dorgon, and Shunzhi was about to be abandoned in the name of a new Manchu nativism.

| # Kangxi's Consolidation

THE WAR OF THE THREE FEUDATORIES, 1673–1681

Qing emperors had to grow up fast if they were to grow up at all. Shunzhi had been thirteen when, taking advantage of Dorgon's sudden death, he put himself in power. Shunzhi's son, Kangxi, was also thirteen when he first moved to oust the regent Oboi, and he was fifteen when, with the help of his grandmother and a group of Manchu guard officers, he arranged for Oboi's arrest in 1669 on charges of arrogance and dishonesty. Oboi soon died in prison, and Kangxi began a reign that was to last until 1722 and make him one of the most admired rulers in China's history.

The most important of the many problems facing the young ruler was that of unifying the country under Manchu control. Although in 1662 Wu Sangui had eliminated the last Ming pretender in the southwest, the region had not been fully integrated into Beijing's administrative structure. The enormous distances, the mountainous semitropical country that made cavalry campaigning difficult, the presence of hundreds of non-Chinese tribes who fought tenaciously for their own terrain, the shortage of administrators of proven loyalty—all these made both Shunzhi and Oboi unwilling to commit further Qing forces to the area. Instead, the whole of the south and southwest was left under the control of the three Chinese generals who had directed most of the fighting there in the late 1650s.

These three were named as princes by the Qing court and honored by having their sons married to the daughters of Manchu nobles. Each of the three was granted what amounted to an almost independent domain, and in Western histories they are named the "Three Feudatories." The first, Wu Sangui, controlled the provinces of Yunnan and Guizhou as well as sections

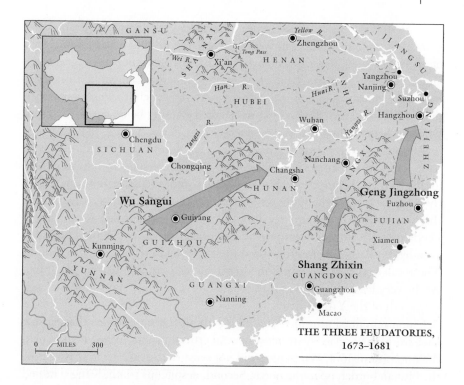

THE THREE FEUDATORIES,
1673–1681

of Hunan and Sichuan; the second ruled Guangdong and parts of Guangxi from his base in Guangzhou; and the third controlled Fujian from the coastal city of Fuzhou.

Together the three men were masters over a region equivalent in size to France and Spain combined. Within these areas, despite the nominal presence of Qing bureaucrats, the Three Feudatories supervised all aspects of military and civil government, the examination systems, relations with the Indigenous peoples, and the collection of taxes. Not only did they keep the local revenues for themselves and control lucrative trade monopolies, they also constantly demanded lavish subsidies from the Qing court as the price of their continued loyalty. By the 1660s, they were receiving more than 10 million ounces of silver every year.

When Wu Sangui threw off his allegiance to the Qing in December 1673, he declared the formation of a new dynasty and started driving his armies deep into Hunan. The other two generals joined the fray in 1674 and 1676, respectively. This War of the Three Feudatories confronted the Chinese in the south and southwest with an agonizing test of loyalties. Those who had survived the years of fighting in the 1640s and 1650s and had made their peace with the Qing now had to decide whether to remain true to that allegiance, or to pin their hopes on Wu's newly named Zhou dynasty. Wu played on their sense of Chinese loyalty by ordering the restoration of Ming customs and the cutting of queues. He also offered Emperor Kangxi an amnesty if he would relocate to establish a new kingdom in Manchuria and Korea. Predictably, Kangxi refused, and to underscore his anger he executed Wu's son, who was being held hostage in Beijing.

With their large standing armies and sound administrative and economic base, Wu and his supporters had a better chance of success than the Ming loyalist princes before them. Furthermore, throughout the south and west, the Chinese loyal to the Qing were surrounded and outnumbered; although there is evidence that many tried to resist service to the rulers of the Three Feudatories—some by fleeing to the mountains, others by feigning illness or even by mutilating themselves—most felt they had no choice but to submit. The result was that the rebellion almost succeeded in destroying the Qing. At the very least, it looked as if the Manchus would lose control of the territory south of the Yangzi River.

China remained a unified country (with all the significance that has for later world history) as the result of several crucial factors. When he first held the initiative in 1674, Wu Sangui did not seize the advantage to drive across the Hunan border, up to the north. Second, despite his youth, Kangxi rallied his court behind him, developed a long-range military strategy, and inspired the courage of a number of Qing generals, who spearheaded the counterattacks. Lastly, the Three Feudatories failed to coordinate and mount a sustained campaign on any one front. They were unable to win the loyalty of many Ming supporters, who were fully aware of the former Ming generals' traitorous collaboration with the Manchus.

Wu Sangui declared himself emperor of the new Zhou dynasty in 1678, but the gesture came too late to be meaningful. He died of dysentery later that year, ending a stormy life. His grandson fought on in his name for three more years, but died by suicide in the Yunnan capital of Kunming when Qing generals trapped him there. Wu's followers were executed, along with the leaders of the other rebellious Feudatories.

At the war's end, in 1681, those who had urged the hard line against the Three Feudatories became Kangxi's close advisers. The emperor was ruthless to those in senior positions who had supported the rebels, but ordered more compassionate treatment to those who had been caught up in the fighting through no fault of their own. As he put it, they had just shown "a natural desire to hang on to life and avoid being killed. If my armies arrive and execute them all, this contradicts my desire to save the people, and denies them any chance to reform." The emperor showed similar sympathy for women and children trapped in the fighting with the "bandits" (as he usually called the rebels): "The women in the bandits' camps were often initially taken there by force—so after the bandits themselves have been destroyed, let the other local people have a chance to identify and reclaim the refugees and their children—don't just arrest everyone indiscriminately."[1]

With the leaders dead, all traces of the Feudatories were abolished. New governors-general and governors—mostly Chinese bannermen—were appointed to the rebellious provinces to integrate them into the Qing realm. Revenues once again began to flow from these areas to Beijing, and with the revenues came a resumption of the examination system in the south and southwest, and the beginning of a trickle of successful candidates. But life had been too seriously disrupted to be speedily repaired. Hunan, Guangxi, Yunnan, and Guizhou all remained peripheral to the main life of China for the rest of Kangxi's reign, and distrust still ran deep. Few men from those provinces were given higher degrees, and even fewer were appointed to high office. Kangxi himself, although a great traveler, never ventured more than a few miles south of the Yangzi. It was the now-prosperous Yangzi delta towns of Nanjing and Suzhou that he referred to as "the South," with the implication that the more truly southern and western provinces remained somehow beyond his range. Throughout his life Kangxi reminisced about how shaken the war had left him, and how bitterly he regretted the loss of life that had followed his decision to let the leaders of the Three Feudatories "retire." But he never regretted the decision itself.

TAIWAN AND MARITIME CHINA

The integration of Taiwan into China's history dates from the mid-seventeenth century. In the later years of the Ming dynasty, Taiwan was still largely unknown: dangerous seas, typhoons, and sand shoals protected its coasts; flat, malarial plains along the west, backed by inhospitable mountain ranges, sealed its isolation. Taiwan's Indigenous populations further discouraged exploration or settlement by outsiders. But a few Chinese traders from the harbors of Guangdong and Fujian braved the dangers and made a decent profit from Taiwanese deer hides and crushed deerhorns (believed to be a potent aphrodisiac), and established small settlements in the southwest of the island. Chinese and Japanese pirates also found havens along the same coast.

In the 1620s Taiwan began to feature in global politics. At one time, shipwrecked sailors and missionaries had been the island's only European visitors. The Portuguese then explored the island and gave it the name of "Beautiful Isle" ("Ilha Formosa"); but they withdrew, deciding to keep Macao as their main base of operations in East Asia. Not so the Spaniards, who established a small base in the north at Keelung, nor the Protestant Dutch, who in 1624 established a fort they named Zeelandia in the town of Anping (present-day Tainan) in the south. By the 1640s the Dutch had driven out both the Spaniards and the last Japanese pirates, and a profitable trade developed among the island, the Dutch Empire in the East Indies (now Indonesia), and the merchants and administrators on China's east coast. Drawn by the island's possibilities, clusters of Chinese settlers congregated around first the Spanish and then the Dutch enclaves, while others came to drain and farm the land on Taiwan's western plains. The Dutch encouraged Chinese traders, though initially few settled permanently; they would return to the mainland coast in the winters, leaving the Dutch to work out their own economic and organizational system by a divide-and-rule strategy with the island's native inhabitants.

The Dutch stayed largely aloof from the fighting by the Ming loyalists in the 1640s and 1650s, but the development of the coastal war and its interconnections with loyalists in Taiwan eventually made Dutch isolation impossible. The fighting escalated when the leader of the powerful Zheng family, a pirate and trader who plied the waters between Fujian, Taiwan, and southern Japan, was made an official by the desperate Ming. Although he defected to the Qing court in 1646, his impetuous son, Zheng Chenggong, refused to do so. Instead he made his troops and ships available to the fleeing Ming, and continued to support them in name and deed even after they had been driven inland.

This remarkable naval warrior, known to history as Koxinga,* had been born in 1624 to a Japanese mother, and his upbringing reflected the polyglot world of international trade and cultural relations. His father's trade networks extended from Nagasaki to Macao, and at their fortified home near Xiamen (Amoy) was a chapel with both Christian and Buddhist images, as well as a bodyguard of Black slaves, fugitives from the Portuguese in Macao.

Koxinga's fleets fought the Manchus along China's east coast all through the 1650s, and under his control Xiamen became an international entrepôt. He organized ten trading companies that dealt in sugar and luxury goods, in exchange for the naval supplies and gunpowder needed to keep his fleets in fighting shape. It was not until he tried a decisive frontal assault on Nanjing in 1659 that he was seriously defeated. As the Qing armies closed in on his main base, Koxinga made the bold decision to attack the Dutch fortress of Zeelandia. Probably aided by a former Chinese interpreter who had worked for the Dutch and knew the details of Zeelandia's defensive system, Koxinga pressed the siege. Although he conquered the surrounding countryside easily

---

* The Ming gave him their imperial surname, a title pronounced in Fujian dialect as "Kokseng-ia," transformed by Westerners into the word *Koxinga*.

enough, the Dutch defenders of the fort held out for an astonishing nine months. Only in February 1662 did they surrender, leaving Koxinga trade goods and cash estimated to be worth over 1 million ounces of silver.

Koxinga did not enjoy his success for long. The news that his father and brothers had been executed in Beijing because of his intransigence (his Japanese mother had been killed long before by Qing troops) perhaps exacerbated his already unstable mental condition. He began a destructive pattern of abusing his subordinates and directing passionate rages against his own children, and died later in 1662.

Despite the cruel efficiency of their policy of removing the Chinese coastal population, initiated in 1661, the Oboi regents failed to bring Taiwan into submission. They did form a brief alliance with the Dutch to smoke out the last Zheng family holdouts on the Fujian coast, but two expeditions against Taiwan planned in 1664 and 1665 both fizzled out. The Manchus were inexperienced at naval warfare and, after 1673, were largely preoccupied with the civil war of the Three Feudatories. This allowed the Zhengs in Taiwan to continue developing a prosperous trade and commercial empire: first Koxinga's sons and then his grandson supervised a Chinese population that swelled

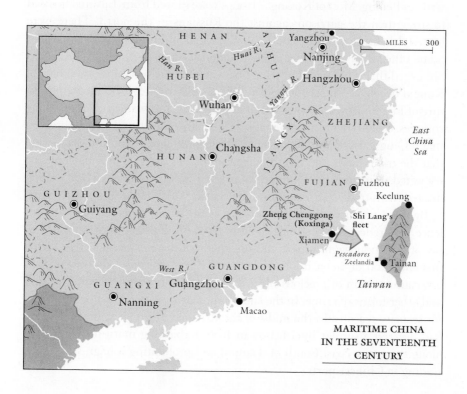

MARITIME CHINA
IN THE SEVENTEENTH
CENTURY

through emigration and flight from the mainland to over 100,000, produced large quantities of rice and sugarcane, and conducted considerable business in salt, refined sugar, and shipbuilding.

Even after the war of the Three Feudatories was over, Kangxi still found it hard to assemble the necessary forces to capture the island from the Zheng family. The emperor's final strategy was to appoint one of Koxinga's father's former admirals, Shi Lang—who had surrendered long before, in the 1650s—to be the senior admiral of an expeditionary force. The choice was an excellent one. Not only was Shi Lang a fine commander, but his father, brother, and son had all been vengefully killed by Koxinga when Shi joined the Manchus. He could be counted on to push the battle to its limits.

Shi Lang planned methodically for his campaign, and the scale of his fleet—300 war vessels—reminds us of the Qing's strong potential as a sea power, even though its naval resources were not usually exploited. Leading his fleet from Fujian province in early July 1683, Admiral Shi won a crushing victory in the Pescadores over the last Zheng forces.

Taiwan surrendered three months later, and Kangxi, perhaps wearied by the bloodbaths of the earlier civil-war period, treated the fallen Zheng family and their leading officers graciously, ennobling some and allowing them to settle in Beijing. Most of Koxinga's troops were moved from Taiwan and used to strengthen the garrisons against the Russians in the north. There were heated debates at the Qing court about what should be done with the island. Some officials suggested that it be abandoned altogether, whereas Admiral Shi urged that it be made a fortified base against the warships of the Dutch. Kangxi decided to incorporate Taiwan into his empire. It became a prefecture of Fujian province, with a capital at Tainan, and was divided into three counties, each under a civilian magistrate. At the same time, Kangxi ordered that a Qing garrison of 8,000 troops be left permanently on the island, and that the tribal lands and hunting grounds of the Indigenous inhabitants be respected. Further Han Chinese emigration to Taiwan was to be carefully limited, with trade restricted through licensing rules and limits on ship sizes.

By these rather conflicting responses, Kangxi was reflecting the ambivalence his predecessors had felt about overseas trade and colonization. They saw it as conducive to unrest and disorder, and feared it would lead to the dissemination of secret information about China's defenses to foreign powers, cause a drain of precious silver from the country, and encourage piracy and other forms of crime. In the late Ming, maritime trade had been banned for security reasons. In the midst of the Koxinga insurgency, the Qing state had decreed a similar interdiction in 1656, forbidding maritime commerce along the entire coast (south of Tianjin) and prohibiting foreign ships from trading in Chinese ports.

After the Zheng family's final defeat, Kangxi consulted at length with his advisers about the prudence of rescinding the ban and assessed the suitability of different methods for taxing and regulating maritime commerce. In 1684, the emperor was persuaded that the advantages outweighed the perils. He decreed that all coastal ports would be opened to private trade, allowing all his subjects (eventually including Manchus and bannermen) to join the vigorous entrepreneurial world of the east coast and the commercial networks extending throughout Southeast Asia. Four provincial customs offices (one each in Guangdong, Fujian, Zhejiang, and Jiangsu) with 150 branch stations enforced an across-the-board tariff of 20 percent on foreign imports. In addition, purchased monopolies functioned as a licensing system, in which merchants regulated themselves in exchange for submitting a fixed cut of the revenues to the government.[2]

Despite these regulations, illicit profits flowed into the hands of the senior bureaucrats in charge of the maritime and coastal trade. A Chinese bondservant in the early 1680s allegedly paid bribes well in excess of 10,000 ounces of silver in order to win the post of governor-general of Guangdong and Guangxi, which would allow him to supervise most of the trade out of Guangzhou. In a massive relocation of the population back to the coastal regions, this man, with the aid of commissioners appointed to the task, reassigned almost half a million acres of land to more than 30,000 people. The fortune accumulated by this one merchant-official apparently exceeded 400,000 ounces (taels) of silver.

WOOING THE INTELLECTUALS

The protracted resistance of the Ming claimants, the support given to Koxinga and his descendants, the swift spread and near success of the Three Feudatories: all these pointed to a lack of support for the Qing among its Chinese subjects. From the beginning of his reign, Emperor Kangxi addressed himself to this problem by trying to strike a balance between reassuring the Manchus of his martial vigor and political firmness on the one hand, and trying to convince the Chinese of his respect for their traditional culture on the other.

Appealing to the Manchus turned out to be comparatively simple. Kangxi was a strong young man whose survival of a childhood bout of smallpox was a factor that led to his being chosen as Shunzhi's heir. He early developed a passion for hunting and for archery, and his skill at riding meant he could go on long excursions into the ancestral homelands of Manchuria. The elite guards-officers and Manchu nobles who accompanied him on these journeys were bonded in loyalty to their ruler, and though there were serious differences of opinion over national policy, they stood behind him in all his early crises. His doting grandmother, Hong Taiji's widow, was also a powerful political figure through her family connections. Kangxi was meticulous, too, in carrying out ceremonies at the Manchu shamanic temples in Beijing, in promoting Manchus to high office along with the Chinese, and in holding back eunuch power by balancing their roles against those of Chinese bondservants and the Manchu nobles placed in charge of the imperial household.

Appealing to the Chinese was more complex. The Manchus claimed that they had entered China in 1644 to avenge the Ming emperor Chongzhen, but numerous Chinese did not accept this. Even if they did, the ties of loyalty to one's ruler were so strong that many killed themselves when they heard of Chongzhen's death; others took up arms, though certain that resistance would ultimately prove fatal; and many more simply removed their talents from the Qing state, refusing to serve the government in any form.

This refusal to serve was rationalized on grounds of Confucian principle, and it was on these grounds that Kangxi chose to meet the opposition. The teachings of Confucius had an undisputed place in Chinese society, although by the mid-seventeenth century there was considerable difference of opinion about what those teachings meant. In essence, during the fifth century B.C.E. Confucius had been the spokesman for the values of morality and dignity in private life and in government. He had argued for the importance of righteousness and loyalty, reinforced by correct rituals that would place individuals in proper relationships with the cosmos and with contemporaries. He had stated that worthy men should not serve unworthy rulers and must be ready to sacrifice their lives, if necessary, in the defense of principle.

A collection of conversations that Confucius held with statesmen and students, known as the *Analects*, portrayed him as a shrewd and vigorous man, constantly testing himself and those around him for flaws of character while never losing faith in the possibilities of virtuous action. His belief in the powers of moral example and in the central importance of education was absolute. Some centuries after Confucius's death, five of the works attributed to his editorial hand were designated as the "Five Classics" of the Confucian canon. One of these works was on rituals, two were on history, one on poetry, and one on cosmology and divination. Subsequently, in the twelfth century C.E., the *Analects*, along with the sayings of Confucius's later follower Mencius and two selections from the ritual classic that dealt with human nature and moral development, were grouped together as the "Four Books." Cumulatively, these nine works were believed to contain the basic precepts for leading a moral life, and to offer a record of an earlier utopian historical period that had reached its apogee of enlightened government and social harmony during the early Zhou dynasty, some 1,500 years in the past.

A portrait of the emperor Kangxi at his studies
Through his study of the Confucian classics, Kangxi took on the aura of a "sage ruler."

Over the ensuing centuries this body of material was swollen by floods of commentaries and reinterpretations, and modified in subtle ways by elements drawn from Buddhism—which flourished in China after the fifth century C.E.—and from other traditions within Chinese philosophy. At the same time, this diversity of "Confucian" material was turned into "doctrine," and the Four Books and Five Classics became the basis for the state examinations that qualified aspiring scholars for government service. Confucianism was now construed in a rigidly hierarchical way and used to support the rights of parents over their children, of husbands over their wives, and of rulers over their subjects. This hierarchy was reinforced by restricting the examinations to male candidates and by not allowing women to serve in the bureaucracy. The prevailing school of Confucianism in the Qing emphasized the force of principle (*li*) in the world but placed it outside and above life energy (*qi*), leading to a dualistic interpretation of human nature and of the whole metaphysical structure of the Chinese world.

From the moment he imprisoned the regent Oboi, Kangxi showed the utmost respect for this complex legacy. In 1670 he issued a series of sixteen maxims, designed as a summation of Confucian moral values. Known as the "Sacred Edict," these maxims emphasized hierarchical submission in social relations, generosity, obedience, thrift, and hard work. Kangxi subsequently named a team of Manchu and Chinese tutors, with whom he read meticulously through the Four Books and then the Five Classics. In the official court diaries, one can chart his progress from chapter to chapter and watch him debate knotty points with his teachers. Judiciously "leaked" to the court, the news of these studies, along with Kangxi's intensive work on Chinese calligraphy, gave the young monarch the aura of a "sage ruler." At the same time, popular versions of the Sacred Edict, rendered in a colloquial style, ensured the wide dissemination of Kangxi's ethical views to the people as a whole.

One of the great powers of the Chinese state lay in its control of the examination system. The Qing government perpetuated this dynamic by adopting the Ming examination curriculum. In the Kangxi reign the exams were held every three years—even during the civil-war period of the Three Feudatories. But the emperor was vexed at the number of accomplished scholars who refused even to sit for the examinations, on the grounds that to do so would be a betrayal of the Ming dynasty. As an ingenious solution to this predicament, in 1679 Kangxi asked for nominations from the provinces for a special examination—separate from the triennial national exams—to be held for men of outstanding talent. Although some still refused to participate, the venture was a success. Fifty special degrees were awarded, mostly to scholars from the Yangzi delta provinces. In a tactful gesture to their past loyalties, these scholars were put to work helping compile the official history of the fallen Ming dynasty.

Three scholars stand out for both their actions and their writings in this period. One was the Hunanese Wang Fuzhi, who spent years with the fugitive court of the prince of Gui before returning home in 1650. He devoted much effort thereafter to attacking the philosophical trends that had been influential in the mid-Ming, claiming that the preoccupation with individual conscience had wrecked the moral fiber of the time. Wang Fuzhi also wrote a history of the prince of Gui's court as well as critical appraisals of former "barbarian" regimes, which would have led to his execution had they been discovered. The second scholar, Huang Zongxi, a Zhejiang native whose father had been killed in 1626 on the orders of the eunuch Wei Zhongxian, was a passionate partisan of the Donglin Society. Huang Zongxi fought for years alongside the Ming claimants on the east coast. Finally, after 1649, he retired to a life of scholarship. In addition to writing biographies of major Ming figures, he also analyzed the structure of government, critiqued dynastic rule, and advocated for systemic reform.

Most famous of the three scholars was Gu Yanwu, born in 1613 in Jiangsu and raised by his widowed foster mother, a remarkable woman of great moral rectitude who was determined that Gu follow correct Confucian ethical precepts. In the late Ming, Gu Yanwu passed the lower-level examinations. In 1644 he served briefly with the prince of Fu against the Manchus, and was deeply moved by the example of his foster mother, who starved herself to death rather than submit to the new conquerors. In her dying words to Gu, she declared, "To perish with the [Ming] dynasty is no more than my duty. Do not serve another dynasty."[3]

Though Gu declined to emulate her action, he took her words to heart and spent the rest of his life (he died in 1682) in travel, reflection, and scholarship. He developed a new kind of rigorous and pragmatic scholasticism, to counter what he saw as the moral hollowness and pretension of the dominant schools of Confucianism, with their emphases on metaphysical dualisms and intuition. In his voluminous writings, Gu focused on such themes as government, ethics, economics, geography, and social relations, and paid special attention to philology, which he saw as a fundamental tool for evaluating the meaning of China's earlier scholarly legacy. Despite growing fame, he refused all invitations to serve the Qing. After his death, Gu was revered by many scholars who saw him as a model of scholarly precision and integrity, and in the eighteenth century, his works came to have a profound influence on Chinese thought.

It was not only soldiers and scholars who resisted the Manchus. Many early Qing painters used their art to show their agitation and lack of faith in the regime. Through boldly innovative and eccentric brushwork, and the use of empty space in their compositions, they portrayed a world that was bleak or out of balance. Lone and twisted pine trees, desolate, angular mountain ranges, images of tangled foliage laid on paper in thick, wet strokes—such were the subjects these artists often chose. Some of the most brilliant of these painters, like Shitao or Bada Shanren, were related to members of the fallen Ming ruling house and retired to isolated monasteries in the conquest period. Bada Shanren (a self-selected name, meaning "one who dwells in the eight great mountains") made silence his gesture of defiance. After writing the character for "dumb" upon his door, he refused to speak, though he would still laugh or weep extravagantly when drunk or caught in creative fever. But Shitao slowly edged back into society, began to mingle with other scholars and artists even if they had served with the Qing, accepted occasional commissions designing landscape gardens for wealthy urbanites, and ended up on the outer edges of court circles.

One could, indeed, write a history of the period by tracing the co-opting of the intellectuals by the Qing court. Those who would not serve in administrative office and would not take the examinations could still be lured by the promise of good company and hard cash. Literary compilations especially proved an attractive focus for their energies. Kangxi assembled several groups of scholars and hired them to write dictionaries, encyclopedias, records of imperial tours, and collections of classical prose and poetry. Other senior ministers sponsored geographical studies and local histories, which enabled restless scholars to travel the country in search of material and then to return to a comfortable home base to write. Yet other officials gave promising writers jobs as private secretaries with light duties, which allowed them ample time for pursuing their own creative paths, whether as novelists, poets, or dramatists. The result was a cultural flowering in the later seventeenth century, despite the recent period of warfare and bloodshed.

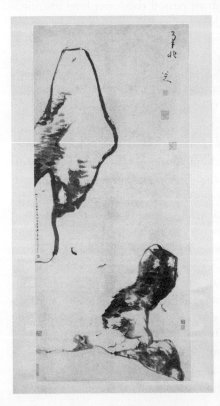

Bada Shenren's "Fish and Rocks," 1699
Bada Shenren and other painters of this period expressed defiance of the Qing obliquely through their art.

Finally, the very act of Ming resistance and loyalty became an accepted topic at Kangxi's court through the artistry of Kong Shangren. A descendant of Confucius in the sixty-fourth generation, Kong was born in 1648, after the Qing conquest. His father had been a prominent Ming scholar, and Kong Shangren became fascinated with the dynasty's fall and the people who had been caught up in it. During his forties, he composed a popular drama, *The Peach Blossom Fan*, about an upright scholar, the woman he loves, and their travails in the Ming court of the prince of Fu. The heroine resists the advances of a wicked minister, attacking him with her fan, which gets spattered with blood. A painter transforms the blood drops into part of a design of peach blossoms, giving the play its title and providing a brilliant metaphor for the mixture of violence and beauty that Kong saw as lying at the heart of late Ming moral and intellectual life. At the play's end, with the Ming resistance in ruins, the lovers agree to take monastic vows, while the surviving virtuous officials retreat into the mountains to escape a summons from the Qing that they take up office. In one of the last scenes, the lovers and a friend join in a grand aria:

> This tale of the southern court will resound forever,
> And tears of blood will swell the streams with woe,
> We raise to Heaven our "summons to the soul"
> As mists obscure the mighty river's flow.[4]

By the 1690s, Kong Shangren's play had become a palace favorite. In an essay written at this time, Kong caught the emotion of the audience:

> Famous aristocrats, high officials, and talented literati gathered in such a crowd that it was impossible to find space for one's legs. The furnishings formed an embroidered universe, and the banquet a landscape of jewelled delicacies. . . . Yet in the midst of this dazzling theater, there were a few who sat quietly weeping behind their sleeves— former officials and 'survivors.' When the lanterns had flickered out and the drinking was over, they uttered sighs and went their ways.[5]

Such men might still be nostalgic, but they had made their peace.

DEFINING THE BORDERS

Foreign pressure, and at least some elements of foreign technology, were becoming commonplace in early Qing China. Even those Chinese with no knowledge or interest in foreign lands could have their lives abruptly changed. Kong Shangren, for instance, had been slowly losing his eyesight for some years before he wrote *The Peach Blossom Fan*; he recorded his resumption of scholarly activity in an ecstatic poem:

> White glass from across the Western Seas
> Is imported through Macao:
> Fashioned into lenses big as coins,
> They encompass the eyes in a double frame.
> I put them on—it suddenly becomes clear;
> I can see the very tips of things!
> And read fine print by the dim-lit window
> Just like in my youth.[6]

Kong gained this clarity of vision, fruit of a European technology exported through Macao, thanks to the Qing decision not to destroy the Portuguese base. During the 1660s, as part of the coastal withdrawal policy linked to the suppression of Taiwan, Qing naval forces blockaded Macao, and all Chinese were ordered to leave. Portuguese ships were banned, and there was a threat that their buildings would be razed. But for reasons of local economic self-interest, Qing officials in charge of carrying out these orders did not do so. Through subsequent diplomatic embassies, the support of the Jesuits in Beijing (now returned to favor), and the judicious gift in 1678 of an African lion—which fascinated Kangxi—the Portuguese persuaded the Qing to allow them to retain Macao as the base for their East Asian trade.

The same tolerance was not extended to the Russians. Late Ming officials and advisers to Emperor Shunzhi were aware of the spread of Russian hunters and settlers into the northeast border region. A Russian embassy had negotiated with the Qing for permission to send trade caravans, but Kangxi, too, was uneasy about the influence the Russians were having on the allegiance of the border tribes, who paid tribute-taxes to the Qing. An attempt to withdraw several border tribes south of the Russian line of advance and to establish a buffer zone was abandoned as too costly and impractical.

Kangxi had in fact been preparing for some years to launch an attack on the Russian outpost of Albazin, on the Amur River. When Taiwan was finally captured by the Qing in 1683, as we saw above, some of the surviving Zheng family troops were sent to the north to participate in the campaign against the Russians. The maritime skills of the Zheng troops proved useful navigating the northern rivers. With the southern wars safely over, Kangxi ordered a concerted assault on Albazin, which, after stiff fighting, was seized by Qing forces in 1685. Abandoning the town—really more a large, fortified stockade in those days—and pulling back as the emperor had instructed, the Qing commander inexplicably disobeyed the order that he destroy the abundant crops planted by the Russian settlers in the area. Accordingly the garrison commander of

Nerchinsk, the second Russian trading base located to the west, sent men to gather in the crops before the winter and to reoccupy the city.

Furious, Kangxi ordered a second attack on Albazin in 1686, which met stiff Russian resistance. The Russian rulers were worried, however, over their ability to hold the huge territory in the face of determined Qing opposition and decided to sue for peace. The two sides—a Russian delegation of 1,000 and a Qing entourage of more than 10,000—met at Nerchinsk in 1689. With the aid of Jesuit missionaries who used their knowledge of Latin and Manchu to act as interpreters, they negotiated a treaty that, in its long-term effects, was one of the most important in China's history, fixing the northern border in substantially the same place it is today. In the most disputed area, the north-south demarcation line between the countries was fixed at the Gorbitsa and the Argun rivers. Albazin was to be abandoned by the Russians and destroyed, and the whole watershed area of the Amur River was to be part of the Qing domain.

Much of the impetus for the Qing to sign a treaty with Russia had come from the danger posed by the Zunghar confederation of Western Mongols in the northwest: the Qing feared that the Russians might ally themselves

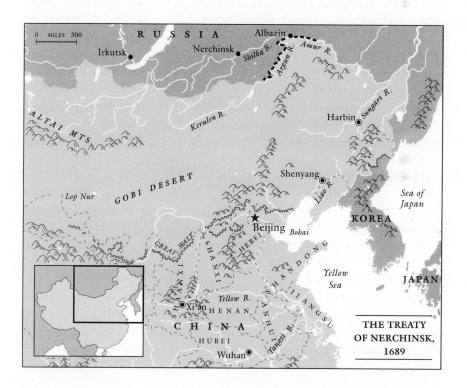

THE TREATY
OF NERCHINSK,
1689

with these dangerous nomadic warriors. Under a brilliant leader, Galdan, and drawing added unity from their deep devotion to the Dalai Lama in Tibet (whom they regarded as their spiritual leader), the Zunghars expanded across the regions now known as Outer Mongolia and Qinghai. In the late 1670s, Galdan emerged triumphant from fratricidal conflicts and moved farther west, seizing the rich oasis towns of Kashgar, Hami, and Turfan in turn, and gaining control over the prosperous caravan routes linking Central Asia and the Mediterranean. The tribes hostile to Galdan and defeated by him in battle fled eastward, pressing into the Qing province of Gansu as they plundered for food, stole horses, and killed. The disturbances posed by this massive migration of warriors deeply worried the emperor, who feared the possibility of a Russian-Zunghar alliance.

But such an alliance was not made, and after the Treaty of Nerchinsk was signed Kangxi sent an army (under his own brother) to attack Galdan. After several more years of inconclusive fighting between Galdan and rival tribes to his east, Kangxi decided to lead a major campaign in person, apparently prompted to such daring by his feeling that it was he—not his generals—who had correctly conceived the successful Russian war. In a massive deployment, some 80,000 men advanced westward on three fronts; Kangxi's army crossed the Gobi and pushed the Zunghars north of the Kerulen River, where Galdan was cornered and defeated in 1696. He died the following year, abandoned by most of his followers.

This successful campaign marked the pinnacle of Kangxi's career as emperor. Now forty-two years old, he took delight in the excitement and danger of the war; after it was over he wrote back to his court favorites in Beijing that the sparkling weather, the new foods, the unexpected scenery—all filled him with joy. "Now Galdan is dead, and his followers have come back to our allegiance," the emperor wrote in a letter in the spring of 1697. "My great task is done. . . . Heaven, earth, and ancestors have protected me and brought me this achievement. As for my own life, one can say it is happy. One can say it's fulfilled. One can say I've got what I wanted. In a few days, in the palace, I'll tell you all about it myself. It's hard to tell it with brush and ink."[7]

But the power politics of the region were not resolved by Galdan's death, and Kangxi found himself drawn into complex struggles with other Zunghar leaders when the Dalai Lama was murdered and an improperly chosen successor was named in his place. This gave Kangxi the opportunity to invade Tibet in the name of righteous retribution (just as the Manchus had entered China in 1644); he dispatched two armies, one of which entered Tibet through Koko Nor, the other through Sichuan province. In the autumn of 1720, the two armies joined forces in the Tibetan capital of Lhasa, and a new

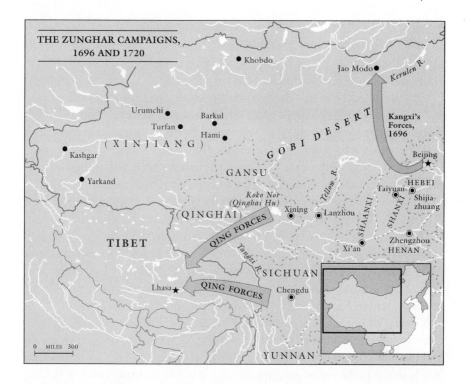

THE ZUNGHAR CAMPAIGNS, 1696 AND 1720

Dalai Lama, loyal to the Qing, was installed. Thus began the Chinese military intervention in the politics of Tibet.

At about the same time, the unsettled nature of life in Taiwan and misgovernment there by the Qing prompted a Fujian native named Zhu Yigui, who had traveled to the island as an official's servant, to raise a flag of revolt along with some fifty blood brothers. Aided by the turbulent conditions of the time and by the fact that he had the same surname as the former Ming imperial family, Zhu Yigui attracted hundreds of followers and seized the prefectural capital, declaring himself king of Taiwan. His reign lasted only two months, until he was apprehended by an expeditionary force led by a son of the Admiral Shi Lang, who had first captured the island thirty-eight years before.

The Qing had shown that they could respond with alacrity and efficiency to two crises on distant fronts, even if they had not solved some of the basic problems that made trouble endemic. When Kangxi died, in 1722, the Tibetan and Taiwan campaigns extended Qing power to the southwest and east. With the Treaty of Nerchinsk holding firm and Manchuria securely engrafted as their ancestral homeland, the Qing empire had reached a depth and extent of territorial conquest unmatched in China's previous dynastic history.

A MIXED LEGACY

Kangxi owed much of his fame to the firmness and vigor of his foreign policy. Priding himself on his decisiveness, he often overruled his senior advisers, both Manchu and Chinese, and when he was successful, he claimed the credit. In several important ways, however, the results were less happy, and he left a tangled legacy to his successors. This was especially true in three areas: the dispute surrounding Yinreng, the heir apparent to the throne; relations with the Catholic missionaries; and rural administration.

From early in his reign, Kangxi clearly wanted to avoid a repetition of the regency interlude that had led to the domination of the court by Dorgon in the 1640s and by Oboi in the 1660s. Accordingly, when his first empress gave birth to a son, Yinreng, in 1674, Kangxi moved rapidly to name the boy heir apparent. Since Yinreng's mother died in childbirth, his birth had an aura of fate around it and set Yinreng even further apart from his many half brothers, whom Kangxi fathered with other consorts or concubines.

Yinreng's upbringing was designed to combine the precepts of moralistic Confucian education with Manchu virtues. Venerable tutors were chosen, and the heir's progress was watched with close attention. He was introduced slowly to the problems of governance, and was left as acting ruler in Beijing while Kangxi was away on the long campaigns against Galdan in 1696–1697. Kangxi even announced his intention of abdicating early so that Yinreng could take over the kingdom as emperor.

But on his return from the west, Kangxi began to hear disquieting rumors about his son's behavior: Yinreng showed signs of being erratic, violent, and cruel. When the emperor took his various sons with him on imperial tours—to the west, to Manchuria, or to the once again prosperous towns on the Grand Canal and on the Yangzi River—Yinreng again began to disturb others with his willful behavior.

One difficulty Kangxi faced was getting accurate information about the situation. Not surprisingly, factions began to develop at court around either Yinreng or one of the seven other sons who were old enough and shrewd enough to be possible rival candidates for the throne. In these conditions, few courtiers and officials were willing to speak frankly. To cut through the haze of rumor, Kangxi began to use a new communications system.

Information for the emperor from his officials came, most commonly, in the form of "memorials." These were carefully written documents that were carried to the court by government couriers and processed in the Grand Secretariat, where they were copied and evaluated before being passed on to the emperor with suggestions as to the responses he might suitably make. But

The Kangxi Emperor's Southern Inspection Tour (detail) by Wang Hui and assistants, c. 1698
Dignitaries of the city of Tai'an gather around an altar, awaiting the arrival of the emperor.

this was a relatively public system, and Kangxi, in the 1690s, had begun to develop a secret system of "palace memorials," which would be delivered to the palace by the writers' own couriers, brought sealed to the emperor, and read, annotated, and sealed by him in private. The route was then reversed, the writers' couriers carrying the memorial, which now bore the emperor's rescript in vermilion ink, back to the original writer.

Kangxi had first used this system in an informal way, telling certain trusted bondservants stationed in the provinces to send him lists of current grain prices, so that he could check the accuracy of his senior officials' reports. Early in the eighteenth century Kangxi began to expand the system; by 1707, a handful of trusted advisers were using palace memorials to tell the emperor secretly the details of Yinreng's conduct. They reported how Yinreng preened himself on his future role as emperor, how he tyrannized his subordinates, and how he ordered his agents to buy both boys and girls in the south and to bring them to his palace for his sexual pleasure. Though it took Kangxi a long time to act, by 1708 so much negative evidence had piled up that he could delay no longer.

Enraged, Kangxi ordered Yinreng disbarred forever from his heir-apparent status and placed under house arrest, to be guarded by Kangxi's fourth son, Yinzhen. Several of Yinreng's close friends, as well as senior courtiers involved in his misdeeds, were executed.

What followed was an anguished circle of indecision, guilt, and recrimination on the emperor's part. Believing that Yinreng could not be guilty as charged and instead had been bewitched, Kangxi released him in 1709. But in 1712 fresh evidence—including the spread of the news that Yinreng had been planning to assassinate the emperor—led Kangxi to order his son's rearrest. Thereafter, for the remaining ten years of his reign, Kangxi refused to name another heir and punished any officials who urged him to do so. The court was awash with rumors, factions grew around Kangxi's other sons, and the future of the Qing dynasty was clouded with uncertainty.

The problems with the Catholic missionaries also involved questions of imperial power and prerogative. Ever since he overthrew the Oboi regency, Kangxi had favored the Jesuits in court: he placed them once again in charge of the astronomy bureau, used them as advisers in matters of cartography and engineering, and allowed them opportunities to practice their religion in Beijing and the provinces. The emperor was drawn to the ideas of missionary-science, and surviving sources show how Kangxi performed his scientific mastery with vivid examples for both his courtiers and the missionaries.[8] Especially for a decade after 1692, when the emperor issued an edict granting toleration to the Christian religion, the Jesuits began to hope that they had a real chance for mass conversion. Kangxi insisted, however, that the Jesuits agree to abide by his stipulation that the Chinese rites of ancestor worship and public homage to Confucius were civil rather than religious ceremonies and, thus, could continue to be practiced by Christian converts. Since this requirement concurred with the position taken by the famous Jesuit missionary Matteo Ricci in the late Ming dynasty, a majority of the Jesuits in China found nothing controversial in it.

However, many other Catholic clergy and missionaries from different religious orders, both in East Asia and in Rome, disagreed profoundly. They believed that Kangxi was essentially claiming paramountcy in matters of church doctrine and that the Jesuits were fatally weakening the integrity of the Christian faith. To investigate, Pope Clement XI dispatched a trusted emissary, Maillard de Tournon, to Beijing. In a series of meetings between legate and emperor held during 1705 and 1706, it became clear how strongly the two men disagreed. When de Tournon forbade Catholic missionaries to follow Kangxi's orders, under pain of excommunication, the emperor responded with an order of expulsion against those who refused to sign a certificate accepting Kangxi's position. Though most Jesuits in China signed, more than a dozen Franciscan, Dominican, and other missionaries refused to do so and were duly expelled. This mutual hard line gravely undermined the position of the missions and severed a key channel that brought knowledge of Western science to China.

In the crucial realm of taxation and rural administration, finally, Kangxi failed to make constructive changes. One lone exception seems to have been Kangxi's decision to make significant grants of money to selected banner organizations. Banner officials were expected to invest this money, through merchant bureaus, in pawnshops or urban trading and long-range commerce; after returning the principal to the emperor, any profit could be used by banner families for their own weddings or other festivals. This practice, termed "procuring profits through entrepreneurial operation," was encouraged from the year 1703 onward and undoubtedly helped many military families.[9] But such innovation was rare, and in general the emperor seems to have accepted the position that no comprehensive new survey of landholdings was possible under existing social circumstances; he also perpetuated the late Ming system in which the taxes formerly paid in kind and through labor services were commuted to silver. But only a small amount of this money stayed in the counties to pay for the salaries of magistrates and their staffs, and for relief and construction. Local officials sought to supplement their resources with a wide range of extra surcharges, much of which they pocketed for themselves, gave to their superiors as gifts, or sent as presents to Beijing to make sure that the relevant ministries did not investigate their conduct too closely. This laxness coincided with a prolonged period of economic depression in which both land and crop prices dropped sharply. Contemporary Chinese agonized over the deflation and stagnation that made Shunzhi's reign appear, in retrospect, as an economic golden age.[10]

As a consequence, despite Kangxi's dramatic successes in political consolidation and territorial conquest, life in the rural areas remained a grim struggle for millions of people. Gangs of bandits could roam freely in many parts, since there was no paid and armed militia to oppose them. Corrupt junior staff from the magistrates' offices could bully farming families into paying a variety of taxes, for which receipts were never issued. Legal battles over land contracts dragged on for decades, and there was little recourse for minors or widows when harassed by the men of their clans. Private feuds led to violence and homicides that harried officials had neither the time nor the staff to investigate.

Perhaps because he recalled the strong support that Koxinga had received from the local Chinese in his 1659 campaign or because the area was regarded as the heartland of Confucian culture, Kangxi was particularly lax about prosecuting tax delinquents in the rich provinces of Jiangsu and Zhejiang. To preserve an appearance of harmony, he urged leniency in delinquency cases and gave generous tax rebates to areas that were not suffering serious hardship. Although he did continue to enforce the "law of avoidance," which stipulated that senior officials could never serve in their home provinces (so as to prevent their abusing their positions while in office), he often ignored confidential reports that pointed to flagrant abuses by the family members of his favored officials, or by those who had retired home after years of service in the capital.

Paradoxically, in the last decade of his reign, Kangxi seems to have genuinely believed that the restoration of rural prosperity was complete, and that the bureaucracy could handle its responsibilities with the resources at hand. The court itself appeared comfortably solvent, since along with the land-tax revenues it received considerable income from monopoly control over salt, ginseng, and jade, from allegedly "voluntary" payments by wealthy merchants, and from transit dues on commerce. Since Kangxi also believed that the country's prosperity was measured by the size of its population, and that the true size of that population was being hidden by local officials who feared that if they reported rising numbers the Ministry of Revenue would raise their tax payments, he decided to take dramatic action. In 1712 he froze the assessments of able-bodied men registered as working a given area of agricultural land and decreed that no matter how much the population increased, the state would not thereby raise that area's taxes. Local officials could thus report population increases accurately, without fearing the burden of a raised assessment at a future date.

Since Kangxi—like Shunzhi before him—had given up on attempting a national survey of landholdings, the land-tax system was now doubly frozen: land in the provinces remained registered according to the last reasonably full survey, made in 1581 during the Ming emperor Wanli's reign, and the numbers of per capita units subject to tax assessment were henceforth based on the 1712 figures. This would seriously impede attempts by Kangxi's successors to rationalize national finances. Although higher population estimates did begin to flow into Beijing, gratifying the emperor with a sense of his empire's prosperity, the underlying fiscal inefficiencies had not been eliminated.

"Now that I am ill I am querulous and forgetful," Kangxi told his courtiers and officials in a self-revelatory edict of 1717, "and terrified of muddling right with wrong, and leaving my work in chaos. I exhaust my mind for the country's sake, and fragment my spirits for the world."[11] Kangxi lived on for another five years after these melancholy words, the longest rule in the history of China up to that time, but longevity brought him diminishing solace. He had still not publicly named an heir when he died in December 1722, of natural causes. It is hard, in retrospect, to gauge the level of despair that had led him to neglect such a fundamental obligation.

| # Yongzheng's Authority

ECONOMIC STRUCTURES

The brief reign of Emperor Yongzheng, successor to Kangxi, was stormy, complicated, and important. It was clouded in controversy from the first, when Yongzheng himself announced that he was the dying emperor's choice as heir. Since his other brothers and half brothers were not present at the scene, and since Yongzheng's close friend was commander of the Beijing guards, there was no one to dispute his claim publicly. But throughout his reign (1723–1735), he was troubled by charges that he was a usurper.

There is little evidence that he had usurped the throne, however, and some evidence to show that Kangxi had trusted Yongzheng more than he had most of his other sons. Kangxi and Yongzheng (then known by his family name of Yinzhen) frequently discussed policy matters together and shared mutual entertainments. As we've seen, for a time Yongzheng served as the jailer of his elder half brother, the deposed heir apparent—a delicate and dangerous task.

Once installed as emperor, Yongzheng expended considerable effort cementing his position by arresting the brothers whom he believed most resented his rule. (He had quieted their suspicions by promoting them first!) The former heir apparent, Yinreng, and two other brothers died in prison shortly after their arrests (whether they were killed or died from mistreatment is not known). Several others were put under house arrest or close surveillance. Yongzheng completely trusted only Kangxi's thirteenth son, Yinxiang, whom he promoted to the highest positions.

Whether one interprets these actions as evidence of a guilty conscience or as practical steps taken to prevent later trouble, Yongzheng proved deeply committed to the craft of government. He had a passion for detail and a willingness to spend long hours every day at work, usually reading history texts from

4:00 A.M. until 7:00 A.M., when he breakfasted, meeting with his advisers into the early afternoon, then reading documents and commenting on them, often until midnight. He took neither lengthy hunting excursions to the north nor leisurely tours of the Yangzi delta cities, as his father had loved to do. His main recreation seems to have been the practice of Buddhism, of which he was a devoted and scholarly adherent, and relaxing in the scenic garden of his palace in northwest Beijing. Whereas his father had often written in Manchu, and had written Chinese slowly and carefully, Yongzheng seems to have preferred Chinese. His calligraphy, clearly written with great speed, was accurate and idiomatic.

But this apparent routinization of imperial life should not blind us to the fact that Yongzheng's China was still far from being a fully integrated or homogenous country. In the vast expanses of the Qing empire there were endless variations in such areas as pace of economic change, types of lineage organization, efficiency of transportation, religious practices, sophistication of commerce, and patterns of land use and landholding. A complete history would ideally include information on all these variables on a district-by-district basis, so that precise patterns of change could be charted and connected with political decisions made at the center.

Daunting though this task is, various studies have shown that it is feasible. In particular, by analyzing late imperial China in terms of units of economic integration rather than through political divisions, we gain a different perspective on the society based on data that was not available to the rulers and bureaucrats of the time. Scholars employing this approach have identified nine "macroregions" (as they term them), each embracing parts of several provinces. Each macroregion had a "core" defined by heightened economic activity in major cities, high population density, and comparatively sophisticated transportation networks. And each core was surrounded by a "periphery" of less populated and developed areas, which also provided a loosely policed area where illegal sects or bandit elements could develop in comparative freedom.[1]

Of these nine macroregions, one was in the northeast, in the area coterminous with southern Manchuria, the Qing's preconquest homeland. Two were in the north, in the Xi'an region of Shaanxi and the Beijing–western Shandong area. Three extended at different points along the Yangzi River— one on the east coast around Nanjing, one halfway upriver around Hankou, and one deeper up the river in Sichuan. A seventh was on the lower east coast in the Fujian region. An eighth was in the far southeast, centered around Guangzhou. The last was in the southwest, in the provinces of Yunnan and Guizhou. Without launching a detailed exploration of all nine macroregions,

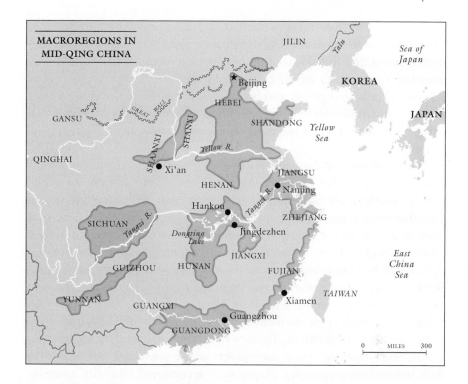

MACROREGIONS IN
MID-QING CHINA

we can take a brief look at three of them to determine what kinds of factors were affecting their patterns of social and economic development in the eighteenth century.

First, the northern macroregion—centered around Beijing and western Shandong, and extending into Henan and northern Jiangsu—was, despite the presence of the capital, less urban than most other macroregions. Flooding was common, brought on by the silt-filled Yellow River, but flood-relief measures and emergency grain distribution in times of famine were more effective than in regions farther from the capital. Cotton was becoming a valuable cash crop of this macroregion as both spinning and weaving techniques grew more efficient. Tobacco cultivation was spreading, too, along with glassmaking, coal mining, and brewing. Shifting social conditions, the presence of the many laborers and boatmen who serviced the grain barges on the Grand Canal, overworked soil, and fragmented landholdings all contributed to make this an area where crime and local violence were common.

By contrast, the middle Yangzi macroregion, with comparatively low population density and untilled land, was at this time experiencing a massive in-migration from other regions. The area developed a population of "sojourners" with divided loyalties to their new base and their old ancestral homes, and of disaffected local minorities pushed off their former lands. The booming Yangzi River city of Hankou, a commercial center with complex systems of banks and guilds, was becoming the focus for interregional long-distance grain trade. To the southeast, Jingdezhen expanded as an industrial city, making porcelain for the export markets of the West as well as for the Chinese elite.

A different series of factors dominated our third example, the lower-east-coast macroregion that centered around Fujian province and incorporated parts of southern Zhejiang and eastern Guangdong. The coastal location gave this macroregion's merchants a host of profitable trade contacts with Taiwan and Southeast Asia, which brought a certain cosmopolitanism and a highly developed system of credit and banking, particularly to the port of Xiamen. Further prosperity came from the rich tea farms of the region. But for a mixture of historical and geographical reasons, this macroregion was also riven by fierce local conflicts. Powerful lineages controlled whole villages, and feuds between them were deadly and frequent. Many richer homes were heavily fortified. Tenancy rates were high, and there were violent tensions involving recent immigrants or the poorer inland farmers on their terraced mountainsides. Strong local accents and mutually unintelligible dialects made contact with outsiders difficult. The region's elite were sliding in the scale of national prestige, as the area produced fewer and fewer holders of the coveted highest examination degree, the *jinshi*. The Qing government identified the region as a potential trouble spot and kept it heavily garrisoned with both Eight Banner forces and local troops known as the Green Standard armies.

Since each of the macroregions had its own internal economic logic, there was always danger that differences with other macroregions might escalate into conflict. If the state proved unable to mediate or control these conflicts, the result might be either fragmentation or civil war. Something close to this had occurred between the 1630s and 1680s, when Li Zicheng's rebels, Ming loyalists, Koxinga's forces, and the Three Feudatories had each found temporary bases in different macroregional cores. The task of the state, therefore, was to bond the macroregions together by ideological and administrative means—backed if necessary by military force. This task would be eased if trade links also developed, as began to happen in the eighteenth century.

Another factor complicating the mid-Qing society and economy was a rapidly growing population. In the mid-Ming (circa 1400) the total population was approximately 65 million; by the late Ming (1630) it had reached a high of 192 million. By the end of the eighteenth century, it had well surpassed the 300 million mark. The growth in population was not steady, for the Ming-Qing transition period of the early seventeenth century had witnessed a catastrophic drop of an estimated 40 million, brought on by invasion, civil war, natural disasters, famine, and epidemics. Considering this massive loss, the population growth that followed is all the more dramatic. The following table shows the fluctuations in population across the country as a whole, from the late Ming to the mid-Qing.

The population growth of the early to mid-Qing period had major social and political implications. During Kangxi's rule, there was a resettlement of the devastated areas of north China and of the war-ravaged parts of once-prosperous Sichuan. Thereafter, new lands were opened up, with settlers venturing into the southwest and the uplands of the Yangzi and Han river drainage areas, or defying government prohibitions to move into southern Manchuria. But while the population nearly tripled from 1680 to 1850, the acreage of arable land only doubled; the size of individual holdings therefore shrank. Moreover, since customary inheritance practice divided the land equally among the sons under the system known as "partible inheritance," new, large landowning families tended not to emerge. Family holdings in the north China–Beijing macroregion, for which we have good figures in the eighteenth century, were only around 2.5 acres on average; a family holding of over 20 acres was rare, and a quarter or more of the rural households were landless.

The families moving onto upland areas along the Yangzi and Han rivers, or into the forests of southern Manchuria, cleared these areas for agriculture without understanding the ecological effects of their actions. Although yields on virgin lands were high, intensive agriculture brought on soil erosion and deforestation. Hillside runoffs into the rivers caused corresponding silting problems and the danger of serious flooding in settled farming areas downstream. Furthermore, with human wastes constituting much of the fertilizer source, exhausted soil in isolated upland areas could not be replenished easily (as, for instance, farms near urban areas could be) and often had to be abandoned.

Population Figures[2]

1630	192,510,000	
1644	152,470,000	−20.1%
1680	150,000,000	−.02%
1776	311,000,000	+107%
1820	383,100,000	+23.2%
1851	436,090,000	+13.8%

Anonymous, the Yongzheng emperor offering sacrifices at the altar of agriculture
This detail of a handscroll shows the Yongzheng emperor performing the springtime sacrifices in Beijing during the ritual start of the growing season.

Much of the country's population growth in the eighteenth century was speeded up by a major ecological change: the introduction of food crops from the Americas. Sweet potatoes, for example, were widespread in coastal China by the mid-eighteenth century, while maize and the Irish potato became common in the north and in the southwest in the same period. Peanuts had spread rapidly in the south and southwest in the late Ming, and were also becoming an important crop in the north. All these crops helped to boost the caloric intake of rural communities. Because the crops also grew well in poor, hilly, or sandy soil, they enabled the population to rise rapidly in areas of otherwise marginal productivity.

Surviving documents from one village of Chinese banner households in southern Manchuria provide a closer look at local population figures and age profiles, and suggest some of the rhythms of family life at the end of the century. In Daoyi village, one-third of the male youth died in their first year of life, and half before they were twenty. The average life expectancy for the men of the village was around thirty-two years, and some 4 percent lived past sixty-five. The age span for women was comparable. The data also indicate that women in their later twenties were the most likely to have children, with the median age of childbirth between 25 and 29. This suggests that some women postponed having children during the early years of maximum female fertility, likely due to scarce food supplies. The subsequent spacing of all childbirths, and the high ratio of recorded male to female births, provides evidence of family planning. Because of childhood illnesses, a less-than-adequate diet, even infanticide in time of famine—and because wealthy men tended to keep several female consorts—there were many fewer marriageable women than men in Daoyi, as in many other areas of China. The effects of this are telling: although almost every woman in Daoyi over thirty was married or widowed, 20 percent of the adult men never married at all.[3] Such single men were typically impoverished and lacked resources to marry. They were not firmly anchored in the social order, and as their numbers swelled with the overall population growth, their discontent would become a factor fueling the rebellions of the nineteenth century.

THE QUESTION OF TAXES

During his brief twelve-year reign Emperor Yongzheng concentrated on a number of key problems in government that were crucial in his own day and have remained so to the present. These included the structure of the bureaucracy and finance in the countryside, the development of an effective and confidential information system, and the strengthening of the central executive branch of the state. These three were (and are) tightly interconnected; success in managing them would go far to ensure more efficient control of China's enormous territory.

From the beginning of his reign, Yongzheng had a clear vision of how to proceed. He was not a child under the supervision of regents when he ascended the throne, as his father and grandfather had been, but an experienced man of forty-five who had watched his father's reign begin to fall apart. The system of secret palace memorials was made to measure for him, and he extended the informal structure that Kangxi had initiated. Apart from routine matters, which were reported, as in the past, in open memorials to the ministries and to the Grand Secretariat, most senior provincial officials now reported confidentially to Yongzheng on the details of their administration and on each other. As the emperor began to realize the size of the tax deficits and the casualness with which the fiscal crisis had been treated in his father's reign, he urged his officials to suggest means of reforming the financial structure, and established a small executive office of financial review to stand separate from and above the Ministry of Revenue. In charge of this office he placed his trusted younger brother Yinxiang.

The financial crisis was too complicated for even an absolute ruler to solve with an edict or two. The central budget in 1723 was about 35 million taels (ounces of silver), of which about 6 million came from commercial taxes of various kinds and 29 million from the "land and head tax" (*diding*). Anywhere from 15 to 30 percent of this 29 million was retained in each province for "local use," while the rest was sent to Beijing; but nearly all of the "local use" percentage was spent on projects that were really national ones, such as military supplies and imperial post stations. Less than one-sixth of the total was available to officials for administration in their own areas. One might have thought it simple to increase income by raising the number of land-tax and head-tax units, but here the obligations of filiality to Emperor Kangxi were too strong, and Yongzheng did not attempt to change his father's 1712 ruling. Moreover, an important premise of Chinese political theory, which the Manchus had also made their own, was that a low tax base was essential to the well-being of the country and the proof of an emperor's benevolence. Qing officials were also convinced that tax increases had been a major cause of the Ming collapse: excessive taxation pushed the rural population below subsistence levels and sparked the popular rebellions that contributed to the dynasty's demise. Wary of repeating the same mistake, Qing political elites opposed increasing rural taxation, which they feared would produce similar unrest.[4]

As a result, the Qing agricultural tax was frozen on the basis of late Ming land and household registries, which were not updated even as the population grew. To cope with chronic funding shortages, local officials invented numerous surcharges and manipulated copper-cash to silver conversion rates. The fees generated were illegal, but the revenue was needed to pay the magistrate's staff and to subsidize local administrative functions, including infrastructure repairs and public security.

Such a system, lacking regulation and transparency, was an invitation for corruption and abuse. Members of the upper class were often wealthy landowners, and, as in Kangxi's time, many of them concealed their tax responsibilities in a maze of false names, misregistrations, transferred holdings, mortgages, and so on, which made it almost impossible to trace their exact holdings. Furthermore, much of the economic power in the countryside was in the hands of small landholders who tyrannized the local villagers. These landholders colluded with the clerks in the magistrates' offices in order to evade paying their own taxes, which forced the poorer farmers to assume a disproportionate amount of the burden for the whole community. In such situations, the farmers had little redress, and money that had been embezzled was counted as being in "arrears"—that is, owed by delinquent farmers.

Between 1725 and 1729, Yongzheng modified his father's approach and made a concerted effort to reform the agricultural taxation system and to break the power of the local intermediate groups. He was determined to extend the power of the Qing state more effectively into the countryside. As he expressed in an edict of 1725, "When the flesh and blood of the common people is used to rectify the deficits of the officials, how can there not be hardship in the countryside? I am deeply concerned about these abuses."[5]

He began by accumulating accurate information through palace memorials and by appointing new men—often Manchus or Chinese bannermen who would be less influenced by the local elites—to the key offices of provincial governor and financial commissioner. Yongzheng then moved to establish an official consensus that a fixed rate of surcharge should be levied on the basic land-tax (*di*) and head-tax (*ding*) quotas, that all of this surcharge should be passed on to the provincial financial commissioners' offices, and that all other supplementary fees and gifts should be declared illegal. The tax money gathered by the financial commissioners' offices would then be reallocated within the province on an equitable basis. Part would be used to give far higher salaries to the local officials than they had ever received before (this was called "money to nourish honesty"), and part would go into county funds for the support of irrigation works, road and school building, and other needs such as the provision of draft animals for disaster victims, jail improvement, city sewers, charity graveyards, examination cubicles, or candles and incense for temples.

In assessing the effects of these reforms, one can get a brief overview of the country's regional variations at this time. The reforms were most successful in the northern macroregions comprising the provinces of Shanxi, Henan, and Hebei, where independent landholding farmers were common, land registration was comparatively easy, and magistrates could be closely supervised and forced to give up their perquisites. Virtually everyone in this region benefited from the reforms except for the corrupt middlemen landlords, clerks, and magistrates. The flat surcharge of 15 to 20 percent on the basic land tax proved much less burdensome to the farmers and even to the larger landholders than the endless rounds of fees that had prevailed. And the new salaries gave the officials a more regular and higher-level income than they had previously enjoyed: 600 to 1,000 taels a year in the case of county magistrates, as opposed to 45 taels before the reforms. Offices were now better-run, business was conducted faster, and there was real local autonomy and initiative for dealing with specific projects.

In the south and southwest macroregions, however, the reforms went much less smoothly. Here the basic tax-quota figures were far lower because there were many recently settled, sparsely populated areas. But since the number of officials was still high, the surcharges did not bring in enough money to pay the same high levels of salary as in the north. The system could be made to work only by granting the local officials some of the tax revenues from such commercial enterprises as mining, salt production, and transit dues. Even so, because of the great distances and expense involved, many magistrates failed to forward all of the surcharge money to the financial commissioners of their provinces, pleading instead to be allowed to withdraw their new salaries and the local expense money *before* they forwarded the rest. Predictably this led to renewed graft and precluded the commissioners from making equitable distributions of revenues.

It was in the central Yangzi provinces, however—especially Jiangsu and Anhui, but also Zhejiang and Jiangxi—that the system ran into the most trouble. Here lived many retired but still powerful former officials and their relatives, whose lands had never been properly registered and who could intimidate the local magistrates through connections in the capital. Kangxi had been especially lenient to the wealthy elites in this area, and they were not about to submit meekly to tougher central control. Opposition to Yongzheng's reform was so obvious and so concentrated that the emperor finally appointed a special Manchu commissioner, backed by a staff of seventy experienced auditors, to push through a thorough examination of the provinces' finances and to make a complete and accurate registration of land.

The malfeasance they found was incredible, and the examples of false and overlapping registrations so complex that they despaired of ever unraveling them. In some cases, the auditors found, landowners had divided their holdings under hundreds of false names, confident that in each of these tiny units the tax liability was so low that no magistrate or clerk would take the time to chase up arrears. The auditors' attempts at on-the-spot examination were met by delays, hostility, blocked roads, cut bridges, even riots and physical assault. Those imprisoned for questioning were rescued by jail-storming crowds. Coded logbooks confiscated by the auditors showed how, generation after generation, local clerks had exempted wealthy families from nearly all their tax obligations in return for payoffs. Yet even with this evidence, the auditors still found it hard to pin down the guilty parties and even harder to collect more than a small percentage of the 10 million taels they estimated was owed to the government.

The very tenacity of this opposition showed that the attempted reforms were a step in the right direction, for the reforms suggested that with persistence, the efforts of honest officials, and the emperor's encouragement, the Qing state could reach a new level of bureaucratic efficiency. In particular, if the center could control and garner the rich resources of the most prosperous provinces, that would surely benefit and strengthen the country as a whole.

THE CENTER AND CHANNELS OF POWER

Rulers are rarely free to concentrate on one problem at a time, and Yong-zheng was never able to give his full attention to the problems of rural taxation and administration in the central provinces. It became necessary again to reinforce Qing power on the borders. Zhu Yigui's rebellion in Taiwan had been swiftly suppressed in 1721, but effective pacification was complex. After lengthy consultations, Yongzheng decided to strengthen local control there by subdividing several of Taiwan's counties into smaller units and adding reinforcements to the military garrisons. Restrictions on Han Chinese migration to the island were temporarily eased by allowing wives and children to join the men, so as to foster a more settled social environment. The Han Chinese were now permitted to rent land on contract from the Indigenous groups, and they increasingly encroached on native land rights.

There was need as well for careful new negotiations with Russia to prevent the Treaty of Nerchinsk from falling apart over arguments concerning the border tribes, trade caravans, and clashes sparked by the discovery of gold in southern Siberia. A senior negotiating team, consisting entirely of Manchus, drew up a supplementary treaty, signed at Kiakhta in 1727. The Treaty of Kiakhta drew a line between the two countries from Kiakhta to the Argun, and stated which tribes should be based in Qing territory. Kiakhta was to be one of two new border trading towns, one Russian caravan was to be allowed to trade in Beijing every three years, and a Russian Orthodox church was to be maintained there. Most members of the small Russian community in the capital had been captured in earlier wars and were now incorporated in the banners. (The treaty specifically stipulated that they were to be encouraged to learn the Chinese language.) Yongzheng also consolidated his hold over the last of the Manchu banners still controlled by Manchu princes and noblemen, and began to take serious note of problems in Tibet and among the Miao tribes in the southwest.

Yongzheng saw the renewed Zunghar threat as the most serious one in the long term, despite their defeat by Kangxi's forces in 1696. He was convinced that the Zunghars could be suppressed only if he prepared a major military buildup in the far west. But the supply lines were immensely long, and it was hard to keep the preparations secret. The court was full of ears, and the emperor's main policy discussion group—the Deliberative Council of

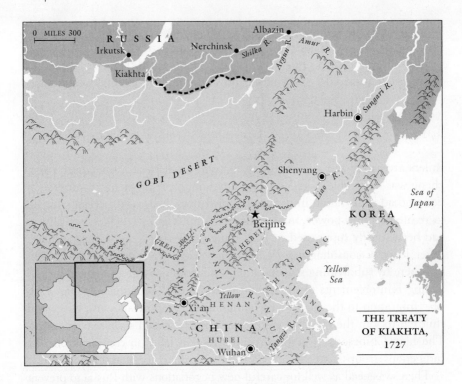

THE TREATY
OF KIAKHTA,
1727

Princes and High Officials—proved unable to keep its proceedings confidential. Beijing was also full of Mongol princes and princesses, banner generals, traveling merchants, and Tibetan Buddhist lamas, any of whom might spread news of Qing intentions. So Yongzheng initially kept much of his military planning private by limiting discussions to a small group of his most trusted grand secretaries, whom he came to call the "inner grand secretaries." (The title distinguished them from those who worked in the "outer" court with the regular bureaucracy.)

The three key members of this group were his trusted younger brother Yinxiang (who was also running the revenue-auditing bureau) and two Chinese grand secretaries, Zhang Tingyu and Jiang Tingxi. Zhang, son of one of Kangxi's most trusted advisers, was fluent in Manchu and had served as minister of revenue; Jiang had also been in charge of that ministry and was a nationally prominent painter as well. Both men also held the senior (*jinshi*) examination degree and had served in the prestigious imperial Hanlin Academy on the basis of their scholarly excellence. They may be seen, therefore, as representing the most talented upper levels of the traditional Chinese bureaucracy who now, more than eighty years after the conquest, were firmly loyal to their Manchu emperor. By 1729 the three men were overseeing a secret new bureau, the Office of Military Finance, aided by a small group of experienced middle-echelon officials, both Manchu and Chinese, and were trusted to be discreet. Not even all the other grand secretaries knew the details of their work, and only in the reign of Yongzheng's son, Qianlong, was this office to gain public notice and prominence as the Grand Council.[6]

So once again, as he had in the matter of finance, Yongzheng created an informal yet efficient network to enhance his own power and to deflect certain information and decisions away from the regular six ministries and their staffs. Why the secretive departure from conventional channels? Part of the answer is probably that Yongzheng and his advisers feared there would be questionable financial dealings in the complicated and expensive logistical preparations for the western campaigns, and wanted to keep their inquiries concealed from the formal ministries. It is also likely that they wanted to keep the scale of their operations secret. Hence we find the Office of Military Finance keeping the most detailed accounts on such items as the number of mules or camels and carts needed to transport the supplies for a given number of troops.

Another reason for these new arrangements was that the inner grand secretaries frequently needed to deliberate over secret palace memorials. In some cases these had to be filed; the emperor, after all, could not keep all these details in his head, and the only safe place to file them was in a specially staffed office under tight security. Yongzheng could also communicate with his generals at the front through so-called court letters drafted for him by the inner grand secretaries, and dispatched swiftly and secretly to the recipient. This saved time for the emperor, who was already responding to fifty to a hundred palace memorials a day, often at great length. With court letters drafted for him in secrecy, the emperor could now take the time to add personal notes to show his frontier generals how he trusted them. "How are you after riding your horse through wind and snow?" the emperor wrote to General Yue Zhongqi, stationed in the far western provinces. "Are the officers, troops and animals in good condition?" Or, again to Yue, "I have made a selection of auspicious days for you to start on your journey from Xi'an to the front, and am sending it to you."[7]

Finally the new measures were prompted by considerations of state security as they related to the safety of the emperor from his own forces. The emperor was well aware of the need to have the firm support of the banner forces, and he greatly expanded the system of commercial investments, begun by his father, until by the late 1720s he had paid out more than 2 million taels to the various garrison commands in both Beijing and the provinces, as seed money for their maintenance.[8] Nevertheless, potential threats abounded. For instance, one of Yongzheng's least trusted brothers had been serving as a general in the Tibetan campaigns when Yongzheng ascended the throne. One of Yongzheng's closest friends, while serving as commanding general in Sichuan and Gansu, had also been implicated in the plots of Yongzheng's brothers and ordered to die by suicide in 1727. And the new commanding general in the region, Yue Zhongqi, though given the just-quoted marks of appreciation by the emperor, was a descendant of Yue Fei, the famous twelfth-century patriot who had been killed in prison by his own Song dynasty rulers. To avoid potential threats like these from his own military, Yongzheng would have had cause to tread cautiously.

The long-planned campaign against the Zunghars went badly. In 1732 General Yue Zhongqi, from his forward headquarters at Barkol, raided the enemy in Ürümchi but could not protect his own forces in Hami from counterattacks. Yue's fellow senior general rashly led his army of ten thousand troops into an ambush near Khobdo; although he escaped, he lost four-fifths of his men and most of his officers. Both generals were sentenced to death by Yongzheng for these failures and related charges of corruption, although he later commuted the death sentences. As a result of these failures, it would take another thirty years to settle the security problems in this region.

Yongzheng also employed some of his new communication channels to coordinate the fighting in the southwest against the Indigenous Miao peoples. Han Chinese settlers had been pressing into the provinces of Yunnan and Guizhou since the suppression of the Three Feudatories, pushing the local valley dwellers up into the hills and disrupting local society by opening silver and copper mines. In 1726 Yongzheng made Ortai governor-general of the entire region. An experienced administrator from a family in the blue banner, and fluent in Chinese as well as Manchu, Ortai kept constantly in touch with the emperor through his palace memorials. These traced his efforts to break the power of the local Miao chieftains, to confiscate their lands, and to have them reregistered and administered as part of the Qing prefectural system. Those who resisted were surrounded and killed by Qing armies; those who submitted still lost the rights to their land but were often reinstated as administrators with their own stipends.

In 1728, in a highly unusual move, Ortai was also named governor-general of Guangxi to speed the suppression of the local tribes there. Yongzheng's long comments on the palace memorials constantly spurred Ortai on, debated knotty problems, and discussed the performance of other officials in the area. In 1732 Ortai, having largely pacified the southwest, was recalled to Beijing to serve concurrently in the Office of Military Finance. He took the place of Prince Yinxiang and Jiang Tingxi, both of whom had

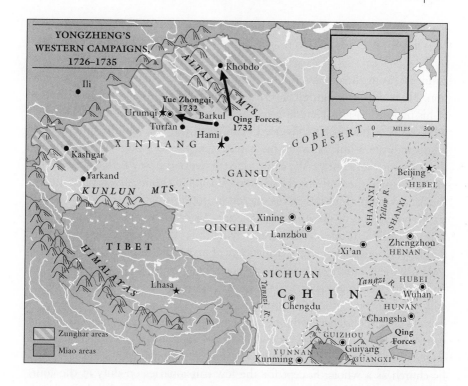

died while Ortai was in the southwest. Thus he and Zhang Tingyu became Yongzheng's most trusted advisers in the capital.

Surveying these developments in the supervision of finance, the communication system, and military affairs, we can see how the Qing empire was developing in terms of unity and autocracy. In the near century since the conquest, the power of great Manchu regents or noblemen had waned. Royal brothers could still be a danger to the emperor, but they could be manipulated or suppressed. The regular bureaucracy was considered useful in many ways but a hindrance in others, especially when speed and confidentiality were required. Yet Yongzheng did not take the route of simply forming an important new office, staffing it with his own men, and insisting on its monopoly over important decision making. Instead he chose a more roundabout way, establishing an undramatic-looking office with a nondescript title, and having those who worked in it hold other jobs at the same time; thus their salaries and official ranks derived from other, more conventional bureaucratic functions. Yongzheng was a remarkable tactician with a flair for—and a belief in—informal and secret structures. Dominance of those structures was, to him, the essence of power.

MORAL AUTHORITY

Emperor Yongzheng's interests took in more than matters of administration. He had a far-ranging concern for moral and cultural values, and many of his major decisions were affected by his moral convictions. He was a man who seems to have been convinced of his own rectitude, and his pronouncements indicate a link between his basic conception of power and his idea of the emperor's superiority. We can gauge this from the way he handled a wide range of issues: the Catholic church, the Lu Liuliang affair, his amplification of the Sacred Edict of his father, his interest in Buddhism, the problems of industrial laborers and of opium addiction, and his emancipation of the so-called "mean people." At one level, he was playing the role of Confucian monarch; at another, he bore the autocratic impatience of his conquering Manchu forebears.

With the Catholic missionaries, Yongzheng was even sterner than his father had been in the later years of his life. Not only was the rites controversy still splitting the Catholic community in China, but at least two Jesuits had been in correspondence with one of the brothers Yongzheng most distrusted, using the Roman alphabet as code. When Yongzheng discovered this, his anger spread to other scholars who knew the missionaries and to the Catholic church as a whole. Except for the few missionaries on duty at the court in Beijing, all the others living in various provinces were ordered to relocate to Guangzhou or Macao; several provincial churches were converted to use as schools or as hostels. Since Yongzheng had committed himself publicly against political in-groups by his often-repeated attacks on the whole idea of "factions," he spoke out angrily against the factional influence of the church. Still, he held back from a final ban. Only one missionary was executed in this period, but as a group they had to be extraordinarily circumspect in their behavior. Their influence waned to the point that their only remaining roles of significance at court were as directors of the astronomical bureau and as painters in the imperial studios.

The Lu Liuliang affair produced a similarly complex imperial reaction, involving both vengeance and compassion. Lu was a bitterly anti-Manchu scholar, medical doctor, and monk who had died in 1683, stipulating in his will that he not be buried in clothes of Manchu design. Some of his writings, containing sneering remarks about Manchus and other "barbarians," circulated in central China and were read by, among others, an impressionable young schoolteacher named Zeng Jing. Fired with anti-Manchu ardor by Lu's writings and believing the rumors that Yongzheng was a usurper, in 1728 Zeng tried to convince General Yue Zhongqi, who was in Sichuan preparing for the Zunghar campaign, to rebel. Yue responded by feigning sympathy until he had unraveled the details of the plot, and then informed Yongzheng of what he had learned.

Checking into the case, Yongzheng was enraged to discover Lu's writings, and how widely rumors of his usurpation had circulated. The imperial response was threefold: to order the exhumation and dismemberment of Lu's corpse and the enslavement or exile of all his surviving family members; to write an angry and detailed rebuttal, attempting to prove that he was indeed his father's chosen successor, which every holder of a state examination degree was required to read; and to make a dramatic gesture of pardoning Zeng with no more than a reprimand on the grounds that he had been young and gullible.[9]

Yongzheng projected this image linking Confucian benevolence to paternal sternness in other ways, including his amplifications to the Sacred Edict of his father. Kangxi had been content to give a brief summary of sixteen moral points to help his subjects lead obedient and peaceful lives. But Yongzheng elaborated on each of the maxims at great length, preparing lectures that were to be delivered by local scholars, twice a month, down to the village level. In his elaborations, Yongzheng emphasized the need for integrated communities that would pay their taxes promptly, avoid feuds, and protect themselves from outlaws; the role of thrift and hard work in an agricultural economy; avoidance of litigation; and the fostering of an educational system that taught moral conduct and orthodoxy while renouncing "false doctrines." All examination candidates at the county level had to commit to memory the expanded maxims and the emperor's commentaries on them. Simplified versions were also prepared by some of Yongzheng's officials, so that the homilies could be delivered by those with limited education and to minority peoples who spoke non-Han languages. It was a thorough attempt at indoctrination, which, Yongzheng believed, would improve people's thoughts and behavior, and intensify their loyalty to the state. Such patterns of moral indoctrination would become a recurrent theme in later Chinese history, both after the great rebellions of the mid-nineteenth century and under the successive governments of the Nationalists and the Communists.

In the realm of Buddhism, one can again see the polarities in Yongzheng's behavior as he played out the dual roles of ardent believer and autocrat. The school of Buddhism that most attracted Yongzheng was Chan, which had first begun to flourish in China a millennium earlier. Chan devotees practiced an austere program of meditation and introspection so that they would ultimately understand that the so-called "practical" world they inhabited was in truth a realm of illusion. They believed, too, that the Buddha nature was immanent in all beings and that enlightenment could be obtained by all individuals with the requisite faith and concentration. True to this set of beliefs, Yongzheng met regularly in his palace with a fourteen-person Chan study group, consisting of five brothers he trusted, select senior officials, one Daoist, and five Buddhist monks. He also authorized a Buddhist press to print sutras—passages from Buddhist scripture. Yet when Yongzheng disagreed with the interpretations that had been put forth by two late Ming monks and were still adhered to by many Chan believers in his own day, he ordered the controversial books burned and compelled their later followers to renounce the monks and their works.

One can see Yongzheng's social values emerge in the area of labor relations as well. The region around Suzhou was famous in the eighteenth century as a center of the silk- and cotton-cloth trades. Among the area's large labor force were men, legendary for their great physical strength, who used huge rollers, weighing a thousand pounds or more, to press and finish the cloth. These "calenderers," as they were called, worked furiously hard for poor wages: it took almost a day to process a 68-foot length of cloth, for which each worker received 11 copper cash (just over one-hundredth of a silver tael), barely enough to purchase rice for one person's survival.

In Kangxi's reign these calenderers went on strike several times, demanding better wages and the right to build a hospital, an orphanage, and a meeting hall. The strikers got nowhere and their leaders were beaten, but the calenderers rose in protest once more in 1723 and again in 1729. Since there were more than eight thousand of these aggrieved laborers around Suzhou, Yongzheng took the matter seriously, but he was more concerned with their possible links to other rebels and agitators than he was about their economic plight. He praised the governor who arrested and interrogated twenty-two of the workers.

Through surviving palace memorials bearing his lengthy interlinear inscriptions, we can see how carefully Yongzheng followed the investigation, which yielded the unsettling news that some of the workers were involved with martial-arts experts, fortune-tellers, brothel owners, and even some alleged allies of a claimant to the Ming throne who had fled to the Philippines. Only when all these elements had been unraveled in 1730 and the conspirators punished did the emperor write his informant the notation: "Good, now you can send a public memorial." In other words, only now would the central ministries and the grand secretaries be allowed to share in the full details that the emperor and a few favored officials had been brooding about for seven years.

In the area of opium addiction, the emperor was on new and untested terrain. Although use of opium for its medicinal and narcotic properties had been recorded since the eleventh century, it was only after tobacco smoking had become popular during the seventeenth century, and after knowledge of opium-smoking techniques had been brought back from Taiwan by the soldiers sent to suppress the Zhu Yigui rebellion of 1721, that opium addiction spread to the southeast coastal provinces. Yongzheng was alerted to the extent of the problem early in his reign and determined to ban opium smoking, but since there was no clear precedent in the legal code, a number of different clauses had to be invoked by analogy. Thus opium dealers were to be sentenced, like those selling contraband goods, to wear the heavy wooden collar called the "cangue" for one month and then to be banished to a military frontier garrison. Those who lured the innocent into their opium dens were to be punished, like those preaching heterodox religions, to strangulation (subject to mitigation after review). Those smoking or growing opium were to be beaten with one hundred strokes in accordance with penalties for those who violated imperial orders.

But in 1729 a long memorial reached Yongzheng and persuaded him to think the problem through with greater care. The memorial concerned an opium seller named Chen, who had been sentenced under the laws to have all his stock confiscated, to wear the cangue, and to be banished. But Chen protested his innocence on the grounds that he had been selling opium as pills to treat various illnesses, not mixed with tobacco for smoking. Reviewing the evidence, Yongzheng acknowledged that this was indeed a valid distinction and that officials should always ascertain motivation in actions under investigation: "If the opium is contraband, then Chen should not be graciously pardoned. If it is not contraband, then why have you stored it in the provincial treasury? This is the hard-earned capital of the common people. How can you deal with an error by committing another error, and thus deprive him of his livelihood?"[10] Here was a concrete example of a situation in which the ruler of the world's largest empire could still keep a close watch on social problems, attempt to enforce a measure of economic equity, and pose as a supreme cultural arbiter.

Yongzheng's most dramatic gesture in this direction was his decision to emancipate the "mean people," a designation applied to several hereditary outcast groups. Among the communities so designated were the "singing people" of Shaanxi and Shanxi, who sang and played music at weddings and funerals; the "fallen people" of Zhejiang; the hereditary servants of Anhui and the hereditary beggars of Jiangsu; the boatmen, oyster gatherers, and pearl fishers from certain tribes who worked in the dangerous seas off the southeast coast; the "hut dwellers" who gathered hemp and indigo on the Zhejiang-Fujian border; and others who toiled as domestic slaves. Perhaps Yongzheng was moved to change their lowly status more from his desire to establish a unified code of public morals than from genuine compassion, but the fact that he issued a series of edicts between 1723 and 1731 to remove their debased legal and social status shows his consistency and tenacity in seeking to end this type of discrimination.

In the short run the edicts had less effect than he hoped. Many of the "mean people" stayed in their lowly occupations out of choice, while others were used to their degraded status and simply accepted it even though the laws had changed. Members of the general public were not eager to accept these outcasts as equals, despite the emperor's edicts. But over the long term his pronouncements had the desired effect, and slowly many of the despised groups were able to take a more settled place in Qing society.

Here, as at other times in his reign, Yongzheng had a chance to learn that human nature could be obdurate, and that public pronouncements of moralistic concern did not necessarily change patterns of behavior, but we cannot tell if he took the lesson to heart. His belief in his own powers of persuasion remained intact, and he continued to exhort his officials and his subjects until the day he died. His practical moralism is a sign of how deeply a Manchu monarch of the Qing state had internalized conventional Confucian virtues.

CHAPTER 5

Chinese Society and the Reign of Qianlong

"LIKE THE SUN AT MIDDAY"

The reign of Qianlong, from 1736 to 1799, was the longest in the history of China. Combined with the almost equally long reign of Kangxi and that of Yongzheng, just three emperors ruled during the span extending from 1661 to 1799—an extraordinary era of stability and continuity. If we examine Qianlong's reign more closely, however, we can see that it was in fact a time of experimentation and change, in which there began to emerge certain signs of stress that were to have important effects on the future life of the Qing dynasty.

Emperor Qianlong began his reign in a spirit of optimism. The fourth son of Yongzheng, he came peacefully to the throne at the age of twenty-five, having been spared the battles that plagued his father's own ascension. Yongzheng had had the foresight to write down his choice of heir in secret and to place the name in a locked box so that there could be no dispute. Qianlong had been carefully groomed for the role of emperor and had no doubts about his abilities or the grandeur of the dynasty over which he presided. But he brought an added dimension to Qing rule by conceiving of himself not merely as the emperor of China, but as the ruler of a multicultural Inner Asian empire. To the political dimensions of rule he added new religious, linguistic, and ethnic elements, which forced a reconsideration of the Manchu heritage and of the nature of power.

Qianlong's most important legacy was the conquest and integration of huge areas of western territory—the region later known as Xinjiang, the "New Territories"—into the Qing state. By doing this he increased the territorial expanse of the empire to its greatest extent, ended the Zunghar threat, and fixed a firm western border with Russia to go along with the northern borders

Qing forces, 1759 Qianlong's conquest and integration of huge territories in the west, now known as Xinjiang, was accomplished at tremendous cost. This engraving shows Qing forces encamped during their drive to take Kashgar and Yarkand in 1759.

settled by treaties at Nerchinsk and Kiakhta. The accomplishment of this task took much time and money, and incurred catastrophic costs in human life.

In 1745, a succession struggle following the death of the ruling Zunghar khan had split the confederation. When a chieftain named Amursana defected to the Qing, bringing with him 20,000 followers, Qianlong saw this as a strategic opportunity to consolidate control over the troublesome border region. But after allying with Qing forces to defeat his rivals in 1755, Amursana declared his intention to become the new khan and turned against the Qing. Enraged, Qianlong directed his generals to "show no mercy": all Zunghar men were to be "exterminated," and the women, children, and elderly were to be taken as slaves and bondservants. More than half a million people were slaughtered on the emperor's direct orders. The scorched-earth policy erased the Zunghars, as a state and as a people.[1]

In pursuit of the Zunghars and their allies, Qing forces moved farther south to invade oasis towns along the Tianshan range and in the Tarim Basin region. The native inhabitants of Ili, Urümchi, Kashgar, and Yarkand were Turkic, Uyghur, and other Muslim groups. To secure and govern this vast territory required a military government backed by 40,000 troops, at an annual cost of 3 million taels. When Qianlong decided to invade and then annex Xinjiang, he did so against the advice of some of his advisers, who considered the region a "wasteland," not worth the colossal expenses of conquest and occupation. The emperor insisted that the security reasons were sufficient to justify the cost; he also confidently projected that Xinjiang would be self-supporting. Qianlong would be disappointed in this regard. Despite imperial monopolies over mining jade and gold, the expansion of trade in copper, saltpeter, and slaves, infrastructure projects to improve transportation and communication, and state farms to produce grain, the revenue generated was not enough to cover the military and administrative costs.

In local governance, the Qing adapted different approaches, depending on the ethnicity and background of the population. In the southern Muslim oasis towns, local chieftain leaders known as *begs* were given responsibilities as mayors, revenue collectors, and judges. The inhabitants retained their own dietary practices and religious leaders, and were excused from shaving their heads and wearing the queue. Elsewhere, nomadic groups were organized into companies and put under the authority of hereditary leaders (known as *jasaks*) who ruled with a degree of local autonomy. Until the nineteenth century, the region was closed to Han Chinese colonization and settlement. For the small numbers of early settlers, the civilian administration mirrored the structure of the inner provinces. At the outset, then, Qing rule over Xinjiang comprised multiple systems designed to manage the diversity of this vast frontier region.[2]

Qianlong's immense campaigns had not been conducted from the small, secretive Office of Military Finance, as Yongzheng's had. Although the office coordinating the campaigns bore the same name, its scope and personnel had vastly expanded, as had its power and visibility in the government as a whole. For this reason, from Qianlong's reign onward the office is translated as the "Grand Council" in English, for it now transcended in power all the ministries and even the Grand Secretariat itself. Among the first of Qianlong's grand councilors were his father Yongzheng's two trusted advisers, Ortai and Zhang Tingyu. They gave continuity to the government, and were gradually joined by a small number of hand-picked ministers, the total remaining at around six or seven during most of Qianlong's reign. The grand councilors were backed by a secretarial staff of 250 or more, who served in rotation and round the clock so that the key offices were never empty.

The Grand Council now became the center for the crucial palace memorials conveyed by senior officials throughout the empire. As these memorials were copied out, evaluated by a wider circle of advisers, and often passed on to the ministries for discussion, both their symbolic and their real functions as special devices bonding official and ruler began to fade. Qianlong's comments in vermilion ink on the memorials were often perfunctory—"Noted," "Read," "Send to the relevant Ministry"—and conveyed little of the sense of warmth and intimacy, or indeed of anger or concern, that had characterized the comments of his father and grandfather.

This is not to say Qianlong was not a conscientious ruler, for he was. He met senior officials regularly in audience, read the documents submitted to him, traveled extensively both to the Yangzi delta cities and in Manchuria, coordinated military campaigns, and issued numerous edicts on important policy matters. It was rather that he left a great deal of the actual decision making to his grand councilors; as a result the sense of dynamic central leadership that had characterized the reigns of his father and grandfather faded away.

This loss of impulse can be seen in his approach to the reform of rural tax collection that had featured so largely in Yongzheng's thinking. Although Qianlong had ordered all candidates for the *jinshi* exams in 1742 to write essays on how revenue should be apportioned between the provinces, and asked the same of his senior officials, slowly—almost casually—the key elements of that tax strategy were abandoned. Wealthy provinces with surplus revenue were made to hand it over to the poorer provinces. The result was that the rich provinces lost the opportunity to take important local initiatives that might have strengthened governance, while the poorer provinces lost any incentive to expand their collection system or reform their economic base. Qianlong compounded the loss of opportunity by a 1769 command canceling the revenue-enhancing practices that his father and grandfather had given to the banner organizations. In the lofty rhetoric that closed the argument, Qianlong reiterated that "it is not in accordance with the system of the country for the government to get involved in entrepreneurial operations."[3]

More and more often, magistrates kept the local tax surpluses to themselves rather than forwarding them to the provincial financial commissioner. Abuses of extra fees, payments, and illegal surcharges crept back in. The Ministry of Revenue gradually instituted a system by which every item of local expenditure had to be approved by members of its Beijing staff before the money could be spent. This led to an avalanche of paperwork and an absurd system in which trivial matters were held up for years and important ones never got done at all. One Ministry of Revenue document of this time from the capital province of Hebei shows that provincial officials had to clear such items as 48 taels to pay some guards on a bridge, 105 taels for sailors' wages, and 12 taels as pension allowance for two widows.

In cultural affairs, Qianlong's approach was similar to his father's. He made a public show of his filial piety, particularly in his ritualized treatment of his own mother, the dowager empress, whom he pampered and flattered to an extraordinary degree. Claiming filial loyalty to his insulted father, he reversed Yongzheng's edict of clemency and ordered the unfortunate Zeng Jing—that inept popularizer of Lu Liuliang's ideas back in 1728—sliced to pieces in the market square of Beijing. He gave additional examinations to scholars of outstanding caliber who had been unsuccessful in the regular state exams, made much of the local lecture systems that promulgated Confucian values and the Sacred Edict, celebrated the aged in special festivals, and praised virtuous wives and widows.

In some areas Qianlong took new initiatives. He expanded the imperial collection of painting and calligraphy enormously, drawing into the court many of the finest works from the previous millennium. (He has been blamed, by later connoisseurs, for writing elaborate poems on great paintings in his neat but undistinguished calligraphy, thus ruining the subtlety of the original compo-

In My Heart There Is the Power to Reign Peaceably Detail of Emperor Qianlong (1736) by Giuseppe Castiglione (Lang Shining)

The Yuan Ming Yuan   The summer palace designed by Jesuits in China for Qianlong was located just outside Beijing. Illustration from "Le Costume Ancien et Moderne" by Giulio Ferrario, published c. 1820s–1830s (colored engraving), Zancon, Gaetano (1771–1816)

sitions.) He patronized a number of Jesuit painters, especially the talented Italian Giuseppe Castiglione, whose royal portraits and large panoramas of hunts and processions marked a unique blend of Chinese composition with Western perspective and coloration. Qianlong employed Jesuit architects and designers to work on a magnificent European-style summer palace, the Yuan Ming Yuan, erected in a lakeside park just outside Beijing. The emperor personally supervised the construction and furnishings of a retirement palace for himself and his closest family members inside the Forbidden City complex. He ordered the compilation of a number of important works—genealogies, histories, accounts of rituals—that would accurately preserve and enshrine the Manchu heritage. And to emphasize the power of the Qing as religious patrons, he had a replica of the great Tibetan lamaist temple, the Potala, built on the grounds of his extensive summer palace in Rehe.

To preserve the greatness of Chinese culture, Qianlong also ordered a massive compilation to be made of the most famous literary and historical works of the past. Known as the *Four Treasuries* from its four main components of classics, histories, philosophy, and miscellaneous literary works, this was not just a selection of passages on given topics; rather, it was a complete anthology, with learned introductions, into which the works selected were copied in their entirety. This collection, which ended up comprising 3,450 complete works and commentaries on 6,750 others, filled 36,000 manuscript volumes and took ten years to assemble. It is one of the great achievements of Chinese bibliography.

Yet compiling the *Four Treasuries* also served the function of a literary inquisition, since private libraries were searched and those people owning works considered to be slighting to the Manchus were strictly punished. Such books, along with volumes of geography or travel containing information considered harmful to the empire's defenses, were destroyed. So thorough was this campaign that over 2,000 works that we know were scheduled for destruction have never been rediscovered. Some senior editors on the *Four Treasuries* project were also able to support the schools of philosophy they espoused by omitting the works of major rivals, or by emphasizing their own philosophical views in their commentaries. On the other hand, during that same literary inquisition scholars were allowed access to many older sources that illumined the histories of the Mongols and Uyghurs, and made major new discoveries in the fields of geography, cartography, and philology. These discoveries enabled the Chinese to develop a new pride in being part of a broader cultural and historical tradition, which was—later in the nineteenth century—to have important effects on the Chinese conception of multiethnic empire.[4]

One can trace, running through many of Qianlong's pronouncements and actions, a faint undercurrent. It is that of a man who has been praised too much and has thought too little, of someone who has played to the gallery in public life, mistaken grandeur for substance, sought confirmation and support for even routine actions, and is not really equipped to make difficult or unpopular decisions. In the midst of Qianlong's many glories, signs of decay were becoming apparent. One of the five classics, the *Book of Changes*, had anticipated this, as any educated Chinese would have known. The fifty-fifth hexagram of the *Changes* is *feng*, meaning "abundance" or "fullness," and its main description says,

> ABUNDANCE has success.
> The king attains abundance.
> Be not sad.
> Be like the sun at midday.[5]

But the ancient commentary on this passage adds,

> When the sun stands at midday, it begins to set; when the moon is full it begins to wane. The fullness and emptiness of heaven and earth wane and wax in the course of time. How much truer is this of men, or of spirits and gods!

EIGHTEENTH-CENTURY CONFUCIANISM

If questioned, Qianlong would surely have insisted that he presided over a Confucian system of government with Confucian means, and there were many ways in which he could have justified such a claim: the works of Confucius were regarded by the emperor and his officials as the key repositories of ethical wisdom; the Confucian classics formed the basic curriculum in schools and were central to the rigorously competitive state examination system; Confucian values of loyalty and filial piety bonded officials to rulers and children to parents, just as lectures on Confucian topics by scholars and officials in the countryside were aimed at unifying the populace in obedience to the state. Yet "Confucianism" was constantly changing as accretions were adopted or swept away. In the eighteenth century, the doctrine began to develop in new directions, paralleling changes in the society and the economy.

During the second half of the seventeenth century, scholars had been absorbed in searching out the reason for the collapse of the Ming dynasty, and many of them found a satisfactory explanation in the extreme individualism and belief in innate moral knowledge that had been popular in the late Ming. Senior scholar-officials under the early Qing emperors Shunzhi and Kangxi— as well as those emperors themselves—sought to counter what they considered decadent Ming trends by reasserting the central values of Song-dynasty (960–1279) Confucianism. They emphasized the Song because it was then that the philosopher Zhu Xi (d. 1200) had given prominence to the view that there were underlying principles (*li*) that explained heaven's actions and guided human conduct. Understanding such principles, Zhu Xi and his later followers believed, would help men to live rationally and in tune with heaven, and would justify the attempts of moral men to find meaning in a public career. Thus there was a state-oriented tilt to Song Confucianism, even though the elaboration of such beliefs demanded multifaceted levels of cosmological speculation as individual thinkers probed for heaven's purposes. Furthermore, the realization that even the most moral of men might never be able to fathom the dictates of heaven and would, therefore, inevitably fail in their duties to state and community led to complex levels of anxiety among Confucian thinkers.

Just as early Qing scholars in state positions had rejected elements of Ming thought and had found security in the earlier texts and interpretations of the twelfth-century Song dynasty, so did later Qing thinkers reject those Song norms and search for certainty elsewhere. By the time of Qianlong, many scholars had begun to find a new security not so much in particular texts as in a methodology. This methodology, which they called *kaozheng*, has been usefully translated as "practicing evidential research," because it involved the evaluation of data based on rigorous standards of precision. *Kaozheng* scholars sought to get away from speculation altogether, to root their studies in "hard facts." They devoted their energies to studies in linguistics, mathematics, astronomy, and geography, confident that these would lead to greater certainty about the true words and intentions of the ancient sages and, hence, to a better understanding of how to live in the present.

The most important precursors of the *kaozheng* movement were men who had lived during Kangxi's reign. One of the *kaozheng* heroes was Gu Yanwu, the Ming loyalist who had sought to defend his home territory against the Manchu forces. As noted in Chapter 3, Gu eventually made a tacit peace with the new Qing dynasty, and spent the last part of his life traveling across north China to study aspects of local technology as well as to track down old steles, from which he took careful rubbings. Gu also kept detailed records of his work with precise notes on texts, rare sources, geographical observations, and ancient artifacts.

Yan Ruoju, a friend of Gu's, applied similar techniques to collating the chronology and linguistic structures of part of the Confucian classic of historical documents. His conclusions, though circulated only in manuscript until the 1740s, had a shattering effect on many scholars of the time. Yan proved, with carefully marshaled evidence, that several sections of this major work (on which generations of state examination questions had been based) were a later forgery and thus did not deserve the reverence ascribed to it.

By the 1740s the examinations as a whole were coming under attack as sterile exercises that failed to select the finest scholars for office, and Yan's work heightened this sense of state Confucianism's weakness. Social tensions further undermined confidence in this system, for by the mid-eighteenth century the state had not increased quotas of examination candidates proportionately to population growth. The consequent pressures on students and the difficulties of finding employment even if one passed the exams brought frustration and disillusionment to many members of the educated elite. (The plight of swelling numbers of unemployed degree candidates, and the corruptibility and pomposity of many self-satisfied scholars, was poignantly and amusingly caught in a novel entitled *Unofficial History of the Scholars*, published in 1768.)

Eighteenth-century scholars used *kaozheng* insights and methodologies to begin a profound exploration of the Confucian past. Many spent much of their time reading texts and commentaries from the Han dynasty (206 B.C.E.–220 C.E.), since these were so much nearer to Confucius's time than the Song texts still used in the state's schools and, hence, were believed to be closer to the true sentiments of the sage himself. Partisans of the Han texts subsequently divided into groups, according to whether they placed more faith in scholarship done earlier or later in the Han dynasty. These were not just abstruse debates, but explorations of the past that began to approach the classics as history and to treat history itself with a sharp and penetrating skepticism. The work of the *kaozheng* scholars also had major implications for eighteenth-century policy, since the "ant-like accumulation of facts"—as one scholar described his studies—brought insights into hydraulics, astronomy, cartography, and ancient texts on government that enabled the evaluation of Qing reality with a shrewder eye.

The influence of *kaozheng* scholarship in the mid-Qianlong reign was supported by an interlocking infrastructure of book dealers and publishers, printers, library owners, and professional teachers of the many skills needed for advanced research of this kind. Often the lines between scholars and the commercial world blurred, since many merchants became patrons of *kaozheng* learning and accumulated libraries that they put at the scholars' disposal. Other *kaozheng* scholars were descended directly from merchant families, reflecting the growth of new urban centers and the blurring of previously sharp occupational categories.

In Emperor Qianlong's compilation project of the *Four Treasuries*, *kaozheng* scholars dominated the editorial process, using their new learning to denigrate speculative Confucian theories of the Song period (even though those theories remained "orthodox" in the examinations) and to boost the reputations of writers working in a *kaozheng* vein. Qianlong, in return, was grateful for the amount of rare material that these scholars made available to him. He ordered officials to write out three extra manuscript sets of the rarest works included in the *Four Treasuries* compendium. These were deposited in libraries at the three main centers of *kaozheng* learning—Yangzhou, Zhenjiang, and Hangzhou—so that scholars could consult them.

One aspect of the eighteenth-century fascination with scholarship was a renewed interest in women's education. The rate of female literacy remained very low in the overall population. (The estimate for the nineteenth century is between 1 and 10 percent, with wide geographical disparities.) For upper class families of the Qianlong period, the education and cultural refinement of wives and daughters enhanced their social status. Grooming a daughter for marriage included training in embroidery, painting, poetry composition, and calligraphy. Most important of all, her moral education, based on the principles imparted in the Confucian classics, must be impeccable. The abbreviated curriculum featured texts considered most appropriate for female learning: *The Analects for Women*, the Han classic *Precepts for Women*, *Instructions for the Inner Quarters* by an empress of the Ming dynasty, and a *Record of Female Exemplars*. Beyond these four selections, other guidebooks proliferated in the eighteenth century, offering additional instructions for educating women, and further advice for literate women.

Women of elite families were bound by gender norms to maintain the separation of the sexes and stay in the "inner quarters." As female writing culture flourished in the eighteenth century, accomplished poets published their works and gained public fame. For many others, writing was a form of private self-expression, to convey feelings of passion or anguish, to voice their worries about the pressures of family life or illness. Yet others sustained long-distance friendships through correspondence and exchanges of verse, embroidery, and paintings in informal poetry clubs. The expansion of women's education and literary culture was controversial. While some prominent male scholars strongly advocated for female learning, other critics debated whether such "frivolous" pursuits undermined the cardinal virtues of womanhood. The public expression of female creativity and imagination, as well as the transgression of the gender divide between the inner female sphere and the outer male realm, provoked anxious discussions about the proper orientation and content of women's education.[6]

Confucianism was not just a matter of moral philosophy. Painting and calligraphy had always been essential adjuncts to the Confucian value system, and here again there were significant eighteenth-century shifts in style and matter. Conventional techniques of painting were made available to just about any moderately educated person in "how to do it" painting manuals like the *Mustard Seed Garden* of 1701. From such a book, one could quickly learn to render a passable branch of plum blossom, a thatched cottage, or a distant mountain range, allowing any member of the educated public to produce a reasonable painting. In response, the literati painters now began to cultivate a greater sense of eccentricity, deliberately violating the norms of composition and color to show an "amateurism" that was in fact highly planned. Such eccentricity had been a feature of Ming loyalist painting in the seventeenth century, when it was used to convey a political position; by the eighteenth century, it showed a more status-conscious face.

Significant changes also took place in calligraphy. *Kaozheng* scholars' discoveries and reprintings of archaic scripts, and the circulation of careful rubbings of stone engravings, enabled the cult of the far past to dominate the present. At some extremes, painters would render the calligraphy on their paintings as if it were carved with a chisel, managing to be evocative and erudite at the same time. Thus as literacy spread by the end of the Qianlong reign, it was perhaps no coincidence that the most highly educated men developed new modes of cultured expression that were out of the reach of almost everyone else.

THE DREAM OF THE RED CHAMBER

The Dream of the Red Chamber, China's greatest novel, was written in the middle of Emperor Qianlong's reign. The author, Cao Xueqin, was descended from one of the Chinese bannerman-bondservants who had enjoyed wealth and influence as a favorite of Emperor Kangxi. But the Cao family, which had lived for years on a grand scale in Nanjing, was subsequently punished for dishonesty and incompetence by Emperor Yongzheng and most of its wealth was confiscated. Cao Xueqin was thus thoroughly familiar with the Sino-Manchu tensions that persisted through the Qing dynasty and, by the time of his death in 1763, had tasted the nectar of luxurious living and the gall of bankrupt gentility.

The Dream of the Red Chamber—often known by its alternate title, *The Story of the Stone*—presents a meticulous description of the Jias, a wealthy extended family who occupy a series of linked mansions in an unnamed city that seems to have some elements of Nanjing and some of Beijing. Many aspects of the fictional Jia family's story are clearly drawn from the history of Kangxi's reign: the Jias are aware of Manchu culture and deportment, carry out confidential assignments for the emperor, and have a favored relationship with the court, where one of the Jia daughters is a secondary consort. Yet the novel is not content to offer a realistic portrayal of Qing life. Each of the novel's two titles points to different and complex elements in the novel's structure: the "dream" that is ascribed to the "red chamber" constitutes an elaborate yet mysterious foretelling of the fates of the main female protagonists who are related or linked to the Jias in some way; the "stone" whose "story" is to be told is a miraculous artifact, empowered by the gods with a magical life of its own, and living out its existence on this earth through the religious mediation of a Buddhist and a Daoist priest.

In simple outline, *The Dream of the Red Chamber* is a love story. The fate of the novel's hero, Jia Baoyu (named "Precious Jade" for the stone found in his mouth at birth), is closely entwined with the lives of two young women, Lin Daiyu and Xue Baochai, each of whom bears one of the elements of his name in her own. The three grow up in the Jia family mansions with a host of other young companions, but their idyllic relations come to a sharp end when Jia Baoyu, who deeply loves Lin Daiyu, is tricked by his parents into marrying the wealthier and stronger Xue Baochai. This deceit leads to Lin Daiyu's death; at the novel's end, Jia Baoyu—although he has just passed the highest level of the state examinations—leaves his young wife and the spacious grounds of his crumbling estate to seek the pure life of a religious pilgrim.

Cao Xueqin had a serious purpose in writing the novel, as well as the simple desire to entertain. Beyond its plot, *Dream* is a story of the quest for identity and for an understanding of the human purpose on earth. The novel also explores the different levels of reality and illusion that lie entwined inside so-called success and failure. In Cao's words in the introduction to the book, "Truth becomes fiction when the fiction's true."[7]

Although this suggests that Cao intends to disavow "realism," so rich are the texture and structure of the novel—which is 120 chapters long and contains hundreds of vividly drawn characters in addition to the main protagonists— that it can nevertheless be seen as a kind of summation of the many elements of mid-Qing elite life, including family structure, politics, economics, religion, aesthetics, and sexuality. Even allowing for the freedoms of the writer's imagination and for the allegorical overtones that pervade the work, a look at each of these six categories can still tell us much about the grandeur of Qing society in the mid-eighteenth century, and about its underside.

In the realm of family structure, Cao Xueqin points to the immense power of the father over his children, especially on questions of their moral growth and education. It is the Jia father who chooses the schoolteacher for the local lineage school, who grills Baoyu over the progress of his studies, and who punishes him for negligence or immorality. So terrible is the father's anger that the mere mention of it reduces the son to abject fear. The mother, in this context, is comparatively powerless; but the matriarch of the family, Baoyu's grandmother, has great economic and intellectual strength, able to moderate family behavior on the basis of respect for her advanced age and generational seniority. Similarly, generational hierarchies give Baoyu prestige over younger siblings or cousins, while forcing him to defer to his elders.

In political terms, the Jias are powerful not just because a member of their family is a consort to the emperor, or because they hold high office in the bureaucracy and undertake imperial commissions. Their power is also local, in that they can use their prestige to bend the judicial system to their advantage. Any county magistrate knows better than to prosecute one of the Jias or their friends—it would be more than his job is worth. The family is thus subject to a kind of corrupting influence, which leads its younger members to believe they can break the law with impunity, even to the extent of hushing up homicides in which family members have been involved. This political power is potentially self-perpetuating, since the web of princely friends and the patterns of examination success will propel the younger men of the lineage into positions of influence, and the young women of the family into powerful marriages.

Economically, the Jia family can call on resources that would be beyond the imagination of most families. Their home is full of silver bullion, bolts of silk, paintings, and scrolls. Their grounds and buildings are spacious, and their coffers constantly replenished with the rents brought by bailiffs from urban holdings and from far-off farms that the Jias own as absentee landlords. They indulge in profitable business deals of great complexity, and gain additional income from carrying out imperial commissions and acquiring exotic goods from merchants who trade with Western countries. They also have scores of indentured servants, male and female, who perform all duties in the family compound and act as retainers whenever the Jias go outside the walls.

In matters of religion, the Jia family are as eclectic as Qing society was. Central to the family's prestige and sense of fulfillment is the meticulous worship, in the Confucian tradition, of their own ancestors. Funerals, like marriages, are occasions for intense, careful pomp and ritual performance.

But the Jias also call, as necessary, on priests of the Daoist and Buddhist religions; they follow the prescribed ceremonies of these religions, and even keep a group of young female Buddhist novices in the purlieus of their own home. The Jias practice both Buddhist and Daoist rites in times of fear or illness, and on occasion have priests conduct exorcisms to expel harmful spirits and malignant influences. Jia Baoyu himself is, for a long period in the novel, immobilized by an enemy's use of black magic, against which not even his jade talisman can protect him. One senior member of the family has withdrawn to a temple to follow his own pattern of religious enlightenment. (He later dies from imbibing too many magical Daoist elixirs of immortality.)

Aesthetically, life in the Jia mansions is a joy, recalling the elegance that typified elite life in the late Ming dynasty. The high level of literacy of the young men and women makes possible an endless array of poetry games and the exchange of erudite jokes and riddles. The clothing, décor, and gardens described are exquisite; the preparation of tea, drinking of wine, and eating of an evening meal are a triumphant blending of taste and artifice. Music and drama are also an integral part of life: the Jia family keeps its own troupe of actors and actresses who, whenever they are requested to do so, perform scenes from now-classic works such as *The Peony Pavilion*, by the Ming dramatist Tang Xianzu.

Finally, in the realm of sexuality, there are few limitations on the behavior of the Jia family members. The children and adolescents may live together in a youthful world where banter is innocent even if full of sexual innuendo, but their elders are lustful creatures, and the children are growing up to be like them. Both men and women use their powers in the family hierarchy to obtain their sexual pleasures. Jealousy goes with adultery; love affairs lead to murders. Servants and bondslaves become sexual objects and are powerless to protest except by flight or suicide. Novice nuns or young male actors are also caught up in seduction and deceit, and in the schoolroom, same-sex liaisons flourish among the young male scholars.

Cao Xueqin had not completed his novel when he died in 1763, and for several decades it circulated in various manuscript editions among his family and friends. Only in 1792 did a "full" version, with lacunae filled in by later hands, appear in published form, and it became an immediate success. One may speculate that the novel's wide readership was composed of men and women from the upper class, of underemployed scholars, and also of those with some education who lived and worked as merchants and traders in the flourishing cities of the largely peaceful mid-Qing world.

Although *The Dream of the Red Chamber* is full of echoes from the great plays and novels of the late Ming and from earlier Chinese poetic traditions, and although we cannot be sure which sections of the last forty chapters were the author's personal work, the novel remains a dazzling and original triumph. The irony, perhaps, is that this great novel adds luster to the reign of Qianlong, although Cao Xueqin's own sharp gaze saw much that was wrong underneath all that grandeur.

QIANLONG'S LATER YEARS

As if echoing the warning note sounded by the *feng* hexagram, a series of crises erupted in Emperor Qianlong's later years. There was no particular pattern to these troubles; a series of government misjudgments coincided with previously unsuspected levels of domestic resentment to produce a tense situation overall. Bungled military campaigns, local rebellions, bureaucratic corruption, and imperial favoritism were all part of the story, which took place in a context of intellectual uneasiness over traditional scholarly values, the state's failure to address pressing financial and administrative needs, and a steadily growing population that put unprecedented pressures on the land.

In public pronouncements, Qianlong prided himself on his sagacity as a coordinator of military campaigns, and he took great satisfaction in the conquest of Xinjiang in the 1750s. But a campaign against Burma in the 1760s was badly mismanaged, in sharp contrast to the efficiency with which Wu Sangui had pursued the last Ming prince in the same region a century before. And the brief war that China waged against Vietnam in 1788 and 1789 threw a sharp light on the inadequacies of Qing policy.

In 1788 the ruler of Vietnam's Le dynasty fled with his family from usurpers who had seized Hanoi. Taking refuge in Guangxi province, he begged for Qing protection. Qianlong responded swiftly, ordering a three-pronged attack on Vietnam, with one army marching south from Guangxi under General Sun Shiyi, a second southeast from Yunnan, and a third transported by sea from Guangdong. The Qing armies under General Sun entered Hanoi in December 1788 and declared victory and the restoration of the Le dynasty. Qianlong at once promoted General Sun to ducal rank. But just one month later, while Sun and his troops were in Hanoi celebrating the lunar new year festival, the rebels counterattacked, killing over 4,000 of Sun's troops and forcing his ignominious flight back to Guangxi. Qianlong pragmatically commented that the Le had been fated to fall, and he acknowledged the succession of the victor as Vietnam's legitimate ruler. The conferral of ritual title papered over the humiliating defeat and the weakness of Qing military leadership. (This misadventure marked the end of China's attempts at direct military involvement in Vietnam until an equally unsuccessful invasion in 1979.)

On the other hand, victories over the Gurkhas of Nepal, who attacked Tibet in 1790 and 1791, demonstrated that some Manchu generals were highly skilled in

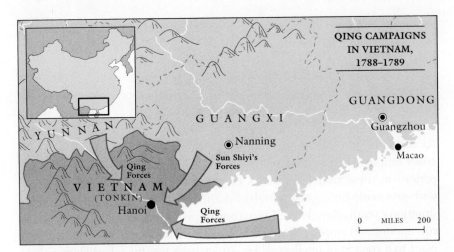

military strategy and tactics. Qing troops reached Tibet in 1792 and defeated the Gurkhas in a series of battles, forcing them back into Nepal through the Himalayan passes. In this case, the Qing military deftly navigated the challenges of logistics and fighting in some of the harshest terrain in the world. In the ensuing peace treaty, Nepal agreed to send tribute to the Qing every five years, a promise that they kept up until the year 1908. But the campaign had been extremely expensive, and a great deal of the money expended was never accounted for satisfactorily. The man in charge of writing up the accounts was that same General Sun Shiyi who had bungled the Vietnam campaign. Despite Sun's failure there, Qianlong had transferred him to Lhasa, demonstrating more the strength of the emperor's will than the shrewdness of his judgment of character.

These long-range campaigns against foreign states were conducted in an unsettling context of domestic rebellions, which began to occur in different parts of the Qing empire during the later eighteenth century. Some of these uprisings were more imaginary than real, and served to demonstrate the emperor's suspicious nature rather than any genuine threat to the throne. Such was the case with the sorcery scare of 1768, in which the emperor grew convinced that a group of plotters were clipping the queues of hair from unsuspecting victims in order to develop magical potions that could steal away a man's soul and conjure up armies of spirit troops. Only after scores of arrests and many interrogations under torture—from which many innocent vagrants died—did the emperor decide that he had been misled and that no plot against him existed. Other cases, however, were more serious and fully grounded in reality. One such major uprising took place not far from Beijing, in Shandong province near the city of Linqing, a key point on the Grand Canal grain transportation route. This was an area near the periphery of the northeast macroregion, where population had been rising sharply and where disaffected farmers mingled easily with the barge pullers and coolies who kept the Grand Canal in operation. In 1774 rebels under the leadership of a martial-arts and herbal-healing expert named Wang Lun rose up against the Qing, invoking the support of an "Eternal Venerable Mother" goddess. In this way the revolt showed its links to a tradition of underground or sectarian White Lotus folk-Buddhism, which venerated the same female deity and was based on a millenarian view of earthly catastrophe that reached back at least five centuries. Wang drew his followers from a wide variety of occupations: many were farmers or other rural laborers, but there were also traveling actors, carters, fish sellers, monks, vegetable-oil retailers, and a moneylender. We cannot say that Wang Lun had a firm political agenda: he never talked of abolishing rent, or helping the poor, or dividing the land equally. His followers rose in rebellion not in response to some specific political program for social and economic amelioration, but from general feelings of antagonism to the dominant forces of society, reinforced by spiritual convictions.

Wang Lun's teachings convinced the rebels that they could withstand all Qing attacks. As he told them, "If I call on Heaven, Heaven will assist me; if I call on Earth, Earth will give me magical strength. Their guns will not fire. What men will dare impede me?"[8] In early fighting, some of Wang's predictions seemed correct: he captured several small towns and parts of Linqing city, and many Qing troops sent against him fled or deserted. But the state called up massive forces; Wang Lun and his various "soldiers," armed mainly with spears or knives, could not withstand the coordinated attacks of Qing troops. Despite brave street fighting, often house to house, the rebels were pinned down and slaughtered with their families. A vivid rendition of Wang Lun's final apocalypse was given to Qing authorities by a captured rebel who fled his leader's burning headquarters. Wang Lun, he testified, met his death wearing a long purple robe and two silver bracelets, his dagger and double-bladed sword beside him. He sat cross-legged in the corner of the room, motionless, his clothes and beard aflame.

Wang Lun's uprising was more important as a symptom of deep underlying discontents than for its immediate effects, and it should be considered along with other rebellions that erupted elsewhere, often with no precisely stated grievances or goals. In the 1780s, members of a group known as the Heaven and Earth Society (often called the Triads) rose in revolt on Taiwan, seizing several cities and declaring a new dynasty. The uprising seems to have been as much a battle between different groups of emigrants from Fujian province for dominance over Taiwan's economy as it was an assault on the Qing state, but the government responded swiftly. The rebels were suppressed and their leaders executed in 1788.

Also in the 1780s, in Gansu province, there were two major revolts of the Muslim communities, sparked by adherents of a fundamentalist "new sect" who opposed the local Muslim officials appointed by the Qing. Both Muslim uprisings were suppressed after heavy fighting, as were a series of revolts by Miao tribes in the southwest. But the fighting was costly to the Qing, who despite their victories did not eradicate the underlying causes of religious, economic, and ethnic resentments. In 1799, as Qianlong's reign ended, rebels claiming the same White Lotus affiliation that had animated the followers of Wang Lun were rising up all across central China and were actively fighting Qing troops in many areas of Sichuan, Hubei, Shaanxi, and Henan.

Can one link these outbreaks to specific Qing policies that alienated the people? The evidence is not clear on this, but it is certain that in the late eighteenth century many government institutions began to falter: the emergency granaries were often empty, sections of the Grand Canal silted up, regular banner troops behaved with incompetence or brutality, efforts to stop ecologically dangerous land-reclamation projects were abandoned, the bureaucracy was faction-ridden, and corruption ran deep. This last was proved when investigation of the Gansu uprisings revealed an astonishing network of dishonesty and collusion in the ranks of the Qing civilian and military authorities. Emperor

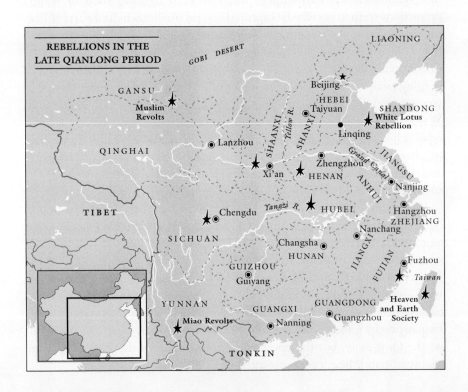

REBELLIONS IN THE
LATE QIANLONG PERIOD

Qianlong himself compounded the problem by demanding tens of thousands of taels as "penitence silver" to be paid directly into his own privy purse by officials who had been found guilty of graft. It is also possible that Qing reluctance to create new county governments in areas of new settlement or dense population put impossible stresses on officials in the bureaucracy. Moreover, the intense pressure for jobs meant that those who had finally obtained office sought a swift return for all their waiting and anxiety, pressing those in their jurisdictions for speedy tax payments and for supplementary charges. The White Lotus insurgents of the 1790s, for instance, stated categorically that "the officials have forced the people to rebel."[9] It is also true that in the conduct of the border campaigns, as in the suppression of local rebellions, Qing officials indulged in an unusually high level of graft. This was made possible by collusion between high figures in military and civil government, who often hid the real situation from the emperor. And Qianlong, having allowed the secret palace memorial system of his father Yongzheng to become impersonal and routine, now had no reliable, confidential sources from which to learn of his officials' malfeasance.

There is no doubt that this pattern of corruption grew worse after 1775, when a young Manchu guards officer named Heshen became entrenched as the elderly emperor's court favorite, although he was not responsible for everything that was going awry. At that time Heshen was twenty-five and the emperor sixty-five, and the following year the favorite received an extraordinary series of promotions: Qianlong named Heshen a deputy lieutenant general of the Manchu plain blue banner, a minister of the imperial household, vice-minister of revenue, and a grand councilor. There were no parallels in Qing history for giving so many powerful appointments to a young man, and Qianlong later piled honor on honor. Heshen was made minister of revenue (and, for a time, minister of civil office), a grand secretary, a director of the *Four Treasuries* compilation project, commanding officer of the Beijing troops, supervisor of transit dues, and a baron. His son was married to the emperor's favorite daughter in 1790.

It is not surprising that rumors swirled around the emperor's relations with his favorite. A sexual liaison was implied in popular stories, such as one suggesting Heshen was the reincarnation of one of Emperor Yongzheng's concubines, with whom Qianlong had been infatuated as a youth. A Korean diplomat on a visit to China, perhaps influenced by such rumors, described Heshen at thirty as "elegant in looks, sprucely handsome in a dandified way that suggested a lack of virtue." In 1793 Lord Macartney, who—as we will see in the next chapter—was visiting as ambassador for King George III, described Heshen as "a handsome, fair man about forty to forty-five years old, quick and fluent."[10]

There is, in fact, no clear evidence about the relationship one way or the other. Certainly Qianlong trusted Heshen for the rest of his life. It is possible that Qianlong initially wanted Heshen to be the emperor's "ears and eyes," similar in range and competence to the bondservants and officials who used the palace memorial system in the days of Kangxi and Yongzheng. Thus in 1780 the emperor sent Heshen on a confidential mission to Yunnan province to investigate corruption charges against the governor-general there, and in 1781 sent him to assist in suppressing the Muslim uprisings in Gansu. But Heshen, who was often ill, mainly stayed in Beijing as Qianlong's chief minister and confidant. Heshen's physicians concluded that his "symptoms were owing to a malignant vapour or spirit which had infused itself into, or was generated in his flesh, which shifted itself from place to place," and stated that they were unable to help him. Turning to Western medicine as an alternative, Heshen summoned Lord Macartney's Scottish doctor Hugh Gillan for a consultation. Gillan found that Heshen was suffering from acute rheumatism and a serious hernia, conditions that had plagued him since childhood, and arranged for him to be fitted with a truss.[11]

In various comments on Heshen, both Macartney and Gillan described him as forceful and intelligent, if evasive. Moreover, miscellaneous Chinese sources also show that Heshen possessed a lively intelligence, keen curiosity, tact, and a high level of literacy. But he used those skills and his offices to make prodigious amounts of money for himself and his cronies. He took on nearly imperial pretensions, coerced favors, and demanded fees for all services. He raked in extra millions by misreporting the needs for supplies and services on the numerous military campaigns conducted during Qianlong's later years, especially the protracted, savage, and badly executed forays against the White Lotus rebels. By all these actions, Heshen compounded the problems of the time and contributed to a growing demoralization among the bureaucracy and the people.

Heshen's dominance was even stronger after 1796. In that year, Qianlong abdicated the throne as a "filial" gesture to show that he did not consider himself worthy to reign longer than the sixty-one years of his grandfather, Kangxi. But Qianlong did not allow his son to exercise power, and during this twilight period, even though Qianlong's name was not used in dynastic titles, his will was manifested through Heshen's continuing power. When Qianlong died at last in 1799, Heshen's base crumbled. He was charged with corruption by Qianlong's son and forced to kill himself. It was a melancholy yet somehow fitting end to one of the richest centuries in China's long history, an end that highlighted the mix of strength and weakness that was now emerging as lying at the heart of the Qing dynasty. It used to be generally accepted that Qianlong's reign marked a pinnacle in our assessments of the long span of the Qing dynasty. But as we learn more, we can also see that roots of future problems were becoming glaringly apparent, and that the dynasty was going to be forced to adjust to the troubles it was facing, whether for good or ill.

CHAPTER 6

China and the Eighteenth-Century World

MANAGING THE FOREIGNERS

The Qing managed its relations with foreigners using a variety of strategies and institutions, which took into account the specific political circumstances and security threats of diverse regions. These flexible arrangements, well-suited for the Qing empire in the eighteenth century, would be forcefully challenged in the nineteenth century by formidable European powers that operated with different assumptions about the conduct of foreign affairs.

In the northern and western border regions, relations with the Russians, Mongols, and Tibetans were handled mainly by the Lifan Yuan (the Office of the Administration of Outer Provinces), which had been founded by Hong Taiji in 1638. Staffed by Manchu and Mongol officials, with Han Chinese permitted only to serve in clerical positions, the Lifan Yuan's task was to keep things quiet along the frontiers that had produced repeated threats to the empire. To this end, the office in the capital and its extensive field staff were responsible for military preparedness and civilian administration. Equally crucial was orchestrating the participation of chieftains and other leaders in the imperial hunt, as confirmation of their continued loyalty to the Qing. The marriages of imperial daughters to influential Mongol princes formed a protective network of personal alliances, bolstered by Qing garrisons located at strategic points. Muslims, some of whom were of Central Asian origin and others Chinese, were watched with care but generally allowed to practice their religion in peace. The variety of tasks coordinated by officials in the Lifan Yuan gave them considerable breadth of experience in dealing with foreign policy and border problems.

European missionary contact with China was supervised mainly by the imperial household in Beijing. This agency managed a wide range of the emperor's affairs, including his finances, the provision of favorite foods and delicacies for the imperial family, and the maintenance of imperial estates and palaces. It was most commonly the bondservants in the imperial household—often men of considerable wealth and power—who dealt directly with the missionaries and escorted papal embassies. Their general role in missionary business underlined the prevailing view that this dimension of foreign affairs was an aspect of the court's prestige rather than of national policy. The Jesuits especially found their work much constricted by this arrangement and tried to emphasize their independence in letters back to European colleagues. Some of the Jesuits, along with other Catholic missionaries and Chinese priests, worked in secret, sheltered by their converts. All faced serious punishment if caught by the authorities.

Interactions with countries such as Korea, Burma, Thailand, Vietnam, Japan, and the Ryukyu Islands were supervised by the Ministry of Rituals. Some of these countries, such as Korea and Vietnam, shared many of the values of Chinese culture, such as the practice of Confucianism and Buddhism, writing systems based on classical Chinese, similar types of food and dress, and the outlines of Chinese bureaucratic organization. Others, such as Burma and Thailand, had developed under the influence of Indian culture and religion, and were more distant in cultural terms. Regardless of the degree of cultural affinity, diplomatic contact between the Qing court and these neighboring countries was based on their deference to Qing claims of superiority, with correspondence conducted using Chinese language and the rhetoric of submission. As they had in the Ming (and dating back as far as the Han dynasty), these "vassal" states sent regular emissaries, who were expected to pay homage to the emperor with a ritual of three kneelings and nine prostrations, known as *koutou*. The emissaries brought tribute gifts such as native products or exotic animals, which the imperial court reciprocated with extravagant generosity as validation of its superior status. In addition, such tribute missions were allowed to bring other goods to trade at designated locations and with selected merchants. The lucrative profits from these exchanges were a major incentive for the visitors to abide by the compulsory ritual protocols. Occasionally, some intrepid foreign merchants arrived bearing credentials and gifts from fictitious states, scheming for access to sought-after Chinese luxury goods.

Within this system, there was considerable flexibility. The most frequent missions were those from Korea, which came every year; Korean visitors mingled freely with Qing scholars and officials, and left vivid accounts of the social and cultural life in Beijing. Embassies from Japan, however, had completely ceased during the later Ming. Japan's refusal to acknowledge the Qing's ritual superiority, combined with the Tokugawa government's decision to restrict foreign residence and trade to Nagasaki, meant that its formal ties with the Qing were minimal. In the Ryukyu Islands, there was a curious case of divided loyalties. The islanders were in fact controlled by the southern Japanese lords of Satsuma, but on ritual occasions continued to profess themselves tributary subjects of the Qing. Contemporary eighteenth-century accounts show Japanese ships retreating discreetly out of sight when Qing diplomatic missions visited the islands, only to return upon the departure of the visitors.

Apart from finessing the conduct of diplomatic relations, officials and scholars applied their skills of evidential research (*kaozheng*) to studying the geographical and linguistic features of border regions and foreign countries. Deciphering the confusing tangle of place names across different languages required philological expertise and patient analysis. Information collected during the western military campaigns needed multilingual teams to translate and interpret intelligence provided by local informants and traveling merchants. The Qianlong court also commissioned mapping surveys of Xinjiang, sending cartographic teams of Han Chinese officials, Jesuits, high-ranking bannermen, and imperial bodyguards on monthslong expeditions for field research. Ethnographic studies documented the customs of minority groups living in the southwest and in Taiwan, and ranked their level of progress toward a Chinese cultural ideal, reflecting the patronizing assumptions of a civilizing mission. In the 1790s, to put on display the magnificent linguistic pluralism of his empire, Qianlong commissioned a pentaglot dictionary of five languages—Manchu, Tibetan, Mongolian, Chinese, and Chagatai Turki (related to modern Uyghur).

As research on the Qing frontiers blossomed through official channels and private scholarly networks, the eagerness for knowledge extended to lands beyond the imperial domain. Some descriptions of foreign countries continued to contain an exotic blend of mystical tales and fantasy in which foreigners were likened to animals or birds, or were described in deliberately belittling language. But other scholars opened rigorous inquiry about the geopolitical conditions of "Hindustan" (India), Afghanistan, and the Ottoman and Russian Empires.[1]

This body of Qing beliefs and practices began to clash with those of the European powers, especially after the newly expanding states of Britain, France, and Holland developed major overseas empires at the expense of the earlier dominant partners, Spain and Portugal. One can trace this process of opposition through the gradual emergence of a structure commonly known as the Canton system. In the early Qing, Dutch and Portuguese embassies both tried to establish broad trading privileges with China but had to be content with the status of "tributary nations," permitted to send trade missions only at stipulated intervals. British ships sporadically appeared off the east China coast beginning in 1635, and under the Qing, British merchants were permitted to trade in Zhoushan, Xiamen, and Guangzhou. All the European countries benefited when Kangxi ended the coastal trade-restriction policy in the 1680s and the idea of their tributary status was generally dropped.

Regulations implemented after 1684, when Kangxi opened all ports to foreign trade, required vessels to register at customs stations and pay the requisite tariffs. Guangzhou (Canton) quickly became the dominant port of call for European traders. Its location on the Pearl River connected the southern entrepôt to a transportation network providing easy access to markets in the middle and lower Yangzi regions and in the north. Soon Chinese merchants specializing in foreign trade congregated in Guangzhou. In 1725 the Yongzheng emperor designated responsibility for managing trade with Europeans to an organization of these merchants known as the Cohong.

Then, in the mid-1750s, a series of parallel developments altered coastal trade conditions. Intent on monopolizing profits, local officials and merchants in Guangzhou successfully lobbied the Qing state to close all rival ports to European traders. The discovery of a rash of illegal Christian activity sounded the alarm about possible antigovernment sectarian activity in collusion with foreigners. (In several cases, priests had entered through the coastal ports and ventured into the interior to preach, gathering with Chinese converts secretly to worship.) Further regulations followed: each European ship arriving in the port was required to secure the guarantee of a Cohong merchant; Europeans would be allowed to reside in Guangzhou only during the trading season of October to March. Called the "Canton system" (for the romanized name of Guangzhou), these conditions singled out European traders for unfavorable treatment; other traders, such as those from Batavia (Dutch East Indies), Vietnam, or Thailand, were subjected to fewer constraints. Meanwhile, commerce in the northwestern corridor expanded, with welcoming policies that invited Central Asian, Indian, and Russian traders to visit the marketplaces of the Qing's new dominion. In the northeast, towns situated between Manchuria and Korea profited from lively cross-border commercial exchanges.[2]

The British East India Company, founded in 1600 and granted a monopoly of East Indian trade by the British government, was now rising rapidly from a small operation to a position of global significance as it attracted sizable new investments and started to conquer territories in the subcontinent of India. During the Qianlong reign, its directors began to chafe at Qing restrictions, as did the British government itself. In 1741, the British discovered the importance of having a base of operations (as the Portuguese had in Macao and the Spaniards in Manila) when Commodore George Anson of the Royal Navy tried to seek refuge in Guangzhou. Sent to attack Spanish shipping in the Philippines, Anson's fleet had been damaged by severe storms. His flagship survived and put in to the harbor at Guangzhou, in dire need of supplies and repairs. After local officials refused to help and merchants charged him outrageous prices for shoddy materials, Anson left in anger. *A Voyage Around the World*, his published account of his alleged mistreatment, was widely circulated and translated into several European languages, contributing to a groundswell of anti-Chinese feeling in Britain and elsewhere in the West.

The East India Company tried to enlarge the scope for trade and negotiation in 1759 by sending James Flint, a company trader who had learned Chinese as an orphan in Guangzhou, to convey their requests to the emperor. With the help of his Chinese teacher, Flint wrote a petition asking for investigation of the senior customs official in Guangzhou (known as "the Hoppo" to the foreign community) for corruption. He also requested permission to trade in Ningbo, a port where the British had previously conducted business. Flint sailed from Macao with a small crew and stopped in Ningbo, where he was not permitted to disembark. Heading north, the party arrived at the gateway to Tianjin, where they met the same reception. One official, however, suggested that for a suitable fee, Flint's ship could be described as having been blown off course by storms, rather than arriving without permission or with the intent of breaching Qing law. The payoff secured Flint's passage to Tianjin, where he was received politely, with his petition sent on to Beijing. The emperor's response focused on the allegations of official misconduct. Qianlong ordered Flint to leave his crew and ship behind and accompany an imperial commissioner back to Guangzhou by land; he was to provide evidence for the investigation of the Hoppo there. In the end, the corrupt official was duly removed, but Flint himself was imprisoned for three years—for venturing where foreign ships were prohibited and for submitting a petition directly to the throne in violation of the protocol governing imperial communication. His Chinese teacher was arrested as an accomplice and executed for abetting a foreigner's crimes.[3]

Despite the harsh lesson, the British appetite for trade in China continued to grow. In some instances, British merchants formed enduring business relationships with Chinese counterparts, to their mutual benefit. A triangular trade developed, with profits from British textile businesses in India invested in Guangzhou and used to purchase tea, which was then transshipped back to the European markets. But overall, Qing restrictions were exasperating to Europeans accustomed to dictating the terms of commercial exchange. Tensions increased after the 1770s as British traders, worried by the trade deficits that forced them to offer hundreds of thousands of pounds' worth of silver bullion each year in exchange for Chinese silks, porcelains, and teas, began to ship Indian opium to southern Chinese ports to offset the imbalance. The stakes became higher each year as the passion for tea drinking grew in both Britain and America: by 1800, the East India Company was buying over 23 million pounds of Chinese tea at a cost of £3.6 million. From 1784 onward, merchants in the newly independent United States began to send their ships, eager for a share of the lucrative China tea market; they were subjected to the same restrictions that bound Europeans.

Near the end of Qianlong's reign, the British East India Company, acting in agreement with King George III's government, decided to try to rectify the situation in a direction they believed was consonant with the dignity of Britain as a world power. They selected as their emissary Lord George Macartney, a politically well-connected peer and experienced diplomat from Northern Ireland. The British embassy traveled in a man-of-war of sixty-six guns, with two support vessels, each loaded with expensive gifts designed to show the finest aspects of British manufacturing technology. Macartney was accompanied by a retinue of almost 100, including scientists, artists, guards, valets, and Chinese language teachers from the Catholic college in Naples.

Leaving London in September 1792, Macartney's ships touched briefly at Guangzhou in June 1793. They were allowed to proceed to Tianjin and land there since they claimed to be saluting Qianlong on his eightieth birthday. Once ashore, the embassy was escorted to Beijing with much pomp but with the official status of tribute emissaries. The protocol for the imperial audience became a point of contention. Macartney was most concerned about how his conduct would be regarded in Britain after his return—if he performed the ritual prostration as dictated by Qing decorum, he could expect to be publicly pilloried for his obeisance. Proceeding to the northern summer palace of Rehe, Macartney was courteously received in September 1793 by Heshen and by the emperor. In his own account Macartney was careful to note that he refused to prostrate himself before the emperor in the ritual *koutou*; other British and Chinese accounts suggest that he did. In his audience, Macartney asked for British rights of diplomatic residence in Beijing, an end to the restrictive Canton trading system, new ports opened to international commerce, and fair and equitable tariffs.

Neither the Qing emperor nor his minister would yield to any of the British requests. Instead, they lavishly entertained Macartney and his entourage, in the process learning bits and pieces about British colonial expansion. As both sides recognized their basic disagreement over diplomacy and trade policy, negotiations stalled. Macartney had no counterforce to employ. He could only leave by the designated land route back to Guangzhou, taking as many notes about the country as he could along the way. Meanwhile, Qianlong

The approach of the Emperor of China to his tent to receive the British emissary Lord George Macartney, from a 1793 engraving by William Alexander (1767–1816)

instructed the governors of the coastal provinces to make defensive preparations and to organize a show of military force synchronized to the embassy's journey south: "England is stronger and fiercer than the other countries in the Western Ocean. Since things have not gone according to their wishes, it may cause them to stir up trouble."[4]

Macartney carried back to London the emperor's reply to King George. Qianlong explained his rationale for refusing the British demands: they were impractical as well as contrary to dynastic precedent and current practice; granting them would invite a barrage of similar requests from other nations. In an often-quoted line from the letter, the emperor dismissed the gifts Macartney brought: "We have never valued ingenious articles, nor do we have the slightest need of your country's manufactures."[5]

It was not an auspicious opening to the era of face-to-face diplomatic relations, although Macartney himself did nicely. He had negotiated for an annual allowance of £15,000 before undertaking the venture and cleared a profit of over £20,000 from the mission. Back in London, British merchants and diplomats with vested interests in the China trade drew a different conclusion. They fixated on Macartney's purportedly principled refusal to prostrate himself before the Qing emperor as the reason the mission failed to secure its objectives, and as illustrative of the clash between "Western rationalism" and

"Oriental despotism." Thus the word "kowtow" entered the English language, as a loaded term meaning obsequious deference—different from the Chinese term *koutou*, meaning paying homage to one's sovereign or respect to one's parents.[6]

FOREIGNERS AND CHINESE LAW

One of Lord Macartney's more interesting acquisitions was a copy of the Qing dynasty's legal code. This copy of the code was brought back to England and later translated by a scholar who had learned Chinese as a member of Macartney's retinue. It made clear what had seemed probable to British traders—namely, that the Chinese and the Europeans had different views of what constituted the law and, accordingly, that recourse to legal expedients might exacerbate rather than lessen international tensions.

Although based on a wide range of prior experience and precedent, Qing law was codified and interpreted by the state. There was no independent judiciary either in the provinces or in the capital: the county magistrate acted as the local representative of justice. A series of reviews by the prefect and the judicial intendant of a given province could bring a case to the Ministry of Punishments. Appeals by plaintiffs were also possible but only within a hierarchy that culminated in a "court" of senior officials. Death sentences were reviewed by the magistrate's superiors, and technically the emperor himself passed final judgment on all crimes meriting execution. But that was not always possible in practice and often arbitrary. In local insurrections, rebels were customarily executed immediately to discourage their followers; in cases involving foreigners, summary executions were also common.

The county magistrates acted as detectives, judges, and jury. They accumulated the evidence, evaluated it, and decided the sentence. Punishments for particular crimes were prescribed in the legal code, which magistrates had to follow. Although these officials often relied on a member of their staff who was allegedly a legal expert, there was no independent profession of law and no lawyers. Suspects were routinely treated with great harshness in jail, and often beaten or tortured with wooden presses if they refused to confess. Since the beatings, with a heavy wooden pole sometimes used to extract confessions from suspects, could lead to severe injury or death, it is not surprising that many Chinese feared the legal structure, although they did use the magistrates' courts in serious property or inheritance disagreements. Those threatened with lawsuits in such cases might well pay to hush a case up. The junior personnel of the magistrate's staff supplemented their meager incomes by accepting bribes to keep matters quiet. With gifts or payments to the magistrate and his staff, those accused of committing serious crimes would try to buy their way out of trouble.

The Qing penal system also maintained Confucian social hierarchy. Crimes against the emperor and his family were the most serious, and crimes against officials or state property were also severely punished—by execution or prolonged periods of exile. Within the family structure, fathers committing a crime against their sons were punished more lightly than the reverse, and the same was true of husbands harming their wives, or older relatives their younger ones. In one case in which a father killed his son by burying him alive, the Ministry of Punishments reviewed the facts and concluded that the governor had erred in sentencing the father to be beaten for the crime. Fathers who killed sons should be beaten only if they had acted "unreasonably," argued the ministry. In this case, the son had used foul language at his father, an act that deserved the death penalty: "Thus, although the killing was done intentionally, it was the killing of a son who had committed a capital crime by reviling his father."[7] The father was acquitted.

Had the Ministry of Punishments not intervened, the father could have avoided punishment nonetheless. After trial and sentencing, many punishments could be commuted for cash—depending on the severity of the offense, from 0.50 tael for twenty blows with the bamboo, to 720 taels for banishment in perpetuity, and 1,200 taels or more for a death sentence. Such sums were comparatively trivial to the wealthy; for the poor they might constitute many months or years of income. Furthermore, scholars who passed the lower-level state examinations were exempt from corporal punishment and escaped the fearsome beatings that often forced confessions from terrified commoners. In these ways the legal system favored the wealthy and the educated.

The Qing judicial structure received reinforcement from a community mutual-responsibility system known as the *baojia*. A *bao*, a group of 1,000 households, consisted of 10 *jia*, each of which contained 100 households. All households were supposed to be registered in *jia* and *bao* groups and supervised by a "headman" chosen from among their own number on a rotating system. These headmen were responsible for the accuracy of the household registration forms, and for local law and order. They also supervised community projects such as dike repairs and militia operations, and they were expected to enforce prompt tax payments from their members. Their job was difficult, frustrating, and sometimes dangerous; in many communities, the system grew moribund because no one wanted to serve as headman. But of most importance to the foreigners who studied the Qing legal code was the concept represented by the *baojia*—because members of a community were collectively responsible for the good order of that community, neighbors or friends of guilty parties might also be held liable and punished for any illegal acts. The concept (and foreign misunderstandings) of "collective responsibility" would become a flashpoint of contention in the Qing state's prosecution of Westerners accused of breaking the law.

Although the Qing penal system was harsh, its standard of law and order was comparable to that prevalent in Europe or the United States at the time. Like other early modern empires, the Qing insisted on enforcing the sovereignty of its legal code, but could permit some modifications in cases involving foreign subjects. In China, as we have seen, in routine matters foreigners fell within the jurisdiction either of the Lifan Yuan, the Ministry of Rituals, the Hoppos, or the imperial household. If they violated the law, the assumption was that they would be handled by Qing courts in the conventional way.

Several cases in which the crews of foreign ships accidentally killed Chinese show that the local Qing authorities were initially willing to accept cash payments in restitution. In Kangxi's reign, Qing authorities demanded 5,000 taels after the crew of a British ship killed a Chinese near Guangzhou in 1689. When the British counteroffer of 2,000 taels was rejected, the ship abandoned its trading plans and sailed away. At the end of the reign, in 1722, the captain of the King George paid 2,000 taels after his gunner's mate accidentally killed a Chinese boy while out hunting. In 1754, when a Frenchman killed an English sailor in Guangzhou, Qing officials showed their determination to intervene in cases occurring within their jurisdiction even when no Chinese were involved. All trade with France was stopped until the French officers yielded up the killer. (The killer was released shortly thereafter because Emperor Qianlong, to celebrate the twentieth year of his reign and the Qing victories in the Zunghar wars, had ordered a general amnesty for all convicted criminals.)

More ominous for Westerners were a number of legal cases that occurred in the later years of Qianlong's reign. In 1773 the Portuguese authorities in Macao tried an Englishman who had allegedly killed a Chinese; they found him innocent and released him. But Qing officials, insisting on their right to intervene in homicide cases in which the victim was Chinese, retried the Englishman and executed him. Seven years later, Qing authorities successfully reasserted their right to intervene in cases in which foreigners killed foreigners on Chinese soil: a Frenchman who had killed a Portuguese sailor in a fight was forced out of his refuge with the French consul and publicly executed by strangulation.

The cases that made the greatest impact on Western thinking about dealing with the Qing in international diplomacy were those involving two trading vessels, the Lady Hughes and the Emily. The first of these incidents occurred in 1784, nine years before Lord Macartney arrived in China. The Lady Hughes, a private British ship under license to the East India Company, was anchored at Huangpu (known as Whampoa), twelve miles from Guangzhou. When the ship's gunner fired a salute for another vessel's departure from the harbor, the discharge from the shot killed two Chinese men in a boat nearby. The ship's captain and representatives of the East India Company blocked the Qing investigation of the deaths. They insisted that it had been an accident and claimed that the gunner and other witnesses had fled the scene. (There was in fact evidence that the captain willfully disregarded a warning about the possible danger to the nearby boat; the gunner was hiding in the ship.) After the British refused to allow investigators to search their warehouses and ships, Qing authorities took the business manager of the *Lady Hughes* into custody for questioning and suspended trade in Guangzhou. The detention of the business manager caused an uproar, as the British interpreted the act as an egregious application of the Qing legal concept of "collective responsibility." They immediately rallied their European colleagues and a newcomer—the first China-trade venture from the United States—to send their ships with armed crews into the port at Guangzhou. Seeking to defuse a tense situation, the Qing governor invited the foreign representatives—excepting the British—for a meeting. He persuaded them to withdraw their ships and lifted their trade embargoes when they did so. Meanwhile, the British held out for another two days before turning the gunner over to the Qing authorities. He was sentenced to death by strangulation a month later.

The case of the United States merchant ship *Emily*, which occurred in 1821, was the first to involve American interests in a central way. Francis Terranova, an Italian crew member on the *Emily*, caused the death of a boatwoman named Ko Leang-she during a quarrel. From his perch on the ship, Terranova was buying fruits or liquor from Ko in her small boat when he allegedly threw an earthenware jar in anger, striking her on the head. She fell overboard and drowned. Like the British in the *Lady Hughes* case, the Americans refused to turn the suspect over. After lengthy negotiations, conflicting testimony from witnesses who likely perjured themselves, and the Qing government's threat of suspending trade, the ship's captain finally handed Terranova over to the Qing authorities. The captain was likely quite concerned about the opium in his cargo hold. Terranova was tried, found guilty of homicide, and executed by strangulation.

Both cases tested the resolve of the Qing government to hold foreigners accountable for criminal acts and to enforce its own laws. Had the same crimes been committed in Britain or the United States, the culprits could have been charged with negligent homicide. To make the claim that Westerners should be exempt from Qing jurisdiction, the British and the Americans characterized its legal system as primitive, barbaric, and arbitrary. Propelled by an aggressive sense of cultural superiority, they felt no compunction about obstructing the investigations, lying, or threatening violence. If they could compel the Qing to yield legal jurisdiction over foreign nationals, in the future they would be able to conduct business without the constraint of local laws. To that end, the *Lady Hughes* and the *Emily* would be repeatedly invoked by foreign traders and diplomats throughout the nineteenth century as cautionary tales, and used to justify Western demands for extraterritoriality—both immunity from Qing legal jurisdiction and the right to apply the laws of Western nations in China.[8] The issue of extraterritoriality would become a lightning rod for Chinese nationalism in the twentieth century.

It was not only foreigners who began to protest that Chinese law was inadequate. From a diametrically opposite point of view, Chinese elites and commoners grew exasperated by Qing officials' weakness in the face of foreign demands for certain exemptions and special treatment. When in 1807 brawling sailors from the British ship *Neptune* killed two Chinese, Qing officials and the British trade supervisor worked out a compromise by which a scapegoat was produced. They subsequently charged him with accidental homicide and permitted him to redeem his sentence for 12.42 taels, in accordance with the commutation table of the Qing code. In what seems to have been a concerted campaign, placards were posted all over Guangzhou accusing the Qing of selling out to the "foreign devils." The initiators of that campaign are unknown, but they were sounding a theme that was to become central in the gradual emergence of a new force in Chinese history: antiforeign nationalism.

OPIUM

The captain of the *Emily*, in offering up the sailor Terranova to Qing justice so that the ship's cargo of opium could be safeguarded, was very much a figure of his times. Over the previous century, the growing demand in Europe and America for Chinese teas, porcelain, silks, and decorative goods had not been matched by growth in Chinese demand for Western products such as cotton and woolen goods, furs, clocks, tin, and lead. The result was a serious balance-of-payments problem for the European and American traders, who had to pay for Chinese goods mainly in silver. This steady flow of silver into China—one of the causes of the general prosperity in Qianlong's reign—became a source of alarm especially to the British government. In the decade of the 1760s, for example, silver flow into Qing China exceeded 3 million taels; in the 1770s, the total grew to 7.5 million, and by the 1780s, 16 million. By the late eighteenth century, the British had developed an alternative product to exchange for Chinese goods: opium. Although the trade was subject to fluctuations, figures for opium sales show the overall trend with bleak clarity. Each chest contained between 130 and 160 pounds of opium; by the 1820s enough opium was imported to sustain the habits of around 1 million addicts. When one adds to this supply domestically grown opium (although this was still on a small scale), one can begin to sense the extent of opium consumption.

For opium to sell steadily, several factors were necessary: the narcotic had to be available in large quantities, there had to be a developed means of consuming it, enough people had to want to consume it to make the trade viable, and government attempts at prohibitions had to be ineffectual. At the same time, the scale of trade between Westerners and Chinese had to be steadily expanding, so that profits were possible for both parties, even though many of the Cohong merchants were almost consistently in debt.[9] The conjunction of all these elements brought China into this particularly agonizing cycle of its modern history.

The British conquest of large areas of India first spurred the organized production and sale of opium. Between 1750 and 1800 the British had gained control of much of northern India, from Bombay in the west to Calcutta in the east, with additional bases in the south at Madras. Eager to find a cash crop that would earn revenue through export sales, the British discovered that the opium poppy grew especially luxuriantly in certain areas of India. Moreover, there was an abundant supply of labor to collect the sap from the incised poppy pods and to process it (by boiling) into the thick paste that was best for smoking.

The East India Company established a monopoly for the purchase of Indian opium and then sold trade licenses to selected merchants known as the "country traders," preferring this indirect means of profit making to getting directly involved in narcotics trafficking. Having sold their opium in China, the country traders deposited the silver they received in payment with company

British Sales of Opium to China[10]

Year	Number of chests
1729	200
1750	600 (est.)
1773	1,000
1790	4,054
1800	4,570
1810	4,968
1816	5,106
1823	7,082
1828	13,131
1832	23,570

agents in Guangzhou in exchange for letters of credit; the company, in turn, used the silver to buy tea, porcelain, and other Chinese goods for sale in Britain. Thus a triangular trade of goods from Britain to India, India to China, and China to Britain developed. At each step high profits could be made.

The consumption of opium was perhaps a simpler aspect of the process. History offers examples of many ways of taking opium derivatives—from steeping them in potions or smoking them mixed with other herbs, to the concentrated morphine tablets of the late nineteenth century and the heroin injections of our own day. The style of opium smoking favored in China— heating a tiny globule of refined opium paste over a flame and then smoking it from the bowl of a long-stemmed pipe—may have been initially popular because tobacco smoking had become a craze in the early Qing. Tobacco plants had been introduced into Korea and Fujian province from Latin America. It had spread swiftly from there to Shandong and other parts of China, despite being banned as a toxic substance by both the Qing and the Ming rulers, who punished tobacco smoking or sales of leaves with harsh beatings and even execution. In scrolls from Kangxi's reign, scores of Chinese smoking tobacco pipes can be seen strolling down city streets, and the brand names of popular varieties were displayed in front of stores. The practice of smoking opium mixed with tobacco probably came to China in the 1720s, brought by troops returning home from Taiwan after suppressing Zhu Yigui's rebellion of 1721. By the middle of Qianlong's reign, detailed accounts of the drug and how to prepare it for consumption were available to anyone who could read. Small public rooms where, for a few coppers, people could get a pipeful of opium and smoke it as they reclined in comfort brought the drug in reach of urban dwellers and the poor.

Why did the Chinese of the mid- and late Qing begin to smoke so much opium? Opium derivatives have the effect of slowing down and blurring one's perception of the world, of making time stretch and fade, of shifting complex or painful realities to an apparently infinite distance. Opium appealed initially to groups confronting boredom or stress: eunuchs caught in the webs of court politics, Manchu officials with sinecures or virtually pointless jobs in the bureaucracy, women in wealthy households forbidden to travel outside the walls of their homes, soldiers on their way to combat, secretaries in the harried magistrates' offices, students preparing for—and even taking—the state examinations. Over time, the practice spread from the coast to the north and the interior and became part of a consumption culture among the leisure classes. Opium also acquired a reputation as a potent aphrodisiac, adding to its appeal.

Later in the nineteenth century, opium smoking became "a hobby among the high and the low in officialdom."[11] The cultivation of domestic opium made available less expensive alternatives to foreign imports. Laborers began to smoke it, to overcome the drudgery and pain of hauling huge loads day after day. (Ruthless employers, observing that workers could carry heavier loads if they were under the influence of opium, even made the drug available to them.) By the end of the nineteenth century, many subsistence farmers also became addicts, particularly those who themselves had begun to grow the poppies as a cash crop to supplement their incomes.

The Qing government was not sure how to handle the problem. As we saw previously, Yongzheng, the first emperor to pronounce on the narcotic, was aware that there was a legitimate need for its use as a medicinal drug but that nonmedicinal uses seemed harmful. His uneasy compromise strictly punished those who "pushed" the drug to potential users and operated opium dens, while "medicinal" sales were permitted.

During the eighteenth century, most of the wholesale opium purchases were handled by licensed Cohong merchants. The trade became more indirect after 1800, when an edict forbade both opium imports and domestic opium production, and especially after 1813, when further edicts banned opium smoking altogether. Chinese smokers could be punished with 100 blows of the bamboo and with the public wearing of the "cangue," a heavy wooden collar, for a month or more. The Cohong merchants no longer dared deal in opium, but foreign traders found that if they anchored at selected spots off the coast, there were plenty of Chinese adventurers willing to come out and purchase their opium stocks. Large fortified hulks anchored off Lintin Island in the bay below Guangzhou also formed a convenient distribution point for the drug. Sailing or rowing in swift, shallow-draft boats, Chinese dealers could elude attempts by the Qing naval forces to intercept them. Thereafter they distributed the opium through a network of local trade routes, by road, river, and track.

As the Qing government tried to enforce its ban by punishing dealers severely and rigorously questioning smokers as to their sources of supply, those involved in opium sales grew more circumspect, covering their trail through numerous intermediaries. The 1831 transcript of an arrested court eunuch's testimony illustrates this:

> At first we bought the opium we smoked in small quantities directly from the Muslim Zhu Da. Then I learned that when the sea vessels came into Tianjin the opium pills got cheaper, so I asked Kekesibuku for a loan of 100 strings of local cash, and I also sold my mule cart for money. I took my servant Qin Baoquan with me to Tianjin, and got Qin's old friend Yang Huiyuan to act as my agent. Yang bought 160 ounces of opium from Zhang for 240 strings of cash. I gave Yang a commission of 3.8 strings of cash.[12]

If the Qing authorities ever did pursue this case with vigor, they might have gotten past the two intermediaries and reached the local dealer, Zhang. But Zhang himself was probably only a minor figure in the network, and by the time he was arrested the larger distributors and the vessels that supplied them would long since have gone on their way.

WESTERN IMAGES OF CHINA

Until the middle of the eighteenth century, China generally received favorable attention in the West. In large part this stemmed from the wide dissemination of books and published correspondence by Catholics, especially the Jesuits, who saw in the huge population of China a potential harvest of souls for the Christian faith. Although mindful of some of the country's problems, most Catholic observers followed the example of the Jesuit missionary Matteo Ricci, who had lived in China from 1583 to 1610. Ricci had expressed admiration for the industry of China's population, the sophistication of the government bureaucracy, the philosophical richness of its cultural traditions, and the strength of its rulers.

The French Jesuits, who dominated the China missions late in Kangxi's reign, presented an even more laudatory picture, one deliberately designed to appeal to Louis XIV and to persuade him to back the missionaries with money and personnel. Central to these flattering presentations was the idea that the ethical content of the Confucian classics proved the Chinese had once practiced a form of monotheism not so different from that found in the Judeo-Christian tradition. With a little effort, therefore, the Chinese could be brought back to the true values they had once espoused and did not have to be forced to convert. As part of this plan for cultural acceptance within Europe of Chinese philosophical and moral values, Catholic missionaries, with the help of Chinese scholars, had translated the Analects of Confucius into Latin. The Latin version was completed in the 1680s, and by 1687 had been made available in libraries in Paris and Oxford.

Although the Jesuits lost influence in China during the last years of Kangxi's reign, and declined in prestige in Europe until they were suppressed altogether in 1773, their books on Chinese government and society remained by far the most detailed available. The German philosopher Gottfried Wilhelm von Leibnitz read them and became deeply interested in the binary structure of the hexagrams in the *Book of Changes*. Even the anticlerical philosopher Voltaire was intrigued by what he read about China. Intent on attacking the power of the Catholic church in eighteenth-century France, he cleverly used the information provided by the Catholics. If, argued Voltaire, the Chinese really were so intelligent, ethical, and well governed, and if this was largely attributable to the influence of Confucius, it followed that, since Confucius had not been a Christian, it was possible for a country to get along admirably without Catholicism.

In a series of influential works written between 1740 and 1760, Voltaire expounded his ideas about China. Notably, in an unusual historiographical gesture, Voltaire *began* his review of world history with a lengthy section on China. He did this to emphasize the values of differing civilizations and to put European arrogance in perspective: "The great misunderstanding over Chinese rites sprang from our judging their practices in light of ours: for we carry the prejudices that spring from our contentious nature to the ends of the world."[13] Unable to find a "philosopher-king" in Europe to exemplify his views of religion and government, Voltaire believed Emperor Qianlong would fill the gap, and he wrote poems in the distant emperor's honor.

Voltaire's praise for Chinese institutions appeared in a cultural context that was intensely sympathetic to China. During this same brief period in the mid-eighteenth century, Europe was swept by a fascination with China that is usually described by the French word *chinoiserie*, an enthusiasm drawn more to décor and design than to philosophy and government. In prints and descriptions of Chinese houses and gardens and in embroidered silks, rugs, and colorful porcelains, Europeans found an alternative to their neoclassical architecture and baroque design. The popular manifestations of *chinoiserie* could be found everywhere in Europe: "Chinese" designs on the furnishings that graced middle-class homes, pagodas in public parks, latticework that surrounded ornamental gardens.

The Audience with the Chinese Emperor   A chinoiserie view of China from the eighteenth century, by French painter François Boucher (1703–1770)

Yet this appreciation of China, whether intellectual or aesthetic, faded swiftly as angry accounts like George Anson's became available. Voltaire's enthusiasms made him the object of sarcasm and mockery as other French Enlightenment philosophers began to find his picture of China unconvincing. Jean-Jacques Rousseau and the Baron de Montesquieu worried that the Chinese did not enjoy true liberty, that their laws were based on fear rather than on reason, and that their elaborate educational system might lead to the corruption of morals rather than to their improvement. Other writers declared that China did not seem to be progressing and indeed had no notion of progress; from this it was but a short step to see the Chinese as retrogressing.

Reflecting on these arguments, some leading European thinkers labored to assess China's prospects. One of these was the Scottish philosopher Adam Smith in *The Wealth of Nations*, first published in 1776. Smith's analysis of the productive capacities of different countries invoked China for comparative purposes, especially with the nations of Europe and the developing societies of North America. Examining population growth as an index of development, he concluded that in contrast to steady growth in Europe and rapid advancement in North America, China had reached a stage where continued population growth brought serious economic repercussions, exacerbated by its refusal to engage fully with the world economy.[14]

In the early 1820s, the German philosopher Georg Wilhelm Friedrich Hegel synthesized the critical analyses of Rousseau, Montesquieu, and Smith to portray "Oriental Civilizations"—China preeminent among them—as an early and now bypassed stage of history. Hegel's concept of "Asiatic Society" was to have a profound influence on the young Karl Marx and other later nineteenth-century thinkers. History, to Hegel, was the development of what he called the ideas and practices of freedom throughout the world. Freedom was the expression of the "World Spirit," and that spirit was reaching its fullest manifestations in the Christian states of Europe and North America. Optimistic about his own society, he developed a theory that denigrated China's past and present as dominated by despotism. In a series of bleak conclusions, Hegel consigned the Chinese permanently to a space outside the development of the World Spirit and therefore "outside of the World's History."[15]

Embedded with Eurocentric assumptions, the polemical analysis of such thinkers would have an insidious influence on European views of Qing China as inert and unable to modernize. These perspectives were further amplified by developing theories of racial hierarchy and geographical determinism, which positioned "the West" as the engine of dynamism and progress, and "the East" as hopelessly behind. And in time, Chinese restrictions would be interpreted as an obstinate refusal to engage in "free trade" with the rest of the world, thereby providing cynical justification for the predatory behavior of European nations.

CHAPTER 7

The First Clash
with the West

PROPOSALS FOR REFORM

Even before the death of Emperor Qianlong in 1799, Confucian scholars were becoming aware of the severity of the domestic and foreign problems confronting the dynasty. From within the *kaozheng* tradition of evidential research new trends began to emerge. Some scholars began to advocate for more attention to current needs and administrative problems; others began to speculate boldly on the country's future and to wonder if, in the Confucian tradition itself, elements encouraging change could be found. Yet others thought that the *kaozheng* school was growing sterile and formalistic, and they worked to develop a new political focus for their writings.

Still, it remained dangerous for anyone to direct criticism at the ruling Qing. One who learned this was Hong Liangji, a tenacious examination taker who failed the top-level *jinshi* exams four times before finally passing at the age of forty-four. Hong spent three years as commissioner of education in Guizhou province, which enabled him to add knowledge of problems in local governance and society to his ongoing analysis of politics in the capital. In a series of essays written in the 1790s, he discussed a number of problems facing China. One of these was unchecked population growth and the difficulties that would follow as the population outraced the country's productive capacity. Hong also addressed the growth of luxury in the cities, the spread of government corruption, and the problems attendant on the attempts to suppress the White Lotus and other rebels. In 1799, as part of debates about reforms encouraged by Emperor Jiaqing (ruled 1799–1820),* Hong wrote a scathing letter denouncing

---

* Jiaqing technically began his reign in 1796 when his father abdicated, but as we saw previously, Qianlong did not relinquish power until he died in 1799.

high-ranking officials for the woeful state of civil administration. In addition to naming the prominent bureaucrats and military commanders he felt were responsible, the letter also criticized the policies of the just-deceased Emperor Qianlong and his favorite Heshen. For this audacity, Hong was fired from his position and sent into exile in Ili in the far northwest.[1]

A year later, Emperor Jiaqing, who had been investigating the web of corruption surrounding Heshen, pardoned Hong and allowed him to return to a life of scholarship and writing in Anhui. Hong died in 1809, but the kind of probing yet practical work for which he had become known was continued by many others. One of the best known was He Changling, who compiled a massive collection of documents on Qing statecraft. This was not just a theoretical work, but one that included the finest memorials of earlier and contemporary Qing administrators, and ranged widely over such fields as personnel evaluation, salaries, banditry, taxes, the *baojia* mutual security system, granaries and famine relief, salt monopolies, currency, folk religions, and flood control. When the full edition of He's work appeared in 1827, many contemporaries read its descriptions with a real sense of urgency about a faltering dynasty.

He Changling was an exponent of statecraft thinking and also an administrator of experience and insight. To circumvent the decaying Grand Canal system, he developed a plan to transport government grain supplies from central and southern China to the north by sea. In 1826, on his advice, 4.5 million bushels of rice were shipped successfully in this way, on a fleet of over 1,500 ships. But He's plan was soon canceled, mainly in response to the vested interests of those who worked on the Grand Canal system.

Other scholars sought a theoretical justification for change. One of these was Gong Zizhen, born in 1792 to a wealthy official family in the beautiful Zhejiang city of Hangzhou. Initially Gong followed the mainstream scholarly trends of his time, studying texts of the "Han Learning" school with evidential research methods. But his critical feelings about Chinese society and government drew him to the Gongyang commentaries on *Spring and Autumn Annals*, one of the Confucian classics. Unlike most Chinese historical texts, which implied a cyclical view of history, the Gongyang commentaries posited a theory of historical development through a sequence of three ages: an age of chaos, an age of ascending peace, and a final period of universal peace.

Gong Zizhen was an emotionally complex and cantankerous man who in some ways echoed the behavior of the early Qing "eccentrics": he paid no attention to dress or deportment, wrote wild calligraphy, consorted with all social classes, gambled recklessly, and insulted his elders. The range of his social commentary was wide. Gong attacked official corruption, court rituals such as the *koutou*, and the clichés of the state examination system. He also underlined the sense that China was currently in the lowest of the three epochs—the age of chaos—with his criticisms of the judicial system, the unequal distribution of wealth, foot-binding of women, opium smoking, and all trade with foreigners.

On the redistribution of wealth, Gong was eloquent. In some forgotten early period, he wrote, rulers and subjects had been like guests at a feast to which all have contributed and in which all share alike. But in the Shang and Zhou dynasties (some three thousand years ago), "it was as if people were sitting around a bowl of soup; the rulers filled a dish as their share, the ministers used a large spoon, the ordinary people a small one." Pursuing the metaphor, Gong pointed to the development of a society in which those with large and small spoons began to attack each other, while the ruler tried to appropriate the entire kettle. Not surprisingly, the kettle "often dried up or toppled over." Now the time had come once again to spoon things out fairly.

[For] when the wealthy vie with each other in splendor and display while the poor squeeze each other to death; when the poor do not enjoy a moment's rest while the rich are comfortable; when the poor lose more and more while the rich keep piling up treasures; when in some ever more extravagant desires awaken, and in others an ever more burning hatred; when some become more and more arrogant and overbearing in their conduct, and others ever more miserable and pitiful until gradually the most perverse and curious customs arise, bursting forth as though from a hundred springs and impossible to stop, all of this will finally congeal in an ominous vapor which will fill the space between heaven and earth with its darkness.[2]

If scholars like Gong moved from evidential research to blunt social criticism, others took a more indirect route. One of China's finest satiric novels, *Flowers in the Mirror*, was written between 1810 and 1820. Its author, Li Ruzhen, was a Confucian scholar whose first intellectual passion was for phonetics. But the crises of his times led Li to reexamine not only the world of philosophy and its relation to politics, but also the particularly sensitive question of the relationship between the sexes. In central sections of his novel, he presented a world in which conventional gender roles were completely reversed. In a chapter entitled "Country of the Women," it is the man who must taste the life of humiliation, pain, and subjugation as he has his ears pierced with needles, endures the agony of binding his feet, and spends hours over his make-up to please his female lords. Although other writers had toyed with such ideas before, no one had pursued them as vigorously as Li.

Li's sense of social dislocation must have been common among scholars living in Jiaqing's reign, who found it difficult to pass the state examinations or to find a job. Despite the swelling numbers of educated men in the early nineteenth century, the government did not increase examination quotas or enlarge the size of the bureaucracy. If these scholars had no private incomes, no interest in reform, and no great artistic or literary talent, their lives took on a certain melancholy. One such man, Shen Fu, in a poignant memoir written around 1807, gives a haunting picture of what it was like to be educated and without prospects. Born in Suzhou, Shen had drifted through a number of roles as part-time scholar, part-time merchant, part-time secretary. His memoirs, appropriately entitled *Six Records of a Floating Life*, show him wandering in search of patrons, subordinate to his dictatorial father or the whims of various employers.

Not that Shen's life was entirely somber. He saw something of the world on his business trips, traveling as far south as Guangzhou. He had a loving wife, his companion for twenty-three years until her death, with whom he shared aesthetic, sensual, and culinary joys. She was a good poet, imaginative and gentle, and did everything she could to stretch their small and erratic income. Shen's portrayal of their life together shows that it was indeed possible to have a close and affectionate marriage despite the rigorous views of the superiority of husband to wife that had become part of the Confucian tradition. Ultimately, however, the couple were worn down by their poverty and his failures, though to the last Shen could not understand why fate did not allow them to be happier. "Why is it that there are sorrows and hardships in this life?" he asked. "Usually they are due to one's own fault, but this was not the case with me. I was fond of friendship, proud of keeping my word, and by nature frank and straightforward."[3] But in the society he was living in, there was little material reward for those quiet virtues.

TRADE AND OPIUM

Apart from some British sparring to make sure Macao did not fall into French hands, there was a respite from foreign pressure during Jiaqing's reign. The reason was the Napoleonic Wars in Europe, which left the British and French few resources for an expansive policy in East Asia.

Within a year of Napoleon's defeat at Waterloo in 1815, the British East India Company dispatched another embassy to China under the leadership of William Pitt, Lord Amherst. Whereas twenty-three years earlier George Macartney had asked for permanent British diplomatic residence and additional ports opened for trade, the Amherst mission had a different set of goals. Relations between British traders and Qing officials in Guangzhou had soured in recent years. The War of 1812 had brought conflicts between British and American ships to the Chinese coast, with warships and armed trading vessels exchanging fire. Local Qing authorities threatened to suspend trade with both parties, to no avail. Frustrations further accumulated after the numbers of Cohong merchants licensed to trade with foreigners were reduced, and the governor-general of Guangdong-Guangxi refused to accept communications written in Chinese from the East India Company. Lord Amherst intended to appeal to the emperor in person, in the hopes that once informed of his officials' obstruction, he would discipline them and smooth the way for better trade relations. Amherst also planned to request a direct communication channel to Qing officials in the capital, and for permission to trade with other Chinese merchants besides those licensed in the Cohong.

He never got the chance to ask. Negotiations for the imperial audience were first derailed by arguments over protocol, with both sides citing Macartney as precedent: Qing officials insisted the former emissary had performed the ritual *koutou*; the British insisted he had not. After receiving word of Amherst's refusal to *koutou*, the Emperor instructed his officials to be flexible on this issue. Thus Qing officials were ready to admit Lord Amherst and his retinue to an imperial audience, but it was to take place immediately upon their arrival in Beijing, at dawn. Having traveled through the night covering the final twelve miles of the journey, Amherst was exhausted and disheveled. He asked for time to rest and refused to be escorted before the throne. A physical altercation broke out between Qing officials and the British visitors; weapons were drawn. The imperial audience was canceled, and the British were sent on their way. In the meantime, the embassy's main ship completed a surveying mission along the northern coast and sustained storm damage when it sailed south. Denied permission to approach Guangzhou for repairs, the ship's captain forced his way up the river and fired on the fort guarding the entrance to the city. Forty-seven Qing soldiers were killed.[4]

Although this episode was used by the British to show that the Qing were unwilling to deal rationally with foreigners, in fact the political complexities of relations with the West were becoming apparent to imperial officials. One indication of this was the growing importance that began to attach to Guangzhou and to the officials who governed the Guangdong-Guangxi region. The sums of money circulating in the southeast because of the opium trade brought heightened corruption. At the same time, state revenues increased from transit dues and from taxation of legitimate foreign trade, such as in tea and silk. The Cohong merchants were forced to make immense "donations" to the court and to local officials in order to assure continued imperial favor. Their base of security was always frail, and many of them ran up enormous debts by buying on credit from foreign firms, or went bankrupt altogether, to be replaced by new—often reluctant—nominees.

Whether to take a hard or soft line on the problem of opium addiction also became a central issue in managing foreign affairs and the domestic economy. Moreover the controversy began to affect the formation of factions and alliances

View of the Hongs at Guangzhou
Western merchants created their own small world in a restricted area southwest of
Guangzhou, where they were permitted to reside. Danish, Austrian, American, Swedish,
British, and Dutch flags label the factories in this painting of the harbor.

within the metropolitan and the provincial bureaucracies. Emperor Daoguang, Jiaqing's successor who reigned from 1821 to 1850, seems to have been
a well-meaning but indecisive ruler, with a habit of demoting and punishing officials who incurred his wrath, then pardoning and reinstating them.
The prohibitions that Jiaqing had imposed on opium dealing in 1800 and
1813 had not been effective, and Daoguang now sought a more successful
alternative.

By 1825, Daoguang was receiving many alarming reports about the amount
of silver going to pay for Indian opium, to the detriment of the national economy. Although this phenomenon was still mainly restricted to the southeast
coastal regions, its effects were being felt far inland. The situation worsened in
1833 when the British Parliament ended the East India Company's monopoly
of trade with Asia. The action threw open the China trade to all comers, with
a predictable rise in opium sales and in the numbers of foreign traders from
elsewhere in Europe and from the United States. The crisis for China was
exacerbated by a worldwide silver shortage that caused foreigners to use specie
less frequently when buying Chinese goods. The net outflow of silver intensified in the 1830s. A string of 1,000 copper cash had been roughly equivalent
to 1 tael of silver in Qianlong's reign; by Daoguang's era, the conversion rate
had grown to 2,700 to 1 in one province. Since taxes were paid in silver while

copper coins were used in everyday transactions, the rise in the value of silver meant in effect steadily higher taxes. The currency crisis and deflationary spiral generated cascading problems of bank failures and unemployment. With declining state revenues, critical infrastructure maintenance and repairs were neglected; military preparedness was scaled back. Catastrophic floods in the 1820s had already precipitated both rural and urban unrest.[5]

The 1834 arrival in Guangzhou of Lord Napier, the British government's first superintendent of trade in China following the end of the East India Company monopoly, led to new confrontations. A veteran of the Napoleonic Wars, Napier had no experience in trade or diplomacy and little knowledge of China. Despite receiving explicit instructions from the British prime minister to adopt a conciliary attitude and to exercise "the most careful discretion," Napier was primed for conflict, armed with the conviction that "every act of violence on our part has been productive of instant redress and other beneficial results." Representing the British crown, he felt justified in refusing to abide by the longstanding protocols that East India Company representatives had followed. After sailing into Guangzhou, taking up residence without permission, and insisting on communicating with local officials rather than dealing with the Cohong merchants, Napier ignored the Guangdong-Guangxi governor-general's order to leave. Mutual insults and threats followed; Qing authorities then shut down British trade and blockaded their warehouses. In response Napier summoned two gunboats to head toward Guangzhou as a show of force, and they engaged in a long exchange of cannon fire with the defensive forts at the Bogue (the main entrance to the river). Some British traders, anxious to reopen trade, asked the belligerent superintendent to leave. When Napier finally gave up and departed Guangzhou, he was ill with fever and soon died of malaria.[6]

Lord Napier's death became ammunition for British war hawks, who demanded action to avenge the insults to Napier, the king, and the British empire. Meanwhile, opium imports to China continued to rise, passing 30,000 chests in 1835. In 1836 Emperor Daoguang asked his senior officials to advise him on the issue. The advice was split. Those who advocated legalization of the opium trade pointed out that it would end corruption and bring in a steady revenue through tariffs. It would also allow the cheaper domestically grown product to gradually displace Indian opium. Many officials, however, considered this view pernicious. They argued that foreigners were cruel and greedy, and that the Chinese did not need opium, domestic or foreign. They thought the prohibitions issued by Emperor Jiaqing, far from being abandoned, should be pursued with even greater rigor. A small minority advocated for a zero-tolerance policy, with the death penalty for users.

In 1838, after evaluating the evidence, Emperor Daoguang made his decision. The opium trade must be stopped. To enforce this decree he appointed a Fujian scholar-official named Lin Zexu as imperial commissioner for the suppression of opium, and sent him to Guangzhou. On paper, the choice was a fine one. Lin was a *jinshi* degree holder of 1811 who had served in the Hanlin Academy—the prestigious center for Confucian studies in Beijing—and in a wide range of provincial posts. As governor-general of Hubei and Hunan, he had launched vigorous campaigns against opium smokers. One of his confidants was the outspoken scholar Gong Zizhen, who wrote in a letter to Lin that he believed all smokers, dealers, and producers of opium should be punished by death.

When he reached Guangzhou in March 1839, Commissioner Lin (as the British came to call him) first mobilized the forces and values of the Confucian state. In public proclamations, he emphasized the health dangers of opium consumption and ordered all smokers to turn in their drugs and pipes within two months. Lin instructed education officials to double-check whether any degree holders were opium smokers; those who smoked were punished, and the rest were organized into five-person mutual-responsibility teams—like miniature *baojia* units—pledged to abstinence. In an ingenious adaptation of the traditional examination system, Lin summoned over 600 local students to a special assembly. There, in addition to being asked questions on the Confucian

Lin Zexu

classics, they were asked to name—anonymously, if they so chose—the major opium distributors and to suggest means of stopping their trade. Similar groups were formed among military and naval personnel. Lin also mobilized the local gentry to form an expanded version of the *baojia* system to spot addicts in the community. By mid-May 1839, over 1,600 Chinese had been arrested and about 35,000 pounds of opium and 43,000 opium pipes had been confiscated. In the following two months, Lin's forces seized a further 15,000 pounds of the drug and another 27,500 pipes.

With the foreigners, Lin used a similar combination of reason, moral suasion, and coercion, and we know from numerous statements that he was wary of provoking armed conflict. He moved first against the Cohong merchants, interviewing them personally in March. Lin scolded them for posting false bonds in which they stated that certain prominent British merchants—such as William Jardine and James Innes—were not opium traders, when everyone knew they were. He ordered the merchants to pass on a command to the foreigners to hand over the thousands of chests of opium they had stored, and to sign pledges that they would cease all further trade in opium. Foreign residents in Guangzhou were also told to state in writing the number of weapons they owned. Lin did not wish to move rashly against foreign ships but felt he could bring enough pressure to bear on the local foreign community to force them to yield. He did not offer compensation for the opium they were to hand over.

Lin also tried to reason with the foreigners, urging them to stick to their legitimate trade in tea, silk, and rhubarb, and to desist from harming the Chinese people. The Guangdong-Guangxi governor-general, with whom Lin cooperated closely, had already optimistically told the foreign traders that "the smokers have all quit the habit and the dealers have dispersed. There is no more demand for the drug and henceforth no profit can be derived from the traffic." In a carefully phrased letter to Queen Victoria (who acceded to the British throne in 1837), Lin tried to appeal to her moral sense of responsibility. "We have heard that in your honorable nation, too," wrote Lin, "the people are not permitted to smoke the drug, and that offenders in this particular expose themselves to sure punishment. . . . In order to remove the source of the evil thoroughly, would it not be better to prohibit its sale and manufacture rather than merely prohibit its consumption?"[7] Opium in fact was *not* prohibited in Britain and was taken often in the form of laudanum; some regarded it as less harmful than alcohol. But Lin's moral exhortations had no effect, for his letter never reached Queen Victoria.

Facing the crackdown, panic-stricken Cohong merchants begged the foreign traders to yield. They in turn explained that they handled opium on consignment for others and were not empowered to hand it over, and then offered to give up a token 1,000 chests. Lin, furious, ordered the arrest of Lancelot Dent, one of the leading British opium traders. When the foreign community refused to yield up Dent for trial, on March 24, 1839, Lin shut down foreign trade completely. All Chinese staff and servants were ordered to leave foreign employ; and the 350 foreigners in Guangzhou, including the senior British official, Superintendent Charles Elliot, were blockaded in their warehouse quarters. Although food and water were available and extra goods and messages were smuggled in, it was a nerve-wracking time, with long days of boredom made worse by the din of gongs and horns that Qing troops kept up throughout the nights. After six weeks, the traders gave up and surrendered more than 20,000 chests of opium. The blockade was lifted, and all but sixteen foreigners were allowed to leave.

Lin had carefully supervised the transfer of this vast amount of opium, even living on a boat in April and May to be near the action and to prevent cheating and theft. He was now faced with the challenge of destroying close to 3 million pounds of raw opium. His solution was to order the digging of three huge trenches, 7 feet deep and 150 feet long. Thereafter, 500 laborers, supervised by 60 officials, broke up the large balls of raw opium and mixed them with water, salt, and lime until dissolved. Then, as large crowds of Chinese and foreigners looked on, the murky mixture was flushed out into a neighboring creek, and so reached the sea.

In a special prayer to the spirit of the Southern Sea, Lin apologized for filling its domain with the noxious mixture and, he wrote in his diary, advised it "to tell the creatures of the water to move away for a time, to avoid being contaminated." As for the foreigners who had lived through the blockade and now watched the solemn proceedings, Lin wrote in a memorial to Emperor Daoguang, they "do not dare show any disrespect, and indeed I should judge from their attitudes that they have the decency to feel heartily ashamed."[8]

BRITAIN'S MILITARY RESPONSE

Commissioner Lin Zexu and Emperor Daoguang were conscientious, hard-working men who had fully internalized the Confucian structures of hierarchy and control. They acted from the conviction that the people of Guangzhou and the foreign traders there would respond to firm guidance and statements of moral principles set out in simple, clear terms. The reality was unfortunately more complex, as plenty of their contemporaries saw. Even before the opium had been washed out to sea, one Qing official had dared to point out that Lin had not really solved the opium problem, just one of its immediate manifestations. And a British opium trader, reflecting on his experiences during the blockade, noted dryly to a friend that the blockade "is even fortunate as adding to the account for which we have to claim redress."[9]

The buildup toward war between China and Britain was now gaining momentum. Some of the broader causes have been noted already: the social dislocations that began to appear in the Qing world, the spread of addiction, foreign refusal to accept Qing legal norms, changes in international trade structures, and the ending of European intellectuals' admiration for China. Other elements were more precisely tied to the background of Lin's negotiations, with ramifications that he could not have anticipated. One of these was the fact that the foreign dealers, having followed the Qing debates at court between 1836 and 1838, were convinced that opium consumption was about to be legalized. As a result, they had stockpiled large amounts and had placed additional orders with Indian growers. When the prohibitions of 1838 began to take effect, the market diminished and dealers found themselves oversupplied.

A second source of tension was the new post of superintendent of trade in China, now held by a deputy of the British crown, not by an employee of the East India Company. If the Chinese crossed the superintendent, they would be insulting the British nation rather than a business corporation. But neither the emperor nor his officials fully understood the close linkages between British imperial power and private interests. The superintendent, in turn, lacked clear legal authority over the British traders and had no control over nationals from other European nations or from the United States. He could, however, call on the aid of the British military in times of serious trouble.

The third element in the picture on the British side was a crucial combination of these previous two: British opium dealers, suffering from a glut of the unsold drug, had handed their supply over to Superintendent Charles Elliot. In turn, Elliot had handed it over to Lin Zexu. Thus, far from being "ashamed" as their opium drifted out to sea, the merchants could anticipate putting pressure on the British government to make sure that they received compensation.

The unfolding events were monitored as closely in England as time and distance allowed. In the early summer of 1839, Elliot sent messages to London asking for assistance. Foreign Secretary Lord Palmerston, initially unsympathetic to British merchants who would not abide by Qing laws, now swung in their favor. As Palmerston wrote in a letter addressed to "The Minister of the Emperor of China," he had heard "with extreme surprise" that "violent outrages" had been committed against the British residents "living peaceably" in Guangzhou. Although the queen did not condone opium selling, she "cannot permit that her subjects residing abroad be treated with violence, and be exposed to insult and injustice."[10]

After news of the blockade and opium seizures reached England, China trade interests and chambers of commerce in the larger manufacturing areas launched intensive lobbying efforts to pressure Parliament into taking retaliatory action. The opium merchant William Jardine cut short his retirement journey and hurried back to England to add his voice to the chorus, and to ensure that the moral objections to the opium traffic being raised by various Protestant missionary societies did not gain too wide an influence. Parliament did not, however, declare war on China. Instead it authorized the dispatch of a fleet and the mobilization of further troops in India in order to obtain "satisfaction and reparation" and, if necessary, to "hold in custody the ships of the Chinese and their cargoes."[11] The total force, under the command of Charles Elliot's cousin, Admiral George Elliot, consisted of 16 warships carrying 540 guns, 4 newly designed armed steamers, 28 transports, and 4,000 troops, along with 3,000 tons of coal for the steamers and 16,000 gallons of rum for the men.

Indeed, Lin vastly underestimated the violent force of the British response. He regarded the opium traders as profit-seeking merchants whose wicked behavior must be unknown to their young queen—when she learned the full range of their misdeeds, surely Victoria would repudiate them. Based on these assumptions, Lin interpreted intelligence reports of British military preparations as rumors or the "empty bluster" of greedy merchants. Meanwhile, the cleansing of Guangdong province continued. Arrests and investigations of addicts and dealers went on apace, with opium now commanding "famine prices" of up to Mex$3,000 a chest instead of the usual $500.* When the British merchants refused to sign bonds pledging that they would never again traffic in opium, Lin had them ousted from Macao as they had been from Guangzhou. In response to this expulsion order, Charles Elliot inaugurated a new phase in East Asian history by settling his group on the almost deserted rocky island of Hong Kong. Trade in Guangzhou by no means came to a standstill, since the Americans especially were delighted to profit from the opportunity to operate as middlemen for the British. The U.S. vice consul let his countrymen sign bonds promising not to violate Qing regulations. As one American merchant explained, "We Yankees had no Queen to guarantee our losses," and even if the Chinese closed other ports of access, he would continue "retreating step by step, but buying and selling just as long as I found parties to operate with."[12]

As tensions escalated, Commissioner Lin issued orders for defensive preparations: fortifying the waterways into Guangzhou, buying new cannon for the forts and immense chains to block the channel, and commencing the training and drilling of his forces. The British who had retreated to Hong Kong were harried by the local Chinese, who poisoned many wells and refused to sell the foreigners food. Armed clashes between British and Qing war vessels in Hong Kong harbor and near Guangzhou occurred in September and October 1839, with casualties on both sides. The possibilities of further negotiation faded. Lin even encouraged mobilization of local "braves" against the British, who had grown even more unpopular after a group of drunken seamen had killed a Chinese villager on Kowloon, across from Hong Kong Island. Elliot had refused to hand the accused over to the Qing courts. "Assemble yourselves together for consideration," ran one proclama-

---

* The Mexican silver dollar was now widely circulated and accepted as standard silver currency in China.

tion; "Purchase arms and weapons; join together the stoutest of your villagers and thus be prepared to defend yourselves."[13]

The full British fleet under George Elliot arrived off Guangzhou in June 1840. To Lin's chagrin they did not try to storm his new defenses. Instead, Elliot left four ships to blockade the harbor entrance and sailed north with the bulk of the force. In July, the British blockaded Ningbo with two ships and seized the main town on the island of Zhoushan off the Zhejiang coast, from which they could interdict sea traffic to the Yangzi delta region. Leaving a garrison force on Zhoushan with a missionary-interpreter standing in for the Qing magistrate (who had killed himself), the fleet sailed unopposed to the mouth of the White River, near the Dagu forts that guarded the approaches to the city of Tianjin. Here, in August and September 1840, negotiations began with Qishan, governor-general of the region and a Manchu grand secretary trusted by Emperor Daoguang. Qishan persuaded the British to return to Guangzhou to complete the negotiations, for which he was lavishly praised by the emperor and named governor-general of Guangxi and Guangdong. Lin Zexu, who had been named to that post earlier in the year, was dismissed and banished to the western territory of Xinjiang, blamed for provoking the war and losing it.

In January 1841 Qishan reached an agreement with the British in which he ceded Hong Kong, agreed to pay Mex$6 million in indemnities, allowed the British direct official contacts with the Qing state, and promised to reopen the Guangzhou trade to them within ten days. When he learned of these terms, Daoguang was so enraged that he ordered Qishan executed. The sentence was commuted to banishment, which lasted a year before he was pardoned.

Lord Palmerston was equally furious with Charles Elliot for not exacting better terms. In a blistering letter of April 1841, he dismissed Elliot and refused to ratify the agreement. Palmerston was especially angry that Elliot had given up Zhoushan, had not insisted on repayment for the opium destroyed, and had merely gotten modified rights over Hong Kong, "a barren island with hardly a house upon it." To his new plenipotentiary, Sir Henry Pottinger, Palmerston demanded that the new agreement must be with the emperor himself. "Her Majesty's Government cannot allow that, in a transaction between Great Britain and China, the unreasonable practice of the Chinese should supersede the reasonable practice of all the rest of mankind."[14]

With these instructions, Pottinger reached China in August 1841 to find the situation even more volatile. There had been renewed fighting in the countryside around Guangzhou, much of it by aroused bands of local militia, and British troops had been killed and wounded. The British had responded by destroying the Bogue forts, sinking Chinese vessels, razing part of the waterfront, and occupying sections of Guangzhou. Although the British occupying troops subsequently withdrew after officials paid them Mex$6 million, there was no agreement about whether this sum was a "ransom" to save the city, a response to the sum named in Elliot's earlier convention with Qishan, or recompense for the opium destroyed two years before. From Beijing, the emperor's view of the war's progress was distorted by his commanders and officials, some of whom underreported bad news, downplayed intelligence that cast their conduct in a negative light, or invented fictitious victories.

In late August 1841, Pottinger proceeded north with the British fleet, seizing Xiamen and Ningbo, and recapturing Zhoushan. When reinforcements arrived from India in late spring 1842, he launched a campaign to force Qing capitulation by cutting the main river and canal communications routes. The British captured Shanghai in June and took Zhenjiang in July, even though Qing forces fought bravely. Scores of Qing officers at the Manchu banner garrison died by suicide with their families when defeat was certain. The traffic on the Grand Canal and lower Yangzi was now blocked. Pottinger, ignoring Qing requests for a parley, pushed on to the former Ming capital of Nanjing, taking up attack positions outside the walls on August 5. The Qing sued for peace, and on August 29 the terms of the Treaty of Nanjing were signed by the Manchu commissioners and the governor-general of Liangjiang.* Daoguang accepted the treaty in September, and Queen Victoria ratified it at the end of December.

Before turning to the precise stipulations of this treaty and its supplements, it is worth reemphasizing that in military terms the Opium War of 1839–1842 marked an important historical moment. It was not only the most decisive reversal the Qing had ever received, but it also saw innovations in Western military technology and tactics. The emergence of the steam-driven vessel as a considerable force in naval battles was perhaps the most important of these, as shown by the British ship *Nemesis*. The *Nemesis* was an iron steamer that used sails in favorable winds and six boilers fired by wood or coal for making seven to eight knots even in heavy seas. Drawing only five feet, the ship could operate in shallow coastal waters in virtually any wind or tidal condition. In the Guangzhou Bogue campaigns, the *Nemesis* roamed the shallows firing shells and rockets, ferrying troops, and towing other sailing vessels on calm days. In the Shanghai campaign, the ship towed the men-of-war with heavy guns within firing range of the city and served as a transport that could unload soldiers directly onto the docks.

---

* The name of the administrative unit comprising the three provinces of Jiangsu, Anhui, and Jiangxi.

**THE OPIUM WAR,
1839–1842**

The firepower of the *Nemesis* provided stark evidence of the lethal capabilities of Western technology, in contrast to the Qing military's woeful inadequacies. While still in Guangzhou, Commissioner Lin had set up a translation bureau to cull information from foreign newspapers and scholarly works of international law and geography. To defend the city, Lin had bought guns and an old British ship mounted with thirty-four cannons, but these measures were no match for the war machinery of the most powerful navy in the world. As the British proceeded with their campaigns in 1842, they found evidence of the speed with which Qing officials adapted new technology. In Xiamen, for instance, there was a nearly completed replica of a British two-decker man-of-war with thirty guns; it was almost ready to sail, and work on several other similar vessels was well under way. Elsewhere they discovered five new paddle-wheel boats armed with newly cast brass guns and seized sixteen beautifully made eighteen-pound ship's guns, perfect in detail down to the sights cast on the barrels and the pierced vents for flintlocks. And as the British threatened Beijing, Emperor Daoguang hurried his officials to build new warships, and to share information about experiments with cannons and other innovations.[15] In these cases, the foreign challenge proved to be a stimulus as well as an outrage.

THE NEW TREATY SYSTEM

The Treaty of Nanjing was signed on August 29, 1842, aboard Her Majesty's Ship *Cornwallis* moored in the Yangzi River, and ratified in Hong Kong ten months later after formal approval by Queen Victoria and Emperor Daoguang. It was the most important treaty settlement in China's modern history. The treaty contained twelve main articles that cumulatively had significant ramifications for Qing commerce and society:

Article 1. Stipulated peace and friendship between Britain and China, and "full security and protection for their persons and property within the dominions of the other."

Article 2. Determined the opening of five Chinese cities—Guangzhou, Fuzhou, Xiamen, Ningbo, and Shanghai—to residence by British subjects and their families "for the purpose of carrying on their mercantile pursuits, without molestation or restraint." It also permitted the establishment of consulates in each of those cities.

Article 3. "The Island of Hong Kong to be possessed in perpetuity" by the British and ruled as they "shall see fit."

Article 4. Payment of Mex\$6 million by the Qing, calculated as the value of the opium delivered to Lin Zexu.

Article 5. Abolition of the Cohong system and permission at the five specified ports for British merchants "to carry on their mercantile transactions with whatever persons they please." The Qing were to pay Mex\$3 million in settlement of outstanding Cohong debts.

Article 6. Payment of a further Mex\$12 million for expenses incurred in the recent fighting, minus any sums already received "as ransom for cities and towns in China" since August 1, 1841.

Article 7. The total indemnity of Mex\$21 million was to be paid in four installments before the end of 1845, with a 5 percent interest charge per annum on late payments.

Article 8. Immediate release of any prisoners who were British subjects, whether Indian or European.

Article 9. An unconditional amnesty for all Qing subjects who had resided with, dealt with, or served the British.

Article 10. At the five treaty ports listed in Article 2, all merchants should pay "a fair and regular Tariff of Export and Import Customs and other Dues." Once those fees were paid, only fair and stipulated transit dues should be paid on goods conveyed to the interior of China.

Article 11. Instead of terminology such as "petition" or "beg" that foreigners had previously been forced to use, nonderogatory and nonsubordinate

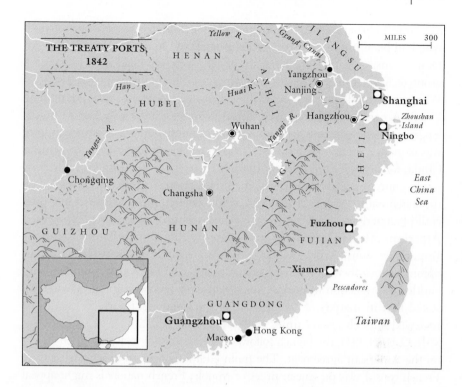

THE TREATY PORTS, 1842

terms of address were to be used in future official correspondence between the British and Qing governments.

Article 12. On receiving the first installment of the indemnity money, British forces would leave Nanjing and the Grand Canal. Troops would continue to hold Zhoushan until all money was paid and the named ports opened to British merchants.[16]

Apart from the stipulation of a Mex\$6 million payment as compensation for the opium destroyed in 1839, the narcotic was nowhere mentioned in the treaty, nor was it discussed in the supplementary tariff agreement of 1843, which fixed the rates for tea, silk, cotton, woolens, ivory, metals, and spirits. Opium was again ignored in the complicated procedures agreed to for conducting foreign trade in the five ports. In private talks with the chief Manchu negotiator Qiying, Pottinger mentioned the British hope that the Qing would allow a legalized opium on a barter basis—to end the outflow of silver. When Qiying replied that he dared not raise the question, Pottinger said that he, too, had been ordered not to press the matter.

The clauses of the Treaty of Nanjing and its supplements were studied carefully by other powers. In 1843, President John Tyler dispatched Caleb Cushing, a Massachusetts congressman, as minister plenipotentiary. Arriving at

Macao in February 1844, Cushing at once began negotiations with Qiying, who had been promoted to governor-general of Guangdong and Guangxi. Despite tensions caused by the death of a Chinese who had tried to assault a group of Americans, Qiying and Cushing moved rapidly to sign the Treaty of Wangxia (named after the small village near Macao where it was concluded).

The American treaty followed the same lines as the British, but was much longer and had a number of important additions. Article 17, for instance, was of great potential importance to Protestant missionaries eager to work in China, for it gave Americans in the five treaty ports the right to build hospitals, churches, and cemeteries. The jurisdictional question was settled by the statement in Article 21 that Americans who committed crimes in China could be tried and punished only by the consuls or other duly empowered American officials "according to the laws of the United States." Rejecting Britain's evasions, Article 33 stated that any Americans "who shall trade in opium or any other contraband" would be subject to Qing law, without being entitled to protection from the United States government. Finally, Article 34 stated that in matters of "commerce and navigation," the treaty should be reviewed in twelve years' time.[17]

In October 1844, the French followed with their own treaty, modeled closely on the American agreement. The main additions were to stipulate that if no French consul was present in times of trouble, French nationals might appeal to the consuls of any friendly nation, and to reemphasize the principle of extraterritoriality—the right to be judged by one's own national law in criminal cases on Chinese soil—with even greater force than had Caleb Cushing. Yielding to French pressure, Qiying obtained an imperial rescript ensuring full toleration to the Catholics and reversing Yongzheng's edicts against missionaries; a supplementary proclamation of 1845 extended the same rights to Protestants.

So within six years of Lin Zexu's appointment as imperial commissioner, the Qing had lost control of vital elements of its commercial, social, and foreign policies. A host of other nations followed where Britain, the United States, and France had shown the way. The British did not have to worry about these other negotiations, because any new concessions came also to them. An ingenious article included in their own supplement treaty of 1843 had stipulated a "most-favored-nation" clause, which claimed for the British all additional privileges or immunities the Qing granted to any foreign country. The Qing had agreed to this clause in the belief that it would limit foreign pressures, but in fact this provision prevented the Qing from forming alliances or playing off one nation against another in the years to come.

Surprisingly, however, the short-term commercial results of the Opium War turned out to be disappointing for the British and most other foreign merchants. Although the five treaty ports had been carefully chosen, trade at

Fuzhou and Ningbo grew so slowly that there was talk of trying to swap them for other cities with better prospects. In Xiamen, Europeans and Americans found it difficult to penetrate the robust trade conducted with Taiwan and the Philippines. Only traffic in human labor brought some profit when British ships began to transport Chinese laborers to work in the sugar plantations of Cuba. Guangzhou had held the promise of enormous profits once the Cohong monopoly was abolished and trade was opened to all. But local antipathy to the British and other foreigners proved to be so strong that they found it impossible to establish residence or open consulates in the city. The 1840s and early 1850s were marked by a cycle of rural militias and urban mobs attacking the British, met in turn by British reprisals.

Of the five new treaty ports, only Shanghai became a boomtown when extensive "concession" areas of marshy and largely uninhabited countryside were made available for British, French, and other foreign settlements. By 1850, with the land drained and the riverbanks shored up, over 100 merchants resided there, supported by consular staffs, five physicians, and seventeen missionaries, many of whom were married. Whereas 44 foreign ships had entered the port in 1844, the number for 1849 was 133, and by 1855 it was 437. The silk trade expanded prodigiously, reaching a value of over Mex$20

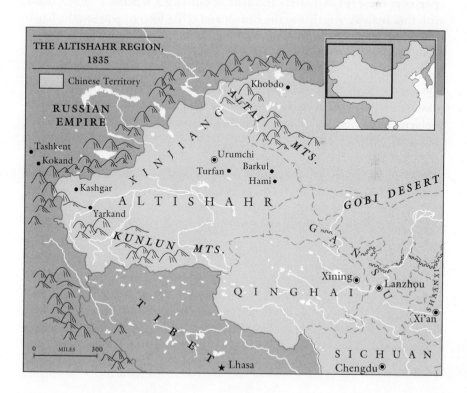

THE ALTISHAHR REGION, 1835

Chinese Territory

RUSSIAN EMPIRE

Khobdo

ALTAI MTS.

XINJIANG

Tashkent
Kokand
Kashgar

Urumchi
Turfan   Barkul
         Hami

GOBI DESERT

ALTISHAHR
Yarkand

KUNLUN MTS.

GANSU

TIBET

QINGHAI
Xining   Lanzhou
         Xi'an
SHAANXI

0   MILES   300

★ Lhasa

SICHUAN
Chengdu

million by the mid-1850s. Opium, though still illegal, was coming in at a rate of at least 20,000 chests a year.

The Qing attitude to the new treaty-port structure was ambiguous. Governor-General Qiying's view, shared by many at court, was that the Westerners' prior motivation was commercial greed and that they could probably be stalled on most other demands if their trade kept moving. In their confidence about this and their feeling that even concessions such as extraterritoriality were insignificant, they drew on recent precedents from Qing foreign policy in Central Asia. During the 1830s, similar allowances had been made to deal with the aggressive khanate of Kokand.

As he might have done with unruly potentates in Central Asia, Qiying continued to woo Henry Pottinger well after the Nanjing treaty and its supplements had been signed: he bestowed the status of honorary adoption on Pottinger's son, fed sugarplums with his own hands into the astonished plenipotentiary's mouth, and created a new word—*yin-di-mi-te* in Chinese—to indicate that Pottinger was his "intimate" friend. The two also exchanged keepsakes, including pictures of their wives. But to Emperor Daoguang, Qiying confided that this was his way of "subduing and conciliating" the British. He was not going to "fight with them over empty names"; instead, he would "pass over these small matters and achieve our larger scheme."[18] The trouble with this analysis was that to the British and other foreign powers, the hard-won treaty stipulations were far from being "empty names." They were the very stuff of international and commercial life. For the ruling Qing, however, there were other, far more pressing preoccupations—the "larger scheme" was now nothing less than the survival of the dynasty itself. To those holding power in China, the mounting pressures of domestic discontent made all problems of foreign policy appear, indeed, peripheral.

CHAPTER 8

The Crisis Within

SOCIAL DISLOCATION NORTH AND SOUTH

The damaging defeats inflicted on Qing China by the British during the first half of the nineteenth century were part cause and part consequence of the country's growing domestic instability. Many of the elements of that instability have been discussed previously: the growing population that put new pressures on the land, the difficulty the educated elite found in gaining official employment, the mounting incidences of opium addiction and the outflow of silver that widespread addiction entailed, the waning abilities of the military, the demoralization in the bureaucracy caused by Heshen and his faction, the wide-scale suffering that accompanied the spread and eventual suppression of the White Lotus rebellion.

Other abuses, already apparent in the late eighteenth century, became more serious in the early nineteenth century. The enormous bureaucracies responsible for managing the Yellow River dike works and the Grand Canal grew ineffective, swelling their ranks with sinecure appointments and using allotted government funds for private purposes. The consequent silting up of stretches of the Grand Canal, and the failure to regulate water levels on the Yellow and Huai Rivers at the points where they crossed the Grand Canal, crucially weakened the system of government rice transport from the south. That disruption, in turn, led to trouble with the workers along the canal who pulled the government barges for a living. Many of these workers banded into their own secret associations, both to protect their jobs and to tyrannize the local farming communities.

The massive system of salt distribution also became riddled with problems. Salt sales were, in theory, a government monopoly in which the Qing supervised production and sold the product to licensed merchants, who in turn transported the salt for sale to designated areas. By the early nineteenth century, inefficiencies and corruption in this system had led to a phenomenal rise in salt smuggling. These economic and organizational problems spurred the growth of competing factions within the post-Heshen bureaucracy, as vested interests contended for profits. Many senior officials began to form their own bureaucratic subnetworks of clients and assistants, whose salaries they paid by further exploiting public sources of income.

During these same years, there was also a great increase in local para-military or formally organized militia units, led by scholars or landlords who sought to protect their communities from marauding groups of pirates, sectarian rebels, or the jobless and the desperate. In other areas, local leaders formed secret societies to spread religious doctrines and to defend themselves. Some of these initiatives were encouraged by officials, especially in situations where they could not call on the resources of the central government for protection.

In much of China, private interests were encroaching on formerly governmental spheres. When he assumed power in 1799, Emperor Jiaqing quickly realized that the rot of corruption exemplified by Heshen had infested the entire civilian bureaucracy. To root out the problem would have required cleaning house at the cost of disrupting government functions at every level. Bound by filial piety, the new emperor also could not overtly repudiate the policies and legacy of his late father or imply that Qianlong was in any way responsible. Thus Heshen was demonized as the "primal evil," even while Jiaqing made examples of the chief coconspirators and removed them from office. In addition, to curb some of the worst systemic abuses, the emperor announced a strict prohibition on gift-giving within the bureaucracy, limited the purchase of official titles, and reorganized the Imperial Household Department and the Grand Council—two institutions that Heshen had manipulated for his personal gain.[1]

In the short-term, the reforms of the early nineteenth century helped stabilize the Qing empire. However, for Daoguang, Jiaqing's successor, such improvements were inadequate to meet the simultaneous challenges posed by economic depression, foreign pressures, and domestic rebellion. By the end of Daoguang's reign (1821–1850), a series of popular uprisings began that were to last for twenty-three years—and almost bring about the fall of the Qing dynasty.

But just as those uprisings must be seen in the context of China's foreign-policy problems, so must they be considered as the culminating stage in a pattern of protest that began with the White Lotus and continued through less dramatic but still significant crises in both north and south China. One such uprising was led by Lin Qing in 1813. Lin was born in 1770 in a village about

ten miles from Beijing, and his early life suggests a case study of the rootlessness endemic to the portion of Qing society that hovered just above the urban
poverty line. The son of a local government clerk, Lin Qing took an apprenticeship in an herbal-medicine shop, but he worked at this trade for only a
short period before being fired and becoming a night watchman. When his
father died, Lin managed to get himself appointed clerk in his father's place;
thereupon he embezzled some Grand Canal repair funds stored in this office
and used the money to open a tea shop. Gambling away the shop's profits, he
moved north to Manchuria, where he held a construction job for a time. Still
restless, he traveled south to Suzhou, where he worked first as attendant
to a local grain official, then on the junior staff of a magistrate's office. He
returned north, earning money as a laborer pulling grain boats up the Grand
Canal. Back home near Beijing, he ran a business selling songbirds.

Now equipped with some knowledge of the world, Lin Qing joined the
religious sect known as the Eight Trigrams, that drew its beliefs from millenarian Buddhism. Lin was able to inspire confidence in hundreds of local
villagers and—more surprisingly—in a number of poverty-stricken Chinese
bannermen and bondservants, as well as eunuchs in palace service. "He was
very convincing," his nephew later told Qing officials. "He said that making
contributions was the same as sowing seeds for future blessings and that in
the future such gifts would be multiplied tenfold. So people believed and gave
him money. I never saw him give any back."[2] Some of the promises were dramatic: 100 copper cash given to Lin brought a promise of 100 *mou* of land in
the future. (Equivalent to around 16 acres, 100 *mou* would have represented a
munificent estate to any poor person in the nineteenth century.)

Growing more grandiose as he allied with other sectarian leaders, Lin
began to term himself the future Buddha, sent by the Eternal Mother to prepare the faithful to survive the catastrophes of the coming *kalpa*, the new
great cycle of human history. Rhymes recited by his followers suggested that
an anti-Manchu element was also becoming stronger: "We wait only for the
northern region to be returned to a Han emperor / Then all-that-is will again
be under a single line."[3] By 1813, Lin Qing had laid plans to move on the capital and kill Emperor Jiaqing.

At this point the plot began to unravel. Officials were warned of trouble
by a lower degree holder from Shandong and by two fathers worried about
their sons' involvement in the illegal sect. Arrests of some sectarians, interrogations under torture, and sporadic clashes followed during that summer.
Late in 1813, a handful of Lin's disciples launched the planned attack on the
palace, but it was a disastrous failure. Oddly fatalistic, Lin Qing stayed at
home in his village during his "uprising," and it was there that local police
officials arrested him. Emperor Jiaqing was so curious about this unknown

man who had sought to kill him that he summoned him to a private inter-rogation. Lin refused to give any further explanations and was executed by slicing. His severed head was displayed in Henan as a warning to his follow-ers, who were still holding out in rebellion there.

In south China there was also simmering discontent, but with a differ-ent focus. Here the dominant force was the Triads, also called the Heaven and Earth Society, comprising groups with their own blood oaths, religious rituals, and brotherhoods. The Triads developed in Taiwan and Fujian in the later eighteenth century—though they were to claim much earlier ori-gins once their power grew—and then gathered strength in Guangdong and Guangxi. Many early Triad members were sailors; others were poor city dwellers. They often engaged in criminal activities—extortion, robbery, and kidnappings—all the while protecting themselves through society members in the magistrates' own offices. By the 1830s, Triad lodges were also attract-ing numerous poor recruits, perhaps because in south China, where power-ful lineages often controlled entire villages, the Triads offered an alternative form of protection to those living on the edge of destitution. Women were recruited into Triad ranks, as they were into the White Lotus, giving them a prestige and function in society otherwise largely denied to them. According to some accounts, women who joined Triad lodges in advance of their hus-bands might claim precedence within the household over their own spouses. Others were members without their husbands' knowledge.

The Triads also claimed it as their cause to oust the Qing and restore the Ming. Their anti-Manchu stance was probably fueled by the inability of the Qing to control the foreigners in Guangzhou, and the repeated occupa-tions of that city by foreign troops. These pressures in turn made it hard for the court to mobilize for drastic action against potential rebels among its own people. And since the more dangerous rebel groups tended to assem-ble in rugged, hard-to-control border regions such as that between Guangxi and Guangdong, local officials could not easily coordinate their suppression activities.

The Triad lodges, and their affiliates in the local bureaucracy, enhanced their power through involvement in militia organizations. Lin Zexu had encouraged the formation of such groups to defend Guangzhou against the British, just as gentry in the late Ming had done to protect their bases against rebels and the invading Manchus. The Guangzhou militia groups became complicated mixtures of gentry leaders, local thugs, poor farmers, members of other martial arts organizations, and groups of tradesmen. In May 1841, such a mélange of forces had confronted a British patrol outside Guangzhou at the village of Sanyuanli. Armed with spears and hoes—some even with guns—they had forced the British to retreat, killing one British soldier and wounding fifteen others. The "Sanyuanli Incident" became a symbol for the possibility of a united resistance to foreign pressures.

Emperor Daoguang tried to think this through when responding to the attacks on the British in the Guangzhou region, which reached a pinnacle during 1848: "The only important thing is to appease the people's emotions. If the people's loyalties are not lost, then the foreign bandits can be handled."[4] The trouble was that appeasing popular violence was a dangerous gamble for the Qing.

THE TAIPING HEAVENLY KINGDOM

In the immense upheaval known as the Taiping Uprising, which ravaged much of China between 1850 and 1864, we see many elements similar to those just mentioned: the restlessness and religious self-identification of a man like Lin Qing, the underlying social discord in the southeast, the growing strength of secret-society organizations among the poor, and the dislocation caused by the opium trade. But at the same time, one individual's life story gave the Taiping movement its distinctive shape. This was Hong Xiuquan, one of those who had such a difficult time trying to latch on to the lowest rung of the ladder of Qing gentility. Hong was born in 1814, the fourth of five children in a rural family of Guangdong. His parents were from the Hakka minority (the so-called "guest peoples" who had migrated southward from central China), and they sacrificed to give Hong an education that would win him a place in the local elite. But even though he passed the initial examinations permitting him to qualify for the licentiate's *shengyuan* degree, by the early 1830s he had failed in his first two attempts to obtain the degree.

For any ambitious young man, such failure could be humiliating, but for Hong it seems to have been unusually so. He took solace only in the chance to travel and study in Guangzhou. In 1836 he was just about to enter the examination hall there, in pursuit of the elusive degree, when a Chinese Protestant evangelist pressed a collection of translated Bible passages called "Good Words for Exhorting the Age" into Hong's hands. Such a moment was possible because of new historical circumstances that were to distinguish Hong's uprising from all those that had come before. Western Protestant missionaries—mainly British and American—had been working since the early 1800s to translate the entire Bible into Chinese, and had printed numerous copies, which they distributed while traveling up the coast and in the interior. They and their Chinese converts also tried to distill the message of the scriptures into simple tracts like the "Good Words," which reached even more readers.

Hong Xiuquan
Left: Statue of Hong Xiu-
quan, leader of Taiping
Heavenly Kingdom. Right:
A Taiping decree.

Hong Xiuquan neither studied the tracts nor threw them away. Instead he seems to have glanced at them quickly and then kept them at home. He initially made no connection between these tracts and a strange dream and delirium he experienced after a third examination failure in 1837. In those visions, Hong conversed with a bearded, golden-haired man who gave him a sword, and a younger man who instructed him on how to slay evil spirits and whom Hong addressed as "Elder Brother." For six years after his visions, Hong worked as a village schoolteacher and tried once again to pass the examinations. But after he failed for the fourth time, he opened the Christian tracts and read them fully. In a sudden shock of realization, Hong saw that the two men in his dreams must have been the God and the Jesus described in the tracts, and that therefore he, Hong, must be the Son of God, younger brother to Jesus Christ.

Like Lin Qing in north China thirty years before, Hong was able to per-suade people of his spiritual powers through a charismatic manner and a strong religious conviction. But unlike Lin, Hong did not work in secret. He began to preach his message publicly; he baptized converts and brazenly destroyed Con-fucian and ancestral shrines. Although these activities prompted local anger, which caused Hong to flee his village temporarily, they did not provoke the local authorities, and he continued to teach. In 1847 he returned to Guangzhou and studied the Bible with Isaacher Roberts, an American Baptist. Late that year Hong left for Guangxi to join a close friend, one of his first converts, who had formed a Society of God Worshippers in a rugged area called Thistle Mountain.

Hong's rhetorical passion drew a devoted following. Among his closest advisers were an illiterate charcoal maker from the Thistle Mountain area who proved to be a brilliant military tactician, and a member of a wealthy local landlord lineage who persuaded most of his relatives to throw in their lot with Hong, bringing an estimated 100,000 taels into Hong's treasury. Another important group of converts was the local miners, whose skills with explosives and tunneling were later to be used in the demolition of city walls. Many others contributed a variety of areas of expertise: pawnbrokers (who ran the treasury), legal clerks (who developed bureaucratic structures), former soldiers of the Qing forces or local militias, as well as at least two well-known women bandit leaders and several gangs of river pirates.

By 1850 Hong's recruits surpassed 20,000. His movement was now sufficiently organized to drill troops, manufacture arms, and assemble military tables of organization; it enforced rigorous rules against corruption, sensuality, and opium smoking; conducted ceremonies of Christian worship; pooled all money and valuables in a central treasury; convinced the men to abandon their queues and wear their flowing hair long; and segregated the women into a separate camp run by female officers. Through these actions, the God Worshippers attracted enough notice to be singled out from the scores of other bandit groups that roamed different parts of the country.

In December 1850, Qing forces sent to oust Hong from the Thistle Mountain area were badly defeated, and their Manchu commander killed. On January 11, 1851, Hong Xiuquan declared himself the Heavenly King of the Taiping Tianguo—"Heavenly Kingdom of Great Peace," commonly abbreviated to Taiping. Forced out of their base by larger government armies, the Taiping

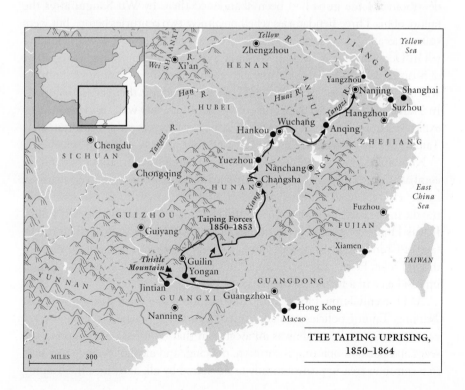

THE TAIPING UPRISING,
1850–1864

campaigned on the Guangxi-Guangdong border until autumn 1851, when they swung north and seized the city of Yong'an along with great stores of cash and food. New recruits swelled their numbers to 60,000 or more.

The Taiping next attacked the Guangxi capital of Guilin, which they failed to capture despite the heroic exploits of their new regiments of Hakka women, who fought fiercely and courageously. (Used to a life of hard farming, Hakka women had never bound their feet as other Chinese women did.) In the summer they crossed into Hunan but were frustrated in their two-month attempt to take Changsha. Here the Taiping proclamations became more fiery in an attempt to win fresh recruits: "Can the Chinese still consider themselves men? Ever since the Manchus poisoned China, the flame of oppression has risen up to heaven, the poison of corruption has defiled the emperor's throne, the offensive odor has spread over the four seas, and the influence of demons has distressed the empire while the Chinese with bowed heads and dejected spirits willingly became subjects and servants."[5]

A breakthrough came in December 1852, when the Taiping army entered Yuezhou on the east side of Dongting Lake almost unopposed. Yuezhou was a wealthy town, unlike the poorer areas through which the Taiping had hitherto ranged, and here they seized 5,000 boats and stockpiles of arms and gunpowder. (Some of the guns had been abandoned there by Wu Sangui after the failure of his Three Feudatories rebellion almost two centuries before, but were still serviceable.) Thereafter an incredible string of successes followed: Hankou fell in December and Wuchang in January 1853, bringing Hong a large fleet of boats and 1.6 million taels from the provincial treasury. Anqing fell almost without opposition in February 1853, further swelling the Taiping's coffers. In March Nanjing—defended by only a small force, its walls undermined by explosive charges, its center bombarded by artillery, its streets infiltrated by Taiping soldiers disguised as Buddhist or Daoist priests—fell to the rebels.

Nanjing's Manchu population of some 40,000, of whom about 5,000 were combat troops, retreated into the city's inner citadel but were overwhelmed by the charges of wave after wave of Taiping troops. All Manchus who did not die in the battle—men, women, and children—were systematically killed. It was Hong's way of showing that the "devils" would be driven from the face of China. At the end of March, wearing a crown and an embroidered dragon robe, Hong was carried into the city in a golden palanquin, and took up residence in a former Ming palace.

As Heavenly King, Hong Xiuquan ruled for eleven years (1853–1864) from Nanjing. Taiping policies were, on paper and often in practice, startlingly radical. One facet of their rule was an asceticism that required segregation of the sexes and bans on opium, prostitution, dancing, and alcohol. Money was held in a common treasury, theoretically to be shared by all, and since the Taiping had acquired more than 18 million taels along their route of march and within Nanjing itself, their prosperity seemed assured. Examinations were reinstituted, based now on Chinese translations of the Bible and on the transcribed versions of Hong Xiuquan's religious revelations and literary works. Women, organized into special residential and administrative units, held supervisory offices in the bureaucracy and could sit for their own examinations.

Most remarkable was the Taiping land law, which, linked to a local system of military recruitment, constituted perhaps the most utopian, comprehensive, and authoritarian scheme for human organization ever seen in China up to that time. All land was to be divided among all families of the Taiping and their supporters according to family size, with men and women receiving equal shares. After keeping the produce they needed for their own sustenance, each family would place the rest in common granaries.[6]

Yet for all their military and ideological passion, the Taiping failed to overthrow the Qing and were ultimately eliminated, with terrible slaughter. Why did the Taiping not succeed—after achieving so many triumphs, with such speed and in the name of such a utopian ideology?

One reason was the failure of collective leadership. From the original brotherhood, Hong Xiuquan had gone on to name some key followers as "kings," who ruled jointly under his supervision. But two of the most talented leaders were killed in early campaigns, and the most brilliant survivors—especially Yang Xiuqing and Shi Dakai—ultimately lost faith in him. Yang, who had arrogated enormous powers to himself, was assassinated in a murderous palace coup in 1856 on Hong's orders. Shi, who lived up to his early promise and became a great general, left Nanjing the same year, after his wife and mother were killed. He tried to set up an independent kingdom in Sichuan but was trapped and killed there by Qing troops in 1863.

Shorn of his most talented advisers, Hong faltered as a leader once he had won a measure of power. In Wuchang he had missed a chance to strike north to Beijing; after his seizure of Nanjing he also failed to push the initiative. Instead he withdrew into his palace, surrounding himself with concubines and perusing the Bible for references to himself and his mission, which he found underlined everywhere from the Book of Genesis to the Book of Revelation. He did not exploit the potentially popular issue of an anti-Manchu crusade and squandered his reputation as a serious religious leader.

Hong's failure to appeal to anti-Manchu sentiment was symptomatic of the Taiping's isolation, even when they held power in Nanjing. If they had maintained the city as a thriving metropolitan center, and if Hong had established himself there on a firm base of popular support, the Taiping might have been unbeatable. But the Han Chinese residents of Nanjing found the occupiers—many of whom were Hakkas with unfamiliar dress, accents, and large-footed women—as bizarre as any foreigners or Manchus. The residents resented the Taiping for their alterations of economic life, their attempt to establish a common treasury and regulate markets, their segregation of the population by sex and occupation, and their attempt to enforce a strict code of conduct. Passive resistance to the Taiping was endemic, and flight, spying, and defections to the Qing common.

Beyond Nanjing, the Taiping failed in the countryside, where plans for a common treasury and an equitable system of landholding remained largely unrealized. Even though they controlled large areas of Jiangsu, Anhui, and Zhejiang for years, and territories farther north and west intermittently, they lacked the commitment or personnel to push through their dramatic land reforms, and ended up as yet another tax-collection agency on the backs of poor farmers. The constant need for food and supplies to maintain huge armies meant that Taiping foraging squads scoured the country for hundreds of miles. These logistical demands, when coupled with the constant fighting with Qing forces—who also needed food and lodging—left large areas of what had once been China's most prosperous region as barren wasteland.

Nor did the Taiping manage to enlist Western sympathy in their cause. Foreigners, especially missionaries, had been initially excited by the prospect of a Christian revolutionary force that promised social reforms and the defeat of the intransigent Qing dynasty. But the eccentricities of Hong Xiuquan's Christianity soon became apparent to the missionaries, and traders came to fear the Taiping's zealous opposition to opium. Finally, the Western powers decided to back the Qing in order to prevent a Taiping seizure of Shanghai, which might threaten their newly won treaty gains. In the closing years of the conflict, a foreign-officered mercenary army fought alongside Qing forces against the Taiping. This was called the Ever-Victorious Army, led first by the American adventurer Frederick Townsend Ward, and after his death by Charles Gordon, a British artillery officer.

The Qing cause was also bolstered by the tenacity and courage of senior Chinese officials, who fought on against the Taiping even though the Manchu-led banner armies seemed unable to defeat the enemy. These Confucian-educated scholars were alarmed by the threat to their ancestral homes and distraught at the Taiping's use of Christianity to attack the whole structure of Chinese values. The greatest of these leaders was the Hunanese official Zeng Guofan, who had first raised local troops to defend his own estates when he was on mourning leave from the court in 1852. Zeng went on with his brothers to raise an army of tough conscripts officered by local gentry. Given the weakness of the Qing banner forces in the region and the ineptitude of the local bureaucrats in maintaining militia forces, Zeng's troops formed a

Qing Victory over the Taiping   In 1854, Qing forces finally suppressed Hong Xiuquan's Taiping uprising. This painting, honoring Zeng Guofan and his armies, shows the Qing victory on Dongting Lake in Hunan, July 1824.

crucial addition to the state's defensive resources. Named the Xiang Army after the river that cuts through Hunan, this army became one of the Taiping's deadliest enemies and played a critical part in the recapture of Nanjing.

The fatal inflexibility of Hong's regime is evident in the failure of a bold attempt to alter and "Westernize" Taiping rule. The author of this venture was Hong Ren'gan, a younger relation of the Heavenly King who had also studied with missionaries in Guangzhou and been a member of the first God Worshippers. During the early years of the uprising, Hong Ren'gan lived and worked in Hong Kong, and became familiar with Britain's colonial government there. In 1859 he made his way overland to Nanjing and was enthusiastically received by Hong Xiuquan, who named him prime minister. Hong Ren'gan prepared an elaborate document entitled "A New Treatise on Aids to Administration," which he presented to the Heavenly King in late 1859. His program called for the development of legal and banking systems; the construction of highways, railways, and steamships; the introduction of a postal service; the publication of newspapers; and the abandonment of geomancy and infanticide. Hong Xiuquan endorsed all these proposals (except for the suggestion of newspapers), but no concrete steps were taken to initiate the reforms. And once Hong Ren'gan's attempt to develop a new strategy to regain the upper Yangzi failed, and a massive counterattack against Suzhou and Hangzhou was beaten back, the last elements of popular support for the Taiping were dashed.

As Zeng Guofan told the Qing emperor, "Now when the people hear of the rebels, pain and regret pierce their hearts, men as well as women flee, and kitchen fires no longer burn. The tillers do not have harvests of a single grain, and one after another they abandon their occupations. When the rebels travel through a territory without people, it is like fish trying to swim in a place without water." Yet when the end came in July 1864, after Hong Xiuquan's death—either by suicide or from illness, it was never made clear—and Qing troops stormed into Nanjing, Zeng wrote to the emperor in some awe: "Not one of the 100,000 rebels in Nanjing surrendered themselves when the city was taken but in many cases gathered together and burned themselves and passed away without repentance. Such a formidable band of rebels has been rarely known from ancient times to the present."[7]

The scale of the destruction wrought by the civil war was staggering. An estimated 20 to 30 million people lost their lives over the course of nearly fifteen years. As contemporary accounts and memoirs described, the Taiping were not the only or primary instigators of violence. The forces that fought on behalf of the Qing committed numerous atrocities; local villagers feared the militias, mercenaries, and regional armies formed ostensibly for their protection as much as they feared the "long-haired" insurgents. In the aftermath, travelers passing through once prosperous provinces reported going for days without seeing anything other than rotting corpses, the smoldering remains of villages, and stray dogs. Areas directly affected by the upheaval lost 40 to 80 percent of their populations. Overall, the upheaval took a devastating toll on the legitimacy of the Qing dynasty and the morale of the survivors. For the people who limped home to rebuild their communities, the Taiping civil war was a searing, traumatic experience that colored everything else that followed.[8] It would take years to locate lost relatives, repair the broken infrastructure of cities and towns, and reclaim abandoned fields. Postwar reconstruction would be a colossal and expensive undertaking.

FOREIGN PRESSURES

One of many factors that helped the Qing defeat the Taiping was the assistance of foreigners in the early 1860s, whether in the form of customs dues on trade passed over to the Qing government or in the form of the Ever-Victorious Army. The reasons for that support had mainly to do with international affairs, in which, once again, the primary actors were the British. Disappointed at the results of the Nanjing treaty and frustrated by continued Qing intransigence, the British reacted with scant sympathy when the Qing were threatened by the spread of the Taiping threat. Instead the British made the highly legalistic decision to invoke the "most-favored-nation" clause in response to the American treaty of 1844, which had stipulated a renegotiation of the terms in twelve years. By applying that renewal stipulation to their own agreements with the Qing, British authorities forced them to renegotiate in 1854.

The British foreign secretary saw the speciousness of this argument, but he nevertheless suggested that the Qing be presented with a formidable list of requests: British access to the entire interior of China or, failing that, to all of coastal Zhejiang and the lower Yangzi up to Nanjing; legalization of the opium trade; cancellation of internal transit dues on foreign imports; suppression of piracy; regulation of Chinese labor emigration; residence in Beijing for a British ambassador; and reliance on the English version rather than the Chinese in all disputed interpretations of the revised treaty.

Despite some caution because of their involvement in the Crimean War against Russia, the British moved jointly with the Americans and French to press for treaty revisions, which the beleaguered Qing continued to oppose. The British finally took advantage of an allegedly illegal Qing search of a ship formerly of Hong Kong registry, the *Arrow*, to recommence military actions in late 1856. After some delays in getting reinforcements—the Indian mutiny was now raging, and the idea of another war in east Asia was not popular with the British people—the British seized Guangzhou in December 1857. Sailing north in a near repeat of the 1840 campaign, they took the strategic Dagu forts in May 1858 and threatened to seize Tianjin. In June, with the way to the capital now open to the British forces, the Qing capitulated and agreed to sign a new treaty.

The Treaty of Tianjin of 1858 imposed extraordinarily strict terms. A British ambassador was henceforth to reside in Beijing, accompanied by family and staff, and housed in a fitting residence. The open preaching of Christianity was protected. Travel anywhere inside China was permitted to those with valid passports, and within thirty miles of treaty ports without passports. Once the rebellions currently raging in China were suppressed, trade was to be allowed up the Yangzi as far as Hankou, and four new Yangzi treaty ports would be opened. In the meantime, six additional treaty ports were to be opened immediately: one in Manchuria, one in Shandong, two on Taiwan, one in Guangdong, and one on Hainan Island in the far south.

The Tianjin treaty also stipulated that all further interior transit taxes on foreign imports be dropped upon payment of a flat fee of 2.5 percent. Standard weights and measures would be employed at all ports and customshouses. Official communications were to be in English. The character for "barbarian" (*yi*) would no longer be used in Chinese documents describing the British. And British ships hunting pirates would be free to enter any Chinese port. A supplementary clause accompanying the various commercial agreements stated explicitly, "Opium will henceforth pay thirty taels per picul [approximately 130 pounds] Import Duty. The importer will sell it only at the port. It will be carried into the interior by Chinese only, and only as Chinese property; the foreign trader will not be allowed to accompany it." This condition was imposed despite the prohibition in the Qing penal code on the sale and consumption of opium. Virtually the only British concession was to pull back from Tianjin and return the Dagu forts to Qing control.

The British evidently expected China's rulers to abandon the struggle at this point, but the Qing would not, and showed no intention of following the treaty clause that permitted foreign ambassadors to live in Beijing. In June 1859, to enforce the new treaty terms, the British once more attacked the Dagu forts, now strengthened and reinforced by Qing troops. Fighting was heavy and the British were beaten back, even though the American naval commodore Josiah Tattnall (despite his country's declared neutrality) came to the aid of the British with the ringing cry, "Blood is thicker than water."[9] Repulsed from the Dagu forts, the British sent a team of negotiators to

Interior of the Dagu forts, August 1860 (photograph by Felix Beato)
Continuing to resist European incursions even after signing the Tianjin treaty (1858), the Qing repulsed British forces at the strategic Dagu forts in 1859, but succumbed to Anglo-French attacks the following year. This is the earliest "news photo" taken in China.

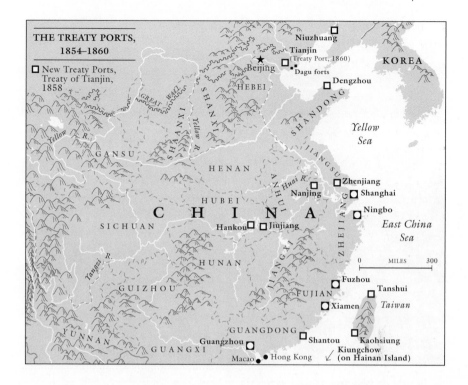

THE TREATY PORTS,
1854–1860

☐ New Treaty Ports,
Treaty of Tianjin,
1858

Niuzhuang

Tianjin
(Treaty Port, 1860)

★ Beijing
Dagu forts

KOREA

HEBEI

Dengzhou

GREAT WALL

SHANXI

SHAANXI

Yellow R.

Yellow R.

GANSU

SHANDONG

Yellow
Sea

JIANGSU

HENAN

HUBEI

ANHUI

Huai R.

Zhenjiang

Nanjing

Shanghai

C H I N A

ZHEJIANG

Ningbo

SICHUAN

Hankou ☐ ☐ Jiujiang

East China
Sea

JIANGXI

Tangzi R.

HUNAN

0   MILES   300

GUIZHOU

Fuzhou

FUJIAN

Tanshui

YUNNAN

GUANGDONG

☐ Xiamen

Taiwan

GUANGXI

Guangzhou

Shantou

Kaohsiung

Macao ● ● Hong Kong

Kiungchow
(on Hainan Island)

Beijing by a different route in 1860, but they were arrested by the Qing and some were tortured or executed. Determined now to teach the Qing a lesson they could not ignore, Lord Elgin, Britain's chief treaty negotiator, ordered his troops to march on the capital. On October 18, 1860, following Elgin's orders, the British burnt to the ground the Yuan Ming Yuan—the exquisite summer palace in the Beijing suburbs built for Qianlong's pleasure. The British, however, spared the Forbidden City palaces, calculating that destruction of those hallowed buildings would be a disgrace so profound that the Qing dynasty would fall.

The emperor Xianfeng had already fled the city and named his younger brother, Prince Gong, to act as negotiator. But there was little left to negotiate, and on the very day the summer palace burned, Prince Gong reaffirmed the terms of the 1858 Tianjin treaty. In an additional "Beijing Convention," the emperor expressed his "deep regret" at the harassment of the British queen's representatives. He also promised a further 8 million taels in indemnity, permitted Chinese emigration on British ships, made Tianjin itself a treaty port, and ceded part of the mainland Kowloon peninsula to Hong Kong. Thus did the "treaty system" reach its fruition.

Ruins of the Yuan Ming Yuan, c. 1875
On October 18, 1860, Britain's Lord Elgin ordered his troops to destroy the summer palace.

THE NIAN REBELLION

The outbreak of the Nian rebellion is usually dated to 1851, the same year as the formal declaration of the Taiping Heavenly Kingdom. But the origins of the Nian can be traced back to the 1790s among roving groups of bandits who operated north of the Huai River, especially in the area at the borders of Shandong, Jiangsu, Henan, and Anhui provinces. The name *Nian* probably referred to the rebels' status as mobile bands, although the ambiguity of the term is such that it can also refer to the martial disguises they sometimes adopted, or to the twisted paper torches by whose light they robbed houses at night.

Unlike the Taiping, the Nian had no clear-cut religious affiliation, political ideology, strategic goals, or unified leadership. Yet for the first fifty years of the nineteenth century, they steadily grew in numbers and strength. Some Nian had connections with White Lotus groups, Eight Trigrams followers, or the Triads, while others were linked to salt smugglers. But most were subsistence farmers struggling to survive in a bleak environment of exhausted soil, harsh winters, and unstable river systems subject to flooding. The prevalence of female infanticide in the area also meant that there was a profound imbalance in the region's sex ratios.

After 1851, when serious floods in northern Jiangsu brought fresh hardship, affiliation with Nian groups rose dramatically. In 1855, two years after the Taiping seized Nanjing, the Yellow River climaxed a long series of floods by breaking out of its main restraining dikes east of Kaifeng and carving a new channel into the gulf north of Shandong. The ensuing misery brought ever more recruits to the Nian. At the same time, its organization tightened: in 1852 leaders of eighteen Nian groups had proclaimed as their head Zhang Luoxing, a landlord from Anhui who had run a salt smugglers' protection racket. The Nian forces organized themselves into five main banners, named for different colors, each of which grouped together rebels of common surnames from neighboring communities.

The veteran forces of Nian warriors may have numbered only 30,000 to 50,000 troops, but their effect was disproportionate to their size. Many of them were cavalrymen, many had firearms, and they could cut at will across the lines of communication between Beijing and the government forces besieging Nanjing. By developing strongly walled or moated communities often armed with cannon, they established dozens of secure bases in the area north

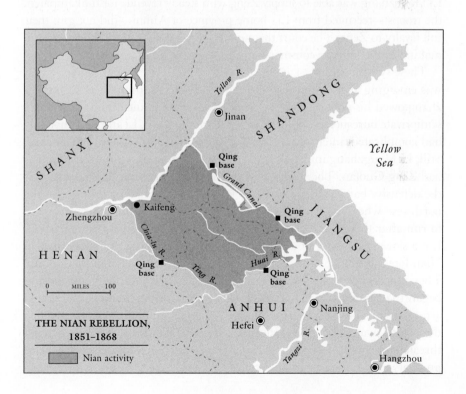

THE NIAN REBELLION,
1851–1868

Nian activity

of the Huai River. Other villages and market towns also fortified themselves to keep the rebels *out*, so that much of the region became crisscrossed with defensive communities. Although Zhang Luoxing was killed in combat, other able Nian leaders soon emerged to replace him. They developed a successful guerrilla strategy, and often conducted a grim scorched-earth policy, luring Qing forces into areas where all the crops had been rooted up, houses and boats burned, and wells filled with stones.

The Qing court's response was to appoint Zeng Guofan, hailed as a great victor after the fall of Nanjing, as supreme commander for Nian suppression. But Zeng could not finish off the Nian, despite a careful plan that involved the formation of four military bases—one each in the provinces of Jiangsu, Anhui, Henan, and Shandong. The plan also entailed the digging of canals and trenches to curb the mobility of the Nian cavalry, and a systematic attempt to win local villages back to Qing allegiance by means of conciliatory policies and the selection of new headmen. The strategy failed in part because the governors of the four provinces could not cooperate fully, and because Zeng had disbanded many of his best Xiang Army troops after recapturing Nanjing. Accordingly he was dependent on soldiers from the army of his protégé Li Hongzhang, who had been appointed governor-general of Liangjiang. While Li Hongzhang was able to supply Zeng with steady revenue for the campaign, the troops—recruited from Li's home province of Anhui—did not give their full loyalty to Zeng. The court thereupon switched the offices of the two men, making Li the military commander and Zeng the governor-general.

These switches emphasized the complexity of the new political world that was emerging as more power devolved to regional commanders. Li Hongzhang owed his political career to Zeng, who had recruited him for his own semiprivate bureaucracy while Li was still a young man. Li and Zeng not only had complicated, interlocking careers, they ran their own military systems. Still, Li Hongzhang initially had as difficult a time suppressing the Nian as had Zeng Guofan. The rebels seemed always to elude him, breaking across the defensive barriers, even roaming as far afield as Shaanxi province in the northwest, where they entered the cities of Xi'an and Yan'an. "Our troops had to run after them," as Li put it, "while they moved as freely as mercury."[10] But a slow, steady war of attrition brought the collapse of the now divided Nian forces by 1868. Li's armies were well paid and generally loyal to him. They used rifles and artillery they had purchased from the foreigners, and began the systematic use of gunboats on the northern waterways. Foreign armored ships—two of them named the *Confucius* and the *Plato*—patrolled the coastal waters off Shandong to prevent a Nian breakaway that might threaten foreign trade, now flourishing under the terms exacted by the Tianjin treaty and the Beijing Convention.

In August 1868, after heavy fighting brought final Qing victories in Shandong and the execution of the cornered Nian survivors, the court offered sacrifices of thanks to heaven in the temples of their ancestors and the god of war. Li Hongzhang was ennobled and given the honorific title Grand Guardian of the Heir Apparent. Like Zeng Guofan, who had been named to the highest possible honorific rank after recapturing Nanjing, Li Hongzhang had consolidated his career on the backs of defeated rebels. Zeng did not have much time to enjoy his fame and prestige, as he died in 1872, but Li Hongzhang was granted a long life. For the next thirty-three years he was to be one of the most powerful officials in China.

MUSLIM REVOLTS

There had been settlements of Muslims in China since the Tang dynasty (618–907 c.e.), both at the termini of the central Asian trade routes in Gansu and Shaanxi, and in certain southeast coastal towns of Fujian and Guangdong frequented by Arab traders. By the late Ming period, so many Muslims had intermarried with Chinese families that there were large settled communities of Chinese Muslims (known as Hui), which added another level of complexity to local administration. During Qianlong's reign Chinese Muslims had launched several uprisings; and the jihads (holy wars) declared by the khans of Kokand during the early nineteenth century had diluted Qing control of Kashgar and Yarkand in the far western area of Xinjiang. In the more settled agricultural areas of north China ravaged by the Nian rebellion, there were also sizable Muslim communities, containing perhaps 1 million or more of the faithful. Discriminatory legislation protected Chinese involved in violence with Muslims, and religious feuds were commonplace.

The areas of greatest Muslim concentration, besides Gansu-Shaanxi, were in the southwest, particularly the province of Yunnan. The Muslim settlements here dated back to the time of the Mongol conquest of China in the thirteenth century, and friction with other Chinese settlers pushing into the region had been endemic. In Yunnan in 1855, as the Taiping strengthened their hold on Nanjing and the Nian began to organize their alliance, a third major conflict erupted. The triggers for this uprising were the heavy land taxes and extra levies imposed on Hui Muslims, whose plight was exacerbated by disputes over the gold and silver mines that gave the province much of its scarce wealth. The Han Chinese, having exhausted their own mines, tried to oust the Muslims from theirs. As the violence escalated, Han attackers pillaged Hui villages and destroyed mosques; thousands were murdered. Qing officials did little to stop the bloodshed, and some overtly encouraged the

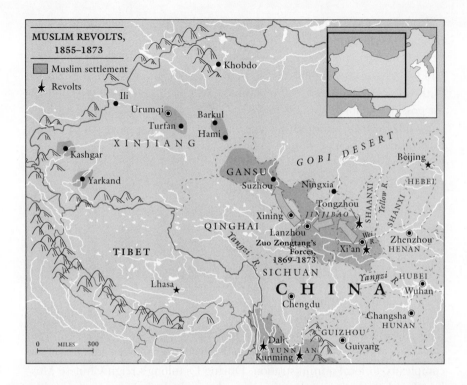

attacks. Over a three-day period in May 1856, Han Chinese militias killed 8,000 Hui and destroyed the Muslim quarter in Kunming, the provincial capital. A cascade of violence swept across Yunnan as Muslims fought back. In September they seized the city of Dali in the west of the province and killed the ranking Qing official and his family.[11]

Consolidating their victory, disparate Hui groups selected Du Wenxiu as their leader and Sultan. He established the Kingdom of the Pacified South (a variation of the Taiping Heavenly Kingdom), which was to last for more than fifteen years. From Dali, Du's forces established control over much of western Yunnan and thwarted early attempts from the Qing military to put down the rebellion. It was only after the final defeat of the Taiping that the imperial court directed its attention and resources to Yunnan. A cohort of generals with a force of 60,000 began to take back cities in the province, leaving heavily fortified Dali for last. As the Qing military encircled Dali at the end of 1872, Du Wenxiu took a dose of opium calculated to be fatal and surrendered, asking for mercy for his followers. The Qing commander who received Du's corpse decapitated it and sent the head as proof of victory to Beijing. Du's plea for mercy was in vain—in the final assault on Dali, "neither man, woman nor child who was Muslim was spared." More than 10,000 were slaughtered.[12]

At the height of the Dali Sultanate, another Muslim rebellion broke out far to the north—in Shaanxi and Gansu. Several areas of Gansu and southern Shaanxi had sizable Muslim populations, many of them followers of the "New Teachings" derived from the central Asian mystical school of Sufism. Following a series of Muslim uprisings between 1781 and 1783, the Qing attempt to ban these New Teachings had deepened resentment.

The northwest revolt of 1862 arose first from local tensions between Han Chinese and Muslims, rather than from any particular religious or anti-Qing focus. A volatile situation of rioting and harassment was intensified by Taiping forays into the area, and by feuds within Hui communities. Following the pattern now long established in east and north China, the local population responded to the threat by forming militias to defend their homes, with Muslim groups in some areas and Han groups in others. Since most banner troops had been drafted away to fight the Taiping and the Nian, and since many of the local garrison Green Standard troops were themselves Muslim, Qing authority in the region was weak. The revolt began with a tiny incident—a quarrel between a group of Muslims and a Han Chinese merchant over the price of some bamboo poles. Arguments led to blows, Chinese crowds gathered and, with gentry leadership, attacked and burned Muslim villages along the Wei River, killing innocent Muslim families. The Muslims in turn formed armed bands, retaliated against the Han Chinese and against their coreligionists who refused to take up arms. In June 1862 they besieged two prosperous cities in southern Shaanxi.

A murky sequence of pitched battles, trickery, false surrenders, and reprisals followed throughout 1863 and 1864. Rumors circulated that Xinjiang's military governor had issued an order to round up and kill all Hui Muslims, to prevent the spread of unrest to his jurisdiction. The Hui organized to attack Han civilians and the weakly defended Qing garrisons. By 1866 gunpowder supplies and fuel had run out. Local rice and wheat prices soared, and horses died for lack of fodder. Many civilians starved or died by suicide.

In desperation, the Qing court turned to Zuo Zongtang, who had emerged as one of the most effective anti-Taiping leaders. Like Zeng Guofan, Zuo was born and raised in Hunan province. In 1830, when he was eighteen, his father died, and he spent some time studying with the powerful official and statecraft scholar He Changling. Although he was a conscientious scholar, Zuo failed the *jinshi* examinations three times and decided never to try for them again. Instead he worked as a tutor, studied the geography and history of China's western regions, and experimented with tea and silk production. During the Taiping uprising, he emerged as a talented military leader, fighting first in his native Hunan—where he raised, trained, and equipped a volunteer army of 5,000 men—and subsequently in Anhui, Zhejiang, and Fujian.

Zuo approached the task of defeating the northwest Muslims, which had baffled his predecessors, with a practical and patient mind. He took advantage of his geography studies and benefitted from talks with Lin Zexu, after Lin's return from post–Opium War exile in Ili. Zuo also received advice from a local scholar who had served as Lin Zexu's secretary and had long lived in Shaanxi. This man told Zuo Zongtang, "You must take your time. Advance only when you have plenty of food and well-trained soldiers. . . . Once you are ready to strike, hit the meanest Muslim leader hard. Deal with him firmly, without mercy. When the others become quite frightened by the punishment he receives, then you can accept their surrender."[13]

From Zuo's subsequent actions, we can tell that he fastened on Ma Hualong as that "meanest Muslim leader." Ma had established a strong base in the region of Jinjibao, south of Ningxia. He was revered as a leading exponent of the New Teachings and regarded by many of his followers as an incarnation of the holy spirit, equal in power to the prophet Muhammad. Accordingly, the Muslims fought with devoted tenacity. Even after Zuo had assembled and supplied adequate troops, the siege of Jinjibao took sixteen months. Only when the Muslim defenders had been reduced to eating grasses, then hides, and finally the bodies of dead comrades did Ma Hualong surrender in March 1871. He and his family were executed by slicing; more than eighty of his officials were killed; thousands of Muslim merchants, women, and children were forcibly removed to other cities or exiled to northern Manchuria. From Ningxia, Zuo Zongtang marched his forces westward along the well-traveled caravan trade route to Lanzhou, where he established an arsenal and military farms to feed his armies. He prepared with meticulous calm for the final assault on the northwest Gansu city of Suzhou, which he took in November 1873, killing most of the defenders.

After Zuo Zongtang completed the bloody pacification of Ningxia and Gansu, his plan to pursue the Muslim rebels who had fled farther west was delayed. There, in Xinjiang, a charismatic leader from the Kokand khanate named Ya'qub Beg had established an independent state and controlled major oasis cities in the region. But in Beijing, there was a protracted debate among senior officials about the relative priority of coastal versus frontier defense. Which presented the greater danger to the Qing dynasty—the British or the Russians? Where should resources be allocated? The demands on the imperial treasury were substantial—from mounting debts in the form of foreign indemnities, to expenses associated with post-Taiping reconstruction. When advocates of frontier defense finally prevailed in the debate, the court appointed Zuo Zongtang the imperial commissioner for Xinjiang military affairs and allocated funds for the campaign from other provinces and from the customs service. Zuo was also authorized to borrow 8.5 million taels from the Hong Kong and Shanghai Banking Corporation.[14]

From their base in Gansu, Zuo's forces moved into northern Xinjiang in the summer of 1876. The reconquest of Xinjiang was completed with astonishing speed—in the final stage, Zuo's Xiang Army covered more than six hundred miles in seventy days. The campaign received an unexpected boost when Ya'qub Beg died suddenly in 1877; allegations of betrayal soon unraveled the alliance of Muslim factions. (The cause was probably a stroke, but at the time many insisted he had been poisoned, with suspicion widely cast). When the last of the rebels surrendered Khotan in January 1878, Zuo succeeded in subjugating a restive region that had been sliding from Qing control for decades. He did so against the sharp objections of critics—powerful officials both in the imperial court and in the provinces—who decried the financial cost, which amounted to one-sixth of the central government's expenditures every year.[15] Nonetheless, when Zuo returned triumphant to Beijing, the Qing had finally managed to overcome the series of uprisings that had challenged its rule across the empire, at the extraordinary price of millions of lives.

CHAPTER 9 | # Restoration through Reform

CONFUCIAN REFORM

What was truly remarkable, after this long series of challenges, was that the Qing dynasty did not collapse right away, but managed to survive for the rest of the nineteenth century and on until 1912. In partial explanation, Qing statesmen described this survival as a "restoration" (*zhongxing*), a venerable phrase frequently applied to other dynasties that had managed to weather waves of crises and restore order to the empire. The idea of restoration had both a nostalgic and a bittersweet ring to it: although significant, those past restorations had been impermanent, for each of the "restored" dynasties had eventually passed away. Unlike those of the past, moreover, the Qing restoration took place without strong imperial leadership. Emperor Tongzhi, whose name is given to this restoration period, was only five years old at his accession to the throne in 1861, and he died in 1875 before having had a chance to exercise personal power. His "reign" was presided over by his mother, Cixi, acting as regent; by his uncle Prince Gong; by one or two influential grand councilors; but above all by an exceptional group of provincial officials who had risen to prominence fighting the Taiping, the Nian, or the Muslim rebels. Zeng Guofan, Li Hongzhang, and Zuo Zongtang were the best known of these, but there were scores of others of comparable skill. Acting sometimes in concert and sometimes independently, these officials managed to reinvest the Qing dynasty with a sense of purpose, shore up the economy, and develop significant new institutions. This was a remarkable achievement in the context of what had appeared to be a state on the verge of collapse.

Qing officials, as we have seen, had explored all varieties of military mobilization in order to crush challengers to the dynasty. They had used the Eight Banner and Green Standard armies, local gentry-led militia, and semiprivate regional armies; they had also developed military-agricultural bases as well as defensive perimeters of waterways and forts, and had made selective use of Western mercenaries. But all that was mere preamble to what was considered the great central task: the reestablishment of the basic values of Confucian government.

The most important representative of this restoration attitude was the scholar-general Zeng Guofan. Born in 1811 to a minor gentry family of modest means in Hunan, Zeng studied for the civil service examinations tenaciously and obtained the *jinshi* degree in 1838. He was admitted to the Hanlin Academy and soon became known as an expert on problems of ritual and deportment. Zeng lived a simple life on a small salary, often having to borrow money from the wealthier Hunanese in the capital to pay for the expenses of his household and for the education of his younger brothers. It was only when he was appointed to supervise the provincial examinations in Sichuan that he became financially well off: so many eager families gave him "gifts" that he was able to pay off his debts.

The doctrine that Zeng espoused was an austere yet eclectic one that sought to reconcile three approaches to Confucian truth. One approach insisted on the primacy of moral principle and personal ethical values acquired through education; one espoused the methods of textual scrutiny and rigor that had come to dominate *kaozheng* thinking in Qianlong's reign; one believed in the "practical" learning of statecraft thinkers like He Changling, seeking a sturdy foundation on which to rebuild a sound and honest government.

Zeng arrived at this synthesis after years of study and reflection during the dark days that followed the Qing defeat in the Opium War. Over these years, he engaged in long periods of meditation and kept a meticulous diary in which he jotted notes on his readings along with reflections on his own behavior and attitudes. A sample passage shows the frankness of Zeng's self-assessments:

> Got up too late, and felt restless all day long. Read the *Book of Changes*, but could not concentrate. Then I decided to practice quiet sitting. But after a little while, I fell asleep. How could I have become so lazy? Some friends came in the afternoon to show me some of their literary work. I praised them very highly, but deep in my heart I didn't think they were well written at all. I have done this many times lately. I must be sick. How can people value my words anymore if I praise them every day? I have not only deceived my friends but have also deceived myself. I must get rid of this bad habit. At night, read the *Book of Changes*. Wrote two poems before going to bed.[1]

The endless demands of the Taiping war destroyed the pattern of moral reflection and scholarship to which Zeng would have liked to devote his life, and he was now forced to think through his values in a new way. Convinced that a kind of spiritual collapse was the chief source of the mid-Qing crises,

Zeng's approach to restoration was to rebuild schools and reinstitute a strict Confucian curriculum. He wished to encourage able students to take the conventional exams rather than purchase degrees and titles from the Qing government, which had been selling them by the thousands to raise more revenue to meet military costs. He compiled and published lists of those who had died opposing the Taiping, so that their example of martyrdom would live on for future generations. Like other provincial leaders of the time, he also tried to restore order to agricultural work. His plan was to return ousted landlords to their original holdings and reassess land taxes, while attempting to prevent exploitation of long-term tenants. He aimed also to resettle the millions of refugees whose lives had been wrecked over the years by countermarching armies. So great had been the devastation in east and central China that for decades thereafter, what had been densely populated and prosperous regions were drawing numerous emigrants from western and northern provinces.

These policies had the general support of the imperial court in Beijing, but since revenues were short and many problems clamored for attention, Zeng and his colleagues in the provinces were left a free hand. Still there was an obvious coherence to their programs, since many of these officials owed their careers to Zeng Guofan. He had originally hired some to help him manage his Xiang Army and others to assist in local administration. Zeng had developed a careful system of personnel evaluation: he tried to gauge the applicants' honesty, efficiency, and intellectual prowess before employing them; he always rejected those who were opium addicts, boastful, shifty-eyed, or coarse in speech and manner. By the 1870s,

Ren Bonian (1840–1895) Portrait of a Down-and-Out Man The artist served in the Taiping army. Here he portrays a friend's plight as a low-paid, minor government official.

dozens of his former staff had been promoted by the central government to substantive offices. It was a tribute to Zeng's loyalty to the Qing that he did not try to exploit this situation and seize power in his own name.

Despite the weight Zeng placed on traditional scholarly and moral values, he was not a simple-minded conservative. For instance, he was also quick to see the value of making selective use of Western technology. The first person to present Zeng with convincing arguments for such a policy was the scholar Feng Guifen. The two men had a good deal in common, since Feng was also a *jinshi* degree holder (class of 1840) who had served in the Hanlin Academy. Feng's experience of warfare had developed during the mid-1850s, when he led a volunteer corps against the Taiping in defense of his native Suzhou; in 1860 he had moved to Shanghai, where he was impressed by the firepower wielded by the Westerners.

In a series of essays written in 1860, Feng argued that China must learn to "strengthen itself" (*ziqiang*) by including foreign languages, mathematics, and science in the curriculum: students excelling in these subjects should be granted the provincial examination degree. China was 100 times larger than France and 200 times larger than England, Feng wrote, so "why are they small and yet strong? Why are we large and yet weak?" The answer lay in the greater skills of foreigners in four main areas: utilizing all their labor resources, exploiting their soil to the full, maintaining close bonds between ruler and subjects, and the "matching of words with deeds." In order to start strengthening China, Feng argued, the Chinese needed to learn from the foreigners how to build "solid ships and effective guns." This could be achieved by establishing shipyards and arsenals in selected ports, and by hiring foreign advisers to train Chinese artisans. Those who mastered the technology should be rewarded with degrees in the examination system commensurate with their achievement. Since Feng felt that "the intelligence and wisdom of the Chinese are necessarily superior," the conclusion was clear: China would first learn from foreigners, then equal them, and finally surpass them.[2]

In a diary entry of June 1862, Zeng Guofan recorded that he had told his staff members, "If we wish to find a method of self-strengthening, we should begin by considering the reform of government service and the securing of men of ability as urgent tasks, and then regard learning to make explosive shells and steamships and other instruments as the work of first importance."[3] Later that year, Zeng directed the staff at his military camp at Anqing to experiment with building a small steamboat. Its performance was disappointing, but Zeng did not give up. He sent thirty-five-year-old Yung Wing (Rong Hong)* to the United States, with instructions to buy the

---

* This is the Cantonese romanization that Yung himself used during his life.

machinery necessary for establishing an arsenal in China. The choice was a shrewd one, for Yung, born to a poor family near Macao and educated at missionary schools there and in Hong Kong, had first traveled to the United States in 1847. After three years of preparatory school in Massachusetts, Yung had worked his way through Yale and received his B.A. in 1854, becoming the first Chinese to graduate from an American university.

True to his proven methods of assessing character, Zeng had begun his first interview with Yung by simply staring at him, in total silence, a slight smile on his face. But once he had decided to trust Yung, Zeng went all the way, giving him 68,000 taels to purchase the tools needed to establish a machine shop in China. After Yung Wing had traveled to Europe and made preliminary estimates and enquiries—en route he saw the Suez Canal being built and realized how much it would speed travel to China—he continued to the United States, which he reached in the spring of 1864.

With the Civil War raging, it was hard to find an American firm that would fill the order, but at last the Putnam Machine Company in Massachusetts agreed to take on the work. Leaving an American engineer he had met in China to supervise the technical details, Yung attended his tenth Yale class reunion and, as a naturalized U.S. citizen, volunteered his services to the Union in the Civil War. His offer was courteously declined. He then arranged for the shipment of the machinery from New York to Shanghai, while he traveled via San Francisco, Hawaii, and Yokohama. Yung's circumnavigation of the globe while on official business marked a new stage for a Qing employee.

After the equipment Yung purchased arrived in Shanghai, it was combined with other acquisitions and installed at a new arsenal. The machines were first used to make guns and cannons; by 1868, with the help of Western technicians and special grants from the foreign customs dues, a Chinese-built hull and boiler were successfully combined with a refurbished foreign steam engine, and the SS *Tianqi* ("The Auspicious") was launched. A second arsenal and shipyard was established at Fuzhou in Fujian province by Zuo Zongtang shortly before he was transferred to the northwest to suppress the Muslim rebels. At both arsenals, schools for the study of mechanical skills and navigation were founded under the direction of foreign advisers, and translation projects for technical works were started on an ambitious scale.

An English visitor to the arsenals, despite a sarcastic note, could not conceal his surprise at the success of these ventures and their applicability to China's needs in both peace and war: "Already several transports carrying guns, and gunboats, have been successfully launched from the dockyard, and others are rapidly approaching completion. The former vessels have been employed in carrying the imperial grain to the north, and although they are manned and officered by natives, it is noteworthy that no accident has yet befallen any of them."⁴ It seemed as if a methodical program of such self-strengthening might indeed combine with Confucian core values to produce a revitalized state and economy.

DEFINING FOREIGN POLICY

After the events of the 1850s had forced Qing leaders to acquiesce to pressures from foreign countries, they gradually developed a number of devices to help them interact with a changing world. The first of these had been the foreign-managed Inspectorate of Customs, created in 1854 as a response to the threat of Taiping attack on Shanghai, and designed to collect tariffs and generate new revenues for the Qing from the import dues on foreign goods. The allied British and American occupation of Beijing in 1860 and the court's flight necessitated a second institution that would provide formal means of negotiating with foreigners. The Qing solution, after protracted debate, was to establish a new agency in 1861: the General Office for Managing Affairs of All Foreign Countries, usually known by its abbreviation, the Zongli Yamen. This was the first significant institutional innovation in the central bureaucracy that the Qing had made since Emperor Yongzheng created the nucleus of the Grand Council in 1729.

The Zongli Yamen was supervised by a board of five senior officials (initially all Manchus), among whom the emperor's uncle, Prince Gong, was the de facto leader. In their discussions on establishing the new agency, Qing officials reiterated that it was to be a temporary institution, maintained until the current crises had passed. Prince Gong had also assured the emperor that he would keep the premises modest. So although foreigners would be conducting business there, the new Zongli Yamen would carry, in Gong's words, "the hidden meaning that it cannot have a standing equal to that of other traditional government offices, thus preserving the distinction between China and foreign countries."⁵ In keeping with this decision, the building chosen was a small and dilapidated one, located in the eastern part of the imperial city. But with an imposing new front gate added to reassure foreigners that the Zongli Yamen would indeed perform important functions, the structure was opened for business on November 11, 1861.

Prince Gong, the most important Manchu to emerge as a reformer in the Tongzhi Restoration period, was at this time only twenty-eight. Bitterly anti-foreign as a youth, he had moved gradually to a position of patient wariness and eventually to open respect for the West. As an uncle of the reigning boy emperor Tongzhi and a trusted adviser to the empress dowager and regent Cixi, he endowed the new Zongli Yamen with considerable prestige. The bulk of the brainwork, however, was carried out by his talented second-in-command, Wenxiang, a *jinshi* degree holder who served concurrently as grand councilor and minister of war.

Two early examples of Prince Gong's and Wenxiang's work in the Zongli Yamen show different aspects of the Qing's new foreign-policy methods, and how much things had changed since the era of the *Lady Hughes* and the *Emily*: one, the hiring of the Lay-Osborn Flotilla, was something of a disaster; the other, the adjudication of rights over Prussia, was a considerable triumph.

The Lay-Osborn Flotilla had its origins in 1862, when Taiping victories in coastal Zhejiang made the Qing court fear it might lose control at sea to the insurgents. The Zongli Yamen was ordered to purchase a fleet in England and to hire the necessary officers and crew. As intermediary, the Zongli Yamen chose the current head of the Inspectorate of Customs, Horatio Nelson Lay, and made available to him a sum of 1.295 million taels. With this money Lay arranged the purchase of seven steamers and one store ship, to be commanded by a captain of the Royal Navy, Sherard Osborn.

Captain Osborn reached Shanghai with his fleet in September 1863, but was confronted at once with a complex problem. Prince Gong instructed Osborn to serve as assistant commander in chief of the fleet, under the direction of a Qing admiral. In tactical operations, Osborn was to obey the orders of the Qing field commanders—who at this time were Zeng Guofan and Li Hongzhang—although Osborn himself would be in control of all foreigners within the fleet. The trouble here was the initial agreement with Lay, signed in England and assumed to coincide with Qing intentions, which stipulated that Osborn was "to have entire control over all vessels of European construction" and to attend only to orders from the emperor.[6]

The result was an impasse, since none of the parties would yield. Osborn was a man of high principles who felt he had been made a firm promise of command. Lay was a man of immense conceit and arrogance. And the Zongli Yamen could not afford to be seen as weak. After weeks of inconclusive bargaining, the Zongli Yamen acknowledged the hopelessness of the situation by paying off Captain Osborn and his crews and sending them home. Both the Americans and the Qing shared fears that the ships might fall into the wrong hands—either to the Southern Confederacy or to the Taiping. Accordingly the British undertook to sell the ships to their own merchant companies. Lay was given a generous cash settlement and dismissed from his service with the Inspectorate of Customs.

The second experiment of the Zongli Yamen in the realm of international sovereignty was more successful. Since its publication in 1836, Henry Wheaton's *Elements of International Law* had become a standard text in the Western diplomatic community. In 1862 the Zongli Yamen studied a translation of the section on foreign legations. One year later they were offered a draft of the entire work, translated into Chinese by W. A. P. Martin, a missionary from Indiana with long service in Ningbo and Shanghai. After some discussion, they accepted the translation, although Prince Gong ordered his staff to revise it stylistically into a more elegant literary form.

Prince Gong, discussing the translation with the court, observed that he had told the Westerners "that China had her own institutions and systems, and did not feel free to consult foreign books." He took this line, said Gong, "to forestall their demand that we act according to the said book."[7] But when a conflict from the other side of the world—the Prussian-Danish War of 1864—spread into Chinese territorial waters with the seizure by a Prussian warship of three Danish merchant ships at the Dagu anchorage, Prince Gong and his colleagues used Wheaton to good effect. By combining their new knowledge of the accepted definitions of a nation's territorial waters with an examination of the Qing dynasty's existing treaties with Prussia, they forced the Prussian minister to release the three Danish ships and to pay compensation of Mex\$1,500. Now noting that although "the said book on foreign laws and regulations is not basically in agreement with the Chinese systems, it nevertheless contains sporadic useful points,"[8] Prince Gong put up 500 taels to publish Wheaton and distributed 300 copies to provincial officials. Perhaps from fear of conservative backlash, he declined to write a preface to the volume in his own name.

In 1862 Wenxiang and Prince Gong also obtained the court's permission to open a school to train interpreters in Beijing. Its small body of students, aged fourteen and under, would be chosen from each of the eight banners and paid a stipend to learn English and French. (Russian had been taught for many years in the capital in a small separate school.) The decision to draw students from the eight banners reflected ongoing attempts to provide reassurances that Manchus would continue to have a guiding hand over foreign-policy work. But in fact the system spread rapidly and was not confined to Manchus. New government-sponsored language schools opened in Shanghai, Guangzhou, and Fuzhou, and in 1867 Prince Gong and Wenxiang began a campaign to transform the school for interpreters into a full-fledged college. They proposed adding to the curriculum such subjects as mathematics, chemistry, geology, mechanics, and international law, and hiring foreigners as instructors. Despite vigorous protests from conservative officials that there was no need for foreign teachers to instruct them in "trifling arts," and that even the great emperor Kangxi 200 years before had "used their methods [but] actually hated them," the reformers carried the day. The college, with its new curriculum, opened in February 1867 under the direction of Xu Jiyu, a pioneering geographer and historian.

The choice of Xu again showed that a new kind of thinking was gaining ground. Xu had learned much from American missionaries in Fujian in the 1840s, and had been one of the earliest appointees to the Zongli Yamen staff. He had written glowingly about the United States, with its curious, kingless government: "The public organs are entrusted to public opinion. There has never been a system of this sort in ancient or modern times. This is really a wonder." Xu had also praised George Washington as "an extraordinary man," superior even to China's own cultural heroes in valor and strategic cunning.[9] Not surprisingly, the Americans in China were delighted at his appointment, which seemed an excellent omen for future diplomatic relations. The United States' minister to China, Anson Burlingame, gave Xu a copy of Gilbert Stuart's famous portrait of Washington, and Xu's praises of Washington were inscribed on a block of granite and placed at the 300-foot level of the Washington Monument. When Xu retired for health reasons in 1869, he was succeeded by W. A. P. Martin, the missionary scholar who had translated Wheaton's *International Law* in 1863.

Because it provided much needed funds, the parallel development of the Qing Imperial Maritime Customs was essential to these projects. Under the direction of the capable Robert Hart, who had served in the British consulates at Ningbo and Guangzhou before transferring his services to the Qing, the Imperial Maritime Customs was erected on the foundation of the small foreign Inspectorate of Customs of 1854. In the 1860s the customs service became an internationally staffed bureaucracy with outposts in all the treaty ports. Hart was able to make large sums of money available to the central government, some of which supported its modernizing projects. Equally important, his staff accumulated statistics on trade patterns and local conditions all over China.

After so many years of warfare and misunderstanding, the later 1860s seemed to be promising ones for cooperation between China and the foreign powers. With revision of the Tianjin treaty of 1858 stipulated to take place in 1868, the Zongli Yamen officials (with the court's cooperation) moved carefully and skillfully in their discussions with the British, who were represented by Rutherford Alcock. Both Alcock and Hart submitted position papers to the Zongli Yamen on the types of change they thought the Qing should undertake in administration, education, and budgetary planning. The ministers of the foreign diplomatic community moved peacefully into spacious quarters in Beijing, and the question of ritual for imperial audiences was shelved by the simple fact that Tongzhi, because of his youth, gave no audiences. (The issue was solved in 1873, without crisis, when the Qing allowed the foreigners to follow their own customs in paying homage to the emperor.) A group of senior Qing officials traveled to Europe with Hart to observe government systems there, and the imperial court assigned Anson Burlingame, the former U.S. minister to China, as the Qing representative in treaty discussions in the United States and Europe.

Many difficult questions remained, however, concerning missionary and trading rights, the building of railways and telegraphs, the control of opium sales, the status of foreign courts on Chinese soil, and the navigation of internal waterways. After the opening of the Suez Canal in 1869, China was suddenly much nearer to Europe, and old greeds and antagonisms that had seemed to slumber appeared once again. To the anger and disappointment of both Alcock and the veteran Zongli Yamen official Wenxiang, their compromises for treaty revision were rejected by a majority vote in the British House of Commons in 1870, wasting years of work. Hart was dismayed and Alcock depressed. Alcock went to call on Wenxiang, to whom he complained of accusations by the British merchant community that he was too pliable with the Chinese. With the Zongli Yamen's own plans also lying in ruins, Wenxiang responded, "Yes, no doubt; I see what your newspapers say sometimes. I, too, am accused of being a renegade and only wearing Chinese clothes."[10]

THE MISSIONARY PRESENCE

Throughout the 1860s, as officials from the Zongli Yamen adjusted to their new world, violence against Western missionaries formed a harsh accompaniment. In Sichuan, Guizhou and Guangdong, the commercial city of Yangzhou, and the barren hills of Shaanxi, missionaries and their converts were harassed, beaten, and occasionally killed, and their property threatened or destroyed. Finally, in the summer of 1870 in Tianjin, the city that had given its name to the 1858 treaties, the violence burst into hideous prominence.

For months rumors had spread through Tianjin that Christians had been maiming and torturing children, and practicing every kind of sexual aberration. The Catholics, whose imposing new church had been built—despite public protest—on the site of a former imperial park and temple, came in for the worst abuse. Seeing himself as the Catholics' main protector, the French consul Henri Fontanier protested several times to the city officials. But they did little to calm the agitation, and large crowds of Chinese continued to menace the foreigners. Frustrated and angry, Fontanier, two pistols tucked into his belt and accompanied by an aide with a drawn sword, rushed into the magistrate's office. Furious at the official's prevarication, Fontanier drew one pistol and fired. The shot missed the magistrate but killed a bystander. A crowd assembled outside the office exploded with their own rage. Fontanier and his aide were killed, along with several French traders and their wives. The church was burned. A mob broke into the convent of the Catholic Sisters of Mercy and killed ten nuns. By day's end, sixteen French men and women were dead, along with three Russians whom the crowd had thought were French.

The French demand for vengeance came swiftly, and the Qing were forced to respond. Involved in the investigations were Prince Gong and officials of the Zongli Yamen, along with the ailing Zeng Guofan, who as governor-general of the Hebei region had titular jurisdiction over Tianjin, and Li Hongzhang, who was to succeed Zeng. After investigation under torture, sixteen Chinese were found guilty of the attacks and executed. The exact matching of the number of these "criminals" to the French dead was too neat, suggesting the concept of "an eye for an eye" rather than any thorough search for proof of guilt. The Qing government also agreed to pay reparations of 250,000 taels, the money to go in part to the rebuilding of the church and in part to the families of the dead civilians. The prefect and magistrate of the Tianjin region were condemned to exile for life on the Amur River, and the Qing agreed to send a mission of apology to France.

The Tianjin Massacre, as the foreigners called it, was but the bloodiest example of a series of clashes that continued throughout the century. These violent outbreaks revealed the deep fissures that lay between the Christian effort at conversion and the Chinese gentry's sense of their authority and responsibility. It was often well-educated Chinese who wrote the scurrilous, provocative posters and pamphlets attacking the missionaries, and who assembled the crowds prior to many incidents. Behind exaggerations of Christian excesses lay a complex web of truths that made their exhortations effective: the Christian missionaries did preach a new doctrine at variance with Confucianism, they did seek to penetrate ever deeper into China's interior, they protected Chinese converts engaged in lawsuits with non-Christian Chinese, they developed their own educational system, and they misrepresented real-estate deals in which they adapted private homes to churches. Furthermore, in their zeal to save souls, missionaries often accepted, or even sought out, fatally ill babies abandoned by their parents, so that they could baptize them before they died. When the burial grounds of these infant corpses were dug up by hostile Chinese, it inevitably led to highly charged emotional responses.

Yet the story of the Christian mission movement in China was not just one of exploitation, misunderstanding, and hostility. The missionaries represented a wide range of nationalities and religious backgrounds. Besides the Jesuits, other Catholics, and members of the mendicant orders, there were a bewildering number of Protestant groups—over thirty by 1865. Cumulatively, the Catholics and Protestants had deep and subtle effects on Chinese society, particularly in relation to education and in their efforts to raise the status of women.

In education, the impact of the mission movement came through the spread of Christian texts, the publication of general historical and scientific works, the development of schools, and the introduction of new medical techniques. Christian texts spread swiftly in parts of China; we have seen how the future Taiping leader Hong Xiuquan found inspiration from the tracts he received in Guangzhou. Preliminary Chinese translations of the Bible had been finished as early as the 1820s. Careful revisions, supervised by groups of missionaries, were circulating widely in China by 1850, along with a full Manchu version of the New Testament. Special editions of the Bible, in romanization, were prepared for use in the Ningbo, Xiamen, and Fuzhou dialect areas and among the Hakkas of the southeast. The wide circulation of works on Western government and history began in the later 1830s, often by way of missionary journals printed in Guangzhou and Shanghai. These works systematically placed China in a world context and made it possible for Chinese scholars to view their country's history in new ways.

The introduction of scientific and technical texts in translation was given extra impetus by the training schools that were developed along with the new arsenals opened during the first phase of the self-strengthening movement. In 1865 Zeng Guofan wrote an approving preface to Euclid's *Elements of Geometry*, translated jointly by the Chinese mathematician Li Shanlan and the British missionary Alexander Wylie. Zeng noted that this work completed the pioneering translation of Euclid's first six books done by the Jesuit Matteo Ricci over 250 years before—the complete translation provided a crucial supplement to existing Chinese works on mathematics. During the 1860s, Wylie and various collaborators also wrote, or translated into Chinese, treatises on mechanics, algebra, differential calculus, astronomy, and logarithmic tables. Equally productive was the long collaboration between the English missionary John Fryer and the Chinese scholar-mathematician Xu Shou. Working patiently together over decades, they compiled and published a systematic rendering of the entire vocabulary of chemistry into the Chinese language, backing this labor up with study guides and a journal, and making rapid growth possible in many areas of industrial applied chemistry. By the late 1870s, other Western scholars had prepared Chinese texts on electricity, the steam engine, photography, lathes, trigonometrical surveying, and navigation.

The number of mission schools in China increased steadily throughout the nineteenth century, spreading upcoast and inland with the opening of each new treaty port. Often run by individual missionaries or by a tiny handful of teachers, these schools not only prepared young Chinese for English-speaking jobs in the treaty ports, but were designed to lead Chinese children to an understanding of Christian principles and, if possible, to convert the youngsters and train them for later work alongside the Western missionaries. Although viewed with suspicion by traditional Chinese teachers, these schools offered basic education to the children of the poor, both boys and girls. Reciprocal benefits were also achieved. By working closely with Chinese collaborators, the Scottish missionary scholar James Legge completed the first full translation of the Four Books and Five Classics into fluent and accurate English, immeasurably aiding the growth of Sinological studies overseas.

Because the mission schools were unfamiliar and the object of local fears, the missionary-teachers often had to lure students with offers of free food and housing, medical care, and even clothing and cash subsidies. Such was the case at the mission school in the early treaty port of Ningbo, which admitted thirty boys in 1844 and managed to graduate a first class of eight in 1850. Of these eight, one stayed to teach in the school, one went on to study medicine, and four were hired to work with the Presbyterian printing press. Yung Wing, later to become Zeng Guofan's assistant in buying foreign machinery, had been tutored from the ages of seven to twelve by a missionary's wife in a mixed primary school in Macao. He then enrolled in a Macao missionary school at the age of thirteen to study English, Chinese, geography, and arithmetic with five others. By 1847, when he was twenty, Yung was well prepared enough to travel to the United States, which he did with funds provided by local Western merchants and free passage on a tea clipper.

Like other young Chinese of his day, Yung Wing had been impressed by what he saw of Western medicine and initially hoped to become a doctor. Missionaries were quick to note the impact of medical expertise and knowledge, and they had the greatest early successes in gaining converts by providing treatment. It was not that China lacked medical sophistication of its own—there was a long tradition of diagnosis by study of the pulses, and of treatment through extracts of plants, animal derivatives, minerals, and acupuncture—but by the early nineteenth century the West had much greater knowledge of anatomy and more sophisticated skills in surgery. Although there were always some fatalities, which could cause local hostility or lawsuits, Western doctors proved especially successful in removing tumors and curing eye diseases such as cataracts. By the 1860s, both missionary and unaffiliated doctors were beginning to build hospitals with money given by Western philanthropists or raised by subscription from local Chinese. Initially, these buildings were concentrated, of necessity, in the treaty ports, as were such accompanying centers as homes for the blind, for lepers, and for the insane. Other missionaries introduced new seed strains to Chinese farmers, and new varieties of fruits and plants; some also applied their energies to reforestation projects, attempting to halt the serious erosion that had been causing havoc on China's now barren hillsides.

Through their texts, presses, schools, and hospitals, the efforts of missionaries affected Chinese thought and practice. The strength of that influence
is impossible to calculate, but the missionaries did offer the Chinese a new
range of options, a new way of looking at the world. The same was true in
the broader world of family structures and the roles of women. Several early
missionaries were women, and the wives of male missionaries also played
active roles in their communities. Yung Wing recalled his first teacher, a
white woman with strong, assertive features and deep blue eyes: "Her features taken collectively indicated great determination and will power. As she
came forward to welcome me in her long and full flowing white dress, . . . sur-
mounted by two large globe sleeves which were fashionable at the time and
which lent her an exaggerated appearance, I remember most vividly I was
no less puzzled than stunned. I actually trembled all over with fear at her
imposing proportions—having never in my life seen such a peculiar and odd
fashion. I clung to my father in fear."[11]

Yet the fear could be transcended. Thousands of Chinese learned to
study from, work with, be treated by, even become friends of missionaries.
The Western women presented options of public work and careers that had
seemed impossible to Chinese women. As mission families moved deep into
the interior, they created their own versions of domestic worlds and values.
They shared these with Chinese women, introducing them to new ideas of
hygiene, cuisine, and child raising. They protested foot-binding, commiser-
ated over opium addiction, offered religion and education as sources of solace
and change. Some of the bolder ones offered a new perspective on social
hierarchies and female subordination. And some American women—such as
Pearl Buck's mother—encouraged their children to live with Chinese girls
and to become fluent in their language. Pearl Buck's fictional renderings of
life in China won her the Nobel Prize for Literature in 1938.

Young foreign men also made their own arrangements. Robert Hart, later
the inspector-general of the Imperial Maritime Customs, had kept a Chinese
mistress when he was a young man in Ningbo and Guangzhou. It was "a common practice for unmarried Englishmen resident in China to keep a Chinese
girl," he wrote later in a confidential legal deposition, "and I did as others
did."[12] When it came time for him to wed a lady of good British family, he
paid off the Chinese woman with $3,000 and shipped their three children off
to England, so they would not be an embarrassment to him. Yet such double
standards did not always prevail in personal relations between Westerners
and Chinese. Yung Wing married an American woman from Hartford,
Connecticut; their two children both attended Yale University. In his memoirs Yung recalled vividly how his first formidable Western teacher had also
helped three blind Chinese girls learn to read in Braille, doing everything

Dr. Ida Kahn, a Chinese mission-school graduate who earned her medical degree at the University of Michigan, with a Methodist mission group

she could to save them from the bleak life that otherwise would have been their probable lot. By century's end, the options for some Chinese women had become broader than either Yung Wing or Robert Hart could have foreseen. In 1892 two young Chinese mission-school graduates, who took the names Ida Kahn and Mary Stone, sailed to the United States and earned their medical degrees at the University of Michigan. By 1896 they were back in China and had opened their own practices. The success of these women and the faith that inspired it were a tribute to the power of one side of the missionary dream.

OVERSEAS CHINESE

Tens of millions of Chinese were killed or left homeless in the waves of domestic rebellions and the accompanying famine and social dislocation that marked the mid-nineteenth century. Yet the pressures on the land continued to be unrelenting. The population had reached 430 million by 1850, and even though it dipped sharply during the civil wars of the 1860s, it began to climb once more in the 1870s.

One response to the scarcity of arable land was internal migration, but the Chinese had no alternative as straightforward as that of the westward migrations to the Great Plains and the Pacific Coast that marked the same period in U.S. history. Chinese settlers moving west or northwest came either to the high, arid plateaus of Tibet or to the vast deserts of Xinjiang, which was incorporated as a province in 1884 but remained forbidding territory. Those moving southwest encountered hostile mountain tribes or the settled borders of already established kingdoms in Vietnam and Burma. Millions chose to move northeast, first to the settled arable regions of Liaodong—the staging area long before for the Manchu conquest—and then, defying bans by the Qing state, north again into the wooded mountains and bitter cold of what is now Jilin and Heilongjiang provinces. Others braved the short sea passage to swell the number of immigrants on Taiwan, which had become thoroughly opened to Chinese settlement by the 1850s and was named a province in 1885. And some chose to leave the countryside and try their luck in the expanding cities—such as Hankou, Shanghai, and Tianjin—where new industries and the need for transport workers offered chances for employment, even if at pitifully low wages.

The other main response to the demographic crisis was to move out of the known Chinese world altogether and to try one's fortunes elsewhere. Those who made this choice were mostly from southeast China, and used Guangzhou or Macao as their points of debarkation. Some were destitute farmers, some fugitives from rebel regimes, some the ambitious children of large families who saw few opportunities for advancement in Qing society. Most were men who often married just before they left China and dreamed of returning someday to their native villages, loaded with riches, so they could buy more land and expand their families' waning fortunes. They tended to focus their hopes initially on three main regions: Southeast Asia and Indonesia, the Caribbean and the northern countries of Latin America, and the west coast of the United States.

Emigration to Southeast Asia was cheapest and easiest, and many Chinese settled quickly into rice-farming or fishing communities, or into retail and commercial businesses. Even though the upper levels of economic life were dominated by the British, the French, or the Dutch (according to the region), Chinese emigrants found ample room for their entrepreneurial skills. They branched out successfully into tin mines, rubber plantations, and shipping. Under Dutch rule in Indonesia, the Chinese served profitably as tax collectors, working under contract, and as managers of the Dutch-controlled opium monopoly.

Because so many of these new settlers came from Fujian or the Guangzhou delta region, local community bonds and dialect groups remained important,

with migrants from similar neighborhoods clustering together and supporting each other. The Triads and other secret-society groups also flourished, setting up protection rackets, channeling opium sales, arranging cheap passages
on credit, and running prostitution rings; as late as 1890, there were still few
married Chinese women in the Southeast Asian communities. Despite their
uneasiness about the extent of emigration, the Qing set up a consulate in Singapore in 1873 so that they could keep closer watch on the half million or more
Chinese settlers in that area. They also tried to retain the loyalty of the richer
emigrants by selling them honorary titles in the Qing hierarchy.

Latin America, too, drew large numbers of Chinese settlers, especially
after 1840, when several countries in the region experienced rapid economic
growth. Along with increasing opposition there to the use of slave labor and
the availability of cheap passages on steam vessels, this rapid development beck-
oned to the Chinese with the promise of jobs. Close to 100,000, for instance,
had come to Peru by 1875, often lured by promoters and handbills promising
them great riches. Instead of making their fortunes, most of these workers laid
railway lines, toiled on cotton plantations, and labored in guano pits, where
conditions were particularly vile and often led to illness and premature death.
Others worked as domestics, cigar makers, and millers. Many had signed labor
contracts without understanding their full implications, and those who fled
were, if caught, forced to work in chains. There were many suicides. In Cuba,
where tens of thousands of Chinese were working on the sugar plantations
by the 1860s, conditions were equally bad. The Chinese were often treated
more like slaves than free labor, forced to work inhuman hours on docked pay,
and were similarly punished if they fled their workplaces or argued with their
employers. Conditions were little better on the sugarcane and pineapple plantations of Hawaii, where thousands of Chinese had also settled.

In 1873 the Zongli Yamen initiated a new phase of Qing foreign-policy
activism by authorizing commissions to investigate the conditions of life and
work for Chinese in both Peru and Cuba. (Yung Wing, who had just successfully concluded a purchase of weapons for the Tianjin arsenal, was a delegate
on the Peruvian commission.) The two commission reports gave startling
evidence of the abuses that existed in working conditions and in the labor procurement process. Thousands had clearly been tricked into signing up or
been cheated once they had done so. A great many had been kidnapped and
held incommunicado in hulks at Macao or Guangzhou, before being shipped
off to suffer abysmal conditions during the passage. From 1876 on, mainly in
response to these reports, the worst abuses of the contract-labor practices were
abolished and shipping procedures were more carefully regulated.

The first great impetus for Chinese emigration to the United States came
with the gold rush of 1848–1849 in California. But few Chinese arrived in time

to make lucrative strikes, and most of them, after working over mines already abandoned by less tenacious forerunners, moved into other lines of work. They flourished as market gardeners, storekeepers, and laundry workers, spreading along the coast from Los Angeles to Seattle. Thousands worked on the final stages of the railway-building boom that extended the lines from California to Utah in the 1860s. The Chinese migration eastward across the United States subsequently coincided with the later stages of the American move west: travelers on the Oregon Trail recorded in their diaries seeing chopsticks used as eating utensils for the first time. Portland had a large Chinese population by 1880, while other settlements arose in the mountains of Wyoming Territory and along the Snake River in Idaho. After the Civil War, plantation owners lured Chinese to Mississippi, Alabama, and Tennessee and tried to induce them to work fields abandoned by former slaves. By the late 1880s, Chinese were working in shoe factories in Massachusetts, cutlery plants in Pennsylvania, and steam laundries in New Jersey, and there was a sizable group of Chinese merchants in Boston.

The process of Chinese settlement in the United States echoed the experiences of many other immigrant groups—opportunity intertwined with discrimination and racism. White Americans disliked the strangeness of Chinese social customs, mocked the unfamiliar sounds of their speech, and condemned the skewed gender ratios of Chinese communities as unnatural. The queues that many of the men wore looked bizarre; the gambling or opium-smoking habits of some gave the Chinese as a whole a reputation for depravity and vice. Yet at the same time, their industrious work habits caused them to be envied for making a profit where others had failed. There was a common belief among white workers that the willingness of the Chinese to work for low wages dragged

The California Railroad
The first great impetus for Chinese immigration to the United States came with the California Gold Rush of 1848–49. In the 1860s, thousands of Chinese worked on the final stages of the great railroad-building boom that extended the lines from California to Utah.

down wages across the board. Although there was little truth to that assertion, there were occasions when employers used the Chinese as strikebreak-
ers. Knowing little or no English, the Chinese were often unaware of the
social and economic battles into which they had been projected.

Because many Chinese wished to work for only a few years in the United
States and then return home, they were denigrated as "sojourners" rather than
true immigrants. Anti-Chinese discriminatory legislation concerning housing, schooling, work permits, and eating establishments forced them into ethnic enclaves (the first "Chinatowns") and kept them there. Redress was not
easy to find. Chinese in many states were not allowed to testify against white
citizens in court and were forbidden to hold public-service jobs. Most had to
struggle for even basic educational opportunities.

Within a few years of the first settlements in 1849, underlying tensions burst
into open violence, deliberately fanned by the racist rhetoric of white workers and their political supporters. The worst examples were in California
and Wyoming. In October 1871, after two policemen had been killed trying
to intervene in a battle between feuding Chinese gangs, a crowd smashed
through the Chinatown in Los Angeles, looting shops and burning houses.
The crowd ultimately killed nineteen Chinese men, women, and children and
injured hundreds before the civic authorities checked them. (By a macabre
coincidence the Chinese fatalities in Los Angeles exactly matched in number the French and Russians killed in the Tianjin Massacre of 1870.) Fourteen years later in Rock Springs, Wyoming Territory, groups of white miners
first beat a Chinese miner to death with a shovel, then burned the camps of
Chinese migrant workers and killed at least twenty-eight. Two months later,
white mobs terrorized Chinese migrants and expelled them from Washington Territory; more than a hundred communities joined the rampage of vigi-
lantism. Scores of other incidents occurred in the same period, playing an
integral and violent part in the "opening of the West."[13]

Unaccustomed to recognizing the rights of Chinese who moved overseas,
the Qing government reacted slowly, although officials in the Zongli Yamen
were aware of the kinds of problems that existed. In 1867 they obtained the
services of the former American minister Anson Burlingame as ambassador-
at-large. The next year Burlingame passionately pleaded the cause of the
Chinese in his tour across the United States and Europe. "The present
enlightened Government of China has advanced steadily along the path of
progress," Burlingame told his audiences. "She says now: 'Send us your wheat,
your lumber, your coal, your silver, your goods from everywhere—we will take
as many of them as we can. We will give you back our tea, our silk, free labor
which we have sent so largely out into the world.'" His power of persuasion
led the United States to sign a treaty in 1868 guaranteeing continued Chinese

rights of immigration. But Burlingame also muddled the issue by promising that the Qing state was ripe for conversion to Christianity: it would be only a short while, he declared, before China invited Western missionaries "to plant the shining cross on every hill and in every valley, for she is hospitable to fair argument."[14] Following up on Burlingame's initiative, the Qing sent diplomatic representatives to France and England in 1871 and had a full ambassador in the United States by 1878.

But political pressures against the Chinese spread from California to Washington, D.C. In a series of closely contested electoral battles between Democrats and Republicans, there was growing preoccupation with the need to limit Chinese immigration. In 1875, the Page Act denied entry to contract laborers from Asia and Chinese women suspected of harboring "lewd or immoral purposes." President Rutherford B. Hayes vetoed an 1879 congressional bill to limit Chinese emigrants to fifteen per ship, but the following year he pressured the Qing to sign a new treaty that gave the United States the right to "regulate, limit or suspend" Chinese immigration. Finally, the 1882 Exclusion Act barred Chinese laborers for ten years and banned all Chinese immigrants from obtaining citizenship.

Despite its name and intent, Chinese immigration to the United States did not fully cease with the 1882 Exclusion Act. Exempt from the legislation, diplomats, merchants and their families, students, and tourists could enter, as could "return immigrants"—those who had resided in the United States before 1880. Nonetheless, the Exclusion Act represented a milestone—the first time the United States government restricted immigration on the basis of race and class. Successive American presidents confirmed and continued these policies. Grover Cleveland in 1888 proclaimed the Chinese "an element ignorant of our constitution and laws, impossible of assimilation with our people, and dangerous to our peace and welfare," and endorsed new legislation that forbade reentry to Chinese laborers who had returned to China on temporary visits.[15] Benjamin Harrison, accepting the Republican nomination in the same year, spoke of the "duty to defend our civilization by excluding alien races whose ultimate assimilation with our people is neither possible nor desirable." After his election, Harrison chose as secretary of state a man committed to the view that the Chinese had brought with them "the seeds of moral and physical disease, of destitution, and of death."[16] Americans were now choosing to make judgments about Chinese inferiority that were as harsh and comprehensive as any that Qing statesmen had made about the rest of the world in the days of Qing glory.

| New Tensions
in the Late Qing

SELF-STRENGTHENING AND
THE SINO-JAPANESE WAR

The Confucian statesmen whose skill, integrity, and tenacity helped suppress the rebellions of the mid-nineteenth century saved the Qing dynasty from collapse. Under the general banner of restoring order to the Qing empire, they had developed new structures to handle foreign relations and collect custom dues, to build modern ships and weapons, and to start teaching international law and modern science. "Self-strengthening" had not proved an empty slogan, but an apparently viable road to a more secure future. Progressive-minded Chinese and Manchus worked together in order to preserve the most cherished aspects of their traditional cultures by adapting elements of Western learning and technology to China's needs. There remained complex problems of continuing rural militarization, local autonomy over taxation, landlord abuses and bureaucratic corruption, and bellicose foreign powers with their military, diplomatic, and missionary encroachments. But with forceful imperial leadership and a resolute Grand Council, it appeared that the Qing dynasty might regain some of its former strength.

Unfortunately for the survival of the dynasty, forceful leadership was not forthcoming. Tongzhi, in the name of whose rule the "restoration" had been undertaken, died suddenly at the age of eighteen in 1875, shortly after taking up power in person. His young empress was pregnant when he died, but seems to have been excluded from the crucial meetings called by Tongzhi's mother, the empress dowager Cixi, to decide on the imperial succession.

The only way for Cixi to preserve her own power was to continue in her role as regent; accordingly, she appointed as emperor her three-year-old nephew Guangxu, thus assuring herself of many more years as the power behind the throne. The success of this stratagem was secured when Tong-zhi's pregnant wife died that spring, her baby still unborn.* The choice of Guangxu, however, violated a fundamental law of Qing succession: he was from the same generation as Tongzhi, not from a later one, and so could not properly perform the filial ancestral ceremonies in Tongzhi's memory. Cixi silenced overt opposition on this point by promising that when a son was born to Guangxu, that son would be adopted as Tongzhi's heir and be able to perform the necessary rites. One official killed himself outside Tongzhi's tomb to protest the decision, but no others made as dramatic an issue of their discontent. Senior bureaucrats on the whole were silent, apparently resigned to another protracted period of indirect rule by the powerful female regent.

Cixi was a complex, capable woman—and ruthless when she considered it necessary. She was the only woman to attain a high level of political power during the Qing, and was consequently blamed for many of the dynasty's woes by men who thought she should not have been in power at all. Born in 1835, Cixi was named one of Emperor Xianfeng's consorts in 1851 and became his favorite when she gave birth to a son five years later. Xianfeng discussed policy matters with her and allowed her to read incoming memorials. She accompanied him when he fled the advancing British and American troops in 1860. After Xianfeng's death, she formed an alliance with Prince Gong, her brother-in-law, and outmaneuvered powerful Manchu nobles and Han Chinese officials to become coregent. From 1861 to 1889, she ruled succes-sively as coregent for her son Tongzhi and for her nephew Guangxu. She also was the ultimate political authority while Guangxu languished in palace seclusion—on her orders—from 1898 to 1908. Highly literate and a com-petent painter, Cixi kept herself well informed on all affairs of state as she sat behind a screen (for propriety's sake) and listened to her male ministers' reports. Politically conservative and financially extravagant, she nevertheless approved many of the self-strengtheners' ventures; at the same time, she tried jealously to guard the prerogatives of the Manchu imperial line.

It was unfortunate that Cixi ended up clashing with Prince Gong, who had emerged in this period as a capable and progressive leader in the imperial court. The reasons were personal: Cixi considered Prince Gong responsible for the execution of a favorite eunuch, who had been convicted of abusing his power; she also resented Prince Gong's opposition to her lavish plans to rebuild the Summer Palace. Thereafter Cixi found ways to demote Prince Gong and deprive him of various imperial titles and privileges. Further dilut-ing the strength of the Qing, the powerful statesman Zeng Guofan died in

---

* It is probable that the pregnant widow of Tongzhi was driven to suicide by Cixi, but the evidence remains disputed.

1872, the skillful Wenxiang died in 1876, and Zuo Zongtang remained pre-occupied with the suppression of the Muslims in the northwest. The grand councilors in Beijing, though worthy enough men with distinguished careers behind them, tended to be conservative and lacked the skill or initiative to direct the dynasty on a new course. Although self-strengthening programs continued during the last decades of the nineteenth century, a disproportionate number of them were initiated by one man, Li Hongzhang. Li was trusted by Cixi; after the suppression of the Taiping and Nian, he was posted to north China in the dual capacity of governor-general of the Hebei region and trade commissioner for the northern ports. More than any other person, he put his imprint on the closing years of the century.

Li Hongzhang's political endeavors fell largely into three broad areas: entrepreneurial, educational, and diplomatic. As an entrepreneur he built on the foundations laid during the earlier phase of the self-strengthening movement and sought to diversify enterprise into areas that would have long-range effects on the country's development. These initiatives involved the Qing government and individual merchant capitalists in joint operations under a formula called "government supervision and merchant management." One such project was the China Merchant Steamship Navigation Company, founded in 1872 and designed to stop the domination of coastal shipping by foreign powers. With Li Hongzhang as a principal shareholder, the company drew much of its income from contracts to transship government taxation grain from central China to the capital region. After 1877 Li ordered the expansion of the Kaiping coal mines near Tianjin to provide fuel for the growing

navy, and founded a sizable cotton mill at Shanghai. In the 1880s he built arsenals in Tianjin and developed a national telegraph system. He also directed the construction of a seven-mile stretch of railway line to carry coal from the Kaiping mines to a nearby canal, where the coal was shipped to Tianjin for use by the Qing fleet. Originally the rail cars were pulled down the tracks by mules; in 1881 one of Li's

Li Hongzhang

assistants used scrap parts to build China's first steam engine, which was employed successfully on the line.

Li Hongzhang carried forward earlier efforts at educational reform as well. He originally supported the proposal for an educational mission in the United States, an idea first formulated by Yung Wing and backed by Zeng Guofan. The court gave its consent, and in 1872 the first group of Chinese boys, aged twelve to fourteen, were sent to Connecticut. They lived with American families in Hartford and studied a general American high school curriculum that also included elements of Chinese studies. By 1875 there were 120 students in all. To the dismay of Qing officials, in the school and social environments of this American city, the boys began to dress in Western-style clothing. Several cut off their queues under pressure or mockery, and many were attracted to Christianity.

The final blow to the educational mission was the belated discovery that the United States government would not permit a select group of the students, after completing their high-school education, to enroll in the naval and military academies at Annapolis and West Point, as Li Hongzhang had hoped. In 1881 he acquiesced to the decision made by Qing officials to bring the students home, and they returned to China by sea from San Francisco in August 1881. Their final triumph on American soil was their defeat of the local Oakland baseball team, which had expected a walkover but was routed by the wicked curveball of the Chinese pitcher. Upon their return to China, many of the students became influential in the armed services, engineering, and business, but Li Hongzhang henceforth dispatched the most promising students to France, Germany, or Great Britain, where the governments did not object to their receiving technically advanced military and naval training. He also established both a naval and a military academy in Tianjin itself.

The world of international diplomacy was even more inhospitable to the Qing. Here Li Hongzhang worked—sometimes on his own, sometimes in conjunction with Maritime Customs Inspector-General Robert Hart or the Zongli Yamen—to handle a wide range of difficult problems. In the 1870s this included competition with Japan as it began to assert a more aggressive stance in East Asia. Beginning in 1868, the sweeping economic and institutional reforms of the Meiji Restoration meant that Japan could bring superior military force to bear on its East Asian neighbors.

The first occasion for conflict was a Japanese military expedition, sent to Taiwan in 1874, to avenge the deaths of fifty-four sailors from the Ryukyu Islands. The sailors had been killed by Indigenous people after their vessel shipwrecked on the southern coast of Taiwan. In seeking redress on behalf of these victims as Meiji subjects, Japan staked a claim to sovereignty over the Ryukyus, a domain long in the Qing orbit of influence. Japanese forces withdrew from Taiwan after the Qing agreed to pay a small indemnity in a negotiated settlement. In 1876, the Japanese sent four warships and a full battalion to Korea in a show of force that compelled the Korean king to acquiesce to a treaty. Three years later, the Japanese annexed the Ryukyu Islands and incorporated them as Okinawa prefecture. The Qing court was unprepared to respond to the expansion of Japanese power in this period.

In 1876 Li Hongzhang also had to conduct complex negotiations with the British after one of their consuls, Augustus Margary, was killed in an ambush in Yunnan. Margary had been on assignment with a British survey team exploring the feasibility of road or railway routes from Burma into Yunnan. Representing the Qing, Li agreed to pay an indemnity of 700,000 taels, to send a mission of apology to Queen Victoria, and to open four more treaty ports.

More beneficial to China's interests were the negotiations with Russia conducted in the late 1870s by the Zongli Yamen and Zeng Guofan's son, now the Qing minister to Great Britain. By the Treaty of St. Petersburg of 1881, the Russians agreed to abrogate an earlier unequal treaty and to return sections of Ili that had been under Russian occupation since the outbreak of the Muslim rebellions. Although Russia still held huge areas of former Qing territory north of the Amur and Ussuri rivers, the St. Petersburg treaty assured Qing control of its far western borders, a sovereignty confirmed when Xinjiang was declared a province in 1884.

The creation of Xinjiang province was the culmination of a process begun after Zuo Zongtang's suppression of the Muslim rebellions in the 1870s. Officers of Zuo's Xiang Army, recruited from his home province of Hunan, took charge of the reconstruction project. They brought a vision of moral reform to the far northwest of the Qing empire, and they started to implement a program of assimilation intended to transform the Muslim population into obedient Confucian subjects. In place of the former system of indirect rule (in which local leaders such as clerics and *begs* had played crucial roles), an administrative structure of prefectures and counties was established, mirroring the organization of the interior provinces. Han Chinese officials—more than half of them from Hunan—dominated the bureaucracy. While a military force of 30,000 remained permanently stationed in Xinjiang, thousands of demobilized soldiers were shifted from military duty to agricultural settlement. Confucian schools, established starting in the early 1880s, provided a mostly free education to Muslim boys, with the goal of changing "their peculiar customs" and assimilating them to "our Chinese ways."[1]

The successful diplomatic negotiations with Russia and the subsequent confirmation of Xinjiang's provincial status generated a sense of confidence at court and among Qing scholar-officials. When the French expanded their colonial empire by occupying Hanoi and Haiphong in 1880—despite Qing claims to special rights in the area—and began to pressure for new concessions in Vietnam, Li Hongzhang urged caution. But his pleas were swept aside by the excited urging of belligerent Chinese and Manchus, who insisted that the Qing take a strong stand on this matter of principle. While Li was attempting negotiations with France in 1884 to avoid an outbreak of hostilities, those in favor of strong measures continued to fight with the French in Annam and in neighboring Tonkin. The admiral in command of the French fleet in the region responded to these intermittent hostilities by moving his forces into the harbor at Fuzhou and anchoring near the Qing fleet.

Li Hongzhang had urged a negotiated settlement with the French because he understood the fragility of the newly developed Qing navy. When negotiations broke down in August 1884 and the French fleet in Fuzhou opened fire, Li was catastrophically proved correct. The Qing flagship was sunk by torpedoes in the first minute of battle; within one hour every ship was sunk or on fire and the arsenal and docks were destroyed. Although the Qing subsequently won some indecisive land battles in the southwest, French control over Indochina was now assured. A year later the British emulated French aggressiveness and declared Burma a protectorate.

Li Hongzhang could have sent the northern fleet of the navy to reinforce the southern fleet in Fuzhou; instead he chose to conserve those forces and to use them to bolster his own power base. Besides bearing testimony to his power and prestige, the most important task of this fleet was to hold open the sea lanes to Korea. The Qing had created a new senior post in Seoul. This official was charged with the difficult task of maintaining warm relations with the Korean court and ensuring that Japan did not gain a permanent foothold there. During the 1890s tensions heightened as Japanese designs on the peninsula became apparent. In 1894, when the outbreak of a domestic rebellion threatened the Korean king, both the Qing and Japan seized the opportunity to send troops to protect the royal family. Japanese forces arrived first, seized the Korean palace on July 21, and appointed a "regent" loyal to their interests.

That same day the Qing commissioned a British transport to convey 1,200 reinforcements to Korea. Intercepted by a Japanese cruiser and refusing to surrender, the transport was fired on by the Japanese and sunk; fewer than 200 men survived. By the end of the month, Japanese land troops had defeated Qing forces in a series of battles around Seoul and Pyongyang; in October the Japanese crossed the Yalu River, moving the battles of the Sino-Japanese War into Qing territory. The following month another Japanese army seized the harbor at Lüshun, massacring many residents of the city. Japan's land forces were now poised to enter through Shanhaiguan, as Dorgon had done two and a half centuries before.

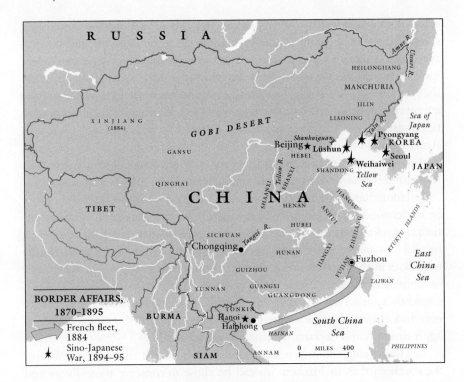

The northern navy, despite Li's efforts to conserve it, now suffered a fate similar to its southern counterpart, with yet more damaging consequences. And just as Li had previously declined to send reinforcements to help in the battle against France, he received little support from the central and southern commands. Li's northern fleet had already been badly damaged by the Japanese in a September battle and had retreated to the heavily defended port of Weihaiwei on the northern side of the Shandong peninsula. In a brilliant maneuver carried through in January 1895, a massive Japanese force marched across the Shandong promontory, seized the Weihaiwei defensive forts from the landward side, and turned the guns on the Qing fleet. Confronting defeat, two Qing admirals and the senior commandants of the forts all killed themselves.

Desperate, the court turned to Prince Gong to help with negotiations, just as it had thirty-five years before when the summer palace had been burned during the disastrous Tianjin treaty negotiations. The prince sadly told a Western diplomat that he had been given the job of "piecing together the cup which the present ministers have smashed to the floor."[2] To assist Prince Gong the Qing chose the most visible of those ministers, Li Hongzhang, and sent him to Japan in person to negotiate with the victors.

The terms of the Treaty of Shimonoseki, finalized in April 1895, were disastrous for the Qing dynasty. They would have been even worse had a Japanese assassin not fired at Li, wounding him in the face below the left eye and shaming the Japanese government before the world. The treaty stipulated "the full and complete independence and autonomy of Korea," which, under the circumstances, effectively made Korea a Japanese protectorate. The Qing also promised to pay Japan 200 million taels in indemnities, opened four more treaty ports, and ceded to Japan "in perpetuity" Taiwan, the Pescadores, and the Liaodong region of southern Manchuria. The Japanese were also to be allowed to build factories and other industrial enterprises in any of the treaty port areas. Russian, German, and French protests forced the Japanese to relinquish the claim to Liaodong in exchange for an additional 30 million taels, but all the other treaty stipulations were confirmed. Many of China's brightest young scholars, assembled in Beijing for the triennial *jinshi* examinations, braved the court's wrath by passionately denouncing the Treaty of Shimonoseki and calling for a new, bolder program of reform. But the Qing court seemed paralyzed. It was a dark conclusion to the brightest hopes of the era of self-strengthening.

THE REFORM MOVEMENT OF 1898

During the closing decade of the nineteenth century, China was in a curious, ambiguous position. Elements of old and new existed side by side. At many levels the pace of change seemed overwhelming and irreversible. Steamboats plied the Yangzi River, imposing new banks lined the Shanghai waterfront, military academies were training young officers in Western tactics, scientific textbooks were rolling off the presses, and memorials flashed by telegraph from the provinces to the Grand Council. Victorious in a series of wars, foreign powers had imposed their presence on China and were now investing in the country, especially in mines, modern communications, and heavy industry. The impact of imperialism was profound, intensifying tensions already generated by the self-strengthening movement.

Yet much of this apparent change was confined to the treaty port cities and within them to the foreign concession areas. Penetration of the countryside by even the most aggressive foreign businesses was slow, and in nearly all cases Chinese-merchant intermediaries—the so-called compradors—played crucial roles in opening up markets for their products through the traditional trade and distribution routes. Grand councilors were indeed learning how to transmit memorials by telegraph to provincial officials, but the messages still had to be hand-carried from the Forbidden City to the telegraph dispatch office. For most young Chinese men from well-to-do families, the patterns of education remained unchanged: they memorized the Confucian classics and labored to obtain the local *shengyuan* degrees before proceeding to the provincial *juren* and national *jinshi* examinations. In town and country, girls still had little access to formal education, their feet were still bound, and their marriages arranged by their parents. In the fields, sowing and harvesting were done by hand, the produce laboriously carried to market. Foreigners, if seen at all, were regarded as exotic or menacing. Qing diplomats, posted overseas, received little prestige from the appointments and were often humiliated on their return and forced into early retirement.

Where a true combination of tradition and change occurred, it was often a long-term, almost invisible development. Farmers attuned to new domestic demands for tobacco or cotton could make much greater profits than before, but they were also more vulnerable to local market swings. Those growing tea or producing silk were in fact responding to world market demands, and sudden unexplained swoops of prosperity and dearth were the effects of global price fluctuations. The refined technology of machine silk weaving in Japan and the United States required a greater evenness of thread, which meant that rural families, who for generations had spun silk thread by hand from the cocoons, faced a shrinking market for their product. The technology of the printing press and the spread of a new urban readership spurred the growth of journals and newspapers. These began to introduce their readers to political commentary and to paid advertisements for health and beauty products, providing a new awareness of options for the individual. A growing sense that China was just one country among others began to lead to the view that it was also a nation among nations, and that no nation could survive without engaged citizens, both men and women. The first regularly printed newspapers began to champion these views, which found a ready response among scholars shamed and disheartened by the Japanese war and the terms of the Shimonoseki treaty.

In the years after the Sino-Japanese War, a formulation became widespread that gave philosophical reassurance to those worried about the value of self-strengthening: Chinese learning should remain the essence, but Western learning should be used for practical development. Generally abbreviated as *ti-yong* (from the Chinese words for "essence" and "practical use"), this was a culturally reassuring position in a time of ambiguous, often painful, change. This formulation affirmed that there was indeed a fundamental structure of Chinese moral and philosophical values that gave continuity and meaning to the civilization. Anchored by that belief, China could then adopt quickly and dramatically all sorts of foreign practices.

This was the favorite formulation of the Confucian scholar-official Zhang Zhidong, once a forceful voice among bellicose conservatives. Zhang capped a distinguished civil-service career by serving for almost eighteen consecutive years as the governor-general of Hunan and Hubei provinces. After Li Hongzhang, he was perhaps the most effective of the provincial reformers. Zhang pressed successfully for the development of a railway line from Hankou to Beijing—funded with foreign loans—and built up the first major coal, iron, and steel complex in east Hubei. At the same time, he ingratiated himself with the empress dowager Cixi and her advisers by his pronouncements on the need for gradual reform and his ringing declarations on the essential values of the Confucian ethical system.

Echoing Zhang Zhidong's *ti-yong* stance, many of the brightest and most successful of the younger generation of Confucian scholars collaborated in indignation after learning the terms of the Treaty of Shimonoseki. They presented a long memorial to the throne, urging continued resistance to Japan and requesting a wide range of economic, industrial, and administrative reforms. These men, assembled in Beijing for the spring 1895 *jinshi* examinations, were coordinated by two scholars of great intelligence and courage: Kang Youwei and Liang Qichao. Kang, a brilliant classical scholar of thirty-seven from the Guangzhou region, had gained fame but also drawn criticism for his eccentric approach to Confucian scholarship. In earlier writings, Kang had used his classical learning to argue that Confucius had not resisted social change and that Confucianism did not negate the basic ideas of human development and progress. In this he was influenced by the ideas of Confucianism first made popular by scholars studying the Gongyang commentaries early in the nineteenth century. Liang Qichao, the second scholar, was twenty-two years old and had been a student of Kang's. He was already actively involved in provincial academies and newly formed national societies that advocated an accelerated program of radical reform. Despite his radicalism, he, like Kang, was also seeking the *jinshi* degree, which remained the most prestigious route to elite status.

Influenced also by Buddhism, and of a highly emotional frame of mind, Kang Youwei saw himself as a new sage capable of saving the Chinese people. His visits to Hong Kong and Shanghai, where he saw manifestations of Western technical and urban development, when coupled with his readings on physics, electricity, and optics, convinced him of the possibilities of a true *ti-yong* synthesis. Liang shared that confidence and sense of excitement. They were overjoyed when the long reform memorial, after being shunted from bureau to bureau by worried officials, was at last read by the emperor himself. Now aged twenty-four, Guangxu was just emerging from the shadow of his

Kang Youwei (left) and Liang Qichao (right)

aunt Cixi, who had gone into semiretirement in the rebuilt summer palace. He had a strong interest in reform and was moved by the words of Kang, Liang, and the other candidates.

The *jinshi* candidates' memorial of 1895 raised many pressing issues. Their petition called on the government to raise taxes, modernize the army with advanced firearms and artillery, develop industry and a state banking system, establish a railway network, build a commercial fleet, and install a modern postal system. Training schools to improve agriculture were needed, as were centers to foster industrial innovation and encourage the kind of creative ingenuity that led inventors in the United States to apply for over 13,000 patents a year. Resettlement programs in poor rural areas should be implemented to lure back the thousands of emigrants leaving every year. Previously such far-reaching changes had been espoused by the Taiping leader Hong Ren'gan, but now the brightest Confucian youth were exploring the same ideas.

As aspiring examination candidates, these would-be reformers did not have sufficient rank to petition the emperor directly. Their bold act violated the protocols and challenged the hierarchical basis of imperial rule. The immediate effects of their demands were negligible. The young emperor Guangxu, even though he seemed interested, had no overt political power, and senior bureaucrats made sure that the proposals were safely filed away. But by the 1890s, demands for change could not be confined to these comparatively orthodox and polite channels. Others, such as the young Sun Yat-sen,* took a different path. Sun, from a poor rural family in the Guangzhou area, had none of the advantages of education and status held by the Kang family. Instead, like thousands of poor Chinese in the southeast, some of the Suns had emigrated to California and Hawaii in the nineteenth century. Sun Yat-sen joined an elder brother in Hawaii in the early 1880s and received an education in the mission schools there before moving to Hong Kong to study medicine. With great ambitions and a deep sense of alarm over China's impending fate, Sun offered his services to Governor-General Li Hongzhang in 1894 as an adviser to help with defense and development. Distracted by the crises in Korea and elsewhere, Li ignored him.

Sun was disappointed and frustrated. The British did not consider his training good enough to practice medicine in their dominions, nor did the Chinese seem adequately to admire his skills. Sun's response was to form the Revive China Society in Hawaii in late 1894, which pledged itself to the overthrow of the Manchus and to the establishment of a new Chinese ruler or even a republican form of government. Raising some money from his brother and other friends, he moved to Hong Kong and tried to combine with local secret societies near Guangzhou to stage a military uprising against the dynasty. Badly organized, hampered by poor security and inadequate weapons and funds, the plan was discovered by Qing authorities and the local ringleaders executed.

Sun fled from Hong Kong to Japan, and eventually to San Francisco and London. In this last city he settled and began to read widely in Western political and economic theory. His studies were interrupted in 1896 when the staff of the Qing legation in London made a clumsy (but nearly successful) attempt to kidnap him and ship him back to China for trial and execution. Sun became a famous figure when this dramatic story was widely written up in the Western press. Returning to the East and setting up a series of bases in Southeast Asia and Japan, Sun continued to labor, through secret societies and his own sworn brethren, to achieve a military coup against the Qing.

Sun Yat-sen found support among restless, adventurous Chinese who felt little allegiance to the Qing and had tasted some of the opportunities and risks of life overseas. One such backer was Song Jiashu, known by his chosen English name Charlie Soong, whose children were later to play significant roles in twentieth-century Chinese politics. Soong grew up on the

---

* This is the romanized style in which the Cantonese form of Sun's name was generally written.

southern island of Hainan and lived for some time with relatives in Java. In 1878 he shipped to Boston, where he was apprenticed to a Chinese merchant family. Bored by his life there, Soong ran away to sea, enlisted as a crewman on a U.S. revenue-service cutter, and was finally passed on by the ship's captain to generous friends in North Carolina who put him through college and prepared him for life as a Christian missionary. Returning to China, he found a focus for his entrepreneurial energies and made a substantial fortune by printing Bibles for missionaries to disseminate. Before long he branched out into the factory production of noodles and moved into a comfortable foreign-style house in the suburbs of Shanghai. At this point, through secret-society contacts, he also began to funnel money to Sun Yat-sen's organization.

By the late 1890s, politically minded Chinese could find inspiration in a range of potential models, from Japanese Meiji reformers to George Washington, Napoléon Bonaparte, and Peter the Great. Chinese language newspapers and didactic histories proliferated, extolling various Western thinkers of the past and holding up as warning examples such countries as Poland, Turkey, and India, which had been respectively partitioned, economically ruined, and politically subjugated. Simultaneously, foreign powers, now including Japan, intensified their demands for economic and residence rights in China—often called "the scramble for concessions"—which placed the Qing in greater jeopardy. In this context, the emperor Guangxu, who undoubtedly had a wider view of the world than any of his predecessors and had even been studying English, decided to

assert his own independence as ruler. Between June and September 1898 he issued an extraordinary series of edicts, earning for this period the name "Hundred Days' Reforms."

Most of the edicts issued in Emperor Guangxu's name dealt with proposals that had already been raised by self-strengtheners and by the *jinshi* protestors of 1895. But there had never before been

Charlie Soong, one of Sun Yat-sen's earliest supporters Soong's three daughters married Sun Yat-sen, Chiang Kai-shek, and the Guomindang finance minister, H. H. Kong.

such a coherent body of reform ideas presented on imperial initiative and backed by imperial prestige. Among the changes, Guangxu decreed that the content of the examination system would shift from the classics to current affairs. The Beijing college would be upgraded and established as an imperial university, with the addition of a medical school. Old academies and Buddhist monasteries would be converted to modern schools offering both Chinese and Western learning, while vocational institutes would focus on the study of mining, industry, and railways. The emperor also ordered the creation of new central bureaus for commerce, industry, and agriculture; the expansion of railway and industrial projects; and the elimination of sinecure positions.

In developing this reform program, several important personnel changes were made. Li Hongzhang had steadily lost influence since the Japanese war disasters and was now removed from the Zongli Yamen. Guangxu's own tutor was also dismissed, caught in the crossfire between factions. Prince Gong had recently died at the end of May. To replace them, several reformist thinkers, among them Kang Youwei, were appointed to the Grand Council or the Zongli Yamen. Kang was granted an imperial audience and submitted two works of historical analysis to the emperor: one on the fate of Poland, the other on the triumphs of Japanese reforms in the Meiji Restoration. But many senior officials, viewing Guangxu's reform program with a jaundiced eye, saw it as detrimental to their personal prospects, the interests of the Qing dynasty, or both. Guangxu seems to have mistakenly thought that the empress dowager Cixi would support his vision and would help him override this opposition.

Although the evidence is contradictory, it seems that a number of reformers feared there might be a coup against the emperor, and accordingly approached some leading generals in an attempt to win their support. There were also rumors of counterplots to overthrow the Manchus or assassinate Cixi. News of the scheming was reported to the empress dowager, and she suddenly returned to the Forbidden City on September 19, 1898. Two days later, she issued an edict claiming that the emperor had asked her to resume power. She put Guangxu under palace detention and arrested six of his reputedly radical advisers. Before they could be tried on the vague conspiracy charges, her order of execution was carried out. Kang Youwei had left Beijing on assignment just before the palace coup, but his younger brother was among the victims. Now with a price on his head, Kang Youwei fled to Hong Kong and from there made his way to Japan and then to Canada. Liang Qichao also fled and began a life of exile. Their dreams, for a coherent program of reform led by the emperor, had ended in disaster.

THREE SIDES OF NATIONALISM

During 1898 and 1899, as part of the general wave of imperialist expansion, foreign powers intensified their pressures and outrages on China. The Germans used the pretext of an attack on their missionaries to occupy the Shandong port city of Qingdao and to claim mining and railway rights in the countryside nearby. The British took over the harbor at Weihaiwei on the north of the Shandong peninsula and forced the Qing to yield a ninety-nine-year lease on a large area of farmland on the peninsula north of Hong Kong, which the British henceforth called "The New Territories." The Russians stepped up their presence in Manchuria and occupied Lüshun, where they erected massive fortifications. The French claimed special rights in the Tonkin border provinces of Yunnan, Guangxi, and Guangdong, and on Hainan Island. The Japanese, already masters of Taiwan, continued to pressure Korea and intensified their economic penetration of central China.

Preoccupied with its own colonization of the Philippines, the United States did not plant its flag on Chinese territory. Instead Secretary of State John Hay's "Open Door" notes proposed a policy of equal opportunity in trade and investment, in which all countries would give others access to their spheres of influence. Under the guise of protecting the Qing's territorial sovereignty and promoting international commerce, this version of the "most-favored-nation" clause asserted rights for the United States on par with the more powerful nations that had staked out zones of economic dominance. Some Chinese began to fear that their country was about to be "carved up like a melon."

In this atmosphere of hostility and fear, a vigorous force began to develop. The many guises in which it appeared can be encompassed under the blanket term *nationalism*, which for the Chinese meant a new, urgent awareness of their relationship to foreign forces and to the Manchus. It also carried the sense that the Chinese people as a unit must be mobilized for its own survival. One can see the growth of this phenomenon in three examples: the Boxer Uprising of 1900, the publication of *The Revolutionary Army* by Zou Rong in 1903, and the anti-American boycott of 1905.

The Boxers United in Righteousness, as they called themselves, began to emerge as a force in northwest Shandong during 1898. They drew their name and the martial rites they practiced from a variety of secret-society and self-defense units that had spread during the previous years, mainly in response to the provocations of Western missionaries and their Chinese converts. Some Boxers believed they were invulnerable to swords and bullets in combat, and they drew on an eclectic pantheon of spirits from folk religion, popular novels, and street plays. Although they lacked a unified leadership, Boxers found ready recruits in a region decimated by disastrous flooding, followed by a prolonged period of drought. Among the Boxers' main targets were the privileges enjoyed by Chinese Christian converts, and they began to attack both converts and foreign missionaries.

By spring 1900, the year their leaders had predicted as the dawn of a new religious age, the Boxers had expanded dramatically. Perhaps 70 percent were poor, young, male farmers. The rest were drawn from a broad mixture of itinerants and artisans, as had been the case with many previous uprisings against the Qing. The Boxer ranks included peddlers and rickshaw men, sedan-chair carriers, canal boatmen, barbers, salt smugglers, and former soldiers. They were joined by female Boxer groups, the most important of which was named the Red Lanterns Shining—girls and women usually aged twelve to eighteen whose powers were invoked to fight the "pollution" of Chinese Christian women. Their most prominent leader was the "Holy Mother Lotus Huang," daughter of a poor boatman and herself a former prostitute, who was believed to have unique spiritual powers. Other women banded together in teams called the Cooking-Pan Lanterns and fed the Boxer troops from pots that were allegedly replenished magically after every meal.

Still without any coordinated leadership, Boxer groups began to drift into Beijing and Tianjin in early June 1900. Roaming the streets, dressed in motley uniforms of red, black, or yellow turbans and red leggings, and with white charms on their wrists, they harried—and sometimes killed—Chinese converts and even those who possessed foreign objects such as lamps, clocks, or matches. The Boxers also killed four French and Belgian engineers and two English missionaries, ripped up railway tracks, burned the stations, and cut telegraph lines. Provincial officials wavered, as did the Qing court, sometimes protecting foreigners, at other times condoning or even approving the Boxer show of antiforeign "loyalty." The Boxer slogan of "Revive the Qing, destroy the foreign" emphasized that they were not anti-dynastic rebels.

On June 17, two dozen foreign ships assembled at and seized the Dagu forts. Two days later in Beijing, the German minister was shot dead in the street on his way to a meeting at the Zongli Yamen, and Boxer forces laid siege to the foreign-legation areas. Praising the Boxers now as a loyal militia, on June 21 the empress dowager issued a "declaration of war" against the foreign powers, which stated in part,

> The foreigners have been aggressive towards us, infringed upon our territorial integrity, trampled our people under their feet. . . . They oppress our people and blaspheme our gods. The common people suffer greatly at their hands, and each one of them is vengeful. Thus it is that the brave followers of the Boxers have been burning churches and killing Christians.[3]

With the empress dowager and senior officials now clearly behind them, the Boxers launched a series of attacks on mission compounds and on foreigners. The attacks were particularly vicious in Shanxi, Hebei, and Henan, with the worst atrocity occurring in Shanxi. There, Governor Yuxian summoned the missionaries and their families to the provincial capital, promising protection. But once they arrived, he ordered all forty-four men, women, and children killed.

In Beijing, the foreign diplomatic corps and their families retreated into an area composed mainly of the British, Russian, German, Japanese, and American compounds, defended with makeshift barricades of furniture, sandbags, timber, and mattresses. Had the Boxers been better organized or had large numbers of Qing army troops joined in the attack, there would have been many more casualties. But the attack was not pressed with coordinated vigor, the Qing armies stood outside the fray, and the governors-general of central China such as Zhang Zhidong stalled for time and refused to commit their troops to the conflict.

On August 4, 1900, an allied expeditionary force of 20,000 troops from eight countries left Tianjin, with Japanese soldiers comprising about half of the force. Boxer resistance quickly crumbled, and key Qing commanders died by suicide. The foreign troops entered Beijing and raised the Boxer siege on August 14. As they came into the city from the east, the empress dowager and the emperor fled to the west, establishing a temporary capital in the city of Xi'an more than 600 miles away. For the next eight months, a bloody campaign led primarily by the Germans launched punitive raids on towns and villages across north China, to ferret out Boxers in hiding and to punish those suspected of harboring them. Meanwhile, it took a year to complete negotiations between the fugitive court and the foreign powers seeking vengeance. With Li Hongzhang and Robert Hart playing mediating roles, a treaty known as the Boxer Protocol was signed in September 1901.

In this protocol, the Qing agreed to erect monuments to the memory of the more than 200 foreigners who had died, to ban examinations for five years in cities where antiforeign atrocities had taken place, to forbid all imports of arms into China for two years, to allow permanent foreign guards and emplacements of defensive weapons to protect the legation quarter in perpetuity, to make the Zongli Yamen into a full Ministry of Foreign Affairs, and to execute the leading Boxer supporters, including the Shanxi governor Yuxian. They also agreed to pay an indemnity of 450 million taels (around U.S.$333 million at the then-current exchange rates), a staggering sum at a time when the government's entire annual income was estimated at around 250 million taels. The indemnity was to be paid in gold, on an ascending scale, with 4 percent interest

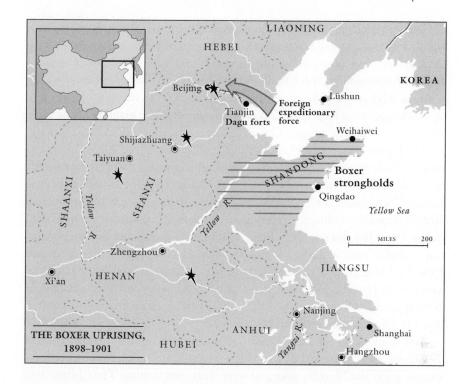

LIAONING

HEBEI

KOREA

Beijing

Lüshun

Tianjin
Dagu forts

Foreign
expeditionary
force

Weihaiwei

Shijiazhuang

Taiyuan

SHANDONG

Boxer
strongholds

Qingdao

Yellow Sea

SHAANXI

SHANXI

Yellow R.

Yellow R.

0   MILES   200

Zhengzhou

JIANGSU

Xi'an

HENAN

Nanjing

THE BOXER UPRISING,
1898–1901

ANHUI

Shanghai

HUBEI

Yangzi R.

Hangzhou

charges, until the debt was amortized on December 31, 1940. With all interest charges factored in, total payments over the thirty-nine-year period would amount to almost 1 billion taels.

In January 1902, the empress dowager and the emperor returned to Beijing, where Li Hongzhang had just died from illness at the age of seventy-eight. Cixi reestablished her residence in the Forbidden City, which for over a year had been the headquarters for the allied expeditionary force. At the end of that month, in a gesture of reconciliation, she received the senior members of the foreign diplomatic corps in person at her palace; on February 1, in another unprecedented action, she held a reception for their ladies. But Emperor Guangxu was still not allowed to play any open political role.

The two exiled reformers, Sun Yat-sen and Kang Youwei, both tried to exploit the disruption caused by the Boxer Uprising by launching their own attacks against the Qing during 1900. Kang's took place in Hubei and Anhui in August and Sun's in Huizhou in October. Kang's goal was to restore Guangxu to power as a constitutional monarch, whereas Sun wanted to establish a Chinese republic. Neither plan was well financed or well coordinated, and both were suppressed by Qing troops without difficulty.

The forms of protest now passed back to the manipulators of the written word. The most articulate of these turned out to be an eighteen-year-old student named Zou Rong, whose work provides a second case study of the new forms of nationalism. Zou Rong was one of a growing number of young Chinese who, in the years after the Sino-Japanese War, had gone to Japan to study the source of its power. Zou grew dismayed at the inability of the Qing to react forcefully in a time of crisis. Like certain secret-society and Taiping leaders before him, he singled out the Manchus for blame, but unlike those earlier rebels he moved beyond slogans to draw up a lengthy indictment. He was able to do this because he had returned from Japan to live in the International Settlement, a foreign-concession area of Shanghai administered by a British-American council. According to agreements concerning extraterritoriality, Qing law did not apply there; Chinese residents (and foreigners without consular representation) accused of crimes were tried before a "Mixed Court" of foreign and Chinese judges. In the International Settlement and other treaty port concession areas, residents could write, and disseminate their writings, with a freedom impossible to those living in ordinary towns supervised by Qing magistrates and police.

Zou Rong drew his anti-Manchu ideas together in a short book entitled *The Revolutionary Army* (1903). In ringing language, he called on his countrymen to reject the Manchu yoke and seize their own destiny. The Chinese had become a race of slaves, declared Zou, and such men as Zeng Guofan, destroyer of the Taiping, were Manchu lackeys who butchered their own countrymen. The Chinese should learn from Western examples that it is possible to overthrow domestic tyranny and free a country from foreign domination if the people are conscious of their unity and struggle together. As Zou wrote,

I do not begrudge repeating over and over again that internally we are the slaves of the Manchus and suffering from their tyranny, externally we are being harassed by the Powers, and we are doubly enslaved. The reason why

Zou Rong, author of The Revolutionary Army *(1903)*

our sacred Han race, descendants of the Yellow Emperor, should support revolutionary independence, arises precisely from the question of whether our race will go under and be exterminated.[4]

And he called dramatically on his Han countrymen to reclaim their destiny:

You possess government, run it yourselves; you have laws, guard them yourselves; you have industries, administer them yourselves; you possess armed forces, order them yourselves; you possess lands, watch over them yourselves; you have inexhaustible resources, exploit them yourselves. You are qualified in every way for revolutionary independence.[5]

These challenging calls, inserted in the midst of other demands for such reforms as elected assemblies, equality of rights for women, and freedom of the press and assembly, made an exciting mix. *The Revolutionary Army* spread widely; Sun Yat-sen seized on it as a means to outflank the more cautious Kang Youwei, distributing thousands of copies to his supporters in San Francisco and Singapore. Qing officials pressured the foreign concession authorities in Shanghai to yield up Zou and others who had collaborated with him to publish articles calling for the overthrow of the Qing; one such article mocked the emperor as a "little clown." The police of the International Settlement took Zou and his accomplices into custody but refused to surrender them to the Qing government. After six months of legal and diplomatic wrangling, in 1904 Zou was tried in the Shanghai Mixed Court on a charge of distributing inflammatory writings. There he received a two-year sentence, whereas a Qing court would certainly have sentenced him to death. But by a cruel irony, Zou fell ill in prison and died in 1905. Even though he was only nineteen, he had managed to make an extraordinary mark on his times.

During the period of Zou's trial, another wave of protest against foreign abuses had been building. Ever since the passage in the United States of the 1882 Chinese Exclusion Act, Americans had performed numerous hostile acts against Chinese immigrants. Immigration officers broke into Chinese homes in American cities allegedly to check registrations; harassments and deportations were common; and Chinese arriving at United States ports—including the delegation coming by invitation to the St. Louis Exposition in 1904—were roughly handled and abused. Further bitterness developed when America's exclusionary policies were extended to Chinese residing in Hawaii and the Philippines.

By 1905, a new sort of response was developing in China, providing a third expression of nationalist feeling. To protest the mistreatment of Chinese in the United States, the newly established Qing Ministry of Foreign

Affairs refused to renew the immigration treaty with the United States. To strengthen China's position, in May 1905 the Shanghai Chamber of Commerce called for a national boycott of American goods, services, and employers. There had been such boycotts before, most notably by merchants in Hankou in the 1880s, but nothing so widespread and ideologically charged. The call to action reached more than twenty cities and towns, drawing support from diverse groups of students, laborers, merchants, and urban residents. Amid the agitation, a young man—who had recently been denied entry to the United States—killed himself in front of the American Consulate in Shanghai by drinking poison. Between late July and September the protests escalated; the boycott was effective in many cities, especially in north China ports. Supported by funds from Chinese communities in California and Oregon, and by the patriotic excitement of students—many recently returned from Japan—merchants refused to handle such goods as American cigarettes, cotton, kerosene, and flour. Only in late September did their solidarity crack as the threat of government suppression loomed. Although it was not as dramatic on the surface as Boxer violence or Zou Rong's fiery rhetoric, this attempt to respond to national humiliation by means of concerted economic action marked a new kind of popular movement in Chinese history.

EMERGING FORCES

The growing strength and complexity of nationalism was but one aspect of a new search for self-identity that cut across many segments of society in the late Qing. Economic, political, educational, and social pressures now began to impinge on virtually everyone in China, except perhaps for those bound to traditional patterns of rural toil far from the cities. Even such poor farmers, however, learned that their taxes were increasing to pay for new reforms, and they gathered in protest in many parts of the country only to be roughly suppressed by Qing troops or the agents of newly founded police forces. Among those who once would have been ignored but who now made their voices heard with ever greater effect in the closing years of the dynasty were the overseas students, women, merchants, and urban workers.

After the recall of the Qing student mission from Hartford, Connecticut, in the 1880s a new surge of Chinese students left for Europe, where Britain and France were especially popular destinations. A pioneer of this movement was Yan Fu, who had been educated in the school affiliated with the Fuzhou shipyard and sent in 1877 to England, where he enrolled in the naval schools at Portsmouth and in Greenwich. There he studied British naval technology, still the best in the world despite a vigorous challenge by the Germans. He also spent much time examining Western legal practices and began a broad reading of Western political theory. In the course of this he developed an interest in Social Darwinism—the application of Charles Darwin's theories of species evolution to the fate of social units.

Such theories, which spoke of the "survival of the fittest" and the need for creative adaptation to avoid extinction, had a sharp relevance for China's plight. Yan Fu's translations of such works circulated widely. After his return to China in 1879, Yan also worked as an academic administrator in Li Hongzhang's Beiyang naval academy, becoming superintendent in 1890. In addition to his many other duties, he embarked on a series of translations of such influential works as Thomas Huxley's *Evolution and Ethics*, John Stuart Mill's *On Liberty*, Montesquieu's *Defense of the Spirit of the Laws*, and Adam Smith's *Wealth of Nations*. Through these works, Yan introduced an electrifying range of ideas to China's students.

When the Qing court ordered the abolition of the Confucian examination system in 1905, the way to a successful intellectual or academic career was thrown wide open. One young man, Zhou Shuren, who subsequently became a celebrated writer under the pseudonym Lu Xun, was caught up by these new currents. Initially trained in local Confucian schools in Zhejiang, Lu Xun read Yan Fu's translations in his late teens and joined the great exodus of students to Japan, which had become a magnet for young Chinese. A closer and more affordable destination than the United States or Europe, Japan offered an attractive model after its defeat of the Qing in 1894 and became even more enticing after its victory in the Russo-Japanese War of 1904–1905. The means by which the Japanese had managed to graft a constitutional structure onto the existing imperial system deeply interested reform-minded young Chinese. From Japanese periodicals they discovered a new vocabulary of concepts such as "human rights," "constitutions," "democracy," "representation," and "parliament." Since the Japanese writing system used Chinese characters, these new linguistic coinages could be transferred to China with apparent ease, even though in reality the original Chinese characters used in these neologisms often had their own resonance that conflicted with the intended new meanings. Japanese law and medical schools, military academies, departments of political science and economics—all seemed to offer new hope at a time when Chinese "essence" seemed every year more fragile in the face of the overwhelming power of foreign imperialism.

While studying medicine in Japan in 1905, Lu Xun was shocked by a lantern slide he was shown of triumphant Japanese executing an alleged Chinese traitor while a large, apathetic circle of Chinese watched. He resolved then to give up medicine and concentrate on literature, which he believed could shock the people into an awareness of their plight and into action. He began translating important works of European and Russian social realism, so that China's students would understand the great issues that had dominated other parts of the world over the preceding half century.

The thousands of Chinese students in Japan could be only loosely supervised by the Qing authorities, if at all, even though many were supported by government stipends and could be sent home for improper behavior. In their excitable, energetic ranks, Sun Yat-sen found ready recruits for his anti-Qing organizations, and in 1905 he allied his group with a number of others to form the "Revolutionary Alliance" (Tongmenghui). The alliance tried to infiltrate student members back into China, there to work toward eventual military insurrection. Its ideology was a mixture of Sun's republican ideas—developed during his period of European study and in subsequent reading—and socialist theories on land-tax equalization and the need to control capitalist development. Sun Yat-sen's bold vision for revolutionary activism was steadily becoming more compelling than Kang Youwei's more cautious call for constitutional monarchy.

Among the students in Japan were many young women, and this reflected a drastic change in Chinese social and political life. Although some male "revolutionaries" brought their bound-footed concubines to Japan, many independent young women were, with the encouragement of their parents or brothers, unbinding their feet and struggling to obtain an adequate or even advanced education. They found moral and social support in sisterhoods that provided economic help if they remained unmarried, in groups of men who pledged to marry young women with the still unfashionable "large feet," and in schools that actively encouraged their pursuit of learning. These women now had new role models like Joan of Arc, Mme. Roland, Florence Nightingale, and Catharine Beecher, whose biographies were translated, printed, and reprinted in magazines. There were also stark new images such as that of the young Russian radical Sophia Perofskaya, whose successful assassination of Tsar Alexander II, even though it led to her arrest and execution, made her a model for female intransigence and courage in the face of autocratic misrule.

Although the scale was still small—by 1909, only around 13,000 girls were enrolled in schools in the whole of China, and a few hundred more overseas—for these young women this was a period for the development of literary skills and reflection on China's weakness and the restrictions of family life. A vivid example of the literal acting out of the more revolutionary female goals was offered by Qiu Jin, a young woman from the same part of Zhejiang as the writer Lu Xun. Married young, by her parents' arrangement, to a merchant's son whom she disliked, she had two children before suddenly leaving her family and sailing alone for Japan in 1904. There, supporting herself by selling her jewelry and assisted by friends, she began to study a wide range of Western subjects and to speak out publicly on the need for reform.

Drawn to the orbit of Sun Yat-sen's Revolutionary Alliance, Qiu Jin liked to dress in men's clothes on occasion and to experiment with explosives. Returning to China in 1906, she became a radical teacher in a small school in Zhejiang, keeping up her contacts with the Revolutionary Alliance and meeting members of secret societies. Often practicing military drills and riding her horse astride, she drew criticism from more conservative townsfolk, but she managed to retain her teaching position. At her school, she tried to launch an uprising against the Qing in July 1907, acting in concert with a revolutionary friend in Anhui. Local troops captured her with little trouble. After a brief trial she was executed, leaving an example of courage and initiative in the face of deep national frustrations.

The commercial world of China's merchants was also swept with change during this period. We have noted that "self-strengthening" statesmen had sought to expand the national economic base by developing "government-supervised merchant-managed companies" and that some had succeeded in fields such as shipping and mining. But problems of overlapping jurisdiction and lack of capital slowed these efforts. By the 1890s there had come to be greater interest in "official-merchant joint-management companies," such as several new spinning and weaving mills, capitalized at 500,000 taels or more. Since the Qing court, the metropolitan bureaucracy, the provincial officials, and the merchants each had their own interests and constituencies, it proved impossible to develop the kind of coordinated economic policy that had been so successful in Japan during the Meiji Restoration. Some leaders at court made gestures in that direction, however. Prince Chun, for example, Emperor Guangxu's brother, met large numbers of overseas Chinese merchants during his diplomatic journey to apologize to the Western governments for the massacres in the Boxer Uprising. He returned to China a strong backer of vigorous economic intervention by the state.

Partly on the urging of Prince Chun, the Qing in 1903 founded a Ministry of Commerce to facilitate industrial and commercial development and at the same time ensure government supervision of new ventures. The new ministry encouraged the formation of chambers of commerce in major cities across the country. Although intended as a means of bolstering business-government cooperation and as a conduit for government control, the chambers of commerce would become forums for merchant autonomy and collective action, as we saw in the anti-American boycott of 1905.

These new forms of commerce and industrial development became, like foreign imperialism, sources of dislocation in the lives of urban workers. Scattered records allow glimpses of the responses of these workers. In the earlier Qing period, there had been examples of labor strikes among such workers as the porcelain furnace men in Jiangxi and the grain-barge pullers on the

Grand Canal. But a letter of 1897, written in Shanghai by a twenty-five-year-old American salesman for the Winchester Repeating Arms Company, shows urban tensions escalating in the midst of new social realities, and how swiftly foreigners could become involved.

The writer described a conflict in late March 1897 over a decision by the Municipal Council of Shanghai to raise the tax on wheelbarrow coolies from 400 copper cash to 600 copper cash a month. In protest, the coolies managed to organize and get all wheelbarrows off the streets by April 1. When one lone coolie, a few days later, tried to cross from the concession area administered by the French to the International Settlement with a wheelbarrow full of offal, a crowd of workers beat him up and smashed his wheelbarrow. A policeman tried to intervene and was beaten in turn. Other foreign bystanders ran to help him, and police reinforcements soon arrived. The coolies fought the policemen's drawn swords with poles and bricks pulled from nearby walls. Four blasts from the ship's siren on a British gunboat brought "volunteers" to the scene in twenty minutes, and the coolies were dispersed, leaving behind three of their number dead and having wounded two policemen. Within thirty minutes, "Blue Jackets" from several foreign ships had arrived and occupied key bridges and public spaces. Peace returned to the streets, and the Municipal Council decided to postpone the tax increase until July.[6]

Hankou was also undergoing dramatic industrial development, with over 10,000 workers employed in modern industrial plants by the 1890s. Here, too, an expansion of resident foreigners and the opening of foreign-concession areas heightened social tensions. Labor conditions were bleak, wages low, and housing conditions atrocious as rural workers migrated to the already crowded city in search of employment. Copper workers struck in 1905, mint employees in 1907, and thousands of street vendors, hawkers, and stall keepers, along with piece-goods shop assistants, struck in 1908. In other large cities, the new cotton mills, cement works, cigarette factories, iron works, and paper mills that were being built—often with foreign capital—all showed the prospects of exploitation and unrest.

No larger patterns in these industrial protests were yet perceived by most people, but news of the attempted Russian Revolution of 1905 had a strong impact in East Asia. Japanese radicals close to Sun Yat-sen drew a new kind of Russo-Chinese parallel and put Sun in contact with Russian revolutionaries. As one Japanese explained it with graphic simplicity, China and Russia were the two greatest autocracies in the world, and the repression they enforced was a block to freedom everywhere. The solution was clear: "For the advance of civilization it was necessary to overthrow these autocracies."[7]

CHAPTER 11

The End of the Dynasty

Between 1860 and 1900, the Qing court and provincial officials had tried to adapt a wide range of Western techniques and ideas to China's proven needs: artillery, ships, the telegraph, new schools, factories, chambers of commerce, and international law. Although the focus constantly shifted, the goal was always to learn selective practices from the West that would strengthen China against the pressures and demands of those same foreigners. In the aftermath of the Boxer Uprising, the heavy price exacted by the punitive settlement intensified the urgency of reform as a matter of survival for the Qing dynasty. While still in exile in January 1901, the empress dowager Cixi issued an edict in the emperor's name, directing all senior officials to "reflect carefully on our present sad state of affairs," to thoroughly scrutinize Chinese and Western governmental systems, and to submit detailed proposals for change within two months:

> Duly weigh what should be kept and what abolished, what new methods should be adopted and what old ones retained. By every available means of knowledge and observation, seek out how to renew our national strength, how to produce men of real talent, how to expand state revenues, and how to revitalize the military.[1]

The proposals that flooded in were the beginning of evolving efforts to resuscitate the Qing dynasty in what would prove to be its final decade. Collectively known as the "New Policies" (*xinzheng*), the reforms ranged from local initiatives to central directives. Although encompassing different strategies that implied conflicting visions, they shared the aspiration to fortify and transform China in a time of crisis. As in the previous self-strengthening movement, powerful provincial governors played crucial roles in both policy proposal and implementation. Liu Kunyi, the governor-general of Jiangnan, and Zhang Zhidong, his counterpart in Hunan-Hubei, jointly submitted three memorials that enumerated twenty-seven areas in need of improvement, ranging from transport, law and punishment, and industry, to schools and the postal service. Many New Policies reprised ideas put forward and resoundingly rejected in 1898—but this time, the efforts received stronger and more consistent support from the imperial court. However reluctantly, the empress dowager Cixi also opened the door to the possibility of fundamental changes to the political system by consenting to reforms in constitutional governance and education.

CONSTITUTIONAL REFORM AND EDUCATION

Qing scholar-officials had been ruminating on ideas for constitutional reform since the mid-nineteenth century. While some expressed admiration for the American political system and the French Revolution, for many the idea of a republic that would entail the demise of the Qing dynasty was too radical to contemplate seriously. A constitutional monarchy seemed an attractive compromise. Great Britain, the world's paramount industrial and military power, was one obvious model for possible emulation; another was Germany, rapidly rising to global prominence; and a third—and most dramatic—was Japan, which in less than twenty years since the establishment of a joint imperial and parliamentary structure had transformed its economy, industry, military, and system of landholding. The incontrovertible proof of the strength these changes brought Japan were its victory over the Qing in the war of 1894 and over Russia in 1904–1905.

The empress dowager Cixi made the first gesture in the direction of constitutional reform in 1905, when she ordered the formation of a group to travel abroad to study foreign governments. Some radical Chinese nationalists, alarmed that the mission might strengthen the Qing state to the extent that it would be impossible to overthrow, resorted to terrorist tactics in an attempt to stop this initiative. One young revolutionary tried to blow up the train carrying the constitutional mission as it was leaving Beijing station in September. The explosion was mistimed, killing the would-be assassin. Two of the commissioners were injured, delaying matters until substitute commissioners could be named.

The revised mission, divided into two groups, visited Japan, the United States, Britain, and other European countries. Upon returning to China in 1906, the commissioners recommended to the empress dowager that some kind of constitutional reform be implemented and suggested Japan as the most effective model, since there the reigning imperial family had maintained power. In November 1906, Cixi issued an edict promising to prepare a constitution, convene a national assembly, and reform the central government administrative structure by reshaping the existing ministries and establishing new ones. Only eight years prior, Emperor Guangxu and his supporters had been prevented from pushing through much milder measures. But the crisis was now so clear that both Manchu and Chinese officials accepted the empress dowager's decision.

Even before these policy decisions had been made at the central-government level, a reassessment of local government and its accessibility to the people was underway. In response to Cixi's call for reform proposals, in 1902 the governor of Shanxi, Zhao Erxun, suggested redesigning the *baojia* mutual-security system into a local government network spanning small towns or groups of villages under carefully chosen headmen. This would create much smaller administrative units than the current counties controlled by magistrates, and would allow greater popular participation in local administration. Other proposed reforms were to establish women's schools, to develop an urban police system, and to redirect funds from community organizations—such as temples or lineages—to the needs of local governance and education. The newly formed Bureau of Government Affairs officially publicized these efforts, and in 1905 the court formally encouraged subcounty administrative offices.

Also in 1905, an imperial edict announced a seismic change: the abolition of the civil service examination system, which had served as the cornerstone of state ideology and bureaucracy for more than a millennium. In its place, a national school system would prepare the next generations to meet the challenges of an increasingly perilous world. Different iterations of the new education system had already been announced in the previous three years, moving toward greater standardization and state oversight. A government-regulated network of primary schools, middle schools, teachers' colleges, and universities would incorporate new subjects influenced by Western and Japanese models. Although many of the new schools that emerged retained the Confucian classics in the curriculum or absorbed former charitable and private academies, the official termination of the examinations shattered the aspirations of both young and old men. For students and "expectant officials" (who had earned degree titles but held no actual positions), this meant forfeiting the investment they and their families had made in many years of study; tens of thousands of teachers lost their jobs in the transition. Painfully for some, the change signaled that the values and ideals they had absorbed through studying the Confucian classics would soon be considered obsolete.[2]

In one sense, the new schools could be seen as offering greater opportunities to the talented of all social classes and occupational groups, broadening avenues of upward mobility. But in fact, it was primarily the sons (and occasionally the daughters) of the traditional elite groups who had the money to enroll in the new schools. Constitutional changes that demanded fairly advanced education as a criterion for the vote or for officeholding also perpetuated the privilege of wealthy families. The new schools, meanwhile, inflicted heavier tax burdens on local communities, to pay for expensive facilities, equipment, and teachers qualified to provide instruction in technical subjects. In the many villages and towns that could not muster the funds to establish a modern primary school, the new-style education proved to be less accessible to those from poorer backgrounds than the academies they replaced.

The problems that became manifest in such reform attempts suggest the difficulty of establishing new institutions in an unprepared context. Members of the educated elite, whether officeholding, landholding, or involved in trade (and in some cases the same family was engaged in all three), enjoyed dominance in the countryside and the cities. Their power had long been stabilized by various state institutions, including the bureaucratic hierarchies, the *baojia*, and the system of rural taxation. Constitutional change would not necessarily diminish the power of this elite; indeed, their power might be sustained or increased if the elite could monopolize the new educational system or gain control of the new organs of government. A case in point was the "law of avoidance," which forbade Qing officials from serving in their own native provinces so that they could not use their office to bolster personal economic interests. But if, as the governor of Shanxi had proposed, local men were appointed to local office, there could be more potential for them to abuse their power in their own communities.

In Tianjin, which had emerged in the late Qing as a cosmopolitan center for foreign trade and the headquarters of the northern military and naval units, the reformist governor Yuan Shikai proposed a different path for local change. Unlike the Shanxi reformers, his plan was to abolish *baojia* systems altogether and institute a police force, so as to strengthen local control. Experiments with education, penal administration, public health interventions, vocational training, and promotion of industry further established Yuan's reputation as a leading reformer. Yuan and his staff were strongly influenced by Japanese models. In interpreting Qing decrees on local government, they moved swiftly to set up a "self-government bureau" to explore the possibilities of limited representation in administration. By 1906, Yuan had set up local self-government schools to educate urban residents for the changes that lay ahead, and in 1907 authorized an election for a council in Tianjin.

Elsewhere in China, with varying degrees of speed and thoroughness, the country edged toward constitutional change. In late 1908 the court announced that full constitutional government would be established over the next nine-year period, the same time span for change after Japan's Meiji Restoration of 1868. Although the Qing emperor was to maintain almost total power in areas ranging from the new parliamentary structure and the budget to the military, foreign policy, and the judicial system, the need for a working system of electoral government at the central, provincial, and local levels was now accepted. The death of the empress dowager Cixi in November 1908, which followed by one day the death of the unfortunate emperor Guangxu—still under palace detention after his failed reform attempt of a decade before—did not deflect the general direction of reform. If anything it increased the sense of urgency. The regents for the new emperor, Puyi—a baby at his accession, like his two predecessors—formed an advisory cabinet packed with Manchus, failing to see that this would heighten Chinese suspicions that constitutional reform was going to be manipulated to protect the ruling dynasty.

The provincial assemblies, which met for the first time in October 1909, were a startlingly new institution and had a volatile effect on the political life of the country. Although these were still elite bodies, open only to males, with narrow criteria as to age, wealth, and education, they drew together in public forums men who cared deeply about the fate of their country. Election turnouts were high for such a thoroughly new institution. The Chinese state had always looked with disapproval on public gatherings, especially those with a political flavor, as was shown by the late Ming treatment of the Donglin party or Kangxi's and Yongzheng's attempts to focus political thinking around the Sacred Edict. Now such gatherings received official backing. Moreover the assemblies were immediately suffused with new viewpoints expressed in political magazines and newspapers, and strengthened by the breadth of experience of members who had been trained in military academies or universities overseas, or worked as entrepreneurs in new industries. By early 1910, these provincial assemblies had exerted so much pressure on the Qing court that it agreed to speed up the reform program and convene the provisional national assembly that October.

The range of expertise within these provincial assemblies is apparent in the men who emerged as their leaders. In Guangdong, the locus of foreign contact and trade for much of the eighteenth and nineteenth centuries, the assembly that met in Guangzhou was presided over by a *jinshi* degree holder and former official who had been active in agitations against the Portuguese in Macao. In Fujian, several of the leading assembly members were Protestant Christian converts. It was the church that gave them experience in public speaking and introduced them to new social and organizational forms.[3]

It was impossible to tell precisely how these men and the assemblies they dominated were going to act, but one thing should have been clear: the imperial court had now effectively guaranteed that any actions it undertook in the future to strengthen its position would be met with sustained scrutiny from the very social strata that, in the past, had provided the dynasty with its most trusted supporters.

NEW RAILWAYS, NEW ARMY

Of the new technologies confronting the Qing, the railways proved to be the most troublesome. Many Chinese considered railways disruptive to the harmony of nature, slicing across the land, disturbing its normal rhythms and displacing its benevolent forces. They also put road and canal workers out of jobs and altered established market patterns. Although some mid-nineteenth-century Chinese scholars pointed out that railways had been a main source of Western industrial development, the first short stretch of

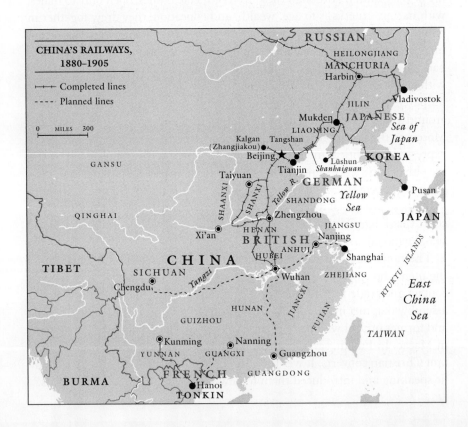

railway built in China, near Shanghai, was bought by the governor and torn out in 1877.

In 1880 Li Hongzhang used subterfuge to get a short length of track laid, in order to move coal from the Kaiping mines at Tangshan to a nearby canal. This stretch of line was extended to Tianjin and adjacent towns in 1888, and into southern Manchuria in 1894, penetrating the pass at Shanhaiguan where Manchu troops had invaded China 250 years before. Despite the expressed willingness of many foreign powers to lend money to the Qing to build a railway network, for a few years little further work was attempted. At the end of 1896 China had only 370 miles of track. By contrast, the United States had 182,000 miles, Great Britain 21,000 miles, and Japan 2,300 miles.

The pressures from foreign powers had been building up ever since Japan's victory in 1894 but reached new levels in the five years following the Boxer Uprising. With the vast Boxer indemnity of 450 million taels to pay on top of all its other debts, the Qing court began to find the proffered railway-development loans attractive, even if they came from foreigners. The most ambitious railway scheme, the Beijing to Wuhan line,* had already failed to lure enough capital from Chinese shareholders, despite its integration with the newly founded Imperial Bank of China. The foreign powers, in turn, were making it clear that they would go ahead and build railways in their areas of influence even if the Qing protested. Germany began to build lines in Shandong; the British drew up plans in the Yangzi valley; the French projected a line from Hanoi to Kunming; the Russians, who had already by treaty agreement driven a line straight across Heilongjiang province to their major port at Vladivostok, added a branch to Lüshun; and the Japanese, as part of their assault on Russia in the war of 1904–1905, drove lines north from Korea toward Mukden. After their victory, the Japanese took control of the main lines in the region and consolidated them as the Southern Manchuria Railroad Company. The results of foreign activity can be clearly seen in the mileage of track completed in this period: 280 miles between 1896 and 1899, and 3,222 miles between 1900 and 1905.

In this expansionist climate, China seemed a good target for railway investors. Through such new banking conglomerates as the British and Chinese Corporation (a key partner in which was the old opium trading firm of Jardine, Matheson), immense sums of money were offered for the development of a comprehensive system, the elements of which slowly began to take focus. The key north-south line, completed in 1905, linked Beijing to Wuhan, with a second stage planned to continue to Guangzhou. From Wuhan, another line was projected to run east to Nanjing and Shanghai, and one west

---

* Wuhan refers to the three linked mid-Yangzi cities of Wuchang, Hankou, and Hanyang.

to Chengdu in Sichuan province. The French-sponsored line into Kunming would be matched by another spur from Indochina up to Nanning, in Guangxi province.

A strong mood of nationalism, however, had been growing in China; elements of it appeared in Zou Rong's polemics, in antiforeign boycotts, and in antimissionary activity. As part of this new groundswell, people in many areas began to press for a "rights-recovery movement." The aim was to raise money through local bonds so that Chinese could buy back the railroad rights made available to foreign investors and thus regain control of their own transportation system. The confidence that suffused the movement partook of other economic and technological advances. One was the growth of new heavy industries run by Chinese entrepreneurs; another, the availability of investment capital among the overseas Chinese in Southeast Asia; a third, the success of a new generation of Western-trained Chinese engineers in handling difficult problems of railway construction in harsh terrain. Nineteen such railroad rights-recovery groups were chartered between 1904 and 1907, covering nearly all provinces.

By 1910 the Qing government had decided that the country's economic development and political stability required a centralized railway network. The court therefore decided to buy out, in turn, the rights to railroad lines from their Chinese investors, and to nationalize the whole system under Qing control. They were drawn to this decision in part because the railways controlled by the new Ministry of Posts and Communications (founded in 1906) were turning a handsome profit of 8 million to 9 million taels a year. The Manchu regents for the emperor had little sense of the volatility of this issue, and were even told by their advisers that the Chinese investors need only be partially recompensed for their investments. The final edict on railway nationalization, promulgated in May 1911, stated in strong language the reasons for the decision:

> The Government must have in all directions extending to the borders of the Empire great trunk lines in order to carry on government effectively, and to maintain centralized authority. Hitherto the methods have been ill-conceived and there has been no fixed plan. . . . How can we contemplate the consequences of such mistakes? We now proclaim clearly to the whole Empire that the trunk railway lines are to belong to the Government.[4]

Only ten days later the Qing, who had just borrowed £10 million (around $50 million) from a British-American banking consortium, signed a new loan agreement with the same consortium for another £6 million to resume work on the Wuhan-Guangzhou and the Wuhan-Chengdu lines. This outraged the many people who believed that each province should have the right to control its own railway development and that foreign powers should not be allowed a dominant role in the process. Within weeks of the May 1911 decision, protests as angry as any once held against foreigners were mounted against the Qing. Popular anger remained unabated throughout the summer, especially in Sichuan, where leaders of the provincial assembly and prominent stockholders vowed not to pay further taxes to the government and to fight for retention of their rights.

In the railway agitation of 1910 and 1911, the officers and soldiers of the newly reformed army played a prominent role. Many of these troops were deeply patriotic and felt that the Qing were selling out the nation's resources to foreigners. At one railway rally, an army officer cut off his finger in protest. At another, a soldier wrote a letter in blood to the Qing railway company, urging it to restore local control. In Sichuan, when a general ordered those of his troops who were members of the antigovernment Railway League to step forward so they could be identified and expelled from the ranks, all the soldiers stepped forward in a show of solidarity, and the general had to rescind his order.

The officers and men in these armies represented a new element on the scene, one that both built on and rejected much of the Eight Banner structure. The last comprehensive attempt to reform the banners had been made by Emperor Qianlong in the 1750s and 1760s, when he transferred many of the Chinese bannermen out of the army and left them to succeed in civilian life as well as they could. But the Manchu bannermen in general had lost their martial skills, and many of their military duties had already been passed over to local military groups known as the Green Standard forces. During the 1850s, officials like Zeng Guofan had formed locally recruited armies, enhancing their military efficiency and moral rectitude by offering them decent wages. Zeng also instilled in them a code of conduct designed to end the popular conception of soldiers as the scourges of the countryside in which they fought. In the Beiyang (north China) armies developed by Li Hongzhang and others, with officer-training schools, foreign instructors, and up-to-date armaments, the genesis of a modern army was firmly in place.

Starting in 1901 the Qing court made a concerted attempt to reorganize the armed forces and to develop what was termed "the New Army." Just as they had with the railway system, the Qing rulers tried to standardize and control the New Army on their own terms. Accordingly the various provincial units were concentrated into thirty-six divisions under the direct control of the Commission for Army Reorganization. With each division projected at 12,500 troops, this would give the government a centrally directed force of 450,000 men. In 1906 the Qing also reorganized the Ministry of War, putting it under the direction of a senior Manchu officer assisted by two Manchu deputies. In 1907 a new position was created—comptroller of the army—and once again the incumbent was a Manchu. That same year the two most powerful Chinese governors-general, Yuan Shikai and Zhang Zhidong, were transferred to Beijing to be grand councilors, a technical promotion that severed them from their troops. The Qing court clearly wished to show that final authority rested with the Manchus in Beijing rather than with the Chinese in the provinces.

At many levels, the military reorganization was effective, with New Army divisions stationed at strategic locations across the country. Qing troops had some dramatic successes in 1910 and 1911, most notably in a series of campaigns in Tibet, where Qing influence had been waning in the face of the assertive independence of local princes and the maneuverings of the British in northern India. Qing forces dispatched to the region overcame the logistical and transportation problems posed by the difficult terrain and conquered portions of eastern Tibet, which were reconstituted as a new province called Xikang. Qing troops also occupied Lhasa, unseated several recalcitrant princes, garrisoned several towns, and forced the flight of the spiritual leader of Tibetan Buddhism, the Dalai Lama, to India. Qing soldiers then advanced to the borders of Nepal, Bhutan, and Sikkim to warn the British to ease their pressures on the region.

But many problems remained for the Qing military. The command structure was still fragmented, especially in north China, where Yuan Shikai maintained a loyal following in the Beiyang army. In an attempt to dilute his power, early in 1909 Yuan was removed from office on a trumped-up excuse of illness, which left him angry and his senior officers disaffected. Among the New Army officers were many men who had embarked on military careers after the abolition of the traditional exams in 1905, since the army seemed to offer a swift channel of upward social mobility. Ambitious and restless, such men were actively involved in the agitations of the provincial assemblies, and New Army ranks were infiltrated with members of the revolutionary societies affiliated with the exiled Sun Yat-sen.

As the troops and officers of the New Army adopted the drills, the khaki uniforms, and the modern weaponry of the European and Japanese troops they sought to emulate, certain customs seemed outdated. The practice of bowing in greeting was replaced by a crisp military salute. Of symbolically greater importance, the long queue of braided hair that the Manchu regent Dorgon had forced the Chinese to adopt in 1645 looked ridiculous in combat situations. Soldiers first tucked their queues under their caps, then received permission to shorten the length of the braid. Soon some grew emboldened to cut it off altogether. With Taiping in the 1850s, the cutting of the queue had been proof enough of rebellion against the state. Now, in the first decade of the twentieth century, the court took note but decided that no disciplinary action could be appropriately taken.

In Nanjing, soldiers of the Revolutionary Army cutting the queues that symbolized the old Manchu order

NATIONALISTS AND SOCIALISTS

In the years between 1905 and 1911, as the Qing edged toward constitutional reform and tried to strengthen control over the New Army and the railways, dissent continued to grow. Having tasted the excitement of new opportunities, assembly members, overseas students, women, merchants, urban workers, and New Army troops pushed both local authorities and the central government to respond more forcefully to their calls for reform. The government's failure to meet their varied demands provoked ever sharper criticisms, within which new concepts of China as a nation began to emerge.

The Manchus' position was extraordinarily difficult. With the banner garrisons cut back or reassigned to civilian occupations and the planned New Army not yet under complete central control or up to full strength, the Qing had no clear military dominance over the country. Each fresh initiative—schools, public-works projects, diplomatic missions—brought rocketing expenses. When the Ministry of War drew up its first detailed budget in late 1910, it calculated that the expanding army would require expenditures of 109 million taels the following year (not including naval expenses), of which 54 million taels would go to the New Army units. In 1911, army expenditures represented almost 35 percent of the projected national budget of 338 million taels. This total was already 40 million taels higher than the deficit budget of 1910. The advisory national assembly, meeting in Beijing, responded by slashing some 30 million taels from the army budget. Even so, to meet the deficit agricultural taxes were increased, along with new duties on tea, wine, salt, and tobacco, higher transit and customs dues, and special taxes on land transactions.

Aspects of these taxes angered almost everyone. Even when the Qing government was on the side of the angels—as, for instance, with its decision to stamp out opium smoking—it ran into problems. Opposition to the effort no longer came from the British, but from Chinese cultivators of opium, who resented the plowing under of their poppy fields. British opium sales had by now been thoroughly undercut by domestic production, which had expanded from Yunnan and Guizhou to become a vast enterprise in Sichuan, Shaanxi, and the coastal provinces of Zhejiang and Fujian. The Qing anti-opium drive antagonized people across a range of social strata, including distributors, transporters, opium-den managers, and the addicts themselves, many of whom were from the wealthiest classes. As if these problems were not enough, the weather conspired against the Qing. Torrential rains in the Yangzi and Huai valleys during 1910 and 1911 caused catastrophic flooding, ruined millions of acres of crops, drove up grain prices, led to hundreds of thousands of deaths, and forced millions of refugees into major cities. The natural disasters also cast into sharp relief the ecological effects of deforestation and the vulnerable state of the hydraulic infrastructure, destabilized by funding cutbacks.

The power of the state was nevertheless still strong within China itself—except in the treaty ports and concession areas—and it remained difficult for concerted political opposition to flourish. As before, much of the most effective political criticism came from Chinese living overseas, whether voluntarily or in exile. Among those offering significant critiques of the Qing, and backing them with their own original political programs, were the constitutional monarchists who followed Kang Youwei, the nationalists influenced by Liang Qichao, various groups of anarchists and Marxists, and those held together in the Revolutionary Alliance directed by Sun Yat-sen.

Of all these critics, Kang Youwei enjoyed the greatest prestige among educated Chinese at home and overseas. A distinguished classical scholar, he had earned the *jinshi* degree (in 1895) and had been a personal adviser to Emperor Guangxu on the 1898 reforms. Right up to 1911 he continued to urge the Qing to reform the government and to modernize the country. He formed various organizations to expound his views, the most important of which were the Society to Protect the Emperor and the Society for Constitutional Government. But as anti-Manchu sentiment grew stronger, Kang's position began to seem eccentric even to his strongest supporters, while his financial backers wondered where all their money had gone. Kang was both financially extravagant and inept. He traveled in style with a young female companion, bought an island off the coast of Sweden as a summer retreat, and invested his funds in shaky ventures in Mexico, where they were lost in the Mexican Revolution. His writings on politics, executed in elegant classical Chinese, seemed increasingly out of place in the twentieth-century world.

One of Kang's most loyal disciples who had sat for the same *jinshi* examinations in 1895 was Liang Qichao. Liang was less emotionally attached than Kang to the Qing ruling house, and explored a greater range of political options. For a time he was even drawn to extreme ideas that prescribed "the medicine of liberty" as the cure for the "corruption and degeneration" of China. Yet he shied away from the violence of the French Revolution, noting that "the sacrifices of 1793 in France were rewarded only in 1870, and the rewards did not measure up to the expectations. If we now seek to purchase liberty at the price of infinite suffering, it may not be attained after seventy years, and even if it is, what will have happened to our ancestral country?"[5]

Liang worried, too, that the Chinese people were unprepared to assume democratic responsibilities. His pessimism was amplified by what he saw of life in America's Chinatowns during a visit in 1903. Chinese behavior there seemed to him disorganized or cowardly, and the social conditions deeply unsatisfactory. Liang used his forceful writing style to push for a stronger nation that would draw on all its people, including women, and develop an informed citizenry under the initial tutelage of tough leaders. To achieve this ideal of an active and unified community of citizens, China needed someone of iron discipline to curb its weaknesses, he wrote, like the Spartan leader Lycurgus or England's Oliver Cromwell, and should forget about the Rousseaus or Washingtons of the world for the time being. But Liang could not condone Cromwell's execution of the English king, and he continued to extol the virtues of constitutional monarchy if it could go hand in hand with progress and economic development. He saw the Italian reunification movement of the nineteenth century as a possible model: in Italy military heroes, constitutional advocates, and skilled diplomats had joined forces to oust foreign occupiers and to reassert a new national identity. Liang's political ideas, which he expressed in novels and plays as well as in essays published in a wide range of newspapers and journals, circulated widely within China and among overseas Chinese communities, spreading a sense of disillusion about the Manchus' ability to lead the nation to revitalization.

Far more radical, although less influential, were the feelings of a considerable number of Chinese who were drawn to various themes within European socialism and anarchism. The development and radical application of Marxist thought had been vigorous in Europe during the nineteenth century and continued after Karl Marx's death in 1883. In 1889 a broad spectrum of socialist parties and trade unions were federated into the Second International, based in Brussels. Although this body supported the concept of parliamentary democracy, it also pledged to exploit the possibilities of international social upheaval brought about by warfare and to use every opportunity to advance the cause of socialist revolution. Members of the Second International accepted Marx's main premises concerning the inevitability of social revolution.

The first discussion of Marx in a Chinese publication appeared in 1899, erroneously describing him as English. The article summed up his messages as saying that the poor would "continue to have many strikes to coerce the rich," and as believing that "the power of the rich will extend across state boundaries to all of the five continents."[6] The attempted Russian Revolution of 1905 was exciting to those who saw the tsars as parallel autocrats to the Qing emperors, and stimulated new interest in Marxist theories, which seemed to offer an opportunity to jolt China into the modern world. Several Chinese began to study an 1899 Japanese work, *Modern Socialism*, which had been translated into Chinese and stated that Marx "used profound scholarship and detailed research to discover an economic base" and that "socialism is easily grasped by the working people and receives the thunderous support of the majority."[7]

In 1906 a summary and partial translation of Marx's *Communist Manifesto* appeared in Chinese, with a rather more poetic touch than in the English or German versions. The famous conclusion to the *Manifesto*, "The proletarians have nothing to lose but their chains. They have a world to win. WORKING MEN OF ALL COUNTRIES, UNITE!" emerged in Chinese as "Then the world will be for the common people, and the sounds of happiness will reach the deepest springs. Ah! Come! People of every land, how can you not be roused?"[8]

Although there was no organized Chinese socialist party until 1911, by 1907 the classical scholar Jiang Kanghu, whose reading abilities included Japanese, English, French, and German, began the scientific study of socialism. Jiang had served as educational adviser to Yuan Shikai and was an ardent feminist. In 1909 he attended the Congress of the Second International when it met at Brussels. Other Chinese were drawn to anarchism, specifically to the theories of Bakunin and Kropotkin, which criticized the contemporary structure of ideas about the state and stressed the role of the individual and the importance of popular participation in all revolutionary processes. A group of Chinese living in Paris founded the anarchist New World Society in 1906. Most of its members were also connected to Sun Yat-sen's Revolutionary Alliance, but they were fortunate enough to have their own source of funding, since one of their number owned a bean-curd factory and a restaurant–tea shop. The anarchists' goals were lofty: to abolish political authority, the military, all laws, class distinctions, private property, and capital. They advocated various ways of advancing toward revolution: written propaganda, strikes, boycotts, mass uprisings, and assassinations when undertaken out of moral commitment. Another Chinese anarchist group flourished in Tokyo at the same time; this one focused more on the plight of women and embraced an antimodernist, agrarian position. Their hero was Tolstoy, and they took seriously the role of the peasantry in revolution, discussing such topics as communitarian life in the countryside and the possibilities of combining agriculture with industry in a rural economy.

Finally there was Sun Yat-sen, since 1905 the head of the broad spectrum of anti-Qing groups that were loosely organized as the Revolutionary Alliance. Some of his adherents were drawn to terrorism and advocated assassination as a tactic; most were committed to the idea of a republican revolution. They implacably opposed the Manchus and as nationalists they sought China's release from what they considered the economic stranglehold of foreign imperialism. Some were also determined socialists who wanted to move China away from what they saw as its "feudal" past into an advanced level of development that would avoid the ills of the capitalist system. A good many members of Sun's alliance were women with powerful aspirations for strengthening the roles of women within a new Chinese state. Sun had strong contacts with secret societies in southern China—he had been inducted into the Hawaii branch of the Triads in 1904 and had relied on Triad support in the United States and Canada.

Sun also consistently sought the overthrow of the Qing with armed force. Between 1906 and 1908, the Revolutionary Alliance directed or instigated at least seven uprisings against the government; three took place in Guangdong province, where Sun's contacts were strongest. Even though each of these uprisings was suppressed by the Qing, Sun remained a charismatic figure to the overseas Chinese, attracting a steady stream of donations from a network of supporters in the United States, Canada, and Singapore, where he had strong backing from several wealthy entrepreneurs. Sun also sold bonds to those who supported his future regime, promising them a tenfold return if they would help him attain power. (Although Sun may not have realized it, Lin Qing had followed a similar strategy in his rebellion a century before.)

Despite his vague planning and many failures, Sun's energy, persuasiveness, and the virulence of his hostility to the Qing sustained the Revolutionary Alliance. By the summer of 1911, the number of active members had grown to almost 10,000, from around 400 in 1905. Many of these were students, recruited in Japan by Sun or his affiliates, who returned to their home provinces to continue secret agitation against the state. Some had risen to be members of the new provincial assemblies, and others were soldiers or officers in New Army units, where they canvassed for support with revolutionary rhetoric and by offering material inducements. The mix of anger, frustration, dreams, and hard cash was an explosive one.

QING FALL

The specific series of events that led to the fall of the two-and-a-half-centuries-old Qing dynasty was triggered by an accidental bomb explosion in Hankou, one of the three cities that composed the area of Wuhan, on October 9, 1911. This explosion might well have remained an isolated and forgotten incident, however, had it not been for the heightened agitations over constitutionalism, railways, the armies, Manchu power, and foreign encroachments.

Since at least 1904, groups of radical young Chinese—many of them students who had lived in Japan and a few of whom were affiliated with the Revolutionary Alliance—had formed revolutionary cells in Hankou and the neighboring city of Wuchang. These two cities, along with Hanyang—the third linked city, with large numbers of industrial workers and boatmen, modern schools, New Army units, and Qing governmental staff—made the Wuhan tricity complex an exciting area for political and social experimentation. The long-range goal of the revolutionaries was to overthrow the Qing state, "to avenge the national disgrace" (as they termed it), "and to restore the Chinese."[9] Their shorter-term strategy was to infiltrate the New Army units and to coordinate political activities with secret society members in the region. The revolutionaries' infiltration of these groups and recruitment of new members were carried out under cover of literary or fraternal societies, which enabled small meetings to be held and individual prospects to be approached. When a particular society was investigated by local authorities, the participants would disband and later regroup in another area under another name. By the fall of 1911, these various societies in the Wuhan area

Revolutionary troops, Hankou, 1911

had attracted 5,000 to 6,000 of the Hubei New Army troops, about one-third of the total force.

The explosion on October 9 occurred while a group of revolutionaries were making bombs at their meetinghouse in the Russian concession of Hankou. Like earlier anti-Qing agitators in Shanghai, they had learned that foreign imperialism could provide a measure of protection, but on this occasion the size of the explosion brought the Russian authorities to investigate. As the most seriously injured conspirators were rushed to the hospital, Qing investigators who had been alerted by the Russians raided the headquarters and found three other revolutionaries, who were executed immediately. They also obtained the membership rosters of the soldiers and others enrolled in the revolutionary societies. The revolutionaries understood that unless they could launch an uprising rapidly, their organization would be unraveled and many more members would lose their lives.

The first troops to take action were in the Wuchang Eighth Engineer Battalion; they mutinied on the early morning of October 10. They were joined by transport and artillery units stationed outside the city. These troops launched a successful attack on Wuchang's main forts, and by day's end soldiers from three other New Army regiments had come to their support.

After trying in vain to muster troops to defend the governor-general's offices, both the governor-general and the divisional commander retreated from the city. On October 11, members of the revolutionary societies launched an uprising in Hanyang, and, along with troops from the First Battalion, seized the arsenal and ironworks. The Hankou troops mutinied on October 12.

It now became imperative that a prestigious public figure take over titular leadership of the mutinous troops and guide the revolutionary movement. Since Sun Yat-sen was overseas and there were no senior members of the Revolutionary Alliance in the area, the rebellious troops approached the president of the provincial assembly, who cautiously declined. They then named a commander of a Hubei New Army brigade, Li Yuanhong, as military governor. Although initially he had to be forced at gunpoint to take the assignment, Li seemed a good choice because he was popular with the soldiers, had been an activist in the railway agitations, was well liked by the provincial assembly leaders, and spoke English, which reassured the large foreign community in Wuhan.

The Qing court responded vigorously to the crisis, ordering the Minister of War to coordinate a counterattack on Wuhan with two divisions of the Beiyang army. At the same time the Manchus, swallowing their pride, summoned Yuan Shikai back from the "retirement" to which they had banished him in 1910. They believed that Yuan, with his long history of leadership over the Beiyang army and his strong personal ties to many of its senior officers, could muster those troops behind the Qing. But Yuan was too canny to accept the appointment as military commander until he had a better sense of how the situation might develop.

Events now moved too swiftly to be controlled by any individual or political group. On October 22, 1911, the New Army mutinied in both Shaanxi and Hunan provinces: in the Shaanxi capital of Xi'an, large numbers of Manchus were massacred, and in Changsha, commanders loyal to the Qing were killed. In both cases the leading members of the provincial assemblies expressed their support for the revolution. During the last week of October, three other provinces rose against the Qing. In Taiyuan, Shanxi, the governor and his family were killed, and the assembly joined with the mutinous New Army units; in Jiangxi province, an alliance of merchants, students, and teachers joined with assembly members and army officers to assert independence from the Qing; and in Yunnan province, the instructors in the officers' school rebelled and joined with New Army units in an attack on troops loyal to the Qing.

The military significance of railways, over which there had been much debate in the late nineteenth century, now became apparent to both sides. While the Qing, using the Beijing-Wuhan railway, sped troops south to quell

THE FALL OF THE QING,
1911

★ Anti-Qing revolts

the mutinies in Wuhan, rebellious units from Shanxi moved down the branch line from Taiyuan to cut that same route, severing the supply lines of the Qing army. At the end of October, a senior northern general rebuffed the Qing order that he lead his troops south by rail. Instead he joined with a number of other commanders to issue twelve demands to the Qing court. The critical components were the establishment of a parliament within the year, the election of a premier to be ratified by the emperor, a general amnesty for all political offenders, and the sharp curtailing of imperial prerogatives. Within a week the Qing court had agreed to most of these demands. On November 11, three days after the members of the provisional national assembly elected Yuan Shikai premier, the court issued a decree appointing him to the same office and ordering him to form a cabinet. Yuan complied, naming mostly his own partisans to key positions.

These developments were clearly moving China toward a constitutional monarchy under Manchu direction—as advocated by Kang Youwei and his supporters—rather than toward the republican form of government central to the demands of Sun Yat-sen and the Revolutionary Alliance. But Sun's supporters, although numerous, did not wield unified military strength. Sun himself was fund-raising in the United States during the events of late 1911;

he read the news of the Wuchang uprising in a Denver newspaper while en route to Kansas City. Sun saw his first priority as securing European promises of neutrality in the coming conflict, and accordingly traveled to London and Paris to confer with the governments there before returning to China. In an important political success, he persuaded the British not to advance any more major loan payments to the Qing government.

Throughout November, Yuan Shikai performed a delicate balancing act, using his influence over the Beiyang army to pressure Manchus and revolutionaries alike. Qing forces managed, after heavy fighting, to recapture both Hankou and Hanyang (though not Wuchang), but this was not much solace to the court as province after province declared allegiance to the revolution. Sun's Revolutionary Alliance turned out to have a startling degree of mass support, which its leaders skillfully exploited. Expanding its organization and focusing its goals, the alliance played a critical role in three provinces that went over to the revolution: Jiangsu (which declared its independence from the Qing on November 3), Sichuan (November 22), and Shandong (December 12). Elsewhere, the alliance remained part of a broader coalition of anti-Qing movements that continued to draw leaders mainly from the New Army, the provincial assemblies, and, in some cases, local merchants.

The Qing court's position was immeasurably weakened when Manchu and loyalist troops were defeated in Nanjing in early December after several weeks of heavy fighting. Nanjing had been the Ming capital in the fourteenth century, and since that time had carried a special symbolic importance. Its fall now reminded Chinese of the failures of the prince of Fu's forces there in 1645 and of the great Taiping victory in 1853. Nanjing thus provided a potentially national base for the Revolutionary Alliance to consolidate its position.

The mother of the five-year-old emperor now moved to the front of negotiations. She pushed through the resignation of the Manchu regent and authorized Yuan Shikai to rule as premier, while the emperor would continue to preside at audiences and state functions. But to many, this seemed like a return to the days of the empress dowager Cixi, and the compromise was not a popular one.

Sun Yat-sen returned to Shanghai from France on Christmas Day, 1911. Four days later, delegates from sixteen provincial assemblies met in Nanjing and elected Sun "provisional president" of the Republic of China. He assumed office in Nanjing on January 1, 1912. On that same New Year's Day, Sun sent a telegram to Yuan Shikai that acknowledged the weakness of his own military power base. In this message, Sun stated that even though he had accepted the presidency for the time being, "it is actually waiting for you, and my offer will eventually be made clear to the world. I hope that you will soon decide to accept this offer."[10]

China now had both a republican president and a Manchu emperor, an impasse that required resolution. Later in January 1912, a series of assassination attempts nearly took the lives of Yuan Shikai and several senior Manchu princes and generals. At the end of the month, a bomb killed the strongest remaining exponent of a tough Manchu line. The final blow to the Qing came at the end of January 1912, when forty-four commanders of the Beiyang army sent a telegram to the Beijing cabinet urging the formation of a republic. While the most intransigent Manchu princes retreated to Manchuria, where they tried to coordinate a resistance, the emperor's mother and her advisers negotiated frantically with Yuan Shikai for a settlement that would guarantee their safety and financial security. The final agreement stipulated continued residence for the emperor and his family in the Forbidden City, ownership of its great imperial treasures, a stipend of $4 million a year, and the protection of all Manchu ancestral temples. The court announced Emperor Puyi's abdication on February 12, 1912. Refusing to recognize Sun Yat-sen's claims, a brief accompanying edict gave Yuan Shikai full powers "to organize a provisional republican government" and to establish national unity with the Revolutionary Alliance and the other anti-imperial forces in central and south China.

With these few simple words, more than two millennia of China's imperial history were brought to a close. And with almost no experience in the arts and institutions of self-government, the Chinese people were presented with the challenge of devising their own future in a watchful and dangerous world.

CHAPTER 12

The New Republic

EXPERIMENT IN DEMOCRACY

The state of China as the last Qing emperor abdicated in February 1912 bore many parallels to the country's position when the last Ming emperor hanged himself in April 1644. With a depleted treasury in Beijing and little money coming in from the provinces, the national finances were in disarray. Groups of scholars and bureaucrats had expressed a wide range of dissatisfactions with the defunct regime, and this discontent now had to be addressed. The army troops occupying the capital were numerous but hard to control, of doubtful loyalty, and liable to mutiny or desertion if their pay fell too long in arrears. In addition, natural disasters had devastated the countryside, causing ruined harvests and starvation, and creating masses of refugees just when financial shortages made it difficult for local governments to provide relief. Many supporters of the defeated ruling house remained loyal and could be the focus for future trouble. Foreign pressure was intense, the possibility of invasion imminent. There was a strong chance that separatist regimes would emerge in several regions, further weakening central authority.

There were also, of course, numerous differences between the two transitional periods, of which four were probably the most significant. First, in 1912 there were at least seven predatory foreign powers with special interests in China, not just one, and China was already heavily in debt to them. Second, in 1912 the entire economic infrastructure of the country was being dramatically transformed by new modes of communication, transportation, and industrial development. Third, the significance of Confucianism as a central philosophical system had been called into question. And fourth, although in 1912 many Chinese still favored a strong, central authority, the institution of the emperorship along with the compromise arrangement of a constitutional monarchy had been rejected by most educated Chinese. The most influential forces in the country sought to establish some type of republican government.

In this period of heightened tension, violence was unpredictable and common, and nobody could guess exactly where the nation was heading. It is therefore not surprising that the two men who were to become China's pre-eminent leaders in the second quarter of the century, and whose battles with each other were to affect the direction and shape of the Chinese revolution, both had their first taste of violent conflict and political activity at this time. One of these men, Mao Zedong, born in 1893 to a farming family in Hunan province, served with local student volunteer forces in the area of Changsha. He witnessed the speedy collapse of the Qing armies firsthand, cut off his queue, and had the grim experience of seeing the murdered bodies of two prominent Revolutionary Alliance leaders lying in the city street. They had been killed not by Qing troops, but by republican supporters of the provincial assembly president, who sought a more moderate path. Mao served briefly as a private in the Hunan republican army, and there came across pamphlets by the socialist thinker Jiang Kanghu, who founded the first Chinese Socialist party in November 1911. But Mao's own political stance was still cautious: he later told an interviewer that he had hoped for a government with Sun Yat-sen as president, Kang Youwei as premier, and Liang Qichao as foreign minister.

The second man, Chiang Kai-shek,* had been born in 1887 to a salt-merchant family near the foreign treaty port of Ningbo in Zhejiang province. Following the route of many ambitious young men of some means, he had gone to Japan to study in a military academy, where he stayed from 1908 to 1910. Chiang joined the Revolutionary Alliance, through which he became a close associate of the Zhejiang leader Chen Qimei; when Chen became military governor of Shanghai in November 1911, Chiang was promoted to be one of his regimental commanders. He served courageously in the attack on Hangzhou and in the effort to win the city over to the revolutionary cause. According to various accounts, Chiang's baptism of personal violence came when he instigated or performed the assassination of a dissident member of the Revolutionary Alliance who opposed both Sun Yat-sen and Chiang's mentor Chen Qimei.

The restoration of order to China required that Yuan Shikai link his Beijing base and Beiyang army support to the Revolutionary Alliance and the

---

* This was the common romanization of his name. Drawn from the local dialect, it was used throughout his life by virtually all Western writers, and Chiang himself used it in his English-language publications. It is retained here, rather than the *pinyin* form of Jiang Jieshi.

Sun Yat-sen (center) in 1912

Nanjing forces. It also hinged on the integration of the New Army units and the provincial assemblies into a national polity bound by a legitimate constitution. The first steps toward these goals were halting ones. Since his troops were no match for Yuan's, Sun Yat-sen, hailed by his supporters as provisional president on January 1, 1912, relinquished claims to the title just over a month later, on February 13, the day after the Qing emperor's abdication. Yuan Shikai assumed the office in Sun Yat-sen's place. Leaders of the Revolutionary Alliance and their supporters stipulated that Yuan Shikai govern from Nanjing, which would move him from his northern military base and mark an important symbolic step toward the formation of a viable civilian regime. But Yuan chose to remain in the north, claiming that the unstable military situation demanded his presence there. A series of mutinies and outbreaks of violence in Beijing, Tianjin, and Baoding during March 1912 seemed to confirm his view, although some cynics observed that it was probably Yuan who had instigated the trouble in the first place to prove his indispensability. Sun Yat-sen, for his part, showed his sincerity by traveling to Beijing, at Yuan's invitation, and drawing up a vast (and visionary) blueprint for the transformation of the railway system.

The task now was to create a meaningful constitution, under which valid elections would be held across China for the new two-chamber parliament. The initial step toward this goal had been the convening of the National Assembly in Beijing in October 1910. This was a one-chamber house, with its members either elected by the provincial assemblies or selected by the Manchu regent. The National Assembly at once joined with the provincial assemblies to press for a full parliament before the 1917 date originally envisioned by Empress Dowager Cixi. In November 1910, the Qing court agreed that a fully elected parliament should be convened in 1913.

Although a creation of the Qing court, the National Assembly swiftly moved to a position of importance for the future of constitutional government. On October 30, 1911, as the Manchus fought for survival, they authorized the National Assembly to draft a constitution, and the assembly produced the first version on November 3. Five days later, the assembly elected Yuan Shikai as China's first premier, conferring a form of democratic legitimacy on his rule. Overlapping with these developments, however, came the meetings of various groups of provincial delegates—first in Shanghai, then in Hankou, and finally in Nanjing. Three delegates from each province were formally convened as the Provisional Senate in Nanjing on January 28, 1912. Sun Yat-sen had stipulated that this body would ratify Yuan's election as provisional president, which it did at his urging on February 14.

Yuan Shikai's ascent to the top of the republican structure had come with dizzying speed. Born in 1859 into a lineage that had produced several successful officials, Yuan Shikai had twice failed the state examinations before he purchased a minor official title. Thereafter he served for over a decade in various military and commercial posts in Korea, during which time he had ample experience with Japan's expansionist aims in that

country. After the Sino-Japanese War of 1894–1895, Yuan Shikai was appointed by the Qing to train the officers for China's first new modernized army corps, which gave him an important nucleus of military protégés. It is almost certain that he helped the empress dowager overthrow Emperor Guangxu and the Hundred Days' reformers in 1898. On the other hand, he refused to support the Qing's endorsement of the Boxers and suppressed the uprising

Yuan Shikai took office as president of the republic on February 13, 1912, after Sun Yat-sen relinquished claims to the title.

in Shandong. After 1901, as governor-general of the Hebei region, he built the Beiyang army into China's finest fighting force—five of its seven divisional commanders and all the other senior officers were his protégés. Yuan showed a real interest in reforms that strengthened his region, including development of local self-government, education, and a police force. Yuan's achievements in late Qing political life offered hope that as leader of the republic he could respond successfully to the challenges confronting the nation.

In his own letter of resignation as provisional president, Sun had attached two conditions: the Provisional Senate in Nanjing was to prepare the constitution of the provisional government, and "the new president must obey it."[1] In accordance with these procedures designed to ensure the formation of a legitimate republican government, the senate promulgated a new draft of the provisional constitution on March 11, 1912. It guaranteed all Chinese and minority peoples equality and protection of persons and property under the law, as well as freedom of worship and assembly. A full parliament must be convened within ten months. At that time the Provisional Senate would be dissolved, and Yuan would resign so that new presidential elections could be held. The senate, with its representatives now increased to five from each province, voted on April 5 to move the seat of government to Beijing, making China a united republic for the first time in word as well as deed. The Republic of China would use a new national flag featuring five horizontal stripes of equal width—representing the Han, Manchus, Mongols, Tibetans, and Muslims, and symbolizing the multi-ethnic basis of the nation. A new calendar likewise signaled a sea change: the years would be counted from the birth of the republic, not according to imperial reign periods.

Under the rules of the provisional constitution, preparations began for the first national elections. There were to be two chambers in the Parliament: a Senate comprised of 274 members serving six-year terms, chosen by the provincial assemblies, with ten members from each province and the remainder representing the overseas Chinese, and a House of Representatives, with 596 members serving three-year terms, drawn more or less proportionately according to population, on a basis of one delegate for each 800,000 people.

With the Qing dynasty at an end, Sun Yat-sen directed the Revolutionary Alliance to transform itself into a political party that would run candidates for office in the December 1912 elections. The organization of this now renamed Nationalist Party (Guomindang*) was placed in the hands of Song Jiaoren, one of Sun's most capable lieutenants. Song, only thirty years

---

* Also romanized as Kuomintang and abbreviated as KMT.

old in 1912, proved a skillful political organizer, although his arrogant self-confidence alienated many. His main interest was to ensure that the powers of the president be limited and that the powers of the Parliament, with its elected representatives, be properly protected. It was clear to most observers in mid-1912 that Yuan Shikai completely dominated the cabinet he had named and wished to amplify presidential power. Traveling to many parts of China in 1912, Song Jiaoren made this point vehemently and in terms that often seemed directly critical of Yuan Shikai's ambitions. Song and other members of the Guomindang approached the December elections with an edge over their three main rivals: the Progressive Party headed by Liang Qichao; the Republican Party, which was strongly nationalistic in tone; and the Unification Party. Over 300 other small political groups or parties contested one or more seats in the elections.

Although the national elections drew more attention, political developments in the countryside were equally important. In the general discussion over local self-government during the last years of the Qing, there had been worries that the reform councils would merely serve to entrench the conservative gentry, who would now add official administrative power to the influence they already wielded because of their education and landholdings. This fear was borne out in the months after the imperial abdication, as old scores were settled and powerful local incumbents took over a range of new posts designed to bring the authority of the central government much deeper into the countryside than the former Qing magistrates had ever been able to do. Unless this trend were checked, it could undermine hopes for a working democracy. But in the excitement of the national race, this problem seemed peripheral and was not directly addressed by the Guomindang or their rivals, although the Guomindang platform did include remarks about the need to develop structures of local self-government.

New electoral regulations promulgated in 1912 gave the vote to men over twenty-one who met one of the following criteria: owned property worth $500, paid taxes of at least $2 the previous year, or held an elementary-school graduation certificate. Approximately 40 million men—around 10 percent of the population—could meet the requirements. Illiterates, opium smokers, bankrupts, and those who had a mental illness were disqualified. Women also failed to win the right to vote, despite their growing assertiveness in the late Qing, the support of several prominent intellectuals, the participation of many women as members and financial supporters of the Revolutionary Alliance, and the experiences of some as soldiers with the revolutionary armies or as nurses on the front lines. The Revolutionary Alliance had previously espoused commitments to gender equality and women's suffrage; to win the support of conservatives, its successor Nationalist Party now abandoned those commitments. In March 1912, suffragists surrounded the Senate as it met in Nanjing to lobby for a statement on gender equality and on women's right to vote in the new constitution. Rebuffed, the women forced their way into the meeting chamber, shouting and jeering; they were unceremoniously evicted. Two days later, sixty protestors returned, carrying weapons and threatening the delegates: "We know how to make bombs and we know how to throw them." When the politicians left Nanjing to reconstitute the new government in Beijing, the suffragists followed. At the Nationalist Party's inaugural convention in August, three women interrupted the proceedings and took the stage. Two suffragists slapped Song Jiaoren in the face with their fans; the other threatened to shoot him.[2] Although activists continued to fight for women's right to vote, underlining the hypocrisy of a constitution that promised equality, the electoral laws were not changed.

The results of China's first national election were announced in January 1913, and they spelled a clear but not overwhelming victory for the Guomindang. In the House of Representatives the party won 269 of the 596 seats, with the remainder divided among the other three main parties. (In this initial election, many politicians maintained allegiance to several parties, so the seats claimed cumulatively exceeded 596.) In the Senate, of the 274 incumbents, 123 were Guomindang members. Under the provisional constitution, the Guomindang would now have a dominant role in selecting the premier and cabinet, and could proceed to push for the election of the president in a fully supervised parliamentary setting.

In the spring of 1913, the newly elected representatives began to travel to the Parliament in Beijing. The victorious party leader, Song Jiaoren, went with his friends to the Shanghai railroad station on March 20. As he stood on the platform waiting to board the train, a man walked up and shot him twice at close range. Song was taken at once to the hospital but died two days later—two weeks before his thirty-first birthday. It was widely believed that he would have been named the premier. It was also widely believed that Yuan Shikai was behind the assassination, since the trail of evidence led to the secretary of the cabinet and to the provisional premier. But the main conspirators were either themselves assassinated or else disappeared mysteriously, and Yuan was never officially implicated.

When the other delegates assembled in Parliament, they pressed to rein in Yuan Shikai's ambitions, to develop a permanent constitution, and to hold a full and open presidential election. The Guomindang members, in particular, were intensely critical of Yuan's handling of national finances: instead of addressing tax-collection problems directly, he had taken out another huge loan of over £25 million (approximately $100 million) from a consortium of foreign banks. Yuan interpreted these criticisms as personal attacks and resolved to strike back. In early May 1913, he dismissed the leading pro-Guomindang military governors. In heavy fighting that summer, troops loyal to the Guomindang were routed by Yuan's forces. In September, General Zhang Xun, with soldiers who still wore queues, took Nanjing for Yuan. In October, Yuan forced the members of Parliament to elect him president for a five-year term. (It took three ballots before he won a majority, however.) Finally, calling the Guomindang a seditious organization, he ordered the dissolution of the party and the eviction of its remaining members from Parliament. At the end of November, Sun Yat-sen left for Japan, driven once more into exile, his republican dreams in ruins.

THE RULE OF YUAN SHIKAI

Foreign powers watched developments in China closely. They had realized that there was no sense in trying to keep the Qing dynasty alive in order to preserve the treaty rights they had won since 1842. As a result they followed a policy of neutrality in 1911 and 1912, while alerting their troops and ships to protect foreign nationals and guard a corridor from Beijing to the sea, to prevent any recurrence of Boxer-like antiforeign outbreaks. The main priority of the foreign powers was to protect their investments in China, which totaled almost $788 million in 1902 and reached $1.61 billion by 1914. Foreigners were, therefore, likely to accept any government that created an economic climate favorable to their interests.

FOREIGN INVESTMENTS IN CHINA, 1902 AND 1914[3]

	1902		1914	
	Millions of U.S. dollars	Percent of total	Millions of U.S. dollars	Percent of total
Great Britain	260.3	33.0	607.5	37.7
Japan	1.0	0.1	219.6	13.6
Russia	246.5	31.3	269.3	16.7
United States	19.7	2.5	49.3	3.1
France	91.1	11.6	171.4	10.7
Germany	164.3	20.9	263.6	16.4
Others	5.0	0.6	29.6	1.8
Total	787.9	100.0	1,610.3	100.0

Although foreign investments were concentrated mainly in Shanghai and southern Manchuria, they covered a wide spectrum of enterprises. Britain's approximately $608-million stake included the Hong Kong-to-Guangzhou railway, shipping, public utilities (gas, electricity, and telephone), tramways, coal mines, cotton mills, sugar refineries, silk filatures, a rope factory, cement works, and real estate. Japan's $220-million investment reflected a similar range. American interests were much smaller, estimated at around $49 million in 1914, primarily in mission properties (including hospitals and schools) and in Shanghai real estate.

Japan and the European powers were initially skeptical about Yuan Shikai's new regime and held off from diplomatic recognition of the republic. In the United States, however, opinion was more favorable both to Yuan and to the idea of the new republic. A large number of the more reform-minded leaders had been educated in mission schools. Sun Yat-sen was a Christian. Yuan Shikai was not, but he cleverly played on pro-Christian sentiments by asking American Protestants to pray for China in their churches as the new parliament convened in April 1913. The request made the headlines in American newspapers and received favorable attention. President Woodrow Wilson observed that he did not know when he had been "so stirred and cheered"; the *Christian Herald* hyperbolically compared Yuan's action to Constantine's and Charlemagne's "in subjecting pagan nations to the yoke of Christ."[4] In May 1913, the United States extended full diplomatic recognition to Yuan's government.

The British minister in Beijing considered the American action "outrageous," since Yuan had not yet given formal guarantees on the preservation of foreign rights and investments. Britain was also anxious to ensure the autonomy of Tibet, which Yuan claimed—following late Qing precedent—was a Chinese dependency. Britain's intransigence on the matter was resented by the Chinese; but on October 7, 1913, Yuan acknowledged Tibetan autonomy, although his decision was not ratified by either the cabinet or Parliament. That same day Britain extended diplomatic recognition to the Chinese republic. Japan extended recognition after Yuan's government agreed to further large-scale railway deals, and Russia did the same after receiving acknowledgment of the autonomy of Outer Mongolia.

The fact that Yuan Shikai had now won foreign recognition for his regime did not mean that his government was secure. China's constitutional arrangements were in shambles. As a prelude to purging the Guomindang members from the Parliament in late 1913, Yuan had ordered his police to conduct house-to-house searches of those representatives and senators believed to be Guomindang affiliates. The searches yielded up 438 members with Guomindang party cards, who were then banned from the Parliament. Since the Parliament now lacked a quorum, in late November the speakers of both houses announced an indefinite adjournment. In January 1914, Parliament was formally dissolved, and a month later similar dissolution orders were issued for the provincial assemblies and for local government organizations.

To give a semblance of legality to his regime, Yuan now convened a body of sixty-six men from his cabinet and from various posts in the provinces. In May 1914 these men produced a "constitutional compact," replacing the provisional constitution and giving Yuan as president virtually unlimited power over war, finance, foreign policy, and the rights of citizens. In explaining his action to one of his close advisers, Yuan observed: "Parliament was an unworkable body. 800 men! 200 were good, 200 were passive, 400 were useless. What had they done? They had not even agreed on procedure."[5] It was a suitably sardonic comment on the destruction of China's democratic hopes.

Deprived of any mass base of financial support, Yuan's government lived largely on loans. By 1913 only 2 million yuan or less were coming in from provincial land taxes, and the government was running a deficit of 13 million yuan each month. The revenue from tariffs on foreign trade was also mainly out of Yuan's reach, since in response to the unrest of the revolution, the Maritime Customs (now under Robert Hart's successor, Hart having died in 1911) deposited the customs revenues in foreign banks so they could be used to pay off the interest on China's rapidly accumulating foreign debts. Even the salt taxes were now under foreign supervision; they were either used to pay off debts or manipulated to put political pressure on Yuan.

Despite this trickle of funds, Yuan Shikai was ambitious, both for the nation and for himself. Even as he subverted the constitution, paradoxically he sought to build on reforms enacted in the late Qing and to develop institutions that would build a strong and stable government. To prepare some of his reforms, he relied on a team of foreign advisers that included an Australian foreign-policy expert, a Japanese railway specialist, a French military attaché, and a Belgian jurist; most of these advisers, however, were by their own admission overpaid and underused.

Yuan continued to work for the development of an independent judiciary, not because he had any abstract love of justice, but because a firm, impartial system of courts would be the best tool for ending the hated system of extraterritoriality. The Supreme Court—established in 1906 by the Qing dynasty—took vigorous steps forward in such areas as commercial law and married women's rights. Changes to the process and qualifications for judicial appointments were attempts to clean up abuses in the legal system. To reform the penal system, Yuan authorized an active prison-building program, featuring facilities with improved sanitary conditions and workshops. In education, Yuan pushed for the nationwide expansion of primary schooling for boys, which would be compulsory and free, and supported experimentation with alphabetized manuals and with teacher training. He insisted that, along with the new skills needed by China's citizens, the primary school curriculum should include study of Confucius.

To strengthen the economy, Yuan launched a series of modernization projects in industry, transportation, mining, and agriculture. Monetary reforms centralized the national currency and established a silver standard based on coins featuring the president's likeness (colloquially called the "Yuan Big Head" silver dollar, referring to the size of his head). The minting of other nickel and copper coins was strictly controlled, and millions of depreciated banknotes in the provinces recalled. Yuan also made an intensive effort to maintain the suppression of opium smoking and production that had begun in the late Qing. So effective was this plan—all county magistrates were evaluated according to their success at opium suppression—that opium dealers retreated into the foreign-concession areas, where they would be protected by foreign law.

It was to Yuan's initial advantage as he built his dictatorship that the First World War had erupted in Europe in August 1914, leaving France, Britain, Germany, and Russia too distracted to press for any more gains in China. Furthermore, in their desperate need for troops on the Western front, these foreign powers summoned home all their able-bodied nationals from China. This gave a new generation of Chinese entrepreneurs and managers a golden opportunity to take over the key functions in business and administration, to build up their private fortunes, and to gain invaluable financial experience. Unfortunately for Yuan, however, Japan was more than ready to pick up the slack. With formal ties of alliance to Great Britain that dated back to 1902, Japan declared war on Germany in August 1914 and immediately followed up by attacking the German concession areas in Shandong province.

In January 1915, Japan dealt China an even harsher blow when it issued Yuan's government the Twenty-One Demands. In these, the Japanese demanded far more extensive economic rights for their subjects in Manchuria and Inner Mongolia, joint Sino-Japanese administration of the Han-Ye-Ping iron and coal works in central China, nonalienation of any Chinese ports or islands to other foreign powers, the stationing of Japanese police and economic advisers in north China, and extensive new commercial rights in Fujian province. Chinese hostility to these moves was expressed in nationwide anti-Japanese rallies and in a boycott of Japanese goods that was far more extensive and successful than the anti-American boycott of 1905. Still, Yuan felt he had to yield, although he did manage to negotiate slight modifications to some of the conditions.

As Yuan's prestige and popularity sagged, his own intransigence hardened. His critics were harassed or silenced under the terms of censorship regulations imposed in 1914 on all newspapers and other publications; these regulations carried stiff penalties for anyone printing material "harmful to the public peace."[6] To build up additional support for his authority, Yuan had already begun to reinstitute elements of Confucian belief as China's state religion. He assumed the role of chief participant in rituals at the Qing Temple of Heaven, taking on the trappings of emperor. Indeed, in late 1915, Yuan moved firmly in that direction, floating rumors that people wanted him to revive the institution. In November a specially convened "Representative Assembly" voted— allegedly with the astonishing unanimity of 1,993 votes in favor and none opposed—to beg Yuan to become emperor. He accepted, inaugurating his new dynasty as of January 1, 1916.

Yuan Shikai and his advisers (one of them, Frank Goodnow, a professor from Columbia University and former president of the American Political Science Association) believed that the Chinese people yearned for a symbol of central authority transcending the president and that, therefore, the restoration of the emperorship would be welcomed. But they had miscalculated. Many of Yuan's close political allies abandoned him, and the solidarity of his former military protégés was shattered. Throughout China there were mass protests matched by open actions in the provinces. The military leader in Yunnan declared that province's independence in December 1915; Guizhou followed in January 1916, and Guangxi in March. The foreign powers were aloof or openly hostile and did not give Yuan the support he expected. He responded to the outcries by declaring that he would cancel the monarchy. But Yuan's prestige was now shattered, and province after province continued to declare independence. He died of uremia—compounded, many thought, by anger and humiliation—on June 6, 1916, at the age of fifty-six.

The successor to the now tarnished presidency was Li Yuanhong, the reluctant ally of the Wuhan revolutionaries in 1911, who had been serving since 1913 as the ineffective and equally reluctant vice president. Li's power base was far weaker than Yuan's, and he had no army behind him—only a sea of disaffected or independent provinces and an almost bankrupt treasury. Li's most important acts were to recall the members of the Parliament (who had been recessed over two years before), reconstituting a representative government, and to reaffirm the provisional constitution of 1912 as the binding force on the nation. But both these steps were controversial: since the representatives had been elected in December 1912 to a three-year term, their status was unclear; and since the 1912 provisional constitution had been replaced by Yuan's of 1914, it was not certain that it still had priority.

Li Yuanhong had been in office just over a year when a military coup occurred, linked to yet another attempt at restoring the emperorship. This time the instigator was General Zhang Xun, who had fought for the Qing in 1911 and had remained a Manchu loyalist throughout Yuan's presidency. In mid-June 1917, allegedly acting as mediator between President Li and other feuding generals, Zhang led his army into Beijing and declared the restoration of the abdicated Qing emperor Puyi, now a boy of eleven. As bemused Beijing residents searched for old Qing imperial banners to hang outside their houses, and foreign diplomats considered how to handle this new development, a small group of former Qing officials and scholars—among them the late Emperor Guangxu's loyal supporter Kang Youwei—hurried to the Forbidden City in official robes to serve the restored emperor.

But the restoration never got off the ground. Other generals in the capital region marched on the palace, and two aviators—in what may well have been China's first aerial action—dropped a bomb on the Forbidden City, killing three men. In mid-July, the troops of rival generals stormed Beijing and defeated Zhang Xun, who was given political asylum in the Dutch legation. Emperor Puyi was deposed once again, although not penalized except by the order of the new president that he be given a modern education under Western tutors. He continued to live in the Forbidden City until 1924, when another warlord evicted him and forced him to seek safety in the Japanese concession in Tianjin. The Forbidden City was thereafter made into a public cultural and historical museum, as it has remained to this day.

With the collapse of General Zhang's insurrection at the hands of a group of rival generals, all pretense of real strength in the central government was gone. From now on both the presidency and the Parliament became the playthings of the militarists; although able, intelligent men were willing to serve in the government, they rose and fell at the behest of these outside forces. Democracy had vanished, and the era of "warlordism" had begun.

MILITARISTS IN CHINA AND CHINESE IN FRANCE

The men known as "warlords," who now controlled much of China, had a wide range of backgrounds and maintained their power in different ways. A number had risen through the ranks of the Beiyang army and had once been protégés of Yuan Shikai; others had served in the provincial armies and had risen to positions as military governor or senior officer in late 1911 or early 1912. A number were local thugs who had seized opportunities to consolidate small bases. Some dominated whole provinces and financed their armies with taxes collected by their own bureaucracies; others controlled only a handful of towns with "transit taxes" collected at gunpoint or through confiscation. Some warlords were deeply loyal to the idea of a republic, continuing to hope that one day they would be reintegrated into a valid constitutional state; others believed that Sun Yat-sen and the Guomindang represented China's legitimate government. Out of choice or necessity, a number worked closely with foreign powers, whether it was the British in Shanghai, the Japanese in Manchuria, or the French in the southwest. Some controlled extensive lengths of railway line, drawing their revenues from passenger and freight services, and from the commerce of cities on the line. Some reinstituted opium growing in their domains and tapped the drug trade for revenues.

In character as well, the warlords differed greatly. Some, like the warlord who for a time dominated Shandong, were capable of a ferocious and erratic cruelty. Many others were educated men who tried to instill in their troops their own vision of morality, which might be a kind of modified Confucianism, Christianity, socialism, or the curious amalgam concocted by the warlord of Shanxi, Yan Xishan, who drew on an array of heroes from Europe and the United States in pursuit of his ideal image. As Yan stated proudly, he had constructed a perfect ideology, one that combined the best features of "militarism, nationalism, anarchism, democracy, capitalism, communism, individualism, imperialism, universalism, paternalism, and utopianism."[7]

No matter whether individual warlords were cruel or generous, sophisticated or muddleheaded, the fragmentation of China would make future attempts to unify the country even harder than it had been for those who inherited the mantle of leadership from the Qing. Nevertheless, a certain apparent coherence adhered to the government because the warlords in north China never completely destroyed what remained of the presidency and the premiership. Instead, they placed their own supporters in these positions, so that whatever prestige the offices preserved would redound back to the militarists themselves.

One man who assumed leadership under these conditions was Duan Qirui, who became premier in 1916. Born in the aftermath of the Taiping civil war, Duan in 1881 was among the first group of cadets to enroll in the Beiyang military academy. Graduated top of his class, he was spotted by Li Hongzhang and sent to Germany to study military science. Thereafter, the course of his career mirrored the new opportunities and dislocations of China itself. His next sponsor, Yuan Shikai, made Duan head of the New Army's artillery battalion. Duan served with Yuan in Shandong during the Boxer Uprising and was promoted to division commander in the Beiyang army. His next appointment as head of the staff officers' college provided an opportunity to build up a coterie of followers, just as he had been a member of Yuan's group of protégés. He commanded the Second Army Corps in Hubei during the 1911 revolution and was named military governor of Hunan and Hubei as a further reward for his loyalty to Yuan. In 1912, he was appointed as minister of war and served as acting premier during the 1913 purge of the Guomindang from the Parliament. With Yuan's death in 1916, Duan—who had

Chinese workers living in close quarters at the gunpowder factory in Saint-Fons, France, 1914

opposed Yuan's imperial-restoration attempt—became premier with the crucial backing of other senior Beiyang commanders.

As Duan consolidated his power base, World War I began to reach its most crucial stage in Western Europe. Duan and his advisers were intrigued by the possibilities of joining France and Britain in their fight against Germany, arguing that if Germany were defeated, then the strategically important German concession areas in Shandong province could be reclaimed by China. Duan was further pressured toward an anti-German declaration from two directions. One was from the United States, which in early 1917 was preparing to enter the war; the other was from the Japanese, who had abandoned various attempts to encourage separatist regimes in Manchuria, Mongolia, and southern China, and had tried to bribe Duan's regime into recognizing Japan's standing in north China at Germany's expense.

China's military strength was trivial compared to that of the European belligerents or of the United States, which had entered the war on the side of Britain and France in April 1917. But China had one crucial resource that the Allies needed—namely, manpower. The slaughter in the European battlefields had been terrible. The Allies realized that if Chinese laborers could be used on the docks and on construction projects in Western Europe, it would free more European men for active combat. Pursuing this harsh but accurate line of reasoning, the British and French had begun to negotiate with Duan's government as early as the summer of 1916, well before the Chinese declaration of war. The result was the establishment of a processing plant for

Chinese laborers in Shandong province, near the British naval base of Wei-haiwei, with a second added later at the port of Qingdao. Crassly referred to by the British as their "sausage machine,"[8] the processing system screened tens of thousands of Chinese volunteers, who were driven by the poverty of the region and lured by the wages offered. If accepted after thorough medical examinations—and about 100,000 made it through the screening—they were issued dog tags with serial numbers, which were sealed with metal rivets on bands around their wrists. Then they were sprayed from head to foot with disinfectant and urged to remove their queues, which many had kept. Each volunteer received an embarkation fee of 20 yuan, clothing, and meals, followed by 10 yuan a month paid to his family.

An initial boatload of Chinese laborers, traveling across the Indian Ocean and through the Suez Canal in 1916 on contract to the French government, was sunk by German submarines in the Mediterranean; 543 Chinese lives were lost. New recruits were thereafter shipped over the Pacific to Canada, across Canada by train, and then reshipped in fleets accompanied by antisubmarine patrols for the journey across the Atlantic. Although their employment had been protested by many French and British, particularly by labor-union members, the Chinese were soon at work, most of them in northern France. They were given such tasks as unloading cargo, building barracks and hospitals, digging trenches, and handling ammunition in the railway marshaling yards. They worked ten-hour days, seven days a week, with some time off allowed at the traditional Chinese festivals. The laborers remained nonbelligerents even after China's declaration of war, since Duan's regime could not finance an army in Europe.

The presence of so many Chinese men in France—54,000 by late 1917, 96,000 by late 1918—brought both dangers and opportunities. Some of their camps were bombed by German planes or shelled, and on occasion they retaliated for their dead comrades by killing German prisoners of war. Some Chinese were blown up by unexploded mines when clearing battlefields or digging trenches. Many fell ill from the unfamiliar diet and the intense damp and cold, and on occasion they mutinied against their French and British employers or ransacked local restaurants in search of food. Sample sentences from a Chinese phrase book, prepared by the British army for use by its staff in the camps, hint at the levels of irritation or discrimination the Chinese labor corps experienced: "I want eight men to go over there quickly." "Why don't you eat this food?" "The inside of this tent is not very clean." "You must have a bath tomorrow." "This latrine is reserved for Europeans and is not available to Chinese."[9]

The most significant response to the bleak conditions came from representatives of the Young Men's Christian Association (YMCA), who saw a major opportunity for service. They focused on recreational activities and on education, designing special textbooks and teaching techniques to spread literacy among the workers. With the aid of such educated Chinese staff, as many as 50,000 letters a month were mailed from France to China, where they were read and reread aloud to the villagers. Brief, simple in vocabulary, and censored for military secrets by the Allies, these letters are nevertheless important signs of the growing literacy among Chinese workers. One surviving letter ran as follows:

> For the inspection of my elder brother. I have come many ten thousand *li* since I saw you.* I am doing well and you need not have anxiety about me. I am earning three francs per day, but as living is expensive I cannot send many home yet. As to my quarrelling with you, that day at Yaowan, before I left, forget it! I did unworthily. Please take care of our parents and when I return in three or five years, I will bring enough money to help support them the rest of their days.[10]

The Chinese contribution to the war was not without its cost. In addition to the 543 lost at sea, almost 2,000 Chinese workers died in France and Flanders, and were laid to rest in special cemeteries. There the long lines of gravestones, each neatly incised with their Chinese names and the serial numbers given to them, still bear mute testimony to China's first involvement in such a global conflict. More complex was the legacy of the tens of thousands of workers when they returned home, literate and wise in the ways of the world, often with a decent balance of cash stored up with their families. They would be in position to play new roles in politics, as some Chinese socialists observed.

After the armistice of November 11, 1918, ended the war with Germany's defeat, anticipation in China ran high. There were triumphant parades in Beijing, and an exuberant crowd demolished the memorial that the Qing had been forced to raise in honor of the Germans killed by the Boxers. The government was now headed by yet another Beiyang-faction president and premier. Duan Qirui had resigned in October 1918, but before doing so he had used Japanese loans to enhance his own military power and had negotiated secret deals with the Japanese. The Chinese delegation to the postwar treaty negotiations at Versailles was headed by five capable diplomats who had never been fully briefed on what to expect. They were greeted at Versailles by the shattering announcement of the chief Japanese delegate that early in 1917, in return for Japanese naval assistance against the Germans, Great Britain, France, and Italy had signed a secret treaty ensuring "support [of] Japan's claims in regard to the disposal of Germany's rights in Shandong" after the war.[11]

---

* A *li* is one-third of a mile.

As if that were not bad enough, the Japanese also announced that they had come to secret agreements with Duan Qirui in September 1918, while he was still premier. These agreements granted the Japanese the right to station police and to establish military garrisons in Jinan and Qingdao, and also mortgaged to Japan, in partial payment for its loans, the total income from two new Shandong railroads the Japanese planned to develop. The Chinese delegates seem to have been genuinely unaware of these secret agreements. President Woodrow Wilson, who had earlier been sympathetic to China's desire to recover its Shandong rights, now felt that Japan had staked out a firm claim to them on the basis of international law. On April 30, 1919, he agreed with the British and French representatives to transfer all of Germany's Shandong rights to Japan.

As the nature of this new betrayal grew clear, urgent telegrams flew between Paris and Beijing, and the Chinese public was aroused as rarely before. China's delegates at Versailles were bombarded by petitions and protests from political and commercial groups, from overseas Chinese communities, and from Chinese students at universities abroad. On May 1, the news arrived that the Chinese delegates acknowledged their case as hopeless because of the prior agreements. This news sparked mass protests in Beijing on May 4, which were followed by demonstrations in cities all over the country. While the government dithered, pressure on the Versailles delegates not to sign the treaty was unrelenting. The president did at last telegraph an instruction not to sign, but the telegram was sent too late to reach Versailles before the June 28 deadline. However, Chinese students and demonstrators had surrounded the delegates in their Paris hotel and forcibly prevented them from attending the signing ceremony. The Versailles treaty ended up without China's acceptance.

The formative years of the early Republic had sown seeds of bright hope for constitutional government and representative democracy in China. As those hopes foundered on the shoals of militarism, and in the aftermath of Versailles, a new generation of young activists, disgusted by the betrayal of the promises of the Republic and the duplicity of Western nations, directed probing questions at the nature of Chinese and Western moral values. And the date of May 4, 1919, on which the citizens and students of Beijing protested publicly in the streets against the Versailles treaty, was to give its name to a new movement, one in which the juxtaposition of nationalism and cultural self-analysis took the Chinese people in yet another new direction.

CHAPTER 13

"A Road Is Made"

THE WARNING VOICE OF SOCIAL DARWINISM

The fragmentation of authority under Yuan Shikai, the failure of the fledgling republic, and the betrayal of Versailles—all served to deepen a fear that had been latent among Chinese since the late Qing: that China was about to be dismembered, that it would cease to exist as a nation, and that the 4,000 years of its recorded history would come to a jolting end. At the same time, analytical tools for probing the nation's plight had been made available by the spreading popularity of Social Darwinism, and even if the theories gave little solace to Chinese thinkers, these ideas nevertheless helped to bring some sense of method into a despairing debate.

The evolutionary theories of Charles Darwin, whose *On the Origin of Species* was first published in England in 1859, explained how the adaptive processes of natural selection determined which species managed to thrive and which were doomed to extinction. From the observations that he made while sailing to the Cape Verde Islands, Chile, the Galápagos Islands, New Zealand, and Australia, Darwin realized that those organisms best fitted to survive slowly ousted those that were less well fitted. Through the laws of heredity, furthermore, the degree of adaptation achieved by a species would be maintained or improved.

The British sociologist Herbert Spencer made his own creative adaptation of Darwin's theories and applied them to the development of human societies. Spencer's arguments that the "survival of the fittest" governed social as well as biological evolution were then modified by the scientist Thomas Huxley, and encapsulated in 1893 in his book *Evolution and Ethics*. Yan Fu, a product of China's naval-school system during the self-strengthening period and later a student in England, read Huxley's book and translated it into Chinese in 1896—with his own added commentary and interpretations—under the title *On Evolution*. Partly because Yan Fu chose to give the work a nationalistic emphasis not evident in the original, it had an immense impact on Chinese scholars in the late Qing and early republic.

Yan Fu's message was that Spencer's sociological writings were not merely analytical and descriptive, but prescriptive as well, offering means to transform and strengthen society. Yan Fu summarized Darwin as follows:

> Peoples and living things struggle for survival. At first, species struggle with species; then as [people] gradually progress, there is a struggle between one social group and another. The weak invariably become the prey of the strong, the stupid invariably become subservient to the clever.[1]

Spencer, Yan Fu continued, "based himself on the theory of evolution to explain the origins of human relations and of civilization." Other late Qing thinkers, such as Liang Qichao, were quick to see the significance of these ideas. In advocating the 1898 reforms, Liang observed hopefully that evolutionary theories allowed "the possibility of influence and change that can cause the species to steadily improve"; thus, the Chinese could strengthen their race to engage in the struggle for survival.[2] Pondering the problems of race and racial strength, other reformers combined the theories from the West with the writings of seventeenth-century anti-Manchu nationalists like Wang Fuzhi, which now attracted a revival of interest. "A nation with spirit will survive," a Chinese scholar wrote just before the 1911 Wuhan uprising; "a nation without it will perish. But where does the 'national spirit' lie? In national studies."[3]

The 1911 revolution briefly raised hopes that Social Darwinist ideas of harsh social competition were now discredited. Just as his reorganized Guomindang won the 1912 elections, Sun Yat-sen wrote:

> Before the twentieth century, the nations of Europe invented a newfangled struggle-for-existence theory, which for a time influenced everything. Every nation assumed that "the survival of the fittest" and "the weak are the meat of the strong" were the vital laws on which to establish a state. They even went so far as to say that "might is the only right, there is no reason." This kind of theory in the early days of the evolution of European civilization had its uses. But, from the vantage point of today, it appears a barbaric form of learning.[4]

But by 1913, Sun was writing sadly of a world dominated by struggles for survival from which no government or industrial enterprise could be exempt. As for Yan Fu, he lost his enthusiasm for the theories he had helped to popularize, writing that the failures of the Chinese republic and the bloodshed of World

War I in Europe showed that "three hundred years of evolutionary progress have all come down to nothing but four words: selfishness, slaughter, shamelessness, and corruption."[5]

Such pessimism might well lead to a refusal to strive for social change, as indeed happened among Social Darwinists in the United States. This possibility lent added urgency to China's radical thinkers. As Chen Duxiu, later a cofounder of the Chinese Communist Party (CCP), wrote to a friend just after Yuan Shikai's death, "The majority of our people are lethargic and do not know that not only our morality, politics and technology but even common commodities for daily use are all unfit for struggle and are going to be eliminated in the process of natural selection."[6] If that happened, China would die.

Elements of these strains of thought came together in the mind of another future leader of the CCP, Mao Zedong. In 1917, when he published his first essay, Mao was twenty-four years old. He had rebelled against his father, rejecting both the rural life on the family farm in Hunan province and the marriage his parents had arranged for him with the daughter of a neighboring family. Instead, after serving briefly in the republican army in 1911, he had plunged into a haphazard and eclectic life of study in Changsha. After making his way through Yan Fu's translations of Mill, Montesquieu, Rousseau, and Spencer, as well as a wide range of Chinese political philosophers, Mao enrolled at the well-known First Normal School in Changsha, where he studied ethics as his major field. This deepened his knowledge of the works of Spencer and Rousseau, and introduced him to Kant, as well as to the ways that such thinkers could be usefully compared to figures from China's own past.

Mao's first approach to the problems of national weakness was a literal-minded one. If China was weak, it was because the Chinese were weak. If the Chinese were weak, it was because their culture concentrated on building up the mind and neglected strengthening the body. Mao toughened his own physique by swimming and exercising; in his essay "A Study of Physical Education," published in the journal *New Youth* in April 1917, he urged others to do

Mao Zedong, c. 1919

the same. "Our nation is wanting in

strength; the military spirit has not been encouraged," Mao wrote. "The physical condition of our people deteriorates daily. . . . If our bodies are not strong, we will tremble at the sight of [enemy] soldiers. How then can we attain our goals?" Students disliked exercise for many reasons, the primary ones being social norms that valorized literary accomplishments and "fine deportment" while despising violent exertion. All that had to change—"When the body is strong, then one can advance speedily in knowledge and morality." In his essay, Mao outlined a six-part regimen with thirty different exercises and emphasized the need for perseverance and concentration of strength. Young people should strive for a "savage and rude" attitude in their physical training: "To charge on horseback, amidst the clash of arms, and to be ever victorious; to shake the mountains by one's cries, and the colors of the sky by one's roars of anger."[7]

As was true of many young Chinese at this time, Mao's main ideas were Darwinist, idealistic, and tinged with anarchist belief, but as yet not deeply affected by influences from Marxist-Socialism. As Mao wrote, he admired the anarchist Kropotkin more than Marx, for the key values in society were "mutual aid" and voluntary unions.[8] In a series of nine articles published in a Changsha newspaper in November 1919, Mao showed that he had combined his thinking on the need for collective struggle with the kinds of reflections on women and their rights that had been advocated by Liang Qichao, Qiu Jin, and others in the late Qing. They had argued that the energy of women should be harnessed to strengthen the nation, enabling China to face the world with its full complement of 400 million people, rather than with the resources of only its 200 million men. Mao's articles "On the Suicide of Miss Zhao" addressed an event that had occurred in Changsha. A young woman from the Zhao family had been betrothed without her consent to a young man from the Wu family. Such arrangements were common; what was unusual about Miss Zhao was that she objected so violently to the marriage that she slit her own throat inside the sedan chair, en route to the marriage ceremonies. Her death was followed by a tussle between the Wu and Zhao families as each tried to give the other responsibility for burying the bride.

Writing with both passion and acuteness, Mao observed that this tragedy could have been avoided if any of three conditions had been different: if Miss Zhao's family had been more sympathetic, if the Wu family had not insisted on the letter of their marriage contract, and if the society of Changsha (and, by implication, of all China) had been braver and more open. Miss Zhao's death mattered, wrote Mao. "It happened because of the shameful system of arranged marriages, because of the darkness of the social system, the negation of the individual will, and the absence of the freedom to choose one's own mate." Yet Mao could not condone the act of suicide, even in such a state of despair. If the Chinese refused to confront reality, they would achieve nothing. People died by suicide because society deprived them of hope, but even in a position of complete hopelessness, Mao wrote, "we should struggle against society in order to regain the hope that we have lost. . . . We should die fighting."[9]

"We should die fighting." The words were bold ones, but the real difficulty lay in deciding who was the main enemy. Was it an apathetic local society? Was it the warlords who controlled Hunan? Was it the corrupt politicians in Beijing? Was it the gunboats of the voracious foreign powers, or the foreign businesses that were making ever further inroads into China? Or was it perhaps something even more complex: the whole structure of Chinese beliefs, and the economic system that went with it? For the young men and women of Mao's generation, the problems were baffling, but they had somehow to come up with a program for solving these difficulties if China was not to succumb to despair.

MARXIST STIRRINGS

Before the Bolshevik Revolution of 1917 in Russia, there was not much interest in Marxism in China. Almost none of Marx's work had been translated into Chinese, except for sections of *The Communist Manifesto*. Marxism did not seem a useful analytical tool for solving the nation's problems. Marx's view of a progression for human societies—from primitive communalism through an era of slavery to feudalism and capitalism—did not appear to fit China's historical experience. And since China could hardly claim to be a capitalist society even in embryo, Marx's theory that the overthrow of capitalism was a prerequisite for the new era of socialism seemed to make that transition indefinitely remote.

So despite Chinese press reports of the victories of the Petrograd workers' soviet led by Trotsky and the formation of Lenin's revolutionary Soviet government, the news did not initially attract much attention. But slowly some began to realize that the events in Russia went beyond the experiences of France in 1789, and for many observers it was electrifying to see how the entrenched Russian autocracy, with all its embedded institutions, had turned out after all to have contained the seeds of the Soviet Union. Sun Yat-sen, who had returned from exile after the death of Yuan Shikai, sent a personal message of congratulation to Lenin.

As the seriousness of the Bolsheviks' ongoing struggle with the conservative White Russian forces became apparent, and as hostile reactions from the other Allied powers became more open once Lenin had made peace with

Germany, greater numbers of Chinese began to reflect on the significance of what had occurred and to try and draw lessons for their own society. At the vanguard of this attempt was the head librarian at Beijing University, Li Dazhao. Born in 1889 to a poor farming family in Hebei province, Li had sold what little property he owned to go to a modern school. From 1913 to 1916 he studied political economy in Japan, earning a reputation there as a fine writer and editor. Because of these skills, in February 1918 he was appointed librarian of what had become China's most prestigious university.

Li felt that Russia was approaching a great surge of development: Britain and France had risen to splendid heights and were now sinking; Germany was at its peak and would soon begin to fade; but Russia, "because of its comparative slowness in the evolution of civilization," had "surplus energy for development."[10] Might not China also make such a leap? Within six months, Li had established an informal study group at his office, where a dozen or so students and faculty would meet to discuss political developments. By the end of 1918, this group had acquired a semiformal identity as the "Marxist Research Society," with Li leading analytical discussions of Marx's *Capital*.

As interest grew, Chen Duxiu, who was dean of Beijing University,* as well as editor of the most influential journal of the day, *New Youth*, decided to run a special issue on Marxism with Li Dazhao as general editor. Originally scheduled for publication on May 1, 1919, printing delays kept the issue from the public until the fall. Most of the articles were scholarly analyses of specific Marxist concepts, and several were critical of Marx's methodology. But Li's essay, "My Marxist Views," gave the most careful analysis of the concept of class struggle and the problem of capitalist exploitation that had yet been published in China. Because of the journal's reputation, the message was immediately spread to an influential readership across the country. Moreover, the fledgling Soviet Union advertised its anti-imperialist position with promises of relinquishing tsarist claims and treaties, including indemnities due from the Boxer Uprising and control of the Chinese Eastern Railway. Although these promises were later retracted, the early gestures made a strong impression.

By 1919, Li Dazhao's study group had attracted a broad circle of students. Some were wealthy, urban members of Beijing University's elite student body, but others came from different backgrounds. One regular was Qu Qiubai, a young student from Jiangsu province who was a devout Buddhist and a fine classical scholar. Born to a gentry family, Qu had enjoyed a comfortable childhood and received a good education. When Qu was in his teens, his father abandoned the family, leaving his mother to raise six children on her own;

* In March 1919 he was forced to resign by conservative opponents.

she killed herself when he was sixteen. Qu managed to complete his secondary schooling, but he could not afford to attend Beijing University. Instead he enrolled at the Russian language institute of the Ministry of Foreign Affairs, which was tuition-free and offered a small stipend. Another participant in Li's Marxist study group was Zhang Guotao, son of a Hakka landlord from the Jiangxi-Hunan border. As a teenager, Zhang had smuggled guns for Sun Yatsen's revolutionary organizations and later became an activist against Yuan Shikai.

Despite the initial enthusiasm these young men and other students showed for Bolshevism and Marxism, the need remained—if Marxism was to have any relevance to social conditions in China—to reformulate its basic premises. Most vexing was the problem of the central role Marx ascribed to the urban proletariat and to the Communist party as the vanguard of that class, since China had such a small industrial sector. But it was encouraging that Russia did not fit any Marxist model either, and by a certain intellectual sleight of hand, Li Dazhao developed an interpretation that brought China into a Marxist arena of dialogue as a "proletarian nation." China, he observed, was at the mercy of foreign imperialist forces that had exploited all Chinese people in ways similar to those in which capitalists exploited their workers—by owning the means of production and seizing the workers' surplus value for themselves. Therefore, Li concluded that "the whole country has gradually been transformed into part of the world proletariat."[11]

Li Dazhao also wrote powerfully on the need for intellectuals to redeem themselves through labor and to escape from the corrupting powers of city life by working alongside the farmers in the fields. By going to the countryside, educated youths could gradually repair the wreckage of the constitutional system, for the students could explain the workings of the electoral system to the villagers and urge them to participate in the democratic process. By early 1920, Beijing University students were traveling to the neighboring countryside in groups, trying to live out Li's ideas.

The experience was not a mere academic exercise. In 1920 and 1921, five provinces in north China (Hebei, Shandong, Henan, Shanxi, and Shaanxi) were caught in a devastating cycle of famine caused by severe droughts in 1919. In villages where the average density of people per square mile was 1,230, the combination of withered crops and inadequate government relief was disastrous: at least 500,000 people died, and out of an estimated 48.8 million in these five provinces, over 19.8 million were declared destitute. Refugees crowded the roads and railway lines; many lost limbs or were killed trying to force their way onto overcrowded trains. Tens of thousands of children were sold as servants or, in the case of girls, as prostitutes and secondary wives. In one village, sixty households out of a hundred had no food, and villagers were reduced to eating straw and leaves. Epidemics—typhus being the most dreaded and the most prevalent—decimated those already weakened by hunger. Those students who followed Li's call had an opportunity to learn something of the desperation and poverty that was endemic in their own society, and from which they had been sheltered. And some of them, as they pondered such misery and its context of governmental corruption and incompetence, began to wonder about the alternatives open to them personally, and to their country as a whole.

THE FACETS OF MAY FOURTH

Both the growing discussion of Social Darwinist ideas and the rise of interest in communist ideology were symptomatic of a cultural upheaval that was spreading throughout China. This upheaval is often called the May Fourth movement, since in important ways it was intricately connected to the events that occurred in Beijing on May 4, 1919, and to the effect that those events had on the country as a whole. The term *May Fourth movement* is therefore both limited and broad, depending on whether it is applied to the demonstrations that took place on that particular day or to the complex emotional, cultural, and political developments that followed.

The student representatives from thirteen area colleges and universities who met in Beijing on the morning of May 4, 1919, drew up five resolutions: one protested the Shandong settlement reached at the Versailles conference, a second sought to awaken "the masses all over the country" to an awareness of China's plight, a third proposed holding a mass meeting of all Beijing residents, a fourth urged the formation of a Beijing student union, and a fifth called for a demonstration that afternoon in protest of the treaty terms.

The fifth resolution was acted on at once. Defying a police order forbidding the demonstration, about 3,000 students assembled in front of the Forbidden City complex at Tiananmen Square—then a small walled park rather than the gigantic open space into which it was later transformed—and began to march toward the foreign-legation quarter. At the head of the procession fluttered two funeral banners on which were written the names of the most hated pro-Japanese members of the cabinet. As they marched, the students handed out broadsheets to the watching citizens, written in easy-to-read vernacular Chinese, explaining that the loss of the Shandong rights to Japan meant the end of China's territorial integrity, and calling on people of all occupations and classes to join in protest. Barred from the legation quarter by foreign guards and Chinese police, the students marched instead toward the home of the minister of communications, who had been responsible for negotiating loans with Japan.

Students protesting at May Fourth demonstration, 1919

Although the minister was away, some students broke into his house and set it afire while others accosted another prominent politician and beat him into unconsciousness. There were several violent clashes with police; one student, badly injured, died in a hospital three days later, the only fatality. The demonstrators had almost all dispersed by early evening, when police reinforcements arrived, arresting thirty-two of those still in the streets.

In the days that followed, the Beijing students and some of their teachers proceeded to implement the rest of the resolutions that had been passed on the morning of May 4. They moved swiftly to establish a student union that combined the city's middle-school, high-school, college, and university students. An important aspect of this new union was that it included women and gave formal support to the principle of coeducation. (The first female students were admitted to Beijing University in 1920.) The idea of broad-based student unions spread swiftly. In June 1919, delegates from student unions in over thirty cities formed a Student Union of the Republic of China.

The student protesters were also successful in spreading their message to a wide circle, once more reasserting the prestige of the scholarly elite that had been such a central part of education under the Qing dynasty, now clothed in modern garb. The rash of student strikes and mass arrests led to a wave of national sympathy for the students' cause. Support came from merchants and businessmen grouped in chambers of commerce in major cities, from individual industrialists, from shop owners, and from industrial workers. Although there was no central labor union organization at this time, and precise figures are hard to find, as many as 60,000 workers in forty-three enterprises staged some form of work stoppage or sympathy strike in Shanghai alone. Work actions took place in textile plants, print shops, public utilities, shipping concerns, paper mills, petroleum works, and tobacco factories. Much of this agitation was stimulated by socialist clubs and study groups that had spread across the country during 1919.

Tied to the swelling protest against China's international position was the growth of a large number of new periodicals and newspapers. Often written in simple vernacular style accessible to those with limited education, these publications carried articles about a wide range of social and cultural problems. They pointed to the growth of a new force that bridged class, regional, and occupational lines, and drew millions of people together in a search for coherence and meaning in an apparently fragmenting world. Although many of these "May Fourth" journals did not last, their names still echo the excitement of the time: *The Dawn, Young China, New Society, People's Tocsin, The New Woman, Plain People, Upward, Strife*.[12]

The romantic poet Guo Moruo, recently returned from Japan, expressed all the explosive excitement of China's youth with the lines he wrote in 1919:

> I am the light of the moon,
> I am the light of the sun,
> I am the light of all the planets.
> I am the light of *x ray*,
> I am the total *energy* of the entire universe.

In his Chinese verse the words "x ray" and "energy" were printed in English script, giving the requisite touch of exoticism to the flamboyantly personal message.[13]

It was as if the far-off events at Versailles and the mounting evidence of the spinelessness of corrupt politicians coalesced in people's minds and impelled them to search for a way to return meaning to Chinese culture. What did it now mean to be Chinese? Where was the country heading? What values should one adopt to help one in the search? In this broad sense, the May Fourth movement was an attempt to redefine China's culture for the modern world. In the attempt, not surprisingly, reformers followed different avenues of thought and conduct. Some May Fourth thinkers concentrated on launching attacks against reactionary or irrelevant "old ways" such as Confucianism, the patriarchal family, arranged marriages, or classical education. Some focused on reform of Chinese writing by using contemporary vernacular speech patterns in works of literature, as an overt challenge to the elitism of the intensely difficult classical language. Some had a deep interest in traditional Western art and culture, while others looked to the avant-garde elements of that culture, such as surrealist and cubist painting, symbolist poetry, graphic design, and realist drama. Some sought to infuse Chinese traditional arts with a new spirit of nationalism by borrowing Western techniques. Those intrigued by the theories of Sigmund Freud searched in Chinese vocabulary for ways to express such ideas as "Oedipus complex," "penis envy," and "hysteria." And some sought a complete liberation of the human spirit: the realization of human potential through a kind of promethean leap of romantic faith.

Those writers who advocated a problem-solving approach sought to develop techniques from such disciplines as sociology, economics, history, and philosophy in order to analyze China's problems and find solutions to them. Others took a similarly pragmatic approach but thought the answer was to develop a sophisticated awareness of the achievements of Western science, engineering, and medicine. In a sea of possibilities, there emerged sharp disagreements about the path forward. The pragmatists clashed with those who held more ideologically oriented views of the world that drew inspiration from socialist, Marxist, or feminist critiques of society, and sought to change the world swiftly by radical activism. The arguments could be vicious and turn personal. In a disingenuous tactic to attract readers and stir controversy, the editors of *New Youth* published fabricated letters from invented adversaries and heaped abuse on these "opinionated fools spewing utter drivel."[14]

Despite the occasional vitriol, most of these reformers shared a central patriotic ground: they wished for a rejuvenated, unified nation that would have the means to cope with the problems of warlordism, an exploitative landlord system now often described as "feudal" in nature, and foreign imperialism. For some, the respect for Western technological power blended with a yearning to retain some essence of Chinese culture—as it had sixty years before in the minds of the Confucian scholar-officials of the Tongzhi Restoration.

Although the May Fourth movement in this broad sense spread among the educated elite across the country, the formative thinking that lay behind the movement originated to a large degree with the faculty and students at Beijing University. In the early years of the republic, Beijing University had risen rapidly to prominence as the leading center of learning, research, and teaching. This rise was attributable in part to the courageous leadership of the scholar-translator Yan Fu, who had served as the first president of the modernized institution in 1912. When the university faced severe budget cuts that year, Yan Fu had persuaded the relevant government ministries to maintain funding at a high level. As Yan wrote, "In today's world, every civilized country has many universities ranging in number from tens to many hundreds. If we cannot preserve even one, especially one already in existence, it is unfortunate indeed."[15]

Yan Fu's success can be gauged by examining the lives of three men who achieved special prominence in the May Fourth movement: Yan's successor as president of the university, Cai Yuanpei; the dean of the university, Chen Duxiu; and the professor of philosophy, Hu Shi. Although no single person can encapsulate the turbulence and excitement of the movement, the backgrounds and activities of these three provide a useful index to a China in flux, show how widely perceptions of the nation's priorities varied, and demonstrate how the West could be both distrusted and revered, depending on the elements in view.

Cai Yuanpei, the oldest of the three, had built up the most distinguished record: he had earned the *jinshi* degree in 1890, when he was only twenty-two, and been a member of the Hanlin Academy. In the last years of the Qing he had served as an educational official in his native Zhejiang, and then as a teacher and sponsor of radical schools and anti-Qing societies. He joined the Revolutionary Alliance, but was studying philosophy in Germany when the Wuhan uprisings began. Returning to China in 1912, he served briefly as the minister of education under both Sun Yat-sen and Yuan Shikai before traveling again to Germany and to France, where he helped establish a work-study program for Chinese students. Appointed president of Beijing University in 1917 after the retirement of Yan Fu, Cai took a brave line with the military and civilian leaders who controlled the government. He defended the rights of his faculty and students to speak out, claiming that they were all seeking "education for a world view" and that the function of a university president was to be "broad-minded and encompass tolerance of diverse points of view."[16] Four days after the May Fourth demonstration, Cai resigned to protest the arrest of his students. He was reappointed in late 1919 and continued as president of the university until 1922, guiding its students and faculty through stormy years and remaining a staunch defender of human rights and freedom of intellectual inquiry.

Chen Duxiu was of a different nature—volatile and emotional, an intuitive rather than an intellectual supporter of the underdog. Born to a wealthy official family in Anhui in 1879, Chen trained initially as a classical scholar but failed the province-level *juren* exams in 1897. (He later wrote a caustic and amusing memoir about the dishonesty and the incompetence that he felt pervaded the examination system.) Chen spent two extended periods of study in Japan, where he helped found radical political societies; he refused, however, to join Sun Yat-sen's Revolutionary Alliance, which he regarded as racist. Prominent in opposition to Yuan Shikai's imperial ambitions, he founded the journal *New Youth* in 1915 and joined the Beijing University faculty as dean in 1917. As editor of *New Youth*, which rapidly became the most influential intellectual journal in China, he espoused bold theoretical investigation, a spirited attack on the past, and a highly moralistic approach to politics through the cleansing of the individual character.

In leading an all-out attack on Confucian vestiges through the pages of *New Youth*, Chen argued that the key flaw in Confucianism was that it ran counter to the independence of individuals that lay at the center of "modern" life. To build a new state in China, said Chen in late 1916, "the basic task is to import the foundation of Western society, that is, the new belief in equality and human rights. We must be thoroughly aware of the incompatibility between Confucianism and the new belief, the new society, and the new state."[17] In other writings he urged the abandonment of the classical language in favor of the vernacular form, and espoused two concepts that he termed "Mr. Democracy" and "Mr. Science." Chen was swiftly caught up by the enthusiasms of the May Fourth demonstrations and was jailed for three months on a charge of distributing inflammatory literature. After his release he left Beijing for Shanghai, becoming ever more interested in Marxism and eager for swift social change. In 1920 he became one of the first members of the new CCP.

Hu Shi, also from an Anhui official family, had originally been a close friend and collaborator of Chen Duxiu. But though Hu also advocated both democracy and science, he later came to see Chen as an extremist who embraced "isms" of all kinds without giving them adequate thought. He traveled to the United States in 1910, when he was nineteen, on one of the scholarships funded with Boxer indemnity money to bring bright students to American schools. Hu took his B.A. in philosophy at Cornell University and then enrolled at Columbia University to study philosophy with John Dewey, among others. He began a thesis on the development of logical method in ancient China, but had not completed the dissertation when he returned to China in 1917 and was named by Cai Yuanpei to be a professor of philosophy. Hu became a strong backer of the movement to write in the vernacular cadences of ordinary speech. He also became an accomplished scholar of literary history, investigating the novels of the past as a source for narrative clarity and flexibility in language. In the early 1920s he published a pioneering study of the eighteenth-century novel *The Dream of the Red Chamber* by Cao Xueqin.

Hu Shi

As a member of a transitional generation, Hu Shi felt he had obligations both to the past and to the future, and was doomed to make sacrifices for both. His boldness in some cultural and historical matters existed side by side with his caution over speedy solutions. He followed his teacher, the pragmatist philosopher John Dewey, in seeking an "ever-enduring process of perfecting" rather than perfection. In the summer of 1919, he wrote a celebrated attack on Chen Duxiu and other radical intellectuals, which he entitled "Study More Problems, Talk Less of 'Isms.'" As Hu put it,

> We don't study the standard of living of the ricksha coolie but rant instead about socialism; we don't study the ways in which women can be emancipated, or the family system set right, but instead we rave about wife-sharing and free love; we don't examine the ways in which the Anfu Clique might be broken up,* or how the question of north and south might be resolved, but instead we rave about anarchism. And, moreover, we are delighted with ourselves, we congratulate ourselves, because we are talking about fundamental "solutions." Putting it bluntly, this is dream talk.[18]

Hu Shi stayed on at Beijing University after the May Fourth demonstrations. As he grew more politically conservative in the early 1920s, he tried to find a middle way between competing factions. Like other May Fourth intellectuals, Hu found it difficult to resolve the tensions inherent in his visions of a new China. On the one hand, he stayed with his wife from an arranged marriage, even though he had no great affection for her. On the other hand, he pressed for freedom from marriage constraints for others, and he acted as the interpreter for the American feminist and birth control activist Margaret Sanger when she visited China on a lecture trip in 1922.

Sanger's visit highlighted the new issues that were constantly impinging on China. She was one of many foreigners whose visits in this period had enormous influence on May Fourth thinkers. The British philosopher Bertrand Russell traveled extensively in China in 1920 and 1921. Russell's brilliant expositions of mathematical logic enthralled his audiences, while his ideas on pacifism also found ready listeners. John Dewey lived in Beijing during 1919 and 1920, taught several courses, traveled and lectured widely, and later wrote an influential account of China's intellectual life during the May Fourth movement. En route to Japan, Albert Einstein was invited to China in late 1922, just after completing his first work on general relativity theory. A little later, in 1923, Rabindranath Tagore, the Nobel Prize–winning Indian poet, gave a Chinese lecture tour to present his views on aesthetics, nonviolence, and the construction of rural communities based on principles of self-sufficiency and cooperative labor.

Through the force of such characters and ideas, the May Fourth movement brought changes in consciousnesses that in turn opened new possibilities for life and action in China. Another powerful influence in this regard was the Norwegian dramatist Henrik Ibsen, whose plays were widely performed and

---

* A group of militarists and politicians who played a prominent role in Beijing politics at this time.

admired in China at this time. In 1918, a special issue of *New Youth* devoted to Ibsen made a generation of young people aware of the playwright's fundamental criticism of bourgeois hypocrisy and his powerful advocacy of women's emancipation. A full translation of Ibsen's play *A Doll's House* was printed in the 1918 issue, and the central figure, Nora, who decides at the play's end to leave her husband and seek her own destiny, became a cultural and personal symbol to young Chinese women.

The writer Lu Xun observed what he called "the Nora phenomenon" with sympathy but also with some anxiety. In a 1923 address at a women's college, he posed the question: "What Happens after Nora Leaves Home?" He warned his listeners not to forget the realities of the society in which they were still living. Women could overthrow the shackles of marriage and home, but until they gained a level of economic independence and equality, their sense of freedom would be a sham. For their part, men would not yield their economic control lightly, he pointed out. "I have assumed Nora to be an ordinary woman," Lu Xun added shrewdly. "If she is someone exceptional who prefers to dash off to sacrifice herself, that is a different matter."[19]

Lu Xun had emerged as the most brilliant writer of the May Fourth movement, and his words were guaranteed an attentive audience. After many years of failed endeavors—as a medical student and a translator in Japan, as a minor bureaucrat and antiquarian in his native Zhejiang province and in Beijing—he found his full voice in 1917, when he was thirty-five years old. Most of his greatest stories were published between that year and 1921, including the famous "True Story of Ah Q," which portrayed the 1911 revolution as a muddled and inconclusive event, one controlled by charlatans and resulting in the deaths of the ignorant and the gullible. Lu Xun saw it as his task to direct the searching beam of his critical gaze onto the cultural backwardness and moral cowardice of the Chinese people. He was harsh in his criticisms and often pessimistic in tone, even though his stories are full of compassion. He had come to understand his mission as a writer, he told a friend, through this image: he was a man standing outside a great iron box in which the people of China had fallen asleep. If he did nothing, they would all suffocate; if he banged and banged on the outside of the box, he would awaken the sleepers within, who might then be able to free themselves. Even if they could not escape, they would at least be conscious of their fate. The central idea here was not far from Mao Zedong's in his essays on Miss Zhao, but whereas Lu Xun believed that through his work the Chinese at least would die thinking, Mao had insisted that they die fighting.

Lu Xun hated the Confucian legacy and attacked it with bitter satire. He constantly reiterated the "Ah Q" theme, that the "revolution of 1911" had changed nothing of significance but had just brought a new set of scoundrels into office. He felt that revolutionary political activism might one day bring about constructive social change, but he feared that the admixture of progressive thought with superstition and apathy made that possibility remote. Lu Xun lamented the difficulties of speaking across class lines, and of keeping any hope alive in a fragmented society. In the beautiful ending to one of his finest stories, "My Old Home," published in 1921, he mused aloud that "hope cannot be said to exist, nor can it be said not to exist. It is just like roads across the earth. For actually the earth had no roads to begin with, but when many people pass one way, a road is made."[20]

This was as much a central statement of May Fourth movement thinking as Hu Shi's, although more ambiguous and perhaps more pessimistic. But like other prominent figures in the movement who were aged thirty or older, Lu Xun largely confined his actions to the domain of words. When Chen Duxiu began passing out forbidden words with his hands and was arrested for it, this marked a new stage of activism. Younger students with bolder visions of the future seized on this activist strain and claimed the need to expand it further. For them, it was gratifying that their predecessors had believed they could "overturn the earth with their pens." But for these younger radicals the true meaning of May Fourth lay in the recognition that the time had come "to struggle against the forces of darkness with our bare fists."[21]

THE COMINTERN AND THE BIRTH OF THE CCP

If China's youth were going to fight the forces of darkness with their bare fists, they would need a carefully thought-out plan of attack. The outline for one such plan was slowly becoming visible through the labors of the Communist Party of the Soviet Union, even though the Russian revolutionaries had encountered difficulties enough to dismay all but the most determined. Fighting against White Russian forces was bitter and protracted following the Bolshevik seizure of power in 1917. The hostility of many foreign nations was unremitting. Economically, the new Soviet Union was in chaos. Perhaps most disappointingly, workers' movements in Germany, Hungary, and Turkey were savagely suppressed, and there was no succeeding wave of socialist revolutions elsewhere in the industrial world, as many theorists had posited there would be.

In an attempt to encourage socialist revolutions in other countries, Lenin established the Third International of the Communist party (the Comintern) in 1919, and its first congress was held in March that year.[*] Even though

---

* The Second Socialist International, with which Sun Yat-sen had been affiliated, had dissolved in 1915.

all the delegates were Russian or European, they issued a manifesto to the "proletarians of the whole world" in which they praised the Soviet form of government, urged other Communist parties to fight strongly against non-Communist labor movements, and expressed support for all colonial peoples struggling against imperialist powers, including the Chinese seeking to resist Japanese encroachments. During this period, when postwar territorial settlements were fueling nationalist movements in Europe and Asia, the strategic choice facing Lenin and the Comintern leaders was between supporting all efforts at socialist revolution overseas, even if that meant weakening a particular anti-imperialist nationalist movement, or supporting strong nationalist leaders, even if they were bourgeois reformers. At the second Comintern congress, held in July 1920, Lenin took the position that the capitalist stage of development need not be inevitable for backward nations if they were aided by the Soviet Union. Peasant soviets would be encouraged in such cases, along with "a temporary alliance" with bourgeois democratic parties.

Even before the second Comintern congress met, Lenin dispatched two agents—Grigori Voitinsky and Yang Mingzhai—to China to investigate conditions there and explore the possibility of setting up a Communist party. Voitinsky, aged twenty-seven, had been arrested by anti-Bolshevik troops and imprisoned on Sakhalin Island; there he achieved fame leading a successful prisoners' rebellion, and was subsequently posted to the Siberian Comintern headquarters at Irkutsk. Yang was from a Chinese family that had emigrated to Siberia; he had spent the last decade of the tsarist regime living and studying in Moscow. Voitinsky and Yang reached Beijing in 1920 and contacted a Russian émigré who was teaching the Russian language at Beijing University. On his advice they visited Li Dazhao, who in turn advised them to meet with Chen Duxiu.

After serving a three-month jail sentence for his role in the May Fourth demonstrations, Chen Duxiu had settled in Shanghai's French Concession. He continued to edit *New Youth*, which had become politically leftist and been abandoned by many of its former supporters like Hu Shi. When Voitinsky and Yang met Chen Duxiu in May of 1920, he was in a restless intellectual state, exploring a wide range of socialist options, including Japanese theories of model village formation, Korean-Christian socialism, Chinese proposals for "work-and-learning mutual assistance corps," and John Dewey's guild socialism. The Comintern agents gave Chen a clearer sense of direction and the techniques to bind together a political organization from the uncoordinated mixture of socialist groups that already existed in China. They urged Chen to commission a friend to undertake the first complete translation of *The Communist Manifesto* into Chinese, which was subsequently published late in 1920. It was also on Comintern initiative that a nucleus of potential Communist party members met in May that same year. Drawn from a spectrum of socialist, anarchist, progressive, and Guomindang groups, they named Chen Duxiu secretary of their provisional central committee.

Over the next few months the movement took important steps forward. Two front organizations, a Sino-Russian news agency and a foreign-language school, were formed as covers for recruiting activities. Yang and Mrs. Voitinsky, who had accompanied her husband to China, tutored a number of young Chinese in Russian; after gaining proficiency in the language, they were sent to the Soviet Union for advanced training as revolutionary organizers. The Comintern agents also formed a socialist youth league and founded a monthly magazine. From these beginnings, the circles spread steadily outward. Under the direction of Mao Zedong, a Communist group was formed in Hunan; others were formed later that year in Hubei, in Beijing, by Chinese students in Japan, and by work-study students in France.

The French group was to be particularly important to the CCP over the ensuing years. In 1919 and 1920, more than 1,000 young Chinese students volunteered for the work-study programs, which had grown out of a range of earlier programs (several developed by Chinese anarchists) that sought to mix advanced education with a morally rigorous, even ascetic, lifestyle. Among the group that traveled to France in late 1919 were several of Mao Zedong's closest friends from the Changsha region of Hunan. They had been active in labor agitations, in anti-warlord and anti-Japanese protests, and in follow-ups to the May Fourth demonstrations in Beijing. Among those who went to France a year later was Zhou Enlai, leader of the May Fourth student protesters in Tianjin, who had been jailed for his raid on a local government office earlier in the year. The youngest member of the French contingent was sixteen-year-old Deng Xiaoping, from Sichuan province. In later years both Zhou Enlai and Deng Xiaoping were to become key leaders of the CCP.

In France, these students lived mainly in or near Paris, with some congregated at the university in Lyons. They studied French in special classes; when there were openings, some took jobs in factories—such as the Renault auto plant—where they were introduced to French labor organization and socialist doctrine. The most radical students, the ones from Hunan and Sichuan, ran their own underground journals, attended demonstrations, and worked as political activists in other ways. One of the Hunanese students in France, Xiang Jingyu, a young woman who had been a close friend of Mao's in Changsha, was active in the fight for women's rights as well as for socialism. Xiang contracted a "revolutionary" marriage with another Hunanese working in France: the two young lovers announced their union by being photographed together holding a copy of Marx's *Capital*.

The students were constantly plagued by financial problems and by arguments between rival ideological groups. A series of demonstrations outside the Chinese legation in Paris against low pay and poor work conditions was broken up by the police, and there followed in September 1921 an attempt by crowds of angry Chinese radicals to occupy the university buildings in Lyons. One hundred and three protestors were arrested and deported. Among those who were able to stay on were Zhou Enlai and Deng Xiaoping, both of whom joined Communist youth groups in France and recruited successfully among the ranks of Chinese in Europe.

Mao Zedong himself might well have gone to France had he had the contacts or the money, but he had little of either. Instead, for much of 1920 he drifted around Beijing and Shanghai, discussing *The Communist Manifesto* and other Marxist books that had just been translated into Chinese, and working for some months as a laundryman. Mao then returned to Changsha and was appointed director of the primary school there. He now had the money to marry his former teacher's daughter, Yang Kaihui, which he did that fall, the same time that he established a Communist cell. Mao began to play a prominent part in local politics as a writer, an editor, and a leader of workers struggling to achieve better labor conditions through the city's guilds. Because his name was now well known to party leaders, he was invited to be the delegate from Hunan at the first plenary meeting of the CCP, held in Shanghai in July 1921.

The dangerous political climate of the time forced the CCP delegates to meet secretly. At first they met in the French Concession, on the top floor of a girls' school that was closed for the summer. After suspicious visitors began snooping around, they moved to a boat on a lake in Zhejiang, where they continued their discussions. For various reasons neither Chen Duxiu nor Li Dazhao could attend the meetings. Since Voitinsky had left the country, the leading role was played by another recently arrived Comintern agent, a man working under the alias Maring. Maring and the thirteen Chinese delegates, who represented the approximately sixty CCP members in China, discussed the crucial issues of the day and worked to draw up a statement that would be in line with the Soviet Union's basic positions. Chen Duxiu was elected secretary-general of the CCP *in absentia*. The delegates then returned to their hometowns to share the conclusions with their comrades, to implement their findings where feasible, and to recruit new members. Since the thirteen delegates were drawn from a wide geographical range—Guangdong, Hunan, Hubei, and Shandong, Beijing and Shanghai—they were able to spread the word swiftly. Even so, the CCP remained a tiny force on the national scene. By 1922 it counted around 200 members all told, not including those overseas.

That same year many of the Chinese Communists in France returned home, bringing welcome new strength to the CCP ranks. One of them, Xiang Jingyu, proved particularly adept at organizing women factory workers. She thus brought a new dimension to the party's activities and identified another important source of party support, since the women (and child) laborers in the large spinning and weaving mills were among the most cruelly exploited workers. But whereas her husband was swiftly elected to the newly formed Central Committee, Xiang was only briefly appointed as an alternate member and then stayed in sideline positions connected with women's activities. Since she also had two children—one born in 1922 and one in 1924—she could not devote all her attentions to party work; her case underlined the fact that CCP policies were directed almost exclusively by men.

In January 1922 the leaders of the Soviet Union invited about forty Chinese delegates to participate in a meeting of the "Toilers of the Far East" convened in Moscow. Despite the terrible conditions in Moscow and a serious shortage of food, the representatives from China, along with those from Mongolia, Korea, Japan, Java, and India, met at least ten times in plenary session. They were addressed by Grigory Zinoviev as spokesman for the Comintern. He told them that only a united world proletariat could overcome the forces of the capitalist powers: "Remember that the process of history has placed the question thus: you either win your independence side by side with the proletariat, or you do not win it at all." When one Chinese delegate, who was in fact a member of the Guomindang, suggested that the Soviets seemed now to be saying what Sun Yat-sen had been saying for twenty years, he was scolded by a delegate from Soviet Turkistan. "The Guomindang has done great revolutionary work," he was told, but in essence it was a "national democratic movement." As such, it was essential to the "first phase" of the revolutionary movement, but its struggle was not the true "struggle for the proletarian revolution."[22]

Nevertheless, the question of allying in some way with Sun's Guomindang surfaced more and more frequently. Back in China, Maring pushed for the alliance, and it was adopted as part of the CCP's manifesto at their summer 1922 congress in Hangzhou. Here the CCP announced they would seek a temporary alliance with the Guomindang in order to fight "against warlords of the feudal type." Once the democratic revolution had been successful, however, the stage of alliance would be over and the proletariat would "launch the struggle of the second phase," which would seek to achieve "the dictatorship of the proletariat allied to the poor peasants against the bourgeoisie."[23] In the eyes of those making these dogmatic and provocative statements, the amorphous preoccupations and slogans of the May Fourth movement were taking on a specific shape and focus.

CHAPTER 14

The Fractured Alliance

THE INITIAL AGREEMENT

From the time of his return to China in 1916 through the early 1920s, Sun Yat-sen barely managed to keep his hopes for political power alive as he shuttled between Shanghai and Guangzhou according to the vagaries of the military situation. While in exile he had restructured the Guomindang as a hierarchical political party bonded to him by personal loyalty and had strengthened his own leadership prerogatives. The revolution would be conducted in three stages, the first two directly under Sun's control: the first would be military, the second, one of "tutelage" for the Chinese people. Only when the tutelage phase was completed, Sun felt, would the people be ready for self-rule under a republican constitution. For a period in 1921 and 1922, under the protection of the Guangdong warlord Chen Jiongming, Sun had been named "president" of a newly announced government by members of the former parliament who had moved south. But Chen disapproved of Sun's plans for using Guangzhou as a base for a national unification drive and ousted him from that city in August 1922.

Before his ouster, the Comintern agent Maring had visited Sun in Guangzhou in 1921. Although their talks led to no specific agreements, Sun seems to have regarded the new economic policies launched by Lenin that year as a turn away from rigid state socialism on the Soviet Union's part, a step that he found promising. And Sun, who had long sought help from other foreign governments and failed to get it, was interested in the Comintern offer of financial and military aid. In the fall of 1922, with Sun settled in Shanghai, the Comintern dispatched more agents to China, and Sun agreed to allow Communists into his party. Finally in January 1923, he held extended meetings with Adolf Joffe, a Soviet envoy. The two men issued a joint statement that, despite its guarded language, marked the emergence of a new policy both for the Soviet Union and for the Guomindang:

> Dr. Sun Yat-sen holds that the Communistic order or even the Soviet system cannot actually be introduced into China, because there do not exist here the conditions for the successful establishment of either Communism or Sovietism. This view is entirely shared by Mr. Joffe, who is further of the opinion that China's paramount and most pressing problem is to achieve national unification and attain full national independence, and regarding this great task, he has assured Dr. Sun Yat-sen that China has the warmest sympathy of the Russian people and can count on the support of Russia.[1]

Only a month later, so dizzying were the power shifts that Sun was back in Guangzhou, where a new consortium of militarists had ousted Chen Jiongming. One great irony here was that during his tenure Chen had instituted local elections in areas he controlled. He had also advocated a federalist solution to the country's fragmentation, rather than unification through military force. Sun saw this as a threat to his own leadership, and on this point he was backed by the Communists, who dismissed Chen's federalist dreams as "feudal."[2] On his 1923 return to Guangzhou, Sun resumed office as head of the military government. Among his subordinate generals were militarists who controlled their own armies, drawn from Guangdong, Yunnan, Guangxi, Hunan, and Henan. Sun's government consisted of ministries for domestic and foreign affairs, finance, and national reconstruction. There was no longer any attempt to coordinate political decisions with the rump members of the old parliament. Most of them had returned to Beijing, where their presence was sought by successive presidents eager to acquire a façade of legitimacy by convening a parliamentary quorum. By 1923 the parliamentarians were being paid $20 for each meeting they attended to discuss a new constitution, and a bonus of $5,000 if they voted as requested.

To stabilize the Guangzhou military government, Sun needed assistance, and the Soviet Union decided to provide it. The strategic thinking behind this Soviet position emerged from the tension between its twin desires to foster world revolution and to ensure the safety of its own borders. In east Asia, the greatest danger to Soviet security clearly lay with Japan, a staunchly anti-Communist society that had already defeated Russia in the war of 1904–1905 and was now becoming the dominant force in Manchuria, on the Soviet southern frontier. It was therefore in the Soviet Union's interest to expedite the establishment of a Chinese national government that would be friendly to its interests and strong enough to check Japan's ambitions. To the Soviets, Sun Yat-sen had the necessary stature; he had also expressed support for joint Sino-Soviet management of the Chinese Eastern Railway, which ran across Manchuria and provided the main Russian link with Vladivostok. Although the Soviets continued to negotiate with other northern warlords, they were not confident that anyone in the cohort of militarists was strong enough to unify the country. In May 1924, the Soviets signed an agreement with the existing government in Beijing to restore full diplomatic relations.

The CCP too needed the alliance. With only around 300 members in 1923, the party was still in a formative stage. Among the CCP's four priorities—national unification, organization of the urban proletariat for socialist revolution, redress of the terrible poverty and exploitation in the countryside, and eradication of foreign imperialism—it made sense to address the national-unification problem first. The Comintern made the decision to work with the existing Guomindang organization, which had national prestige because of Sun Yat-sen's name, and to strengthen it. In this "united front" tactic of forming a cross-class alliance, CCP members would keep their own party membership and also join the Guomindang, so that at some future time they could use the latter organization for their own purposes.

In addition, the nature of China's industrial labor force was in great flux at this time and made CCP goals to organize workers difficult to achieve. Although increasing numbers of people were drawn as laborers to the burgeoning new enterprises, the vast majority of China's 450 million people still worked the land. Each year half a million or more farm workers temporarily migrated into Manchuria, where they produced such cash crops as soybeans for the world market, forming a kind of mobile rural proletariat. Most of the workers that we might term industrial, furthermore, were artisans of traditional handicrafts and were either self-employed or loosely bonded into guilds. Other workers, such as rickshaw pullers and barge laborers, can only tangentially be called members of the proletariat, although some did form organizations and attempt strikes.

Every year a significant number of Chinese—perhaps a quarter of a million by 1922—were leaving the land or artisanal careers to find work in the new factories, docks, or railways of industrializing cities. Wages were generally low, hours extremely long, lodging conditions ghastly, and medical help usually nonexistent. Harassment and bullying by supervisors on the shop floor were constant. Wages were docked for trivial reasons, kickbacks often demanded. Women workers frequently outnumbered men, forming 65 percent of the labor force in some textile factories, and their wages were even lower than that of their male counterparts. In many industries, but especially in the weaving mills, child labor was common. Girls as young as twelve were often set to work at such tasks as plucking the silk cocoons out of vats of near-boiling water with their bare hands, which led to terrible skin infections and injuries.

The strikes that many workers called in 1919 in support of the May Fourth student activists marked an important new development. Thereafter protesters regularly made effective use of strikes as a tool against injustice, even if initially on a fairly small scale. From mid-1921 onward, the fledgling CCP occasionally got involved, but often independent groups of workers took action on their own. The pattern of small-scale strikes was sharply interrupted by a massive work stoppage that occurred in January 1922 in Hong Kong and Guangzhou. Led by Guomindang activists, nearly 30,000 seamen and dockers struck, immobilizing over 150 ships that were carrying among them 250,000 tons of cargo. By March 1922, when the number of strikers—now joined by sympathetic vegetable sellers, tramway workers, and electricians—had risen to over 120,000, the owners capitulated. The seamen won raises ranging from 15 percent to 30 percent and, along with other material benefits, the recognition of their union's right to exist.

Shortly thereafter, in May 1922, two young Communists—Li Lisan (who had just returned from France) and Liu Shaoqi (who had been among the first students sent to Moscow after the CCP first congress)—began forming "workers' clubs" as fronts for unions among the Anyuan coal miners and the Daye steel foundry laborers. A host of similar clubs soon spread in scattered cities. Often with direct CCP leadership, these clubs were organized among lead miners, cotton balers, printers, rickshaw pullers, and railway workers, to name just a few examples.

The costs of mounting a strike could be desperately high. Strikers were fired, threatened, savagely beaten, or killed in clashes with police. One grim example occurred among the strikers on the Wuhan-to-Beijing railroad, which was controlled by the warlord Wu Peifu. Wu drew much of his income from freight on the line, as did the British who ran mines serviced by the railroad. The CCP had actively encouraged the line's sixteen separate workers' clubs to form one general union, which was achieved on February 2, 1923. Harassed by the police on Wu's orders, the new union called a strike on February 4 and effectively shut the railway down. After the workers ignored Wu's orders that they return to work, on February 7 he ordered two of his subordinate generals to lead their forces against the strikers. Thirty-five workers were killed and many more wounded. That same day the leader of the union's Wuhan branch, Lin Xiangqian, was arrested at his home and told to order his union members back to work. When Lin refused, the workers were assembled on the platform and he was beheaded in front of them. Despite a scattering of sympathy strikes from other unions, the railway men returned to work on February 9.

This grim outcome to the strike helped convince some wavering Communists of the need for an alliance with the Guomindang. The coalition strategy was feasible because, in 1923, senior Guomindang politicians were sympathetic to the Soviet Union. Hu Hanmin, for instance, the chief counselor to Sun's government, felt that Lenin's anti-imperialist arguments formed an admirable basis for nationalist ideology. Hu also applauded the materialist conception of history and had attempted to find precedents for aspects of Marxist-Leninist ideology in earlier schools of Chinese thought. In the draft manifesto that Hu and Wang Jingwei wrote for the Guomindang at Sun's request in late 1922, they spoke of "the unequal distribution of property" as the critical defect in American and European societies, and pledged that China would "share in the new world era ushered in by the revolutionary changes in the rest of the world."

The CCP leader Chen Duxiu was more nervous about the alliance. He was just getting the party organized and was skeptical of how useful or trustworthy the Guomindang might be as an ally. Chen remarked that "an alliance between the parties would confuse the class organizations and restrain our independent policy." Li Dazhao, however, backed the alliance: he was less confident than Chen about the presence of a large Chinese urban proletariat ready for socialist revolution; he had also been expanding his concept of China as a "proletarianized" nation to one in which race was a central issue. Li felt that "the class struggle between the lower-class colored races and the upper-class white race is already in embryonic form," and that at such a moment Chinese solidarity against white imperialism was essential.[3]

The cementing of the united front alliance and the reorganization of the Guomindang were both facilitated by the arrival of the Comintern agent Borodin, who reached Guangzhou on October 6, 1923. Sun named him "special adviser" to the Guomindang a week later. Born Mikhail Gruzenberg to a Russian Jewish family, Borodin grew up in Latvia. He began to work secretly for Lenin in 1903. Exiled after the failed 1905 revolution, he moved to the United States, took courses at Valparaiso University in Indiana, and became a schoolteacher for immigrant children in Chicago. After Lenin's seizure of power in 1917, Borodin returned to his homeland and undertook a number of secret assignments for the Comintern around the world. By 1923 he was a veteran operative.

In China, Borodin negotiated skillfully with all concerned. He convinced the CCP leaders that the policy of joining the Guomindang was in their own long-term interests and in the short run would allow them greater flexibility in organizing both urban and rural workers. At the same time, taking advantage of the imminent danger that Chen Jiongming's troops might recapture Guangzhou, Borodin pushed Sun Yat-sen towards a more radical stance. Workers and peasants would swiftly rally to Sun's armies, argued Borodin, if he backed a program for an eight-hour workday and a fair minimum wage, and promised to confiscate landlords' holdings and redistribute them.

Borodin proceeded to strengthen Sun Yat-sen's position and the general disciplinary structure of the Guomindang. Sun Yat-sen's Three Principles of the People—anti-imperialist nationalism, democracy, and socialism—were declared the official ideology, and Sun himself was named party leader for life. Borodin introduced the Soviet concept of "democratic centralism," under which any Guomindang decision, once reached by a majority of members of the relevant committees, would be binding on all party members. Meanwhile, as the flag of his regime, Sun Yat-sen replaced the five-color banner of the Chinese republic (adopted in 1912) with a bright red one, featuring the Guomindang symbol of a white sun on a blue background.[4]

Newly energized, Guomindang organization expanded into major cities and actively recruited members. Union organizing especially was intensified, and Communist members of the Guomindang began to propagandize actively in the countryside. Mao Zedong, the young communist activist from Hunan, joined the Guomindang at this juncture. At the first Guomindang party congress held in January 1924, ten communists were elected to the Central Executive Committee, including Mao as an alternate.[5] Meanwhile, Guomindang members joined the flow of Communist students going to study in the Soviet Union. Chiang Ching-kuo, the son of Chiang Kai-shek, would be among the cohort that enrolled in Sun Yat-sen University of the Toilers of China, established in Moscow in 1925 by the Comintern to train Chinese revolutionaries.

Just as important as these organizational changes was the Soviet decision to strengthen the Guomindang military. The island of Huangpu (Whampoa), ten miles downriver from Guangzhou, was chosen as the site for a new military academy. Chiang Kai-shek, who had just spent several months in Moscow studying military organization as a member of a Guomindang delegation, was appointed as its first commandant. To balance between Guomindang and CCP influences in the academy, Zhou Enlai, a CCP member just returned from France, was named director of the political department. The first cadets were mainly middle-class youths from Guangdong and Hunan— the admission requirement of a middle-school graduation certificate excluded nearly all workers and peasants. Using good modern equipment, they received rigorous training from highly skilled Soviet advisers such as Vasily Blyukher (known by the alias Galen).

The cadets of the Huangpu Military Academy were also given a thorough indoctrination in the goals of Chinese nationalism and in the Three Principles of Sun Yat-sen. Although several of the cadets were already Communists or were recruited into the CCP—for instance the young Lin Biao, who graduated in 1925—the majority were not sympathetic to communism and became fiercely loyal to Chiang Kai-shek. This group of tough young officers were to exert considerable influence in upcoming power struggles, and they gave the first proof of their efficacy on October 15, 1924. On that day the first class of 800, under Chiang's command and backed by soldiers from regional armies, routed a force of the Guangzhou Merchant Volunteer Corps. To protest a commercial tax imposed by Sun's military government and the seizure of an arms shipment they had imported from Europe, the merchants of that city had called strikes throughout the summer. They also deployed their self-defense militias (over 10,000 men) in a series of confrontations with Sun's government. In October, the Huangpu cadets proved their mettle as Guomindang forces put down the insurrection.

The suppression of the Merchant Volunteer Corps made Sun deeply unpopular in Guangzhou. The following month, he accepted an invitation to join a "national reconstruction conference" in Beijing. Traveling with his wife, Soong Qingling, and accompanied by Wang Jingwei and Borodin, he first visited Shanghai to meet with party loyalists. A side trip to Japan was abruptly terminated by illness, and he hastened to Beijing. Doctors operated on Sun in January 1925 and found he had terminal liver cancer. He died on March 12, aged fifty-nine, leaving a brief last will and testament. Wang Jingwei drafted this will for him, but it was not clear if Wang would inherit his mantle of leadership. Indeed it was unclear whether anyone could, since Sun's prestige had been a personal kind, accrued after long years of building a revolutionary organization.

Sun's death, along with that of Lenin, whom Sun had himself eulogized just fourteen months before, did not stop the momentum of the strategies they had developed. Even as Sun was dying, in February 1925, Chiang Kai-shek's army—led by Huangpu Military Academy graduates, advised by Vasily Blyukher, and supplied with recently received Soviet rifles, machine guns, and artillery—won a series of victories over the warlord Chen Jiongming near his base in Shantou, which Chiang's forces then captured in March. Three months later, in another remarkable victory, they routed two other warlords who had tried to seize Guangzhou; on this second occasion Chiang's troops took 17,000 prisoners and obtained 16,000 guns. They were now beginning to perform like an army ready for national endeavors.

Once again it seemed that a new spirit of patriotism and determination was in the air, a feeling heightened by events that erupted at Shanghai in May 1925. This particular crisis was sparked by a group of Chinese workers who had been locked out of a Japanese-owned textile mill during a strike. Angry at the lockout, they broke into the mill and smashed some of the machinery. Japanese guards opened fire, killing one of the workers. In a pattern that was now familiar in China, the death was followed by a wave of public outrage, student demonstrations, further strikes, and a number of

A poster depicting the fate of Chinese patriotism at the hands of warlords and foreign imperialists in the aftermath of the May Thirtieth Incident (1925)

arrests. On May 30, in the Shanghai International Settlement, thousands of workers and students assembled outside the police station in the main shopping thoroughfare of Nanjing Road. They were there to demand the release of six Chinese students who had been arrested by the British and to protest militarism and foreign imperialism. The situation was an inflammable one. Initially the demonstration, though noisy, was not violent. As more and more people converged on the police station and began to chant—"Kill the foreigners" according to some witnesses, harmless slogans according to others—the

British inspector in charge of a detachment of Chinese and Sikh constables shouted at the crowd to disperse. Just ten seconds later, before the crowd could possibly have obeyed his instructions, he ordered his men to fire. They did so, firing a murderously accurate salvo of forty-four shots that killed eleven of the demonstrators and left twenty more wounded.

The outrage at the massacre was immediate and spread swiftly around the country. At least twenty-eight other cities held demonstrations in solidarity with the "May Thirtieth Martyrs," and in several of these there were attacks on the British and the Japanese. A general strike was called in Shanghai, prompting the foreign powers to bring in their marines and form volunteer corps to patrol the foreign concessions.

The tragedy of May 30 was compounded by events in Guangzhou the following month, when Communist and other labor leaders combined protests against the Shanghai killings with the launching of a major strike in Hong Kong directed at the British. On June 23 British troops fired on a rally of protestors as the demonstration passed close to the foreign concession area on Shamian Island. The rally had been formed from over one hundred different contingents of college students, industrial workers and farmers, schoolchildren and boy scouts, and Huangpu cadets. The indiscriminate firing in Shamian killed 52 Chinese and wounded over 100. One foreigner was killed when some of the Chinese fired back.

The rage all over China was immense, and the strike in Hong Kong—which was to last sixteen months—grew in anger and intensity, backed by a massive boycott of British goods. There were echoes of May Fourth in the way May Thirtieth also became a symbol and rallying cry. But now, in 1925, conditions were different from those in 1919. Both the Guomindang and the CCP, or the combination of the two, stood ready to channel the rage and frustration of the people into their own party organizations. Indigenous nationalism could now call on Soviet expertise and funding to build meaningful political action. Perhaps that was Sun Yat-sen's true legacy.

LAUNCHING THE NORTHERN EXPEDITION

In 1924, as the Guomindang-Communist alliance in Guangzhou was beginning to produce its first results, the situation in Beijing also entered a new stage. The warlord who controlled Manchuria was Zhang Zuolin, a freelance soldier of the late Qing who had consolidated his power between 1913 and 1917 after fighting other militarists. Zhang was a tough, wily operator who had already shown the skills necessary to maneuver between the Russians and the Japanese

Wu Peifu (left) with staff officers   Peifu's stronghold, Wuhan, fell to Guomindang forces
in the Northern Expedition.

in order to protect his domain. In October 1924, after a coup in Beijing had
cut into the power base of his primary rival, Wu Peifu, Zhang Zuolin sent his
troops south through the pass at Shanhaiguan. Although it appeared unlikely
that he would be able to use this preliminary Manchuria-to-Beijing offensive
as the basis for conquest of the whole country—as Dorgon and the Manchus
had—his forces swiftly advanced south into the Yangzi River region. This
success, when coupled with Zhang's establishment of a base around Beijing,
gave the Guomindang forces an additional sense of urgency. Their concern
was heightened after 1926, when Zhang tightened his hold over north China

through a new alliance with his former enemy, Wu Peifu, and began to take a strong anti-Soviet stand. Wu Peifu, in turn, solidified his hold on central China.

Many intellectuals now despaired of seeing an end to the chaos. The writer Lu Xun, a sardonic observer rather than a political activist, was among those deeply moved. He was teaching in Beijing on March 18, 1926, when several of his students were shot and killed in a demonstration against the Chinese politicians who had accepted Japanese demands for additional economic privileges in the northeast. In all, forty-seven young people died that day. Badly shaken, Lu Xun moved with his young wife, first to Xiamen and then to Guangzhou, in search of some kind of security. As he wrote in a bitter essay: "I am always ready to think the worst of my fellow countrymen, but I could neither conceive nor believe that we could stoop to such despicable barbarism." He added sadly, "As for any deeper significance, I think there is very little; for this was only an unarmed demonstration. The history of mankind's battle forward through bloodshed is like the formation of coal, where a great deal of wood is needed to produce a small amount of coal."[6] Liang Qichao, who as a young man had been such a powerful spokesman for nationalism in the late Qing, as a fifty-one-year-old mournfully watched these events from his home in Tianjin. Liang wrote to his sons, who were studying in the United States, that Beijing was "like an enormous powder keg, just waiting for something to set it off."[7]

The problem of how to take effective action toward uniting the country was widely discussed by the Guomindang, the CCP, and their Comintern advisers. If they launched a military campaign, they would face the fundamental problems of logistics, manpower, weaponry, and protecting flanks and rear in the advance. But theirs would also be a political campaign, and the problems of ideology and propaganda had to be considered with equal care. The Guomindang could not move too far to the left politically or it would lose its main supporters, many of whom were landlords or industrialists and were not sympathetic to demands for lower rents and taxes, nor to worker agitation for higher wages.

With hindsight it is clear that any appearance of leftist domination of the Guomindang was deceptive; at least four important indicators showed a countertrend. First, among the Huangpu cadets themselves a new group formed—the Society for the Study of Sun Yat-senism. This innocuous name initially concealed the fact that although these cadet members were nationalists and anti-imperialists, they were also strongly anti-Communist. Their view of a strong, united China rejected the Soviet model, and as they were appointed to new posts, they spread anti-Communist sentiment. Second, the strongly leftist flavor of Guangzhou after the middle of 1925 drove many businessmen and former Guomindang backers out of the city, to reestablish themselves in Shanghai or Beijing. Third, the success of the Huangpu-led armies in Guangdong province began to bring newly surrendered warlord troops into the Guomindang's National Revolutionary Army (its name from 1925 onward). Most of these troops lacked discipline and training. They were prone to desert if sent on dangerous missions; some were opium addicts. Although their presence made the Guomindang force look stronger on paper, they weakened the goal of building an ideologically charged and technically trained elite force. Finally, the disaffected members of the Guomindang formed their own faction in late 1925 to try and steer their party off its leftward track. Called the "Western Hills" group from the area near Beijing where they first met, they vowed to get the Communists out of the party, oust Borodin, and move the party headquarters to Shanghai. They preferred Hu Hanmin, who had been moving steadily to the right politically, to any of the other current Guomindang leaders.

On March 20, 1926, another incident occurred in Guangzhou that showed the frailty of the Communist position and the dangers inherent in the alliance. A gunboat, the *Zhongshan*, commanded by a Communist officer, suddenly appeared before dawn off Huangpu Island. No one ever learned who had ordered it there, but the move was interpreted by Chiang Kai-shek and some of his supporters as the prelude to an attempt to kidnap him. Chiang at once invoked his powers as garrison commander and arrested the ship's captain, put Guangzhou under martial law, disarmed the workers' pickets, and arrested the more than thirty Russian advisers in the city. A number of senior CCP political commissars were held at the Huangpu Academy for "retraining," and the publishing of CCP-affiliated newspapers was suspended. Within a few days Chiang eased the pressures, and by early April he declared that he still believed in the alliance with the Soviet Union; but no one was sure how to interpret these statements.

Chiang Kai-shek, 1927

Borodin had been away from Guangzhou since February, holding a series of secret conferences on Comintern strategy with Russian colleagues in Beijing. In late April he returned, and over the next few days he and Chiang reached a "compromise": in the future no CCP members could head Guomindang or government bureaus, no CCP criticism of Sun Yat-sen's Three Principles of the People was permitted, no Guomindang members could join the CCP, the Comintern had to share its orders to the CCP with a Guomindang committee, and a list of all current CCP members was to be given to the Guomindang Executive Committee. Borodin accepted these terms on Stalin's orders. In Moscow, Stalin was just entering a critical power struggle; he could not afford the blow to his prestige that would be caused by the failure of the united front alliance that he had championed.

With a centrist position now staked out politically, Chiang and the other Guomindang leaders developed plans for a military campaign for national unification. The strategy for the Northern Expedition called for three armed thrusts: one up the completed sections of the Guangzhou-Wuhan railway to the key Hunan city of Changsha, one up the Gan River into Jiangxi, and one up the east coast into Fujian. If all went well, the armies would then have two options: to push on north to the Yangzi River and consolidate in Wuhan or to move east by river or railway to Nanjing and the rich industrial prize of Shanghai. A series of alliances would be worked out with various warlords along the way, and, where feasible, their troops would be incorporated into the National Revolutionary Army.

Communist and Guomindang party members would move ahead of the troops, organizing peasants or urban workers to disrupt hostile forces impeding the line of march. This would have to be done, however, in such a way that it did not alienate potential allies, as had occurred in response to the efforts of Peng Pai, a Communist organizer in Haifeng County on the coast to the east of Guang-zhou. From 1923 onward, Peng Pai created a number of peasant associations that formed self-defense corps and developed social services such as medical care, edu-cation, and agricultural improvements; he pushed for dramatic rent reductions— up to 25 percent in many cases. But such policies had provoked a savage backlash from local landlords and were too drastic for most Guomindang supporters.

The Guomindang and Communists also had to plan to provide large num-bers of transport laborers to carry military supplies over the great areas of coun-try where there were neither railways nor adequate roads. Many of these men were recruited from among the Guangzhou strikers, others from the peasantry on the line of march who were enticed by decent treatment and a high daily rate of pay. Railway workers were also organized to disrupt service on enemy-controlled railroads or to cut off the enemies' retreat by sabotaging the track.

Two other central components in the planning were money and military manpower. The money problems had been greatly eased by the skills of T. V. Soong, Sun Yat-sen's brother-in-law. After graduating from Harvard University and working three years at the International Banking Corpora-tion in New York, Soong was appointed head of the Guangzhou Central

Bank in 1924, where he built up reserves by skillful management. Promoted in 1925 to finance minister, he quadrupled revenues in the Guomindang-controlled areas by such devices as taxes on shipping and kerosene and floating bond issues to raise money for the government.

A series of changes in the military situation in Hunan during April and May 1926 gave added urgency to these hopes for a successful drive for national unification. The feuding among the Hunan generals grew so intense that the northern warlord Wu Peifu began actively campaigning against them to protect his own southern flank. When one of the leading Hunan commanders agreed to ally with the Guomindang and incorporate his troops into the Northern Expedition force, the time for action had clearly come. The Guangzhou government thereupon named Chiang Kai-shek commander in chief of these hybrid forces in June 1926, and the official mobilization order for the Northern Expedition was issued on July 1. The broad purpose of the expedition was defined as follows by the Guomindang Central Executive Committee:

> The hardships of the workers, peasants, merchants and students, and the suffering of all under the oppressive imperialists and warlords; the peace and unification of China called for by Sun Yat-sen; the gathering of the National Assembly ruined by Duan Qirui—all demand the elimination of Wu Peifu and completion of national unification.[8]

The obvious omission of Zhang Zuolin's name from this declaration was presumably an invitation to that wily general to attack his erstwhile enemy from the north while the Guomindang advanced from the south. The Communists under Chen Duxiu were not happy over the timing of the Northern Expedition. Chen believed that the key goal should be to consolidate Guangdong itself against the "ruination from the force of the anti-red armies."[9] But it was impossible to check the new momentum, and on Comintern advice the Communists muted these criticisms and actively participated in the campaign.

As the troops commanded by Chiang pressed northward, their new Hunan allies fought a path through to Changsha, which they captured on July 11. Chiang Kai-shek reached the city in early August. Despite flooding, cholera, and transportation problems that hampered its progress, the National Revolutionary Army pressed northward until it caught up with the retreating enemy forces along the Miluo River. With more troops drawn to his ranks from Guizhou warlords impressed by the army's success, Chiang decided on a bold strike across the river before Wu Peifu could send reinforcements south to bolster his allies. In Chiang's words to his generals, the battle would decide "whether or not the Chinese nation and race can restore their freedom and independence."[10] Between August 17 and August 22 the National Revolutionary Army brought off the gamble. Cutting

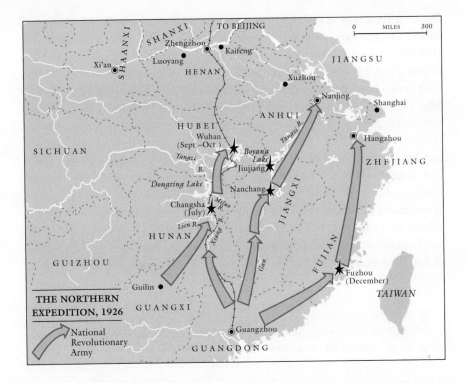

THE NORTHERN
EXPEDITION, 1926

National
Revolutionary
Army

across the Miluo River in two places, they severed the rail links to Wuhan
and surrounded the tri-city area.

In heavy fighting during the last week of August, the Nationalists seized
the bridgeheads—heavily fortified with barbed wire and machine guns—that
guarded the approaches to Wuhan. Wu Peifu had now reached the front and tried
to rally his forces by making an example of those who had lost the bridgeheads: he
publicly beheaded eight commanders in the presence of their fellow officers. The
tactic did not work. In early September the tri-cities of Wuhan, where Wu Peifu
planned a determined stand, began to fall. Hanyang capitulated first, betrayed
by its own commander, who joined the Nationalists. Hankou followed, with
its prosperous businesses and its large foreign concessions (despite his anti-
imperialism, Chiang pledged to protect all foreigners in the city).

While defenders in Wuchang (the third of the tri-cities) held out behind
massive walls, the Nationalists suddenly faced the threat of defeat from the
warlord who controlled Jiangxi. His well-armed troops not only won several victories, but shattered Guomindang and Communist sympathizers by
rounding up known radicals, beheading them, and displaying the severed
heads on stakes. To be considered "radical" it was enough for either male or

female students to have cut their hair short, in what was considered the Russian style. But these acts of terror backfired. The Wuchang commander, with his city full of civilians near starvation, opened the city gates on October 10. While some Nationalist troops occupied the city, others pressed the counterattack back into Jiangxi. Fifteen years to the day after the original mutinies in 1911, the Wuhan tri-city area had ousted its military overlords and welcomed once again the forces of an unpredictable revolution.

SHANGHAI SPRING

In late 1926, the Guomindang and the Communists began to consolidate their hold over Wuhan, and Chiang Kai-shek shifted his attention to the Jiangxi campaign. The fighting was heavy, with key cities lost and taken several times. By mid-November, at a cost of 15,000 casualties, the National Revolutionary Army had firm control over Jiujiang, on the Yangzi River, and Nanchang, the key road and rail junction on the west of Boyang Lake. Chiang made his new base in Nanchang, joined by several members of the Guomindang Executive Committee. Other senior Guomindang leaders, especially the Communists and those sympathetic to the leftist cause, settled in Wuhan. Despite heavy fighting, in mid-December 1926 the troops of the National Revolutionary Army entered the Fujian capital of Fuzhou. The Nationalists now controlled seven provinces in south and central China, achieved through battlefield victories or negotiated agreements. The total population of these provinces was around 170 million.

These victories brought the debate over the next phase of Guomindang strategy to a head. From his Nanchang base Chiang Kai-shek had decided on a drive to Shanghai by two routes—one east along the Yangzi River, one northeast through Zhejiang. The Guomindang leaders in Wuhan, agreeing with Borodin, who was ensconced there, supported instead a northern drive up the Wuhan-Beijing railway. Their forces could then effect a junction with several northern warlords believed to be sympathetic to their cause, followed by a concerted assault on Beijing and the strongholds of Wu Peifu and Zhang Zuolin. Tense arguments took place in January between the rivals. Chiang traveled to Wuhan on January 11, 1927, to state his case. He was not only rebuffed, but also publicly insulted by Borodin and other leftists. He returned, angry, to Nanchang.

The spring of 1927 was henceforth to be dominated by the fate of Shanghai, but the outcome depended on the interconnections among a considerable number of factors: the reactions of various northern warlords to events in the south, the strength of the local labor movement, the nature of the antilabor forces in the city, the attitudes and actions of the foreign community and troops in the concessions, the position of the Guomindang leaders in Wuhan, and the long-range strategy for CCP action decided on by Stalin and relayed through the Comintern.

The speed of the Guomindang advance from Guangzhou to the Yangzi gave pause to a number of the northern warlords. They had been engaged in complex maneuverings and alliances in the huge area stretching from Gansu province in the west to Manchuria in the northeast. They had never formulated a common strategy or reached a binding agreement on how to carve up the territory, but all of them saw the Guomindang as a radical, even revolutionary, force. They had to decide how to respond should the Guomindang seek to advance farther north. Yet when this happened, they remained divided. One of the three most powerful northern militarists, Feng Yuxiang, decided after visiting Moscow to join the Guomindang. From his base in Shaanxi, he pushed steadily into Henan province. Wu Peifu, smarting from the loss of Wuhan and the southern terminus of his railway empire, tried to shore up a new base at the railway-junction city of Zhengzhou, but he had been fatally weakened.

Zhang Zuolin, the Manchurian warlord who currently controlled Beijing, had begun to show imperial pretensions—he made ritual sacrifices to Confucius and had yellow earth, symbolic of an emperor's prestige, strewn across the roads he traversed. In late November 1926, he mobilized a force of 150,000 to march south to the Yangzi River to stem the advancing Guomindang armies. But he suddenly countermanded the order. It is possible that Chiang Kai-shek had negotiated secretly both with Zhang and the Japanese to protect his flanks as he attacked Shanghai. In any case, the Wuhan Communists excoriated Chiang for his "crimes" in this regard, and there is no doubt that Zhang Zuolin had become a fanatical antileftist: his headquarters were festooned with the slogan "Absolutely Destroy Communism."[11] In early April 1927, Zhang ordered his troops to raid the Russian embassy in Beijing and arrested all the Chinese who had sought shelter there. Among them was Li Dazhao, the cofounder of the CCP. On Zhang's orders, Li Dazhao was hanged, along with nineteen others.

Despite these losses in the north, the labor movement all over central and southern China had been making headway since the National Revolutionary Army's successes and the formation of a General Labor Union to coordinate workers' actions. By late 1926 seventy-three unions were listed for Wuhan, with a membership of 82,000, and hundreds of thousands of workers were organized in Shanghai, despite the local warlord's hostility toward them. In February 1927 Shanghai labor leaders called a general strike in support of the National Revolutionary Army columns that had just captured Hangzhou to the south. The strikers managed to bring Shanghai to a standstill for two days before warlord forces attacked, arresting 300 strike leaders and beheading 20.

Worker morale and political agitation nevertheless remained extremely high, bolstered by the lingering effects of the May Thirtieth Incident of 1925 and by the persistent efforts of Shanghai-based CCP leaders such as Zhou Enlai and Li Lisan. The General Labor Union continued with plans for a second major strike, organizing 5,000 pickets, hundreds of whom were armed. In Shanghai, organized workers were a volatile force, possibly capable of setting up a revolutionary workers' government, an urban soviet that might then trigger similar uprisings, as had happened during the Bolshevik Revolution in Russia.

There were plenty of people in the city anxious to defuse the growing strength of the labor movement. A loose confederation of factory owners and financiers, who had profited most from the dramatic expansion of the city as an industrial center and international port, stood to lose heavily if the waves of strikes continued. Some of these financial leaders were linked to secret-society organizations such as the Green Gang, which had grown rich by controlling prostitution, gambling rackets, and opium distribution. For a price, Green Gang leaders could assemble squads to break up unions and labor meetings, and even kill recalcitrant workers. Many Green Gang leaders were also successful businessmen with established positions in the community; some had strong links with the Guomindang or had known Chiang Kai-shek in his Shanghai days.

At the end of 1926 the head of the Shanghai Chamber of Commerce visited Chiang Kai-shek at his Nanchang headquarters and offered the chamber's financial support. In other secret meetings, Chiang's intermediaries negotiated with the heads of the powerful Bank of China in the city. They also held discussions with the chief of detectives in the French Concession, a major underworld figure in close contact with the Green Gang.

Since many wealthy Chinese businessmen lived in Shanghai's foreign concessions, they had social contact with the foreigners and sometimes shared their business interests. The foreigners, few of whom spoke Chinese or knew or cared much about the details of the city's life, were primarily interested in ensuring that a reliable source of labor was available to work in their factories and on the docks, and that the social amenities revolving around their lavish clubs and the racecourse were not disturbed. They also wished to protect their investments—now approaching the $1-billion mark—from extremes of Chinese nationalist feeling that might lead to destruction of property or even confiscation.

By early 1927 the foreign community in China was nervous. In January, crowds had burst through barricades into the foreign-concession area of Hankou, causing considerable property damage and leading to the evacuation of all foreign women and children to Shanghai. Similar disturbances took place in Jiujiang the same month. And most dangerously, in March 1927,

Nationalist troops who had seized Nanjing from the retreating northern warlord armies looted the British, Japanese, and American consulates, killing several foreigners. In return, American destroyers and a British cruiser shelled the area around the Standard Oil Company headquarters to allow an evacuation route for foreign nationals, leading to several Chinese deaths. The British had shown, in the May Thirtieth Incident of 1925, that they would fire on threatening crowds; now they and the Americans had shown that they would shell a Chinese city. What they, the French, or especially the Japanese might do in the face of armed Guomindang opposition was unclear. There were by this time around 22,000 foreign troops and police in Shanghai, and 42 foreign warships at anchor, backed by an additional 129 warships in other Chinese waters.

For Stalin, the stakes in the Chinese conflict had assumed a particular intensity. The reasons for this had more to do with Soviet politics than with events in China itself, for by early 1927 Stalin was locked in a power struggle with Leon Trotsky. This battle was being fought in the ideological and bureaucratic arena rather than with troops, and the interpretation and direction given to the Chinese revolution were central to each man's arguments. Stalin insisted that the leadership provided by Chiang Kai-shek and his forces was critical in the "bourgeois-democratic" phase of the Chinese revolution. The CCP, by this reasoning, must "continue building up a four-class alliance of workers, peasants, intellectuals, and urban petty bourgeoisie within the Guomindang" in order to crush the feudal warlords and the foreign imperialists. In practical terms this meant that the CCP leaders must continue to cooperate with Chiang and the Guomindang.[12]

On March 21, 1927, the General Labor Union in Shanghai, under CCP direction, launched a general strike and an armed insurrection against the warlords and in support of the approaching Guomindang forces. Some 600,000 workers were involved. They cut power and telephone lines, seized police stations, and occupied railway stations. The city again came to a standstill. There were strict orders not to harm foreigners, which the insurrectionists obeyed. The next day the first division of Nationalist troops entered the city, and on March 27 the General Labor Union, now with no need for concealment, held a public inauguration of its headquarters in a former guild hall, with 1,000 delegates representing 300 union branches. In all, according to their released figures, there were now 499 unions in the city, representing 821,282 workers. There was also a workers' militia of 2,700 men, well-armed with weapons and ammunition seized from the city's police stations and military depots.

Chiang Kai-shek himself entered the city at the end of March. He issued reassuring statements to the foreign community and praised the unions for their constructive achievements. While the CCP kept the union membership conciliatory and muted, pressed them to disarm, and withdrew demands that the foreign concessions be abolished, Chiang held meetings with Shanghai industrialists, centrist Guomindang figures like Wang Jingwei and former Beijing University president Cai Yuanpei, and leading Green Gang and underworld figures. These Green Gang leaders formed a "Society for Common Progress," headquartered at the house of the chief of detectives in the French Concession. Using this front organization, a force of around 1,000 armed men was assembled. At the same time, Chiang arranged for generous loans from Shanghai bankers and transferred out of the city those army units known to be sympathetic to the workers.

At 4:00 A.M. on April 12, the men of the Society for Common Progress, heavily armed but dressed in civilian clothes, attacked the headquarters of the city's large unions. These paramilitary groups operated with the knowledge (and at times the assistance) of the foreign-concession authorities, and as the fighting wore on through the day they were assisted by troops from the National Revolutionary Army. Many union members were killed, hundreds arrested, and the pickets disarmed. When Shanghai townspeople, workers, and students staged a protest rally the next day, Guomindang troops fired on them with machine guns. Nearly 100 were killed. Arrests and executions continued over the next several weeks, the General Labor Union organizations were declared illegal, and all strike activity in the city ceased. The Shanghai spring was over.

Wuhan Summer, Autumn Disasters

The news of the April 1927 events in Shanghai caused anguished self-examination in Wuhan. Borodin and Chen Duxiu had the difficult task of fitting the killings of Chinese workers into some kind of convincing ideological scheme. To help them, they had only Stalin's late April analysis of the situation. In this, the Russian leader declared that it had been his goal to prevent Chiang Kai-shek from driving the Communists out of the Guomindang while working to remove "rightists" from the organization. In Shanghai, Chiang had shown his true colors as a representative of the "national bourgeoisie." Thus, Stalin concluded, the events of 1927 "fully and entirely proved the correctness of this line."[13]

This meant that the CCP now had to work closely with the left faction of the Guomindang based in Wuhan, which Stalin declared to be the true inheritor of the Chinese revolution. Stalin hoped that these Guomindang members would lead the "masses of farmers and peasants" to crush the militarists, gentry, and "feudal landowners." Although with hindsight this hope seems absurd, many of the non-Communist Guomindang leaders in Wuhan did have fairly radical political views, and one can certainly say that they were to the left of Chiang Kai-shek and Hu Hanmin. The most influential of these was Wang Jingwei, who had won fame as a young revolutionary in the late Qing and had served Sun Yat-sen loyally in Japan and Guangzhou. It was Wang who had been with Sun during his last illness, and who had received the leader's final instructions.

The main goal for the Wuhan-based Guomindang leaders continued to be the establishment of a firm political and economic base. They were not the only power brokers in Wuhan, let alone in Hubei and Hunan, and they had to deal with local warlords—nominally allied with the Guomindang— as well as with the industrialists and wealthy landlords of the region. In an attempt to win greater support for their regime, Wuhan's Guomindang government had also tried to take over the Japanese concession in Hankou. But that effort had been repulsed by machine-gun fire, and foreign warships in a mile-long line were now anchored in the Yangzi. The unrest in the city led to the closing of most foreign shops and factories, throwing thousands of people out of work. Needing 15 million yuan a month to run its offices and feed its 70,000 troops, who were involved in heavy fighting in north China, the Wuhan government could raise only a fraction of that sum and was reduced to printing paper money, which banks refused to accept.

The Communists, had they been given a free hand, might have been able to foment an uprising in the countryside. In late 1926 and early 1927 there had been discernible signs of rural unrest. In some areas poor farmers had seized the land for themselves, formed "poor peasants associations" to run their communities, and publicly paraded, humiliated, and in many cases killed the more hated of the local landlords. Peng Pai had had dramatic success in forming such radical associations near Guangzhou, until they were counterattacked by landlord forces. Mao Zedong, who had risen to become director of the Guomindang's Peasant Movement Training Institute, also had several opportunities in 1925 and 1926 to propagandize CCP views in the Hunan countryside. In February 1927, after the Northern Expedition had passed through the region, he took the time to study what was happening. His excited report on the peasant movement was concurrently published in a Communist weekly in Hunan and a Guomindang journal in Wuhan.[14]

Mao was particularly impressed by the power of the peasantry and predicted that they would soon play a decisive role in the revolution. "In a very short time," he wrote, "in China's central, southern, and northern provinces, several hundred million peasants will rise like a mighty storm, like a hurricane, a force so swift and violent that no power, however great, will be able to hold it back." The CCP, he noted, could take the initiative with these peasant stalwarts if it chose: "To march at their head and lead them? To trail behind them, gesticulating and criticizing? Or to stand in their way and oppose them? Every Chinese is free to choose, but events will force you to make the choice quickly." In Mao's assessment, it would be folly to ignore this immense potential force.[15]

In this report on Hunan and in other writings analyzing the class structure of Chinese society, Mao joined non-Communist intellectuals and reformers in casting China's past as "feudal" and the villagers of the vast countryside as "peasants," the victims of multiple systems of oppression. In the 1920s, under the influence of Marxist concepts, the term *peasant* (*nongmin*) entered Chinese vocabulary as a cultural and political category, displacing *farmer* in the English-language writings of both Chinese and Westerners. Where Mao celebrated the peasantry's revolutionary potential to overthrow "the forces of rural feudalism," others correlated peasants with backwardness, superstition, and ignorance—they were the benighted culprits of the nation's weakness.[16] But in 1927 Mao's populist vision was not practical in the context of Wuhan's political choices, and it did not fit the Comintern line of continued alliance with the petty bourgeoisie. Accordingly the Chinese Communists were told to dampen peasant ardor in order not to alienate the Guomindang and its remaining influential supporters, many of whom were landlords.

The final statement of the Wuhan-based Central Land Committee, issued in early May 1927, was the fruit of compromises among Wang Jingwei, Borodin, Chen Duxiu, and others. It proposed the establishment of local self-government institutions to handle land redistribution problems; land belonging to soldiers in the pro-Guomindang armies would be protected from confiscation. The maximum size of a holding was to be set at 50 *mou* (each *mou* being one-sixth of an acre) of good land or 100 *mou* of poorer land. All those with larger holdings, unless they were revolutionary soldiers, would have the surplus confiscated.

As it happened, local military leaders solved these knotty problems for the leftists. On May 18, 1927, the Guomindang-allied general who controlled the Changsha-Wuhan stretch of railroad mutinied and marched on Wuhan, cutting a swathe of destruction among the members of the peasant associations he encountered. Although he was defeated by Communist and Guomindang troops, his defection freed others to do the same. On May 21 the garrison general in Changsha raided the major leftist organizations there, ransacking their files and arresting and killing nearly a hundred students and peasant leaders. Allegedly acting to forestall an armed attack on the city, he ordered his men into the countryside to round up and kill the peasant forces. Thousands were slaughtered, often with atrocious cruelty, as the recently humiliated landowners— many of whom had seen their own relatives killed not long before—joined with army troops and members of secret societies to exact revenge.

The Wuhan Guomindang leaders seemed to acquiesce in this slaughter and to concentrate on strengthening their ties to those with military power. Still, Stalin responded to Trotsky's criticisms by proposing to deepen the CCP-Guomindang alliance, instead of abandoning it. He sent the Comintern agents Borodin and M. N. Roy a short cable, spelling out the need for the CCP to shift the Guomindang in a leftward direction while pretending to be firm backers of it. "Without an agrarian revolution victory is impossible," ran Stalin's message, received in Wuhan on June 1. "We are decidedly in favor of the land actually being seized by the masses from below." Accordingly, the CCP was instructed to expel "reactionary leaders" and to mobilize 20,000 Communists and 50,000 "revolutionary workers and peasants" for action.[17]

Apparently thinking that this telegram would convince the Guomindang that the CCP was still a power to be reckoned with, and perhaps to steal a march on Borodin, Roy showed it to Wang Jingwei and Soong Qingling, the widow of Sun Yat-sen. Wang, especially alarmed and startled, intensified his moves to dampen peasant insurrections and curb the CCP; he also began a series of negotiations to see if he could heal the rift with Chiang Kai-shek. Although the CCP issued a contrite statement promising to restrain labor and peasant activities even further, the Comintern agents could see the writing on the wall, and both Roy and Borodin began the long journey across the Gobi Desert back to the Soviet Union. Under immense pressure, Chen Duxiu resigned as party leader.

Among those now assigned the task of stirring up revolution in the countryside was Mao Zedong, whose Hunan report had gained little notice and who had spent the summer—in obedience to Comintern orders—making sure that the militarists' lands were not expropriated. As a loyal party member he did his best to re-arouse the peasants who had seen many of their friends and families killed, their homes ransacked, and their crops destroyed. By early September, Mao had recruited an army of around 3,000 in the countryside and launched attacks on several small towns near Changsha. But his poorly equipped army, composed of peasants along with disgruntled miners and Guomindang deserters, was a pale echo of the 100,000 he had hoped to raise for these "Autumn Harvest Uprisings." They were no match for the combination of the Guomindang armies and local militias allied with landlords. Mao narrowly escaped with his life.

More ambitious, and initially more successful, was a major insurrection in Chiang Kai-shek's former Jiangxi base of Nanchang. Here, in early August, close to 20,000 troops led by Communist generals—one of whom had kept his Communist ties secret for several years awaiting just such an opportunity—seized the city and expropriated the banks "under the banner of the Guomindang left." But they were defeated by a neighboring general whom they had just optimistically invited onto their Revolutionary Committee.

Retreating southward, the remnants of the Communist force settled in the Haifeng area, where Peng Pai had managed to hold onto his rural soviet despite attacks from the local landlords and their backers in Guangzhou.

The setbacks for the CCP continued into the autumn and winter months. In December 1927, the fifteenth congress of the Russian Communist party was meeting in Moscow, and Stalin wanted a definitive victory in China to prove the superiority of his planning over the criticisms of Trotsky, whom he was hoping to crush once and for all. The Comintern passed the orders to Qu Qiubao, the new CCP leader, that there must be an insurrection. Qu directed the CCP to stage an uprising in Guangzhou, where local workers, their ranks swelled by evicted strikers from Hong Kong, seemed primed for revolutionary action. At dawn on December 11, 1927, Communist troops and workers seized the police stations, the barracks, and the post and telegraph offices, and announced the formation of a soviet government.

But the organizers of this insurrection were hopelessly outnumbered and outgunned by anti-Communist troops, who soon rallied. The uprising was suppressed in less than three days. Members of the Russian consulate who had allowed their building to be used as a base for the insurrection were shot, as were all arrested workers and Communists who had participated. After an initial inclination to call this disaster a victory, Stalin and the Comintern accepted it as a serious blow to the CCP, but they also blamed the CCP for having caused it. Among the Chinese Communists, there was plenty of finger-pointing, with bitter recriminations over responsibility for the military blunders and catastrophic losses.[18] The collapse of the united front alliance and the successive failures of urban insurrections would pave the way for a new strategy. As Communist survivors fled to remote base areas in the country-side, the importance of the peasantry in the revolutionary process would be greatly amplified.

CHAPTER 15

The Guomindang in Power

GUOMINDANG GOVERNMENT

These harsh and apparently successful moves to defuse the power bases of the Communist party did not of course mean that the Guomindang had solved all its own problems. National unification remained an elusive goal, and Chiang Kai-shek as commander of the northern expeditionary forces was desperately short of money. The Chinese bankers and industrialists of Shanghai would have been astonished had they known of Stalin's contention that Chiang Kai-shek had shown his true colors by allying with the forces of the national bourgeoisie. In the months after his April 1927 coup against the Communists, Chiang launched a wave of terror against the wealthiest inhabitants of the city. Initially he believed that this was the only way he could raise the funds needed to pay his troops and maintain the momentum of the Northern Expedition. Chiang pressed the chairman of the Shanghai Chamber of Commerce to provide the bulk of a $10-million loan, and confiscated the man's property when he refused, driving him into exile. Other businessmen were coerced into buying 30 million yuan of short-term government bonds. The children of industrialists were arrested as "counterrevolutionaries" or accused of being Communist sympathizers, and released only after their families gave "donations" to the Guomindang.

In June 1927, responding angrily to new Japanese pressures in Shandong, Chiang sponsored a League for the Rupture of Economic Relations with Japan, and began to arrest and harass merchants for violating the boycott. Fines as large as 150,000 yuan each were levied in the cases of one piece-goods dealer and one sugar merchant. Green Gang agents, aided by beggars acting as spotters, made these arrests and acts of extortion possible. Through a newly created Opium Suppression Bureau, the racketeers and the Guomindang divided up the profits from the sale of the drug and from the "registration fees" paid by known addicts. At the same time, the Guomindang actively encouraged the formation of nationalistic merchant associations, which were especially strident in the anti-Japanese boycott.

The influx of money was still not enough, and the Northern Expedition inevitably suffered from the effects of the split between Wuhan and Chiang's Nanjing regime. In July, warlord forces soundly defeated Chiang's troops at the battle for the strategic rail junction of Xuzhou. This, combined with the persistent hostility of Wuhan leaders and perhaps his own personal exhaustion, prompted Chiang to relinquish his posts in August. He used the time he gained to court the youngest daughter of the influential Soong family, Soong Meiling, a 1917 graduate of Wellesley College. Her father, Charlie Soong, had been one of Sun Yat-sen's early supporters in the Revolutionary Alliance. And since Meiling's two elder sisters were respectively Sun Yat-sen's widow and the wife of the financier H. H. Kong, Chiang secured important personal connections through these in-laws.

The Chiang-Soong wedding, celebrated in Shanghai in December 1927, encapsulated many of the crosscurrents of Chinese society. One traditional aspect of the event was that Chiang was still married to his first wife; their eldest son had gone to study in Moscow and remained there, despite the rupture of the alliance with the CCP. Although the Soongs were a Christian family, they apparently agreed to the bigamous marriage because Chiang promised "to study Christianity." In Shanghai, two ceremonies were performed. David Yui, the general secretary of the YMCA in China, officiated the Christian ceremony in the Soong home. Cai Yuanpei, former president of Beijing University, now minister of education, presided over the Chinese ceremony in the grand ballroom of the Majestic Hotel.

In the meantime the other Guomindang leaders had discovered that they could not raise money without Chiang. Sun Fo (son of Sun Yat-sen), who had moved from the Wuhan regime to Nanjing as minister of finance for the reunited Guomindang, found it impossible to persuade the business community to make further large loans, and had to be content with small sums grudgingly provided. The Shanghai Chamber of Commerce became independent again, bonds were not paid up, and opium revenue dropped to zero. Unpaid troops barracked in Shanghai refused to march north to continue the battle against Zhang Zuolin's forces.

In January 1928 Chiang was once again named commander in chief and a member of the standing committee of the nine-person Central Executive Committee. He brought in his new brother-in-law, T. V. Soong, to run the government's finances. By a mixture of strong-arm methods and financial acumen, Soong was able to get Chiang what he needed to resume the stalled Northern Expedition: 1.6 million yuan every five days.

Now Chiang worked to reactivate an alliance with the two most powerful warlords sympathetic to his reunification goals: one was Feng Yuxiang, the formerly Soviet-backed general who had played a pivotal role in the 1927 negotiations and who was now based in Henan, where he had defeated Wu Peifu; the other was the independent ruler of Shanxi province, Yan Xishan. The leading Guangxi generals, who had backed the Northern Expedition from its early days and played a critical role in the capture and purging of Shanghai, were now on campaign in Hunan and not disposed to shift their forces to the north.

Heavy fighting began in late March 1928, with the Beijing base of the Manchurian militarist Zhang Zuolin as the ultimate goal. Chiang's troops entered Jinan in Shandong province on April 30, 1928, and it seemed that final victory would soon be his. But at this point a severe setback occurred. The Japanese had 2,000 civilians residing in Jinan. Remembering how their concessions had been attacked by Guomindang troops in Hankou and Nanjing, the Japanese cabinet decided to send 5,000 soldiers to Shandong to protect their nationals. Five hundred of these troops were already in position as the Nationalists entered the city. When Chiang arrived and asked the Japanese to withdraw, it seemed at first that they would comply. But on May 3 fighting broke out, and the skirmish grew into a devastating clash with appalling atrocities committed by both sides. The Japanese ordered up reinforcements and drove the Chinese troops from the city on May 11. While appealing to the League of Nations, Chiang decided to reroute his men across the Yellow River west of the city and regroup on the north bank. But a bitter sense of the hostility between Chinese and Japanese lingered after the confrontation.

The plans designed by Chiang and Feng Yuxiang called for a joint attack on Tianjin to cut the railway that offered an escape route for Zhang Zuolin's troops, stationed in Beijing. But Tianjin was the site of five foreign concessions with their accompanying investments, and the foreigners wanted no trouble there. Accordingly the Japanese took the lead in assuring Zhang Zuolin that if he abandoned Beijing and retreated back to Manchuria, they would prevent Guomindang armies from pursuing him beyond the Great Wall. After frantic attempts to think up other options, Zhang Zuolin gave in and on June 2 left Beijing with his staff in a luxury railcar.

As he approached Mukden (Shenyang) on the morning of June 4, a bomb exploded, killing Zhang. The assassination was carried out by Japanese officers garrisoned in southern Manchuria, who disagreed with the more measured policy of the government in Tokyo. Their goal was to provoke a crisis that would lead to widespread mobilization and an extension of Japan's power base in northeast China. Instead the Shanxi general Yan Xishan occupied Beijing,

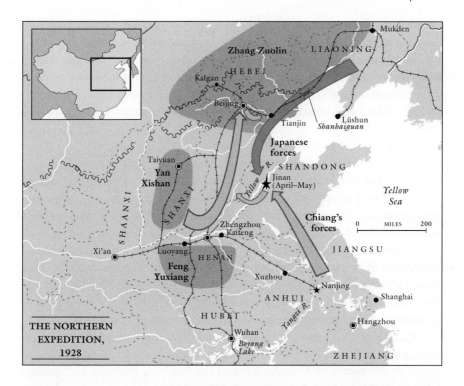

THE NORTHERN
EXPEDITION,
1928

as planned by the Guomindang, while one of his subordinates occupied Tianjin. The Guomindang then pressed for an agreement with Zhang Xueliang, who succeeded his murdered father. While yielding to Japanese demands that he maintain the "autonomy" of Manchuria, Zhang also accepted an appointment in the new national government formally proclaimed at Nanjing on October 10. At the end of 1928, the Guomindang flag flew from Guangzhou to Mukden, realizing Sun Yat-sen's dream of national unification.

The Guomindang's task was now to establish a political and economic structure that would consolidate this achievement. Since Sun Yat-sen had already laid down guidelines for the period of "tutelage" that would follow the military consolidation of the nation, there was little need for Chiang Kai-shek to worry about the trappings of democracy. Chiang's own title was chairman of the State Council, the ruling body of sixteen that constituted the top level of government. Five of the councilmembers served as heads, respectively, of the five main yuan (branches)* among which government tasks were divided: Executive, Legislative, Control, Judicial, and Examination. These represented the "five-power constitution" propagated by Sun Yat-sen, although

* The character for *yuan* (government branch) is different from that for *yuan* (dollar), but they are rendered the same in English.

establishing them in this hurried way, without true elective or popular support, ran counter to some of Sun's ideas about the value of the system.

The Executive Yuan, the most important of the five, directed the central ministries, economic planning, the military, relations with the provinces, and appointment of local officials. Under Tan Yankai, its first head until his death in 1930, it had real prestige. Tan had risen steadily since the days when he had headed the Hunan provincial assembly at the end of the Qing, and was a fine administrator. But as the government was then constituted, Tan still had to follow instructions from the State Council.

The Legislative Yuan also had an extensive role as a legitimizing device; the main job of its approximately eighty members was to debate and vote on new legislation. It also voted on proceedings of the Executive Yuan, especially as they pertained to budgets and foreign-policy matters. Under its first head, Hu Hanmin, it also had some prestige, but its ill-defined tasks and the erratic attendance of its members steadily reduced its power. The duties of the other three yuan, much like those of the former Qing Ministry of Punishments and the examination bureaucracy, were to supervise the selection and behavior of civil-service members and the proceedings of the judicial system.

Chiang Kai-shek's power base remained in Nanjing, now named the capital in place of Beijing.* This had been Sun Yat-sen's original goal in 1912, to diminish the power of Yuan Shikai and the northern generals. In Nanjing, Chiang established the Guomindang Central Political Institute and cadre training schools, the members of which would be firm in their personal loyalty to him. He entrusted the ideological molding of the students to two Chen brothers, nephews of his mentor Chen Qimei, who had helped launch his career. (Chen Qimei himself had been assassinated in 1916, apparently on orders of Yuan Shikai, whose imperial ambitions Chen had opposed.) The basis of the training was an anti-Communist, anti-imperialist nationalism, into which was injected strong doses of a kind of reinterpreted Confucianism, concentrating on the virtues of order, harmony, discipline, and hierarchy. Since one Chen brother was in charge of the Control Yuan and the other of the Investigation Division focused on anti-Communist counterespionage, the power at their disposal was enormous.

In all these aspects of his rule, Chiang constantly invoked the closeness of his personal and political relationship to Sun Yat-sen. The building of Sun's mausoleum in Nanjing gave him a perfect opportunity to emphasize these links. Since his death, the leader's body had been lying at a temple in the Western Hills outside Beijing. As soon as Chiang reached Nanjing in spring

---

* In 1928, Beijing's name was changed to Beiping, which means "northern peace" as opposed to "northern capital." In 1949 the city was renamed Beijing. For simplicity, Beijing is retained here.

Sun Yat-sen's funeral procession

1927, he arranged for a whole mountainside outside the city to be acquired as Sun's final resting place, and for a road to be driven through the city linking the Yangzi to the burial site. The following year Chiang visited Sun's temporary bier near Beijing, weeping aloud in a dramatic display of apparently inconsolable grief. In 1929, with the lavish tomb complex completed to imperial specifications, Chiang dispatched a special train to bring Sun's body back to the new capital. In the funeral ceremony at Nanjing in June 1929 Chiang took the leading role, pointedly excluding his most important political rivals from this politically charged symbolic moment.[1]

Despite such extravagant displays of homage to the Guomindang founder, regular income for the government remained as much a problem for Chiang as it had been for Yuan Shikai. Chiang had financed the later stages of the Northern Expedition in part by ruthlessly extorting Chinese industrialists, but that could not be the basis for a permanent policy. T. V. Soong worked hard to convince others that China must establish a central financial authority; he called for an independent budget committee with the power to allocate funds to the different branches of the government. But since the final budgetary decisions were still to be ratified by the State Council, problems of jurisdiction and special influence were bound to remain.

One critical breakthrough occurred in July 1928 with the Sino-American Tariff Treaty, which annulled all previous agreements related to import and export duties and transit taxes. Referring to "an earnest desire to maintain the good relations which happily subsist between the two countries," the United States affirmed that "the principle of complete national tariff autonomy" would apply to China.[2] In 1842, the Treaty of Nanjing had compelled the Qing dynasty to acquiesce to tariffs dictated by the British; successive agreements kept the effective tax rate on foreign imports at below five percent. For a nearly a century, the loss of tariff autonomy sharply reduced government revenues and left domestic industries vulnerable to the onslaught of imported goods. For the Guomindang and the Chinese public in the 1920s, the issue was a potent symbol of national sovereignty. By vigorous negotiations, the Guomindang gained American assent to a revised tariff schedule, with rates set between 7.5 and 27 percent. Similar treaties with other foreign countries followed, with Japan the last to consent in 1930. The higher tariffs provided an immediate boost to the government's finances. Customs revenues rose dramatically, from around 120 million yuan a year to 244 million yuan in 1929 and 385 million in 1931.[3]

While substantial, the increased revenues could not fully allay the central government's budgetary deficits, as the accompanying table shows. There was no income tax, because of collection problems, until 1936. Nor was there a national land tax, since land revenues went to provincial authorities who were not controlled by the Guomindang. And since it was impossible to tax foreign corporations beyond a certain level, the brunt of industrial taxes fell on Chinese entrepreneurs. The paradoxical result was that some previously resilient companies like the Jian family's Nanyang tobacco firm, which had

EXPENDITURES, REVENUES, AND DEFICITS OF THE
NATIONAL GOVERNMENT, 1929–1937[4]

Year ending June 30	Expenditures excluding balances at end of the period, millions of yuan	Revenues, unborrowed, excluding balances at beginning of the period, millions of yuan	Deficit covered by borrowing	
			Amount, millions of yuan	Percentage of expenditure
1929	434	334	100	23.0
1930	585	484	101	17.3
1931	775	558	217	28.0
1932	749	619	130	17.4
1933	699	614	85	12.3
1934	836	689	147	17.6
1935	941	745	196	20.8
1936	1,073	817	256	23.8
1937	1,167	870	297	25.4

successfully competed with the mighty British-American Tobacco Corporation throughout the 1920s, were driven to virtual bankruptcy by constantly spiraling levies.

A further complication was the overreliance of the Guomindang government on revenue generated within the lawless yet financially and culturally ebullient city of Shanghai, the population of which had grown to almost 3 million. Shanghai was divided into zones, two of which, the international and the French concessions—descended from the old treaty port enclaves and protected by the system of extraterritoriality—were home to most of the foreigners and their businesses, as well as to hundreds of thousands of Chinese residents. A third zone was the main Chinese city, now a vast, sprawling metropolis, heavily industrialized; while the fourth was the aptly named "Badlands," west of the Chinese city and the foreign enclaves, where criminal syndicates and a mixed overlay of police forces and paramilitary groups vied for control.

Shanghai was indeed a hybrid, its expanding new industries and bustling international harbor lending impetus to rocketing opium sales and addiction, rampant prostitution, and organized crime. The French had adapted to Shanghai's seamy politics by making one of the leading Chinese racketeers the chief of detectives in their concession area: his job was to keep out all other hoodlums except for those connected with the Green Gang, the city's most powerful criminal group. There had been murky undercurrents of connections between these men and Sun Yat-sen and his supporters. Chiang Kai-shek, for example, had lived in Shanghai on the edges of the criminal world. He was close to Du Yuesheng, who had risen through the opium-smuggling rackets to become an important Green Gang leader in the international settlements. After 1928, Chiang stayed in close contact with the gangsters—some of whom began to pose as conventional businessmen and philanthropists, without changing their true colors—and made massive sums of money for his own supporters by monopolizing opium distribution through licensing operations euphemistically called "opium suppression bureaus."

To achieve a stable political structure, it was also imperative for the Guomindang government to re-establish effective control over the countryside. This task had been too much for the late Qing rulers and for Yuan Shikai, and in the long run it proved too much for the Guomindang also. The administrative system that was attempted left fundamental problems unsolved, and in many rural regions life was little different from what it had been in the Qing. Local administrators were often tyrannical or corrupt, and were more sympathetic to landlords than to the tenant farmers, who often lived in dire poverty. Officials insisted on tax collection and rent payments even in times of natural catastrophe, and used police or military power to enforce their demands. Crops were still sown and harvested by hand, produce was carried to market on human shoulders; infant mortality was high, life expectancy low. Many girls were still made to bind their feet and endure arranged marriages. Education was minimal or nonexistent. The worldwide depression of the late 1920s brought disaster to rural cultivators who had overconcentrated on certain cash crops, and hundreds of thousands—perhaps millions—died when the markets in such crops as silk, cotton, soybeans, or tobacco suddenly plummeted. The need was therefore all the greater for strong political initiative. Rural reform required a plan for crop diversification, with fair divisions of landholdings, reasonable prices paid for produce, some form of local credit structure, improved access to education, and a measure of representative government. Guomindang leaders were aware of these needs and addressed them in sporadic ways. But money was always short, and the government was distracted by foreign pressures and internal dissensions.

As it happened, the main attempts at rural reconstruction were carried out not by the state but by dedicated individuals such as James Yen and Liang Shuming. James Yen received his first challenge as a reformer and teacher working for the YMCA among Chinese laborers serving in France during World War I. Returning to China in 1921 he continued to work for mass literacy, concentrating his efforts in Ding County in Hebei. There, broadening his endeavors, he created a "model village" where the people were taught hygiene and agricultural technology in addition to a basic reading curriculum. By 1929, helped by international donations, James Yen had developed reconstruction programs in education, public health, light industry, agriculture, and self-government for over sixty villages and market towns in Ding County.

Liang Shuming, a noted Confucian scholar whose father had committed suicide in 1918 out of despair at China's plight, had gone on to become a professor of philosophy at Beijing University during the May Fourth period. After experimental work in rural reconstruction in the south, Liang became director of the Shandong Rural Research Institute and attempted to develop Zouping and Heze counties as model communities. Here, in order to obviate the need for class struggle and draw the entire community into a self-governing enterprise, he concentrated on mutual economic assistance and educational projects that involved both the elite and the common people.

CULTURE AND IDEOLOGY

At other levels, in the late 1920s and the 1930s, when the Guomindang held sway, there was immense change to Chinese life. Medical care became more sophisticated, new hospitals were built, schools and college campuses featured sports grounds and laboratories. The extension of roads capable of carrying trucks and automobiles opened up new avenues of social and commercial exchange. New power stations brought electricity to cities; steamer transport expanded on the rivers and along the coast, facilitating interregional trade; faster trains traveled new track; and air transport became possible on certain national routes. Cinemas became a part of urban life; radios and phonographs appeared in the richer homes; and men began sporting business suits, derbies, or cloth caps, the younger women short skirts and high heels. Sophisticated and sexually suggestive advertising grew common in the new popular leisure magazines. Entertainment and shopping complexes grew more lavish, and popular singers and film stars became celebrities. Cigarette smoking became a national fad. For wealthier people, life could be very good indeed, and to a Westerner living in China during this period these were truly "the years that were fat."[5] And yet a pervasive sense of malaise existed among many middle-class Chinese, who should have logically been the Guomindang's most loyal allies.

Ever since the feverish excitement of the May Fourth movement had dissipated amid the shocks of the late 1920s, members of that generation of iconoclasts had assumed different roles: as leaders in the CCP, as spokesmen for the Guomindang vision of an anti-Communist order, as defenders of a middle-of-the-road liberal tradition, as espousers of a rigorous academic methodology, or as proponents of a free-spirited and hedonistic way of life. They could live on the prestige brought by their past classical training, their participation—however remotely—in the drama of late Qing reform movements and the dynasty's fall, or their deep knowledge of one or more foreign cultures. Those who had been teenagers or younger at the time of the May Fourth movement faced the same general range of goals to strive for, but the way toward achieving those goals now seemed less clear. These people felt a deeper sense of dislocation than their elders, for the easier battles had been won; what on earth were they to do with the muddled legacy left to them?

The stakes were high and the issues deadly serious, as can be seen from the case of two young writers: Ding Ling and her husband, Hu Yepin. Ding Ling, born in 1904 to a gentry family in Hunan and educated in the modern schools of Changsha, had been inspired by the dreams for a new China that lay at the heart of the May Fourth movement. She was close friends with many of the students who went off to France in 1919, including several who joined the CCP there. In 1922, Ding Ling traveled first to Nanjing and Shanghai, and then to Beijing. There she lived an emancipated life with the aspiring poet Hu Yepin among a sprawling group of writers and artists, apparently the very model of a Nora who had successfully left home.

In late 1927 Ding Ling published her first major short story. It related the travails of Meng Ke, a naïve country girl who moves gingerly through the world of wealthy Shanghai sophisticates, over-Westernized aesthetes, and dogmatic radicals. She finally settles—by luck rather than good judgment—into a successful career as a movie actress, but in her triumph Meng Ke has been dehumanized, made into an object for the gratification of the male world. In an even more successful story entitled "The Diary of Miss Sophie" and published the following year, Ding Ling presented, through the eyes of the protagonist, a bitter view of loneliness and frustration. Sophie's restlessness is so deep that it makes her physically ill; her petulance alienates even her most loyal friends; she purposefully pursues erotic attachments so as to humiliate herself. In the closing lines of this powerful, dispiriting story, Sophie reflects on what the future has to offer:

> I've defiled myself. Man is his own fiercest enemy. My heaven, how shall I begin to revenge and retrieve all I've lost? Life has been my own toy. I've wasted enough of it away, so it is of no material importance that this new experience has plunged me into a new abyss. I don't want to stay in Beijing and I don't want to go to the Western Hills. I'm going to take the train southward where no one knows me and waste away what's left of my life. Out of the pain, my heart revives. And now I look on myself with pity and I laugh.
>
> Live and die your own way, unnoticed. Oh, how I pity you, Sophie![6]

As Ding Ling's reputation grew, Hu Yepin wrote poetry and short stories, too, which Ding Ling helped him publish with her earnings. Both of them responded to the country's turmoil by moving left politically. Hu joined the CCP first, in 1930, and wrote an emotional, exaggerated novel on the May Thirtieth Incident of 1925, which in fact he had not witnessed. At the end of 1930, Hu determined to go to the Communist base in Jiangxi. In January 1931, just after Ding Ling had given birth to their first child, he was arrested by British police at a secret meeting of the CCP in the concession area of Shanghai and handed over to the Guomindang. There is evidence that a rival faction within the CCP betrayed Hu and his friends. After a brief investigation he was shot, along with twenty-two comrades, at the Guomindang garrison command headquarters near Shanghai. Ding Ling's response was to travel back to her home in Hunan and leave her baby with her mother, before returning to Shanghai and herself joining the CCP.

The young may have sought to further the cause of social justice by joining the CCP, but they found little cultural freedom once they became members. To the contrary: since 1930 the world of leftist creativity in China had been dominated by Soviet views of political aesthetics as transmitted through the League of Left-Wing Writers. The Chinese leaders of this league followed the cultural line laid down by Stalin, which gave its own didactic definitions of how the world should be viewed and where political priorities lay. The basic Stalinist premise was that to be "correct," any depiction of social reality must illuminate class relationships and leave no ambiguities about the direction and purpose of the socialist revolution.

Lu Xun, who of all the May Fourth writers was the most revered among the young, joined the league himself in 1930 but found it and its rules stifling. The Soviet idea of a perfect poem, Lu Xun wrote sarcastically, was

> Oh, steam whistle!
> Oh, Lenin![7]

and the Chinese members of the league, he observed, slavishly followed Russian guidelines while indulging in vengeful backbiting among themselves. Though constantly wooed by the CCP, Lu Xun refused to join its ranks. Instead, right up to his death from tuberculosis in 1936, he tried to encourage younger writers to hold on to a sense of the main issues in Chinese culture, to maintain an acute social conscience, and to never lose their sense of the ridiculous.

Yet many—perhaps most—educated young Chinese did not lose heart and hope. They were absorbed by the intellectual possibilities of the new age, and anxious to make use of their knowledge and skills. As one among other countless examples, we can point to Liang Qichao's son Liang Sicheng, who studied the architectural structures of China's ancient temples and palaces. With his wife, the scholar-poet and art historian Lin Huiyin, he embarked on travels across the country to locate, photograph, sketch—and, if possible, preserve—the choicest items of China's artistic heritage.

It was obvious to Chiang Kai-shek and his advisers that if the students, the intellectuals, and especially the urban workers were to be convinced by Guomindang claims that it was striving to fulfill the mission of national unification and economic reconstruction, some means more compelling than intellectual repression and repeated attacks on the Communists would have to be found. By early 1934 Chiang began to develop such a new ideology, drawing on the doctrines of Sun Yat-sen, the social reform strategies of foreign missionaries, and his own views of the central tenets of Confucianism, especially with regard to loyalty and morality. Chiang named this set of beliefs the New Life Movement, and clearly expected great things from it. He declared that it would create "a new national consciousness and mass psychology"; the revived force of four key virtues—propriety, righteousness, integrity, and sense of shame—would lead to China's "social regeneration."[8]

Chiang launched the crusade for New Life in Nanchang, during what turned out to be the final suppression campaign against the Communist base in the Jiangxi Soviet. From Nanchang, Guomindang party organizations and youth corps spread the movement to other provinces, using mass communications such as lectures, pamphlets, parades, plays, and movies. Hygiene and public health received special scrutiny, with inspectors and police deputized to ensure compliance with rules on cleanliness and orderliness, including detailed expectations of personal conduct—how people should dress, walk, and behave in public. For women, the campaign's messaging emphasized domesticity, frugality, and service, and warned them against blindly following feminist ideas. As the movement progressed, the rhetoric strongly emphasized themes inflected with elements of fascism. Chiang himself repeatedly invoked the need to "militarize" the life of the nation, with the goal of developing the "patriotic and fighting spirit of the people" and increasing their capacity for productive labor. Above all, New Life would forge disciplined citizens willing to sacrifice for the nation.[9]

To implement this agenda, Chiang relied on a network of groups informally known as the Blueshirts, which shared his virulent anti-Communism and admiration for Mussolini and Hitler. (Their nickname indicated a conscious emulation of Italy's "Blackshirts" and Germany's "Brownshirts"). Spearheaded by cadets of the Huangpu Military Academy's earliest graduating classes, the Blueshirts formed a series of secret and front organizations that attained considerable influence in the political and military leadership. Fiercely loyal to Chiang, Blueshirt leaders denounced the pernicious influence of Western culture, singling out May Fourth individualism for fostering decadence and degeneracy. They balanced clandestine operations with prolific output in their own journals and magazines, expounding on aspirations of national rejuvenation based on the combination of militarization and Confucian values. Such publications effusively praised Hitler for successfully establishing a "fascist culture," Mussolini for saving Italy "from near death," and the founding emperor of the Qin dynasty for unifying the country, even if in the process he burned books and buried hundreds of scholars alive.[10] They scorned those advocating for liberal democracy in China, arguing that illiteracy and ignorance rendered the people unprepared to understand even its most basic concepts. "If we were to implement democratic politics immediately," one writer noted, "it would be just like giving a pair of high-heeled shoes to a girl with bound feet from the countryside and then asking her to go out dancing."[11]

With a strong base in the administrative, military, and party machinery, and with its members granted special roles in the anti-Communist campaign and the New Life Movement, the Blueshirt nucleus developed into a disciplined military and secret-police apparatus that could be deployed to neutralize domestic and foreign forces believed to be subversive. Dai Li, a former Huangpu cadet, became head of Chiang Kai-shek's Special Service Section in the euphemistically named Bureau of Investigation and Statistics, where he supervised 1,700 operatives. Dai Li's thugs were believed to have carried out assassinations of those opposed to Chiang, including the head of the Chinese League for the Protection of Civil Rights (in 1933) and the editor of Shanghai's leading newspaper (in 1934).

CHINA AND THE UNITED STATES

Given the realities of the world balance of power, much of the focus of the Guomindang had to be on the international diplomatic arena. Although Japan represented the gravest threat, the United States also played a considerable role in the calculus.

In the chaotic decade that followed the end of World War I, important changes occurred in U.S. foreign policy toward China. The negotiations at the Versailles treaty conference had dramatically confirmed that Japan rather than China now played the dominant role on the international scene in East Asia. President Wilson had been particularly anxious to placate Japanese sentiment because of his hopes for the League of Nations, a global union meant to guarantee lasting peace. But in 1919 and again in 1920, Congress refused to vote for U.S. entrance into the League, dooming Wilson's dream.

Cognizant of Japanese power, and uneasy at the expensive naval arms race that was developing, the United States decided to pursue international agreements that would protect its own position in East Asia and the Pacific, and relieve the growing tensions in the region. Representatives from nine countries convened in Washington in November 1921 and continued their meetings until February 1922. In the Four-Power treaty, the United States, Japan, Britain, and France agreed to consult with each other before taking action in times of crisis; the new arrangement effectively replaced the British-Japanese treaty of 1902. All four countries agreed as well on the "nonfortification" of the Pacific islands they occupied. A follow-up Nine-Power Treaty condemned spheres of influence in China and gave rousing acclamation to the idea of maintaining its "sovereignty, the independence, and the territorial and administrative integrity." A third agreement called for the three primary signatories to maintain a ratio of warship tonnage set at 5:5:3. The United States and Britain would have five units each to Japan's three. Although at first glance this pact seemed to relegate Japan to a second-rank position, in fact, because the American and British fleets were concentrated in the Atlantic and elsewhere, and because of the agreement proscribing armed bases in the Pacific islands, the treaty was likely to assure Japan naval superiority in East Asia. Britain was content because the treaty did not affect existing bases in Singapore, Australia, or New Zealand. The Americans felt they had limited the scope of Japanese expansion and reinforced the status quo in Asian international relations.

Japan appeared to be surprisingly flexible at the conference. On the understanding that its position in southern Manchuria would not be disturbed, Japan agreed to pull back from the Russian maritime provinces and Sakhalin, where its troops had been opposing the Soviets. With respect to China, Japan agreed to back off from the Twenty-One Demands of 1915, and restore management of the Qingdao-Jinan railway and the Jiaozhou "leased territory" (seized from Germany in 1914) to the Chinese government.

Throughout the middle and late 1920s, American investments in China continued to grow steadily, although they still lagged in pace and scale far behind those of Britain and Japan. Despite increased tariffs on foreign trade and the effects of the Great Depression, the profitability of American investments increased. Much of America's involvement in China also represented an expansion of the earlier Christian missionary impulse, which in the late 1920s and early 1930s focused on education, medical care and training, and socially oriented programs such as the YMCA and its counterpart, the Young Women's Christian Association (YWCA). Yanjing (Yenching) University in Beijing, an amalgam of four colleges originally founded by Methodist, Congregational, and Presbyterian sponsors, was famous for its programs in journalism and sociology. On its campus, Chinese students learned to analyze their own society and craft solutions to its problems, whether through business, administration, or rural reconstruction projects. The secular Nankai University in Tianjin was founded by a Chinese self-strengthening activist of the late Qing, who went on to study at Columbia University's Teachers College. Thanks to gifts from private American backers and the Rockefeller Foundation, Nankai developed into a center for economic and social research. At Qinghua College, originally set up as a preparatory school, funds accrued from the returned Boxer indemnity provided scholarships for students aiming to study in the United States. After the Northern Expedition, the Guomindang turned the college into National Qinghua University and added a college of engineering to its already prestigious colleges of letters, sciences, and law.

Medical advances were also considerable, owing in large measure to private philanthropy—in particular the Rockefeller Foundation, which in 1915 made a major commitment to support a medical school. The fruit of this decision, known as Peking Union Medical College, became a renowned center for research and teaching. Although the methodology was Western and the language of instruction was English, the problems addressed were diseases prevalent in or unique to China. Teaching procedures in the college's beautifully equipped hospital were meticulous and expensive: a faculty and staff of 123 foreigners and 23 Chinese oversaw the graduation of 64 Chinese medical students between 1924 and 1930. But with a further grant of $12 million from the foundation in 1928, the college assured its status as the leader in China. The only close runner-up was the Japanese medical college in Manchuria, which was reserved for Japanese students. Meanwhile, Xiangya Medical College in Changsha, Hunan, took a different approach by pooling resources from its benefactors at Yale University with those from the governor and local gentry. Chinese faculty assumed control of the school's administration in 1925. The joint Sino-American team achieved important results in smallpox and cholera research, rat extermination to combat the spread of pneumonic plague, and remedies for opium addiction. One brief moment of glory for Xiangya came in 1926, when two of its doctors (one can imagine them working rather nervously together) extracted a painfully impacted wisdom tooth from Chiang Kai-shek, who was meeting with his generals in Changsha. Several excellent medical colleges for women were established at this time, most of them run by Christian colleges.

American influence also spread through the Chiangs' friendship with individual missionaries, especially once Chiang Kai-shek started his determined attempt to destroy the Jiangxi Soviet. During this period, Chiang and his wife made their summer home in the hills of Kuling (near Jiujiang), which had long been the chosen summer resort for the foreign community. They rented a house belonging to the Methodist church, and Madame Chiang became a close friend of the landlord, William Johnson. Although Chiang's closest foreign adviser was the Australian William Donald, Chiang had lengthy discussions with many of the American missionaries. (He had been baptized as a Christian in 1930.) Later he relied on advice especially from the Congregationalist minister George Shepherd, described as "the one trusted American" in Chiang's "innermost circle."

Another element making for harmonious relations was the muting of problems related to Chinese emigration to the United States. In the late Qing, America's exclusion laws and the Chinese boycotts of 1905 had soured relations between the two countries. But by the late 1920s, despite new American

CHINESE POPULATION IN THE UNITED
STATES, 1890–1940[12]

	Total Chinese in United States	Number of women
1890	106,488	3,868
1900	89,863	4,522
1910	71,531	4,675
1920	61,639	7,748
1930	74,945	15,152
1940	77,504	20,115

laws that forbade Chinese wives of American citizens to enter and excluded Chinese children of couples nonresident in the United States even if they had citizenship, a kind of status quo had been established. The Chinese population in the United States, which had dropped dramatically with the exclusion laws, started slowly to climb again in the 1920s, and the gender imbalance gradually abated as a new generation was born in the United States.

CHINA AND JAPAN

Japanese policy toward China after the beginning of World War I underwent a number of swings. During 1914 and 1915, Japan's seizure of the German concessions in Shandong and issuing of the Twenty-One Demands had shown complete intransigence. The Washington Conference of 1921–1922 saw a more conciliatory stance, with the return of the former German possessions and railways to China. But during 1927–1928 the hard line resurfaced, partly from suspicion that a Guomindang-Communist alliance would exert pressure on Japan's privileged trading position in central China and its dominating military presence in southern Manchuria. The violent clash with National Revolutionary Army troops at Jinan in May 1928 and the assassination of Marshal Zhang Zuolin in June the same year gave ample proof of the new mood.

Tension between the Japanese army and the various governments in China mirrored growing problems in Japan itself. The enormous promise of rapid development that had lasted through the late nineteenth and early twentieth centuries began to waver and fade. Although the granting of full voting rights to all Japanese men in 1925 and the accession of the young emperor Hirohito to the throne in 1926 seemed to augur continued vitality, the imperial-constitutional government had in fact entered a period of decline. Many believed that the government-backed industrial corporations had grown too powerful and corrupt, undermining the integrity of elected politicians and the bureaucracy. Senior officers in the army and navy felt frustrated by international treaties and a foreign policy that seemed to deny them a meaningful role.

There was a pervasive fear of subversion within the country, and even though Japan's Communist party had been ineffectual, tough new "peace-preservation laws" were passed in the late 1920s that gave special powers to the police in their hunt for domestic agitators. A population that had doubled in size since the Meiji reforms, reaching 65 million in 1928, began to face urban unemployment and agricultural depression. Both were exacerbated when the U.S. stock market crash prefigured the collapse of the market for Japanese silks there, throwing thousands of Japanese workers out of jobs and costing farmers their main source of supplementary income. In 1929–1930 silk prices dropped to one-quarter of their previous levels, and Japan's exports to the United States decreased by 40 percent. In the same period, Japanese exports to China dropped by 50 percent.

There was, among many Japanese scholars and politicians, a complicated attitude toward China that combined admiration for its past cultural attainments with patronizing contempt for its current predicaments. Naito Konan, a well-known scholar, volubly articulated these attitudes. On the first day of the Sino-Japanese War in 1894, as a young man of twenty-nine, Naito had written of the new "mission" to spread "Japanese civilization and ways to every corner of the world." Since of all Asian nations China was the largest, naturally it "should become the primary target of Japan's mission." At times, Naito's language could be crudely dismissive: "We no longer need to ask when China will collapse," he wrote in 1919. "It is already dead, only its corpse is wriggling." But more often he tried to spell out Japan's dreams for China by using protracted metaphors of progress and change:

> Suppose, with the intention to open up a huge rice field, you start digging irrigation canals. Eventually, you hit a big rock which must be cracked with a hammer or even blasted by dynamite. What would you say if someone should disregard your ultimate objective, and criticize you for destroying the land?[13]

What this meant for China in economic terms fitted well with what the Southern Manchurian Railway Company, other Japanese industrialists, and the Japanese army were already contemplating or carrying out: "China must in the first place be so reorganized as to become a producing country of crude materials needed for manufacturing."[14] From the conjunction of such views emerged the idea of a Greater East Asian Co-Prosperity Sphere, in which China and Japan, under Japan's vigorous leadership, would claim their rightful place in the world, even if it took war to persuade the Chinese people of the correctness of this course.

Those Japanese army officers who had hoped that the 1928 assassination of Zhang Zuolin would spark a wider war in north China were disappointed. The Tokyo government took a watchful attitude and did not order general mobilization. Instead, Zhang Zuolin's son, Zhang Xueliang, succeeded to the leadership of his father's troops. Born in 1901, Zhang Xueliang had been an undistinguished officer, an opium addict, and a social gadfly despised by many of his father's leading commanders. He could not have initially seemed much of a threat to the Japanese, and was dismissively called "the Young Marshal." But he showed surprising determination in the summer and fall of 1928 by bringing the three northeastern provinces that had constituted his father's domain—Heilongjiang, Jilin, and Liaoning—into nominal unity with the rest of China under the Guomindang. Despite Japanese warnings that they opposed the reunification of Manchuria with the rest of China, Zhang persisted, and pledged loyalty to the Nanjing government in December 1928.

Thereafter Zhang Xueliang began to show an alarming independence. The Japanese had hoped to influence or even dominate him through two of his father's close confidants. Zhang, aware of this plan, invited the two men to dinner in January 1929 and had them shot during the meal. Late that spring, in an echo of his father's 1927 raid on the Soviet embassy in Beijing, Zhang raided the Soviet Union's consulate in Harbin and tried to take over the Soviet-controlled Chinese Eastern Railway. He was forced to retreat from these acts when Stalin ordered a strong military response. But in the fall of 1930, when a coalition in the north tried to oust Chiang Kai-shek from power, Zhang Xueliang ordered his own troops south through the Shanhaiguan pass and occupied northern Hebei province. This move gave him control over key lines of the northern railway network and put the rich Tianjin customs revenues into his pockets.

Chiang Kai-shek, preoccupied with breaking the hostile coalition, accepted Zhang Xueliang's extended base and confirmed Zhang's command over the Northeastern Border Defense Army that now numbered some 400,000 troops. The two men kept up steady pressure on the Japanese, refusing to negotiate new railway deals, actively working for the recovery of existing Japanese rights, and resuming development of a new port facility in south Manchuria to undercut Japanese-controlled Lüshun. The Guomindang also waged a comprehensive economic boycott of Japanese imports, following serious anti-Chinese outbreaks in Korea.

Faced with intensifying violence against Japanese politicians and industrialists, and an economy in decline, members of the War Ministry and the Foreign Ministry in Tokyo began moves to curb the actions of their army in Manchuria. In early September 1931 the Japanese government sent a senior general to Lüshun with orders that "prudence and patience" be used in handling problems in Manchuria. Once such orders had been formally issued, it would have been impossible for the Japanese commanders there to proceed as they wished. Alerted to the purpose of the general's visit by a secret cable from a junior staff officer in Tokyo, Japanese officers in Mukden decided to act before they received the restraining orders.

On the night of September 18, 1931, they set off explosives on a stretch of railway line outside Mukden, selected because it was near the largest barracks

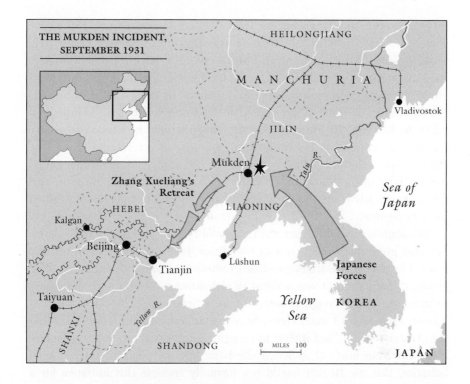

THE MUKDEN INCIDENT,
SEPTEMBER 1931

HEILONGJIANG

MANCHURIA

Vladivostok

JILIN

Mukden

Zhang Xueliang's
Retreat

Talu R.

HEBEI

LIAONING

*Sea of
Japan*

Kalgan

Beijing

Tianjin

Lüshun

Japanese
Forces

Taiyuan

Yellow R.

*Yellow
Sea*

KOREA

SHANXI

SHANDONG

0 MILES 100

JAPAN

of Chinese troops in the region. In the noise and confusion, skirmishes broke out. The senior Japanese staff officer followed up by ordering a full-scale attack on the Chinese barracks and the capture of the walled city of Mukden. The Japanese consul tried to remonstrate but was silenced when one of the officers drew his sword. While the majority of the cabinet in Tokyo was urging restraint, and the Chinese and Americans requested the League of Nations to call for an end to the fighting, the Tokyo chief of staff sent ambiguous messages to his forces in Manchuria. The Japanese commander in Korea independently ordered his troops across the border into south Manchuria, and the Mukden army used current guidelines for self-defense and bandit suppression to extend the scope of its actions. Chiang Kai-shek, who faced a crisis among his supporters, could not afford another large-scale conflict. Instead he ordered Zhang Xueliang not to risk his troops in pitched battles and to withdraw south of the Great Wall. By year's end, Manchuria was under complete Japanese control.

The question of who might lead this potential new "country" was swiftly solved. Since 1925 the former child emperor Puyi had been living in the Japanese concession in Tianjin. Twelve days after the "Mukden Incident,"

Japanese representatives went to Tianjin to confer with him. Talks continued in October, with the Japanese assuring Puyi that they had merely acted against Zhang Xueliang and his troops, and that they wished to help the inhabitants of Manchuria create an independent state. Apparently convinced by these arguments, and perhaps stirred by dreams of restoring his family's imperial glory, Puyi agreed to be smuggled out of Tianjin and taken to Lüshun. In March 1932, after negotiations had failed to secure Japanese agreement to his being the "emperor" of a revived Great Qing, Puyi accepted the title "chief executive" of the state of Manchukuo, which meant "land of the Manchus." A number of former Manchu grandees and Chinese officials from the Qing court came to join him as he established his new regime.

Although it was slow to act, the League of Nations did not let these developments go unquestioned, and in November 1931 it ordered a commission headed by the British statesman Lord Lytton to examine the situation. The United States, though not willing to risk armed intervention, attempted to influence other foreign powers to take a firm stance. President Herbert Hoover's secretary of state, Henry Stimson, announced in January 1932 that the Americans did "not intend to recognize any situation, treaty or agreement" in Manchuria that defied the basic laws of peaceful international behavior. But the British would not formally endorse this initiative for a "nonrecognition" doctrine, as it came to be called, on the grounds that "the present unsettled and distracted state of China" made it impossible to predict what might happen.[15]

"Unsettled and distracted" China might be, but the Mukden Incident prompted deeper levels of anti-Japanese and antiforeign feeling among the people. So serious did the boycotts become in Shanghai that on January 28, 1932, the Municipal Council declared a state of emergency and deployed troops for the defense of the foreign concessions. On that same night Japanese marines, ordered ashore to secure their perimeter, exchanged fire with the Guomindang Nineteenth Route Army in the Chinese residential district of Zhabei. Calling this clash an "insult" to the Japanese empire, the ranking Japanese naval officer ordered Zhabei bombed on January 29.

The bombings—which roused passionate world opinion because of the number of innocent civilians killed—were followed by a full-scale Japanese attack on Shanghai's Chinese defenders. The Japanese committed three entire divisions to the battle, but the Chinese fought back with remarkable courage and tenacity. Their bravery under fire, when coupled with the determined defense of Heilongjiang by another Chinese army in the northeast, renewed foreigners' respect for China's fighting capabilities. And since Japan's aggression was occurring in a context of growing disorder at home—the Japanese

Puyi, the last emperor of the Qing dynasty, became emperor of Manchukuo in 1934.

finance minister was shot and killed during the February elections, the head of the Mitsui corporation was assassinated in downtown Tokyo the same month, and another prime minister was gunned down in his official residence in May—Japanese claims of bringing order to a disintegrating China sounded specious.

The Japanese arranged an armistice in Shanghai in May 1932, forcing the Chinese to accept a neutral zone around the city. Chiang Kai-shek transferred the Nineteenth Route Army, which had fought bravely in Shanghai, out of the city and down to Fujian because he did not trust the loyalty of the army's commander. Later that year the Japanese resumed an aggressive stance, announcing its diplomatic "recognition" of Manchukuo in August. In January 1933, after Japan learned that the Lytton commission report, though conciliatory in tone, was not going to acquiesce in the abandonment of Chinese sovereignty in Manchuria, Japanese troops advanced into Rehe. By April the Japanese had effectively conquered the whole province, consolidating their hold by occupying the strategic pass at the coastal end of the Great Wall in Shanhaiguan.

During February 1933, while the fighting in Rehe was raging, the League of Nations finally held its full debate on the Lytton report. The head of the Japanese delegation argued strongly that the League must understand the Japanese "desire to help China as far as is within our power. This is the duty we must assume."[16] He added a warning that failure to understand the logic of Japan's position might lead to a fateful alliance of a "Red China" with the Soviet Union. Unmoved, all the League countries but one—Siam abstained—endorsed the Lytton report, thus rejecting the claim of Manchukuo as an independent state. When the vote was announced, the Japanese walked out of the League, never to return.

The last stages in this drama of Japan's establishment of a base in northeast China came in May 1933. Finding that they could not consolidate their forces along the north side of the Great Wall unless they cleared its south side of Chinese troops, the Japanese army moved into Hebei province. They attacked Chinese troops in the province, bribed local generals and former warlords to defect or form rival governments, and encouraged resistance by secret-society leaders and paramilitary forces. Setting up a radio station on Chinese military frequencies, they issued fake orders, causing confusion in the Chinese battle plan. And by flying war planes low over Beijing, they terrified the local population.

Routed, demoralized, and divided, the Chinese armies sued for peace at the end of May 1933. In the coastal town of Tanggu, under the guns of a Japanese battleship and destroyer squadron, Chinese negotiators agreed to humiliating terms. The Tanggu Truce stipulated that northeastern Hebei province would be declared a demilitarized zone, to be patrolled only by Chinese police units that must "not be constituted of armed units hostile to Japanese feelings." In return, with the exception of the troops guarding the safe approaches to Beijing, as stipulated long before by the Boxer Protocol, the other Japanese forces would retire back to the Great Wall, maintaining

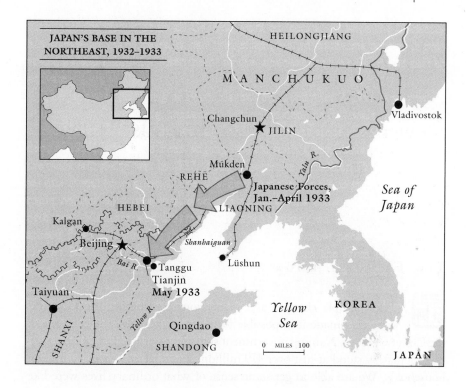

the right to fly spotter planes over the region to make sure there were no Chinese troop movements in violation of the truce.

Within weeks of the Tanggu Truce, the question of Manchukuo's form of government was discussed again—by Puyi and his advisers, the army, and ministers in Tokyo. The commander of the Japanese army in Manchuria told Puyi that there was general agreement on restoring the emperorship. Hearing this, Puyi made arrangements to have the imperial dragon robes of the Guangxu emperor shipped to him from Beijing.

At special ceremonies in March 1934, Puyi donned his borrowed dragon robes to announce his accession at the Altar of Heaven in the eastern suburbs of Changchun, his new capital. He then changed into military uniform for his enthronement. For his new reign title he took the term *Kangde*, meaning "period of virtuous peace." The first syllable of this phrase was intended to evoke the prestige of Emperor Kangxi, who had unified the Qing state 250 years before and consolidated Manchuria's borders against the Russians. But few of the courtiers who were clustered around Puyi can really have believed that the great days of the early Qing were about to be reenacted.

CHAPTER 16

Communist Survival

THE CHINESE POOR

The multiple changes and distractions confronting the Guomindang had made it impossible for them to tackle all the concerns of the Chinese people. Nanjing government statistics assembled in 1936 showed the population stood at just over 479 million, spread across about 86 million households. We are able to get some sense of what ordinary lives were like at this time, since the rapid growth of the social sciences, the proliferation of research institutes, and the compiling of statistics meant that more data than ever before were available on the general population, both urban and rural. One can say with some confidence that conditions were satisfactory to the millions profiting from the continued growth of industry in the larger cities, or benefiting from the rising level of food production through new agricultural techniques and seed strains, and from the continuing expansion of road and rail transportation and distribution networks. At the same time, millions of people—perhaps tens of millions—lived in terrible and humiliating poverty, and were too preoccupied with the daily struggle for survival to look far ahead or brood about the national scene.

Workers with "elite" jobs in industries such as shipbuilding, railway machine shops, electrical plants, silk-weaving mills, and copper-sheet production might make as much as 100 yuan per month, and perhaps even more. But monthly wages in most other industries were far lower, falling to 20 yuan or below in the manufacturing plants for lime, neon lights, cement, alcohol, batteries, and matches. Wages for women and for child labor were lower still, sliding down to 30 cents a day (for child labor in cotton spinning) and 24 cents (for women's work in the match industry). For such workers, even on a six-day week if the work was available, it would be hard to make more than 7 or

UNEMPLOYMENT IN
CHINA, 1935[*1]

Place	Number
Hebei	49,750
Shandong	48,996
Henan	58,010
Jiangsu	411,991
Zhejiang	278,813
Anhui	5,545
Jiangxi	460,300
Hubei	233,391
Hunan	114,756
Sichuan	534,960
Guangdong	1,578,482
Guangxi	1,960
Nanjing	161,476
Shanghai	610,701
Beijing	500,935
Total	5,050,066

* Partial returns only.

8 yuan a month (between U.S.$2 and U.S.$3). Despite the intensive labor agitation of the 1920s, the workday was still long—averaging 9.5 hours in Shanghai (the lowest recorded for any city), 10 hours in Beijing and Wuhan, and rising to 11, 12, or even 13 hours in some provincial industrial centers. Many other conditions made bleak lives bleaker: workers often had to live in company-run dormitories, accept their wages in company notes that could be redeemed for food and necessities only in company stores, or—in the case of women—yield up sexual favors in order to keep their jobs.

Work was not always available, however. As the preceding table shows, even an incomplete survey of Chinese workers, with entire provinces and many large cities not included, calculated over 5 million unemployed in industrial areas in 1935. That same year saw a total of 275 industrial disputes, of which 135 led to full-scale strikes despite a tough government policy against such actions. These were spread across 53 different locations and a wide range of industries; an average of 2,600 workers were involved in each strike for an average duration of almost eight days.[2]

Shanghai remained the city with by far the most industrial workers, and as a result became the area most thoroughly scrutinized by researchers. One study of 390 families conducted in 1936–1937 showed how Shanghai households, categorized by average income and degree of work skill, spent

HOUSEHOLD EXPENDITURES, SHANGHAI, 1936–1937[3]

Workers' degree of skills	Food	Rent	Clothing	Surplus	Total
Skilled (average wage = 45.82 yuan/month)	53.49%	13.50%	9.87%	23.14%	100.00%
Semiskilled (average wage = 29.55 yuan/month)	64.53%	15.85%	8.10%	11.52%	100.00%
Unskilled (average wage = 21.24 yuan/month)	83.26%	18.42%	9.97%	—	111.65%

their money. As a percentage of total income, the surplus expenditure of skilled workers in Shanghai compared well with that of American working-class families in the 1930s. The most common uses of this surplus, which came to around 10 yuan per month, were for recreation, religious offerings, public transport, reading material, medical needs, wine and tobacco, and weddings and funerals. For semiskilled workers, the surplus after meeting their basic monthly expenses was 3.55 yuan, a fraction over U.S.$1. Expenditures for necessities exceeded the average monthly incomes of unskilled workers by 11.65 percent, and the balance had to be made up by borrowing or by part-time work, if available, undertaken by other family members.

Of these 390 Shanghai families, none occupied more than one room. The survey gave a thorough description of one tenement house with a total floor space of 718 square feet. Despite its flat official language, the report still creates a vivid picture of what urban living was like for many of the poor:

> The courtyard has been covered in. The main ground floor room has been cut in two by a partition, and a passageway with a storage loft over made at the side. In the front part, about ten feet square, live the lessor and his family, five persons in all. He customarily pays the rent of the whole house to the landlord, letting out the rest to sub-tenants. In the back portion, about 10 ft. by 8 ft., live three persons. The kitchen has been sectioned off and three more live in a 9 ft.×9 ft. room. Upstairs, the large front room has been divided into two. The front part is the best in the house for it has light and air and runs the full width of the house—it is occupied by two persons. The back part, smaller by reason of the passage, is home to three persons. The room over the kitchen has its advantages because it is secluded; this also is occupied by two persons. This was originally a two storeyed house, but two lofts have been made in the slope of the roof. The front one has a height of only 5 feet in front, 7 ft. 6 in. at the apex of the roof, and is about eight feet deep; it shelters two persons. The back room, about 10 sq. ft., is right under the roof slope, is only 3 ft. high at the back and is occupied by a single person. What was the drying stage has been enclosed, and two more people live in it—about 9 sq. ft.[4]

The same report added that these were by no means the worst conditions encountered. To examine those, one could go to the city's 5,094 huts of straw, bamboo, and reeds, where 25,345 people lived—mostly factory workers— paying anywhere from 40 cents to 3.00 yuan per "room" per month. At the lowest level were the damp and dark shantytowns, often clustered on the edges of the foreign concession areas, where the poor lived under the threat of having these frail shelters bulldozed as "eyesores" in the urban scene.[5]

Just as the cities were coming under studious scrutiny, so was the country-side. A new generation of Chinese sociologists, such as Fei Xiaotong, con-ducted field studies of the rural areas, often at considerable personal risk. On his first research trip, to Guangxi province, Fei was caught in a tiger trap and his wife drowned while trying to get help. He survived to produce a series of studies that analyzed China's rural predicaments in terms of the disinte-gration of a harmonious economic balance between the poor and the state. Fei believed such a balance had existed before foreign imperialism and the growth of global markets brought new financial pressure on rural areas, wrecking the handicraft and other sideline industries that kept families above the poverty level. In the early 1930s, the British scholar R. H. Taw-ney concluded that China's agriculture was beset by two interlocking crises: an ecological one characterized by soil exhaustion and erosion, deforestation, floods, and population pressures; and a socioeconomic one caused by exploit-ative land-tenure systems, abuses by moneylenders, poor communications, and primitive agricultural technology.

Another influential observer was the American missionary John Loss-ing Buck, who was largely self-taught in agricultural economics. (Until their divorce in 1935, he had been married to the novelist Pearl Buck.) After he was appointed to the faculty at the University of Nanjing, Buck wrote a series of field studies based on data gathered by his students when they went home on holiday, and built up a large corps of professional assistants. In 1937 he published the fruits of this research on land utilization, presenting extensive data on 168 locations in 22 provinces, and almost 17,000 farms. Buck's work became a mine for other researchers, even though some of his findings were difficult to interpret and provoked considerable controversy.

The passion for empirical knowledge took on major proportions. A Chinese scholar at Nankai Economic Research Institute in Tianjin—which had been given its start by grants from the Rockefeller Foundation and had gone on to produce some of the finest studies on the Chinese economy—noted in 1935 that no fewer than 102 monographs and 251 periodicals focusing on China's land problems had appeared in the previous fifteen years. Eighty-seven percent of those periodicals had been founded after 1933. Cumulatively, these studies showed the amazing diversity of rural China and the difficulty of reaching judgments or offering solutions applicable to all areas. In certain regions strong lineage organizations dominated and created complex patterns of community mutual support; in others, rural society was fragmented among poor tenant farmers who were easily exploited by absentee landlords. These landlords were backed by the police powers of the Guomindang state, and by the control apparatus of the *baojia* mutual-security system, which was reinstituted after 1934. In yet other areas, particularly in north China, the most successful "peasant" was the managerial farmer, who owned a farm of 20 to 40 acres, and worked it in part by himself and in part with the help of hired hands.

Many of these studies described conditions and even social tensions startlingly similar to those that had prevailed in the late Ming. The data showed striking evidence of terrible poverty among large numbers of farmers in almost every region. Millions of men lived at the subsistence level, working as carters and haulers in the slack season, or as agricultural laborers in the few hectic weeks of sowing and harvesting. At these times they waited in anxious groups with their tools, at 4:00 A.M. or earlier, to see if any work would come that day. Few such men could ever afford to marry. Some of them "escaped" to the factories or became human horses, pulling two-wheeled rickshaws through crowded city streets. These rickshaw men were constantly exploited by racketeers, and returned after each backbreaking day to grim tenements, where they slept in rows, packed side by side, in spaces just vacated by fellow pullers who had returned to work. The life of one such man was powerfully rendered by Lao She in his novel *Rickshaw*, published in 1937.

Tens of millions more (the "poor peasants" of Mao Zedong's and other Communists' analyses) owned farms that were too small to be fully viable economically. These peasants "overemployed" the labor of their family members, while to earn extra cash they hired out their own labor at the busiest moments of the year, even though that was when they were most needed on their own land. Still, many had to sell their children or watch them slowly starve. With the surplus of poverty-stricken labor available, few of the wealthier farmers went to the expense of mechanizing agricultural work. Nor did they invest much in draft animals, since the daily wage paid to a hired laborer was the same as the cost of a day's fodder for a donkey. The man could be laid off when his labor was no longer needed, but the donkey had to be fed and sheltered for the whole year.

Poor women, too, sometimes fled the farms for work in the factories and mills of the big cities. Although they also experienced terrible work conditions as well as the effects of regional and sexual discrimination, some may have had a better life in the city than they would have had in the country, where they were bound to a world of arranged marriages, hard farm labor, child rearing, and handicraft work or silk-cocoon cultivation that filled in every spare moment. Even though they were badly paid in the cities and subjected to exploitation, they banded together in mutual support, sharing resources to make their lives a little brighter, and reinforcing each other in keeping the worst aspects of the male world at bay. Surviving police records from the 1930s contain countless vivid accounts of women and children who ran away or were sold into sexual or household service. The police on the beat were constantly on the look-out at train stations and river crossings for such fugitives, and learned to identify the fake "families" of people being held for sale.

Some of these studies showed how, for the poor, a monotonous diet was an indelible part of existence. Getting food was the point, not its variety. One laborer in a village in Hebei, northeast of Tianjin, recalled his diet as follows:

> In the spring, gruel for breakfast, "dry" boiled millet for lunch, and gruel with vegetable for supper; in the summer, "watered" boiled millet for breakfast, "dry" boiled millet and bean-noodles in soup for lunch, and boiled millet and a vegetable for supper; in the fall, gruel for breakfast, "dry" boiled millet and bean-noodles in soup for lunch, and "watered" boiled millet for supper.[6]

One unexpected consequence of the spread of Japan's power in north China was that highly sophisticated surveys were produced by Japanese researchers, whose data—originally assembled for politico-military purposes—have

SAMPLE FARM INCOMES AND EXPENSES IN MICHANG VILLAGE, HEBEI PROVINCE, 1937[7]

	Managerial farmer	Rich peasant	Middle peasant	Poor peasant
Farm size in *mou* (⅙ of an acre)	133	60	34	13
Adult male farm workers in household	2	3	2	2
Land rented from others (in *mou*)	0	8	7	7
Gross farm income in yuan	2,192	1,117	514	234
Net farm income (gross minus cost of fertilizer, rent, wages, taxes, etc.)	1,200	514	247	56
Fertilizer purchased (in yuan)	152	161	114	53
Fertilizer as percent of gross income	6.9	14.4	22.2	22.6
Rent for land paid to others (in yuan)	0	14	35	38
Rent paid as percent of gross income	0.0	1.3	6.8	16.2
Cash wages and board costs paid to others (in yuan)	550	259	80	66
Wages and board paid to others as percent of gross income	25.1	23.2	15.6	28.2
Taxes paid (in yuan)	113	41	22	6
Tax as percent of gross income	5.2	3.7	4.3	2.6

retained immense value to this day. The first survey teams, drawn from military intelligence staff, the research division of the Southern Manchuria Railroad Company, and Japanese students, were formed in 1935 and began work on twenty-five villages the following year. In early 1937 another group of Japanese researchers (this time without military involvement) selected four villages for more in-depth study, one of which was Michang in Hebei.

The data collected in these surveys rarely can be collated across a long time span for the same locality. It is therefore extremely difficult to know whether the poorer farmers and hired laborers were worse off, doing about the same, or perhaps marginally more prosperous than they had been a decade before. It is equally hard to know how they stood in comparison to farmers of the mid-Qing or the late Ming period. Those analysts who contend that Chinese peasants were getting steadily poorer, and hence that some kind of revolutionary crisis was predictable, tend to rely on one of two main types of explanation. One holds that the callous attitudes of the landlords combined with the pressures of foreign imperialism to worsen exploitation of the peasants. These two developments forced peasants who had formerly owned land to become tenants or hired laborers and subjected them to the effects of erratic world markets. The second explanation suggests that population growth, primitive technology, and soil exhaustion—not the evils of the class structure—were responsible for deepening rural poverty. Neither argument has been able to muster totally convincing evidence, giving rise to a third school, which suggests that with commercialization of agriculture and the changes in marketing and transport patterns brought about by trucks, trains, and steamers, many farmers were doing better by 1920 than in 1900.

What does seem clear is that by the early 1930s, a new wave of rural crises forced many farmers below the subsistence level. Devastating floods on the Yangzi River in 1931 created an estimated 14 million refugees and inundated an area the size of New York state. Japan's seizure of Manchuria broke the habitual patterns of hundreds of thousands of migrant workers, and the Japanese attack on Shanghai caused renewed dislocations in that highly populated area. Changes in the world economy caused by the depression slashed China's exports of cash crops and ruined local handicrafts. Guomindang military campaigns and attempts at institutional and industrial rebuilding led to higher taxes. In the absence of comprehensive data, all one can do is acknowledge that the variations of suffering were endless. Nor can one tell with any precision if these poor peasant families—any more than their urban counterparts—knew or cared much about Communist policies or the threatening clouds of war. But it was in such a context of widespread poverty and frustration that the Communists—who had seemed to be almost wiped out in 1927—were able to regroup, and to rethink their revolutionary strategies.

MAO ZEDONG AND THE RURAL SOVIETS

Because of the failure of the Autumn Harvest Uprisings in 1927 and his abandonment of the attempt to seize Changsha, Mao Zedong was censured by the CCP Central Committee. In November 1927 he was dismissed from his position on that committee, and even from his membership in the Hunan provincial committee. But Mao probably did not learn of these chastisements for several months, since he had fled with other survivors—perhaps 1,000 in all—into the isolated Jinggang Mountains on the border between Hunan and Jiangxi. Just as in the Qing, so in the 1920s the safest fugitive hideouts were in border regions where different administrative zones met, inhibiting coordinated counterattacks by the forces of the state. In this case, the "state" was still a fragmented entity, and Mao's enemies were warlord troops bound by various types of alliance to the Guomindang, as well as the Guomindang itself.

Mao's actions during this period were often dictated by practical rather than theoretical considerations. Just before the Autumn Harvest Uprisings, he had told the Central Committee that he wished to give up all pretense of loyalty to the Guomindang and that he favored the immediate formation of strong peasant soviets and the thorough confiscation and redistribution of land. The Central Committee rejected these positions at the time, but by the end of 1927, following changes in Stalin's stated policies, the Central Committee endorsed all three positions and added that the party should also support uprisings in the countryside. The purpose of these uprisings would not be to establish stable bases, but to keep the masses at a high pitch of revolutionary awareness and to instill that same awareness in the armed forces involved.

By the time the Central Committee had come to these decisions, however, Mao's experiences in Jinggang had led him to abandon essentially all of them. Although he did form communist cells in the five villages within the 250-kilometer circumference that he controlled, order some landlords killed, and try to organize soviets, he ran into sustained resistance from the richer peasants and from the lineage organizations that dominated the communities. In the face of this opposition, he did not try to redistribute land in relation to each person's work capacity. Mao instead buttressed his strength by joining forces with two of the area's bandit chiefs, who were members of secret societies affiliated with the Triads. With their 600 men added to his troops, Mao now led a force drawn from the ranks of the dispossessed and "classless" members of society. Mao had written about these people with his customary forcefulness the year before: "They can be divided into soldiers, bandits, robbers, beggars, and prostitutes," five categories of people with different names and social status, he observed. "Each of them is a 'human being' having five senses and four limbs.

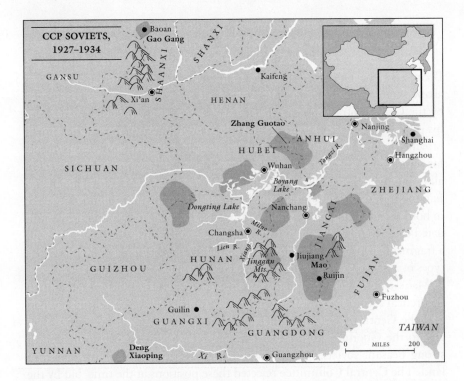

CCP SOVIETS, 1927–1934

They each have their different ways of making a living.... But to the extent that they all seek to make a livelihood and get food to eat, they are all one. They lead the most precarious existence of any human being." The number of such "vagrants" was "fearfully large, probably more than 20 million," Mao added. "These people are capable of fighting very bravely, and, if a method can be found for leading them, they can become a revolutionary force."[8]

Although Mao's Jinggang forces were greatly strengthened by the arrival of Communist fugitives from the fighting in south China in 1927, they suffered constant attacks by Guomindang armies, and often had to send precious troops to aid in CCP battles elsewhere. This was in line with the policies endorsed by the sixth CCP congress, which met in Moscow in the summer of 1928 because conditions in China itself were so dangerous. That congress, echoing Stalin's instructions, had stated that even though at present there was no revolutionary rising tide, armed insurrections must continue, and more soviets must be formed under the leadership of the proletariat. Such orders were essentially meaningless, since union members loyal to the Communists now numbered fewer than 32,000 in the whole country, and only 10 percent of the CCP were proletarians, according to Zhou Enlai. By 1929 the figure had dropped to 3 percent.

At the end of 1928 the sustained level of Guomindang attacks forced Mao to abandon the Jinggang Mountains. After moving steadily eastward, first across Jiangxi and then into western Fujian, the fugitives finally settled in a mountainous area between the two provinces. Here they made the town of Ruijin their new base and the center of a new regime, the Jiangxi Soviet, which was to endure until 1934.

It should not be imagined that Mao, with preternatural cunning, had seized on the two places in China where speedy formation of soviets was possible, nor, on the other hand, that the whole of rural China was seething with peasant hatred of landlords. It is true that during the 1920s and early 1930s there were thousands of incidents in which the poor used violence against local authorities—either in small or large groups, out of anger or desperation. But these attacks were mainly against the representatives of the state: the civil and military officials who gouged them with high taxes and surcharges, conscripted their labor without adequate compensation, compulsorily purchased their land for public-works projects, or forced them either to plant or uproot their opium-producing poppies, depending on the vagaries of the local and national drug trade. There were, comparatively, far fewer cases of violence against landlords, although these did occur. Since most resident landlords depended for their rents on some degree of tenant prosperity and contentment, such anger was usually directed against absentee-landlords' managers or bailiffs when they tried to extract high rents in hard times. The skill of organizers like Mao lay in transforming a largely fiscal discontent into class warfare, allowing them to push effectively for revolutionary change.

In late spring 1930 Mao Zedong greatly strengthened his knowledge of rural conditions by undertaking a meticulous examination of Xunwu county in Jiangxi. From this report we can see how far he had advanced in analytical sophistication since he had written the excited Hunan report on the peasantry in February 1927. Now, in the Xunwu, Mao probed for details of everyday life and searched for precise gradations within the complex layering of rural work and landownership. Broad generalizations about "the proletariat" and "expropriation" gave way to painstaking analysis of the variety of businesses in small county towns, and of the income derived from them. Mao studied salt, cooking oil, and soybean sales; butchers and wine makers; cigarette, umbrella, and fireworks peddlers; furniture and bean curd makers; boardinghouse keepers, ironsmiths, watch repairers, and prostitutes. He observed the rhythms of local markets, the relative strengths of different lineage organizations, and the distribution and wealth of Buddhist and Daoist temples and other religious associations, as well as the number of active Christian proselytizers (there were thirteen—ten Protestant and three Catholic).

Mao also tried to gauge levels of exploitation so that he could analyze class tensions more accurately. He computed the number of prostitutes in Xunwu city and discovered that there were about 30 in a total population of 2,684. He sought out poor peasants who had been forced to sell their children to pay their debts, and found out the prices and ages of the children when they were sold. His investigation revealed the callousness of creditors: "On hearing that a borrower has sold a son, lenders will hurry to the borrower's house and force the borrower to repay his loan. The lender will cruelly shout to the borrower: 'You have sold your son. Why don't you repay me?'"[9] Mao also examined land-owning and tenancy practices, conveying his results in a detailed table with categories based on rental income and means of subsistence, rather than simply on acreage of individual holdings.

In the past, temples, lineage organizations, and other groups had owned 40 percent of Xunwu's land, landlords owned 30 percent, and peasants owned the remaining 30 percent. Mao showed an acute sense of the criteria that should be used in land redistribution. While noting that in a revolutionary situation most land was allocated on a per capita basis, he was aware of the arguments for distributing some land based on the ability to work. He also recognized the needs of women, who often contributed more than men to the land; the problems posed by former monks and other categories of the needy; and difficulties in deciding how to divide up houses, fishponds, and mountainous or forested areas.

In the area of military planning, too, Mao grew more experienced. His main teacher was Zhu De, a Sichuanese soldier of fortune and former opium addict. After mending his ways, Zhu had gone to study in Germany before returning to China to command a Guomindang officer-training regiment. He had kept his Communist affiliation secret until the Nanchang uprisings in 1927, when he had been defeated and forced to flee, eventually joining Mao in the Jinggang Mountains. The "Red Army," as the two structured it, now became a fast-moving guerrilla force. Although only about 2,000 Red Army troops were left by early 1929, Mao and Zhu vigorously opposed fragmenting their forces further by scattering them across the countryside to foster uprisings. As they wrote to the party leader Li Lisan,

> The tactics we have derived from the struggle of the past three years are indeed different from any other tactics, ancient or modern, Chinese or foreign. With our tactics, the masses can be aroused for struggle on an ever-broadening scale, and no enemy, however powerful, can cope with us. Ours are guerrilla tactics. They consist mainly of the following points:
>
> Divide our forces to arouse the masses, concentrate our forces to deal with the enemy.
>
> The enemy advances, we retreat; the enemy camps, we harass; the enemy tires, we attack; the enemy retreats, we pursue.

To extend stable base areas, employ the policy of advancing in waves; when pursued by a powerful enemy, employ the policy of circling around.

Arouse the largest numbers of the masses in the shortest possible time and by the best possible methods.[10]

Their very success in consolidating and expanding the Red Army in Ruijin paradoxically led to the Central Committee's optimistic view that their troops had grown strong enough to fight outside the soviet area in conventional positional warfare. So in 1930, Mao and Zhu received direct orders, which they could not disobey, to attack Nanchang. These orders were part of an ambitious plan by Li Lisan to launch a revolutionary surge; assaults against Wuhan and Changsha were planned at the same time. All three uprisings failed, although Communist forces held Changsha for ten days before the Guomindang retook it. When Mao and Zhu, defeated at Nanchang, were ordered to go to Changsha to help recapture the city, they reluctantly agreed, but faced with the annihilation of their forces, they withdrew from the battle without permission and returned to Ruijin.

As well as concentrating on aspects of economic and military change while he was in Jiangxi, Mao paid attention to social reform in areas such as women's rights. Since writing about the suicide of Miss Zhao in 1919, Mao had shown a continuing awareness of the economic and family pressures that prevented any semblance of equality between the sexes in China. He had reiterated these feelings near the end of his 1927 report on the Hunan peasant movement, writing that although men suffered under three forms of authority—political, clan, and religious—women also had to endure the weight of masculine authority. Mao felt that masculine authority was weakest among the poorer peasants, because "their womenfolk have to do more manual labor than the women of the richer classes and therefore have more say and greater power of decision in family matters." With the rise of the peasant movement, women formed their own associations: "the opportunity has come for them to lift up their heads, and the authority of the husband is getting shakier every day."[11]

One of Mao's important acts in the Jiangxi Soviet was to promulgate regulations (in 1931 and 1934) that forbade arranged marriages, encouraged free choice of spouses, and prohibited polygamy, child brides, and "all purchase and sale in marriage contracts." The legal age of marriage was set at twenty for men and eighteen for women. The law also codified the unilateral right to divorce at the request of either spouse. A major exception was stipulated for the wives of Red Army soldiers, who were required to secure the soldier-husband's consent for divorce (unless he had not been in contact with the family for two or more years). This provision underlined the precarious balancing act of introducing radical reforms without losing the support of the army's enlisted men. Families who depended on the contributions of daughters-in-law to household labor also objected to the divorce provision. The implementation of the marriage law was complicated and incomplete. In some places, women were still forced into arranged marriages or sold as brides; CCP cadres found themselves mediating conflicts over extramarital affairs or opposition to petitions for divorce. Despite the messiness, the incidence of divorce rose. One survey of two counties in the Jiangxi Soviet showed that in a period of three and a half months, 4,274 divorces were registered, 80 percent of them at the request of one spouse, and that 3,783 marriages were registered for the same period. In nine cases the couple married *and* divorced on the same day.[12]

Mao was sympathetic to the plight of poor peasant men—those who feared losing their wives, and those who looked to the Communist government to help them find the wives that they could never have afforded under the system of arranged marriages. The result was that some women in the Jiangxi Soviet were coerced into marrying—or possibly having physical relationships with several men—against their will. Widows were reportedly pressured into remarrying within a few days of their spouse's death. "Teams of laundresses" dispatched to certain units and used in recruiting suggest also that the Communist authorities countenanced a fair amount of not-very-clandestine prostitution.

By 1930, the attacks by the Guomindang and its allies on the Communists in the cities were becoming more savage and more successful. Attempts by the Communists to recoup their fortunes by sending assassination squads to murder former comrades who had defected to the enemy backfired. The Guomindang secret service successfully infiltrated many of the CCP's urban networks. (After 1932 Nationalist terror squads were also directed against those who collaborated with the Japanese.) The labor organizations, in disarray, were subverted by Guomindang agents, and their organizing efforts were often wrecked by harassment or violence from secret-society members in the pay of the industrialists. Attempts at large-scale urban insurrections ordered by Li Lisan all failed. New leaders dispatched by Moscow to remedy the situation were ineffectual. They were young, inexperienced, and doctrinally dogmatic, known sardonically as the "returned Bolsheviks." In 1931 a series of arrests and betrayals compelled a growing number of CCP leaders to abandon Shanghai and join Mao in the Jiangxi Soviet. The more important "returned Bolsheviks" did the same in 1933. Upon arrival they temporarily pushed Mao into eclipse, accusing him of being too "rightist" in his policies of accommodation with the richer peasants. According to some sources, he was under house arrest during 1934 for his erroneous policies. In fact, his obituary had already been published in the main Comintern journal in March 1930, suggesting that at least some senior party members wished him dead.

In the face of the Guomindang's military superiority in terms of conventional forces and modern weapons, the CCP attempted a different strategy for survival, one in which it temporarily gave up its urban bases and reconsolidated deep in the countryside. Living among poor peasants, on whose support they now depended, CCP leaders had to adjust their thinking. Chiang Kai-shek also had to rethink his strategies and priorities. His Guomindang had won the cities and defeated or allied with the strongest northern militarists. But to win over the countryside would take a massive and concerted military, political, and economic effort. To help in this endeavor, Chiang turned to Germany for aid and expertise, hiring several of their specialists for their expertise in logistical and long-range military planning. In 1932 Chiang became chief of the General Staff and chairman of the National Military Council, which commanded the army, navy, and air force. To speed the destruction of the Communists in their rural soviets—two major military campaigns in 1931 and 1932 had failed to dislodge them—Chiang established a Bandit Suppression Headquarters, with himself as its commander in chief and empowered with complete civil, military, and party control in areas where Communists were active. He was also able to allocate funding for the military as his priorities dictated: in the early 1930s direct military costs and accrued debt interest combined to account for 80 percent or more of the annual government budget.

At the same time, the Guomindang put new demands on the people in the form of conscripted labor and heavy surtaxes as—following the Germans' strategic suggestions—they began an ambitious program to build airfields and an encircling network of roads in the war zones. The Guomindang also set out to construct a line of sturdy stone or brick block houses around the Jiangxi Soviet area. The block houses consolidated an economic blockade and acted as defensive points, supply storehouses, emergency field hospitals, and the bases for forward operations. These tactics not only reflected German advice based on their World War I experience but were designed partially in emulation of Zeng Guofan's suppression of the Nian rebels seventy years before. To back up the fourth and fifth suppression campaigns undertaken in 1933 and 1934, 1,500 miles of new roads and 14,000 block houses were built.

Although a number of German officers were active in these campaigns, Chiang Kai-shek felt the need for a senior adviser whom he could really trust. The man he chose was General Hans von Seeckt, a distinguished World War I commander who had been responsible for building the German army into a disciplined, spirited, well-equipped force. Seeckt reached Chiang's headquarters near Nanchang in May 1933, and had several days of intense talks with him. Though Seeckt declined Chiang's request to become the permanent senior adviser of an expanded German mission, he agreed to write a detailed study of China's military needs. He emphasized that the Guomindang army must be qualitatively excellent and led by a professional officer corps, so that it could provide the "foundation of the ruling power." Chiang had too many troops, Seeckt wrote; an army such as the one he suggested need be no more than ten divisions. An elite training brigade should be developed first, to serve as a strike force in its own right. To achieve this and the logistical reform to go with it, Chiang "must ensure that the influence of the German advisers in fact prevails."[13] These advisers would build up an armaments industry for China using their own selected contractors. Seeckt broached the idea also of exchanging Chinese raw materials for the munitions and other goods that China would need from Germany.

The first step in this direction was taken in January 1934, when the German Military and Finance Ministry approved the formation of a single private corporation to handle military-industrial dealings with China. Seeckt made a second visit to China in the summer of 1934 as a lavishly feted guest with a monthly stipend of U.S.$2,000. ("I am seen here as a military Confucius," the German wrote to his sister.)[14] A "strictly secret" treaty was signed, with the provision of a credit of DM 100 million to build an iron and steel complex and to obtain ore-processing machinery and modern arsenals from Germany. Seeckt had pointed out that the arms currently being made in China were "from 75 to 90 percent unusable." In return, the Germans would receive "high-quality ores" such as antimony and tungsten, essential to modern warfare. Germany lacked both metals, while China produced 60 percent of the global supply of antimony and half of the world's supply of tungsten. And as the Guomindang and the Germans began to move their collaboration to an even higher level of exchange, the Communists secretly made their own decision to abandon their Jiangxi base altogether.

THE LONG MARCH

By mid-1934 the Guomindang economic blockade combined with a military encirclement had made the position of the Communists in the Jiangxi Soviet extremely difficult. In August that year, the four men most dominant in military planning—commander in chief Zhu De, the leading member of the returned Bolshevik group Bo Gu, Zhou Enlai, and the Comintern agent Otto Braun—reached general agreement that the soviet should be abandoned. They disagreed, however, about the timing of the move, how many people should be left as a rear guard, and the ultimate destination. Mao

Zedong, demoted in party councils because of disagreements over land policy, was not in the inner circle of decision-makers at this time.

Because the only hope of breaking through the Guomindang blockade hinged on the element of surprise, the planning took place in great secrecy, with most of the local CCP commanders given only a faint idea of what was to be expected of them. There was, furthermore, no chance of coordinating plans with the Soviet Union or the Comintern leadership—in a raid in Shanghai the Guomindang police had seized the broadcasting equipment used by the CCP to keep in touch with Moscow. Evacuation plans were spurred by the information that Chiang Kai-shek was planning a renewed offensive to take place in late autumn, and by the news that a Guomindang commander in Guangdong might be willing to negotiate with the CCP.

Probes by Communist troops suggested that the southwest corner of the Guomindang military blockade was the weakest, although there were still four lines of defenses to be breached, spread across 150 miles. But the local troops defending this zone were not as tenacious as those in the elite units; furthermore, if the Communists escaped through the southwest, they would have a running start over Guomindang troops campaigning in the northern areas of the Jiangxi Soviet. Accordingly in September, the Communist troops were readied for a breakout to the southwest. Food, ammunition, clothing, and medical supplies all had to be prepared and allocated, documents and files packed or destroyed, and personnel winnowed to see who would join the marchers and who would stay behind.

The withdrawal strategy was coordinated by Zhou Enlai. Veteran troops of the First and the Third Army corps led the evacuation, commanded by two of the CCP's finest generals. The First Corps was led by Lin Biao, a former Huangpu cadet, now aged twenty-seven, and the Third Corps by the thirty-six-year-old Peng Dehuai. Lin had around 15,000 combat troops in his corps and Peng had 13,000, but they could not be armed adequately because of the Guomindang blockade. Each corps was equipped with only 9,000 rifles (each with fewer than 100 cartridges), 2 field guns, 30 light mortars firing homemade shells, and 300 machine guns. Most soldiers also carried 1 or 2 hand grenades.

Behind these two army corps came the bulk of the Jiangxi Soviet personnel. The command column, with Central Committee members, intelligence staff, cadets, and a small anti-aircraft unit, was followed by the support column, with more party and government personnel, field-hospital units, supplies of silver bullion, machinery for making simple arms and ammunition, and printing equipment and political pamphlets. With hundreds of recently recruited pack carriers, these two columns, comprising around 14,000 men (only 4,000 of whom could be considered combat troops) were slow and cumbersome to move. Three other smaller and less well-equipped army corps defended the flanks and rear of the columns, making a total for the breakout of some 80,000 men, each carrying about two weeks' rations in rice and salt.

There were also about thirty-five women in these two columns, including He Zizhen, Mao Zedong's second wife, who was pregnant, and Zhu De's fourth wife. (Of Zhu's three previous wives, one had died after childbirth, one had been killed by warlords, and one had been executed by the Guomindang. Mao's first wife, Yang Kaihui, had also been captured and executed by the Guomindang in 1930.) Several thousand other women were incorporated into other army divisions, to work as nurses or in administrative tasks. But the majority of the women and the children had to be left behind at great personal cost and suffering during the Guomindang recapture of the area.[15]

Also left behind was a rear-guard force of some 28,000 troops, of whom as many as 20,000 were wounded and unable to make the necessary forced marches. Their goal was to fight as guerrilla units to retain scattered areas of the former Jiangxi Soviet, and to form an underground network for a possible CCP return. With this group was Mao Zedong's brother Mao Zetan as well as Qu Qiubai, the party leader ousted in 1927, who had tuberculosis and was too ill to travel. Mao Zetan was later killed in action by Guomindang forces, and Qu Qiubai was captured and executed.

The breakout from Jiangxi began under cover of darkness on October 16, 1934. Thus began the "Long March," one of the central heroic sagas in Chinese Communist history. Prompted by tactical defeats, what began as a desperate retreat ended as a strategic victory after the remnants of the Communist forces reached Shaanxi province, having trekked across almost 6,000 miles of hazardous terrain in the span of 370 days.

The initial phases of the march went almost as planned. The Third Corps rapidly broke the second defensive line, although the First Corps took severe casualties. With both regional and Guomindang armies in close pursuit, Communist forces adopted a round-the-clock policy of four hours' marching and four hours' rest, breaking through the third defense line on the Wuhan-Guangzhou railroad. Held up by bulky baggage and by the desertion of many carriers, plagued by poor maps and by atrocious or nonexistent roads, the Communists were almost trapped as they crossed the final defense line, along the Xiang River, in mid-December. Although the Guomindang and their allies had made it impossible for the main Jiangxi army to link up with other Communist forces in Hunan, they could not prevent their onward movement into Guizhou.

Over the next few weeks, Communist troops seized several Guizhou market towns, where they restocked their supplies and reorganized their columns after abandoning much of the heavy equipment, including artillery for which

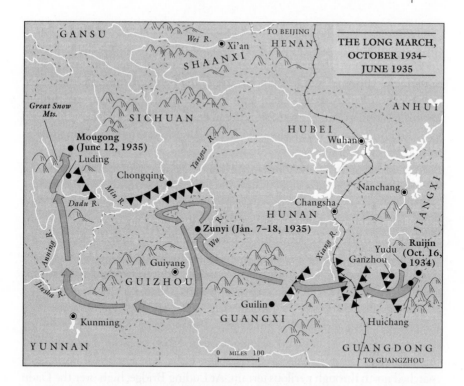

THE LONG MARCH,
OCTOBER 1934–
JUNE 1935

no more ammunition was available. Opposition was growing fragmentary. After the First and Third Corps' daring river crossing on bamboo rafts, they overcame the Guizhou defenses of the Wu River. On January 7, 1935, Communist advance troops entered the city of Zunyi, where they seized supplies of badly needed food and clothing, though the stores of ammunition were disappointingly low.

As the troops rested in Zunyi, CCP leaders moved to make the city the focus for radical change. They evoked some of the excitement of their previous campaigns by holding mass meetings, discussing land reform, distributing confiscated goods to the poor, and forming revolutionary committees. It was also in Zunyi that a tense and important meeting of the highest-level leadership took place from January 15–18, 1935. The conference was attended by eighteen men: six members of the Politburo, four alternate members, seven senior army leaders, and the Comintern representative Otto Braun. During four days of protracted discussion they thrashed over the reasons for the loss of the Jiangxi Soviet and examined the options. The resolutions issued after the conference criticized the Jiangxi Soviet leadership for having followed a policy of "pure defense" instead of a "mobile war," and for having conducted in early 1934 a "desperate, aimless fight against the enemy" that resulted in a withdrawal—"a flight in panic and a sort of house-removal operation."[16] Since these resolutions largely represented Mao Zedong's views, the Zunyi conference marked an important step in his rise in the leadership. Mao was named a full member of the Standing Committee of the Politburo, and the chief assistant to Zhou Enlai for military planning. The "returned Bolshevik" Bo Gu lost his position as "the person with overall responsibility in the Party Center," as he had been termed, and along with Otto Braun lost the controlling role in military decision making.

In the aftermath of the Zunyi conference, Mao gradually moved to take over military leadership from Zhou Enlai. For the Communist forces it was a period of dangerous drifting across northern Guizhou province, northern Yunnan, and southern Sichuan, where they faced opposition from the warlords who still controlled most of those provinces, and from regular Guomindang troops. Some of the time Chiang Kai-shek coordinated the counterattacks personally, and used the Communist presence in the southwest to build up his political strength there at the expense of the local warlords.

The Communist troops avoided the fates that had long ago overcome both the prince of Gui and Wu Sangui in these mountainous regions by making a daring move into Sichuan and Xikang (eastern Tibet) in early May. After taking eight days to ferry their forces over the Jinsha River in small boats, they marched north through perilous terrain. At Luding Bridge, high over the Dadu River, a group of soldiers performed a daring military action that is celebrated as a symbol of the "Long March Spirit" and is so recorded in revolutionary lore. According to the legend, the only crossing of this swift, wide river was by a chain suspension bridge with wooden planks. Enemy troops had removed most of the planks and commanded a clear field of fire over the bridge. Twenty Communist soldiers, carrying grenades, crawled 100 yards across the chains, stormed the position on the other side, and routed the defenders. Even if the story has been embellished, it was a remarkable maneuver that enabled the rest of the Communist forces to cross the river by the end of May 1935.

There followed a grim march across the "Great Snow" mountain ranges, during which Mao, sick with recurrent malaria, had to be carried in a litter at times; Lin Biao endured fainting spells from the thin air; and many soldiers suffered frostbite that later required amputations. Harassed by Tibetan troops, sporadically bombed by the Guomindang air force, and climbing over terrain that reached 16,000 feet in places, the Communist troops at last reached the northern Sichuan town of Mougong on June 12, 1935. Their original number had been halved to around 40,000.

In north Sichuan, the Jiangxi Soviet group joined forces with Zhang Guotao, who had abandoned his soviet areas in eastern Sichuan to lead 50,000 troops to a new base. The union should have been joyful, for Zhang and Mao had known each other long before at Beijing University. Both had attended the founding meetings of the CCP in 1921 before going on to build their own base-area governments. But after weeks of strategic discussion the two leaders could agree only to disagree. Mao insisted on continuing farther north and east to Shaanxi or Ningxia; Zhang wished to build an isolated and defensible base in the Sichuan-Xikang border region. In a compromise, the two armies were blended and redivided. Mao was given command of the reorganized "eastern column," which consisted of the survivors of Lin Biao and Peng Dehuai's First and Third Army Corps along with two of Zhang's corps. Zhang got Mao's former Fifth and Ninth Corps to add to his own forces, and also the services of Zhu De.

The Communist forces now split up again. Zhang moved southwest to rest his soldiers and prepare supplies for the coming winter, while throughout late August and early September Mao's exhausted column struggled across the bleak marshlands of the Qinghai-Gansu border region. Dramatic Communist records and memoirs describe how the driving rain and hail, quicksand-like bogs, lack of food, and the impossibility of sleeping on the saturated ground except standing up, led to thousands of deaths among the marchers. By day they groped their way forward, guided by thin grass ropes laid along the ground by advance scouts. Leaving the swamps, Mao's forces ran into renewed opposition

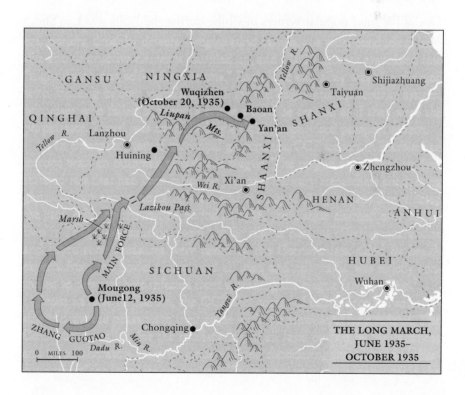

THE LONG MARCH,
JUNE 1935–
OCTOBER 1935

as the column crossed below the western bend of the Yellow River and moved through the Liupan Mountains. At last, on October 20, at Wuqizhen in northern Shaanxi, Mao's troops met up with the north Shaanxi Communist guerrilla forces. About 8,000 to 9,000 of the 80,000 troops who had originally left Jiangxi were still with Mao. Over the course of the following year, survivors from Zhang Guotao's and Zhu De's "western column" straggled into the same area after suffering heavy casualties in vicious fighting.

Summing up the experience in December 1935, Mao wrote, "The Long March is the first of its kind in the annals of History. It is a manifesto, a propaganda force, a seeding-machine.... It has proclaimed to the world that the Red Army is an army of heroes, while the imperialists and their running dogs, Chiang Kai-shek and his like, are impotent."[17] Brave words indeed, but they could not hide the fact that the CCP had lost virtually its entire structure of southern and eastern bases, urban and rural. Fifteen years of revolutionary endeavor appeared to have come to nothing, and rebuilding the shattered edifice would be profoundly difficult.

CRISIS AT XI'AN

One of the most popular writers in China during the 1930s was Lao She, a Manchu who had lived and worked in England for six years before returning home. An admirer of Charles Dickens, D. H. Lawrence, and Joseph Conrad, Lao She was influenced by these writers as he constructed his own novels, which were satirical yet rooted in reality. *Cat Country*, published serially in late 1932 and 1933, pointed out the follies and the miseries of the ongoing civil war, in which the struggle between the Communists and the Guomindang absorbed the nation's energy while the Japanese built up their strength for further blows against Chinese sovereignty.

Cat Country was a transparent enough satire, presenting the story of an astronaut, referred to as Mr. Earth, who crash-lands on Mars. There he finds the country of cats (China) quarreling amongst themselves, even as invaders (the Japanese) from another part of the planet attack. The narrator details the social and political divisions that separate factions of the cat people, preventing them from uniting against the aggressor. Their society is sadly dysfunctional, full of "suspicion, pettiness, selfishness, and neglect." In the schools, every child immediately becomes a university graduate on the first day of attendance. "Everyone considered education to be useless anyway," and with this "innovation" Cat Country could boast the highest number of university graduates of any nation on Mars. Since schools no longer serve any pedagogical purpose, the administrators and teachers battle each other constantly.

The students become accustomed to barbarity, such that "now it is a very common occurrence to see students butchering teachers, professors, chancellors, and principals."

In a sharp caricature of politics, Mr. Earth describes Everybody Shareskyism, the ruling ideology whose adherents speak gibberish and worship "Uncle Karl" as a deity. They depose the cat-emperor, but grandiose programs of revolutionary change result in violence and mass slaughter, which end when the leader of Everybody Shareskyism becomes the new emperor. Lao She lampooned the Communists and directed his acerbic commentary at the Guomindang as well. "War follows in the wake of every revolution," Mr. Earth remarks in a passage applicable to both, "but it is the victorious ones who are helpless. Understanding only how to tear things down, they lack the imagination and ardor necessary to build things up again. And the only result of the revolution is to increase the number of soldiers in arms and the number of corrupt officials preying upon the common people. In this kind of situation the common people will go hungry whether they work or not." Cat Country would soon perish: the "death of a state" represents "a cold and ugly fact; it is the steel logic of history."[18] At the end of the chilling novel, the remaining cat people tear each other to death as enemy soldiers watch.

Patriotic Chinese students responded to the harsh vision presented by Lao She. They had attempted anti-Japanese demonstrations during the 1930s, and the CCP had tapped into such nationalist sentiments by "declaring war" on Japan from the Jiangxi Soviet in 1932. When they reached Shaanxi in 1935, the Communists reiterated the need for a "united front" against Japan. Attacking the "closed-doorists"—as he called those in the CCP who damned all bourgeoisie as "entirely and eternally counter-revolutionary"—Mao Zedong built on the line of argument that he had presented in Sichuan during the Long March. He called for a flexible approach that would draw together all those opposed to Japanese aggression, whether they were the wealthier urban classes, intellectuals, rich peasants, members of the government, or warlords. In taking this stance, he was echoing the position of the Comintern as it struggled to find allies against the rising fascist powers in Europe.

One powerful figure who agreed with this position was Zhang Xueliang, "the Young Marshal" of Manchuria, whose father had been blown up in his train by the Japanese in 1928 and whose own army had been driven out of the northeast in 1931. After recovering from his morphine addiction and taking a leisurely European tour, Zhang Xueliang returned to China in early 1934 and offered his military services to Chiang Kai-shek. Chiang gave him the task of wiping out the Communist soviet in the Hubei-Henan-Anhui border region, which Zhang accomplished. But the Young Marshal was dismayed that, at the very time he was using his troops to exterminate the Communists, the Japanese launched a new series of military threats. They were now planning to establish an independent regime in Inner Mongolia, and to extend the demilitarized zones established by the 1933 Tanggu Truce to include all of Hebei province. In November 1935 the Japanese took decisive control over eastern Hebei through a Chinese general who agreed to collaborate.

Despite the Guomindang's efforts to keep protesters quiet, on December 9, 1935, thousands of students rallied in Beijing to protest Japanese encroachments. Police forces, by locking the city gates, turning water hoses on the demonstrators in the freezing weather, and clubbing or arresting those they could reach, tried to intimidate the students and prevent further protests. But the "December Ninthers," as they were swiftly dubbed, had touched a national chord: just over a week later, more than 30,000 marched in a second demonstration, while thousands more protested in the Nationalist capital of Nanjing and in other cities. Communist organizers, active in many of these demonstrations and in coordinating follow-up activities, tried to broaden the base of the December Ninth movement by appealing for support from women, peasants, and even—on patriotic grounds—the police themselves.

Zhang Xueliang, who had in the meantime been sent to Xi'an to coordinate the attacks on the CCP base in Shaanxi, was among those instrumental in getting the arrested demonstrators released. He was clearly moved by appeals for united action against the Japanese, even as he continued to follow Chiang Kai-shek's orders on "bandit suppression." In January 1936 the Communists appealed directly to Zhang's troops—most of whom were in exile from their Manchurian homeland—to join "the workers' democratic government and the Red Army" and "fight the Japanese jointly."[19] By February Zhang had held at least one meeting with Communist negotiators, and in a successful propaganda move the CCP released all of the Manchurian army prisoners they had captured and indoctrinated with united-front anti-Japanese attitudes. In the spring of 1936 Communist agents, with Zhang's tacit acceptance, organized an influential group of his staff and army officers into a Society of Comrades for Resistance against Japan. And in late April or early May, Zhang Xueliang traveled to the CCP base area in northern Shaanxi, where he met Zhou Enlai to discuss the possibility of concerted actions against Japan.

Although aware of these growing sentiments, Chiang Kai-shek continued to be tenacious in his desire to finish off the Shaanxi Communists before making any moves against Japan. He used the occasion of a visit to Xi'an in late October 1936 to lash out at those who did not agree with him that "the communists are our greatest traitors." But the audience was no longer convinced by this familiar rhetoric, and Chiang returned to Nanjing with matters unresolved.

In late October and November 1936 troops from Japanese armies stationed in Manchukuo, as well as various Mongolian units, launched a full-scale invasion of the northern province of Suiyuan. Chinese troops electrified the country by their heroic resistance. Elsewhere, Chinese workers went on strike in Japanese-owned factories, and leaders of the self-styled National Salvation Movement conducted vigorous campaigns in Shanghai. On the international scene, the signing of the Anti-Comintern Pact between Japan and Germany in late November generated fears that Chiang Kai-shek, with his reliance on German military advice, might now become more pro-Japanese. The landing of Japanese marines in the former German leasehold city of Qingdao—where they helped enforce a lockout of striking workers, occupied public buildings, and arrested agitators—inflamed the situation further.

In early December, Chiang Kai-shek flew back to Xi'an, despite warnings from close friends and others that it was a dangerous thing to do. There he conducted a series of private interviews with the generals in Zhang Xueliang's army to test their loyalty and moved decisively to break the Communists once and for all. Chiang ordered troops whom he could trust transferred to the Xi'an region and brought air-force bombers into the area, demanding that "eight years of bandit suppression . . . be accomplished in two weeks, within a month at most." He remained adamant when thousands of Xi'an students rallied in the city on December 9, 1936, to mark the first anniversary of the December Ninthers. They tried to march on Chiang's headquarters but were turned back by police who fired on their ranks, wounding two students. Determined now to force Chiang to take an anti-Japanese stand, Zhang Xueliang and his senior officers held a tense, protracted meeting on December 11. At dawn the next day, units of Zhang's army stormed Chiang's headquarters in the hills outside the city. They killed most of his bodyguards and captured the shivering, injured generalissimo, who had escaped in his night clothes, scaled a back wall of his compound, and hidden in a cave before being discovered.

Later in the morning of December 12, Zhang and his supporters issued a telegram to all central and provincial government leaders, the press, and various mass organizations. It listed their eight key demands to Chiang: to reorganize the Nanjing government into a broadly representative body, to stop the civil war, to free the patriotic protestors arrested in Shanghai, to release political prisoners elsewhere, to encourage patriotic movements, to guarantee political freedoms of assembly, to carry out the will of Sun Yat-sen, and to convene at once a National Salvation Conference.

The next two weeks witnessed complex and delicate negotiations, with Chiang's fate hanging in the balance. The government in Nanjing, torn between military reprisal or conciliatory negotiations to rescue Chiang, finally decided on both courses. The army and air force mobilized for a major assault

Communist leaders in Yan'an, 1937: from left, Zhou Enlai, Mao Zedong, and Bo Gu

on Xi'an, while Chiang's adviser, the Australian W. H. Donald (who had formerly been an adviser to Zhang Xueliang), was sent to Xi'an. There he was joined by Madame Chiang, her brother T. V. Soong, and the Blueshirt leader Dai Li. Most of Chiang's warlord allies sat on the fence, waiting to see how events would develop. In contrast, a group of 275 young army generals, all graduates of the Huangpu Military Academy and claiming to speak for 70,000 other graduates and students, sent a dramatic telegram to Zhang Xueliang. In it they vowed that, if anything happened to their leader, "we, the alumni, swear that we shall deal with you with all our strength that is within us, and that we shall never live under the same sky and sun with you and with anyone related to you."[20]

In the CCP's Shaanxi base area, the news of Chiang's kidnapping caused excitement and confusion. As in the Nanjing government, there were divided opinions. Some saw this as a golden opportunity to have Chiang killed; others saw it as a chance to rally the country behind a united-front policy of anti-Japanese resistance and at the same time to strengthen the position of the CCP. While they debated, a telegram, believed to have been drafted by Stalin himself, reached the CCP leadership. Stalin supported a united national front but did not think Zhang Xueliang had the power or talent to lead it, the telegram explained. Despite everything that had happened during and since 1927,

Chiang Kai-shek remained the only man with the prestige for such a mission. Stalin urged the CCP to try to secure Chiang's release. And in a surprising comment, he suggested that the whole "Xi'an Incident" might have been engineered by the Japanese to drive China deeper into a civil war.

Negotiations continued until Christmas Day 1936, when Chiang Kai-shek, who had refused to issue any written statements since his kidnapping, offered a "verbal agreement" that he would review the situation. After more discussion, the generals allied with Zhang Xueliang agreed to let Chiang leave Xi'an that afternoon. To prove the sincerity of his motives, and to remove any suggestion that he had been a "mutineer," as well as to hold Chiang to his word, Zhang Xueliang volunteered to fly out with him. The group left Xi'an around 2:00 P.M. After various stopovers to refuel, Chiang reached Nanjing on December 26, to a rapturous greeting from a crowd of 400,000. The kidnapping and his own steadfastness had revived Chiang's popularity as a national leader.

At some levels, however, the subsequent events were anticlimactic. Zhang Xueliang was court-martialed for insubordination, tried, and sentenced to ten years in prison, soon commuted to house arrest. The Xi'an armies hostile to Chiang, after attempting further coups, were transferred to other regions, while troops of proven loyalty were substituted. The CCP dramatically offered to submit its military forces to Guomindang leadership if a full national front against the Japanese were announced. After extended meetings in February 1937, however, the Guomindang plenum refused to make a full commitment to the united front.

Yet things *had* changed. The heat was now off the Shaanxi base area, where the Communists moved to consolidate their forces in the caves around the mountain-girded city of Yan'an. The country as a whole knew that Chiang Kai-shek had implicitly given his word to change the direction of his policies. There was now, suddenly, a chance that Lao She's direst fears would not prove true, and that the cat people might unify to confront their attacker before they clawed each other to death.

CHAPTER 17 | World War II

THE LOSS OF EAST CHINA

During the spring of 1937 there was a period of calm, a deceptive respite before the cataclysm. While the Guomindang and the Communist Party sparred for the propaganda initiative in embracing the united front, the Japanese watched warily. Arguments and tensions within the Japanese cabinet and army led to a change of government in early 1937. The new premier was General Hayashi Senjuro, previously an effective and forceful war minister who nevertheless claimed during his inaugural address, "I have no faith in a pugnacious foreign policy." Hayashi's newly appointed foreign minister stated publicly that to "avert a crisis at any time" with China, Japan had simply "to walk the open path straightforwardly."[1] During this lull, Chiang Kai-shek continued preparations to strengthen his military for the coming conflict, while buying time and trying to avoid an all-out collision. Although improved by several years of German training and fortified by purchases of German equipment, China's troops were far from ready to confront Japan's superior forces and firepower. Meanwhile, surging public sentiment demanded armed resistance against Japanese encroachment, excoriating Chiang and the Guomindang for failing to defend the nation.

A number of large and small events then came together in what—cumulatively—turned out to be a fateful way. When Hayashi failed to get his economic policies through the Japanese parliament, he was replaced by the influential but indecisive Prince Konoe. Japan's commanding general in north China suffered a heart attack and a less experienced subordinate stepped in. And Chinese troops in the vicinity of the "Marco Polo Bridge" (Lugouqiao) decided to strengthen some shoreline defenses on the banks of the Yongding River. This bridge—about ten miles west of Beijing—had once been famed

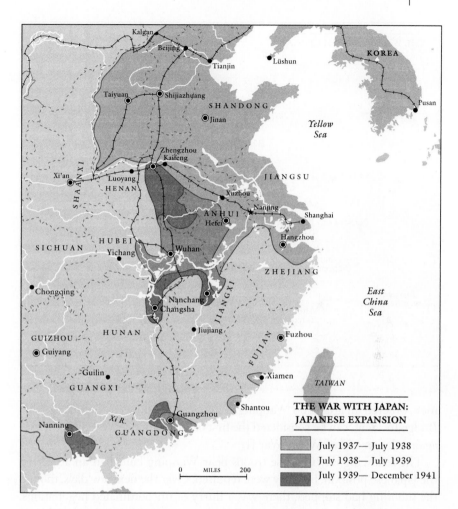

Map legend:

SHANDONG, JIANGSU, Yellow Sea, KOREA, SHAANXI, HENAN, ANHUI, HUBEI, SICHUAN, JIANGXI, ZHEJIANG, East China Sea, HUNAN, GUIZHOU, FUJIAN, GUANGXI, TAIWAN, GUANGDONG

THE WAR WITH JAPAN:
JAPANESE EXPANSION

July 1937— July 1938
July 1938— July 1939
July 1939— December 1941

0   MILES   200

for its beauty; Emperor Qianlong wrote a poem on the loveliness of the setting moon when viewed there in the first light of dawn. Now a strategically
important railway bridge was built next to it, linking the southern lines with
the junction town of Wanping. An army holding Wanping could control rail
access in three directions. For this reason the Japanese troops in north China
often conducted maneuvers in the area, as they were entitled to do by the Boxer
Protocol of 1901.

On July 7, 1937, the Japanese chose to make the bridge the base of a night
maneuver during which the troops fired blank cartridges to simulate combat conditions. At 10:30 P.M. the Chinese fired some shells into the Japanese
assembly area without causing casualties. But when one Japanese soldier was
missing at roll call, the commander, thinking the Chinese had captured the

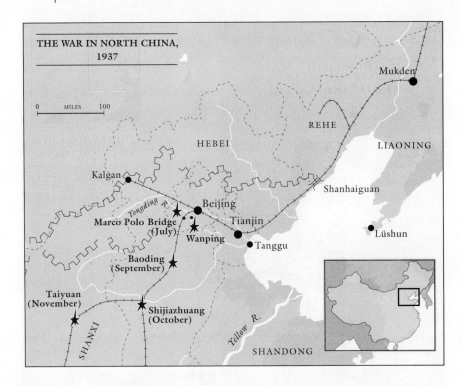

THE WAR IN NORTH CHINA,
1937

0   MILES   100

REHE

HEBEI

LIAONING

Mukden

Shanhaiguan

Kalgan

Beijing

Marco Polo Bridge
(July)

Wanping

Tianjin

Tanggu

Lüshun

Baoding
(September)

Taiyuan
(November)

Shijiazhuang
(October)

SHANXI

Yellow R.

SHANDONG

Yongding R.

man, ordered an attack on Wanping. This assault, known as the Marco Polo
Bridge Incident, can be considered the first battle of China's War of Resistance
against Japan and of World War II.

The following day Chinese troops near Wanping launched an attack on
the Japanese position, but they were repulsed. Over the next few days, though
the shooting had stopped, there was a flurry of uncoordinated negotiations,
statements, and counterstatements. These came from the regional and local
military commanders on both sides, the Chinese and Japanese authorities in
Beijing, and the governments in Nanjing and Tokyo. Feelings began to run
high, with troop mobilizations on both sides. In a press conference, Prince
Konoe insisted that the incident was "entirely the result of an anti-Japanese
military action on the part of China," and that "the Chinese authorities must
apologize to us for the illegal anti-Japanese actions." From his summer home
in Kuling, Chiang Kai-shek vowed not to make further concessions: "If we
allow one more inch of our territory to be lost," said Chiang, "we shall be
guilty of an unpardonable crime against our race."[2]

On July 27, just as the local military commanders seemed to be working
out withdrawal arrangements, more fighting erupted around the Marco Polo
Bridge. Japanese troops seized the bridge and dug in on the left bank of the

Yongding River. By the end of the month, they had consolidated their hold over the entire Tianjin-Beijing region. Hearing of the Chinese defiance, Prince Konoe called for "a fundamental solution of Sino-Japanese relations."[3] At a meeting of the National Defense Council on August 7, senior Guomindang leaders reviewed the situation and weighed the risks of confrontation. Compared to the Japanese, Chiang said, "it's not that we are not 10 percent as prepared, we're not even 1 percent as prepared." The long road of resistance would demand enormous sacrifice. He posed the challenge: "So, comrades, we need a decision. Do we fight, or shall we be destroyed?" Chiang declared this to be the "key moment which will decide whether our country survives or perishes." The answer was abundantly clear.[4]

Chiang Kai-shek now moved to open a second front in Shanghai and to activate his best German-trained divisions for the battle. He had also taken the precaution of constructing a defensive perimeter in the area of Wuxi, should retreat become necessary. In early August, the Japanese ordered the mobilization of troop reinforcements and deployed ships to Shanghai. Tensions rose in the city, with panicked civilians streaming into the foreign concessions in search of refuge. As skirmishes broke out and escalated on August 13, Japanese warships aimed cannon fire at Zhabei, the Chinese district, while the marines moved into action. The next day, the Chinese air force began bombing the Japanese fleet and marine headquarters, aiming to knock out the flagship *Izumu* anchored on the Huangpu River. In a tragic catastrophe, three Chinese planes released aerial torpedoes far from the intended targets, and instead the bombs hit crowded areas in the International Settlement and the French Concession. On a hot Saturday afternoon, when the streets were full of people, more than 1,000 were killed, with hundreds more wounded.[5]

With the "war" still undeclared, the Japanese government sent fifteen new divisions to north and central China. Chiang ordered his troops to overcome the Japanese in Shanghai at all costs, but they failed in their early attempts to break the Japanese defensive perimeter. In late August and all through September and October, the Chinese, now on the defensive, fought with extraordinary heroism. The casualties absorbed were staggering. As many as 250,000 Chinese troops were killed or wounded—almost 60 percent of Chiang's best divisions—while the Japanese suffered 40,000 or more casualties. In early November, the Japanese made a bold amphibious landing at Hangzhou Bay to the south, and breached the defense at Suzhou Creek, putting their army in position to threaten the Chinese position from the rear and the right flank. On November 11 Chinese troops began to retreat westward, but in such disarray that they failed to hold the defensive emplacements at Wuxi. Instead they streamed back toward the capital of Nanjing.

Over the centuries, Nanjing had endured its share of armed attacks: the Manchus in 1645, the Taiping in 1853, the Qing regional armies in 1864, the republican forces in 1912. Now, in 1937, Chiang Kai-shek pledged that his capital would never fall. He entrusted its defense to a Guomindang politician and former warlord, Tang Shengzhi, who had supported the Northern Expedition in the summer of 1926 with his troops in Hunan. Several divisions of Chinese forces, including survivors from the recent battles in Shanghai, dug in and fought hard. As terrified civilians fled into a "safety zone" organized by foreigners, Tang rejected a Japanese demand for surrender. But on December 12, surrounded on three sides by the Japanese army, the general abandoned the city. Since Tang had vowed publicly to fight to the last breath, there were no clear plans for the evacuation, and his departure worsened the confusion. Some 70,000 troops had already been killed in defending Nanjing; many more died in stampedes or drowned in the Yangzi River in desperate attempts to escape. On their way out, Chinese soldiers set buildings on fire, to leave nothing for the enemy.

The Japanese army entered the city on the morning of December 13. There followed in Nanjing a period of terror and destruction that must rank among the worst in the history of modern warfare. For almost seven weeks Japanese troops unleashed on the Chinese soldiers and the helpless civilian population a storm of violence and cruelty that has become known as the Nanjing Massacre. Eyewitness accounts recorded indiscriminate killings, mass executions, rapes numbering in the tens of thousands, prisoners of war tortured and buried alive, looting, and arson. The Japanese military refused to honor the safety zone, claiming that Chinese soldiers were hiding amongst civilians. The number of people killed and the brutality of what transpired remains the subject of intense controversy. Although the exact number of casualties is impossible to tally, most Chinese sources cite 300,000, while a postwar tribunal estimated 200,000.

While the violence raged in Nanjing, the surviving Nationalist armies withdrew to the west and consolidated in Wuhan, site of the opening salvos of the birth of the republic and later seat of the Communists' brightest hopes. Here the Guomindang regrouped to establish a new base for defending the central Yangzi region, and a functioning administration for a temporary wartime capital. As refugees poured into the tri-city area, the metropolis flourished with political experimentation, a free press, and creative output in cultural fields. Over one hundred thousand students converged there, enlivening the streets with their patriotic energy. United in purpose, Wuhan drew international attention as a symbol of heroic resistance against fascism.[6]

Meanwhile, intense fighting continued in central China throughout the first half of 1938. The string of Japanese victories was checked occasionally,

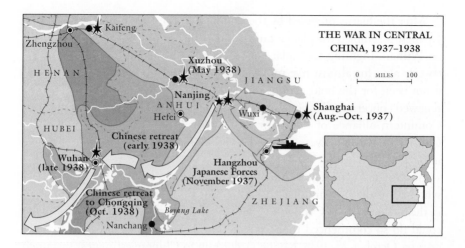

as at the Shandong town of Taierzhuang near the major railway junction of Xuzhou. Here in April, General Li Zongren fought a brilliant battle, luring the Japanese army into a trap and killing as many as 30,000 of its combat troops. But Li could not sustain the momentum and had to retreat. Xuzhou fell in May.

As the Japanese advanced yet farther west to the ancient capital of Kaifeng, which would win them control of the crucial railroad leading to Wuhan, Chiang Kai-shek ordered his engineers to blow up the dikes of the Yellow River. The ensuing giant flood stalled the Japanese for three months and bought the Nationalist army time to withdraw and fortify Wuhan's defenses. The short-term gain, however, exacted an enormous human cost. At the time, the scale of the destruction could not be precisely gauged, though Chiang and his subordinates who carried out the operation knew that it was immense. Postwar investigations revealed that the floodwaters inundated 32 percent of the cultivated land in twenty Henan counties, including 45 percent of the villages in eastern Henan. More than 325,000 people perished, and more than one million were displaced. There were also dire consequences for the longer term, as the destruction of the dikes changed the course of the Yellow River. Since the 1850s, the river had flowed into the Yellow Sea north of the Shandong peninsula. Now the waters again followed the southerly course and flowed across the northern part of Jiangsu before reaching the ocean. Local communities scrambled to build dikes along the new course, but the hastily constructed levees were no match for the river's unpredictable movements, or for the siltation that clogged tributaries and reduced drainage capacities. For years after the initial cataclysmic event, floodwaters would continue to burst through and inundate communities in Henan and nearby provinces.[7]

After the hiatus provided by the flooding, in the late summer of 1938 the Japanese assembled the planes, tanks, and artillery needed for the final assault on Wuhan. Fighting took place at scores of locations north and east of the tri-city area for almost five months. Wuhan might have fallen sooner had it not been for the bold actions of the Russian pilots sent by Stalin, whose renewed concern for Nationalist China's survival could be traced to the anti-Comintern alliance of Germany and Japan. From a base in Lanzhou in Gansu, the Russian flyers inflicted severe damage on the Japanese air force in pitched air battles.

But by late October 1938 much of Wuhan was in ruins. Chiang Kai-shek, who had readied yet another base, this time deep beyond the Yangzi gorges in the Sichuan city of Chongqing, flew to safety there, while those troops who could do so commenced their retreat. The Japanese took over the ravaged area on October 25, 1938, having (according to Chinese estimates) sustained 200,000 casualties and lost more than 100 planes. Only four days before, Japanese marine and naval units had landed and seized Guangzhou. Chiang Kai-shek had now lost de facto control over the whole swathe of eastern China stretching from the passes at Shanhaiguan to the rich ports in the semitropical south, along with all the commercial and industrial cities in between. The area encompassed the most fertile of China's farmland, the ancient cultural heartland of the country, and the primary sources of the Guomindang's tax revenues.

CHINA DIVIDED

By 1938 the great expanse of territory that had once been a unified empire under the Qing was fragmented into ten separate major units: Manchukuo, the Inner Mongolian Federation, northeast China south of the Great Wall, east-central China, and Taiwan—all controlled in varying degrees by Japan—as well as the Guomindang regime in Chongqing, and the Communist base in Shaanxi. In addition, much of Shanxi province remained in the hands of the warlord Yan Xishan. Japanese-occupied Guangzhou constituted yet another separate zone of authority, as did the far-western expanse of Xinjiang. Here the predominantly Muslim population was controlled by a military governor who nervously sought aid and sponsorship first from Soviet Russia and then from the Guomindang. Tibet, too, had reasserted its independence.

Although China since 1911 had grown used to political fragmentation and civil war, this partial reconsolidation into large units, many as big as or bigger than whole countries, renewed the threat that foreign imperialism had posed in the late nineteenth century—that China might end up permanently

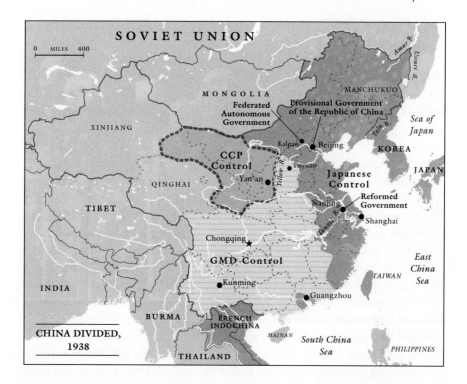

SOVIET UNION

0 MILES 400

MONGOLIA

MANCHUKUO

Federated
Autonomous
Government

Provisional Government
of the Republic of China

XINJIANG

Kalgan • Beijing

CCP
Control

Taiyuan

Yan'an

Japanese
Control

Reformed
Government

Nanjing

Shanghai

Chongqing ★

GMD Control

Kunming

Guangzhou

INDIA

TIBET

QINGHAI

BURMA

FRENCH
INDOCHINA

CHINA DIVIDED,
1938

THAILAND

HAINAN

KOREA

JAPAN

Sea of
Japan

TAIWAN

East
China
Sea

South China
Sea

PHILIPPINES

divided. The solidification of such a group of new states would be a return to the situation that had prevailed before the Qin conquests of 221 B.C.E., during the so-called Warring States period, when ten major regimes controlled the country; or it might bring a recurrence of the shifting patterns of authority and alliances that typified China's history from the third to sixth century C.E., and again from the tenth to the thirteenth.

The fall of Wuhan in late 1938 marked the end of Japan's first concerted assault on China. The Japanese War Ministry's plan to hold a ceiling of 250,000 combat troops in China had not proved feasible, and there was now a danger of becoming seriously overextended. Japan's goal in its China operations was to win an extensive base of natural resources that would fuel further industrial development, and to expand the "new order" in Asia under Japan's leadership. There was no intention of a protracted military occupation; rather the plan was to develop a network of collaborationist regimes, on the model of Manchukuo, that would give Japan preferential economic treatment, be staunchly anti-Communist, and provide troops to garrison and patrol their territories in Japan's name. Japanese planners also hoped to undermine China's financial stability by further fragmenting its economy, especially by weakening the comparatively successful *fabi* currency that the Nationalists had set up in 1935. Without a decent economic base, the Chongqing regime would surely capitulate.

Manchukuo, established in 1932, underwent rapid industrial and military expansion. The formation of a second collaborationist regime in Inner Mongolia had initially been stalled by Chinese resistance. But after the Xi'an Incident in 1936 and the attack on Shanghai in 1937, the Japanese strategy of appeasing a rising Mongolian nationalism culminated in the formation of a Federated Autonomous Government under the leadership of a Mongol prince, aided by a Japanese "supreme adviser." In mid-December 1937, while the Nanjing Massacre was occurring, the Japanese moved to consolidate the various "councils" and "autonomous governments" in north China into the Provisional Government of the Republic of China. To serve as chairman of the new government's executive committee, the Japanese installed Wang Kemin, a former Qing dynasty *juren* degree holder, diplomat, and banker. With its base in Beijing, this government worked closely with the newly formed North China Development Company to oversee industries that had previously been managed by Japanese corporations, and took over responsibility for the region's iron and coal mines, steelworks, and harbors. Once Nanjing fell, the Japanese installed a collaborationist government for central China. It was hard to find any Chinese leaders of caliber willing to take the job. But eventually another Qing *juren*-degree holder, Liang Hongzhi, accepted the post as head of the Reformed Government, with a corollary Central China Development Company.

In Taiwan, a Japanese colony since the Shimonoseki Treaty of 1895, the integration of economic and political life with mainland Japan occurred far in advance of the other regimes. Now Taiwan was supplying Japan with great amounts of industrial products, from wood pulp and chemicals to copper and foodstuffs. Its already impressive network of airfields was being expanded, as were ports and the railroad network. Children on Taiwan were thoroughly indoctrinated in the customs and values of Japanese life, and encouraged to learn the Japanese language rather than their own. Although the Taiwanese were thwarted in their attempts to set up a political assembly with its own representation and prevented from running independent newspapers, the island's economy was prospering under colonial rule.

The Chinese now living under either the Beijing or the Nanjing regime, if they knew anything about Taiwan, might have seen it as a preview of their future fate. Those who wanted to preserve their freedoms faced the choice—however risky—of joining one of the other regimes that had established new temporary bases: the Guomindang in Chongqing, and the Communists in Yan'an. The calls for unified resistance issuing from those two centers were powerful and emotionally compelling. Hundreds of thousands of people chose to make the long and dangerous journey to either Sichuan or Shaanxi. Workers carried the machinery and spare parts of factories across the country. Whole classes of university students from Beijing and Tianjin trudged 1,500 miles or more, with their books and personal belongings, to settle in Kunming at the Southwest Associated University, which for the time being provided sanctuary from the war.

Millions of other refugees had no specific destination, only the goal of fleeing Japanese assaults and bombing raids. As the battlefront migrated from north China to Shanghai, to Nanjing, and to Wuhan, a mass exodus emptied out cities in east and central China. In the autumn of 1937, an estimated 16 million people fled the battle zones in and near Shanghai. In Suzhou the population dropped from 200,000 to 50,000; in nearby Wuxi, 10,000 remained from 300,000 residents. Successive waves of refugees followed the fall of Nanjing in December 1937, the battle for Xuzhou, the breaching of the Yellow River dikes, and the fall of Wuhan in 1938. When the battles ended and some semblance of calm was restored, some refugees returned home, while others remained in temporary camps or continued on the move. The mass displacement of tens of millions (by the end of the war, numbering an estimated 60–95 million) had a profound impact on the social landscape of China. For formerly well-to-do families or educated individuals, the unraveling of comfortable lives of privilege was a disorienting experience. For those who were already poor and struggling to survive, wartime dislocation introduced new forms of trauma, rupturing the ties to family and native place that had provided measures of security. All kinds of people congregated in refugee camps and mingled on packed trains and ships—old and young, rich and poor, merchants and farmers, widows with young children and single men, Shanghai natives and Cantonese speakers. With these shared experiences of hardship, the refugee crisis brought opportunities for interactions across linguistic and social divides.[8]

But most people in north and east China did not flee; they had not the strength, the resources, or the will. They saw no great merit in the policies and the political practices of the Guomindang or the Communists, and chose to face an uncertain future with the Japanese. This was true of industrial workers, as well as of villagers in both north and south China. If they left their jobs or their land and took to the road, they had no guarantees of finding any work, unless they were conscripted into the armed forces. For their part the intellectuals had seen too much of the vindictiveness of the Guomindang and the Communists, however obscured for the moment by the rhetorical veneer of the united front.

Those who opted to stay and live under Japanese occupation often confronted agonizing choices. The question of whether to work for the Japanese directly, or for the collaborationist government in charge, was very difficult. Many people needed jobs. Some prominent writers and filmmakers were singled out and "invited" to produce pro-Japanese propaganda. If the goal was survival, it was not an option to decline. Lu Xun's brother, Zhou Zuoren, became one of the most conspicuous intellectual collaborators. (Lu Xun himself had died in 1936, so he was spared from having to make these kinds of choices.) His brother, also a well-known writer, was teaching at Beijing University in 1937 when the war broke out. Zhou Zuoren was the most prominent member of the faculty to stay. He had a large family to support, some very young and some elderly; he could not bring them along, and he refused to abandon them. He managed to avoid working for the Japanese for two years, but eventually, under duress, Zhou Zuoren agreed to serve as the minister of education in the north China collaborationist government.[9]

CHONGQING AND YAN'AN, 1938–1941

While the Japanese consolidated their hold over north and east China through the various collaborationist regimes, both the Communists in Yan'an and the Nationalists in Chongqing faced similar problems: how to protect their domains from further assaults, how to establish some form of viable governmental structure, and how to strengthen the loyalty of those living in the areas they ruled. Overlapping with these immediate needs each side had a longer-range goal—to build up support, through guerrilla forces or other means, inside the Japanese-dominated areas, so that later they might add these territories to their main centers of control.

Of the two, it was probably the Guomindang in Chongqing who had the harder time with these tasks, for they had lost more than the Communists. They faced a formidable problem of isolation, since they had no previous base of support in Chongqing, which was still in most ways a traditional city with little experience of modern industry or administration. If railways can be taken as one index for economic growth and integration, then the distance between Chongqing and any major railway line in 1937 shows the extent to which the central government was now cut off from the patterns of development that this form of transportation had made possible (refer to the map on page 339).

Since 1935, when Guomindang forces had entered Sichuan while pursuing the Long March fugitives, the Nationalist government had sought to break the power of local warlords and implement reforms that would bind Sichuan more strongly into the national fabric. A civilian provincial government was formed with centralized tax-collection powers, and magistrates were transferred into the province to supervise administration. The Nanjing government paid off provincial bonds with a gold loan worth 70 million yuan, issued 30 million yuan of the new *fabi* notes to redeem the variety of local currencies in circulation, simplified taxes, launched a road-building program, and conducted an intensive opium-suppression campaign.

These reforms were undermined, however, not only by resistance from local militarists, but also by a series of catastrophic droughts that hit the province in 1936, causing the loss of most of the winter food crops. Women and children dodged police patrols to eat the bark of Chongqing's ornamental trees. In early 1937 the police buried over 4,000 famine victims until special crematoria were built to speed the process of disposing of the dead. There were food riots in many Sichuan cities, and a predictable rise in banditry. When Chiang Kai-shek finally reached Chongqing on December 8, 1938, having flown from Wuhan via Guilin, it must have seemed a frail base of operations.

One of Chiang's first priorities was to align the neighboring province of Yunnan firmly with his Sichuan base. Yunnan had been run since 1927 as a virtually independent satrapy under warlord Long Yun. Kunming, capital of a province two-thirds the size of France, had a pre-war population of only 147,000; the effect of the 60,000 refugees who streamed into the city in 1937 and 1938 was therefore dramatic. Chiang Kai-shek confirmed Long Yun as governor, and the two worked together in uneasy alliance throughout the war. Long Yun refused to implement the censorship laws of the Guomindang, with the result that Kunming became a vibrant intellectual center, enlivened with the activities of refugee scholars and students at the Associated University.

As the projected terminus for a road being built over the mountains to Burma, Kunming achieved further prominence once the Yangzi was closed to non-Japanese shipping, and after the French caved to Japanese pressure to stop carrying military supplies on the railway line from Hanoi. The Burma

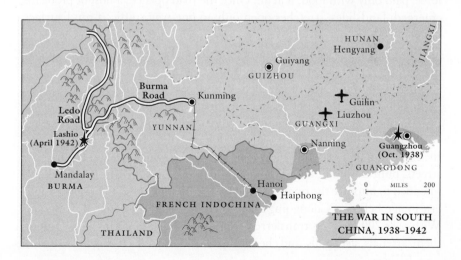

THE WAR IN SOUTH CHINA, 1938–1942

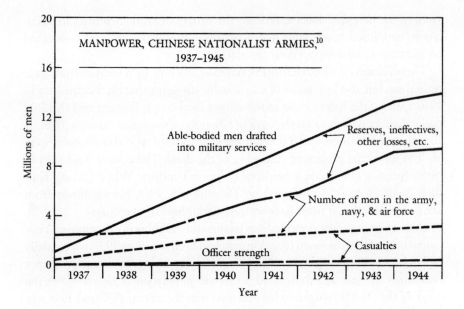

MANPOWER, CHINESE NATIONALIST ARMIES,[10]
1937–1945

Able-bodied men drafted
into military services

Reserves, ineffectives,
other losses, etc.

Number of men in the army,
navy, & air force

Officer strength

Casualties

Millions of men

Year

Road now was the only link to the gasoline and supplies needed to keep Guomindang resistance viable. Running about 715 miles (600 in China, 115 in Burma), the construction of this road, undertaken as the war flared, caught the attention of the world. Hundreds of thousands of Chinese laborers—men, women, and children—worked by hand in the mountains and gorges, hauling rock and earth in baskets, blasting stubborn boulders with bamboo tubes full of gunpowder. Thousands died from accidents and malaria, and surely many others from malnutrition, for this was mainly a conscripted labor force, paid only with food, if at all. Once the road opened, a host of problems emerged: landslides, stretches open only to one-way traffic, a mud surface dangerously slippery in wet weather, and an absence of telegraph centers or gasoline depots. But when the first supplies from Rangoon reached Kunming in December 1938, it marked a significant triumph.

The Burma Road became the lifeline for the Nationalist regime in Chongqing, and for the streams of refugees who arrived from every part of China. As the population tripled, Guomindang officials and municipal reformers worked to transform the city into the nation's wartime capital. They improved the transportation network and public sanitation, widened and renamed the streets, built hospitals, and developed the public health infrastructure—all intended to improve the quality of life for the residents, and to project a modern image befitting Chongqing's status as the anchor of national resistance. With over 200 factories transferred from central and eastern China (among them, arsenals, steel mills, and chemical plants for manufacturing armaments),

Armed only with red-tasseled spears, these young volunteers joined the Eighth Route Army, which became the Red Army, 1939.

Chongqing also became a center of industrial production. The dramatic transformations can be seen in the lives of women—from the 13,000 who worked in the cotton mills, to those who led refugee relief organizations, participated in wartime mobilization efforts, or became activists for child welfare and educational reform. The expanded social mobility of wartime conditions changed women's status, expanded career opportunities for some, and widened the horizons of their expectations.[11]

Paralleling the Guomindang's attempts at consolidation were those of the Communists in their Yan'an base area to the north. By agreements reached between the rival regimes in late 1937, the Red Army was constituted as the Eighth Route Army under nominal Nationalist authority. In September of that year the two sides pledged cooperation in critical areas, with concessions by the CCP: to work to realize Sun Yat-sen's Three Principles of the People; to give up armed rebellion, the forming of soviets, and the confiscation of landlord holdings; to abolish the autonomous government structure of the Shaanxi soviet; and to affirm Guomindang command over the approximately 30,000 troops of the former Red Army. Chiang called this "a triumph of national sentiment over every other consideration,"[12] although the CCP was also here following the practice ordained by the Comintern for all Communist parties internationally.

The astonishing announcement in August 1939 that the Soviet Union had signed a nonaggression pact with Hitler's Germany did not alter this basic united-front policy. Mao Zedong greeted the Hitler-Stalin pact as a positive step that would frustrate the plans of the French and British "international reactionary bourgeoisie," and would "deal a blow against the Chinese capitulators."[13] Nor did this new web of international agreements, despite the earlier Guomindang-Soviet nonaggression pact, mean that the Germans would restore the industrial-military deals that they had projected for China in the earlier 1930s. The Germans were now committed to support the Japanese in their East Asian policies.

Instead of organizing the areas they controlled into new soviets, the CCP announced the formation of two border-region governments. One was named Shaan/Gan/Ning, from the first syllables of the grouping of Shaanxi, Gansu, and Ningxia, and the second Jin/Cha/Ji, referring (less obviously, since these were archaic forms for the relevant provincial names) to Shanxi, Chahar, and Hebei. Japanese power was far stronger in the second border region than in the first; but since neither the Japanese, the provisional north China government, nor the Inner Mongolian Federation had complete control over its terrain, there was ample room for CCP political maneuvers, sabotage, and military recruitment. In addition, the survivors of the Communist forces who at the time of the Long March had been left behind in central China were now reorganized as the New Fourth Army. Since 1935 these guerrilla forces had lived an isolated and precarious life, often sheltered in mountains and forests, operating by their wits, and developing their own ties with the rural poor and those who resisted first the Guomindang and then the Japanese. Drawn together again after a three-year hiatus, this army of 12,000 combat troops was nominally subject to overall Guomindang direction but was actually commanded by experienced Communist officers.

In these early years at Yan'an the CCP tightened its organizational

Communist cadres distributing food in their border region of Shaan/Gan/Ning

CHINESE BATTLE CASUALTIES, 1937–1941[14]

Year	Japanese estimates	Chinese estimates
1937	—	367,362 (July–Dec.)
1938	823,296 (July 1937 to Nov. 1938)	735,017
1939	395,166	346,543
1940	847,000	—
1941	708,000	299,483

form—as the Guomindang had attempted to do—in three main areas: the party, the government, and the army. CCP membership increased dramatically in the period—from around 40,000 in 1937 to an estimated 800,000 in 1940—partly because of sustained recruiting efforts, but also because of the popularity of united-front policies. Temporarily forbidden to pursue land expropriation, the CCP implemented a program of rent reduction, and a graded taxation system that made it uneconomical for rich landlords to keep large holdings and allowed many poorer peasants to increase the size of their holdings. Thus villages could be rallied in loyalty to the CCP and to the anti-Japanese cause without divisive struggles.

The Yan'an government consisted of the central administration with its subordinate ministries, and a network of representative assemblies that ideally—and in some cases actually—reached down to the county level. The united-front agreements were honored by implementation of the "three-thirds system": no more than one-third of positions in government bodies would be held by CCP members; this would leave, in Mao's words, one-third for "non-Party left progressives, and one-third for the intermediate sections who are neither left nor right." Mao believed this system would guarantee CCP dominance, since if Communists of high caliber were chosen for their third of the positions, "this will be enough to ensure the Party's leadership without a larger representation."[15] The Communist military was anchored by the Eighth Route and New Fourth armies, with the Long March veteran Zhu De serving as commander in chief and Peng Dehuai as his deputy. In addition, local, full-time armed forces based in their own home areas were supported by militias of men and women who held regular jobs in farms or the towns, who proved invaluable in gathering intelligence, giving logistical support, and conducting guerilla operations. The CCP devoted much attention to making sure that at all levels its military forces did not exploit the local communities, paid for the food and supplies they needed, and did not molest the local women. Party cadres also worked to gain the support of the secret societies that were strong in north China, and to win them over to an anti-Japanese position. The result was a steadily widening popular base for the CCP.

While dampening social revolutionary forces in their border regions, in 1940 the Communists launched a series of attacks against Japanese strong points and railways in north China. Called the "Hundred Regiments Offensive" and coordinated by Peng Dehuai, more than one hundred units fought 1,824 engagements from August 20 to December 5. With the element of surprise, Communist forces scored numerous victories in the first three weeks of the campaign. When Japanese reinforcements moved in, however, the tide turned. The counterattacks, often of immense cruelty, destroyed whole villages to the last human being, farm animal, and building. As a result of the devastation, the population in the CCP's north China base areas dropped from 44 million to 25 million, and the Eighth Route Army lost 100,000 men to death, injuries, and desertion.

Meanwhile, the wary and fraying military cooperation between the Guomindang and CCP finally tore apart into open conflict. The New Fourth Army's expansion in central China gave the Communists a vital strategic presence in the Yangzi delta, which was the country's richest food-producing area and the focus for much of its heavy industry, now Japanese-controlled. The area was a maze of crisscrossing jurisdictions of Guomindang regular units, local militia, gangs of stragglers and deserters from regular units, and members of the Green Gang and other criminal organizations. Regretting the earlier united-front agreement that permitted some Communist units to regroup south of the Yangzi, the Guomindang generals in the area had been steadily trying to get them to comply with orders to move north. The Communists were reluctant, and in a series of skirmishes and one pitched battle, Nationalist troops trying to enforce the order suffered a serious defeat. In early December 1940, Chiang Kai-shek issued an ultimatum: any Eighth Route Army troops south of the Yangzi must cross to its northern bank by December 31; during the same period the New Fourth Army troops must begin moving northward, and cross over the north bank by January 31, 1941.

Dilatory in carrying out these orders—and possibly not intending to do so—the New Fourth Army command dickered with the Nationalists over their route of march, safe conduct, and the supplies and gold reserves that they had with them. Aware that Guomindang armies were massing against it, the New Fourth Army held public rallies to explain its loyal intentions, even as some units swerved south. In six days of fighting, from January 7 to January 13, 1941, Nationalist forces ambushed the southern wing of the New Fourth Army in the mountains, killing around 3,000. Many more were shot after arrest or taken off to prison camps.

Despite the losses, the incident carried considerable propaganda value for the Communists. They presented the ambush as a plot by Chiang, whose

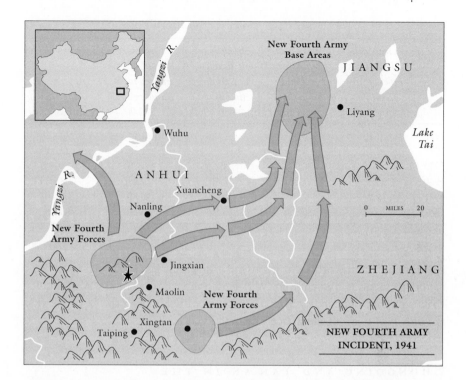

New Fourth Army
Base Areas

JIANGSU

Liyang

Wuhu

*Lake
Tai*

ANHUI

Xuancheng

Nanling

0   MILES   20

New Fourth
Army Forces

Jingxian

ZHEJIANG

Maolin   New Fourth
Army Forces

Xingtan

Taiping

NEW FOURTH ARMY
INCIDENT, 1941

arguments that CCP "insubordination" had to be punished sounded unconvincing. The CCP was also able to regroup the New Fourth Army just north of the Yangzi, and soon reestablished a large guerrilla base to the south of the Yangzi, west of Lake Tai, in the very same area they had been before. The "New Fourth Army Incident," as it was soon termed, did not end the united front, but it certainly highlighted the tensions within it. Thereafter, the Communists and the Guomindang, though continuing to maintain their alliance against Japan, did so with even greater mutual distrust.

Another major rupture in national unity materialized in March 1940, when Wang Jingwei announced his return to Nanjing as the head of a "reorganized" central government under Japanese sponsorship. As Sun Yat-sen's former lieutenant and one time second-in-command to Chiang Kai-shek, Wang was the most prominent and notorious defector. He had escaped to Hanoi in December 1938, and spent the better part of a year in negotiations with the Japanese, hoping for a settlement that would pave the way for national unification and the end of Japan's military occupation. The hopes for Japanese withdrawal were quickly dashed, and the conditions attached to Wang's administration were described as worse than the Twenty-One Demands of 1915. A Japanese

CHINA'S CURRENCY, 1937–1942[17]

	Nationalist-government expenditures (in billions of yuan)	Nationalist-government revenues (in billions of yuan)	Bank-note issues outstanding (in billions of yuan)	December retail-price indices, taking January 1937 as 1.00	Approximate value of yuan in U.S. cents
1937	1.16	0.87	2.06	1.18	.30–.29
1938	2.18	1.31	2.74	1.76	.29–.15
1939	2.80	0.58	4.77	3.23	.16–.06
1940	5.55	1.58	8.40	7.24	.08–.04
1941	10.93	2.02	15.81	19.80	.05–.03
1942	26.03	6.25	35.10	66.20	.03–.02

spokesman stated, without any sense of irony, that Wang's government was as independent as Manchukuo. Widely denounced as a traitor, Wang nonetheless pushed on, convinced that a negotiated peace with the Japanese was the only way to avoid the nation's destruction.[16]

CHONGQING AND YAN'AN IN THE WIDENING WAR

The eruption of World War II in Europe in the summer of 1939 strengthened Japan's hand in China. As in the Great War of 1914–1918, France, Great Britain, and Germany were now all preoccupied on their own fronts and had little time or energy to spare for East Asia. In that first world war, Japan had gained territory and concessions at the expense of Germany, while warily respecting British and French interests in East Asia; in the second, it became clear that Japan might be able to oust both Britain and France from their positions of power in the region. The force of "European imperialism," which had affected China's history so crucially, suddenly began to shrivel.

We have seen how the Japanese were able to pressure the foreign customs service and the once sacrosanct foreign-concession areas in Tianjin and Shanghai, how they closed the Yangzi to foreign ships, and how they forced France to close its railway lines in Vietnam to shipments for the Chinese. Now in July 1940, as Britain tried to recover from the crisis of the Dunkirk retreat and to rally its forces for the aerial Battle of Britain, Prime Minister Winston Churchill announced that he had yielded to a Japanese demand that the Burma Road be closed to all military supplies, trucks, and gasoline for three months. At the end of this period, with the battle against Germany going better,

Churchill ordered the road opened. But Chiang Kai-shek remained bitter, noting that the action had permanently destroyed British prestige in China.

One American adviser now observed that "the situation in China is critical as to morale, since China seems almost alone for the moment, and American action of some sort must not be delayed beyond the point where China's morale would crack."[18] But the United States, preoccupied with Japan's expanding power, did little between 1938 and 1941 but buy stocks of Chinese silver and grant the Nationalists loans in the $25-million to $50-million range. The loans could be used for nonmilitary purchases or price stabilization and were offered against tin and tungsten exports as security. Nevertheless, China's currency began to slide disastrously, as the previous table shows.

One of the Guomindang regime's most serious problems was Japan's air supremacy, which it unleashed on the wartime capital in a campaign of systematic bombing. Between 1938 and 1943, Chongqing endured more than 200 days of bombing, resulting in an estimated 15,000 deaths and more than 20,000 wounded. Incendiary explosives targeted residential districts, hospitals, and commercial thoroughfares. The sustained psychological terror inflicted on residents was intended to weaken the will to resist, destabilize the government, and force the Guomindang's capitulation. To cope with the ferocious air assaults, the municipal authorities built a network of underground shelters, developed a system of air raid alarms, and relied on early warnings from partisans from behind Japanese lines, who radioed when they sighted bombers taking off. But on three separate tragic occasions, hundreds (perhaps thousands) died from asphyxiation in overcrowded shelters or perished in panicked stampedes to escape.[19]

To augment its firepower and air defense systems, the Chinese Air Force purchased planes from the Soviet Union and sought help from the United States. By the end of 1940, a fleet of 160 aircraft could be deployed to defend Chongqing, a figure that increased to 364 a year later. By contrast the Japanese had 968 planes in China—many of them the fast and effective new "Zeros"—and another 120 in Indochina. Help for China also came from Claire Lee Chennault, a retired U.S. Air Force major general and adviser to Chiang Kai-shek since 1937. By informal arrangement so as not to violate neutrality agreements with Japan, Chennault recruited a large number of American pilots and brought them to China as "volunteers," both to fly in combat and to train Chinese pilots. Their feats made them famous as "the Flying Tigers," and they inflicted severe damage on the Japanese in late 1941 and early 1942, earning a bonus of $500 for every plane they shot down.

The Communists in Yan'an were denied even this small morale booster, since the Flying Tigers operated solely within the Chongqing orbit. The New

Fourth Army Incident, which had hit the Communist forces south of the Yangzi hard, was followed by an intensified series of Japanese attacks in the north after the Hundred Regiments Offensive. Chances of receiving help from the Soviet Union diminished following the signing of the Soviet-Japanese neutrality pact in early 1941 and Moscow's pledge to recognize the "territorial integrity" of Manchukuo. The CCP responded to this new blow with brave words: "We must return all the lost land of China. We must fight our way to the Yalu River and drive the Japanese imperialists out of China."[20] But they were in no position to act accordingly. The German invasion of the Soviet Union in June 1941 effectively ended any chance of resources from the Soviet Union until the war in Europe was over.

Yan'an's isolation was compounded by Chiang Kai-shek's decision, following the New Fourth Army Incident, to impose an economic blockade on the Shaanxi border-region government, to stop salt shipments to the region, and to end the subsidies that had been paid to the Eighth Route Army under the united-front agreements. The result was serious shortages in Yan'an accompanied by acute inflation. Desperate for military supplies, the Communists instituted a reward system that encouraged the local civilian population to comb each battlefield for weapons once the fighting was over.

Communist attempts at organizing rural communities in opposition to the Japanese were met with ruthless counterforce under the program given the shorthand term "three-alls," standing for the Japanese army's orders to "kill all, burn all, destroy all" in certain areas. When peasants crisscrossed the ground beneath their villages with mazes of tunnels to avoid discovery, the Japanese responded by pumping poison gas into the underground networks. One documented case of such an action states that 800 Chinese died. Another

details the execution of 1,280 villagers and the burning of every house in an eastern Hebei village. A third describes a "mopping-up campaign" in north China between August and October 1941 that left 4,500 villagers dead and 150,000 homes burnt. Seventeen thousand people from the area were taken to Manchukuo to work as laborers. The purpose of

Mao Zedong exhorting peasants to emulate "labor heroes" during a mass campaign in Shaan/Gan/Ning, 1943

such violence was to deter all Chinese from collaboration with the Communist forces. In many cases, it had that effect, but in countless others, it provoked a deep and bitter resentment of the Japanese that the CCP was able to activate.

The Japanese bombing of Pearl Harbor on December 7, 1941, was greeted with relief in Chongqing, because at last it heralded the full-scale involvement of the United States in the war against Japan. Ever since the Mukden Incident of 1931, Japan had been edging toward such a confrontation, and after the outbreak of the war in 1937, Japan viewed the American Pacific Fleet as a serious threat to its aims. If the U.S. fleet remained able to sail at will, Japan could neither enforce a total blockade of the China coast nor consolidate its hold over Vietnam and Burma. But Japan's attack on Pearl Harbor guaranteed fresh support for the Chinese, whose war now became part of the United States' own struggle. Aid to China came in the form of lend-lease supplies,* which from small beginnings rose to a total of a billion dollars by the end of the war, and large cash credits, which eventually reached a total of U.S.$500 million. This money came even though no one in the United States knew exactly how it was to be used, and Chiang Kai-shek refused to give any guarantees or accept any conditions attached to the funds.

President Roosevelt named a senior army officer, General Joseph Stilwell, to serve as his liaison with Chiang Kai-shek, as commander in chief of the American forces in the China-Burma-India theater, and to have overall supervision of lend-lease materials. Chennault was promoted to general, with his Flying Tigers reorganized as a regular part of the Fourteenth Air Force. Chinese morale was lifted further when Nationalist troops halted a massive Japanese attack on Changsha in Hunan, reemphasizing in a timely way that China was a formidable ally. Despite British reluctance, President Roosevelt accepted China as one of the Big Four powers in the Allied war effort, the others being the Soviet Union and Britain.

The Chinese army was indeed playing a crucial role in the Allied effort, tying down about two-fifths of all the forces available to the Japanese. The importance of China's resistance was made even more vivid by the sudden and almost total collapse of British forces in East Asia. It was not surprising that Hong Kong fell swiftly, since it was virtually indefensible. But Singapore, regarded as an impregnable bastion, fell on February 15, 1942. After only a day's fighting, its 130,000 garrison troops surrendered.

---

* "Lend-lease," as approved by the U.S. Congress in 1941, made military supplies available to Allied powers, stipulating that the supplies need not be paid for if they were used in the common cause against the enemy.

THE DISPOSITION OF JAPAN'S ARMY FORCES, DECEMBER 1941[21]

	China	Pacific and Southeast Asia	Manchuria	Japan	Taiwan and Korea
Army division (50)	21*	10†	13	4	2
Mixed brigade or equivalent (58)	20*	3	24	11	—
Army air squadron (151)	16	70	56	9	—

* Plus one cavalry group army and one army division at Shanghai under the direct command of the Imperial General Headquarters.

† Plus one special column. Of these ten divisions two were shipped from the China theater.

From the Chinese point of view, even worse was Great Britain's inability to hold Burma and defend the supply road it had reopened in late 1940. Unwilling to coordinate their strategy with the movements of Chinese troops or with General Stilwell, the British were outmaneuvered and outfought by Japanese forces. At the end of April 1942, the Japanese seized the key Burmese town of Lashio, once again severing the Burma Road as a crucial supply route for Chongqing. The Burma campaign cost Chiang Kai-shek many of the troops and most of the heavy equipment of the German-trained Fifth and Sixth armies, which constituted about one-third of his strategic reserves. From then on Chongqing would be almost as isolated as Yan'an, its only connection with the outside world being the dangerous air route over the Himalayas to India known as "the Hump."

A debate over military policy now erupted in Chongqing, pitting Chennault against Stilwell on the relative merits of air power versus conventional military power. Chennault argued in favor of air power, pointing out the comparative cheapness of this strategy, and the feasibility of flying in planes from India and supplying them with supplies and ammunition airlifted over the Hump. Stilwell countered with arguments that air forces had to be defended on the ground, and that the Nationalist armies were overofficered, underequipped, and undertrained. It would be far better to develop a smaller, elite Chinese army, and then to work patiently to reopen the land route through northern Burma, so that large-scale supplies could again reach Chongqing.

Chennault's arguments won out—he was both more tactful and more patient than "Vinegar Joe" Stilwell, and his flyers had notched up impressive victories. Stilwell had deep affection for the Chinese soldiers he had encountered. But his contempt for Chiang Kai-shek (whom he referred to in his dispatches by the code name of "Peanut") was matched only by his disdain for most of the Guomindang's commanding officers. So while Stilwell made some progress in developing training programs for Chiang's armies, most of

China's resources went into building up airfields along the eastern edges of the territory controlled by the Chongqing regime, between Hengyang in southern Hunan province, and Liuzhou in Guangxi.

In their border-region governments around Yan'an, the Communists also faced serious problems of revenue raising, social control, and morale. Their response, during 1942 and 1943, was to deepen the intensity of their involvement in the countryside through the mass mobilization of the population. According to some later analyses, the Communist party boosted the production and consumption patterns of a few localities under their control so that they could claim far greater successes than they actually achieved. There is also evidence that they eased a major financial crisis by permitting the peasants to resume opium production, which the Communists then shipped off to both Japanese- and Guomindang-controlled areas. (In financial reports, the trade was disguised by such euphemisms as "special products" and "soap.")[22]

In addition, intellectuals, particularly those in Yan'an, were introduced to the conditions of life in the countryside through campaigns that sent them "down to the villages" to learn from the peasants. From his earliest writings on, Mao Zedong had expressed disdain for the traditionalist elites of China, especially their ignorance of rural poverty and their impracticality. Like Chongqing, Yan'an had become home to thousands of refugees. In an intensive "rectification campaign" in 1942, people living in the Communist-controlled base areas were harshly reminded of the imperatives of socialist revolution. Those singled out for attack were criticized in mass forums for their views, forced to write lengthy self-criticisms, and demoted to lower or menial jobs. Some were physically maltreated or driven to suicide. Among the victims were followers of Mao's main rival for party leadership, Wang Ming, who since his return to China from the Soviet Union had been trying to strengthen his own power base. The Rectification Campaign helped Mao preserve his dominance as party leader and ensured the independence of CCP ideology from Soviet control.

Among the intellectuals sent to labor in the countryside was the writer Ding Ling, whose story "The Diary of Miss Sophie" had so well captured the anomie of China's youth in 1928, and who had joined the CCP after her husband's execution in 1931. Ding Ling had been held under house arrest in Nanjing by the Guomindang but managed to escape and reach Yan'an in 1936. Yet once in Yan'an, she began to write stories that criticized CCP cadres for insensitivity to women workers, and for enforcing an ideological outlook that destroyed individual initiative and opinion. She also argued that the party leadership was using the slogans of national resistance and party solidarity to undermine the recently hard-won rights of women.

In making an example of such people through the Rectification Campaign, Mao affirmed the role of the CCP in defining the limits of intellectual expression and inquiry. To reinforce this role, a number of essays—by Mao, Stalin, and others—were assigned to party members and intellectuals for general reading and discussion. In his own most detailed speeches of May 1942, Mao spoke of the social purpose of art and literature. Those in Yan'an must understand their duty to the masses; they must seek out the "rich deposits of literature and art [that] actually exist in popular life itself." These "deposits" had to be "the sole and inexhaustible source of processed forms of literature and art." Earlier Chinese artistic traditions, said Mao, and the foreign traditions that May Fourth intellectuals had espoused, must be kept firmly subordinate; they need not be completely rejected, but should be used "in a discriminating way . . . as models from which we may learn what to accept or what to reject." Above all, revolutionary writers and artists "must go among the masses of workers, peasants, and soldiers," both to learn from them and to "urge them on in unity and struggle."[23]

WAR'S END

In 1943 and 1944 the main pressures on the Japanese military came from American forces. China's greatest contribution was holding down a large number of Japanese troops, for the Japanese army never achieved its stated goal of using collaborationist troops to guard its areas of influence. Having won a spectacular naval victory in the Battle of Midway (June 1942), American forces were now involved in the slow and bloody ordeal of fighting their way back across the South Pacific, island by island. But as plans for the strategic bombing of Japan were developed by the U.S. Joint Chiefs of Staff, the possibility of deploying the powerful new B-29 bombers on Chennault's forward airfields became feasible and kept China in the minds of the main American, Russian, and British planners.

A number of developments in 1943 showed how decisively Japan's military triumphs—and China's refusal to surrender—had altered the century-old patterns of Western exploitation of China. One important indicator of change was that, following protracted discussions among the Allies, in January 1943 the hated system of extraterritoriality was abolished by common agreement. After a full century of this humiliation, foreigners (except those with diplomatic immunity) would now be subjected to China's own laws.* In August 1943, in a move orchestrated by the Japanese, Wang Jingwei's collaborationist regime in Nanjing took over administration of both the former International Settlement

---

* From June 1943 until the end of the war, however, U.S. service personnel in China were again put under American law.

and the French concession in Shanghai. And in December 1943, Chiang Kai-shek joined Roosevelt and Churchill at the Cairo Conference, where the leaders stipulated the return of Manchukuo and Taiwan to Chinese Nationalist control after the war.

Another indicator of the West's diminished status lay in deliberate Japanese wartime policies. In late March 1943, the foreign community of Beijing (excluding the Germans and a few other wartime allies) were rounded up and marched—loaded down with their baggage, golf clubs, and fur coats—in straggling lines to the railway station. From Beijing the foreigners were transferred to an internment camp at a former missionary compound in Shandong. Americans and Europeans in Shanghai were interned at other camps in central China, but different treatment was meted out to those from Jewish backgrounds. In mid-May, the Japanese moved the majority of Shanghai's 16,000 Jews—refugees from persecution in Europe—to a designated ghetto.* Many Jews, forced to sell their homes and businesses at short notice, were reduced to manual labor or eating in the soup kitchens that local charities kept going; nearly all suffered from malnutrition. But the Japanese did not bow to Nazi proposals that the Shanghai Jews suffer the same terrible program of extermination that had been the fate of their fellows in Europe.

The humiliations of these foreigners occurred during a lull in the heaviest fighting in the China theater, but the military stalemate ended abruptly in 1944. Chennault's vision of fighting the war in the air was implemented, with tens of thousands of Chinese laborers gradually expanding and improving a network of airfields east of Chongqing. In early June 1944, B-29 bombers launched their first significant raid from these new airfields against targets in Bangkok, Thailand. On June 15 they reached the southern Japanese island of Kyushu, dropping 221 tons of bombs on a steel plant there. More raids on industrial targets followed, on the Anshan steelworks in Manchukuo, an oil refinery in Sumatra, and airfields in Taiwan.

As Stilwell had warned, the Japanese struck back, and with massive force. In the summer of 1944, in an operation code-named Ichigo (meaning "Number One"), Japanese troops moved into Henan province to consolidate their hold over the Beijing-Wuhan railway, then moved southward to Changsha. This city, which had resisted so bravely in 1941, fell swiftly. The Japanese army pushed on into Guangxi, seizing the air bases at Guilin and Liuzhou in November. Two columns then swung westward, threatening Guiyang and even Chongqing. At this point the Japanese halted the campaign, apparently content to have smashed the Chinese airfields that had served as bases for the bombing of their

---

* The ghetto order excluded Ashkenazic Jews, mostly from Russia, who had settled in China prior to 1937.

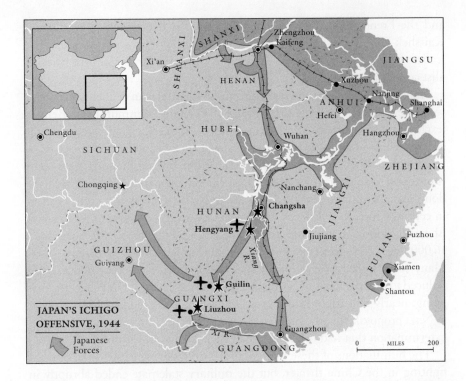

Xi'an
SHAANXI
SHANXI
Zhengzhou
Kaifeng
JIANGSU
HENAN
Xuzhou
Nanjing
ANHUI
Shanghai
Hefei
Chengdu
HUBEI
Wuhan
Hangzhou
SICHUAN
ZHEJIANG
Chongqing ★
Nanchang
HUNAN
Changsha
JIANGXI
Hengyang
Jiujiang
Fuzhou
GUIZHOU
Xiang R.
FUJIAN
Guiyang
Xiamen
Guilin
Shantou
GUANGXI
Liuzhou
JAPAN'S ICHIGO
OFFENSIVE, 1944
Xi R.
Guangzhou
Japanese
Forces
GUANGDONG
0   MILES   200

homeland. At the very moment of this success, however, came fresh proof
that the war was turning against Japan. In late November 1944, an intensive
B-29 bomber attack was launched against Tokyo from American bases in
the newly recaptured Mariana Islands.

Japan's victories in the Ichigo campaigns seriously damaged Chiang Kai-
shek's surviving military forces and severed additional large territories from
his control. At least as important, however, the Japanese victories contributed
to a further deterioration of Chinese morale, and of American confidence in
Chiang's leadership. Wartime Chongqing had long been a center of gossip and
malicious rumor, of stark contrasts of wealth and poverty, of financial speculation and price manipulation, of black-market goods and rumors of treason.
A Chinese poet, in a variant of Western-style free verse, powerfully captured
these contradictions in a 1944 poem that he concocted from movie advertisements, newspaper headlines, and government press releases in Chongqing.
He called his poem "Headline Music":

Tense, Tense, Tense
Bullish, Bullish, Bullish
Four thousand million dollars tumble in the gold market

Change, No change, Don't discuss national affairs
    Every tune grand, elegant, and elevating
    Every scene full of exquisite music and dance
    Sing in honor of schoolmates joining the army
    Dance for benefit of the refugees
A queue tens of miles long, spending the night in the cold wind
Peerless art on creamy artificial ice, spring color in the palace of the moon
Every word is blood and grief, moving the audience to tears
They carried and supported their old and young, we were deeply touched
    Domestically produced great film, a tragedy with costumes in the latest fashion
    The plot touchingly sad, tender, tense
    Ladies, old and young, are respectfully advised to bring more handkerchiefs . . . [24]

At this same time came the news that Chinese farmers in the former Guomindang-held areas had been killing, robbing, and disarming the Nationalist troops retreating from the Ichigo attacks. These were expressions of pent-up rage at the callousness of those same troops a year earlier, when they had enforced tax collections in kind in the midst of terrible famine. American reporters who traveled to inspect the famine-stricken areas of Hunan were shattered by what they saw. "The tear-stained faces, smudgy and forlorn in the cold, shamed us," wrote Theodore White,

> Chinese children are beautiful in health; their hair glows then with the gloss of fine natural oil, and their almond eyes sparkle. But these shrunken scarecrows had pus-filled slits where eyes should be; malnutrition had made their hair dry and brittle; hunger had bloated their bellies; weather had chapped their skins. Their voices had withered into a thin whine that called only for food.[25]

These journalists were outraged when reports of such miseries were cut from their dispatches by Guomindang censors; they blamed the Chongqing regime for both the human and the military dimensions of the catastrophe. Other Americans, including General Stilwell, were equally horrified at the Guomindang army's conscription campaigns, and at the sight of ragged men being led to the front roped together, already weakened almost to death by beriberi or malnutrition. Of the men drafted for active service between 1937 and 1945, approximately 10 percent died before seeing combat.

In the face of this grim situation, it was not surprising that American officers began to look toward the CCP in Yan'an for military cooperation. The Roosevelt administration discussed the possibility of arming the Communists to increase their effectiveness in combat against the Japanese, and contemplated making some lend-lease equipment available to forces that included Communists, if not to individual Communist units. And despite Chiang Kai-shek's irritation, a small U.S. observer group was sent to Yan'an in July 1944. The mission was formally restricted to obtaining intelligence information on Japanese movements, gathering meteorological data, and aiding downed pilots. Although under orders not to engage in "political discussion," the Americans got to know the Communist forces well and gained a high regard for their combat capabilities.

The presence of this American group in Yan'an was mainly the result of the urgings of Vice President Henry Wallace, who visited Chongqing in June 1944. President Roosevelt's special envoy Patrick Hurley, who went to Yan'an in November, pushed further for a rapprochement. In between these two missions Roosevelt himself was becoming insistent that Stilwell be made commander in chief of all troops in China. This was intolerable to Chiang and his senior advisers. After bitter lobbying and recriminations on both sides, Stilwell was recalled to the United States in October 1944 and replaced by General Albert Wedemeyer. Over the next three months, Chiang was also able to deflect further plans for American support to Yan'an.

The CCP were disappointed by this change of heart, but not surprised. They had been fighting on their own for a long time. So while they continued to call publicly for a coalition government that would unite China, and presented in their Yan'an base a smiling face to a growing stream of foreign visitors and journalists, they also worked systematically to deepen their support in the countryside. Their policies became once again overtly radical, even if they showed a certain flexibility in defining class relations in the areas they controlled. Landlords were now viciously attacked, and once again peasants were ranked according to the extent of their holdings.

By Yan'an definitions, "rich peasants" were those who earned more than half their income from the use of hired labor, but it was acknowledged that they might also be exploited as tenants at the same time. Therefore a key element in Communist social analysis and policy again became general living standards and the amount of livestock and tools owned. "Middle peasants" and "poor peasants" were defined in terms of subsistence as well as landownership: technically a "poor peasant" was one who could not reach subsistence level regardless of whether he owned or rented land, and so had to sell some of his labor; a "middle peasant" could sustain himself and his family by hiring other people's labor or occasionally hiring out his own. But who had the greater chance, in local eyes, of living a reasonably happy life? If, according to the community, it was the poor peasant, despite his poverty, and not the middle peasant, then the categories might be reversed. One example of this flexibility was the case of a widow with a five-year-old child. The woman, who owned 3.5 acres of land, three thatched houses, and one pig, was on the surface a landlord. She ended up, however, being classified as a "middle peasant" out of sympathy for her plight as a widow.

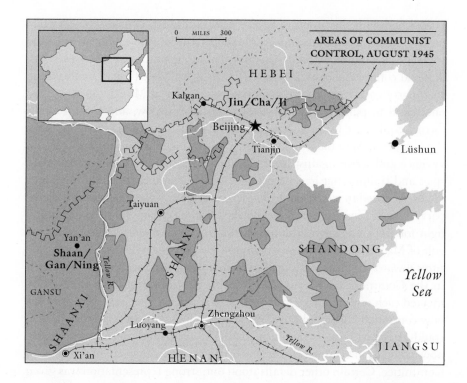

All over north China, in areas interspersed throughout nominally Japanese-controlled territory, and sometimes in areas where Guomindang pockets of resistance still lingered, the CCP continued this complex process of classifying and reclassifying, of analyzing rural social conditions and encouraging the breakdown of age-old patterns of deference through mass mobilization and public criticism. In many communities, it was now the Communist cadres who instituted a version of the *baojia* mutual-security system. This was composed of five-person "mutual guarantee" groups, each group formed voluntarily by those willing to vouch for the behavior of the other members. Not precisely linked to class analysis, this system effectively excluded from the community structure those identified as "socially unreliable" and gave a great sense of solidarity to the majority. Among the "socially unreliable" were those who stole crops, worked as prostitutes, had ties to bandits or opium smugglers, frequented Japanese-occupied areas, were prominent members of secret societies, or had once served in a collaborationist regime. But vaguer categories were also employed, showing how thoroughly CCP investigators questioned villagers about their neighbors. Those same surveys also warned against those who had a "mysterious past," committed adultery, had bad tempers, failed to attend political meetings, smoked opium, or had roving wives.[26]

Satisfied with the growth of CCP power in north China—membership now stood at 1.2 million, and over 900,000 troops were under arms in the Eighth Route and New Fourth armies—Mao Zedong convened the seventh national congress of the CCP at Yan'an in April 1945. (There had been no such party gathering since the sixth congress met in Moscow in 1928.) No one dared to publicly challenge Mao's leadership now, and several of his former rivals were forced to give public self-criticisms. Both before and after the Congress, Mao blamed himself in public for allowing excessive use of violence and terror against loyal Communists, in the frenzied hunting for spies and traitors that had been a part of the Yan'an experience for many. He even bowed in contrition before his colleagues.[27] But the text of the new party constitution acknowledged Mao Zedong Thought as the guiding light for the CCP, laying the foundation for what would later become the cult of Mao. In a report "On Coalition Government" Mao made some gestures toward the Guomindang, but claimed that the government developed in the Communist base areas was the correct form, and one that implemented each of the Three Principles of Sun Yat-sen. Since the Communists now controlled "liberated areas" with a total population of 95 million, Mao could afford to be self-congratulatory. The constitution centralized party power, and Mao assumed the newly formed post of chairman of the Central Committee. Certain other details stood out: strong representation was given to the rural areas, and references to the Soviet Union and the world Communist revolution were dropped. The CCP seemed to be emphasizing its independence.

The seventh CCP congress had been deliberately staged to coincide with the sixth Guomindang congress held in Chongqing. Those sessions conspicuously failed to boost Chiang Kai-shek's position. Instead, sharp criticism of the Guomindang came from the ranks of its own youth-corps members and from rival cliques within the party. Talk of corruption and demoralization was widespread. It was not clear if Chiang could keep the loyalty of even his own most prominent supporters.

Guomindang influence indeed seemed to be slipping not just in China, but overseas as well. Meeting at Yalta in February 1945, Roosevelt, Stalin, and Churchill made no attempt to fill Chiang in on the momentous decisions they made: that the Soviet Union would enter the war in Asia within three months of Germany's surrender; that Russia would regain all territory lost to the Japanese, including Sakhalin and the Kuril Islands; that Russia would be able again to "lease" the naval base at Lüshun and share in the benefits of an "internationalized" city of Dalian; and that it would once more be given a preponderant interest in the former Sino-Russian railways in Manchuria. The last three clauses were all major blows to China's postwar aspirations.

But with the war dragging on, the Guomindang continued to receive large amounts of lend-lease supplies from the United States. General Wedemeyer and his staff labored to improve the combat efficiency of thirty-nine selected divisions of Chiang's forces, with no more unsettling talk of arming or training the Communists. Knowing nothing of the Yalta agreements or the atomic-bomb program—which was shrouded in secrecy—Chiang believed the war would still take years to win. The battle plans charted a slow advance to the east coast and seizure of Guangzhou in late 1945 or early 1946. A march northward toward Shanghai would follow, a plan reminiscent of Chiang's Northern Expedition strategy of nineteen years before. In early August 1945, as an encouraging preliminary, Chinese forces recaptured Guilin and began to move south toward Hainan Island.

Germany's surrender in May 1945 cheered the Chinese but did not change the timetable. But on August 8, in response to the Yalta agreements, Russian forces moved into Manchukuo to attack the Japanese. Only two days before, the United States had dropped an atomic bomb on Hiroshima, followed by a second attack on Nagasaki on August 9. Five days later the Japanese sued for surrender. With an extraordinary suddenness, and in ways no one in China was adequately prepared for, the whole structure of power politics in East Asia had changed.

CHAPTER 18

The Civil War, 1945–1949

THE JAPANESE SURRENDER
AND THE MARSHALL MISSION

In his victory speech broadcast from Chongqing on August 15, 1945, Chiang Kai-shek celebrated the end of the war, thanking the soldiers and civilians who sacrificed their lives, the Allies, and a merciful God. "Right will triumph over might—this great truth which we never once doubted has been finally vindicated," he declared. "Our faith in justice through black and hopeless days and eight long years of struggle has today been rewarded." At the same time, looking to the future, Chiang sounded a sober warning:

> We have won the victory. But it is not yet the final victory.... Peace, when fighting has entirely ceased, will confront us with stupendous and difficult tasks, demanding greater strength and sacrifice than the years of war. At times we may feel that the problems of peace that descend upon us are more trying even than those we met during the war.[1]

From a personal perspective, the toll of eight years of turmoil and the uncertainty of the future weighed heavily on art historian Lin Huiyin. At the time of the Japanese surrender, Lin was seriously ill with tuberculosis. Her husband Liang Sicheng (the son of late Qing intellectual Liang Qichao) worked in cultural preservation for the Guomindang government. Writing to a friend from Kunming, Lin reflected,

> We have all aged greatly, gone through a peculiar form of poverty and sickness, endured long wars and poor communications and are now apprehending a great national strife

and a difficult future. . . . We are torn and shattered. We have emerged through various trials with new integrity, good, bad, or indifferent. We have not only tasted life but been tested by its grimness and hardship. We have lost much of our health though none of our faith. We now know for certain that enjoyment of life and suffering are one.[2]

The mixed feelings of resolve, hope, and exhaustion were widely shared, as China rejoiced in victory while confronting the daunting task of rebuilding the country. The first order of business, accepting the surrender, was a complex operation made more difficult by the intensifying rivalry between the Nationalists and the Communists. By earlier agreement, Chiang Kai-shek and American General Albert Wedemeyer had decided that U.S. forces, once available, would move swiftly to occupy Beijing and Tianjin and five key ports, including Shanghai. A priority was airlifting as many of Chiang's troops as possible from the Chongqing region to north and east China, so that Nationalist forces could accept the Japanese surrenders in person. From August to October 1945, American planes transported over 110,000 of Chiang's best troops to key cities. Japanese commanders were ordered not to surrender to the Communists, and in many cases they continued to clash with Communist forces until the Guomindang army arrived. For their part, Communist commanders tried to compel Japanese officers to surrender directly to them wherever possible, after which the Communists would take on the task of maintaining local law and order.

The surrender operation took months to complete. There were close to 1.25 million Japanese troops in the interior provinces, and another 900,000 in Manchuria, not counting the forces of the collaborationist regimes, armed or partially armed, and over 1.75 million Japanese civilians in the country. The Guomindang army, despite their enormous losses, still numbered 2.7 million troops in 290 divisions. The Communists' Eighth Route and New Fourth armies contained close to 1 million soldiers. The formal and dignified surrender ceremony at Nanjing, between the Japanese commander in chief for the China theater and Chiang Kai-shek, contrasted with the violence in Shanxi, where the warlord Yan Xishan used Japanese troops to help him fight off the Communists and to preserve his power. In the northeast, after arresting the Manchukuo emperor Puyi and accepting the Japanese surrender, Soviet troops allowed the stockpiles of arms and ammunition to fall into the hands of the CCP, whose troops had moved swiftly into the area.

While the military race to claim territory was on, the lack of coordinated advance planning for reconstruction turned out to have serious consequences for the Guomindang. Across China the physical infrastructure was shattered. There were tens of millions of refugees trying to make their way home; 15 to 20 million soldiers and civilians had died—on the battlefield, caught in crossfire, from bombing, famine, or disease. Coming to terms with the scale of destruction, social upheaval, and loss would require patience and compassion. Yet as the Guomindang took back city after city from the Japanese, a pattern of carelessness, inefficiency, and corruption whittled steadily away at the basis of their popular support. Many Chinese were outraged when military officers and politicians who had collaborated openly with the Japanese during the war were allowed to remain in their positions, just to prevent the Communists from expanding their territory. When anti-collaborator regulations were issued at the end of September, they were full of loopholes and promised leniency to those who had performed any patriotic acts during their term of office. The effect of these orders was further nullified by the promotion to senior ranks in the Nationalist armies of numerous officers who had served in Manchukuo, the Inner Mongolian Federation, or the north China collaborationist regime. Yet when it suited their purposes, the Guomindang also accused some people who had not fled the Japanese-occupied areas of having been collaborators, and punished them as such.

The Guomindang also mismanaged the difficult problem of stabilizing the monetary system. It was essential to firm up the exchange rate of the National-ist *fabi* currency, which had been used throughout the war in Chongqing, with the various currency notes issued by different regimes. By not acting decisively or promptly, the Guomindang allowed a chaotic situation to emerge; in one example, occupation currencies traded at 40 to the yuan in Wuhan, 150 to the yuan in Shanghai, and 200 to the yuan in Nanjing. Exchange rates between *fabi* and U.S. dollars also veered sharply, holding for a time at 700 yuan to U.S.$1 in Tianjin and ranging from 1,500 yuan to 2,500 yuan in Shanghai. Speculators shuttled between the cities, buying up U.S. dollars in Tianjin and selling them for a handsome profit in Shanghai. Food prices also began to rise uncontrollably, and no central authority had the power to hold them at a reasonable level.

Crowds in Chongqing celebrating victory over Japan, August 1945

In this dispiriting context, the United States continued to push for a rapprochement that might prevent a civil war. In August 1945, Ambassador Hurley escorted Mao Zedong from Yan'an to Chongqing for negotiations with Chiang Kai-shek. These talks continued until October 10, during the very period in which the two sides were sparring for dominance in east and north China; they resulted in the announcement of a set of principles that seemed a hopeful indication of future cooperation. Mao and Chiang declared that they agreed on the need for democracy, a unified military force, and equal legal status for all political parties. A national assembly or people's congress should be convened promptly, to mark the end of the period of political tutelage that Sun Yat-sen had said would precede the transition to democracy. The government was to guarantee "freedom of person, religion, speech, publication and assembly" and would abolish "special service agencies," leaving law enforcement to duly constituted police and the courts. In principle there would be local government elections, although there was no agreement as to scope or timing.

It was harder to reach a satisfactory compromise over local militias and the Communist-controlled base areas. The Communists, who had already captured Kalgan, the main railway junction of the far north, were content to state that they would pull their troops out of south China. Chiang, on the other hand, was determined to reassert his control over the entire country. In November he launched a fierce attack, sending his best forces into Manchuria, though he had not yet consolidated his hold over the south. As the fighting intensified, Zhou Enlai, who had stayed on as mediator in Chongqing, flew back to Yan'an. And in a surprise move, Ambassador Hurley resigned.

Apparently convinced that mediation was still possible, President Truman dispatched General George Marshall, the highly respected former head of the Joint Chiefs of Staff, as his envoy in December 1945. The U.S. mandate for further involvement in China was unclear now that the war against Japan was over. Nor could the United States honestly claim that it was playing a neutral role, after helping Chiang regain so many cities, advancing fresh credits to his government, and offering military equipment at bargain prices. Nevertheless Marshall convinced both parties to agree to a cease-fire beginning January 10, 1946, and persuaded Chiang Kai-shek to work toward convening the assembly he had discussed with Mao Zedong in the fall.

Accordingly thirty-eight delegates assembled in Nanjing for a "political consultative conference" on January 11. Among the thirty-eight were eight from the Guomindang, seven from the CCP, five from the newly formed Youth Party (which was emerging as a vocal group advocating for peace), and two

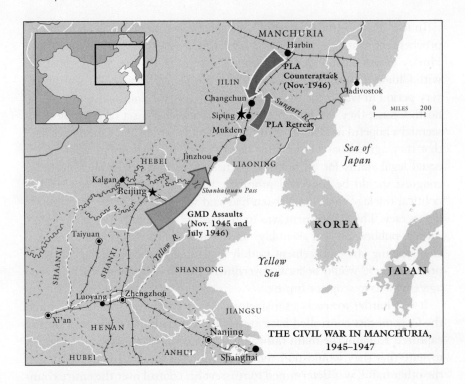

THE CIVIL WAR IN MANCHURIA,
1945–1947

from the Democratic League, which spoke for many liberal intellectuals. The others were from various smaller political associations or were unaffiliated. In ten days of discussion that were widely reported in the press and that led to an upsurge of hope for the future, the delegates seemed to reach agreement on all the most important points concerning constitutional government, unified military command, and a national assembly. In late February a subcommittee announced detailed plans for troop reductions by both sides.

These good intentions came to nothing—indeed perhaps had always been unrealistic. Military clashes between Communists and Nationalists continued in many parts of the country. The Central Executive Committee of the Guomindang made crucial changes to the conference agreements: limiting the veto power of the CCP and the Democratic League in the projected State Council, reaffirming presidential powers for Chiang Kai-shek, and reversing the stand on provincial autonomy. When the CCP and the Democratic League refused to cooperate further unless these changes were rescinded, the Guomindang went ahead anyway, convening in late 1946 a national assembly and drafting a constitution, both without genuine democratic participation.

The whole point of democratic reconstruction had been undermined, and the harassment and even assassination of leftists and liberals resumed. The most prominent victim was the poet Wen Yiduo, a persistent critic of the Guomindang, who was gunned down in Kunming in the summer of 1946. Yet once again, in June 1946, George Marshall managed to get the two sides to proclaim a cease-fire, this time in Manchuria. But even as the cease-fire was theoretically in effect, Nationalist troops were massing for a second assault on Manchuria, which commenced in July. In the meantime, the Communists refused to give up their base areas in north China, reorganized their forces as the People's Liberation Army (PLA), and shifted the focus of land reform from rent reduction and redistribution to confiscation and violent punishment of class enemies.

One exception to the pattern of noncooperation between the Nationalists and the Communists was the mutual effort to rechannel the Yellow River into its northern bed, from which it had been blasted by Chiang Kai-shek's engineers in 1938. In 1947, with aid from the United Nations Relief and Rehabilitation Administration, 200,000 workers moved 22 million cubic meters of soil to close a mile-wide breach and reinforce the hydraulic system.[3] But during this same period the verbal attacks by the CCP against the United States for aiding the Guomindang and interfering in Chinese politics grew in intensity. Several American servicemen were kidnapped by Communist forces, and in July 1946 a convoy of nine supply vehicles and its escort of forty marines were ambushed as they traveled from Tianjin to Beijing. Three American Marines were killed, one died later of wounds, and a dozen others were injured. Such incidents, indicative of new levels of anti-American hostility, promised to make the U.S. position in China untenable.

One further incident aggravated tensions to a breaking point. On Christmas Eve 1946, an American Marine was accused of raping a young woman, while another Marine helped restrain her and stood watch. This shocking incident immediately touched off a firestorm. The victim was a student at Beijing University, and as the news spread, the student community jumped into action, with thousands participating in a three-day strike and a seven-mile march. To the protestors, the rape symbolized the violation of China's national sovereignty. They demanded not only punishment of the perpetrators, but also an open trial, an apology from American officials, and the withdrawal of all U.S. troops from China. Posters and signs vilified American imperialism: "China is not a colony of the United States!" "U.S. soldiers can do nothing but kill and rape." "You are lonely, you are homesick—go home."[4] Members of the Communist Party helped to mobilize student activism and to broadcast the calls for American withdrawal. As outraged letters and editorials echoing these sentiments flooded the press, the furor spread to other cities, culminating in large-scale protests. Student demonstrators shouted down the Guomindang government's clumsy attempts to present the case as simply a personal misfortune. The once cheering crowds that had welcomed Americans as liberators in 1945 now became jeering mobs. If it had ever been possible for the United States to have helped ease the tensions in China, that time was clearly past. President Truman recalled George Marshall in January 1947, marking the beginning of American disengagement. By August, the majority of U.S. forces had withdrawn, leaving the Chinese to resolve or fight out the problems themselves.

LAND REFORM AND THE MANCHURIAN BASE

In the year following the Japanese surrender, the CCP intensified their land-reform program in the areas where they were strong, particularly in northern Jiangsu, areas of Hebei, and Shandong, as well as in its original base area of Shaanxi. Their success with land reform is remarkable considering the much lower incidence of tenancy in these provinces compared with most others. The tenancy rate was as low as 12 percent in both Hebei and Shandong, for instance, but as many as 56 percent of peasants were tenants in parts of the southwest. The Communist message was especially effective in the north, in part because the devastation caused by Japan's "3-all" campaigns came on top of the Guomindang's intentional flooding of the Yellow River and other war-related and natural disasters. But there were also historical reasons for the Communist successes in these areas. The old social order, once bonded by lineage and religious associations, and by local leaders whose prosperity was linked to the community's welfare, had been steadily eroding. The reorganization of local administration, first by the Guomindang and then by the Japanese, had left rural communities institutionally weak, their economic lives fragile, their destinies often in the hands of new types of rural power brokers, whom villagers referred to simply as "local bullies."

The CCP moved fluidly into such fragmented communities. Realizing that their greatest allies were the poorer peasants and the landless laborers, between 1946 and 1947 the CCP instigated a program that sought the elimination of tenancy and the equalization of both land and property within the villages. Violence was an integral part of this process, as old scores were settled with local thugs and personal enemies as well as with landlords. Although figures vary wildly, one source gives a total of 19,307 "instances of struggle" within the CCP-dominated areas of Shandong in 1945; many of these may have led to landlords' deaths. Accounts also show how a whole community could be roused through mass meetings to attack its wealthier members, to kill the most hated, and then to redistribute the confiscated property. The head of the recently formed peasant association in a Shanxi village described the interrogation of a landlord, Sheng Jinghe, against whom over one hundred charges had been registered with local CCP cadres:

> When the final struggle began Jinghe was faced not only with those hundred accusations but with many many more. Old women who had never spoken in public before stood up to accuse him. Even Li Mao's wife—a woman so pitiable she hardly dared look anyone in the face—shook her fist before his nose and cried out, "Once I went to glean wheat on your land. But you cursed me and drove me away. Why did you curse and beat me? And why did you seize the wheat I had gleaned?" Altogether over 180 opinions were raised. Jinghe had no answer to any of them. He stood there with his head bowed. We asked him whether the accusations were false or true. He said they were all true. When the committee of our Association met to figure up what he owed, it came to 400 bags of milled grain, not coarse millet.
>
> That evening all the people went to Jinghe's courtyard to help take over his property. It was very cold that night so we built bonfires and the flames shot up toward the stars. It was very beautiful.[5]

Dissatisfied with the amount of grain that they found, the villagers beat Sheng Jinghe repeatedly and heated an iron bar in the fire to threaten torture. Terrified, he confessed where his money was buried.

The land-reform programs in central and northeast China were subject, however, to a particularly grim corrective. Landlords who had been dispossessed and spared death—or the relatives of those who had been killed—returned whenever possible, to seize back what their families had lost. The threat of such returns would always hang over the CCP as they worked in local communities. In the summer of 1946, for instance, the Guomindang massed 150,000 troops to move on the twenty-nine counties held by the Communists in Jiangsu province. All twenty-nine were retaken by government forces. In the border area of Hebei/Shandong/Henan, where the Communists controlled sixty-four counties in 1946, forty-nine were recaptured by the Guomindang. Those who had sided with the Communists were held under what was euphemistically termed "voluntary surrender and repentance programs." They were jailed unless they could provide ransom money, and many were executed.

Because of the danger of counterattack in central and northern China, Manchuria became all the more important to the future hopes of the CCP. Despite the ravages of war, the region was rich in resources, with a population of over 45 million, large industrial cities, and extensive food reserves. The local topography, much of it forested and mountainous, also offered protection to guerrilla armies. Manchuria had a long history of labor agitation, dating back to strikes in 1906, some launched in conjunction with Russian workers. In the earlier years of the Japanese occupation, a vigorous CCP organization there had pushed through land reform in more isolated areas and carried out guerrilla activities. Arrest records of Communists in Manchuria, kept by the Japanese authorities, show that nearly sixty percent of the members were under age thirty, and represented a wide range of occupations: farmers, factory and railway workers, merchants, teachers and students, soldiers and policemen.

During the war with China, the Japanese—nominally working through the Manchukuo authorities—had become skillful at rounding up Communists in the region. Much of this success came through a ruthless policy of grouping more than 5 million peasants from isolated areas into some 10,000 "collective hamlets," where they lived under police supervision. Their original homes were then destroyed so they could not give shelter to the enemy. The terror had been intensified by the Japanese use of Communist prisoners—or those alleged to be Communists—in live human experiments conducted at secret camps. The prisoners were infected with fatal strains of plague germs, subjected to vivisections, or used in "studies" on the effect of extreme heat and cold on living test subjects.

The scattered remnants of the region's Communist groups resurfaced in 1945, after Japan's defeat and the advance of Russian soldiers into Manchuria. These guerrilla forces regrouped with the arrival in late 1945 of the almost 100,000 Eighth Route Army troops who accompanied General Lin Biao. The guerrillas, by actively recruiting in the countryside, had in the meantime assembled a People's Self-Defense Army of around 150,000 men. Many of these troops were Koreans, fugitives from the Japanese occupiers of their homeland, who had stayed in Manchuria after 1945 when their country was divided, the north now being in the Soviet camp and the south in the American. There were also about 25,000 troops from the Young Marshal Zhang Xueliang's former command, now led by his younger brother.

As soon as Lin Biao's forces arrived in Manchuria in the fall of 1945, they showed a determination to take and hold the key cities. In so doing they moved beyond the CCP's predominantly rural strategy. The Soviet Union held the main industrial cities, the railways, and the mines. With Soviet help the Chinese Communists took stockpiles of Japanese weapons and equipment. But while in Manchuria, the Soviets also seized rich stores of food and machinery for their own use and as reparations for their massive losses in the war against Germany. According to an American investigative team, they were especially thorough in removing power-generation equipment, transformers, electrical motors, laboratories and hospitals, and the best machine tools. The Soviets also took U.S.$3 million in gold and issued profuse runs of short-term bank notes.

Total Japanese investments in Manchuria were estimated at 11 billion yen in 1945. When Soviet troops pulled out in 1946 much of this was seized by the Guomindang, including the Anshan steelworks, the Liaoyang cotton mills, the Fushun coal mines, and many hydroelectric stations. As in Shanghai and elsewhere, the arriving Guomindang officials were ruthless and wasteful in their takeover of industrial plants. Profiteering was common, along with the renting out—for private gain—of public properties. As one newspaper correspondent observed in late 1946, "As for the common people, they feel on the one hand that all under heaven belongs to the southerners and on the other that life today is not as good as it was in Manchukuo times."[6]

The Communists, still too weak to hold southern Manchurian cities against the numerically superior and well-armed Guomindang forces, made their main urban base in Harbin, just north of the Sungari River. This industrial and commercial city of around 800,000 people became their revolutionary nerve center. The personnel to direct the expanding revolution were trained by veteran cadres in special institutes in the city, and all modern means of communication—newspapers, films, magazines, radio—spread the message of communism to the citizens. To ease the task of governing the urban population, the CCP leaders divided the city into six districts, which were subdivided in turn into fifty-eight street governments, each responsible for about 14,000 people. To cope with the large number of transients—laborers, hawkers, porters, droshky drivers—registration campaigns were conducted, bandits and destructive elements rounded up, and 17,000 citizens organized into "night watchmen self-defense teams." Each lane and alley was also charged with forming its own patrols; as with the old *baojia* mutual-security system, witnesses who failed to report a crime would be treated as if they were the perpetrator. Travel was controlled by a rigidly supervised passport system.

In an emergency test of municipal governance, CCP leaders in Harbin had to cope with an outbreak of bubonic plague. The plague was spread by flea-infested rats that had been raised by Japanese military researchers conducting germ-warfare experiments. At war's end in August 1945, the Japanese released the rats. After an incubation period in 1946, the disease claimed over 30,000 lives in 1947. The casualties were not far higher because effective quarantine and inoculation measures were taken by the Communists, aided by health experts from the Soviet Union, and all road and rail traffic was strictly controlled to prevent those infected from spreading the plague farther afield.[7]

From its base in Harbin, the CCP sent teams of cadres into the countryside to draw the peasants to their cause with the promise of land reform. The Communists called for the confiscation of all land owned by the Japanese and by collaborators—a prodigious amount, considering the nature and thoroughness of the Japanese occupation. There were so many large estates in the area that the 12,000 land-reform cadres assigned to the work rarely bothered with landlords holding less than 75 acres—a farm that would have seemed enormous in areas south of the Great Wall. Manchurian landholding featured a number of unique aspects that further taxed the ingenuity of land-reform leaders. One was the so-called "system of dependents," consisting of farm workers who were neither tenants nor day laborers, but people who lived with the landowner's family and worked the land in return for a percentage of the crop. Another was the "assignment system," by which a worker might be given his own land, tools, and house by the landlord, without being charged rent, in return for working a certain number of days per year without further compensation.

While urban and rural reform proceeded in the Communist-controlled areas, Lin Biao continued to build up the People's Liberation Army as a conventional—not a guerrilla—fighting force. The task was not easy. As a result of the Guomindang's assaults in 1945 and 1946, the Communists were pushed north across the Sungari River, while the Nationalists cleared a wide corridor along the coast north of Shanhaiguan, leading through Jinzhou to Shengyang and Changchun (refer to the map on page 374). Lin Biao, however, held onto Harbin, and astonished the Guomindang generals by crossing the frozen Sungari in November 1946 and attacking their armies in their winter quarters. Not allowing the Nationalist troops time to recover, Lin followed this up with a series of attacks across the river in early 1947, culminating in a massive assault on the railway junction of Siping in May with 400,000 troops. Beaten back with heavy losses by a concentration of Nationalist forces backed by air power, Lin regrouped and isolated the key Nationalist-held cities by destroying the railway lines that connected them. Morale among the garrison troops began to crack, and it became apparent how seriously Chiang had miscalculated in moving into the northeast before consolidating his power in north and central China. The Nationalist troops in the campaign abandoned substantial amounts of arms and equipment, which fell to the Communists. Nationalist strategy leaned toward the defensive, opting to dig in behind fixed emplacements rather than pursue Lin Biao's forces.

THE LOSING BATTLE WITH INFLATION

On the surface the most urgent aspect of the crisis facing the Guomindang was the steady loss of territory in the north to the Communists, and the attendant erosion of military morale. But equally important was the alarming growth of inflation, which affected the entire population and undermined the government's plans for reconstruction.

THE COURSE OF *FABI* DEPRECIATION,
SEPTEMBER 1945–FEBRUARY 1947[8]
(SEPTEMBER 1945 = 100)

Month	Shanghai wholesale price index
1945	
October	110
November	288
December	257
1946	
January	269
February	509
March	742
April	748
May	1,103
June	1,070
July	1,180
August	1,242
September	1,475
October	1,554
November	1,541
December	1,656
1947	
January	1,990
February	3,090

The economic crisis confronting the Guomindang in the fall of 1945 had many sources, as we have seen: the muddle and graft involved in the return of Japanese businesses to their previous owners, wide-scale unemployment compounded by defense industry cutbacks and the demobilization of many soldiers, the complexities of multiple currencies in circulation and the opportunities for speculation. The government response to money shortages was to print more banknotes, which contributed further to the inflationary spiral. Taking September 1945 as the baseline, the previous table shows that wholesale prices in Shanghai had increased fivefold by February 1946, elevenfold by May, and thirtyfold by February 1947.

Anyone on a fixed income was disastrously affected by the precipitous rise of prices. Industrial workers protested with special vigor. Despite the Guomindang supervision of all labor-union activities during World War II, soon after the war ended thousands of workers began to go out on strike. In 1946 there were 1,716 strikes and other labor disputes in Shanghai, all mounted in violation of the Guomindang laws requiring arbitration with official mediators

Shanghai citizens desperately trying to reach a bank to change their depreciating currency, December 1948

before work stoppages began. The Communists had successfully infiltrated many unions, and although the information was kept secret at the time, the CCP later revealed the pattern of influence that it had managed to develop in the closing year of the war and immediately afterward. In Shanghai Communist members were covertly installed in the Number 12 Textile Mill; the Dalong Machine Factory; the French Tram, Power, and Water Company; the Number 9 Cotton Mill; the Shanghai Power Company; the customs collection agency; and several department stores. Similar patterns developed in other cities with industrial concentrations, such as Tianjin, Wuhan, and Guangzhou.

The first significant strike of this postwar wave was at the Shanghai Power Company. The strike began in late January 1946 after several worker representatives were dismissed by the company. When fellow workers protested, they were locked out of the plant, but managed to prevent others from going in to keep the power station running. With power cut off, the negotiations had to be conducted by candlelight. Forty local unions joined in a demonstration in early February, which was followed by a show of solidarity involving representatives from seventy enterprises and businesses. The power company eventually yielded.

The government responded to this and other incidents with a softer line than its past record might have suggested, in what was clearly an attempt to

SHANGHAI WHOLESALE-PRICE AND COST-OF-LIVING INDEXES, 1947–1948[9]
(MAY 1947 = 100)

Year	Wholesale-price index	Cost-of-living index
1947		
June	112	107
July	130	122
August	141	131
September	179	146
October	282	208
November	319	226
December	389	290
1948		
January	544	405
February	780	642
March	1,260	923
April	1,460	1,100
May	2,100	1,432
June	7,650	3,022
July	11,100	5,863

buy off the workers. Despite the severe inflation, the government guaranteed to industrial workers wage rates primed to 1936 pay scales, multiplied by the current cost-of-living index. At the same time, the Guomindang tried to undercut the labor movement by disbanding certain unions and re-forming them into fragmented units that would be easier to supervise and manipulate. Unemployment continued to climb in late 1946, reaching around 8 percent in Shanghai, 20 percent in Guangzhou, and 30 percent in Nanjing.

The pegging of workers' wages to the spiraling price index failed to placate labor and displeased employers, who felt that increasing labor costs put them at a competitive disadvantage against other industrial countries. In February 1947 the government tried another tactic—the imposition of price and wage ceilings. Wages were to be frozen on the basis of the January 1947 cost-of-living index, and in all large cities price controls were set on rice and flour, cotton yarn and cloth, fuel, salt, sugar, and edible oil. A meticulous system—at least on paper—stipulated exact amounts of these commodities that would be made available to each worker, along with an allowance of coal briquettes for cooking and heating. The controls had some positive effect during March 1947, thanks to vigorous police supervision, but distribution inefficiencies, hoarding, and the drop in production of certain items (the response by producers to what they considered unprofitable prices) brought a return of inflationary spiral. By April 1947 rice prices were almost double February's level. By May, in the face of mounting protests and evidence of failure, the freeze mechanisms were abandoned.

In the summer of 1947, as Chiang's Manchurian campaign was beginning to falter disastrously, the Guomindang again acknowledged the financial crisis. This time, in July, they attempted to work through the Central Bank of China to offer a program for controlled distribution of food and fuel at artificially lowered prices. The beneficiaries of this plan were to be government employees, schoolteachers and students, factory workers, and those in certain cultural fields. This ambitious program, mainly confined to major cities, did not halt inflation. It did, however, force the cost-of-living index in Shanghai below the wholesale price index, suggesting partial success. Allocations of raw materials for factories, along with coal and imported oil, were rationed among private firms and the public utilities, again with some effect. But the overall price rise continued at an alarming rate through the end of 1947 and into 1948. In the spring of 1948, the government began issuing ration cards for staple foods to residents of the large towns, but this measure also failed to stop the price rises, although it did win the government some popularity for a brief time.

The indexed figures were dramatic enough, but what the inflation meant for the actual use of cash was becoming catastrophic. Even with notes issued in enormous denominations and shopkeepers changing their price cards several times a day, there was little hope of coping with cash transactions. A standard large sack of rice (weighing 171 pounds in Western equivalents) sold for 6.7 million yuan in early June 1948 and 63 million yuan in August. In the same period, a 49-pound bag of flour went from 1.95 million to 21.8 million yuan, and a 22-gallon drum of cooking oil rose from 18.5 million to 190 million yuan. (The summer 1937 prices for the same volumes of these three commodities had stood at 12, 42, and 22 yuan, respectively.)

In July 1948 Chiang Kai-shek met with T. V. Soong and his other senior advisers to discuss a bold plan to stem the chaotic financial slide. The decision was made to switch to a new currency, abandoning the *fabi* yuan and inaugurating a gold yuan, at a conversion rate of 3 million *fabi* yuan to 1 new yuan. Several Guomindang advisers warned that the new currency probably could not hold firm unless the government drastically reduced its deficit spending, much of it the result of the huge military expenses to which Chiang was still committed. (The deficit in 1948 was 66 percent of total expenditures.) And many of them felt that the new measures would succeed only if the U.S. government agreed to provide a large currency-stabilization loan—which in fact the United States refused to do.

Despite these warnings of problems to come, Chiang Kai-shek used his presidential powers to declare a series of emergency measures on August 19, 1948. To inspire confidence in the new notes, the government undertook not to print more than 2 billion of them. Wage and price increases were forbidden, along with strikes and demonstrations. And any gold and silver bullion and foreign currencies held privately by Chinese citizens were to be turned in to the banks in exchange for gold yuan, thus boosting government reserves of specie and foreign exchange. Sales taxes on commodities were sharply increased in order to raise more revenue. Yet, in what many considered a sellout to the wealthy, those with large bank accounts outside China—such as in Hong Kong, the United States, and Switzerland—were not required to exchange those funds for gold-yuan notes. Bank deposits overseas of over U.S.$3,000 were to be reported to the government, but there was no mechanism for assuring that this would be done.

The one place where the emergency laws seemed to have even a faint chance of succeeding was Shanghai. Here Chiang Kai-shek's son by his first marriage, the Soviet-educated Chiang Ching-kuo—who had returned to China in 1937 and worked several years as an administrator in Jiangxi—was appointed commissioner in charge of the reforms. He moved to the task with an immense amount of energy and sincerity, backed by tough implementation measures. In Shanghai, to urge public compliance, Chiang mobilized criticism against hoarders and speculators, ordered the arrest and occasional execution of offenders, and raided warehouses and suspects' homes. He also employed local youth organizations along with the paramilitary forces of the newly established anti-Communist Bandit Suppression National Reconstruction Corps to help him in his task. "Secret-report boxes" were placed in the streets so that citizens could report speculators or anyone who defied the bans by raising prices in their shops. Loudspeaker trucks cruised the streets, reminding people of the new laws. Maximum publicity was given to important arrests. One of them was the Green Gang leader Du Yuesheng's son, charged with black-market stock-exchange trading; other financiers were jailed for foreign-exchange manipulation.

But despite dedication and strenuous enforcement attempts, the gold-yuan plan failed. Shanghai was, in any case, not isolated from the rest of the country, and the more successful Chiang Ching-kuo was, the greater the pressure on Shanghai businesses to sell their goods elsewhere, where prices continued to rise. It also made no sense for farmers to sell their produce in Shanghai at low prices when they could get much more elsewhere. Accordingly the city began to experience shortages of food and manufactured goods. Nor did the government hold firm to its plan. When it imposed new taxes on sales of certain consumer goods such as tobacco, shopkeepers simply closed their doors until they won permission to raise their prices by the same amount as the new taxes. News also spread that the note-printing program was accelerating and promised soon to exceed the ceiling of 2 billion gold yuan pledged by the

Shanghai Wholesale-Price and
Cost-of-Living Indexes, 1948–1949[10]
(August 1948 = 100)

Year	Shanghai wholesale-price index	Shanghai cost-of-living index
1948		
September	106	N.A.
October	118	N.A.
November	1,365	1,170
December	1,921	1,670
1949		
January	6,900	6,825
February	40,825	52,113

government. By October 1948, with shops emptied of goods, restaurants closing, and medical supplies unobtainable, the failure of the reforms was clear.

For a moment in September and October, Shanghai had held firm, allowing hope that the economy could be turned around. What followed next is most simply shown by the figures in the preceding table. The vaunted gold yuan began to follow in the steps of the old *fabi* currency. The Chinese republic had become, for all practical purposes, a barter economy.

Defeat of the Guomindang Armies

It was in this context of a final loss of confidence in the economy and the political policies of the Guomindang that the Communists forged their conclusive military victory. In the spring of 1947, the Nationalists had managed to keep open four strategic corridors in north China: one running north of Beijing through the Shanhaiguan pass to Shengyang and Changchun in Manchuria, one southwest from Beijing to Yan Xishan's armies in Taiyuan, one northwest from Beijing along the Kalgan railway to Baotou, and one within Shandong linking Jinan to the port of Qingdao. They also held the key railway linking Xuzhou to Kaifeng, Luoyang, and Xi'an.

But the Communists now controlled much of the north China countryside. Guerrilla fighters constantly disrupted Nationalist supply lines, making relief of the beleaguered forces slow and dangerous. By May 1948 the situation of the Guomindang armies was becoming hopeless. Both Shengyang and Changchun were surrounded by Communist troops and could be supplied only by air. There were 200,000 Nationalist soldiers in Shengyang supported by artillery and tanks, but their strangulation was assured if the airfields fell.

Yet Chiang Kai-shek refused to pull those troops back south of the Great Wall and fortify his defenses in north China. He had invested too much of his prestige in the Manchurian campaign to back down now. Meanwhile, Communist forces tightened the stranglehold on Changchun, cutting electricity and eventually food supplies. The city of Luoyang, after changing hands three times in seesaw fighting, fell to Communist forces in April 1948, severing Xi'an from the east. Major Communist victories in Shandong cut the Jinan-to-Qingdao corridor, isolating the 100,000 Nationalist defenders in Jinan. The Communists, under Peng Dehuai, also recaptured Yan'an in March, and that spring Peng made a bold move toward Sichuan, although he was beaten back after heavy fighting.

Given added confidence by these victories and by the quantities of vehicles, arms, and ammunition that had fallen into his troops' hands, Mao Zedong announced in 1948 that the People's Liberation Army would shift from a strategy of predominantly guerrilla warfare to one of conventional battles. The Communists had already conducted such campaigns in Manchuria, but now they were directed at Kaifeng, the city on the Yellow River that guarded the railway junction of Zhengzhou. The Nationalists holding the area numbered 250,000 regular troops, supported by 50,000 men in the Peace Preservation Corps. Against them the Communists threw 200,000 veteran troops in five groups. The Communists managed to seize and hold Kaifeng for a week in late June, but pulled back when Nationalist reinforcements counterattacked, aided by air strikes. Suffering 90,000 casualties, however, the Nationalists' apparent victory was hollow. The Communist retreat brought little lasting reprieve to the Guomindang, whose senior military officers made a survey of relative troop strengths and concluded that the Communists were making relentless gains, as the following table shows.

SHIFTS IN GUOMINDANG AND CCP TROOP STRENGTH, 1945–1948[11]

	August 1945	June 1948
Guomindang		
Well-armed troops	1,620,000	980,000
Poorly armed troops	2,080,000	1,200,000
Artillery pieces	6,000	21,000
CCP		
Well-armed troops	166,000*	970,000
Poorly armed troops	154,000	590,000
Artillery pieces	600	22,800

* This estimate is extremely low, given what we know of CCP power in Yan'an at the war's end.

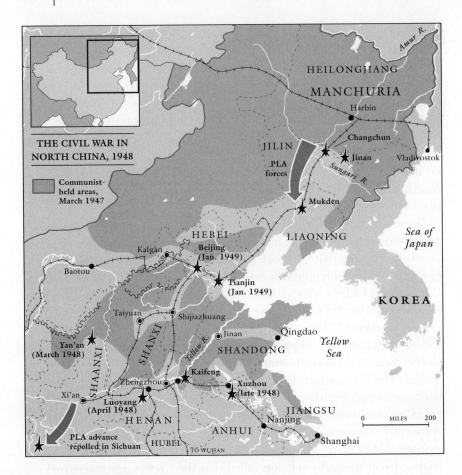

THE CIVIL WAR IN
NORTH CHINA, 1948

Communist-
held areas,
March 1947

This bleak assessment came at a troubled political moment. Chiang Kai-shek had been overwhelmingly reelected president in spring 1948 by the new National Assembly—the one declared invalid by both the CCP and the Democratic League—and had been given wide-ranging powers to bypass the fledgling 1947 constitution, in order to avert imminent danger to state security. But his power was eroding, and his waning popularity suffered further damage in July 1948 with the killing of unarmed students by government forces.

This tragedy had its roots in the constant fighting that was filling north Chinese cities with refugees, of whom the most vocal were students, displaced from their schools by Communist victories, and reassigned by the Guomindang into specified new locations. Given only a small subsistence allowance, such students became homeless transients, sleeping in parks or temples and sometimes turning to petty crime to survive. Five thousand students from

Manchuria, flown south to Beijing in a publicity-conscious gesture by the government, had been reduced to such dire straits. In July 1948, reacting to news of plans to draft them into the Guomindang army, they formed an angry demonstration and marched on the residence of the Municipal Council's president. To stop them, the garrison commander mobilized armored cars and 200 soldiers, who opened fire with machine guns. Fourteen students were killed and over 100 wounded, inevitably reminding people of the May Thirtieth demonstrations against the British in 1925, the killings of Beijing students in 1926, and the protests of the December Ninthers in 1935. By September 1948 the number of student refugees had grown even higher; in Beijing there were 20,000 to 30,000, with another 20,000 in Nanjing and 10,000 in Wuhan.

Shortly after this massacre and the failure of the gold-yuan currency reforms, the heavily garrisoned city of Jinan fell, undermined from within by Communist subversion and troop desertions; thus Chiang lost his last main base in Shandong. A series of tactically brilliant campaigns conducted by Lin Biao in Manchuria during September and October led to the fall of Shengyang and Changchun, and the destruction, surrender, or desertion of 400,000 Nationalist troops. Only 20,000 escaped, evacuated by sea from south Manchuria. In Changchun, the year-long siege resulted in the deaths of an estimated 200,000 civilians.

Noting that the loss of Manchuria was "discouraging," but "relieves the government of a formidable burden, so far as military defenses are concerned," Chiang tried to regroup for a stand in north or central China. Zhu De, commander in chief of the Communist armies, decided to commit 600,000 troops to the seizure of Xuzhou, opposing an equal number of Nationalist troops, who also had air superiority. In a sixty-five-day battle toward the end of 1948, the Communists showed a new mastery of artillery power and emerged victorious by outmaneuvering Chiang's generals. The Nationalist commanders were plagued by the contradictory orders issued by Chiang Kai-shek, and by the massive desertion of their troops. In this complex and protracted campaign, the extraordinary Communist effort at mobilizing upward of 2 million peasants in four provinces to provide logistical support was directed by Deng Xiaoping, once the youngest of the work-study students in France, now a veteran party organizer of forty-five.

In a third campaign overlapping with these two, Lin Biao captured Tianjin for the Communists in January 1949. Turning west with the bulk of his forces and holding an overwhelming tactical advantage, he persuaded the Nationalist general commanding Beijing to surrender after a siege of seven days. When Communist troops entered the old imperial capital on January 31, north China was irrevocably lost to the Guomindang.

As Mao Zedong set out for Beijing in March, he half-jokingly told Zhou Enlai, "Today we are going to the capital to take the imperial exam." Having proved themselves on the battlefield, this would be the litmus test of the CCP's ability to govern. Mao sounded a cautionary note, saying that they must be mindful of the negative example of Li Zicheng, the bandit who deposed the last Ming emperor and pillaged Beijing in 1644. The conquest of so many large cities in rapid succession confronted the CCP with new challenges and marked a fundamental shift, as Mao acknowledged in a report to the Central Committee:

> From 1927 to the present, the center of gravity of our work has been in the villages— gathering strength in the villages, using the villages in order to surround the cities, and then taking the cities. The period for this method of work has now ended. The period of "from the city to the village" and of the city leading the village has now begun. The center of gravity of the Party's work has shifted from the village to the city.[12]

In practical terms this required the CCP to use its Harbin experience to the full and do everything possible to avoid the Guomindang's serious mistakes after their return from Chongqing in late 1945. The CCP insisted that the People's Liberation Army maintain strict discipline in the cities it occupied, that ordinary businesses not be disrupted, and that urban property *not* be redistributed to benefit the poor. Factories were patrolled and machinery guarded to prevent looting. A new "people's currency"—the *renminbi*—was introduced, with only a short term allowed in which to exchange gold yuan notes for the new ones. Thereafter trading in gold, silver, and foreign currency was to be explicitly forbidden.

CCP officials relocated Guomindang officers and soldiers or incorporated them into the People's Liberation Army following a period of political education. Labor organizations were prevented from disruptive strikes by a web of mediation rules and urged to accept "reasonable exploitation" by capitalists in the transition period. Refugees were fed and sent home whenever possible. Schools and colleges were kept open. Stockpiles of food and oil kept in government storehouses helped to stabilize prices. City dwellers were encouraged to save through "commodity savings deposit units," designed to be insulated from inflation. Depositors were promised that their savings would be computed in terms of the prevailing food and fuel costs, and at the time of withdrawal would be adjusted to yield the same amount of food and fuel, plus accrued interest. Not all these measures succeeded at once, but the sincerity of the attempts was praised by both foreign and Chinese observers, regardless of their political sympathies.

Chiang Kai-shek, meanwhile, had roughly the same range of options that had faced the southern Ming court once the Manchus had seized Beijing and the north China plain 305 years before. He could try to consolidate a regime in central or south China, perhaps in Nanjing, relying on the Yangzi River as a natural barrier; he could try to consolidate in the southwest, or establish a coastal base in Fujian or Guangdong; or he could use Taiwan as a base, as Koxinga had done in the seventeenth century.

In 1945, the Nationalist government had reclaimed Taiwan, which had been a colony under Japanese rule since 1895. In reasserting central government power on the island, Guomindang officials behaved in a style similar to the conduct of officials in Shanghai and Manchuria. Often inefficient or corrupt, they failed to build up public support and eroded many of the more satisfactory aspects of Japanese economic development. Chen Yi, the former Zhejiang militarist and Fujian governor, was appointed chief administrator of Taiwan province and roused strong local opposition because of his underlings' behavior. When Taiwanese anger broke out into antigovernment riots in February 1947, Nationalist troops fired into the crowd, killing many demonstrators. Over the following weeks, in a series of ruthless actions that recall Chiang Kai-shek's Shanghai tactics of 1927, Chen Yi attempted to break the spirit of the Taiwanese by ordering the arrest and execution of thousands of prominent intellectuals and citizen leaders.

With the Taiwanese opposition broken, Chiang recalled Chen Yi and replaced him with more moderate administrators, who built up the island as a viable base for the Guomindang. In the months before the fall of Beijing, furthermore, thousands of crates of Qing-dynasty archives were shipped to Taiwan along with the finest pieces of art from the former imperial-palace collections. A force of 300,000 troops loyal to Chiang was based on the island by early 1949, backed by twenty-six gunboats and some planes. The scene was set for the Guomindang's retreat to Taiwan, should Chiang choose the option.

The spring of 1949 marked a waiting period, while the Communists regrouped, rested their troops north of the Yangzi, and formed a provisional people's government for north China. After his resignation in January 1949, Chiang had been succeeded as president by General Li Zongren. From Nanjing, Li tried in vain to persuade Mao Zedong to compromise on the CCP's eight-point program for Guomindang surrender. Mao's eight points were stark: (1) punish all war criminals, (2) abolish the invalid 1947 constitution, (3) abolish the Guomindang's legal system, (4) reorganize the Nationalist armies, (5) confiscate all bureaucratic capital, (6) reform the land-tenure system, (7) abolish all treasonous treaties, and (8) convene a full Political Consultative Conference to form a democratic coalition government.

As Li Zongren was considering these terms, the Communist troops gave dramatic notice that they would not tolerate any involvement in the fighting by foreign imperialist interests. In making their point they echoed the actions of the Japanese, who in November 1937 had sunk the U.S. gunboat *Panay* when it was seeking to evacuate embassy personnel from the threatened city of Nanjing. This time it was the British who were put on notice, when in April 1949 they tried to move their armed frigate *Amethyst* to Nanjing to take supplies to the embassy and evacuate British civilians if deemed necessary. As the *Amethyst* sailed up the Yangzi, it came under heavy fire from Communist batteries on the north bank and ran aground, with seventeen dead and twenty wounded. The British ships sent to the rescue were beaten back.

In April 1949 the Communists gave President Li an ultimatum to accept their eight points or surrender within five days. When he refused, they recommenced their campaign. Nanjing fell without a fight on April 23, and Hangzhou and Wuhan shortly thereafter. Shanghai fell in late May after only token resistance. In the following months the Communist armies moved swiftly to consolidate their hold. Peng Dehuai's forces drove west, seized Xi'an, and claimed Lanzhou in August 1949. Lin Biao's troops took Changsha the same month, and marched rapidly south to Guangzhou as Peng's armies in the northwest drove into Xinjiang. In September the Nationalist armies in

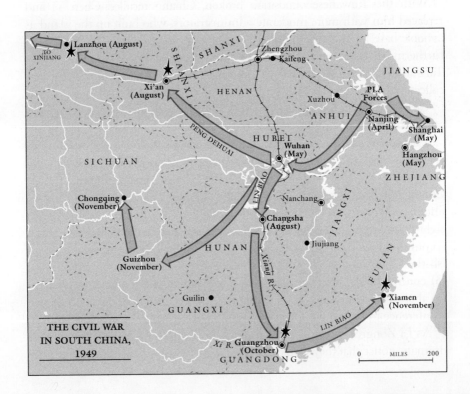

THE CIVIL WAR
IN SOUTH CHINA,
1949

Mao Zedong declaring the founding of the People's Republic of China, Beijing, October 1, 1949

Xinjiang surrendered, along with those in Suiyuan and Ningxia. Lin Biao's troops, who had faced considerable opposition in the southeast, took Guangzhou in mid-October, as well as Xiamen—which was stoutly defended as the last gateway for those retreating to Taiwan. Other Communist forces turned southwest, taking over Guizhou in mid-November, and seizing the Nationalist wartime base of Chongqing at the end of the month.

Anticipating these final victories, Mao Zedong assembled a new Political Consultative Conference in Beijing in late September. Appearing to be true to the declared principles of a "democratic coalition government," delegates from fourteen political parties were invited to attend, including defectors representing the Guomindang. They elected the members of the central government, with Mao as chairman and Zhu De as senior vice-chairman; designated Beijing as the capital again in place of Nanjing; chose the five-pointed gold star with its four subsidiary stars on a red ground as the national flag,* and ordered that each year now be designated in accordance with the Western Gregorian calendar.† At a ceremony on October 1, 1949, from a reviewing stand atop the Gate of Heavenly Peace—once the main entrance to the Ming

---

* The large star represented the CCP, and the four smaller stars the four classes that would constitute the new regime: the national and the petty bourgeoisie, the workers, and the peasants.

† The Guomindang had counted days and months according to the Western calendar but had dated years by their distance from the 1911 revolution—for example, 1948 was the thirty-seventh year of the Republic.

and Qing imperial palace—Mao Zedong proclaimed the founding of the People's Republic of China.

The symbolism was appropriate, even though the violent acts of heroic self-sacrifice that had accompanied the fall of the Ming were absent. True, there had been many tough battles, and some members of Chiang's staff, as well as others deeply loyal to him, died by suicide. But there were few echoes of those seventeenth-century confrontations in which Confucian scholars had brought whole cities flaming down around their heads as they died to prove the rightness of their moral stance. The country as a whole was watchful and nervous rather than in a mood for sacrifice. This had been a long, bloody, complex, and baffling civil war, full of heroism and cruelty, of dramatic social ideals and hideous abuses. We can catch some of the atmosphere of the time through the work of the French photographer Henri Cartier-Bresson, who was in China in late 1949. His black-and-white images caught much of the doubt that flowed through Chinese hearts. The beggarwomen in the streets, the hungry children, the tired People's Liberation Army troops with their white bandoleers of rice rations slung around their shoulders, the equally tired Guomindang officers guarding their piled baggage on the docks, the mobs of refugees, the citizens jammed together trying to reach a bank to change their constantly depreciating paper money, the students hurriedly erecting signboards to welcome their new conquerors—all of these people had become part of the revolution, and would now have to think their way into the new and uncertain future.

CHAPTER 19

The Birth of the People's Republic

COUNTRYSIDE AND TOWN, 1949–1950

In an essay he wrote in mid-1949 titled "On the People's Democratic Dictatorship," Mao Zedong succinctly spelled out the ideas that would permeate the policies of the new Chinese state. The experience of the revolution to date could be analyzed into two basic categories, wrote Mao. The first was the arousing of the nation's people to build a "domestic united front" under the leadership of the working class. This united front included the peasantry, the urban petty bourgeoisie, and the national bourgeoisie, as well as the working class, and would form the basis of a "people's democratic dictatorship" led by the working class. The second category embraced the international aspects of the revolution, including China's alliance with the Soviet Union, the countries in the Soviet bloc, and the world proletariat. This dimension of the revolution had taught the Chinese that they had to "lean to one side" or the other in their allegiances—either to socialism or to imperialism. The triumphs of the revolution had been attained under the leadership of the CCP, which, said Mao, "is no longer a child or a lad in his teens but has become an adult."[1]

Mao then elaborated on some of his main intentions. The new government would establish relations with any country willing to respect China's international equality and territorial integrity. The people's democratic dictatorship, however, would "deprive the reactionaries of the right to speak and let the people alone have the right." In jocular style, Mao imagined critics protesting that he was being dictatorial, to which he would reply, "My dear sirs, you are right, that is just what we are." He would be dictatorial to the "running dogs of imperialism," as well as to "the landlord class and bureaucrat-bourgeoisie" and to "the Guomindang reactionaries and their accomplices." But the rest of the people would enjoy the full range of freedoms, while China developed its potential through the twin policies of socialization of agriculture and "a powerful industry having state enterprise as its backbone."[2]

The constitutional structure that would make these changes possible was laid out in the Common Program, announced by the People's Political Consultative Conference when it convened in September 1949. As was the case with the ill-fated body of a similar name assembled in 1946, the delegates were drawn from a broad spectrum of political interests and parties. But Chiang Kai-shek's party was now castigated as the "feudal, compradore, fascist, dictatorial Guomindang." In line with Mao's statement, the Common Program guaranteed to all, except for "political reactionaries," the freedoms of thought, speech, publication, assembly, association, domicile, movement, and religious belief. It promised equal rights to women and outlined ambitious goals for universal education, the development of heavy industry, and rural reform through rent reduction and land redistribution.[3]

In the first months of the People's Republic, the main focus had to be on the immediately pressing tasks of restraining inflation, building up agricultural production, restoring the dismantled heavy industries, and completing military consolidation around the peripheries. In Xinjiang, PLA troops crossed the Taklamakan Desert on foot in the spring of 1950; in the southwest, armed resistance to the CCP persisted into 1951. If there were to be a drastic remolding of the people's ideology, it would have to wait until the CCP had solidified its territorial control and increased the number of trained cadres it had at its disposal. The initial priority was to persuade the technical and managerial elites to serve the new state, regardless of their political beliefs or affiliations. Similarly, despite the rhetoric of anti-imperialism, foreign technical personnel and large foreign businesses already in China were encouraged to stay and work for the new society.

To cement the revolution in the rural areas, it was essential to complete land reform on a national scale, expanding the process launched in north China and Manchuria during the civil war. In 1948 the CCP leadership had started tamping down the violence unleashed during class struggle sessions, with criticisms of "indiscriminate killings" as errors of "leftist tendencies." The Agrarian Reform Law of 1950 continued the trend of moderation by exempting most of the land owned by rich and middle peasants from seizure. Previous references to "land equalization" were dropped. But the property and assets of landlords were confiscated and redistributed, under a new rubric that calculated the proportion of income derived from exploiting the labor of others, rather than total landholdings.[4]

Work teams comprised of veteran cadres and new recruits fanned out across the countryside to implement land reform, following the practices that had been developed earlier in north China and Manchuria. A supplemental "Decisions Concerning the Differentiation of Class Status in the Countryside" defined parameters to guide the designation of class labels. In villages, cadres worked in conjunction with newly formed peasant associations to identify and isolate the landlords, seeking to break the patterns of deference that were one of the props of landlord power. The work teams soon became familiar with a range of deceptive practices, whether it was landlord families dropping their standard of living to appear poorer than they really were, consuming livestock that could not then be counted as wealth, or withholding fertilizer from land about to be confiscated.

When the work teams tried to apply the classification scheme drawn from land reform experiences in north China, they discovered complex local variables in social and economic conditions, including the extent of commercial development, tenancy rates, population density, and the relative strength of lineages. In the commercialized regions of east and south China, for instance, the categories of landlord, and rich, middle, and poor peasant could not be easily or logically mapped onto local conditions. The majority of the rural population engaged in agricultural production on a part-time basis, with handicrafts and factory work accounting for a large share of incomes. Landlords, many of them absentee, typically owned plots only marginally larger than the average family, while middling peasants routinely rented out their land. In many villages, an ambiguous line of demarcation separated the "exploiting class" from the "exploited," and there was not much extra land that could be redistributed.[5]

Also included in the redistribution calculations were peddlers, monks, and nuns, as well as demobilized soldiers and migrants from the villages who wished to return home. A new marriage law gave unmarried, divorced, and widowed women the right to hold land in their own names. According to an official tally, on a national basis 43 percent of land was redistributed to approximately 60 percent of the rural population by the end of 1952. In the northwest, a family of five might have received up to 2.5 acres, while in the central south the total could have ranged from 1 to 2 acres. Such amounts could not provide complete security, but for many it opened new possibilities of survival, especially for those who had previously lived in dire poverty.[6]

While the economic effects of land reform varied, its political effects were more uniform as well as long lasting. The reforms effectively dismantled the power base of the rural elite. In violent confrontations between landlords and their tenants and hired laborers, the old hierarchies of village life were overturned. Through land reform, the CCP taught the people the language of class struggle and enlisted their participation or complicity in acts of state-sanctioned violence. An estimated one to two million people died during this phase of the revolution. For those whose lives were spared, the class status assigned to their families endured. For the next twenty-five years they would be punished as landlords and as enemies of the people, even as they were reduced to impoverishment. In the years to come, rich and middle peasants would also find themselves in agonizing political trouble for their class backgrounds.

Concurrent with the land campaign, the CCP embarked on a major effort to reform the family. The provisions of the Marriage Law of 1950 drew on precedents enacted in Communist base areas in the 1930s: equality and consent, freedom of marriage and divorce, and the prohibition of "feudal" practices such as bigamy, concubinage, arranged marriages, child brides, interference in widow remarriage, and the exaction of money or gifts in marital arrangements. A eugenic component forbade people with mental disabilities, leprosy, or sexually transmitted diseases from marrying. All marriages had to be registered with the local government and certified as meeting the minimum age requirements (twenty for men, eighteen for women). Despite its many elements aimed at reforming the broader kinship system, and to the dismay of CCP leaders, the marriage law became popularly known as the divorce law. Women who initiated divorce applications, or who sought to exercise their new legal rights, encountered the resistance of in-laws and husbands. When they appealed to the government for help, local cadres did not consistently uphold the law as prescribed. In villages preoccupied with navigating the conflicts of land reform, women's assertion of their new rights threatened to destabilize families. Those determined to leave unhappy, abusive, or arranged marriages circumvented the obstacles by applying for divorce judgments in the courts, or by escaping to their natal homes. Across the country, as the marriage law was implemented in the early 1950s, tens of thousands of women were reportedly killed or died by suicide as a result of family conflicts. While Party leaders sharply criticized violence against women and chastised those who failed to protect them, the distance between central directives and local practices revealed the difficulty of changing social practices and norms.[7]

Whereas class struggle had unleashed terror in the countryside, by contrast in the cities the first tasks for the Communist government were to ensure order, to stabilize the economy, and to establish the administrative infrastructure for urban governance. Throughout 1949, a wave of labor disputes erupted in large cities. Emboldened by CCP rhetoric that promised a leading role for the proletariat in the revolution, industrial workers protested factory closures and demanded payment for back wages. Between June and December, more than 3,000 labor actions occurred in Shanghai alone. The Communist government voiced strong support for unions, but in practice such organizations could not be autonomous and were to remain under the direction of the CCP. Vigilance was also necessary against racketeers connected to criminal networks and Guomindang saboteurs, suspected of fanning discontent to make trouble for the new regime. When negotiations and mediation by cadres failed to placate the Shanghai workers and restore order, the government reconstituted armed militias to "suppress the counterrevolutionaries." And when Nationalist planes from Taiwan bombed Shanghai in February 1950, causing more than 500 fatalities, the emergency provided further justification for tightening public security measures. In seeking to undermine labor radicalism and control unions in the interests of security and stability, the CCP's approach to labor management echoed that of the predecessor Guomindang and invoked a similar rationale.[8]

In the broader landscape of urban administration, the CCP confronted a shortage of personnel, especially the lack of cadres with urban experience. Most of the party's veteran cadres had been peasant guerilla fighters. Some were illiterate, or only semiliterate. Those assigned to accompany the PLA in the drive to take over Shanghai and other points south grumbled about the incomprehensible dialects spoken by the locals, the unfamiliar food, and the unbearably humid weather. As the military campaign advanced, it became urgent to recruit and train new cadres to administer cities as they came under Communist rule. In the spring of 1949, the CCP's East China Bureau assembled 15,000 cadres to move south. Among them was a cohort of one thousand students, hastily trained in Shandong to assume public security duties in Shanghai. Even so, on a national basis the CCP vetted and kept approximately 60 percent of the Guomindang's former police force. After investigation and reeducation to ensure their political conformity, these men and women constituted important components of the new regime's security apparatus.[9]

As the CCP takeover proceeded, the party retained technical workers, clerks, accountants, and teachers in their jobs. Such personnel were needed to jumpstart industrial production, keep schools open, manage the food supply, and register the population. The CCP preserved some aspects of the Guomindang's *baojia* mutual-security system—itself a continuation of the Qing dynasty's method of surveillance—but gave it a new name and eventually developed it into a comprehensive regime of labor control and population management. In 1950–51, using the Guomindang's census records as the basis, the Communist government began to build the *hukou* (household registration) system. Its purpose was to keep track of people, to monitor suspicious activities, and to ferret out potential enemies of the revolution. In later years the *hukou* system would be used to restrict movement between the countryside and the cities. At its inception, however, there were no mechanisms for doing so; the intent was to protect urban public security through population registration.

The goals of security and surveillance were further accomplished through networks of street committees. Composed of residents who lived in a close-knit section of streets and lanes, these committees worked on such tasks as sanitation, dispute mediation, and public health programs. They also had some responsibility for neighborhood security and could be used to enforce curfews or mount local patrols. In contrast to the male-dominated *baojia* system of the past, women were the linchpins of the neighborhood groups. House-wives led propaganda teams, organized political study sessions, and supervised street cleaning, combining voluntarism and grassroots activism with political indoctrination. Partly under the aegis of these street committees, campaigns were launched against prostitution, gambling, and opium addiction. Neigh-bors exerted group pressure against people wearing flashy clothes or provoca-tive hairstyles and makeup. With greater thoroughness than had been possible in the 1930s, some of the elements of Chiang Kai-shek's New Life movement were therefore incorporated within the new Communist state.

Government propaganda stressing the priorities of the new regime reached urban residents through newspapers, the theater, cinema, and radio. In one example, an intensive campaign was launched against financial speculators and on behalf of the new *renminbi* currency in 1949–1950. Mindful of how the disastrous gold yuan reforms in 1948 had contributed to the unraveling of the Nationalist government, the CCP moved carefully to stabilize the urban economy. In May 1949, the government took over all public and private banks in Shanghai and confiscated their holdings of gold, silver, currencies, and other assets. In the conversion to the new currency and despite its name, how-ever, the people did not immediately embrace the *renminbi*. Instead, silver dollars became the currency of choice, with a fluctuating exchange rate that speculators exploited for profit. As commodity prices rose to alarming levels, the government announced a ban on silver dollars and made *renminbi* the only legal tender. The crackdown on profiteers and black-market dealings began with arrests and secret police entrapment, then gained momentum by enlist-ing popular participation. The campaign to denounce speculators, counter-feiters, and rice hoarders drew in students and urban residents to stage street performances, attend public rallies, and organize meetings in neighborhoods and work units. Through the combination of these measures, the CCP won the "silver dollar war," although for some years thereafter the forbidden cur-rency still circulated in rural areas.[10]

Farther south, the takeover process was made more complicated by ten-sions among the stalwart guerilla fighters, newly arrived work teams from the north, and holdovers from the Guomindang government. Local cadres in

Guangzhou were told that they had to learn standard northern pronunciation (termed "Mandarin" in English) in preference to their own local dialects if they wanted to retain their positions. They resented having to work with (or in some cases, work under) their former enemies, having fought for years and at great peril against the Guomindang. Cultural and linguistic differences between the mostly educated and urban youths from the north and the largely uneducated peasant guerillas produced misunderstandings and conflicts. A saying that circulated in Guangzhou at the time highlights the ambiguity that for many lay at the center of this new stage of the revolution: "Old revolutionaries aren't treated as well as new revolutionaries, new revolutionaries aren't treated as well as non-revolutionaries, and non-revolutionaries aren't treated as well as counter-revolutionaries."[11]

THE STRUCTURE OF THE NEW GOVERNMENT

The establishment of an effective national government was Mao's paramount priority. Success here would bolster the Communists' claims to be representing the forces of a new order, and prove that the CCP had accomplished the reintegration of the country, a goal that had eluded Sun Yat-sen, Yuan Shikai, and Chiang Kai-shek, along with the Japanese and their surrogates. The new government was designed around a framework that nominally divided power among three central components: the Communist Party, the formal governmental structure, and the army. This organizational form grew logically out of the Yan'an experience and the experiments of the civil-war period.

Supervising all aspects of ideology, and coordinating the work of the government and of the army, was the Communist party organization. The CCP had 4,448,080 members in October 1949, when the founding of the People's Republic of China (PRC) was announced. The demands of governing the country led quickly to a jump in party membership, which reached 5,821,604 at the end of 1950. CCP members were integrated throughout all the governmental organs, the mass organizations, the judiciary, the educational system, and the army. Regional branches of the party were coordinated at the top by the Central Committee, which had forty-four members in 1949; fourteen of those members constituted the Politburo, which was effectively run by its five-person Standing Committee.

In 1949 this group consisted of Mao Zedong, Liu Shaoqi, Zhou Enlai, Zhu De, and Chen Yun. The greater public prominence of Mao, Zhou, and Zhu De does not mean that the other two figures were of lesser importance; rather it suggests that their careers had focused on party organization and kept them out of the limelight. Liu Shaoqi, aged fifty, had been educated in the Soviet Union in the 1920s. He emerged later that decade and in the early 1930s as a masterful labor organizer; in the early 1940s he became a leading figure in organizing Communist groups in areas under Japanese occupation. Liu's short book *How to Be a Good Communist*, originally delivered as lectures in Yan'an, became staple reading for party cadres in the 1940s and 1950s. The book was an intriguing mélange, blending Confucian traditions of morality and discipline with a standard Marxist-Leninist line, and presenting the whole in fervent revolutionary language. As Liu wrote,

> All those who have succeeded in becoming very good and experienced revolutionaries must certainly have gone through long years of steeling and self-cultivation in the revolutionary struggle. Hence, our Party members can make themselves politically inflexible revolutionaries of high quality only by steeling themselves, strengthening their self-cultivation, not losing their sense of the new and by improving their thinking ability in the course of the revolutionary struggle of the broad masses under all difficulties and hardships.
>
> Confucius said:
>
>> At fifteen, I had my mind bent on learning. At thirty, I stood firm. At forty, I had no doubts. At fifty, I knew the decree of Heaven. At sixty, my ear was an obedient organ for the reception of truth. At seventy, I could follow my heart's desire, without transgressing what was right.
>
>> Here Confucius was relating the process of his steeling and self-cultivation. He did not regard himself as a born "sage."[12]

As a text, Liu Shaoqi's work spoke to a new generation in search of reasons to serve the revolution that had been suddenly triumphant. Liu appealed to the "beauty" of the revolutionary vision and contrasted it to the "ugliness" of the capitalist world. He emphasized selfless service as a goal and an ideal. And he spoke—reassuringly to upper-class intellectuals—of the mixed class backgrounds of party members. Few had ever been members of the working-class "urban proletariat," said Liu, and any class background could be transcended by piercing self-examination and prolonged study of Marxism-Leninism.

The fifth member of the inner group, Chen Yun, born in 1905, was a typesetter and well-known union organizer who joined the party in 1925. Like Liu, he was considered a seminal party theorist, whose works were assigned in the 1942 Rectification Campaign. By 1949 he was the CCP's leading economic planner, charged with the task of rebuilding the nation's shattered economy. Almost as powerful was Gao Gang, born in 1902, who had been one of the architects of the Gansu-Shaanxi soviet in the early 1930s, and thus helped to create the relatively secure base to which the Long Marchers retreated in 1935. He served as political commissar of the Shaan/Gan/Ning border government and as commander of the Jilin-Heilongjiang region during the civil war in Manchuria.

These leaders of the Central People's Government were a formidable group with considerable military and administrative experience. They coordinated their work with the other main central government apparatus, the State Council (or cabinet), of which Zhou Enlai was premier. Under Zhou were twenty-four new ministries, which spanned arenas considered of greatest importance to the nation's development. Of the senior ministers, two (of justice and of public health) were women.

The formal governmental structure overlapped and interconnected with the CCP organization, and both of them extended their influence through mass organizations that were intended to link the entire country across regional lines by dint of some special focus or shared interest: among these in 1949 and 1950 were the federation of literature and arts, the Sino-Soviet friendship association, the federation of democratic youth, and the federation of women. This last was headed by Cai Chang, a young radical from Changsha who had joined the group of work-study students in France in 1919. A specialist in organizing women factory workers, she had served in the Jiangxi Soviet, survived the Long March, and become a prominent figure in Yan'an before being promoted to this important new post.

The power of the People's Liberation Army (PLA) was firmly embedded in Chinese society by the division of the nation into six regions, each with its own unified military command. These were directed by regional party bureaus that held both military and administrative power above the provincial governors. These regions developed out of the CCP's wartime border-government experience, and had some of the geographical and economic unity of the macroregions into which some analysts believe China naturally falls (refer to the map on page 405). These regions were grouped as follows:

1. *Northeast China Bureau*: Heilongjiang, Jilin, Rehe, Liaoning
2. *Northwest China Bureau*: Gansu, Ningxia, Shaanxi, Xinjiang, Qinghai
3. *North China Bureau*: Chahar, Hebei, Shanxi, Suiyuan
4. *East China Bureau*: Anhui, Fujian, Jiangsu, Shandong, Zhejiang
5. *Central-South China Bureau*: Henan, Hunan, Hubei, Jiangxi, Guangxi, Guangdong
6. *Southwest China Bureau*: Guizhou, Xikang, Sichuan, Yunnan

Among the leaders in these regional governments, five men were particularly powerful. First, Gao Gang wielded extraordinary influence in Manchuria (the Northeast China Bureau), where he held four key posts. Gao had close contacts with senior officials in the Soviet Union, and Russian interest in the railways and resources of Manchuria assured the importance of his role. Second, Peng Dehuai, the military commander and hero of the civil war, was both government chairman and military commander in the Northwest China Bureau. That area, too, because of its shared border with the Soviet Union, was of critical importance in Sino-Soviet relations. Third, Rao Shushi, a veteran organizer of the New Fourth Army, held sway in east China. Finally, Lin Biao in the central-south region and Deng Xiaoping in the southwest also obtained regional power bases. Each of these five men was later to fall afoul of Mao Zedong and be purged. We can see with hindsight that despite the impressive restructuring of the government, there were perennial problems embedded within the PRC. Tensions of regional and central authority, of crosscutting bureaucratic lines, and of individual ambitions and power bases, which to different degrees had plagued China since the late Ming dynasty, were not going to be eradicated in any simple way.

THE KOREAN WAR

Even before all Guomindang forces within China had been eliminated, Mao Zedong followed up his statements about "leaning to one side" by traveling to the Soviet Union to meet with Stalin. He reached Moscow on December 16, 1949, just before Stalin's seventieth birthday. This was Mao's first excursion beyond China's borders. He had no firsthand knowledge of any of the countries that had so much influenced the Chinese among whom he had grown up. But now that the PRC was formally established, Mao had to enter the world of international diplomacy. Indeed, many nations—and not just those in the Communist bloc—swiftly granted recognition of the new state.

Mao's experiences in the Soviet Union were baffling and contradictory. The initial meeting between the two leaders on the day of Mao's arrival seemed encouraging. Stalin expressed flexibility over aspects of the Yalta agreement that affected China adversely and offered help with military training. He was cautious over agreeing to provide support for an invasion of Taiwan, but suggested fomenting trouble in Hong Kong to shake up Britain. After the initial reception, apart from attending a banquet in celebration of Stalin's birthday, Mao was left to other Soviet officials to handle. He visited an automobile factory in Moscow and the Hermitage Museum in Leningrad, and he saw doctors for numerous ailments. But mostly Mao stewed in a dacha, furious at being ignored. When Stalin finally summoned him to the Kremlin a month later, negotiations resumed for the terms of the aid package that Mao sought.[14] The Sino-Soviet Treaty of Friendship, Alliance, and Mutual Security, signed in February 1951, promised Soviet support of the PRC in the event of attack by Japan; credits valued at U.S.$300 million, to be paid in equal installments over five years; and Stalin's promise to evacuate Lüshun

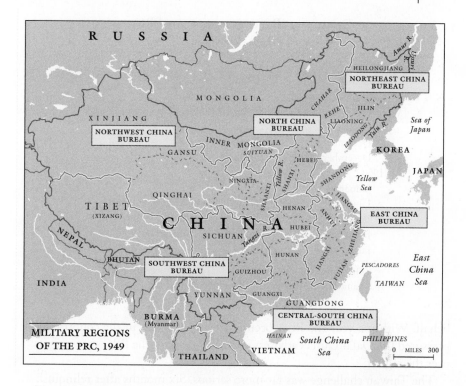

MILITARY REGIONS OF THE PRC, 1949

and Dalian by 1952, when they would return to Chinese sovereignty. In a bitter blow, Mao acquiesced to an independent Mongolian People's Republic, which would remain firmly under Soviet influence. Mao had claimed several times that Mongolia would one day return to Chinese dominance; he now had to abandon hope that the PRC would regain territories similar in extent to those controlled by the Qing at the height of their power.

The broad arena of foreign policy was not, however, of central importance to the PRC leaders in the spring of 1950. With Hainan Island successfully captured by Lin Biao's troops in April, the military felt ready—even without any clear offer of Soviet assistance—to proceed with the two final aspects of territorial consolidation: the conquests of Tibet and Taiwan. The Tibetan operations, though logistically complex, were not expected to offer much challenge to the now seasoned PLA forces, especially since India had become independent in 1947 and the British had lost their interest in maintaining Tibet's buffer status. Chinese Communist troops invaded Tibet in October 1950, claiming to "liberate" the country from "imperialist oppression." Despite the poignant Tibetan protest—"Liberation from whom and what? Ours was a happy country with a solvent government"[15]—the United Nations took no action, nor would India or Britain intervene on Tibet's

DIPLOMATIC RECOGNITION OF THE PRC,
1949–1950[13]

1949
October 2	USSR
October 3	Bulgaria, Romania
October 4	Poland, Hungary, Czechoslovakia
October 5	Yugoslavia
December 9	Burma
December 30	India

1950
January 4	Pakistan
January 6	Great Britain,* Ceylon, Norway
January 9	Denmark, Israel
January 13	Finland, Afghanistan
January 14	Sweden

* The Chinese rejected Britain's January 6 offer, since the British maintained formal diplomatic ties with Taiwan.

behalf. Within a year the PLA occupied the key points in the country and pressured the Dalai Lama's advisers into acceptance of the PRC's sovereignty over the region.

The Taiwan challenge was far more serious. Six months after relinquishing the presidency in January 1949, Chiang Kai-shek had retreated to Taiwan, where the Guomindang had stabilized its power following the riots and massacre of 1947. Taiwan had flourished economically under Japanese colonial administration between 1895 and 1945, and Chiang moved swiftly to reassert his leadership over the island's inhabitants. The PLA commanders were under no illusions that it would be easy to recapture the island. Communist forces had already been rebuffed in an attempt in October 1949 to take the offshore island of Jinmen, one of the worst defeats in the history of the PLA. In February 1950, the general commanding the units of the Third Field Army in Fujian and Zhejiang, which were scheduled to make the assault on Taiwan, gave a frank assessment of the prospects:

I must first of all point out that the liberation of the islands along the southeast coast, especially Taiwan, is an extremely big problem and will involve the biggest campaign in the history of modern Chinese warfare. . . . [Taiwan] cannot be occupied without sufficient transport, suitable equipment, and adequate supplies. Furthermore a considerable number of Chiang Kai-shek's land, sea, and air forces are concentrated there together with a batch of the most intransigent reactionaries who have fled from China's mainland. They have built strong defense works, depending on the surrounding sea for protection.[16]

Because of these difficulties, Mao Zedong and other CCP leaders seem to have been undecided about the correct course to follow. By the summer of 1950 the military consolidation over south China was complete. A large force of veteran PLA troops was moved to the Fujian coastal region but not ordered into action against Taiwan at that time. One possible explanation for the delay is that the CCP leaders were hoping that the Taiwanese themselves might stage an insurrection against the Guomindang. (Stalin had suggested this in December 1949 during his conversations with Mao, as an alternative to Soviet support.) Another possible explanation is that an epidemic of snail fever raged through the PLA troops that summer, rendering many of them unfit for combat duty.

Worried about spiraling military expenses, yet mindful of the problems that the Guomindang had encountered when they deactivated its forces too quickly after the Japanese surrender, the CCP Central Committee decided on a partial and carefully managed demobilization. In the Central Committee's words,

> The PLA, while preserving its main forces, should demobilize part of its troops in 1950, but only on condition that sufficient forces to liberate Taiwan and Tibet are guaranteed as well as sufficient forces to consolidate the national defense and suppress the counter-revolutionaries. This demobilization must be carried out with care so that demobilized soldiers can return home and settle down to productive work.[17]

There was at this same time nothing to suggest that the United States would intervene in the Chinese conflict any further, despite angry Republican party demands for enactment of a generous assistance program to aid Chiang Kai-shek in the eventual recovery of the mainland. In the summer of 1949, at President Truman's request, Secretary of State Dean Acheson had compiled a dossier of all the documents he considered relevant to American involvement in China's wartime and civil-war experience. Acheson wrote in his letter of transmittal: "The Nationalist armies did not have to be defeated; they disintegrated. History has proved again and again that a regime without faith in itself and an army without morale cannot survive the test of battle."[18] Acheson concluded that further U.S. aid or involvement would be as pointless as previous attempts had been. But not everyone agreed. The former Chinese ambassador to the United States, Hu Shi, who had been briefly drawn to Christianity in his youth, jotted in the margin of his copy of Acheson's text the note "Matthew 27:24" ("So when Pilate saw that he was gaining nothing, but rather that a riot was beginning, he took water and washed his hands before the crowd, saying, 'I am innocent of this man's blood; see to it yourselves'").[19]

In the meantime, State Department staff drafted the official statement they intended to issue once Taiwan had fallen into Communist hands. Public declarations by both General Douglas MacArthur, the commander of occupied

Japan, and Dean Acheson now defined the American "defensive perimeter" in the Pacific as running along a line connecting the Aleutians, Japan, Okinawa, the Ryukyus, and the Philippines. The CCP could take note that this definition of American strategic interests did not include Taiwan, nor did it include South Korea, which since 1945 had emerged as an independent state under American patronage, separated from Soviet-dominated North Korea along the thirty-eighth parallel. Once Taiwan was conquered, the PRC expected to take its rightful place in the United Nations, for which it was already actively lobbying.

The apparent harmony of these American and Chinese stances was shattered on June 25, 1950, when a massive force of North Korean troops crossed the thirty-eighth parallel and invaded South Korea. Within a few weeks, North Korean forces had advanced swiftly down the peninsula and captured Seoul. At this time the Soviet Union was boycotting the UN Security Council, to protest its refusal to seat the PRC delegation in the place of Taiwan. With no threat of a Soviet veto, the other members of the Security Council acted swiftly to condemn the North Koreans and to urge UN members to give "such assistance" as "may be necessary." President Truman ordered U.S.

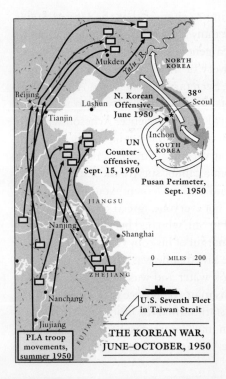

THE KOREAN WAR, JUNE–OCTOBER, 1950

THE KOREAN WAR, NOV. 1950–JULY 1953

forces based in Japan to assist South Korea, joined by troops from fifteen other nations. Fearing that the Chinese might seize this moment to launch an attack on Taiwan, Truman also ordered the U.S. Seventh Fleet to patrol the Taiwan Straits as a "neutralization" move. The PRC now could not invade Taiwan even if it was ready to do so.

Over the next few months, as UN forces won major victories in South Korea, PRC denunciations of "the barbarous action of American imperialism" grew sharper. Mass rallies condemned the United States and its allies for their role in the war, as a menace to peace in Asia and as a threat to China's security. "North Korea's friends are our friends," declared an editorial. "North Korea's enemy is our enemy. North Korea's defense is our defense."[20] General MacArthur, now commander in chief of UN forces in Korea, held cordial talks with Chiang Kai-shek and declared that Taiwan was now part of the United States' "island chain" of air-power bases. Behind the scenes, the CCP leadership debated whether to dispatch troops in support of their beleaguered ally, and if so, on what terms. Mao was a strong advocate of joining the fight—he saw the Korean conflict as an opportunity to prove to the world that new China could be the leading force of communism in Asia. Even so, Mao wanted assurance of Soviet air support before sending troops to North Korea.

The crucial change in the war came in mid-September, when, in a daring amphibious maneuver, MacArthur landed his forces at the harbor of Inchon, to the rear of the North Korean lines. North Korean troops began to break and retreat homeward. U.S. troops in pursuit crossed the thirty-eighth parallel on October 7 and pushed northward toward the Chinese border along the Yalu River. The dramatic reversal in the military situation sharpened the security threat to the PRC and intensified the imperative to intervene. After several rounds of tense negotiations for Soviet air support, Mao issued the order to deploy Chinese "volunteers" to fight in North Korea.[21]

PLA commander Peng Dehuai coordinated his forces superbly. In bitter fighting that December, the Chinese pushed the UN forces back once again to a line along the thirty-eighth parallel. In January 1951 UN troops retreated farther south, as Chinese and North Korean units retook what was left of the burned-out shell of Seoul. Rallying, UN forces regained Seoul, and at this point the battle lines settled along the chains of hills that ran just north of the thirty-eighth parallel. Savage fighting for positional advantage continued, leaving both sides with heavy casualties. The war dragged on for a painful two years, ending with a truce (but no peace treaty) in July 1953.

By that time U.S. casualties had reached over 160,000 (54,000 dead, 103,000 wounded, 5,000 missing), South Korean casualties 400,000, North Korean 600,000, and Chinese between 700,000 and 900,000. The Chinese never

Chinese troops crossing the frozen Yalu River into North Korea, late 1950

released exact figures since they claimed that all their troops in Korea were "volunteers," not regular army personnel. But the staggering losses of close to 1 million men, many of whom were killed in the last year of the war by the superior fire power of the UN forces, gave Chinese military leaders pause. Peng Dehuai, especially, realized that China must develop a more modern, well-equipped army, like the Soviet Union's, to prepare for future conflicts. Among the Chinese who died in the Korean conflict was the elder of Mao Zedong's two surviving sons by his first wife. Mao Anying, born in 1922, had been a student in Moscow and a farm laborer in Yan'an. His body was buried on Korean soil. (Mao's only other son, Anqing, had a history of mental troubles and spent most of his life in institutions.)

The significance of the war for the PRC was profound. Uppermost was the suffering of hundreds of thousands of Chinese troops, who fought in harsh winter weather with inadequate clothing, insufficient food, and little ammunition, against an enemy with overwhelming superiority in air and artillery power. The courageous but costly charges that the Chinese mounted against well-entrenched enemy emplacements amazed the foreign troops who witnessed them. This very courage gave rise to a new mystique of revolutionary endurance and heroism, which was elaborated for domestic audiences by an outpouring of literature, films, plays, and tales of model soldiers. The PRC also drew closer to the Soviet Union, which rewarded its loyalty to the Soviet bloc by making large amounts of military materials available—although the Chinese had to pay for the aid. In addition, the events of the war were used to reinforce Chinese perceptions of the evils of Western imperialism, and particularly to isolate the United States as the prime enemy. State propaganda pointed to American involvement in Korea as clear evidence of its ambitions in East Asia, and of the implacable hatred of the United States for China and the Chinese people.

This led to another domestic effect of the war: the decision to turn against most of the Westerners who had stayed in China for business or religious reasons, and to force them to leave the country. A significant number, including some missionaries, were arrested and prosecuted on charges of espionage. The CCP also conducted mass campaigns to extend the ethos of the war into a zealous hunt for domestic spies and alleged or real enemy agents. This was accompanied by a general hardening of attitudes against all who had previous contacts with the Guomindang or had worked in foreign firms, universities, or church organizations. In rural areas, the land reform campaign also became intertwined with the hunt for counterrevolutionaries, escalating the level of violence against those identified as enemies of the people. Finally, it was abundantly clear that Taiwan would not be easily "liberated" and reunified with the mainland, but would remain the focal point—with conspicuous American support—for hostility to the PRC.

In the United States as in China, the effects of the war were serious, deeply harming the two countries' perceptions of each other. Revulsion and fear of the Chinese was heightened by reports of attempts to "brainwash" American or South Korean prisoners of war. And the fact that the Korean peace talks stalled for nearly two years because the PRC demanded that all Chinese prisoners be returned home, when over 14,000 had begged not to be sent back, showed how swiftly China had developed into a dictatorship. The Chinese finally gave in on this issue, and the 14,000 prisoners were repatriated elsewhere—mainly to Taiwan.

Chinese Communist strength in the field also made Americans look differently at the record of the 1930s and 1940s, much of which was now available in Dean Acheson's lengthy report, published in 1949 as a 1,054-page volume. For those who were drawn to a deep antagonism to communism, the actions of those Americans who had been sympathetic to Yan'an smacked of treason. The corrosive period of domestic American anticommunism, which climaxed in the charges of subversion made by Senator Joseph McCarthy, precluded any clear-eyed look at Sino-American relations for over a decade. Although conducted on a lesser scale than the contemporaneous Chinese hunt for domestic enemies, the campaign of allegation and innuendo launched by McCarthy and others had a profoundly damaging effect. Leading China experts in the State Department, subjected to repeated loyalty investigations, were dismissed or transferred to backwaters of the world scene. It became ever more popular to say that the United States had somehow "lost" China—

whether by treason, misrepresentation, or failure to provide crucial military and financial aid.

In the short run, the CCP probably gained from participating in the Korean War. If the United States had triumphed in October 1950 and been able to establish a unified non-Communist Korean regime, the People's Republic would have had a hostile and powerful neighbor on its crucial northeast border. But the costs were high, as we have seen, and the longer-range tragedy was that hopes evaporated for the "new democracy" that had seemed implicit in the rhetoric and some of the policies of 1949.

MASS PARTY, MASS CAMPAIGNS

The CCP had learned, during the Yan'an Rectification Campaign of 1942, how to force its members into self-criticism, and to use group pressure and intimidation to compel ideological conformity. In the early 1950s these experiences surfaced again in four major campaigns involving the mass mobilization of the people. The first of these was the Resist America and Aid Korea campaign, which focused on foreign presence and influence. The party ordered police searches of alleged spies, confiscated objects such as radio receivers and firearms, and investigated public associations that included or had contact with foreigners—whether these associations were involved in cultural, business, health, or religious pursuits. Foreign business assets were frozen in December 1950, and foreign businesses—although not wholly expropriated—were pressured into selling, often at artificially low prices. Some gave up their assets altogether to meet enormous demands for "back taxes." Workers in foreign-owned factories and businesses aired their grievances against their employers at public meetings, and in some cases mass rallies were held to accuse the foreigners of abusive behavior. In a dramatic confrontation that recalls the anti-Christian agitations in the late nineteenth century, five Canadian nuns who ran an orphanage in Guangzhou were accused of having killed over 2,000 babies entrusted to their care. Other foreigners were imprisoned and forced to confess to espionage. By late 1950 almost all foreigners had left the country. Chinese Christians, most of whom remained, were organized and commanded to abide by the principles of the "Three Self" movement, so named for the commitment to self-administration, self-support, and self-propagation. Foreign influence and control were anathema; in the case of Catholics, this meant the requirement to deny the authority of the Vatican.

Propelled by the anger and excitement of the Korean War, a second mass campaign aimed to "suppress counterrevolutionaries." Millions of people—those who had served in Nationalist armies or were former Guomindang party members—had never been thoroughly investigated. Some of them no doubt harbored pro–Chiang Kai-shek sympathies; a few secretly aided the sabotage expeditions that were sent from Taiwan. At the end of 1950, the CCP leadership launched a campaign against domestic subversion, seeking to expose secret agents, spies, and "active" counterrevolutionaries. As the campaign grew in intensity, it became brutal and terrifying. Regulations issued in February 1951 cast a wide net by expanding the definition of "counterrevolutionary crimes" to include spreading rumors, forging public documents, bribing government officials, and illegally crossing international borders. Local tyrants and "historical counterrevolutionaries who incurred blood debts in the past" became legitimate targets. In April a Central Committee directive set "0.1 percent of the population as a standard," with instructions to "execute half of this figure first, and then wait and see how the situation develops."[22]

The capacious category of counterrevolutionary crime and the quota for execution opened the door to hasty arrests, fabrications, and revenge for personal vendettas. As cadres rushed to meet the target, they conducted mass arrests, and in some cases mass executions, improvising to find enough counterrevolutionaries to fill the quota. For millions of people the violence and humiliation of these days effectively ended any hope that they would be able to live out their lives peacefully under the Communist regime, whatever their past histories might have been. Millions of others witnessed and participated in violent attacks on those identified as enemies of the state. This campaign created a precedent for using quotas as a method of setting goals and measuring compliance, to fatal effects. At the conclusion of the campaign, the deputy minister of public security reported to Chairman Mao that 712,000 had been executed, with 1,290,000 more imprisoned for their counterrevolutionary crimes.[23]

Even before the hunt for counterrevolutionaries concluded, the CCP leadership had already been planning a third political drive—this one against corruption within the party. The Three Anti campaign targeted three sets of vices (corruption, waste, and obstructionist bureaucracy) alleged to be common among three occupational groups (Communist party members, the wider circles of bureaucratic officials, and the managers of factories and other businesses). First launched in Manchuria—perhaps as a trial run—under the direction of Gao Gang, the party chief there, the Three Anti campaign had spread to the rest of the country by the end of 1951. Even though it was not conducted with the violence of the pursuit of counterrevolutionaries, it did lead to thorough investigations and to the humiliation or expulsion of many senior figures. (According to what seems solid evidence, some of them had indeed benefited financially from their privileged positions). The Three Anti campaign was also used to strengthen the government's control over labor.

In cities where job contractors and local bosses had continued to dominate, through mass meetings the CCP educated workers about patterns of discrimination. Enraged workers were then mobilized to turn on their bosses and join in expanded state-supervised labor organizations that would, the party promised, end longstanding practices of graft and influence.

The Three Anti drive drew much of its energy from a fourth concurrent mass campaign—the Five Anti movement, designed as an all-out assault on the bourgeoisie. This was an act of class war that mirrored in scope, rage, and effectiveness its counterpart campaign against landlords in the countryside. The targets of the Five Anti drive were identified as industrialists and businessmen, as well as those who "represented" the capitalist class, a vague definition that could incorporate anyone the state chose to charge. The five vices to be expunged were bribery, tax evasion, theft of state property, cheating on government contracts, and stealing state economic information.

The Five Anti campaign was launched in January 1952, as the Korean War settled into a protracted stalemate. It took place in cities all across China, but the movement in Shanghai can serve as a case study since the city's size and the wealth of its business community meant that coverage of events in press and radio was especially thorough. In tracking the growth of the Five Anti movement, we can see how all the elements of group mobilization and self-criticism—developed in Yan'an and Manchuria and honed in the other mass campaigns—were brought to a smoothly manipulated consummation.

As a preliminary stage in the campaign, CCP cadres in Shanghai had carefully coached workers' organizations to look into their employers' business affairs and search out evidence of tax evasion or other wrongdoing. Propaganda networks were also developed, consisting of trained personnel who could work through the media and small discussion groups to encourage compliance with the government's policies. One function of these cadres and propagandists was to break down the often tight personal, emotional, and family bonds that united workers to their employers, especially in the smaller businesses. Even if wages were desperately low, personal bonds often crossed class lines, and many employers were not dramatically wealthier than their workers. The situation paralleled that in the countryside, where it was hard to get peasants to speak out in public denunciation of people they had known and worked with all their lives.

Business leaders were forced to undergo group criticism sessions and to confess their past economic crimes. Some did admit to actual malfeasance, although many tried to write bland self-criticisms that dodged major issues. To weaken the business leaders' sense of solidarity, they were encouraged by the party to denounce each other. In early February 1952 over 3,000 mass meetings were held in Shanghai, and an estimated 160,000 workers attended one or more of them. Parades with drums and banners, door-to-door visits, and the use of radio and loudspeakers set up at street junctions all over the city mobilized the whole community and put immense psychological pressure on individual business leaders. By March, the pace intensified. Twelve thousand trained cadres were now available for the dramatic phase of the campaign. Five Anti work brigades spearheaded the final identification of victims by assembling the workers for struggle sessions at different plants. In meetings throughout April, business leaders were forced to endure the open meetings and denunciations, and publicly to confess all their "crimes." In China as a whole, the Three Anti and Five Anti campaigns had an immense effect. The CCP revealed that it would no longer protect private businesses or tolerate the maze of semilegal practices that had continued after 1949. In sharp contrast to the Suppression of Counterrevolutionaries campaign, few of the Three Anti and Five Anti victims were killed. Almost all were terrified or humiliated or both, and many had to pay large fines as well as repay money they had allegedly taken in graft or withheld from their taxes; some had their property confiscated and were sent to labor camps.

The techniques of group pressure employed against the Three and Five Antis did not end when those campaigns concluded. On the contrary, worker-employer meetings became a regular feature of most businesses, and the pressures brought by workers and party cadres prevented employers from running their own businesses independently. Meticulous examinations of class status were carried out, with the result that urban dwellers were classified, as the rural population had been in the process of land reform. Among the sixty new categories into which "class" was now divided, one could find such labels as "enterprise worker," "handicraft worker," "pedicab worker," "idler," "urban pauper," "peddler," "small shop owner," "office employee," and so on. Furthermore, a whole group of activists had now been identified by the state. In Shanghai, 40,000 workers who had proven themselves in the Five Anti struggles were enrolled in propaganda corps, ready to serve the state again when needed; large numbers were similarly recruited in other cities. Even those who had never seen a guerrilla unit or experienced life in the countryside now had had at least a taste of revolution.

CHAPTER 20

Planning
the New Society

THE FIRST FIVE-YEAR PLAN

With the first phase of land reform complete, the power of the bourgeoisie broken, and the Korean War over, the CCP began in 1953 to develop an integrated plan for the nation's economic development. The model adopted was that of the Soviet Union, where state-controlled industrial production in a sequence of five-year plans was believed to have been responsible for that nation's emergence as a world-class power in the 1930s, with the ability to withstand and repulse the full force of Germany's attack in World War II. That victory in turn allowed the USSR to expand its influence in Europe at war's end. The PRC's First Five-Year Plan adopted the Soviet system of industrialization and economic planning. Although rarely acknowledged at the time, physical assets and personnel from the former Japanese colonial regime in the northeast and the Nationalist government in the southwest also facilitated the transition to socialist industrialization.[1]

To prepare for the task of restructuring the economy, China's leaders set standards for bureaucratic recruitment and pay scales, introduced regular administrative procedures, and organized the urban population according to the local units in which they worked (*danwei*) to increase the degree and efficiency of social control and indoctrination. In 1954, during difficult discussions at the highest political levels, the structure of the government was reorganized into 21 provinces,* eliminating the six military-political regions into which the country had been divided in 1949. The army was placed under a newly formed Ministry of Defense, itself subordinate to the State Council. For implementation of party decisions, a tightly centralized system of provincial secretaries

---

* Taiwan was listed as the twenty-second.

THE FIRST FIVE-YEAR PLAN, 1953–1957[2]

Indicator (unit)	1952 Data	1957 Plan	1957 Actual	1957 Actual as percentage of plan
Gross output value (in million 1952 yuan)				
Industry (excluding handicrafts)	27,010	53,560	65,020	121.4
Producer sector	10,730	24,303	34,330	141.0
Machinery	1,404	3,470	6,177	178.0
Chemicals	864	2,271	4,291	188.9
Producer sector less machinery and chemicals	8,462	18,562	23,862	128.5
Physical output				
Coal (mmt)	68.50	113.00	130.00	115.0
Crude oil (tmt)	436	2,012	1,458	72.5
Steel ingot (mmt)	1.35	4.12	5.35	129.8
Cement (mmt)	2.86	6.00	6.86	114.3
Electric power (billion kwh)	7.26	15.90	19.34	121.6
Internal combustion engines (thousand hp)	27.6	260.2	609.0	234.2
Hydroelectric turbines (kw)	6,664	79,500	74,900	94.2
Generators (thousand kw)	29.7	227.0	312.2	137.5
Electric motors (thousand kw)	639	1,048	1,455	138.8
Transformers (thousand kva)	1,167	2,610	3,500	134.1
Machine tools (units)	13,734	12,720	28,000	220.1
Locomotives (units)	20	200	167	83.5
Railway freight cars (units)	5,792	8,500	7,300	85.9
Merchant ships (thousand dwt tons)	21.5	179.1	54.0	30.2
Trucks (units)	0	4,000	7,500	187.5
Bicycles (thousand units)	80	555	1,174	211.5

Note: mmt = million metric tons; tmt = thousand metric tons.

supervised the dissemination of Central Committee orders through a chain of subprovincial party offices. At the local level, approximately 2,200 county governments supervised about 1 million CCP branch offices in towns, villages, army units, factories, and schools.

Overall, the First Five-Year Plan achieved a dramatic increase in industrial production across a broad sector of goods (refer to the table above). The plan was designed to cover the years from 1953 to 1957, although exact details were released only in 1955 because of continuing internal debate over procedures. Most of its targets had already been fulfilled by the end of 1956. Even if the output figures for 1952 are considered artificially low because of the long periods of disruption brought about by the Japanese war, the civil war, and

DISTRIBUTION OF GOVERNMENT BUDGET EXPENDITURES, 1950–1957[3]

Expenditure category	1950	1952	1957
Economic construction	25.5%	45.4%	51.4%
Social, cultural, and educational outlays	11.1	13.6	16.0
National defense	41.5	26.0	19.0
Government administration	19.3	10.3	7.8
Other	2.6	4.7	5.8
Total in percent	100.0	100.0	100.0
Total in millions of yuan	6,810	16,790	29,020

the first period of Communist retrenchment, the execution of the plan was still a formidable achievement.

This was the period of closest collaboration between China and the Soviet Union. Thousands of Soviet technical advisers arrived to help with factory building, industrial planning, the development of hydroelectric power, and the extension of the railway network. The Soviet model for industrial growth has been summarized as comprising five elements: an emphasis on high growth across the entire plan period, a focus on heavy industry, high rates of saving and investment to make that growth possible, institutional transformations in agriculture, and a bias toward capital-intensive methods. In all these ways the Chinese followed their Soviet mentors. To sustain the ambitious targets of the First Five-Year Plan, the state requisitioned grain from the countryside, forcing the peasantry to sell more than a quarter of their production at extremely low prices. This policy left the peasants at subsistence level while it enabled the government to guarantee food supplies in the cities and keep wages down.

The government had prepared the economy for the five-year plan by curbing inflation, which was achieved by 1952 despite the pressures for military production brought on by the Korean War. Use of the new *renminbi* currency was enforced throughout China, a process completed when the separate currency that had been circulating in Manchuria was withdrawn in March 1951. The state produced a balanced budget by controlling government spending and reorganizing the tax system to raise rates on urban dwellers. Particularly striking was the decline in the percentage of the budget allocated to the government's own administration, and the effective reduction of military expenses (see the preceding table). The other side of this coin was the low level of investment, averaging about one percent, in public health and welfare during this phase. Despite this small investment, with the conclusion of the wars that had afflicted the country for so long, and the adoption of improved hygiene measures and disease and pest control, the population expanded rapidly. In 1953 the first full-scale census was taken using comparatively modern methods.* The data showed that China's population had grown by well over 100 million since the late Qing, and now numbered 582.6 million; by 1957, the population had risen to 646.5 million.

The government met its budgetary deficits not by issuing new notes—as the Guomindang had—or by borrowing large sums from creditors, but by sale of government bonds and the encouragement of "contributions," stimulated by mass patriotic campaigns. The Bank of China was also able to bring interest rates down dramatically, strengthening faith in the economy. Bank interest rates that had been 70 to 80 percent per annum in December 1949 declined to 18 percent in 1950, and to 3 percent in 1951. To heighten confidence further, all wages were paid out to workers, and savings in the state banks were calibrated to "commodity basket" values—that is, the cost of a typical package of food staples, cloth, coal, and cooking oils. Every seven to ten days, the cost of such a package was announced in all major cities. Those withdrawing from savings would be given the new cash equivalent to the commodity-basket units they had originally deposited, plus accumulated interest. Retail price rises were held to between 1.5 percent and 2.0 percent per year between 1952 and 1957.

China's state planners were often ignorant of basic procedures, and the planning process itself was marred by numerous errors, production bottlenecks, and disagreements between the industrial ministries in Beijing and the local producers. Feeling pressured by production-quota deadlines, many managers built up unofficial stockpiles of goods. Furthermore, there was a minimum of cooperation among industries, and fierce competition for emergency supplies and repair services. Tensions with private firms lessened, however, as state involvement spread to ever more of the private enterprises. This trend continued through the Five Anti campaign and into the First Five-Year Plan, until at the end of 1955 an official shift to nationalization abolished all wholly private enterprises, leaving only two forms of industrial organization: the completely state-controlled and the mixed public and private.

For the urban workers, increases in production brought material benefits and job security but at the cost of personal mobility, as it was difficult to change assigned jobs. Through union organizations and the CCP apparatus, the government controlled the workers more effectively than the Guomindang had ever been able to do. The industrial side of the First Five-Year Plan was, given the nature of the economy, intimately connected with agricultural

---

* Some demographers believe that the 1953 figures may have been undercounted by anywhere from 5 percent to 15 percent, which would make the subsequent rise less dramatic.

developments. Indeed most of the resources needed for industry had to be extracted from the agricultural sector; some of this investment came in the form of taxes and savings, but the great bulk came from state procurement quotas at artificially low prices. Once the first land-reform drives had broken the landlords, the state began to group the rural population into forms of cooperative labor. The first stage was to encourage peasants to join mutual-aid teams, by promoting the heightened productivity that could be obtained by pooling labor, tools, and draft animals. Such teams usually included six or seven households; by excluding rich and even middle peasants, they emphasized the ambiguous and potentially dangerous nature of their position as the more affluent members of their villages. To further underscore this point, the hierarchy of class status followed in the cities was now applied to the countryside. Mao's essays on class analysis were widely circulated to teach people in rural society a new political vocabulary; land-reform experiences from the Jiangxi Soviet, Yan'an, and the civil-war period were examined and discussed. Landlords were given a variety of designations—"hidden," "bankrupt," "enlightened," "overseas Chinese," "despotic"—and middle peasants were subdivided into "old," "new," and "well-to-do." As discussion deepened, the mutual-aid teams, which had initially disbanded after each harvest season, were gradually solidified on a year-round basis.

In 1952 and 1953, the government experimented with bonding peasant workers into larger units of thirty to fifty households. Land as well as labor was pooled in these cooperatives, even though each family kept its title to the plots it contributed. This consolidation gained extra acreage for the cooperative by abolishing the strips that had separated the myriad tiny plots into which rural holdings were divided, led to some improvements in productivity by eliminating travel between plots, and in some cases allowed for use of mechanized techniques. At the end of each year, after the state procurement quotas had been met and some money set aside for investment in the cooperative, the balance was divided between a "land share" (based on the acreage contributed by each family) and a "labor share" (based on the daily amount of work each family performed). This was only a semisocialist arrangement, since richer peasants contributed more land and gained a greater reward. For this reason these were often termed "lower-stage cooperatives."

The steady shift to cooperative organization involved enormously complicated decisions, not only about class status and work methods, but about the ideal size of plots for specific crops, the scope or feasibility of mechanization, and the exercise of authority within the cooperatives. In late 1955, after extensive propaganda campaigns and experimentation in target areas, the state began to reduce gradually the land share and increase the percentage of payout for the labor share. In the next stage of "higher-stage cooperatives," labor became the sole criterion for remuneration. They were also organized on a much larger scale, often including 200 to 300 households. Such cooperatives exceeded the size of most villages and demanded more full-time administrators and party representatives. By 1956 this shift was well under way, as lower-stage cooperatives began to shrink in number and the mutual-aid teams were dissolved.

Peasants, however, still technically held title to the land they contributed to the cooperatives, and they were also allowed to keep private plots for their own use, which preserved a sense of individual ownership and gave them scope for their entrepreneurial skills. Such plots were meant to constitute no more than 5 percent of a given higher-stage cooperative's land area. But peasants tilled them with great fervor since the produce could be sold in rural markets for supplemental income. The plots were generally used to grow vegetables, which could be sold for several times the price of grains. As much as 20 percent to 30 percent of farm income came from these private plots in 1956, and 83 percent of all hogs were raised with feed purchased with this surplus income, supplemented by vegetable scraps. The same combination of foods was used to raise much of the country's poultry. The livestock in turn produced valuable fertilizer, which went to further raise the yields of private plots.

The resulting surge in private production began to alarm Mao Zedong and other party leaders. They feared the reemergence of a two- or three-class system in the countryside, in which a new generation of enriched peasantry might begin to rise at the expense of their less able, or fortunate, or ruthless fellows. In 1956 and 1957 the peasants were eating better than they had in the early 1950s, and their per capita consumption of grain was higher than that of urban workers. At the same time, it is clear with hindsight that the poultry and hogs raised on private plots contributed heavily to the availability of chicken, duck, eggs, and pork that was a conspicuous feature of the industrial worker's fattened consumption basket. There was a paradox in the making, and how the Party responded to the increasing success of private production would be of crucial importance to the next stage in the history of the People's Republic.

UNITY AND CONTROL

In the early 1950s, the Party leadership was largely stable and unified, absent the intense inner-court conflicts that would characterize the CCP in later decades. Still there were sources of tension, which burst into view with the

Gao-Rao affair at the end of 1953, the first purge to occur in the CCP since the founding of the People's Republic. The two main protagonists were Gao Gang, the former political commissar of the northeast region, and Rao Shushi, a leading official from Shanghai. In 1952, Gao became the chair and Rao a member of the key State Planning Commission, which had assumed responsibility for the First Five-Year Plan. Although some details remain murky, Gao apparently became convinced that he had Mao's blessing (or tacit approval) to oust Liu Shaoqi and replace him as the chairman's second-in-command. Gao and Rao attacked Liu's close colleagues in party meetings, meanwhile maneuvering behind the scenes to win support from army leaders, including Peng Dehuai and Lin Biao. Some of those approached reported the "conspiratorial" overtures to Mao. At a meeting of the Politburo in December 1953, Mao denounced Gao's "underground activities," saying that there were now "two headquarters in Beijing"—one headed by himself, and the other "operating underground," stirring up "a sinister wind" and lighting "a sinister fire."[4] Mao then deputized Liu Shaoqi to convene a Central Committee plenum to adjudicate the case. The conspirators faced serious charges and were given a chance for redemption, but their contrition was judged insufficient. Gao died by suicide in 1954, before he could be formally denounced and expelled from the CCP. Rao spent ten years in prison.

While Mao's forceful resolution of the Gao-Rao affair reinforced his control of the senior leadership, the scheming and machinations revealed fault lines in CCP unity. More broadly, control and unity were key goals in two crucial government policies that impinged on the lives of the population with different effects: the *hukou* household registration system and the ethnic minority classification project.

The *hukou* system had been established in the early 1950s with the primary goals of monitoring suspicious activity and maintaining urban public security. *Hukou* registration then became the basis for resource allocation in the cities, with the distribution of food rations, social welfare benefits, and subsidies based on the number of people registered in each household. In 1955 the system was expanded to the countryside; thereafter each person was classified as belonging to an urban or a rural household and registered in a specific place of residence. With the allocation of food, jobs, and housing directly tied to the urban *hukou* system, the government could regulate internal migration, most notably by preventing rural residents from moving to cities. The restrictions on peasant mobility bound them to the land and to evolving forms of collectivized agriculture. By the end of the 1950s, the *hukou* system was comprehensively implemented in the country's Han Chinese regions, creating a sharp divide between urban and rural society that institutionalized significant disparities in standards of living.

The areas with large ethnic minority populations were initially exempt from the more aggressive policies of land reform and collectivized agriculture. In the high mountains of Tibet, the vast grasslands of Inner Mongolia, or the oasis economies of Xinjiang, land was not the primary economic resource. CCP work teams sent to "collectivize" herds and livestock provoked much confusion and resistance, and the Party backed off on swiftly imposing such policies. The 1953 census had tallied some 34 million people as belonging to ten large "nationalities" (*minzu*), including 6.86 million Zhuang and nearly 2.4 million who identified as Manchu. In addition, nationwide the census takers had recorded more than 400 different answers to the *minzu* question, resulting in a bewildering taxonomy of ethnic identity. In Yunnan province alone there were 200 different groups, including 66 with single-digit populations.[5] (The process of classifying, counting, and affirming ethnic categories would take several decades to complete, culminating in 1979 with an official count of 56—the Han majority plus 55 minority groups.)

Establishing a firm taxonomy of ethnic classification had significant ideological and administrative implications. The concept of the PRC as a "unitary, multinational state" was enshrined in the constitution, as were the principles of "regional autonomy" and "self-government" for areas where ethnic minority populations predominated. In 1955 the "Xinjiang Uyghur Autonomous Region" was established, the name reflecting the demographic majority (more than 70 percent) of the province. The further subdivision of 13 "autonomous prefectures" for Xinjiang, however, counterbalanced the numerical advantage of Uyghurs by assigning jurisdictions to Mongols, Kazakhs, Hui, Kirghiz, and others.[6] In 1958 Guangxi province would be designated the autonomous region of the Zhuang *minzu*; the Hui would be given titular recognition of Ningxia, despite accounting for less than one-third of the provincial population. (Inner Mongolia was the pacesetter, having been established as an autonomous region in 1947.)

The rhetoric and administrative framework of regional autonomy promised ethnic minority groups the right to be "masters of their own house," with protection for their languages, religions, and cultural practices, and with assurances of special economic aid from the state. Such promises had been freely made to differentiate the CCP from its predecessor regimes, co-opt minority groups into the project of national integration, and diffuse separatist sentiments percolating in outer peripheral territories. In practice, however, genuine autonomy was limited. Starting in the early 1950s, the CCP began to recruit minority cadres into its ranks and train them for service in local government organs. Such recruits were generally consigned to low-level staff positions, and all autonomous units, from the county to the province, answered to the central government and Party authorities in Beijing.

Nonetheless, the CCP advertised this program as part of promoting "self-government" in minority regions. The admission of the first group of new Tibetan recruits was proudly announced in the summer of 1956. The following year the CCP publicized that it had reached the goal of enrolling 400,000 new members from all minority areas (out of a national membership of 12.72 million). Meanwhile, 600,000 younger recruits had been added to the ranks of the Communist Youth League.

FOREIGN POLICY

In the realm of foreign affairs, China's leaders in the 1950s had a central goal to reestablish the international prestige that had dwindled from the early Republic through the last years of Guomindang rule. As Churchill had warned, China's role in World War II did not echo in reality the great power status the Allies had conferred in words. The Korean War further complicated China's international status by fixing the United States in a position of hostility, which in turn ensured that Taiwan would remain outside PRC control and the PRC outside the United Nations.

China's international prestige nevertheless grew swiftly in the 1950s, at the same time that the First Five-Year Plan was being implemented. This was a period of optimism, and by presenting the PRC as a responsible member of the world community, Chinese leaders modified the sense of extremism generated by their domestic policies. The architect of this foreign policy was Zhou Enlai, who held the dual offices of premier and foreign minister, as well as membership in the standing committee of the Politburo. A seasoned revolutionary and the veteran negotiator at Chongqing during World War II, Zhou Enlai had a remarkable presence as a diplomat that came in part from his prosperous background, in part from the years he spent in France as a young man, and in part from his flexibility in pursuing the desired ends. Initially Zhou concentrated on relations with India and developed a warm friendship with India's post-independence leader, Jawaharlal Nehru. He managed to persuade the Indian government to accept China's occupation of Tibet in 1950 and 1951, and Indian officials acted as the go-betweens for the PRC and the United States during many difficult phases of the Korean War truce negotiations.

The death of Stalin in March 1953, which led the Soviet Union to modify some of its belligerent postures, also broke the impasse over the Korean War negotiations and ended the threat, posed by Eisenhower, that nuclear weapons might be used to conclude the fighting. Zhou Enlai attended

Stalin's funeral in Moscow and was treated with considerable respect by Soviet officials. (Mao Zedong chose not to go, possibly because no senior Soviet leader had yet made a ceremonial visit to the People's Republic.) Zhou was permitted to stand with the new leaders of the USSR instead of with the groups of foreign dignitaries and walked directly behind the gun carriage bearing Stalin's coffin. These meetings bore fruit in late 1954, when Khrushchev visited Beijing to take part in the fifth-anniversary celebrations of the PRC.

Both before and after his 1953 visit to Moscow, Zhou had been working to strengthen relations with the other key Communist states on China's borders, in line with Soviet policies promoting socialist solidarity. In late 1952 he signed an economic and cultural agreement with the Mongolian People's Republic,* as well as a formal agreement with Kim Il Sung to help in post-war reconstruction of the shattered North Korean economy. The PRC forged close ties with the insurgents in Vietnam, building up the road and rail transport system in Guangxi province in order to send supplies to Ho Chi Minh, now involved in the last stages of his struggle for independence against the French. These supplies matched the support that the French were receiving from the United States, and helped Ho Chi Minh's forces survive their protracted war. As the Soviet Union began to show greater flexibility toward neutral countries, Zhou also furthered ties with India and had amicable talks with Prime Minister U Nu in Burma.† He gave eloquent expression to the "Five Principles of Peaceful Coexistence," which the leaders of India and Burma endorsed in a joint statement. The framework encompassed mutual respect for territorial integrity and sovereignty, nonaggression, noninterference in others' internal affairs, equality and mutual benefit, and the endorsement of "peaceful coexistence."

The first great shift in China's diplomatic visibility on the international stage came when Zhou Enlai traveled to Geneva, Switzerland, in April 1954, to attend the meetings convened there to settle the Franco-Vietnamese War. Zhou walked a delicate line between Soviet, French, American, and North Vietnamese demands and counterproposals, and his patience and shrewdness were credited with helping the parties iron out an agreement. During one early meeting in Geneva, Zhou Enlai found himself in the same room with John Foster Dulles, the staunchly anti-Communist U.S. secretary of state. In a confrontation that swiftly became

---

* This agreement was also a de facto acknowledgment of the independent status of Mongolia, and hence of the loss of territory that once had been more or less under Qing control.

† Since 1989 renamed the Union of Myanmar.

famous, Zhou held out his hand in greeting, but Dulles rudely turned his back and walked out of the room. With a shrug of the shoulders at this behavior, Zhou delighted onlookers and made a small victory out of a moment of possible humiliation. He handled with equal aplomb Dulles's insistence that the Chinese delegate never be allowed to chair the Geneva sessions, and furthered the impression of urbanity by having lunch with Charlie Chaplin, who was living in Switzerland after being blacklisted in the United States because of his radical politics.

Of even greater political importance was Zhou Enlai's prominent participation in the 1955 Bandung Conference of the Non-Aligned Movement held in Indonesia. Behind the convening of this conference lay an intricate skein of international relationships. In September 1954 an alliance of anti-Communist countries formed the Southeast Asia Treaty Organization (SEATO). Led by the United States, SEATO aimed to stop the rise of communist revolutionary movements, particularly in Laos and Cambodia. Zhou Enlai complained vociferously that while China was working for "world peace and the progress of mankind," the "aggressive circles" in the United States were aiding the Nationalists on Taiwan and planning to rearm the Japanese. The PRC responded with a sustained shelling of the islands off the Fujian coast that still harbored Guomindang army garrisons, and by flying a reconnaissance plane over Taipei. Taiwan in turn mounted air raids on the mainland, using advanced model U.S. fighter-bombers. The United States subsequently signed a mutual-defense treaty with Taiwan in December 1954.

In response to heightening tensions, the five countries known as the

Colombo Powers—India, Burma, Indonesia, Pakistan (also a SEATO member), and Ceylon (Sri Lanka)—invited the PRC to join a conference in Bandung, Indonesia. When the conference opened on April 18, 1955, President Ahmed Sukarno welcomed delegates from twenty-nine Asian and African nations with these ringing words:

North Korean Foreign Minister Nam Il (left) and Zhou Enlai at the Geneva Conference in April 1954, which ended France's war in Vietnam

For many generations our people have been the voiceless ones in the world. We have been the unregarded, the people for whom decisions were made by others whose interests were paramount, the peoples who lived in poverty and humiliation. Then our nations demanded, nay fought for independence, and achieved independence, and with that independence came responsibility. We have heavy responsibility to ourselves, and to the world, and to the yet-unborn generations. But we do not regret them.[7]

At Bandung, representatives from newly independent states and those still struggling against colonial rule wrestled with the bitter legacies of imperialism and debated issues of self-determination and solidarity in a postcolonial world. Nonaligned countries were eager to find ways to avoid entanglement in Cold War confrontations between the superpowers. As head of the Chinese contingent, Zhou Enlai skillfully positioned the United States as the major threat to the stability of Asia. With the support of Nehru, Sukarno, Gamal Abdel Nasser of Egypt, and others, the conference delegates produced strong declarations in favor of peace, the abolition of nuclear weapons, the principle of universal representation in the United Nations, and arms reductions. The language of the final resolution echoed the PRC's "Five Principles of Peaceful Coexistence." Particularly noteworthy to the assembly was Zhou's remark that "the population of Asia will never forget that the first atom bomb exploded on Asian soil."

One important sideline to Bandung was the PRC's effort to resolve problems arising from the large numbers of Chinese living in Southeast Asian countries. The income that these migrants sent back to their families at home was an important source of China's foreign exchange. But for the large communities of Chinese in countries such as Indonesia (where they numbered more than 3 million), Malaya, Vietnam, and the Philippines, their loyalty to China and their dominant position in many businesses were considered by the host countries as potential threats to national security.

It was in Malaya that this threat seemed most serious. The Malayan Communist Party had been trying since 1948 to destroy the British colonial government there by attacks on planters, police, and their associates, and by clearing "liberated areas" in the countryside. Because more than 90 percent of Malayan Communist Party members were Chinese, it was easy to regard their actions as being orchestrated from Beijing, and to ignore the refusal of most Chinese settlers in Malaya and Singapore to join or help the party. In other areas of large Chinese settlement where local Communist forces were strong, such as the Philippines or Indonesia, the Chinese formed only a minority in the Communist parties and often faced discrimination prompted by the overwhelmingly nationalistic thrust of those insurrectionary movements.

One anomaly in this pattern of feared Chinese Communist subversion was the threat posed by tens of thousands of Guomindang troops who, defeated by the Communists in 1949, had retreated into Thailand and north Burma.

In the mountainous Shan border region of Burma, the Guomindang general Li Mi, a graduate of the Huangpu Military Academy, established a base for his Anti-Communist National Salvation Army. There he recruited guerilla fighters for an invasion of Yunnan, which he carried out in mid-1951 to disastrous results. Li Mi's army was partially supported with American funds and advisers (with supplies airdropped by the CIA), although most of its money came from opium-poppy production and distribution. Over 7,000 of these troops were repatriated to Taiwan in 1953, but at the time of the Bandung negotiations, 7,000 were still ensconced on the Burma-Laos border, and thousands more in northern Thailand.

China's stance had traditionally been that overseas Chinese remained citizens and owed ultimate obedience to the Chinese state, now the People's Republic. But in light of fears of subversion, and after protracted negotiations conducted largely by the Chinese ambassador to Indonesia, in 1955 the PRC government signed its first dual-nationality agreement, in which it authorized Chinese to choose either their own or their host country's nationality during the next two years. In fact, the agreement was not ratified as a formal treaty until 1957, and the promise of harmony was undercut in 1959 when the Indonesian government closed many Chinese businesses and schools and condoned widespread anti-Chinese violence.

But those difficulties lay in the future and did not tarnish Zhou Enlai's image at Bandung as a flexible and open-minded negotiator. Zhou also showed great subtlety over the Taiwan and offshore-islands crisis. As it became apparent that the Americans—and perhaps even the British—would safeguard Taiwan's independent existence if the Guomindang would abandon the Dachen islands off the coast of Zhejiang, which were a potential powder keg, Zhou persuaded the Chinese government to back off from confrontation and let Chiang Kai-shek keep Jinmen (Quemoy) and Mazu (Matsu). In May 1955 Zhou Enlai issued a formal statement declaring that the PRC would "strive for the liberation of Taiwan by peaceful means so far as it is possible."

ARMY REFORM

The PLA performed bravely in the Korean War but took a terrible mauling, with estimated casualties between 700,000 and 900,000. Medical services had been inadequate, food in short supply, and clothing unfit for the Korean winter. Almost 90 percent of Chinese troops reportedly suffered from frostbite in the harsh winter campaigns. Weapons had been a motley assemblage of American, Japanese, Russian, German, and other materials; most infantrymen were each issued eighty or fewer bullets. In 1951, the Soviet Union gradually made MiG fighters available to the PLA, but the Chinese military never had effective naval forces to counteract the formidable sea power of the United States.

Even before the 1953 truce in Korea and the return home of its troops, the PRC began a massive reorganization to develop a professional army that could compete with others in the modern technological world. Peng Dehuai, the PLA commander in Korea who subsequently was named defense minister, believed that the best hope for rebuilding the military lay in continuing to follow the Soviet Union's lead and developing well-armed conventional forces. The rest of the CCP leadership accepted this decision, and in 1953 Mao called for "a tidal wave of learning from the Soviet Union on a nation-wide scale," even though the Soviets had proven at best a grudging friend during the early stages of the Korean conflict. In a pragmatic modification of Mao's earlier dismissal of American imperialists as "paper tigers," a military training manual described the U.S. army as an aggressive force with modernized equipment and fighting power. "To destroy thoroughly such enemy troops" the PLA would need to match its firepower, and every soldier would need to have a "correct understanding" of the character of the American army.[8]

One crucial decision CCP leaders made early on was that the PLA must cut back its numbers and focus on building a well-trained force that could be adequately outfitted and supplied. Even while the Korean War was in progress, the demobilization of large numbers of troops began, as soon as provision had been made for their employment in the cities or in their native villages. By 1953 the size of the PLA was down to 3.5 million from its 1950 peak of 5 million. By 1957 the force had been further reduced to 2.5 million.

In 1954, a new structure of thirteen regional commands was established under the direction of the PLA general headquarters, which now reported to the Military Affairs Commission (with Mao Zedong as chairman) and to the Ministry of Defense (headed by Peng Dehuai). Although these were still large units—a typical military region comprised two or more provinces—the new structure allowed more effective central control. The shape of a professional army began to emerge, especially with the development of technical arms such as the engineering corps, railway and signals corps, and the "ABC" corps, named for its focus on anti-atomic, -biological, and -chemical warfare. The Chinese believed the United States might use all or any of these in the event of an all-out attack.

By integrating its needs with the industrial priorities of the five-year plan, the army was supplied with a wide range of modern infantry weapons, including rifles, machine guns, mortars, rocket launchers, and medium artillery. Because of the cost involved, however, the PLA remained poorly equipped with self-propelled artillery, military transport vehicles, heavy engineering equipment, and tanks. The caliber of officers improved as military academies began to train a new generation in the techniques of modern war. A significant number of Chinese officers were also sent for advanced training at the Soviet Union's military staff college in Kiev.

An adequate flow of personnel into the army was guaranteed by a conscription law, promulgated in 1955 following two years of experimentation. All able-bodied men between eighteen and twenty had to register, except for criminals and those "deprived of their political rights." Local authorities then chose those slated for military service according to a national quota system designed to furnish about 800,000 recruits each year. High-school or college students and those who were only sons could apply for exemptions, but the majority of those selected for military service, especially from poor rural areas, were happy to take the assignment, which offered a prime chance for upward mobility and acquisition of special skills. The huge pool of nonconscripted registrants, along with those who had served their three-year terms, formed reserve units. The CCP maintained a stream of propaganda about the glory of serving in the PLA and issued vivid accounts designed to show how different conditions now were from the days of Guomindang conscription. Nevertheless, army life was tough, and complaints about hardship and unfairness within the military system were widespread.

Because of the length of time needed to acquire technical skills, conscription into the air force meant a term of four years, and into the navy a term of five. Both these arms, considered crucial to national defense after the Korean War experience, had to be built up from a weak base. After initial caution, the Soviet Union began making large numbers of MiG-15 jet fighters available to China in 1951, along with a small number of light jet bombers. However, to avoid an escalation of the Korean conflict, the Soviets did not provide the PRC with long-range bombers able to strike more distant targets. From 1954 onward the Chinese air force concentrated on building a network of airfields along the coast near Taiwan, with the goal of speeding the recapture of the island.

The advancement of military weapons technology received a major boost in the summer of 1955, when the rocketry expert Qian Xuesen (H. S. Tsien) returned to China. Born in Hangzhou in 1911, Qian had studied at MIT and Caltech in the 1930s and served in the U.S. Air Force during World War II. After the war he helped establish the Jet Propulsion Laboratory at Caltech and served on the U.S. government's Science Advisory Board. In 1950 he applied for permission to visit his parents in China, a request that triggered the revocation of his security clearance and accusations of espionage. After five years of virtual house arrest under proceedings of dubious legality, Qian was deported from the United States. Back in China, Qian began assembling the staff to develop a rocket and ballistic-missile program, which he would lead with tremendous success for the next three decades. At the same time, Chinese nuclear physicists were working partly independently and partly in collaboration with Soviet scientists at the Dubna nuclear research institute near Moscow to develop nuclear capabilities, and Soviet leaders promised to provide China a prototype atomic bomb at a future date.

The self-strengthening experts of the later Qing had considered the development of a modern navy central to national defense; in the PRC this was no longer a high priority. The small navy focused its energies on coastal patrol vessels, the main goal presumably being to interdict Guomindang commando squads active on the eastern coast, or to prevent smuggling and the escape of defectors. The Soviet Union also made available some pre–World War II submarines. When the Soviets finally relinquished Lüshun in 1955, as they had promised to do, they handed over some vessels, including two destroyers and five newer-model submarines. But it was obvious that, for a time, the Chinese navy was not going to figure prominently on the world scene.

The growth of professionalism within the PLA had a profound impact on Chinese society and on the CCP itself. Particularly troubling was the reemergence of elitism. In the countryside and in the towns, the protracted and often violent campaigns against landlords and capitalists had stressed equality and cooperative labor. But in the army, where once in guerrilla days decisions were made after group consultation, and ideological mobilization was as important as military tactics, steps in the mid-1950s seemed to move in the opposite direction. The last traces of the old camaraderie vanished as fourteen precise grades of officer ranks were introduced in 1955, along with insignia and uniforms featuring markers of hierarchy. Pay scales became sharply differentiated, with a lieutenant getting ten times more than a private, and a colonel close to three times more than a lieutenant. Higher education and scientific abilities could lead swiftly to promotions.

Even more seriously, the combination of high status with the garrison mentality of troops away from home led to a range of abuses that showed a slide away from the standards of discipline that the Red Army had previously depended on for survival in its guerrilla campaigns. The PLA troops were beginning to act like the Nationalists, or even like Qing bannermen. In the guarded words of the head of the PLA's political department in summer 1955, some officers now felt "no need for the tradition of unanimity of army men and civilians, and support of the government and love of the people."[9] In practical terms this meant that they were requisitioning land, living in a luxurious style, taking over private homes without permission, or using their status to secure perks. The practice of abusing women in the local communities was reportedly widespread.

In response to rising concerns about such abuses, the CCP tried to improve military discipline by mandating that officers and enlisted men contribute to production in the countryside. An elaborate code of behavior, promulgated for all units in 1956, included the obligation to help in agricultural work, the contribution of five to seven labor days a year to local projects, and the expectation of spending holiday time with peasants, hunting down the "four pests" (rats, sparrows, flies, and mosquitoes). In addition, human excrement should be collected and given to cooperatives as fertilizer, and every fifty PLA members must jointly raise one hog. All soldiers were to learn the standard northern "Mandarin" pronunciation and help in local schools.

In many areas the performance of such acts would have surely increased popular support for the PLA. But among some in the army the regulations aroused profound antipathies and even undermined their obedience to the party. One of the most famous quotations from Mao Zedong's works was that "political power grows out of the barrel of the gun." Taken that far, this seemed to confirm Mao as an heir to previous warlords and Guomindang generals. But what Mao had actually said was this: "Political power grows out of the barrel of the gun. Our principle is that the party commands the gun and the gun shall never be allowed to command the party."[10] As PLA officers and troops gained technical skills that CCP cadres had not yet mastered, tensions between army and party had to be reckoned with. It was not clear in which direction the predominant tilt would go.

THE HUNDRED FLOWERS

During the first years of the People's Republic, intellectuals struggled to find solid footing in the new regime. For the generation born in the early twentieth century, the substance and methods of their education had been transformed, with traditional Chinese learning and Western disciplines now coexisting or intermingling in different combinations. Education remained a time-consuming and costly process, and most intellectuals continued to come from families that had made money or inherited wealth from landholdings or business. Those with positions in the government bureaucracy, or who worked in the teaching or legal professions, inevitably had extensive contacts with the Guomindang. Those in universities and the medical and scientific professions had often obtained their advanced degrees overseas or been taught by Westerners in China.

Since such backgrounds were now considered "feudal," "reactionary," or "capitalist," it was incumbent on the intellectuals to show their loyalty to the CCP. Many of them were ready or eager to help the new regime because they had lost faith that the Guomindang could bring enduring, constructive change. The CCP's promise that Guomindang officials might stay on at their jobs had been reassuring. Not only did the majority of the intellectual elite not flee to Taiwan or the West, but distinguished figures living overseas returned to China in late 1949 and 1950 to help build a new society. Among them were many scientists and economists, along with members of the diplomatic corps who had been posted in embassies and consulates abroad. Even those who had seen the faults of both the CCP and the Guomindang were drawn home out of patriotism and a sense of new opportunities. Lao She, author of *Rickshaw* and *Cat Country*—who had been living in New York since 1946 and was famous throughout the United States, where *Rickshaw* had been a bestseller—returned home in 1950, ignoring the warnings of his friends that he might find life there difficult.*

During 1950 and 1951 tens of thousands of intellectuals of all ages were given six- to eight-month-long "courses" at "revolutionary colleges" in an attempt to lead them to a true understanding of their class background. As well as being lectured by veteran CCP cadres on the nature of the revolution, and introduced to the thought of Mao Zedong along with the basic works of Marx, Engels, Lenin, and Stalin, they met in small groups for discussion and self-criticism, and prepared "autobiographies" in which they analyzed their own past failings and those of their parents. This last requirement caused profound crises for many who had been brought up with the tenets of Confucian filial piety, and in general the entire process subjected the intellectuals to severe mental stress. As the process advanced, they moved from an excited appreciation of shared group solidarity, through a period of intense isolation and guilt, followed by fear and insecurity, to a final "resolution" in which they expressed gratitude to the CCP for making their new lives possible.

The eleven-page confession of a distinguished professor of philosophy who had studied at Harvard University before returning to take up his post in China offers a good example. The professor began by criticizing the life of ease he had spent with his "bureaucratic landlord family" and went on to analyze the "crust of selfishness" that enclosed him, to condemn his interest in decadent bourgeois philosophy and his wish to remain above politics, and finally to hail the sense of new purpose granted him by the Communist party and by the "miracles" of the PLA.[11] The most distinguished alumnus of the process—in terms of former rank—was Puyi, the last emperor of the Qing dynasty and the ruler of Manchukuo, who had been captured by the

---

* The best-selling English edition of *Rickshaw* was given an upbeat, romantic ending by its translator, without Lao She's permission. The original novel ended with a pessimistic view of the future.

Soviets in 1945. After he returned to China, Puyi was subjected to "remolding" in a camp for war criminals and began to draft his first full confession in 1952.* It is impossible to tell if such testimonials were sincere or not. The party rejected confessions it regarded as insincere or self-censored, but the use of irony was always hard to catch.

Intellectuals, like other members of society, participated in the confrontations of the Three Anti and Five Anti campaigns. Struggling to prove their loyalty to the new regime, they also volunteered to participate in land-reform teams and worked to promote the party's policies. During the early stages of the First Five-Year Plan, Mao Zedong began to see that the contributions of intellectuals of all disciplines were needed to increase the nation's productive capacities. They had to be taught to conform to the CCP's ideological expectations, but they should not be terrorized into inaction or silence. Cadres were told that they were wrong to "take the ability to grasp Marxist-Leninism as the sole criterion on which to base their judgments." Intellectuals who "are capable of working honestly and of knowing their work" must be encouraged.[12]

Yet when writers went too far in following the logic of these remarks, they met ferocious opposition. The author and editor Hu Feng, a party member who held seats on the executive board of the writers' union and in the National People's Congress, wrote that the control exercised by the CCP over culture "exhausted" people, such that they could no longer think straight. The use of Marxism to judge works of art was "crude sociology" and "not based on reality." "This weapon is frightening, because it can stifle the real feelings of creativity and art."[13] For remarks like these, Hu Feng became the target of a criticism campaign in 1955, and he was dismissed from his posts. As the campaign intensified and spread, the accusations sharpened. Charged first with ideological deviation, he was next accused of being a counterrevolutionary and an imperialist, and finally cast as a Guomindang agent and commander of an anti-Communist underground. Hu Feng became the focus for countless meetings to deepen political consciousness; these sessions were synchronized to the transition from lower-level agricultural cooperatives to higher-level cooperatives in 1955 and 1956. Thus the countrywide search for "Hu Feng-ism" became a way of detecting whether anyone dared overtly oppose the accelerated development of agricultural cooperatives. Hu wrote three lengthy self-criticisms, which the party rejected as inadequate. After a secret trial, he was sentenced to prison, where he would remain (with one short hiatus of freedom) until 1979.

* Because of the complexities of his experiences, Puyi was not released from detention until 1959. In 1960 he was assigned a job at a machine repair shop in a Beijing botanical garden. He died of cancer in 1967.

A complex situation now developed in which the leadership became divided over how to deal with the country's demoralized intellectuals. Of the wide spectrum of positions on the matter, two polar views stood out. One favored continuing the "united front alliance" with the intellectuals, arguing that their skills were desperately needed in the drive to achieve the First Five-Year Plan, and that their loyalty could ultimately be trusted even if they did criticize the party. The other held that Party unity was paramount, and that the CCP could not be criticized from outside without fatal effects.

The tortuous course of what came to be called the Hundred Flowers movement emerged from these political divisions. The decision to launch the movement was part of the attempt by CCP leaders to understand the significance of Khrushchev's attacks on Stalin's memory, made in January and February 1956 at the twentieth congress of the Soviet Communist party, which both Deng Xiaoping and Zhu De attended. Khrushchev's statement that war was not predestined between the great opposing powers reinforced the views Zhou Enlai had expounded at Bandung concerning "peaceful coexistence." In a speech he delivered on May 2 to a closed session of party leaders, Mao elaborated on the idea of "letting a hundred flowers bloom" in the field of culture and "a hundred schools of thought contend" in the field of science.[14]

There followed a lull while party leaders continued to brood about the problem in private. Mao was ebullient at the general successes of his policies, as we can judge by a triumphant poem he wrote in the summer of 1956, after he took three lengthy swims in the Yangzi River to demonstrate his continuing good health—he was now sixty-two—to the country at large. But in the fall, major problems emerged as the attempt to impose cooperative agriculture led to chaos and waste, compounded by poor management and contradictory orders. The rapid growth initially achieved during the First Five-Year Plan was clearly going to be hard to repeat, and economic difficulties loomed. At the eighth party congress in September 1956, Mao's most dramatic plans for faster economic growth in agriculture were shelved in favor of stronger planning controls. And in the new draft of the party constitution all references to the importance of Mao Zedong Thought were dropped, as was perhaps inevitable after the Soviet attacks on Stalin's cult of personality.

In explaining this decision, Liu Shaoqi was quoted as saying that "if one is always repeating something so that people get accustomed to hearing it, it does not serve any purpose." Mao's statements that he might "retire to the second front" implied that he was looking for a peaceful succession to his leadership, a theory reinforced by the introduction into the constitution of a new post—honorary chairman of the Central Committee. The general tenor of the congress opposed so-called united front policies, and favored stricter party discipline and supervision. CCP leaders were also concerned about the

political riots that occurred in Poland that June, and their worries were reinforced in October 1956 by the Hungarian uprisings against the Soviet Union.
At the same time, major demonstrations occurred in Tibet protesting the
presence of PLA troops on Tibetan soil.

Mao had to use all his influence to get a full Hundred Flowers campaign
going. In a free-wheeling speech of February 1957, delivered to a group of intellectual and CCP leaders, Mao tried to instill the idea of flexibility and openness
into the minds of his captive audience, in sharp contrast to what had become the
party's more authoritarian mode—one which he himself had helped to create.
Other party leaders prevented the draft of this speech, "On Contradictions,"
from being published in the party press.[15] Only in late April of 1957, after weeks
of pressure against foot-dragging party secretaries around the country, did the
full weight of the press and other propaganda organs swing in favor of the campaign. It was now couched in the rhetoric of a rectification movement, in which
intellectuals were encouraged to speak out against abuses within the party. The
campaign took aim at the CCP's own "bureaucratism, sectarianism and subjec-
tivism," in a deliberate echo of the 1942 Rectification Campaign in Yan'an. The
language of the campaign directive, however, reassured cadres that they would
be gently treated. This was to be a campaign for unity that would bind all in
common progress. It would be, said Mao,

> a movement of ideological education carried out seriously, yet as gently as a breeze or a
> mild rain. It should be a campaign of criticism and self-criticism carried to the proper
> extent. . . . Comradely heart-to-heart talks in the form of conversations, namely exchange
> of views between individuals, should be used more and large meetings of criticism or
> "struggle" should not be held.[16]

Convinced that permission to air their grievances was now official, intellectuals responded with enthusiasm across a five-week period from May 1
to June 7, 1957. In closed forums attended by CCP delegates, in the state-
controlled press, in posters glued onto the walls of their campuses, and at
rallies in the streets, people began to speak out. Mao and other senior officials tried to lead the way by concentrating on such issues as reintroducing a
measure of constructive physical labor for party cadres to keep them in touch
with the masses, or allowing economic issues to get a proper airing before decisions were made. But the public criticisms immediately broadened the scope
of the dialogue. They protested CCP control over intellectual life, the harshness of previous mass campaigns, the slavish following of Soviet models, low
standards of living, the proscription of foreign literature, corruption among
party cadres, and the fact that "Party members enjoy many privileges which
make them a race apart." The earlier mass campaigns were called "a serious
violation of human rights" by one professor in Hankou. He added, "This is

tyranny! This is malevolence!" The voting system of ratifying party slates was a farce. "Today we do not even know the height or size of a person we elect, let alone his character or ability. We have simply become ballot-casting machines."[17]

"There seems to be an invisible pressure which compels people to say nothing," observed a Shaanxi professor, describing life under the CCP. "It is not true that all the peasants consciously want to join the cooperatives," said a Shengyang teacher. "As a matter of fact, the majority of them are forced to join." Another professor wrote that the administration at his university was "absolutely littered with feudal princes and stinking charlatans." A former friend of Lu Xun's wrote that there had been more freedom of speech for writers in Chongqing under Chiang Kai-shek than in today's Beijing. "The communist party is at the end of its tether," former landlords in Henan allegedly said. "The time for our liberation has come."[18]

In the heart of Beijing University, the students created what they called a "Democratic Wall" and covered it with posters critical of the CCP. Addressing students there in late May, a young woman from another campus defended Hu Feng, blasted the Yan'an campaign for the restrictions imposed on literary and poetic production, and urged students to coordinate their protests with actions occurring in the northwest, Nanjing, and Wuhan. In fact protests had already erupted in many more cities than that, and soon from Chengdu to Qingdao there were reports of excited groups of students rioting, beating up cadres, ransacking files, calling on other colleges and secondary schools to join them in sympathy strikes, and urging new educational policies.

Some of China's most renowned scholars began to publish articles of astonishing frankness. Fei Xiaotong, a pioneering sociologist whose essays and books on rural society had been famous in the 1930s and 1940s, was among the most outspoken. In June 1957 he published an account of his return visit earlier that year to Kaixiangong village in a remote part of Jiangsu, where he had done field work in the 1930s. Fei pointed out numerous problems that still existed in the area, including irrational planning practices, disregard for local industries, failure to raise livestock suited to the environment, and total neglect of children's education. The implication was that in the mid-1950s many aspects of life in Kaixiangong were no better than they had been in the mid-1930s. Fei included several reflective passages that conveyed his uneasiness with current policies:

> To doubt the superiority of collectivization is incorrect. But to recognize the superiority of collectivization and at the same time believe that it solves all problems is in my opinion incorrect as well. The one way is as incorrect as the other. If we think too simplemindedly, we will be in greater danger of error. [19]

The party secretaries in at least nine provinces had never backed the Hundred Flowers movement, and many others were doubtless only reluctant participants. Their backlash began in June. They were supported by those in the capital who had also opposed the campaign but had been temporarily overruled by Mao. Realizing that the tide was now going against him, Mao swung to the side of the hard-liners. He altered the text of his "Contradictions" speech so that it read as if the promised intellectual freedoms were permissible only if they contributed to the strengthening of socialism. This revised version was then widely disseminated. The speech now appeared to censure intellectuals rather than encourage public criticisms, as Mao had originally intended it to be. In July, an intensive assault against critics of the party was mounted in major newspapers, launching the "antirightist campaign." In early August Peng Zhen accused the party's critics of behaving like the "anti-communist, counter-revolutionary 'heroes' Chiang Kai-shek and Wang Jingwei" during 1927. Should the CCP in 1957, he asked rhetorically, behave as then-party leader Chen Duxiu did in the dark days of the Shanghai and Wuhan massacres: "forgive the anti-communist, anti-people, counter-revolutionary crimes . . . and suffer the ferocious onslaughts of the bourgeois rightists?" His answer was preordained: "Very definitely, we cannot."[20]

By the end of the year, over 300,000 intellectuals had been branded "rightists," a label that effectively ruined their careers. Many were sent to labor camps

or to jail, others to the countryside in a punitive exile with no expiration date. Among them was the writer Ding Ling, her Stalin prize forgotten, banished to a farm in remote Heilongjiang. A whole generation of young party activists were similarly penalized, among them some of the country's finest social scientists, scientists, and economists. Fei Xiaotong gave an abject confession to the National People's Congress, which still met occasionally in formal

Ding Ling More than 30,000 intellectuals were branded "rightists" in the campaigns of 1957, and many were imprisoned or sent to labor camps. Ding Ling, the distinguished writer and early party member, was banished to a farm in Heilongjiang.

session, allegedly keeping some form of democratic participation alive. Fei repudiated his Kaixiangong report, and confessed he had been "doubting and opposing the goals of socialism," had "incited a worsening of relations between the Party and the peasants," and "even planned to use these materials to write yet another piece of propaganda for foreigners."[21] Fei lost his various honorific posts, was labeled a "rightist," and was forbidden to teach, publish, or conduct research. Still he was more fortunate than many other professors and students who were driven to suicide by the incessant pressure of public struggle sessions. Three student leaders in the Hanyang First Middle School, who had triggered a protest against the CCP administration of their school, were tried and shot. According to the news report, the executions were carried out at the start of the school year and in the presence of 10,000 people, many of them presumably fellow students. The blooming of the Hundred Flowers had ended with a vengeance, leaving China poised for a new era of sharp revolutionary struggle.

CHAPTER 21

Deepening the Revolution

THE GREAT LEAP FORWARD

The Hundred Flowers campaign was not merely a plot by Mao to reveal the hidden rightists in his country, as some critics later charged and as he himself seemed to claim in the published version of his speech "On . . . Contradictions." It was, rather, a muddled and inconclusive movement that grew out of conflicting attitudes within the party leadership and forced intellectuals to take a public stance on matters of policy and the meaning of their own lives under the CCP. At its center was an argument about the pace and type of development that was best for China, and a debate about the nature of the First Five-Year Plan and its promise for further growth. From those disagreements and the accompanying political tensions sprang the Great Leap Forward.

Despite the speed of compliance with the call for higher-level cooperatives, agricultural production figures for 1957 were disappointing. Grain production increased only 1 percent over the year, in the face of a 2 percent population rise. Cotton-cloth rations had to be cut because of shortages. Although the First Five-Year Plan had met its quotas well enough, it had also revealed disturbing imbalances in the economic system. While industrial output rose at 18.7 percent per year during the plan period, agricultural production rose only 3.8 percent. Per capita grain consumption grew even less, at just under 3 percent per year. With rural markets booming, local purchasers bought up most of the grains, edible oils, and cotton that was for sale, decreasing the amount available for state procurement or for urban consumers. At those levels of agricultural production, it was hard to see how more could be extracted from the peasantry to pay for the industrial growth mandated by the Soviet model, unless China embarked on the same ruthless program of enforced agricultural procurement that had caused such terrible famine in the USSR in the early 1930s. But this was an unlikely measure, since in the 1950s China's per capita grain production was far lower than the Soviet Union's had been in the 1930s. Moreover, CCP membership was almost 70 percent rural (the Soviet party was 70 percent urban) and would not be enthusiastic about such a policy if it led to misery in the countryside.

Mao's emerging response to the disappointing agricultural production on the cooperative farms was to push for a strategy of heightened production through moral incentives and mass mobilization under the direction of local cadres. This vision, which drew on methods used in Yan'an, was endorsed by the top leadership. By decentralizing economic decision making, the strategy was intended to foster even greater CCP power in the countryside and a corresponding decline in the influence of professional economic planners in the ministries. Economic woes would be solved by the spontaneous energizing of the whole nation.

This debate over growth strategy, which unfolded during 1957 and 1958, took place in a period of ambiguous Sino-Soviet relations. The Soviets demanded heavy payments for aid in industrial development, and one reason China needed an even greater agricultural surplus was to meet the terms of Soviet loans. Soviet technology, which had already mastered the production of the atomic and hydrogen bombs, seemed triumphant with the successful testing of an intercontinental ballistic missile in August 1957 and the launching of the Sputnik satellite six weeks later. In early November 1957, when Mao made his second (and last) trip to Moscow, a second Soviet satellite was launched into orbit, this time with a live dog on board.

The Soviet achievement came only a few months after all hopes evaporated for a peaceful reunification with Taiwan. A series of anti-United States riots in Taiwan had been rigorously suppressed by Chiang Kai-shek, who publicly apologized to the Americans for the disturbances. Chiang's government thereafter allowed the United States to use Taiwan as a base from which missiles could deliver nuclear warheads hundreds of miles into Chinese territory. In Moscow, Mao told Chinese students that, weighing the state of international competition, the "forces of socialism surpass the forces of imperialism" and that "the East wind [China and the USSR] was prevailing over the West wind." This conclusion led Mao to the view that in a nuclear war the Chinese would triumph. "If the worst came to the worst and half of mankind died, the other half would remain while imperialism would be razed to the ground and the whole world would become socialist."[1]

Mao Zedong was troubled, however, by the loss of vitality that seemed to be emerging as the Chinese revolution moved into a phase of cautious long-range planning. The core of Mao's radical thinking had always centered on his belief in the voluntaristic, heroic workings of human will and the power of the masses, ideas he had celebrated in his earliest writings forty years before. Then he had seen his friends go off to work-and-study programs that blended intellectual activity with manual labor, and he himself had plunged into the exciting task of organizing labor groups in which unlettered workers were swiftly taught to master new skills and to seize their destinies for themselves from their capitalist exploiters. Following these experiences, Mao had felt the euphoria of working with emerging peasant associations in 1926 and 1927, when illiterate peasants seemed able to grasp complex problems of strategy and politics and to apply them to their own grim circumstances.

But in the disappointing circumstances of China in 1957, as Mao told a gathering of CCP officials in Qingdao, the peasants and rural cadres had fallen into a pattern of "individualism, departmentalism, absolute egalitarianism or liberalism." This was shorthand for saying that peasants were too concerned with gaining a better living after collectivization, that cadres concealed true output figures and exaggerated shortages in order to pay less to the state and get more from it, and that both groups resented the higher living standards of their urban counterparts. This rhetoric was accompanied by police action, as groups of internal security agents fanned out across the country, hunting down those criticizing the government or those whose behavior could in any way be described as "capitalist." Unlicensed traders, peddlers, vagrants, and "delinquents" were all caught in the net, given long sentences in detention camps, and in some cases publicly shot.[2]

On a different tack, but still veering in the same direction, Mao sorted out his thoughts on the idea of continuing revolution. In the Soviet Union the theory of "permanent" revolution had been repudiated as a Trotskyist heresy that denied the validity of correct revolutionary stages and the leadership role of the party. Mao boldly seized on a similar concept with a different label in an attempt to give "continuing revolution" new respectability as a Chinese contribution to revolutionary theory and practice. The idea could draw on all of China's revolutionary experiences to date and could be invoked to mobilize the masses yet again. It is worth quoting Mao's own words, in this instance from a list of "Sixty Points on Working Methods," that he circulated as an internal document in January and February 1958:

> Continuing revolution. Our revolutions come one after another. Starting from the seizure of power in the whole country in 1949, there followed in quick succession the anti-feudal land reform, the agricultural co-operativization, and the socialist reconstruction of private industries, commerce, and handicrafts. . . . Now we must start a technological revolution so that we may overtake Britain in fifteen or more years. . . . After fifteen years, when our foodstuffs and iron and steel become plentiful, we shall take a much greater initiative. Our revolutions are like battles. After a victory, we must at once put forward a new task. In this way, cadres and the masses will forever be filled with revolutionary

fervour, instead of conceit. Indeed, they will have no time for conceit, even if they like to feel conceited. With new tasks on their shoulders, they are totally preoccupied with the problems for their fulfilment.[3]

In elaborating on this idea of continuous revolutionary upsurge, Mao also emphasized the need for all Chinese to be both "red and expert," to forge a true synthesis of their socialist commitment and their technical skills. Mao celebrated the fact that China's 600 million people were "poor and blank," as he phrased it, for "poor people want change, want to do things, want revolution. A blank sheet of paper has no blotches, and so the newest and most beautiful words can be written on it, the newest and most beautiful pictures can be painted on it."[4] From this, as the vision soared, it was a short leap of memory back to the utopian message of Marx's *The German Ideology*, which was frequently quoted in support of Mao's vision. Writing of the future joys of a communist society, Marx had described a world in which

> nobody has one exclusive sphere of activity but each can become accomplished in any branch he wishes, [a society that] regulates the general production and thus makes it possible for me to do one thing today and another tomorrow, to hunt in the morning, fish in the afternoon, rear cattle in the evening, criticize after dinner, just as I have a mind, without ever becoming hunter, fisherman, shepherd or critic.[5]

In late 1957, CCP leaders began to experiment with a new scale of social organization by mobilizing the peasants for gigantic new tasks in water control and irrigation, as if to prove that human will and strength could vanquish all natural and technical challenges. By the end of January 1958, 100 million people had reportedly opened up 7.8 million hectares of land through irrigation work. If the population could be galvanized in this way, surely they could just as dramatically transform agricultural production—it was just a question of finding the right organizational forms and maintaining mass commitment. But the almost military dragooning of labor on the irrigation projects led to new problems as men were taken away from their cooperatives to work at some distance from home. One solution was to persuade women to take a greater role in agricultural labor outside the home. To release them from time-consuming domestic work, centralized childcare and dining halls were established. This centralization of domestic tasks became even more urgent when, to raise industrial production nationwide, party leaders ordered some industries relocated to the countryside. This would enable the peasants to learn new techniques and utilize their productive labor in the slack periods of the farming year.

Thus did the massing of higher-level cooperatives into much larger units become an accepted part of Chinese revolutionary thinking. The goals were to increase rural productivity in order to boost industrial growth, as well as to realize new human potential and flexibility. In the fall of 1957 the Politburo ordered formerly urban-based cadres to go to the countryside and examine conditions there, and work to increase production under the slogan "More, faster, better, cheaper." Cowed by the hunts for dissidents and manipulated by their local political leaders (who were often fighting their own career battles), peasants dared not dispute even the most fanciful claims for higher agricultural yields. The term "people's commune" (*renmin gongshe*) was not used in party journals until July 1958, but as early as April the abolition of private plots and the amalgamation of 27 Henan cooperatives into one immense commune of 9,369 households were carried out.

By the summer of 1958, after an abundant harvest had dramatically raised everyone's hopes, the campaign to end all private plots and to organize the rural population into people's communes began, with extraordinary reports of success. Meeting in August 1958, the Central Committee issued a resounding endorsement of the Great Leap process:

> The people's communes are the logical result of the march of events. . . . The people have taken to organizing themselves along military lines, working with militancy, and leading a collective life, and this has raised the political consciousness of the 500 million peasants still further. Community dining rooms, kindergartens, nurseries, sewing groups, barber shops, public baths, happy homes for the aged, agricultural middle schools, "red and expert" schools, are leading the peasants toward a happier collective life and further fostering ideas of collectivism among the peasant masses.

With the defeat of "advocates of the capitalist road" and "right conservatism," the Central Committee stated, agriculture has "leaped forward," doubling, increasing tenfold, or even multiplying "scores of times." The commune structure, governing all aspects of rural life, would be the "fundamental policy to guide the peasants to accelerate socialist construction, complete the building of socialism ahead of time, and carry out the gradual transition to communism."[6] At their next meeting, held in December 1958, the Central Committee claimed that in the summer of 1958, 740,000 cooperatives had reorganized into 26,000 communes, comprising over 120 million households (more than 99 percent of the rural population). The triumph of agricultural production and industrialization in the communes was such, the Central Committee added, that China no longer need worry about overpopulation, as some had been doing. To the contrary, the forthcoming problem would be "not so much overpopulation as [the] shortage of manpower."[7]

The vision was altogether intoxicating, and seemed a complete vindication of Mao's views on the possibility for accelerated growth through the mobilization of mass will and energy, especially when freed of constraints of overcautious planning and an entrenched bureaucracy. For several months, the

Women belonging to a cooperative look over their rice paddy field made possible by new irriga-tion systems, 1958.

euphoria was self-sustaining as the astounding production figures submitted by local cadres poured into provincial offices, to be relayed to Beijing. The language also was self-sustaining as observers caught the mood that they knew party leaders wanted. One example, from a reporter observing conditions in Jiangxi in the fall of 1958, can serve for myriad others:

> Small red flags fly overhead indicating the sections belonging to the various companies and squads of farmer-steelworkers, who are organized like militia units. The air is filled with the high-pitched melodies of local operas pouring through an amplifier above the site and accompanied by the hum of blowers, the panting of gasoline engines, the honking of heavily-laden lorries, and the bellowing of oxen hauling ore and coal.[8]

It does not belittle the vision—which was as rich or richer than anything expressed in China since the Taiping Heavenly King, Hong Xiuquan, ruled over Nanjing just over a century before—to say that it did not coincide with reality. The grain-production figures had been disastrously overinflated. The announced total for 1958 of 375 million tons of grain had to be revised downward to 250 million tons (Western economists later estimated that actual production was around 215 million tons). Cadres did not dare to report

People collect old pots, pans, and scrap metal for backyard furnaces.

shortfalls of their procurement quotas out of fear of being labeled "rightists" or "defeatists." Many of the best-trained statisticians from state bureaus, having been removed in the 1957 antirightist campaign (along with the most able demographers), were no longer around to issue words of caution even if they had dared. The campaign for steel production had set even more fantastical targets—the goal of reaching 700 million tons a year within a decade was several times the total produced in the entire world. To contribute, people brought whatever metal objects they could find (doorknobs, pots and pans, nails, farm tools) to melt down in "backyard furnaces." But the diversion of resources (such as firewood and cement) to build more than 1 million such furnaces was a waste, for the "steel" produced was useless.

The Great Leap did bring several fundamental changes. The pooling of household, childcare, and cooking arrangements had significant effects on family structure, even as it showed that the nuclear family remained a more popular form of social organization. The massing of huge numbers of rural and city workers for irrigation, terracing, and construction projects changed the face of the landscape and brought prosperity to previously infertile regions. Thousands of peasants, given simple training and instructions, were sent into isolated areas to prospect for uranium and petroleum. The aim was to prove that self-reliance could speed the country's development of a nuclear weapon and end recurrent fuel shortages. In several cases, the prospectors made important finds. Cities were also transformed, sometimes at great aesthetic cost; in Beijing, for instance, the last of the great city walls were demolished to create immense new boulevards, and the city itself was honeycombed with a maze of underground shelters in case of nuclear attack from the United States. The people's militia that was developed during the Great Leap—when 220 million people had allegedly been organized into militia units, and 30 million furnished with firearms—brought new strength to local areas and provided a potential rival to the PLA. The attempt also to mobilize a great leap forward in poetry encouraged millions of men and women, who had always thought poetry to be the preserve of a scholarly elite, to try their hands at it, and spurred the collection of hundreds of thousands of folk tales and songs. Perhaps this aspect of the Great Leap came closest, briefly, to realizing a fragment of Marx's dream about developing fully rounded human beings with access to all their latent talents.

Criticism of the Great Leap strategy, and an attempt to constrain the communes and return to central planning and allocation, had begun even before the Central Committee's December 1958 meeting. The rhetorical flourishes of those proceedings did not hide the conviction of most party leaders that they had moved too far too fast, and that the long-term prospects for the Great Leap were dim. By early 1959 some communes were returning to their earlier cooperative forms, with the subcomponent of the production brigade as the unit of accounting. In many areas, private plots were once again allocated to individual families. Mao stepped down as head of state in early 1959, and in the spring Liu Shaoqi was named to his place. Mao had earlier announced that he might step down, but the timing implied a measure of coercion, even though he kept his other powerful positions as chairman of the CCP and of the Military Affairs Commission.

Despite the chaos caused by the Great Leap, there was only one overt attempt to oppose the extremism of Mao's plan. This criticism came from the army marshal Peng Dehuai at a conference of top leaders held during July 1959. In informal discussions at Lushan in Jiangxi, Peng pointed out some of the Great Leap's problems and observed that Mao's home village in Hunan had received more state aid than Mao realized. Peng had already voiced grave doubts about the accuracy of the enormous grain-harvest figures (375 million tons) reported for 1958. In a private letter he delivered to Mao, Peng spelled out his worries over the misreporting of conditions in the countryside, and its potential effect on the nation.

Instead of treating the letter as a private communication from a trusted colleague, Mao circulated it to the senior cadres at the Lushan conference and launched a personal denunciation of Peng. He accused the marshal of forming a "right opportunist clique" and of "unprincipled factional activity,"[9] and he made it clear that he believed Peng, who had just returned from visiting the Soviet Union, had given negative information about the communes to Khrushchev. The Soviet leader had then used this information in a speech deriding the idea of communes. The venom of the attack startled those in attendance and marked a key juncture in CCP history. Mao now treated criticism of policy within senior party ranks as an attack on his own leadership and foresight. Peng was removed from his post as minister of defense, and other party leaders were cowed into accepting Mao's interpretations of recent events.

In a speech he made at the Lushan meeting, Mao took a bellicose and self-justificatory position on the Great Leap and the communes. Confucius, Lenin, and Marx had all made mistakes, he said, so why be surprised that he had too? If everyone insisted on emphasizing nothing but the negative side, then he would "go to the countryside to lead the peasants to overthrow the government. If those of you in the Liberation Army won't follow me, then I will go and find a Red Army, and organize another Liberation Army." As for the communes, said Mao, "up to now not one has collapsed. We were prepared for the collapse of half of them, and if seventy percent collapsed there would still be thirty percent left. If they must collapse let them." He ended caustically, addressing those at the conference with vulgar language, as if to emphasize that he came from the masses whereas many of the other leaders present did not: "The chaos caused was on a grand scale and I take responsibility. Comrades, you must all analyze your own responsibility. If you have to shit, shit! If you have to fart, fart! You will feel much better for it."[10]

The scatological metaphor was designed to shock the audience, and perhaps to defuse the tension of the moment with laughter. But in the context of the crisis in the countryside, the metaphor was crueler than Mao seems to have realized. At the time he was delivering his earthy remarks, peasants within fifty miles of Beijing, like those in many other parts of China, were starving in their villages. One young party activist, branded as a rightist after the Hundred Flowers movement and exiled to the countryside, recalled later how she combed the mountainsides for apricot pits fallen from the trees, so that they could be pressed for oil or boiled for porridge. The other food of the villagers was rice husks or crushed corncobs, with apricot leaves dried in the sun and ground into "flour" before being mixed with powdered elm-tree bark to make another kind of porridge. Since pigs, too, were starving in the pens, they were let out and allowed to roam. As commune members squatted in open latrines, swollen with malnutrition and constipated from the grim diet, the pigs would jostle them with their snouts, trying to get at the excrement before it had fallen from their bodies.[11]

The victory over Peng Dehuai at Lushan gave Mao renewed confidence in his vision, and a determination to reassert the primacy of the commune system, bureaucratic decentralization, and mass mobilization. The organizational form of the commune was now spread to many cities in an effort to encourage factory workers to reach new heights of production. Far from responding to worries over grain shortfalls by remitting procurement quotas to desperate areas, Mao insisted on increased extraction of the rapidly dwindling agricultural surplus. Still believing the exaggerated reports of grain production, many cadres ordered fields left fallow, to avoid the problem of storage for the anticipated surpluses.

As national investment in industry rose to an astonishing 43.4 percent of national income in 1959, grain exports to the Soviet Union were also increased to pay for more heavy machinery. The average amount of grain available to each person in the countryside, which had been 205 kilos in 1957 and 201 kilos in 1958, dropped to a disastrous 183 kilos in 1959, and a catastrophic 156 kilos in 1960. In 1961 it fell again—to 154 kilos. The result was famine on a colossal scale, which claimed 20 to 35 million lives between 1959 and 1962. The wide range reflects different methodologies for extrapolating from incomplete data, defining a baseline, and calculating excess mortality, total mortality, or mortality plus lost births. But even the estimates at the low end of the range make this one of the largest famines in human history.[12] The suffering was widespread but unevenly distributed, with the highest known death tolls in Anhui, Sichuan, Guizhou, Hunan, Gansu, and Henan provinces.[13] Urban residents experienced hunger and hardship during this period but were relatively insulated by preferential state policies that prioritized their food supply. To survive, peasants in the countryside stole grain from the fields or storehouses; ate tree bark, insects, and clay; or slaughtered draft animals in desperation. Some fled their villages for nearby cities; others migrated to Xinjiang in the far northwest or Heilongjiang in the far northeast.

Among countless personal tragedies, Yang Jisheng's account of watching his father die of starvation is harrowing in its anguished simplicity. In 1959 Yang was a middle school boarding student, living about six miles from his village in Hubei. He was busy extolling the accomplishments of the Great Leap Forward at school when a friend brought the message to return home immediately. Yang hurried back to find the village a "ghost town," with no dogs, chickens, or children in sight. The trees had been stripped of bark and all the roots dug up. At home, his father was barely alive.

> My father was half-reclined on his bed, his eyes sunken and lifeless, his face gaunt, the skin creased and flaccid. He tried to extend his hand to greet me, but couldn't lift it, just moving it a little. That hand reminded me of the human skeleton in my anatomy

class; although it was covered with a layer of withered skin, nothing concealed the protrusions and hollows of the bone structure. I was shocked with the realization that the term *skin and bones* referred to something so horrible and cruel.

Yang tried to feed him porridge made from rice he brought, but it was too late. His father died three days later. Yang grieved deeply yet made no connection between the Great Leap Forward and the famine that ensued. "I believed that what was happening in my home village was isolated, and that my father's death was merely one family's tragedy. Compared to the advent of the great Communist society, what was my family's petty misfortune?"[14]

THE SINO-SOVIET RIFT

Within the CCP leadership, the planning and implementation of the Great Leap Forward, and the subsequent debates about the reasons for its failure, took place at the same time that relations between China and the Soviet Union entered a catastrophic decline. In important respects, indeed, these two events must be linked together, for the Great Leap—the attempt to break through economic constrictions and to reassert the centrality of revolutionary social change—stood in opposition to the Soviet Union's approach to economic development and mass mobilization.

Behind the Soviet-Chinese disagreements that emerged in the late 1950s lay a tangled history of friendship and distrust. Ever since the late 1920s, Mao Zedong had differed from Stalin by asserting his own interpretations of the need for a mass-based rural revolution, whether in Hunan, in the Jiangxi Soviet, in Yan'an, or during the closing year of the civil war. At the same time, he and Stalin had joined in the call for an aggressive wariness in dealing with the capitalist world, which each described—with a mixture of rhetoric and conviction—as the tenacious enemy of socialist development in both China and the Soviet Union.

In its early years, the PRC depended heavily on Soviet technical assistance to develop its industry, communications networks, and power supplies. Soviet influence was also strong in such areas as architecture and city planning, higher education, and the arts and literature. After Stalin died in 1953, Soviet influence continued, and the heavy Chinese losses in the Korean War required an intensified Soviet involvement in building up the army, navy, and air force. This technical interconnection was valued and deepened by Peng Dehuai, commander in chief of the Chinese forces in Korea, and the incumbent minister of defense. Chinese leaders accepted the fact that, for the time being, the Russians were their only shield against the threat of possible nuclear attack by the United States. This point became especially important in 1957, when the United States announced that it would deploy Matador missiles in Taiwan. At the same time, Mao was anxious to advance China's development of an atomic bomb, to reduce what might become a dangerous overreliance on the Soviet Union.

Nikita Khrushchev, one of the leading contenders to succeed Stalin, visited Beijing during 1954. He responded positively to Chinese requests for industrial development assistance and agreed to withdraw from the Lüshun naval base in Dalian, which Soviet troops had occupied since 1945. This "honeymoon period" ended as the Sino-Soviet alliance began to fray in 1956, after Khrushchev launched his attack on Stalin's memory at the twentieth Soviet party congress. The incendiary charges made by Khrushchev in what became known as the "secret speech" had disturbing implications for leaders throughout the Communist world who had venerated Stalin. Khrushchev had made no attempt to warn Mao in advance of what he intended to do. Indeed, General Zhu De, who was in Moscow, had just praised Stalin in a speech at the same congress.[15]

Khrushchev underlined the new approach he wanted for Soviet-bloc relations in June 1956, when he invited Yugoslavia's famous former anti-Nazi guerrilla leader and current Communist chief, Marshal Tito, to visit Moscow. It was hard for the Chinese to accept this offer of an olive branch to a "revisionist" who had held his country aloof from the Soviet Union during the postwar years. Chinese leaders were further dismayed when, in a bid for greater freedom and flexibility, the Hungarians rose in revolt against the Soviet Union that autumn. After weeks of bloody street fighting, the revolt was smashed by the might of Russian tanks.

There was still no overt clash between China and the Soviet Union, even after Mao published the emended version of his ideas on the theory of contradictions in the summer of 1957. By suggesting the inevitability of "nonantagonistic contradictions" even within socialist countries, and the need for their careful resolution, Mao's speech could be seen as a rebuke to the Soviets for allowing the situation in Hungary to get out of control. Khrushchev nevertheless invited Mao to visit Moscow in October 1957 for the celebration of the fortieth anniversary of the Bolshevik Revolution. This journey marked the second and last time Mao traveled outside China; the first had been his trip to the Soviet Union in 1949. On October 15 the two countries signed a secret agreement, in which, Mao later claimed, the Soviets promised to give China "a sample of an atomic bomb and technical data concerning its manufacture." Senior Chinese army officers and scientists conferred with their Russian counterparts to define the details of the assistance, and over the next two years the Soviets helped design and develop uranium mines in Hunan and Jiangxi, construct a gaseous diffusion plant near Lanzhou in Gansu province, and build a nuclear testing site in the Lop Nur desert of Xinjiang. The Chinese in turn reorganized their research structures to speed the independent development of nuclear-weapons and missile programs, should the Soviets decide not to help them after all.

Mao believed that the Communist bloc should now prepare for a vigorous challenge to the capitalist West. Khrushchev, on the other hand, showed no inclination to change the stance he had taken in 1956, when he had reiterated his belief in the "peaceful co-existence of states with different social systems," as well as his faith in the principles previously espoused by India and China at the Bandung conference.[16] True to this spirit, Khrushchev refused to respond aggressively to the United States' dispatch of marines to Lebanon, or to support the Chinese when they began to bombard the offshore island of Jinmen, still occupied by Guomindang troops. He also made it clear that the Soviet Union would not provide the Chinese with a prototype atomic bomb.

Khrushchev's caution angered CCP leaders, who felt imperiled on many levels. The nation's economy was unstable; they faced a Taiwan armed with the latest American weapons; and they confronted a U.S. government that remained unremittingly hostile and, they were convinced, might at any time use nuclear weapons against China. The PRC's isolation from world markets and Western technology left it overly dependent on the Soviet Union. They needed Soviet aid to supplement the Great Leap strategy, yet they found Khrushchev grudging with resources. In 1959 Chinese leaders backed off from their earlier claims, made during the Great Leap, that they were nearing a rapid transition to communism.

Also in 1959, a wide range of global events began to impinge on China just when the country could least muster effective leadership to cope with them. In Laos, a right-wing coup, with U.S. encouragement, thwarted the rise of an elected Communist government. In Tibet, a surge of protests against the Chinese occupation burst into armed rebellion in March. Many Tibetans were killed by PLA troops, and some of the most beautiful monasteries were destroyed. The Tibetan spiritual leader, the Dalai Lama, fled to India, where he was given sanctuary despite Chinese protests. The apparent Chinese military victory in Tibet did not stop the insurgency there, in part because of the activities of the U.S. Central Intelligence Agency, which was training Tibetan rebels at camps in Colorado before flying them back to their homeland.

Meanwhile, a crisis arose in Indonesia when anti-Chinese riots erupted. Thousands of Chinese were killed or injured, and the survivors were forced to flee the country. Finally, the threat of war with India emerged over disputed borders, where Chinese and Indian maps differed. In the summer of 1959 fighting broke out along the southern slopes of the Himalayan mountains and in

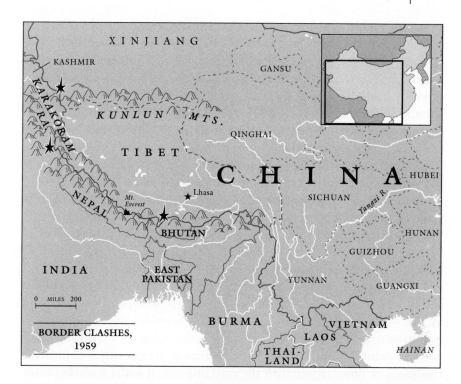

the western part of Tibet. In these conflicts, Khrushchev showed his opposition to the PRC positions by extending generous aid to both Indonesia and India. In the case of the Sino-Indian border clashes, Khrushchev refused to endorse Chinese territorial claims, professed Soviet neutrality, and described the fighting as "sad" and "stupid."

While the events at the Lushan plenum were unfolding in China, Khrushchev followed up on his "peaceful coexistence" initiatives by accepting President Eisenhower's invitation for an official state visit, the first ever extended to a Soviet head of state. Accompanied by his wife and children, Khrushchev was given a red-carpet welcome when he arrived in Washington D.C. on September 15, 1959. He spent thirteen days in the United States, including two days at Camp David for meetings with Eisenhower. Immediately after returning to Moscow, Khrushchev flew to Beijing to attend the celebration of the PRC's tenth anniversary. Although Mao met Khrushchev at the airport, the reception in Beijing was chilly. Tensions surfaced during the brief visit, as the Soviet leader publicly praised Eisenhower for endorsing "peaceful coexistence" and chided his hosts to "do all we can to exclude war as a means of settling disputed questions."[17] In tense meetings, Khrushchev and CCP leaders exchanged sharp words on the Sino-Indian conflicts. For his part, Mao made no public comment on the Soviet leader's American journey or the withdrawal of the atomic-bomb offer. The party journal *Red Flag*, however, had already clarified official policy by remarking that some socialist leaders (i.e., Khrushchev) mistakenly believed that the Americans would "lay down their butcher knife and become Buddhas." In his subsequent public remarks Khrushchev described the talks in Beijing as "cordial and amicable." But in private, he complained about Mao and compared his belligerent attitudes to Trotsky's in 1918.[18]

Throughout 1960 the relationship between the PRC and the Soviet Union deteriorated as the ideological rivalry and battle for leadership of the global communist movement sharpened. Charges and countercharges were bandied about at communist congresses, with Soviet denunciations of Albania standing in for criticisms of the PRC. (Since China supported the Albanians in their bid for independence from Moscow, attacks on Albania were understood to be thinly veiled condemnations of China.) While the Soviet-bloc countries issued statements concerning the horrors of nuclear war and the "annihilation of whole states," the PRC press—echoing the statements made in 1957 by Mao—continued to insist that the Chinese were not frightened. After a nuclear war, ran an essay in *Red Flag*, "on the debris of a dead imperialism, the victorious [socialist] people would create very swiftly a civilization thousands of times higher than the capitalist system and a truly beautiful future for themselves. The conclusion can only be this: whichever way you look at it, none of the new techniques like atomic energy, rocketry and so on has changed, as alleged by modern revisionists, the basic characteristics of the epoch of imperialism and proletarian revolution pointed out by Lenin."[19]

That summer of 1960 the Soviet Union announced the intention of recalling its advisers from the PRC. The threat was carried out immediately, and by September all 1,390 Soviet experts working in China had been summoned home, taking their blueprints with them and leading, the Chinese claimed, to the cancellation of 343 major contracts and 257 other technical projects. Among the departing Soviet scientists were two nuclear-weapons experts who had consistently refused to provide information on atomic-bomb construction, and were derided by the Chinese as "mute monks who would read but not speak."[20] Before they left, the two men tore to shreds all the documents they could not take with them. Painstakingly reconstructing the shredded documents, the Chinese found in them important information on atomic implosion. In November, when the Soviet Union called a meeting of the Communist parties from eighty-one countries, Mao declined to attend and sent Liu Shaoqi and Deng Xiaoping in his stead. After Khrushchev criticized the CCP in a speech, Deng responded by accusing the Soviet leader of "big nation chauvinism." It took a mediating effort by Ho Chi Minh, the leader of the Vietnamese Workers' Party, to broker a temporary truce and avoid an all-out rupture.[21]

The rupture came a year later. In preparation for the twenty-second party congress, to be convened in Moscow, Khrushchev circulated the draft of a new program proclaiming that the Soviet Union would achieve communism by 1980. With the end of class antagonisms in Soviet society, the Communist party would now be "a party of the entire people," with membership open to all. The draft program also reiterated the obligation to prevent nuclear war through peaceful coexistence. In Beijing, these statements verified the suspicion that Khrushchev intended to negate class struggle and the dictatorship of the proletariat as guiding principles—this, to CCP leaders, marked a milestone in Soviet revisionism. When the Soviet party congress opened in October 1961, Zhou Enlai spoke of safeguarding "the unity of the socialist bloc," but the chasm could not be papered over. After an exchange of salvos over Albania, and after Khrushchev delivered a blistering attack on Stalin, the allegories had worn too thin to sustain. Zhou Enlai left Moscow in protest and returned to Beijing.[22]

POLITICAL INVESTIGATION AND SOCIALIST EDUCATION

In the months of 1959 following the ouster of Peng Dehuai and the growth of tensions with the Soviet Union, Chinese leaders jostled for new roles in the ruling hierarchy while famine conditions spread across the country. By late 1960 the Great Leap strategy had been discredited in most eyes; and while Mao "retired from the front line," as he put it, other CCP leaders assessed strategies for recouping the nation's economic losses and rebuilding public morale.

One strategy, which in a sense recalls the days of Mao Zedong's survey of local conditions in Hunan and Jiangxi in 1927 and 1930, was to have individual leaders travel to the countryside to inspect conditions for themselves. In the early summer of 1961, Chen Yun embarked on one of these investigations, traveling to a commune in Qingpu County near Shanghai. Chen had been a union organizer in the 1920s, had joined the Long March and studied in the Soviet Union, and had played a prominent role in the Yan'an rectification campaign of 1942–1944. In 1961 he ranked number five in the Standing Committee of the Politburo. Chen chose this particular commune in part because he had been born in the area and had organized peasants in the county as a young party activist in 1927. During two weeks of intensive discussions with local peasants, Chen quizzed them about their pig-raising procedures, crop-growing patterns, use of private plots, remuneration for labor performed, and involvement in local commerce and handicraft work. He also asked about the state purchase quotas, the behavior of the local cadres, and problems of crime.

Chen Yun was reassured that the peasants remembered his record in the area and therefore "dared speak the truth." This made their disclosures all the more worrying. Even in this commune, which should have been prosperous because of its proximity to the urban market of Shanghai, the peasants did not have enough to eat. Because the collective agriculture had been badly supervised, they had no enthusiasm for it, preferring to work on their own private plots and on "sideline production" for the market. They believed that the cadres in their commune had given wrong orders and then stubbornly refused to change course. And after setting arbitrarily high production quotas and procurement demands for peasants, the same cadres "have failed to participate regularly in work and have led privileged lives."[23]

In a hundred ways, Chen observed, the peasants knew those small details of rural life that were ignored by the cadres, who tried to enforce conformity to national norms and allegedly "logical" plans for collectivized development. It was the local farmers, he noted, who understood how to protect the weakest piglets by attaching them to the sow's third nipple, the one with the richest milk supply. These farmers knew how to keep a sow from heatstroke in summer by using waterweeds as her bedding base, and that combining broad green beans with a single rice crop was far more productive than double-cropping or adding wheat. They knew that if bamboo groves were chopped down to make room for intensive cereals production, then there would be much less fuel and fewer weeding rakes and handles for the simple harrows they all used.

Drawing on these and other observations, Chen came up with five recommendations. Since agricultural recovery would take many years and conditions in the cities were also deteriorating, the 30 million peasants who had drifted into the cities since 1957 should be relocated back to the countryside, and unemployed urban youths should be sent to work there as well. Thousands of inefficient Great Leap industrial enterprises should be dismantled. The principle of collective work should be preserved, but 6 percent of rural land was to be restored to peasants in the form of private plots, and private rural markets reopened. These pessimistic assessments as well as recommendations were conveyed to Mao Zedong by the leaders who outranked Chen Yun: Liu Shaoqi, head of state; Zhou Enlai, premier of the State Council; and Deng Xiaoping, secretary-general of the CCP. Mao agreed to let Chen's views be circulated even though he himself felt that the country was well on the way to economic recovery, and despite his strong opposition to any steps toward dismantling the collectives.

During 1962 and 1963, as the party followed a policy of economic read-justment, more and more evidence showed how bad morale was in the countryside and how frequently cadres abused their positions. The Great Leap famine had sparked this corruption. Given enormous autonomy in decision making to meet unrealistic national quotas, cadres adjusted to famine conditions by protecting themselves and those in their favor, while confiscating grain from the weaker or those they did not favor. Their behavior did not improve after famine conditions eased. Numerous cases were reported of cadres who gambled, traded illegally, or arranged "marriages by sale." Fourteen-year-old girls were sold for 750 yuan; one girl was "married" thirteen times. Many peasants responded by retreating into the banned worlds of "spiritualism and witchcraft," or by concentrating their labor on their own small plots at the expense of the collective.

To address such serious problems, which undermined party control over local cadres and peasants, the Socialist Education Campaign was launched in the spring of 1963. The movement, also known as the "Four Cleanups," initially targeted corrupt practices in the realms of financial management, bookkeeping, granary supplies, and in the system of allocating work points for labor performed in the communes. Rural cadres were accused of embez-zlement, bribery, misuse of public property, and fraud, and were blamed for the "excess mortality" of the Great Leap. As the campaign spread, tens of thousands of urban cadres were relocated into the countryside, both to learn from the peasants by manual labor and to purify the peasants' understanding of the "mass line."[24]

In 1964, the Socialist Education Campaign took a sharp turn. The struggles at the upper levels of leadership moved out into the countryside, as can be seen in the example of Liu Shaoqi and his wife Wang Guangmei. In November 1963 Wang traveled to Taoyuan in Hebei province and stayed there until April 1964. Disguising her identity under a pseudonym and her face under a gauze mask (often worn as protection from dust or germs), she took part in mass meetings and built up a circle of trusted informants. Without telling even the local party officials who she was, she compiled dossiers concerning graft and incipient capitalism, concluding that in Taoyuan "the four uncleans exist universally among the cadres. All of them, big or small, have problems and cannot be trusted." Among the peasants, too, she uncov-ered no fewer than sixty-six forms of incipient capitalism, from selling chickens to building independent family businesses. When she submitted her report to Liu Shaoqi, he instructed her to initiate public struggle sessions against the miscreants. Forty out of the forty-seven ranking cadres in Taoyuan were publicly criticized or removed from office. That summer of 1964, Liu and Wang made a well-publicized tour of central and south China to spread their warnings against party corruption and to urge the need for stern correctives. They found examples of spectacular abuses by "model cadres," especially in Guangdong.

The harshness of Wang's condemnation could be interpreted as an assault on those cadres who had risen to power in the early days of the Communist revolution, and then had consolidated their hold there during the First Five-Year Plan and the Great Leap Forward. Of these cadres, none was more famous than Chen Yonggui, the leader of a production brigade in the mountainous and impoverished Shanxi commune of Dazhai. By the dramatically hard work of its residents and under Chen's leadership, this bleak area had reportedly blossomed, increasing production fivefold, and proving to all the truth of Mao's vision of rural self-reliance and revolutionary zeal as the keys to China's future. Because of his achievements, Chen Yonggui was elected to the county people's congress, and in 1964 he represented Shanxi at the National People's Congress in Beijing. Then followed a dizzying spate of honors: a place in the prestigious presidium of the People's Congress, public praise from Zhou Enlai, a private audience with Mao, and an address to the congress delegates on his chosen theme—"Self-Reliance Is a Magic Wand" for implementing Mao's policies. In late December 1964, Chen's photograph appeared beside Mao's on the front page of *People's Daily*. The caption repeated Mao's declaration of earlier the same year: "In agriculture learn from Dazhai."

What was especially significant about these public gestures was that during late 1964 an investigative work team—similar to the one run by Wang Guangmei in Taoyuan—had been looking into Chen's leadership in Dazhai. The team concluded that many of Chen's dramatic claims were spurious, based on inflated production figures, the underreporting of available land, and exaggerated grain sales figures, and that the people of Dazhai did not have enough to eat. "There are wood-worms in the staff of the red banner of Dazhai. If they are not eliminated, the banner cannot be raised high."[25] In normal circumstances, Chen could have expected to be disciplined or dismissed like the condemned cadres of Taoyuan and scores of other scrutinized communities. But boosted by Mao's declaration of faith, he returned to Dazhai in triumph and it was the investigative work team that retired, discomfited.

A different type of ambiguity was at the heart of Mao's call, issued in late 1963, that in industry China should "learn from Daqing." These oilfields in Heilongjiang, first explored by technicians and squads of peasants in the Great Leap period, had swiftly become one of China's major economic assets. Under the mantra of self-reliance, using primitive equipment and laboring in subzero temperatures, Daqing workers had indeed been models of daring and tenacity. The senior party personnel at the oilfields, however, overemphasized the local people's untrained contributions to the oilfield's development and minimized the crucial role of foreign technology, including prospecting and refining equipment bought on the international market. Ecstatic at their success—by 1963 Daqing produced 4.4 million metric tons of oil, over two-thirds of the national total—Mao began to transfer staff members from Daqing and the Ministry of Petroleum Industries into his top economic-planning institutions. By 1964 these people were well entrenched, helping Mao formulate ambitious development plans that undercut his more cautious planners.[26]

Mao's struggle with Liu Shaoqi over the investigative work teams was a subtle yet important one. Liu believed that correction of cadre abuses was an internal party affair and should be handled by party members themselves, so as to maintain prestige in the eyes of the public. With so many cadres discredited by their ruthlessness or corruption in the Great Leap period, this approach was more essential than ever. Mao felt that if the party showed serious signs of weakness, it should be rectified through open debate and criticism, with the "masses" involved in the process. Thus Mao believed that he was calling for a socialist campaign that would pit the genuine proletariat against the bourgeoisie, while Liu and his supporters were sidetracking the issue by concentrating on the "four cleanups" or comparatively minor economic faults. By using investigative work teams in such a dictatorial manner, and discrediting large numbers of cadres, Liu was in fact working *against* socialism. As Mao phrased it, "Though you repeat day after day that there must be democracy, there is no democracy; though you ask others to be democratic, you are not democratic yourselves."[27]

Deng Xiaoping was equally guilty of this kind of behavior, said Mao in January 1965. By shrouding the investigations in secrecy, by not bringing the common people of the area themselves into the investigative process, Mao insinuated that Deng did not have faith in the judgment of the masses. Of course such a process was unpredictable, but that was what revolutions were all about. As Mao chided another senior party leader who was a close friend of Liu Shaoqi, "When you go out to develop and engage in a mass movement, or to lead a mass struggle, the masses will do as they wish and they will create their own leaders in the course of the struggle. . . . Whether one is a professional or an amateur, one can only learn by fighting." When the party leader concerned argued that cadres must "control the temperature" in such situations to prevent excess, Mao retorted sharply, "It is necessary to give the masses a free hand."[28]

The language about learning by "fighting" came straight from Mao's past as a young radical protesting the tragic suicide of Miss Zhao in 1919; the objection to reducing revolutionary temperature was delivered by one who had seen, in 1927, what happened to the workers of Shanghai and the peasants of Hunan when their excesses were curtailed; the appeals to the innate integrity of the masses were reprises of Yan'an and the euphoric beginnings of the Great Leap. But to China's economic planners, who felt they were getting the country back on track, the rhetoric must have sounded tired. To them, the achievements of the years 1962 to 1965 were palpable. The readjustments proposed by Chen Yun had been accomplished, leading to the removal of millions of unproductive urban workers from state payrolls and the closing of over 25,000 enterprises. Although this led to corresponding drops in coal, cement, and steel production, the 1960 budget deficit of 8 billion yuan was replaced by a 1962 surplus of close to 1 billion yuan. Spared the huge grain procurement demands of the Great Leap period, production teams of 20 to 30 households working within smaller communes were given new economic initiatives and allowed to produce for the open market on their own plots. By 1965 agricultural production levels had returned to around the pre–Great Leap levels of 1957, while the output of light industry was expanding at 27 percent a year and heavy industry at 17 percent. Thanks to the rich deposits found at the Daqing wells in Heilongjiang, domestic oil production was up tenfold since 1957, freeing the country from its long reliance on Soviet oil supplies; natural gas production was up fortyfold. If such steady advances could continue, China might have a chance to enter an era of unspectacular but real economic progress. The party bureaucrats and the planners—not Mao and the masses—would be pointing the way to the future.

| # Cultural Revolution

THE CULT OF MAO AND THE CRITICS

The divided opinions that had surfaced among the leadership of the PRC concerning the Hundred Flowers, the Great Leap, relations with the Soviet Union, and the Socialist Education Campaign left Mao feeling threatened. Liu Shaoqi, Deng Xiaoping, Chen Yun, and Zhou Enlai, veteran revolutionaries all, seemed increasingly disinclined to support his vision of continuous struggle; indeed they barely seemed to need his presence or his inspiration. Mao had developed a personal lifestyle that put him out of touch with many of his political colleagues. He had come to value the trappings of power, whether it was swims in the pool built for him in the Zhongnanhai compound, summoning his staff to meetings at any time of day or night, the pleasant sojourns in various villas (to which he traveled in his special train), or the sexual companionship of a succession of young women—whom he met either at weekly dances or amidst the enthusiastic youthful followers he encountered on his train journeys.[1] But these diversions, and the long periods of reading and reflection in his study, could not disguise the fact that his policies of the late 1950s had failed, and his reputation in the early 1960s was not as high as once it had been.

One man who helped to rebuild Mao's self-esteem was Lin Biao, the veteran army commander from the days of Yan'an and the civil war. Born in 1907 and educated among the first military cadets at the Huangpu Military Academy, Lin had consistently been a loyal party member, although ill health had often kept him on the sidelines of the major political events of the 1950s. After the dismissal of Peng Dehuai, Mao Zedong chose Lin to be the new minister of defense and the de facto head of the PLA.

In the early 1960s, while the economic planners were trying to stabilize the economy after the crises of the Great Leap, within the army Lin Biao moved to strengthen the vision of Mao as a great leader. He did this first by making a compilation of aphorisms from among the writings and speeches that Mao had produced over the previous thirty years and more. By 1963, the "little red book" of *Quotations from Chairman Mao* were being studied and discussed throughout the PLA. Though the ideological significance of this collection, with its exhortations to self-sacrifice, self-reliance, and continuous revolutionary struggle, was not apparent to most CCP leaders, first thousands and then millions of soldiers began to study and memorize Mao's sayings, raising him to a new level of reverence.

In early 1963, Lin Biao intensified the degree of indoctrination by starting a campaign within the PLA to emphasize the values of loyalty and service to the party. At the center of this campaign was a young soldier named Lei Feng, who had recently sacrificed his life for his country. The posthumously discovered *Diary of Lei Feng* emphasized his undying love for the revolution, for the party, for his comrades—and most of all, his unswerving devotion to Chairman Mao. The fact that the diary was fictitious, concocted by PLA propaganda writers, should not minimize its significance, which was to launch an attack against the lack of revolutionary fervor displayed by many intellectuals and writers.

Those writers had been starting once again, especially after the Great Leap, to discuss some of the ambiguities of the revolutionary experience, such as the economic hardship of peasants or the problems that workers and teachers faced in their jobs. Lei Feng, the model soldier pledged to service and obedience, allowed no such ambiguities. His life was presented as honest and sincere, but without great drama except for his family's suffering at the hands of Japanese invaders, Guomindang officials, and rapacious landlords. He died, selflessly but unheroically, in an accident as he was trying to help a comrade in trouble. The study of Lei Feng's diary was introduced into the school system, and Mao consolidated its impact when, in late 1963, he graced the diary's title page with his calligraphy. Mao called on the whole country to "learn from the PLA," placing the military on par with the duty of "learning from the party."

The ideas of self-reliance and sacrifice were again underscored in 1964, when the growing threat that the Vietnam War would spread to China led Mao to order the speedy development of heavy industry, transportation systems, and military facilities in the central and western provinces. Currently concentrated in major coastal cities, the nation's critical infrastructure was highly vulnerable to air raids or a nuclear strike in the event of war. Mao called this massive covert project the "Third Front," which would provide a bulwark against Soviet invasion or American attack. From 1964 to 1972, fifteen million workers (plus one million of their family members) relocated to the southwest and the northwest to build steel, munitions, and cement factories, or to open mines, extend railways, and enlarge dams. As additional precautionary measures, the facilities were hidden in remote regions or deep in the mountains, or had their component parts split up and distributed in different areas.[2]

The development of the Third Front provided China's national security with a "defensive backbone" to reinforce the PLA's frontline capabilities. The Chinese army had performed well in renewed border wars with India in 1962, and scientists working under PLA supervision at secret bases had designed, built, and successfully tested an atomic bomb in October 1964.[*] The nuclear device was exploded just two days after Khrushchev had been toppled from power in a Soviet coup.

The priorities of national defense in a time of global Cold War tensions elevated Lin Biao's standing. Lin had also been extending his power base beyond the army by making important contacts in the internal-security apparatus and in the cultural bureaucracy, and by placing PLA-staffed political bureaus in many schools and factories. Matters of internal security and culture were closely connected in the PRC, just as they had been throughout the Qing and republican periods. It was often through their paintings or literary works that opponents of government policies voiced their criticisms, using historical allegory or poetic allusion to convey negative or sarcastic points that no one could dare issue openly. Lin Biao's attempts to indoctrinate the PLA with Maoist ideology and to control potential dissent through the broader institutional base he was forging made him a formidable force.

A natural ally for Lin was Mao Zedong's third wife, Jiang Qing, who was beginning to play an active part in cultural politics. Born in 1914, Jiang Qing had been an actress in the early 1930s; among her roles was the part of Nora in Ibsen's *A Doll's House*. Traveling to Yan'an in 1937, she soon became Mao's companion and by 1938 was regarded as his wife. (Mao's second wife, He Zizhen, had fallen mentally and physically ill and was sent to the Soviet Union for treatment.) Jiang Qing kept out of politics until the early 1960s. At this time, she later stated, she became deeply disturbed by the "feudal" content of much contemporary Chinese art, including the plays she saw in Shanghai, and was eager to do something about the situation. A third figure, Kang Sheng, shared the same ideological goals. Trained by the Soviet secret service in the 1930s, Kang had emerged as a force in the national security system and had become Mao's

---

[*] The first Chinese atomic bomb was code-named "596," in sardonic reference to the month of June 1959 in which Khrushchev had informed the Chinese that the Soviets would not give them a prototype of the bomb.

closest adviser on problems of interpreting Soviet ideological policies. By the 1960s he also was alarmed about the threat posed by an unhealthy spirit of criticism toward the CCP and even toward Chairman Mao. Kang urged that literature and art return to a "purer" vision of revolution that would draw its inspiration from the ranks of the workers and peasants. Lin Biao's use of Lei Feng's life to inspire the masses fit well with that approach.

The first victim of this group of radical ideologues was Wu Han, the vice mayor of Beijing. An expert on the history of the Ming dynasty, as a young professor during World War II Wu had used historical examples to criticize Chiang Kai-shek and the Guomindang. In the midst of the Great Leap Forward, Mao Zedong invited him to write on Hai Rui, an official who in the sixteenth century had fought for the people's economic rights against short-sighted and conservative bureaucrats. Wu Han concentrated in his first essay on the way that Hai Rui, though a loyal official, rebuked the emperor for wasting the country's resources while the famished population was driven to the edge of rebellion. In September 1959 Wu Han published another essay in the *People's Daily*, this time praising Hai Rui as a man "of courage for all times" who remained "unintimidated by threats of punishment." In contrast, Wu described the emperor whom Hai Rui served as "craving vainly for immortality" and as "being self-opinionated and unreceptive to criticism."[3]

In 1965 both Mao and Jiang Qing were to seize on these essays as Wu Han's attempt to link Peng Dehuai allegorically to the virtuous Hai Rui. But at the time of their initial publication the two essays were not publicly criticized. During the early 1960s Wu Han was one of a number of intellectuals who wrote short pieces in the Beijing newspapers, using historical or other social themes that were obviously critical of CCP policies, and of Mao's isolation from an accurate reading of public opinion. These intellectuals used the joint pseudonym of Three-Family Village, referring to a Song dynasty official who had retired to a village of that name after his dismissal from the government. One of the group, Deng Tuo, was especially sharp in the way he praised the Donglin partisans of the late Ming dynasty for their courage in opposing the court's injustice. As Deng wrote in a poem to the Donglin martyrs' memory,

> Do not think of them as mere intellectuals indulging in empty talk;
> Fresh were the bloodstains when the heads rolled.
> Fighting the wicked men in power with abiding will,
> The Donglin scholars were a stout-hearted generation.[4]

Wu Han's full-length play, *The Dismissal of Hai Rui from Office*, was staged in Beijing in February 1961 and published in the summer of the same year. By this time word of Peng Dehuai's criticism of Mao for the Great Leap had circulated, so the rendering of Hai Rui's words of protest registered a sharp relevance:

> You say the common people are tyrannized,
> but do you know the gentry injures them?
> Much is made at court of the gentry's oppression,
> but do you know of the poverty
> endured by the common people?
> You pay lip service to the principle
> that the people are the roots of the state.
> But officials still oppress the masses
> while pretending to be virtuous men.
> They act wildly as tigers
> and deceive the emperor.
> If your conscience bothers you
> you know no peace by day or night.[5]

The Three-Family Village writings and Wu Han's play were part of a flow of allegorical and critical works that angered many leading political figures. These leaders were, however, unclear about how to forbid the publication of such pieces, which often were carried in party-controlled newspapers and magazines.

In November 1965, controversy erupted over Wu Han's portrayal of the Ming dynasty official, when Yao Wenyuan published a strong attack on the play in Shanghai. Yao was among a group of hard-liners in that city closely allied with Jiang Qing. At her instigation and with Mao's private endorsement—he revised the final draft multiple times—Yao's article alleged that the play was a poisonous weed and its author an anti-Party reactionary. Couched in historical drama, Wu had called for "redressing injustices" in the countryside at the very time that "the peasants of our country have already realized socialism, possess everything, and have established the great People's Communes." According to Yao's analysis, Wu and his supporters wished to "replace the state theory of Marxism-Leninism with the state theory of the landlord and bourgeoisie," and "replace the theory of class struggle with the theory of class harmony."[6]

The publication of Yao's attack in the Shanghai press set off a behind-the-scenes scramble among senior party officials, who were unsure of how to react and whether they should join the condemnation of Wu Han. At this juncture Mao left Beijing for Shanghai; he would spend the next eight months moving between Shanghai and other cities in the lower Yangzi region, laying the groundwork before returning to the capital to ignite a new revolutionary upsurge. Meanwhile, it was twenty days before Yao's essay was picked up by the official press in Beijing, attesting to the uneasiness there over the implications of this first salvo.[7] Now the most powerful political figures in the country were forced to take sides publicly. Were they for or against Wu Han? By implication, for or against Peng Dehuai? And, not so transparently, for or against Mao Zedong and Lin Biao?

LAUNCHING THE CULTURAL REVOLUTION

As the year 1966 began, two different groups met to discuss the Wu Han case and related matters. One was the Group of Five—though its active membership was far larger than the name implies—which met under the direction of Peng Zhen, a veteran party leader who was currently mayor of Beijing and a member of the Politburo Standing Committee. This group included senior staff from the press, academics, and members of the Ministry of Culture, almost all of whom could be regarded as bureaucrats and intellectuals who embraced the status quo and were close to Liu Shaoqi and Deng Xiaoping. The second group met in Shanghai under the general guidance of Jiang Qing, who led a forum to discuss the political purposes of literature and the performing arts. Members of this group may be loosely called radical intellectuals; they were pushing for socialist purification of art and favored dramatic forms untainted by either "feudal" or May Fourth elitist values. They were aware of the opportunities that arose for spreading their views when Lin Biao invited Jiang Qing to coordinate the new cultural policies for the PLA in February 1966.

Peng Zhen's Group of Five tried to defuse the Wu Han case by treating it as an academic debate, rather than as a political matter involving the crucial factor of class struggle. They issued a report critical of Wu Han but urged caution, noting that "we must carry out this struggle under leadership, seriously, positively and prudently," especially since "problems of academic contention are rather complicated, and some matters are not easy to define within a short time." This approach was reinforced by the group's use of language drawn from the more moderate phases of land reform in its calls for "mutual-aid teams" and "cooperatives" of academic workers. They pointed out, in what could be seen as a jab at Mao or Jiang Qing, that "even some staunch revolutionary leftists . . . can hardly avoid saying something wrong."[8] Much as Mao might have disliked this analysis, on February 12, 1966, the Central Committee approved it for distribution as a discussion document.

That same February, Jiang Qing and cultural workers from the PLA were meeting at their Shanghai forum. The delegates saw numerous finished films and the rushes of works in progress, attended three theatrical performances, and joined in group readings of Mao Zedong's works. The chairman's writings on culture, they concluded, marked a "new development of the Marxist-Leninist world outlook." But despite Mao's achievement, the country was still "under the dictatorship of a sinister Anti-Party and Anti-Socialist line which is diametrically opposed to Chairman Mao's thought." They branded Wu Han's work as a perfect example of this politically erroneous writing and warned that the Chinese cultural garden was overgrown with "anti-socialist poisonous weeds." In this fight the PLA—"the mainstay and hope of the Chinese people and the revolutionary people of the world"—would play a crucial role, and help "destroy blind faith in Chinese and foreign classical literature." In warmly endorsing the final report of the forum, which spelled out all these ideas, Lin Biao noted that "if the proletariat does not occupy the positions in literature and art, the bourgeoisie certainly will. This struggle is inevitable."[9]

The lines were drawn for the cataclysmic central phase of what Mao and his supporters called the Great Proletarian Cultural Revolution. This movement defies simple classification, for embedded within it were many impulses at once feeding and impeding each other. There was Mao Zedong's view that the revolution was losing impetus because of party conservatism and the lethargy of the huge and cumbersome bureaucracy, which had lost the ability to make speedy or innovative decisions. Mao declared that many party bureaucrats "were taking the capitalist road" even as they mouthed socialist slogans. There were, too, Mao's sense of his advancing age—he was now seventy-three—and his concern that his colleagues were shunting him aside. There were straightforward elements of factional struggle pitting Jiang Qing and the Shanghai radicals against those in the Beijing cultural bureaucracy who wanted to maintain their dominance. There were those who diverged with Mao over the pace and direction of change, such as veteran party leaders Liu Shaoqi, Deng Xiaoping, Chen Yun, and Peng Zhen. There were the political ambitions of Lin Biao and those who supported his efforts to expand the role of the army in politics.

These factional fires were fueled by students frustrated over policies that kept them from advancement because they had been classified as "bad" elements on account of their family background. There were those, within the largest cities, who were denied access to the tiny number of elite schools that had become, in effect, "prep schools" for the children of influential party cadres. (With the shortage of colleges and the thickets of entrance examinations that were confounding to navigate, only this handful of schools could assure access to higher education.) There were industrial workers who felt trapped in dead-end jobs and were excited by the possibilities for improving their fortunes. And finally there were those who felt that party positions were monopolized by the uneducated rural cadres of the CCP's former guerrilla days, and that these people should now be eased out to make way for more educated recruits.

In the late spring and summer of 1966, events moved to a swift yet unpredictable climax. In May the report of the Group of Five, calling for caution in cultural reform, was repudiated by the Central Committee—clearly at Mao's urging—and a purge of the cultural bureaucracy commenced. Peng Zhen was ousted, other key figures in the Ministry of Culture removed, and attacks launched against the writers of the Three-Family Village articles and against Wu Han and his family.* The protests and criticisms spread throughout the university system after Nie Yuanzi, a philosophy professor at Beijing University, wrote a wall poster excoriating the administrators of her university as "Khrushchev-type" revisionists. Attempts by Deng Xiaoping, Liu Shaoqi, and others to send "work teams" onto the campuses to quell the disturbances backfired as more and more radicals among faculty and students turned on party members. Turmoil spread swiftly to high schools, and squads of students were issued arm bands by the Cultural Revolution radicals declaring them to be "Red Guards"—the vanguard of the new revolutionary upheaval.

To underscore his vigor and health, in July Mao Zedong took a swim in the Yangzi River near Wuhan, where the 1911 revolution had first erupted. The swim was given euphoric coverage in the party press. Back in Beijing, Mao heated up the revolutionary rhetoric even further by declaring that Nie's poster surpassed the significance of the Paris Commune declaration. The Paris Commune of 1871, about which Marx had written with great passion, had been considered a pinnacle of spontaneous socialist insurrection. Now Mao was claiming that the Cultural Revolution would exceed it. Of course there would be hostile forces, he noted, just as there had been in France. "Who are against the great Cultural Revolution? American imperialism, Russian revisionism, Japanese revisionism, and the reactionaries." This will be a test of our resolve and courage, declared Mao; "we must depend on the masses, trust the masses, and fight to the end."[10]

In early August 1966, Mao issued his own big character poster with the incendiary title "Bombard the Headquarters"—meaning the Communist Party itself. Published in newspapers across the country, Mao's call to action denounced "leading comrades from the central down to the local levels," accusing them of enforcing a "bourgeois dictatorship" and trying to suppress "the surging movement of the Great Proletarian Cultural Revolution." Three days later, the Central Committee issued a directive of sixteen points, calling

---

* Wu Han died in 1969 of illness following the brutal treatment to which he was subjected.

for a new stage in the socialist revolution and identifying the enemy: "The main target of the present movement is those within the Party who are in authority and are taking the capitalist road." Having "wormed their way" into positions of power, they could be expected to counterattack, the directive predicted. But by activating the masses to "expose all the ghosts and monsters," and with Mao Zedong Thought as the "guide for action," the Cultural Revolution was "bound to achieve brilliant victory." Even as the rhetoric escalated to "unleash" the masses, still there were enough cooler heads in charge for a sentence to be inserted suggesting that debates should be "conducted by reasoning, not by coercion or force," and that "special care" should be taken of scientists and technical personnel.[11]

As August drew on, Red Guards poured into Beijing and held mass rallies in Tiananmen Square. Mao attended the first on August 16, manifesting himself to more than one million students. Some wept in ecstasy when the chairman appeared atop the rostrum—a moment they later recalled as the happiest of their lives, or a moment of salvation and the beginning of a new life.[12] The Red Guards chanted "Long Live Chairman Mao!" in unison, waved his little red book of quotations, and listened in rapt silence as he instructed them to go forth and wage war on his enemies. Seven more rallies were held in Tiananmen Square through November, attended by 13 million

紧跟毛主席在大风大浪中前进

A poster from November 1969 depicting Mao's appearance at the Red guard rally in Tiananmen Square reads, "Follow Chairman Mao Closely to March Forward in Wind and Waves."

Red Guards. Initially composed largely of students from the elite schools, the Red Guard ranks were now swelled by other disaffected and frustrated students, and by those from the provinces drawn by the revolutionary fervor and their reverence for Mao. Lin Biao heightened the public euphoria with his own declarations. "Chairman Mao is the most outstanding leader of the proletariat in the present era and the greatest genius in the present era," Lin told a Red Guard rally on August 18. What Mao had done was to create "a Marxism-Leninism for remoulding the souls of the people."

In the autumn and winter of 1966, the struggles grew deeper and more intense, the destruction and loss of life more terrible. With all schools and colleges closed for the staging of revolutionary struggle, millions of young people were encouraged by the Cultural Revolution's leaders to demolish the old buildings, temples, and art objects in their cities and towns, and to attack teachers, school administrators, party cadres, and parents. One of the most spectacular examples of Red Guard destruction occurred in Qufu, the ancestral hometown of Confucius in Shandong province. Two hundred eager revolutionaries from Beijing spent one month there in November, searching for and destroying centuries-old artifacts: books, paintings, works of calligraphy, altars, statues, and steles. They defiled 2,000 graves at the cemetery where the descendants of Confucius were buried. After they forced open Confucius's own grave, they were furious to find it empty. Another group of Red Guards traveled to Hainan Island to find the burial place of Hai Rai—the Ming dynasty official who was the subject of Wu Han's play—so that they could desecrate it.[13]

The leaders of the Cultural Revolution called for a comprehensive attack

on the "four old" elements within society—old customs, old habits, old culture, and old thinking—but they left it to Red Guard initiative to apply these terms. In practice what often happened was that after the obvious targets had been identified, Red Guards eager to prove their revolutionary credentials turned on anyone who tried to hold them in check and anyone who had received foreign

Victims wearing dunce caps and signs proclaiming their crimes are publicly paraded through the streets of Beijing by Red Guards.

education or had interacted with missionaries; all intellectuals who could be charged with "feudal" or "reactionary" modes of thinking. The techniques of public humiliation grew more complex and cruel as the victims were forced to parade through the streets in dunce caps or with self-incriminatory plac-ards around their necks, to declaim their public self-criticisms before jeering crowds, and to stand for hours on end with backs agonizingly bent and arms outstretched in what was called "the airplane position."

As for the Party leadership, the purges escalated to higher and higher levels under the direction of a small group of Mao's confidants, along with Jiang Qing and other Shanghai radicals. Both Liu Shaoqi and Deng Xiaop-ing were removed from their posts and subjected to humiliation and tor-ture, along with their families. With euphoria, fear, excitement, and tension gripping the country, violence grew apace. Thousands of intellectuals and others were beaten to death or died of their injuries. Countless others killed themselves, among them Lao She, the author of the novel *Cat Country*, who had written so eloquently in 1932 about a society in the future where people turned on each other. Thousands more were imprisoned, often in solitary con-finement, for years.

The extent of this outpouring of violence and the rage of the young Red Guards against authority figures suggest the depths of frustration at the heart of Chinese society. The youth needed little urging from Mao to revolt against their parents, teachers, and party cadres, and to perform acts of calculated sadism. For years the young had been called on to lead lives of revolutionary sacrifice, sexual restraint, and absolute obedience to the state, under conditions of perpetual supervision. They were repressed, angry, and aware of their powerlessness. They eagerly seized on Mao's words: "To rebel is justified." The natural targets were those who seemed responsible for their cramped lives. To them Mao stood above this fray, all-wise and all-knowing, the "red sun" in their hearts. The disasters of the Great Leap had never been widely publicized, and in any case could be attributed to inept bureaucrats or hostile Soviets and Americans. For millions of students and teenagers, Mao spoke still for hope and freedom. In the absence of any convincing counter-claims, the wild rhetoric about his powers was accepted as true.

Another explanation for the extent of this violence can be found in the nature of Chinese politics and personal manipulation over the previous sev-enteen years. All Chinese were enmeshed in a system that controlled people by assigning class labels to them, by making them dependent on the "bosses" of their particular units, and by habituating them to mass campaigns of ter-ror and intimidation. Such a system bred both fear and compliance.

Embedded within this frenzied activism was a political agenda of great sig-nificance, what might be called a "purist egalitarianism" that echoed the Paris

Commune of 1871 evoked by Mao Zedong. This involved much more than the confiscation or destruction of private property: demands were raised for the complete nationalization of all industrial enterprises, the abolition of all interest on deposits in the state banks, the eviction of all landlords from their own houses, the elimination of all private plots and a restrengthening of the commune system, and the ending of all traces of a private market economy.

The peak of this profoundly radical program came during the first month of 1967, in what has been termed the "January power seizure." Backed by the Cultural Revolution group in Beijing, militant Red Guard organizations attempted to oust party incumbents and take over their organizations all over the country. The campaign was triggered by New Year's Day editorials in the press that called for "worker-peasant" coalitions to "overthrow power holders in factories, mines and rural areas," and urged these worker-peasant groups to ally with "revolutionary intellectuals" in the struggle. Ambitious workers seized on this opportunity to leapfrog up the political ladder into leadership positions. The Red Guards were told to view the Cultural Revolution as the struggle of one class to overthrow another, and to exempt no one in that struggle. Unlike 1949, when the CCP had accommodated the centrists and liberals, in 1967 "everything which does not fit the socialist system and proletarian dictatorship should be attacked."[14]

The result was a bewildering situation in which varieties of radical groups struggled with party leaders and with each other. The battles at the provincial level show this well. One seizure attempt in Heilongjiang province was led by a former opponent of the Great Leap Forward who now tried to prove his loyalty to Mao by an amplified showing of his political zeal. In Shanxi, the vice governor of the province joined with Red Guards to oust the other party leaders. In Guizhou, it was the provincial deputy political commissar who allied with the Red Guards. It was difficult in many such cases to tell if these were real or sham power struggles—whether "the masses" were really seizing power or whether party leaders were merely pretending to cede their authority. This latter was clearly the case in Guangdong province, where the first party secretary, Zhao Ziyang, handed over his seals to a "Red Flag faction" of railway workers, demobilized soldiers, teachers, and students. Having made his gesture, Zhao and his staff continued to run the province.

The word *radical* was used in many ways at this time. In Shanghai, for instance, where the power seizure was defined as successful, a 500,000-strong worker organization known as the Scarlet Red Guards made the strongest demands for better wages and working conditions, as well as the right to participate in "revolutionary experiences" without losing pay. Similar demands were launched by millions of other workers, from pedicab drivers to cooks, from street peddlers to train engineers. Workers on short-term contracts and other temporary laborers were especially vocal in pressing for permanent job status or awards of back pay. But such actions were soon branded by leaders of the Cultural Revolution as "economism." The Scarlet Red Guards' stance was labeled "conservative" by other groups, such as the equally numerous Shanghai Workers' General Headquarters, which claimed the radical label for themselves. During the last months of 1966, battling factions of both student and worker Red Guards virtually paralyzed Shanghai—shipping and railway services disrupted; the city jammed with Red Guards, returnees, and fugitives from the countryside; food supplies falling to dangerously low levels. In this context, the January 1967 "radical" power seizure in Shanghai can also be seen as an attempt to prevent the workers from gaining truly independent power.

This stage of struggle began when one of Jiang Qing's closest allies, Zhang Chunqiao, traveled to Shanghai in early January 1967. After gaining control of the most influential newspapers and ordering the workers to return to their jobs, Zhang held a series of mass meetings and rallies to attack the Shanghai party leadership, who were accused of "economism" for giving in to worker demands. Joined by Yao Wenyuan (who had fired the first major shots against Wu Han the year before), Zhang used the PLA to restore order in the city and to develop the new slogan "Grasping Revolution and Promoting Production." While soldiers guarded airfields, banks, and docks, student Red Guards took the place of workers still refusing to return to their jobs.

Zhang and Yao, however, also had to fight militant student Red Guards who wished to maintain solidarity with the workers. In late January student groups held a struggle session against Zhang and Yao and "arrested" Yao's propaganda staff. Only in early February, with massive military support, was order restored with the Cultural Revolution leaders in charge. On February 5, Zhang announced the formation of the Shanghai People's Commune, which created a truly paradoxical situation. Under the guise of this most revolutionary sounding of titles, those who had so thoroughly purged the party tried now to bolster their own positions as new leaders, and to compel the obedience of the very students and workers who had sought to usher in a new age of freedom.

PARTY RETRENCHMENT AND THE DEATH OF LIN BIAO

In Shanghai, thirty-eight rebel groups had celebrated the inauguration of the people's commune on February 5. One week later, Mao told Zhang Chunqiao to change the name of the governance structure to the Shanghai

Revolutionary Committee. Ten thousand people convened in a mass rally at the end of February to hail the name change. The structure of such revolutionary committees, whether in urban areas, in the communes, or in such institutions as schools and newspapers, was to be a "three-way alliance" of representatives from the masses, PLA members, and those party cadres deemed "correct" in attitude and behavior. In practice, this meant reduction in the representation of industrial workers in the local leadership. Such "power seizures" were often coordinated by central party leaders themselves, as was dramatically shown in Premier Zhou Enlai's ability to manipulate an intricate series of assaults on the various ministries in the central government bureaucracy. In Zhou's attempt to dampen the extent of disruptive violence, students were told to "resume classes and carry on revolution," army personnel were to extend military training into all colleges and schools down to the primary levels, and cadres were permitted "to reform themselves and redeem their mistakes by making contributions." The result was a period in which the more extreme forms of "radical" disruption were muted, although the country remained in a turbulent state.

The PLA in particular, as a key component of the new three-way alliance, began to play an expanded role. Not only were soldiers fully represented on the new revolutionary committees, they also used armed force to suppress militants who tried to disrupt or purge the PLA's own organization. Throughout the Cultural Revolution, Lin Biao and other senior PLA officers had played complicated roles in the struggles. The leaders of the "radicals" and apparently egalitarian in organization and procedure, the PLA was also a professional army committed to defending national security. Thus while seemingly supporting the revolutionary fervor of the Red Guards, the PLA kept its own ranks closed to their interference, along with its military installations, confidential files, and production plants. PLA troops also protected the technical installations at the Daqing oilfields and kept Red Guard units—even one led by Mao Zedong's own nephew—from entering the facilities where physicists were working on the hydrogen bomb. When Jiang Qing attacked the chief of the PLA propaganda department for having "changed the army into an army of bourgeoisie," Red Guards picked up her lead and raided the man's house. This brought an instant response from Zhou Enlai. At a meeting of 900 senior military leaders in late January 1967, Zhou issued a broad criticism of those who sought to "lower the prestige of the Army."

The PLA had been given the task, at the end of January 1967, of disbanding all "counter revolutionary organizations." They interpreted this as a call to break up militant groups that took a line sharply opposed to their own (or their political allies') interests. The numbers of those killed by the PLA in these various confrontations are unknown, but there were eyewitness reports of rivers blocked with bodies, and many corpses washed up on the shores of Hong Kong. The Cultural Revolution leaders in Beijing, in their turn, were dismayed by the severity of the PLA's attacks on those who were, after all, often responding to the CCP center's own call to purify the ranks of the bureaucracy. Numerous instructions went out to the PLA, urging restraint.

The most important clash between the army and the radicals occurred in Wuhan during the summer of 1967. The chaotic proliferation of Red Guard and worker rebel groups had for months produced tense standoffs, which in the spring erupted into armed struggle against a "conservative" coalition named the "Million Heroes." The regional commander of the PLA called out his forces to take control of critical sectors and infrastructure in the city. He had received instructions from Zhou Enlai to "manage production well"—otherwise "there'll be nothing to eat." When the PLA outlawed one of the worker organizations and made thousands of arrests, the clashes resulted in many casualties. (Conflicting reports, both at the time and in later analysis, claimed hundreds to thousands of deaths and attributed the violence variously to the rebels, the conservatives, and the army.) When two senior members of the Cultural Revolution leadership traveled to Wuhan in July and condemned the army for its behavior, one of them was kidnapped from the guesthouse where he was staying by supporters of the PLA. His release was secured with the intervention of Zhou Enlai, but not before he was severely beaten.[15]

Unbeknownst to the dueling factions in Wuhan, Mao was in the city at the time of this insurrection, which added to the intrigue. The "Wuhan Incident" prompted a period of renewed violence and confrontation between the PLA and a wide range of "radical rebel" groups that continued throughout the summer. Opposing worker and student factions persisted in attacking each other, often with deadly results, using arms and ammunition seized from PLA depots. As Mao himself later commented, the country was in a state of "all-around civil war." The violence was especially intense in Beijing and Guangzhou, with confrontations escalating into the upper ranks of the government itself. In August 1967 radicals took over the Ministry of Foreign Affairs, "appointed" diplomats to posts around the world, and set the office of the British *charge d'affaires* on fire.[16]

So serious was the chaos by September 1967 that most leaders seemed to agree that it had reached an intolerable level. Jiang Qing, formerly the spokesperson for the radicals, now denounced "ultra-left tendencies" and praised the PLA as a champion of "proletarian dictatorship." While Red Guard factions continued to battle each other, the leadership turned to workers' organizations as a means of curbing student excesses and returning the campuses to order. PLA propaganda called for an intensive study of Mao's works rather than an all-out assault on "people taking the bourgeois road."

Complex negotiations were carried on with warring factions in several provinces; as agreements to end hostilities were reached, energies previously devoted to conflict were redirected into contests for representation on the revolutionary committees. Following the pattern established at Shanghai in early 1967, these revolutionary committees would each constitute a "three-way alliance" of the PLA, the masses, and "correct" cadres. Membership in the committees would determine who held the deciding voice in communes, schools, and factories, as well as in the centers of provincial government and the central ministries. The winners in those contests would prevail politically until the winds shifted yet again.

Nevertheless it was not until the summer of 1968 that something approaching order was temporarily restored, as Mao dispersed the Red Guards with instructions to "go up to the mountains and down to the countryside." Responding to an initial call for volunteers, they eagerly signed up to relocate to remote regions, as another way of validating their revolutionary zeal. By the end of the year, relocation was compulsory, as Mao ordered, "Educated youth, go to the countryside to receive re-education from the poor and lower-middle peasants: it is a must." From 1968–1980, more than 17 million middle school graduates (about 10 percent of the urban population) were assigned to work in the borderlands of the northeast, desolate areas of the northwest, or on state or military farms in their home provinces. The rationale of this youth rustication movement followed the same logic of previous transfers, but its scale dwarfed the resettlement schemes of the 1950s and early 1960s. Removing the Red Guards from the cities also helped defuse the factional violence that had spiraled out of control and alleviated pressure on urban food supplies. For this generation of "sent-down youths" (known as *zhiqing*), the period of rural exile would range from a few years to the rest of their lives.[17]

The cataclysmic events of 1966–1968 shattered the nation's educational system, placed immense strains on the army, disrupted industrial production, and crucially weakened the party's efficiency and morale. From Beijing, attempts to restore order took the form of another campaign—this time to "purify class ranks." Launched at the end of 1967 and in full swing by the summer of 1968, the campaign focused on the millions of cadres suspected of being "bad elements" because of prior connections with the bourgeoisie, on "renegades and spies," and on landlords and unrepentant rightists. Suspects were investigated by newly formed Workers' Mao-Thought Propaganda Teams drawn from the "revolutionary masses," in conjunction with the PLA and the relevant revolutionary committees.

There was enormous room to maneuver in these investigations, and the balance between one's background, past performance, and current behavior was weighed by the investigative teams. For hundreds of thousands of cadres and intellectuals, these sessions were held at "May Seventh Cadre Schools," so named for a directive issued on that date in 1966 by Mao, as a prelude to the Cultural Revolution. These "schools" combined hard agricultural labor with constant self-evaluation and study of Mao's works, allegedly to instill a deeper understanding of the socialist revolution. In fact they were as much prisons as schools. Families were often split apart, the frail and elderly set to work along with the strong. Living conditions were harsh, with minimal food allowances and the barest of dormitory accommodations. The work, too, was often pointless, since the cadres and intellectuals could not conceivably compete in rural production with the local peasants, on the edges of whose fields their "schools" were often placed. Although the "students" learned much about the bleakness of rural life, it is probable that few had their thinking fundamentally changed. Yang Jiang, a sixty-year-old professor of English in Beijing, was sent to such a school for two years with her husband, the novelist and scholar Qian Zhongshu (whom she called Mocun). She described their departure from their first May Seventh school in southern Henan:

> In the New Year, at the beginning of April on the Qingming Festival Day, the cadre school moved to a new location in Minggang. Before going, our whole brigade assembled in the vegetable garden one last time to tear down everything that had been put up and pull out whatever could be moved. When we had finished, a tractor came and turned the ground over so that not a trace of the fields or trenches was left. As we were about to set out, Mocun and I sneaked back to have one last look: The hut, well-stand, irrigation ditches, fields—everything had disappeared. Even the flat mound of earth over on the bank of the stream had gone. All that was left was a large area of freshly turned soil.[18]

This combination of incessant indoctrination with hard labor was also the norm in villages all over China during the Cultural Revolution. A detailed study done of one community in Guangdong province illuminates this clearly. Chen Village had its share of political tensions and upheavals, which took place at two overlapping levels. One power struggle pitted two farmers, both locally well known, who switched in leadership roles according to whether they could or could not successfully defend their records of loyalty to Mao and the community. (At times no one in the village wanted any kind of leadership position, so volatile had the situation become.) The other struggle was between educated youth "sent down" to live and work in Chen Village and the native villagers. These rusticated young men and women often led the political discussions because of their superior education and used loudspeakers—newly available after the electrification of the village in 1966—to maintain an intense level of political criticism and public awareness. Within these two levels of conflict were countless other small divisions. The victims, those accused as representatives of the "four olds" and "rightists," were isolated in a run-down hut known as the "cow shed" and struggled against at regular intervals.

Amid the political chaos, however, the rhythms of agricultural work and family life with its joys and sorrows continued in Chen Village under the painted wall slogans, the stenciled portraits of Mao, the blare of loudspeakers, and the constant injunctions to "emulate Dazhai." In line with directives that they give up "selfish" or private production, the villagers returned to the general ethos of the Great Leap period and yielded up to communal ownership their fruit trees and small bamboo groves, their fishing nets, even their breeding sows. For a time, too, the small work teams had to forfeit to the higher level of the production brigade their accounting procedures and powers to allocate work points and distribute land. Despite worries about these changes, individual incomes for the best agricultural workers in Chen Village were higher in 1968 than at any time in the preceding four years. And the new resources made possible by their collective labor led to useful diversification that promised higher incomes in the future. In the space of a few years Chen Village built a brick factory, a grain mill, a peanut-oil press, a small sugar and alcohol refinery, and a processing plant for yams.

Before every meal, the Chen villagers held what was almost a religious service for Mao, reciting some of his quotations, singing verses from the Red Guard anthem "The East Is Red," and offering a little prayer aloud:

> We respectfully wish a long life to the reddest red sun in our hearts, the great leader Chairman Mao. And to Vice Chairman Lin Biao's health: may he forever be healthy. Having been liberated by the land reform we will never forget the Communist Party, and in revolution we will forever follow Chairman Mao![19]

The reference to Lin Biao was by no means formulaic. Lin Biao's stock had risen ever higher since 1969, when he was declared Mao's chosen successor at the party congress. That same year, the PLA engaged in serious military clashes with troops from the Soviet Union on the two countries' shared borders. Although the clashes did not lead to full-scale war, around 100 Soviets were killed or wounded, and as many as 800 Chinese. In China, the major impact of the fighting was on domestic politics. News of the battles, dramatically retold, produced an outpouring of popular excitement over PLA heroism, intensified anti-Soviet antagonisms, and made it appear that Lin Biao's troops were literally saving the Chinese people. Lin's prestige seemed at its zenith in Chen Village, as it was throughout the country. It was therefore completely bewildering when in late 1971 village leaders were rushed to the commune headquarters and returned, shocked and initially pledged to secrecy, with the astonishing news that Lin Biao had betrayed Chairman Mao and met his death in a plane crash.

What the Chen villagers did not know was that Mao's doubts about Lin and his command of the PLA had been growing for some time. The chairman was seeking once again to strengthen the party, feeling it had been shaken up adequately. In March 1970, Mao decided to remove the post of chairman of the state, vacant since Liu Shaoqi's arrest, from the draft constitution. This meant that Lin could not succeed to such a post, and that Zhou Enlai as premier would continue to outrank Lin.

In August 1970, Mao put forward new instructions on rebuilding the CCP, dropping the criteria of revolutionary zeal and ideological purity that Lin and the PLA had assiduously propagated since the early 1960s. Over the course of 1971 Mao began to pursue a three-part policy he later referred to as "throwing stones, adding sand to mud, and undermining the cornerstone."[20] The "stones" were aimed at the senior army officers directly under Lin, who were made to issue public self-criticisms. The "sand" was added by removing Lin's supporters from the Military Affairs Commission. The "cornerstone" comprised the armed forces of the Beijing military region, where Mao also replaced key personnel. Still moving circumspectly, Mao stepped up criticism campaigns against "defective work styles" in the PLA.

According to documents later released by the CCP, Lin Biao, driven to desperation by the collapse of his highest political ambitions, sought support among his closest friends for an assassination attempt on Mao. Unable to implement this plan, Lin panicked and fled with his wife and son in a military jet. The party documents added that the plane was heading to the Soviet Union but was inadequately fueled for such a trip. It crashed in Mongolia on September 13, 1971, with no survivors. This story is essentially beyond verification, since the photographs later released are of dubious authenticity, and details on Lin's exact plans and on the other plotters are blurred. But it was clear to all that Lin's political life—and presumably his physical one as well—was now dramatically over.

At the apparent height of his power five months earlier, in an address to the ninth party congress in April 1969, Lin had told the assembled delegates that former head of state Liu Shaoqi had "betrayed the Party, capitulated to the enemy and became a hidden traitor and scab." In 1972 Premier Zhou Enlai announced that it was Lin Biao who had been the "renegade and traitor." Not surprisingly, the Chen villagers were as puzzled as anyone. "I had felt faithful to Mao," one person recalled in a later interview, "but that Lin Biao stuff affected my thinking." As one of the urban youths assigned to live in the village put it,

When Liu Shaoqi was dragged down we'd been very supportive. At that time Mao Zedong was raised very high: he was the red sun and what not. But the Lin Biao affair provided us with a major lesson. We came to see that the leaders up there could say today that something is round; tomorrow, that it's flat. We lost faith in the system.[21]

The bewilderment of the villagers is fully understandable. The credulity of the people had been stretched beyond all possible boundaries, as leader after leader had first been praised to the skies and then vilified. The most violent strains in Chinese society had been given free rein and its organizational structures stretched to the breaking point. The Great Leap Forward at least had a grandiose economic and social vision at its heart. The Great Proletarian Cultural Revolution showed that neither Mao nor the CCP seemed to know how or where the nation should be heading.

CHAPTER 23

Reopening the Doors

THE UNITED STATES AND THE NIXON VISIT

During the early years of the Cultural Revolution, despite the efforts of Zhou Enlai to maintain continuity and to protect senior personnel in the Ministry of Foreign Affairs from criticism and dismissal, the rhetoric of China's foreign policy grew defiantly revolutionary. In 1965 Lin Biao had declared that just as the rural revolutionaries had surrounded and strangled China's cities in 1948 and 1949, so now would Third World countries surround and strangle the superpowers and the rest of the advanced capitalist nations. This statement became a basic formula for Chinese foreign policy during the Cultural Revolution, and was interpreted by many observers to mean that the PRC sought to play a dominant role in creating global upheavals to attack capitalist nations.

But the rhetoric was not backed by any overt military actions and turned out to be largely meaningless. Lin Biao's statement was, however, used to justify outreach to radical opposition groups abroad, to nations in Africa and the Middle East, and to such Arab nationalist groups as the Palestine Liberation Organization, despite their espousal of terrorism. Visionary statements appeared in China's press on the inherent oneness of the Chinese people with the oppressed of the world. Despite its internal turmoil, the PRC continued to give aid to conspicuous development projects in Third World countries. Mao Zedong Thought was held up as an international guide to revolution, and the little red book of Mao's quotations was translated into scores of languages, with millions of copies distributed around the world.

During the late 1960s the PRC also lobbied intensively to win the seat in the United Nations and on its Security Council, held since 1949 by the

Guomindang government on Taiwan. With the help of some nonaligned countries, the claims of the PRC were advanced each year, and the U.S.-backed position of boycotting China slowly eroded, despite heavy American pressure on its own allies. Well before this, the United States had been inching toward renewed contacts with the PRC. For many years, relations between the two had been conducted only through the roundabout means of periodic meetings in Warsaw between the American ambassador to Poland and Chinese diplomats. Some gestures by the Kennedy administration toward rethinking American intransigence to China were halted after the president's assassination in 1963. By 1966 the momentum had resumed, and in the summer the U.S. secretary of state suggested to the PRC government that some Chinese scientists and scholars be allowed to visit the United States. That gesture, coinciding with the opening acts of the Cultural Revolution, was rejected as a propaganda ploy by a hostile superpower.

By 1970 Mao Zedong had grown deeply worried both by the buildup of Soviet troops on China's borders and by Lin Biao's ambitions. Accordingly the CCP leadership began to discuss the idea of reopening some avenues of contact with the United States. Members of the staffs of the Daqing oilfield and the Ministry of Petroleum Industries were also seeking access advanced Western technology. Many of these men, brought in by Mao between 1964 and 1966 to be senior economic planners, had been harried by Red Guards or sent to May Seventh Cadre Schools in the late 1960s. Now, as the oilfields they had developed proved to be one of the only growth sectors of the economy, and Mao began to turn against Lin Biao and the insistent exponents of complete self-reliance, the "Petroleum Group" (as some called them) returned to favor. They knew that if China was to continue to expand oil production at the rate desired by the top leadership, it would require major initiatives in offshore exploration and drilling. For these ambitions China had neither the resources nor the technology. Foreign skills would be essential, and in petroleum technology the United States was the proven world leader.

In January 1970, at the 135th meeting of U.S. and PRC diplomats in Warsaw, the Chinese broke the routine pattern of angry exchanges over the status of Taiwan and mentioned the possibility of having further talks "at a higher level or through other channels acceptable to both sides." After additional behind-the-scenes maneuverings, in April 1971 the U.S. table tennis team, which was competing at the time in Japan, suddenly received an invitation to visit China. The gesture was overt and clear. Within days, the era of "ping-pong diplomacy" was declared to be at hand.

By dint of negotiations that were initially concealed from the public, Congress, and even the secretary of state, President Nixon's national security adviser, Henry Kissinger, traveled to China in July 1971 to meet privately with

Zhou Enlai and plan the details of a presidential visit. Negotiations were aided by decisions to end the ban on the transfer of U.S. dollars to China, to allow American-owned ships under foreign flags to transport goods to China, and to allow Chinese exports into the United States for the first time since the Korean War. On July 15 Nixon made the public announcement of a presidential visit, scheduled for an unfixed date "before May 1972." A small box on the front page of *People's Daily* also made reference to the forthcoming visit.

As Kissinger later noted in his memoirs, "no government less deserved what was about to happen to it than that of Taiwan."[1] Ever since the decision of President Truman to protect Taiwan against a possible PRC invasion in the first year of the Korean War, Taiwan had been a strong ally of the United States, had provided a valuable Pacific base for U.S. missiles, and had also benefited from massive American aid and trade. The issue of Taiwan was volatile in the United States, since a vocal lobby had continued to press for the need to defend "Free China" at all costs against threats from the mainland; any charges of being "soft" on communism could once again rekindle the smoldering ashes of the McCarthy period. Perhaps only a Republican president like Richard Nixon, with a well-documented past of intense—even unrelenting—hostility to communism, could have made such risky decisions in secret and avoided a political confrontation with Congress. But since both the PRC and Taiwan were implacably opposed to a "two Chinas" solution, no easy compromise was going to be possible. Nixon's announcement of his China trip had a foreseeable effect in the UN. In late October 1971 the General Assembly, by a tally of 59 to 55 with 15 abstentions, voted against the U.S.-sponsored procedural motion that would have allowed Taiwan to keep its UN seat. By a separate vote, the PRC was granted that seat, which meant the expulsion of the Taiwan delegation.

President Nixon was not greeted in China, as he had hoped, by large crowds of cheering Chinese who would boost his wavering image back home via American television. Instead, when he stepped onto the tarmac of Beijing airport on the morning of February 21, 1972, and shook hands with Zhou Enlai—to assuage the slight made by Dulles at Geneva eighteen years before—there was only a small line of Chinese officials and a plainly dressed though impressive honor guard. The motorcade to the guesthouse where the Americans were lodged drove down empty streets, and the massive Tiananmen Square was similarly deserted.

Nixon was taken to meet Mao Zedong that afternoon. Mao explained the cautious welcome in part by observing that a "reactionary group" was opposed to any official contact with the United States, and then made it clear that he was referring to Lin Biao, among others. Mao also joked that Chiang Kai-shek disapproved of the meeting as well. When Nixon sought to flatter Mao by saying that Mao's writings had "moved a nation" and "changed the world," Mao responded, "I have not been able to change it. I have only been able to change a few places in the vicinity of Beijing."[2] In a reversal of customary practice, this meeting was filmed, with a ten-minute segment broadcast on Chinese national television and pages of photographs published in newspapers.

The diplomatic substance of the visit was hammered out in long private sessions by Chinese and American negotiators, while President and Mrs. Nixon enjoyed visits to the Great Wall and the Ming tombs, and endured an endless round of banquets. The central issues were how to handle the status of Taiwan and the possible effects of a changed China policy on the Soviet Union, with which an American summit meeting was planned for May. The resulting statement was issued at Shanghai, during Nixon's visit there, on February 28, 1972. Presented in the form of a "joint communiqué," this document marked a major policy shift for both countries and summarized their divergent points of view on global politics without attempting to reconcile them. The "U.S. side," as the document termed it, affirmed the American opinion that the role of the United States in the Vietnam War did not constitute "outside intervention" in the affairs of Vietnam, and reiterated U.S. commitment to "individual freedom." The United States also pledged continued support for South Korea. The "Chinese side" declared that "wherever there is oppression, there is resistance," that "all foreign troops should be withdrawn to their own countries," and that Korea should be unified along lines proposed by North Korea.

On the matter of Taiwan, the Shanghai communiqué continued, there were obvious differences of opinion rooted in the two countries' different "social systems and foreign policies"; complete agreement was not possible. As the Chinese phrased their side of the argument:

> The Taiwan question is the crucial question obstructing the normalization of relations between China and the United States; the Government of the People's Republic of China is the sole legal government of China; Taiwan is a province of China which has long been returned to the motherland; the liberation of Taiwan is China's internal affair in which no other country has the right to interfere; and all U.S. forces and military installations must be withdrawn from Taiwan. The Chinese Government firmly opposes any activities which aim at the creation of "one China, one Taiwan," "One China, two governments," "two Chinas," an "independent Taiwan" or advocate that "the status of Taiwan remains to be determined."

The United States wrote its own interpretation into the communiqué:

> The United States acknowledges that all Chinese on either side of the Taiwan Strait maintain there is but one China and that Taiwan is a part of China. The United States

Government does not challenge that position. It reaffirms its interest in a peaceful settlement of the Taiwan question by the Chinese themselves. With this prospect in mind, it affirms the ultimate objective of the withdrawal of all U.S. forces and military installations from Taiwan. In the meantime, it will progressively reduce its forces and military installations on Taiwan as the tension in the area diminishes.[3]

The closing sections of the communiqué suggested the mutual benefits of increased trade and "people-to-people contacts and exchanges" in science, technology, culture, sports, and journalism. Communication channels should be open; "a senior U.S. representative" should visit Beijing "from time to time." Both China and the United States would work for the "normalization" of relations as a contribution toward "the relaxation of tension in Asia and the world."

It was a remarkable moment in diplomatic history. Mao was struggling to reassert order after the ravages of the Cultural Revolution and Lin Biao's death, and already showing the advanced symptoms of debilitating illness. Nixon was watching his popularity wane in domestic hostility over the Vietnam War, and already displaying that deeply suspicious view of the American opposition that was to plunge him into the Watergate scandal and shatter his presidency. Yet the opportunity for global realignments had been noted by both men, and they decided to seize it. Perhaps the Treaty of Nerchinsk in 1689, the Treaty of Nanjing in 1842, and the Treaty of Shimonoseki in 1895 had produced more dramatic immediate consequences for the Chinese people. But this agreement of 1972, cautious and elliptical though it was, marked a turning point of parallel significance in China's foreign relations.

ATTACKING CONFUCIUS AND LIN BIAO

As if to emphasize the importance of the Cultural Revolution leadership in China's current and future politics, it was Zhang Chunqiao, chairman of the Shanghai Revolutionary Committee, who hosted the farewell banquet for Nixon and his entourage. In his speech Zhang made the claim, which he described as springing from Mao's teachings, that the people of Shanghai were "maintaining independence and keeping initiative in our own hands and relying on our own efforts."[4] This reassertion of the Maoist value of self-reliance was mandatory in the context, but presumably Zhang and his listeners understood that the United States would be used to strengthen China's position in its ongoing hostility to the Soviet Union.

In China's cities and villages, furthermore, political expectations were different from what they had been only a few years previously. When Liu Shaoqi had been ousted in 1966, the news was accepted without question, even though

CCP ENROLLMENT, 1966–1976[5]

Year	China's population	% change	CCP members	% change
1966	750 million (approx.)		18 million	
1969	806 million	7.5	22 million	22.2
1971	852 million	5.7	17 million	−22.7
1972	870 million (approx.)	2.1	20 million	17.6
1973	892 million	2.5	28 million	40.0
1976	925 million (approx.)	3.7	34 million	21.9

Liu had been head of state and one of Mao's close associates for over forty years. But, as the peasants of Chen Village had so clearly stated, the ouster of Lin Biao, and his alleged treason and death, were much harder to understand. Lin had appeared to be at the very center of the Cultural Revolution, Mao's little red book carried Lin's personally written introduction, and the 1969 party constitution had named him as Mao's chosen successor. How was the CCP to vilify him convincingly and still keep its credibility?

The stakes involved in this question were particularly high for Mao, who had lost credibility over the way Lin's death had been presented, as well as for the actions of his wife Jiang Qing and her supporters. The stakes were also considerable for hundreds of thousands of others who had come to power during the same period and millions of new party members. CCP enrollments in this period show a seesaw pattern of rapidly rising numbers of new recruits in the early years of the Cultural Revolution, followed by a purge of those hostile to the movement, followed in turn by a swelling of membership again (see table above). This second jump, in 1972 and 1973, reflected the addition of new recruits and the return to party ranks of previously disgraced members.

The party's response to the difficult task of maintaining its prestige can be traced through the crosscurrents of the campaign against Lin Biao. Initially, in the first months after his death, Lin Biao was not publicly named as a target. Instead the press, party journals, and radio stations began a series of attacks on unnamed people described as "swindlers like Liu Shaoqi" or as "sham Marxist political swindlers." The crime of these "swindlers" was that they "wanted to use the spectre of anarchism to stir up disorder and poison the masses in order to oppose the revolution," and that they "cunningly incited ultra-'left' trends of thought."[6] By early 1973, some leaders of the Cultural Revolution must have realized that such a campaign of vilification would backfire, for the charges sounded as if they applied to the behavior they had practiced themselves. A reversal now warned that the swindlers' line was revisionist, not leftist, and that those same swindlers had "at certain times and on certain issues . . . put on an extreme 'Left' appearance to disguise their Right essence." One goal of these swindlers, among others, was a "counterrevolutionary desire for the restoration of the overthrown landlord and bourgeois classes."[7] Although the charges obviously referred to Lin Biao, it was not until the tenth party congress in August 1973 that Zhou Enlai said so publicly. But Zhou made no convincing attempt to explain exactly what Lin had done and how he had been allowed to do it, which must surely have sounded absurd to most listeners.

At almost the same time that the tenth congress was convening, a new mass campaign was launched, the ostensible target being no less a personage than Confucius. Scholars began to publish articles on Confucius that had clear implications for the Cultural Revolution, the bureaucracy, and the role of labor in society: Confucius was described as a representative of the declining slave-owning aristocracy who hated the emerging feudal landlords. Since in the context of economic and social development in the fifth century B.C.E. it was "progressive" to move from a slave to a feudal society, his opposition to such progress revealed Confucius to be a reactionary. Other essays published in late 1973 linked the attack on Confucius to praise for Qin Shihuang, the first emperor who unified the Qin empire in 221 B.C.E. Though Qin Shihuang had been vilified in the past as a tyrant who brought terrible suffering in the name of centralized order, scholars in 1973 praised him and argued that even such draconian actions as his burning of Confucian books and burying alive of scholars had been necessary to consolidate the "dictatorship of the landlord class." Lin Biao, it was firmly stated (in case anyone had missed the point), was one of "the Confuciuses of contemporary China."[8]

By 1974 the "anti–Lin Biao anti-Confucius" campaign had spread across the country. In ways that recalled the campaign against Hu Feng in the early 1950s, or the assault on Wu Han that led into the Cultural Revolution, attacks on Lin and Confucius were the focus for mass rallies and group discussions in party cells and universities, in the PLA and militia units, in communes and factories. Even if weary or cynical of such campaigns, there was nothing that the people could do but attend the study groups and read along in the required texts. Foreign visitors and academics, now beginning to appear in China in some numbers, were subjected to endless briefings on the importance of the campaign and its significance to understanding recent events in Chinese history.

In a parallel cultural attack, a documentary film made by the Italian director Michelangelo Antonioni was denounced for failing to pay attention to the achievements of the "new" China, and for its focus instead on traditional patterns of farming, old buildings, and primitive housing. Antonioni, who had claimed to admire China, was accused of "using the camera to slander the Cultural Revolution, insult people and attack the leadership."⁹ Foreign visitors in China were startled to see huge banners denouncing the director hanging above the machinery in factories and displayed in communes; the message was all too clear that foreigners were not welcome unless they praised what they saw. But the government could not always anticipate how its propaganda might be used. Some Chinese professors quietly mentioned that they saw the campaign against Confucius as a way to reintroduce classical literature in their classes. Study of such texts had been considered reactionary during the Cultural Revolution. But now, teachers asked in mock innocence, how could the students criticize Confucius with maximum effect if they could not use every nuance of his reactionary language?

Behind these tensions, there also loomed the major problem of restructuring the educational system. Schools and colleges had been reduced to shambles in the early years of the Cultural Revolution, with classrooms closed for years, students deployed as Red Guards or sent to the remote countryside, and administrators and teachers humiliated or dismissed. The reopening of high schools and colleges in the late 1960s and early 1970s, and especially the reinstatement in 1973 of university entrance examinations, were met with mixed reactions among students who had now tasted a different kind of learning. One case, that of Zhang Tiesheng, an educated youth who had been sent to Liaoning province, received national attention when it was reported that he had handed in a nearly blank examination paper to a college admissions committee. In a note to the examiners, Zhang wrote that as the head of his production team, he was too busy working eighteen-hour days on the commune to devote time to academic study, and that he had "no respect for the bookworms who for many years have been taking it easy and have done nothing useful." It was unfair, noted Zhang, that after all the work he had put in for his country "a few hours of written examination may disqualify me for enrollment in college."¹⁰ The widespread publicity given Zhang's case showed that many in leadership positions were trying to protect the policy of admission based on the "revolutionary purity" extolled in the Cultural Revolution.

Even more media coverage was given to a philosophy student named Zhong Zhimin, who withdrew from Nanjing University in his second year. A telephone call from his father, a Long March veteran and senior military cadre, had secured admission to this prestigious college for Zhong, who had worked on a commune and enlisted in the PLA. In his letter requesting permission to withdraw, Zhong wrote of his belated realization about the unfairness of using such "back door influence." He returned to work in the countryside, loaded down with the gifts from admiring friends: the works of Marx, Engels, Lenin, and Mao; a full package of materials on the struggle to criticize Lin Biao and Confucius; and a hoe, a chisel, scissors, and a sturdy pair of straw shoes.[11] One did not have to believe every detail of these two stories to understand the political point that was being made.

The students Zhang and Zhong, with their contrasting approaches to university entrance and their common experience of work in the rural communes, were the most publicized voices to emerge from the immense body of urban youths who had been sent to the countryside during the Cultural Revolution—allegedly to boost production there, but also to ease overcrowding in the cities and to defuse the violence unleashed by Red Guards. Of the over 17 million who were resettled in these years, 1 million were from Shanghai. Yunnan in the southwest had absorbed 600,000 youths from various cities, and Heilongjiang on the Soviet border in the northeast, 900,000. This vast program of relocation led to personal hardship and brought a new range of social and political conflicts into the countryside. Few of those sent to live in impoverished remote regions can have shared the cheery official conclusion that these young people were "growing healthily in the vast and resourceful rural areas."

Defining the Economy, 1974–1975

By 1974 it was clear that there would soon be significant changes in China's leadership. Zhou Enlai was seriously ill with cancer, and although he continued his intensive schedule of work as premier, he was often in the hospital for treatment. Mao Zedong could no longer control the symptoms of Lou Gehrig's disease, never appeared without nurses in attendance, and spoke of "preparing to meet god." Zhu De, the architect of the Red Army, was in his late eighties and had long retired from an active public role.

Among the figures now jockeying for position, the four leaders of the Cultural Revolution constituted a forceful bloc, supported in the provinces and in the state-controlled media by others who had risen to power in the years since 1966. Despite a grudging acceptance of China's partial opening to the West, they continued to push for what can be called a "radical" line. This meant continuing the system of communes as it had been consolidated in the years after the Great Leap Forward. Party cadres enforced production quotas in the communes and controlled the allocation of development funds and heavy machinery, as well as local education, health-care facilities, and militias.

The radical line also meant continued exhortations to "learn from the model of Dazhai," the production brigade in Shanxi province that had survived near demystification in the early 1960s and was once again extolled as the model for heroic initiative. Along with praise for Dazhai as the great example of self-sustaining rural development came continued invocations of the Daqing oilfield in Heilongjiang province, as a model of how a major industrial enterprise should grow. At Daqing, it was alleged, the emphasis was still on self-reliance and on mobilizing the work force to its fullest extent through political training and indoctrination with Mao's thought. Ironically, such self-reliance could be extremely expensive. Reports from the same period noted that while grain was still sold to urban dwellers at 1950 prices, the state was paying communes twice as much for their grain as it had then. This strategy of keeping urban wages low by subsidizing grain sales was costing the state billions of yuan a year.

The radicals also continued to insist on the right of young people from "good class backgrounds," such as those whose fathers had been poor peasants and industrial workers, to be admitted without formal examination to college, where their political correctness would have the chance to flourish. They continued as well the compulsory relocation of educated youth from the cities to the countryside. They fostered further self-reliance in health systems through the use of "barefoot doctors" or paramedic personnel, of whom there were over 1 million by 1974. And in line with Jiang Qing's earliest expressed views about the cultural scene, they kept tight control over the political content of art, drama, and literature so that class lines would not be blurred nor the moral force of the socialist message blunted by ambiguity.

In growing opposition to this rigidly indigenous program for national development were the planners who hoped for a more dynamic economic growth that would draw on foreign technology and expertise while continuing to preserve China's economic and political integrity. Zhou Enlai was a proponent of this strategy, as was Deng Xiaoping, who had maintained a strong group of supporters in the CCP hierarchy despite his disgrace in 1966. Now reinstated as a vice premier, Deng gave a succinct explanation in a speech delivered at the United Nations in 1974. While apparently praising the "self-reliant" aspects of development touted by radicals of the Cultural Revolution, he added important modifications:

> Self-reliance in no way means "self-seclusion" and rejection of foreign aid. We have always considered it beneficial and necessary for the development of the national economy that countries should carry on economic and technical exchanges on the basis of respect for state sovereignty, equality and mutual benefit, and the exchange of needed goods to make up for each other's deficiencies.[12]

Those in the Petroleum Group, though risen from Daqing ranks, were also drawn to interaction with the larger world. Economic development would hinge on "technology transfer," which could be expected to include low-interest loans, international trade, and the employment of foreign experts. Another component of technology transfer was the purchase of entire industrial

Chinese Trade and Complete Plant Purchases[13]
($U.S. millions)

Year	Total exports	Total imports	Balance of trade	Machinery and equipment imports	Complete plant contracts
1966	2,210	2,035	175	455	0
1967	1,960	1,955	5	380	0
1968	1,960	1,825	135	275	0
1969	2,060	1,835	225	240	0
1970	2,095	2,245	−150	395	0
1971	2,500	2,310	190	505	0
1972	3,150	2,850	300	520	0
1973	5,075	5,225	−150	860	1,259
1974	6,660	7,420	−760	1,610	831
1975	7,180	7,395	−215	2,155	364
1976	7,265	6,010	1,255	1,770	185
1977	7,955	7,100	855	1,200	80
1978	10,260	10,650	−390	2,500	6,934

plants, which as the above table shows, jumped from zero to 1,259 contracts in 1973.

The advocates of growth had originally intended to offset much of the cost of importing foreign plants by increasing oil production for export from the Daqing fields and by boosting other exports. What the planners had not anticipated was a combination of worldwide recession and inflation, which by 1974 was beginning to shrink the market for China's exports and dramatically raise the costs of its technological imports. The result was a $760 million trade deficit for China in 1974, which led to a spirited counterattack by the radicals against the "worship of things foreign" and those who followed a "slavish comprador philosophy."

As had been done often in the past, historical "analysis" was used to make the critical point. One such essay, which accused the Qing self-strengthener Li Hongzhang of accepting technology from foreigners and allowing them to run China's factories in the nineteenth century, was clearly directed at Zhou Enlai. Another essay attacking Zhang Zhidong, also a Qing self-strengthener who had popularized the *ti-yong* synthesis ("essence and practical use"), was transparently aimed at Deng Xiaoping. In fall 1975 a number of similar critiques were synthesized in an essay that appeared in China's foremost historical journal under the pseudonym Liang Xiao, the name used by a group of intellectuals who acted as the defenders of the radical policies of the Cultural Revolution leaders. Allegedly referring to the nineteenth century, the article stated,

Politically, "wholesale Westernization" meant loss of sovereignty and national humiliation, total sell-out of China's independence and self-determination. . . . Ideologically "wholesale Westernization" was meant to praise what is foreign and belittle what is Chinese and propagate national nihilism in order to undermine the national consciousness of the Chinese spirit. . . . Economically "wholesale Westernization" was aimed at spreading blind faith in the Western capitalist material civilization so as to turn the Chinese economy into a complete appendage of imperialism.[14]

The scope of the radicals' counterattack can best be seen in the pomp surrounding the First National Conference on Learning from Dazhai in Agriculture, which was convened in Shanxi province in September and October 1975. Among the 7,000 dignitaries in attendance were Jiang Qing and Deng Xiaoping, staunch political enemies who stood for opposite strategies of national development. The keynote speech was made by Hua Guofeng, the former party secretary from Mao's home province of Hunan, recently named a vice premier and placed in charge of national agricultural development. Born in Shanxi in 1920 and posted to Hunan in the early 1950s, Hua had ingratiated himself with Mao through favorable assessments of the Great Leap Forward and by founding a model "Dazhai brigade" in Hunan in 1964. He complemented the achievement by orchestrating Red Guard visits to Mao's home village, which became a shrine to worshipful crowds in the late 1960s, and by overseeing the development of a factory in Hunan that could produce 30 million Mao buttons a year. After playing a prominent role in investigating Lin Biao's alleged plots against Mao, in January 1975 he was promoted to minister of public security.

Part of the success of Dazhai, Hua declared in his speech, lay in its self-reliance and high production yields, and part in its advanced levels of mechanization. Claiming that over 300 counties had now achieved similar levels of mechanization and organization, Hua threw out the challenge that one-third of the country must attain those targets by 1980. Such gains could be achieved only with the steady expansion of the collective sector of the economy, "the dominance of the poor and lower-middle peasants as a class," and a "resolute struggle against capitalist activities." Hua was not referring here to the activities of industrialists or foreigners, but to the acquisitive drive of "well-to-do middle peasants." In other words, there was to be no opening up of the market economy, and no change in the policy of curtailing private plots and the degree of family production from those plots. Modernizing agriculture in this way, noted Hua, would "more effectively push forward and guarantee the modernization of industry, national defence and science and technology."[15] Zhou Enlai and Deng Xiaoping had already suggested that these were the four main areas in which modernization should be concentrated. Hua was positioning himself as an advocate of compromise by invoking Maoist rhetoric while supporting policies for economic growth.

Within days of the closing of the Dazhai conference in October 1975, articles, essays, and broadcasts throughout the country were picking up these themes and hammering home the message. At meetings and rallies, Hua's points were repeated and local production studied with a view to achieving the new goals. At year's end, by means of work teams and propaganda teams at all levels, at least 1 million cadres had been sent "to the front line" in their own communities, and numerous other leaders were reported to be receiving "rectification."

This attempt to resurrect the whole gamut of Maoist revolutionary arguments surged just after two quite different critics of Mao's message had passed from the scene. One was Peng Dehuai, whose career as a military leader had been wrecked in 1959 by his criticism of the Great Leap Forward; the other was Chiang Kai-shek, who had battled the Communist revolutionaries for twenty-two years before leading his Taiwan exile bastion through a successful land reform of its own. Neither man was there to read the glowing press reports of China's retrenchment. Peng Dehuai had died in November 1974 at the age of seventy-six, and Chiang Kai-shek just a few months before the Dazhai conference opened, at the age of eighty-seven.

1 9 7 6 : T H E O L D G U A R D D I E S

Death was now in the air for China's aging revolutionary leaders. Zhou Enlai succumbed first, dying on January 8, 1976, at the age of seventy-eight, from the cancer that he had battled for four years. To the surprise of many, Mao Zedong had not visited Zhou in his last months, nor did he issue a personal message on Zhou's achievements and contributions to the revolution. Mao sent no public condolences to Zhou's widow, herself a formidable revolutionary with a lifetime of service to the party. And he did not attend the memorial ceremony in the Great Hall of the People the following week. Mao himself was ill, although he had been well enough to receive the president of São Tomé and Príncipe two weeks before Zhou's death. Nor was he too ill to meet with Richard Nixon in February, during his second visit to China, this time as the former president of the United States. Perhaps Mao had grown to distrust Zhou in the complex swings of Cultural Revolution politics. Certainly Mao had maintained mixed feelings about Zhou in his last years, and had often humiliated Zhou in the presence of other party leaders and forced him to make demeaning "self-criticisms."

Whatever Mao's attitude may have been, the country as a whole plunged into mourning. Foreign correspondents described Beijing as looking like a ghost town, and the news that Zhou had willed that his ashes be scattered across the rivers and hills of his beloved land, rather than enshrined in a mausoleum, was received with deep emotion. With Zhou gone it suddenly emerged how many people had revered him and regarded him as a symbol of order and decency in deeply troubled times. On January 11, in freezing weather, more than 1 million people lined the route to the cemetery for revolutionary heroes on the outskirts of Beijing, where Zhou was to be cremated. The following day, crowds of mourners waited to see the casket with his cremated remains and placed wreaths and tributes to Zhou's memory in Tiananmen Square.[16]

At Zhou's state funeral on January 15, Vice Premier Deng Xiaoping gave an emotional eulogy with five thousand people in attendance. Though his speech followed the wording of the official Central Committee statement issued on the day of Zhou's death, or else gave a summation of Zhou's political life, near the end Deng offered a personal tribute to the character of the man he had worked with for many years, one that seemed to speak from the heart even while using the rhetoric of a ceremonial state occasion:

> He was open and aboveboard, paid attention to the interests of the whole, observed Party discipline, was strict in "dissecting" himself and good at uniting the mass of cadres, and upheld the unity and solidarity of the Party. He maintained broad and close ties with the masses and showed boundless warmheartedness toward all comrades and the people. . . . We should learn from his fine style—being modest and prudent, unassuming and approachable, setting an example by his conduct, and living in a plain and hardworking way. We should follow his example of adhering to the proletarian style and opposing the bourgeois style of life.[17]

If one wished to, one could see these words as veiled yet biting criticism of Mao Zedong and of the leaders of the Cultural Revolution, for none of them could possibly be praised for being "open and aboveboard," for displaying "warmheartedness," or for their modesty, prudence, or approachability.

Whether Deng's speech intensified already deep antagonisms toward him or whether his political enemies were simply determined to force him once again into obscurity cannot be exactly known. But in the first week of February 1976, after the Central Committee named Hua Guofeng acting premier, the campaign against Deng that had begun in late 1975 intensified. As had happened often in the recent past, it started with wall posters and rallies, and kept the true target in the shadows. Students at Beijing and Qinghua universities, demanding the rights of those from poor backgrounds for advanced education, began to suggest that "revisionists" and "capitalist roaders" were insisting on reinstituting the old intellectual elitism, and were ignoring "experience as the basis for developing science in favor of closeting scientists behind closed doors." In March, a meeting at the Chinese Academy of Sciences denounced a still-unnamed "capitalist roader," while an essay in *Red Flag* directed a vigorous attack against a man who could only be Deng. The content of this essay suggests that it was written on instructions from Jiang Qing, and that she had been aggravated by Deng's dismissal of an opera she staged. The article stated,

> Not only does he still refuse to watch the model revolutionary theatrical works, but also he dislikes the fine works created after learning from the experience of the model revolutionary theatrical works. He watched the film "Spring Shoots" but left half-way through in displeasure, criticizing it as ultra-leftist. As for those works airing an opposing view against the model revolutionary theatrical works or those distorting the image of workers, peasants and soldiers, he loves them at first sight and personally sponsors and supports their production. In short, what the proletariat supports, he opposes; what the proletariat opposes, he advocates.[18]

The campaign had reached this stage when an extraordinary event occurred, one that showed how spontaneous mass emotions and unplanned actions could fuse with decisive significance. It began quietly, in late March 1976, when wreaths and posters paying tribute to Zhou appeared at the Monument to the People's Heroes in the center of Tiananmen Square. Crowds gathered to listen to speeches, some praising Zhou, others attacking the Gang of Four. There were also expressions of support for Deng Xiaoping, such as little bottles (pronounced *xiaoping*) placed on the streets as a reference to his name. By April 4,

"Mourning Zhou Enlai at the Monument to the People's Heroes in Tiananmen Square," 1976

the eve of the annual Qingming festival of paying respect to deceased ancestors, more than two million people had visited Tiananmen Square.[19] In this square in 1966 and 1967 Mao Zedong had saluted millions of Red Guards passing in review; now the people of Beijing used the venue to pay homage to Zhou Enlai with wreaths, banners, poems, placards, and flowers.

The next morning, fresh crowds gathering at the memorial found that all the tributes from the previous day had been removed by the police. Their protests led to scuffles and blows. Police cars were set on fire, and as the crowd swelled to 100,000 or more some people forced entry into several government buildings that surround the square. Most of the crowd dispersed around 6:00 P.M., after a broadcast speech by the head of the Beijing Municipal Committee ordered the "revolutionary masses" to evacuate, warning of "bad elements carrying out disruption and disturbances and engaging in counter-revolutionary sabotage." But a hard-core group of about one thousand remained until 11:00 P.M.[20] At that hour security forces moved in and arrested a reported 388 people, although the actual figure was certainly far higher. Several of those arrested were subjected to a mass "people's trial," and others were sent to prison camps to "reform themselves through labor." Demonstrations in homage to Zhou, although not on this scale, took place in many other areas—as widely scattered as Kunming in Yunnan, Taiyuan in Shanxi, Changchun in Jilin, and Shanghai, Wuhan, and Guangzhou.

Among the provocations that had especially angered the authorities were the demonstrators' shouts and placards claiming that the rule of Qin Shihuang was now over, and demanding a return of "genuine" Marxism-Leninism. Clearly these were criticisms of Mao and the leaders of the Cultural Revolution, and whether or not they had been orchestrated in any way by Deng and his supporters, the Central Committee decided to strike back. On April 7 the state news agency fingered Deng Xiaoping as the unrepentant "capitalist roader" associated with the unrest. A terse announcement removed Deng from all his posts "inside and outside the Party," although he was allowed to keep his party membership. Another announcement named Hua Guofeng first vice chairman of the Central Committee (a position second to Mao) and premier of the State Council.[21]

Over the following months the case against Deng was deepened in nationwide meetings and study sessions. The Tiananmen Incident was likened to the Hungarian uprising of 1956 and the poems posted on the memorial equated with Lin Biao's counterrevolutionary "vicious language." As the campaign spread, it coalesced around charges that Deng believed class struggle was over, that he was attempting to reverse the achievements of the Cultural Revolution, that he desired to restore capitalism, and that he was convinced of the need, if China was to achieve the four modernizations, "to rely on those proficient in technical or professional work and to introduce more and more advanced foreign techniques."[22] Deng had given plenty of ammunition to his enemies by his outspokenness over the previous two years, in which he had attacked Maoist "sectarians," mocked the cycles of political purges, and said sadly of his own land: "Everyone here is scared—the youth, even more the elderly. That is precisely why our technology is so far behind."[23]

While the anti-Deng campaign raged and as Hua Guofeng consolidated his power, it became clear that Mao had not much longer to live. He performed his last official function on May 27, 1976, when he received the prime minister of Pakistan. That June, the Central Committee declared he would receive no more foreign visitors, and there were rumors that a famous neurologist had been flown in from Europe to attend to him. The country's attention was caught at this point by another death—that of Zhu De, which came in early July shortly after his ninetieth birthday. In his role as the new premier, Hua Guofeng delivered the eulogy, which summarized Zhu's extraordinary career as a general, military strategist, and builder of the Red Army in the 1930s and 1940s.

Less than three weeks later, on July 28, one of the worst earthquakes in China's recorded history occurred, with its epicenter in Tangshan, Hebei. The shock waves were so immense that there was heavy damage in Tianjin, 60 miles to the southwest, and in Beijing, 100 miles away. The city of Tangshan was virtually obliterated, and the death toll was later officially reported as 242,000, with 164,000 seriously injured. The initial estimates were far higher: 655,000 dead and 779,000 injured. In either case, it was a colossal human tragedy. True to the spirit of self-reliance, China declined foreign and UN offers of humanitarian aid. Instead, a national relief campaign was launched, spearheaded by fifty-six medical teams that arrived from Shanghai the day after the disaster, followed by medical and rescue teams from virtually every province and autonomous region. The PLA played an important role in the rehabilitation effort, partly restoring an image that had been badly tarnished by the killing of Red Guards in the Cultural Revolution and by the alleged treason of its leader Lin Biao.

The recovery from the disaster—the ability to rebuild the shattered infrastructure, speedily reopen the Tangshan coal mines, and restore and refire the furnaces in the Tangshan steel plant—was cause for national celebration. The occasion of a relief conference convened on September 1 allowed Hua Guofeng, "on behalf of Chairman Mao," to use the earthquake to make a political point. The sequence of bad harvests in 1960 that followed the Great Leap Forward, he pointed out, had been exploited by Liu Shaoqi and Deng Xiaoping as a pretext for expanding private plots, opening free markets, and encouraging household production and small enterprises. In 1976, by contrast, socialist principles had been the key to handling the disaster. It was interesting that Hua should invoke Mao in this context, for in traditional Chinese historiography a cataclysmic event such as an earthquake usually heralded political upheavals leading to dynastic collapse. Such superstitions, of course, were now allegedly consigned to the dustbin of history. But when Mao Zedong died on September 9, many Chinese must have linked the two events in their minds.

A week-long period of mourning was declared, and Mao's body was placed in a casket in the Great Hall of the People for the crowds to file past. Some 300,000 did so, but even though people were shocked and silent, in Beijing there was none of the rush of emotion that had occurred in response to Zhou's death. The expressions of grief and respect from elsewhere in China and around the world were moving, however, the exception being the Soviet Union, which placed the news of Mao's death on the bottom of page 3 in *Izvestia* and refused to send a message of condolence at the "state to state" level. The Chinese rejected the Russian "party to party" message as improper. The Central Committee's public eulogy, and Hua Guofeng's speech before 1 million people assembled in Tiananmen Square, gave fulsome praises to Mao's extraordinary achievements. There was also a direct political message: one of Mao's greatest accomplishments had been the suppression of a series of both right and left "opportunist lines" in the CCP—a list that began with Chen Duxiu, Qu Qiubai, and Li Lisan, and ended with Peng Dehuai, Liu Shaoqi, Lin Biao, and Deng Xiaoping.

The demands for national mourning were made in almost peremptory terms by the Central Committee. As the final ceremonies began at 3:00 P.M. on September 18, people all over the country were to stop their work and stand at attention, in silence, for three minutes. The phrasing of this statement reminds us that despite its over 3,000-mile extent from east to west, all of China is kept on Beijing time, which provides the pulse for the whole nation. At the same moment all trains, ships, military vessels, and factories were to sound their sirens for three minutes. All government organs, factories, army units, schools, communes, and neighborhood groups were to assemble to hear the live broadcasts or watch the televised version of the ceremonies.

Though Hua Guofeng made the final eulogy and thus received the greatest public attention, the four radical leaders of the Cultural Revolution were also plainly visible. Wang Hongwen presided over the final ceremonies, and Zhang Chunqiao was a director of the funeral committee. Jiang Qing, accompanied by her own and Mao's surviving children, was prominent at the funeral, and cameras also focused on Yao Wenyuan. Yet in the final startling event of an already dramatic year, the four leaders were suddenly arrested on Hua

Guofeng's orders. They were accused of having constituted a "Gang of Four" and of persisting in their evil conduct despite stern warnings from Mao himself.

Hua Guofeng's success in routing his political enemies was due less to his political acumen than to the support of senior PLA generals and the key military commander in Beijing, Wang Dongxing. Steadfast in loyalty to Mao Zedong ever since he had joined the Jiangxi Soviet in 1933 as a seventeen-year-old orphan, Wang had served as Mao's bodyguard on the Long March and protected him in Yan'an and during the civil war. After 1949, Wang developed an elite military force known as Unit 8341, which was responsible for protecting top Party leaders. Wang's command of this unit, when combined with his other official posts in the public-security apparatus, gave him enormous power. Unit 8341 had overseen the arrests and confinement of such Cultural Revolution victims as Peng Zhen, Liu Shaoqi, and Deng Xiaoping. Troops from the unit guarded secret party files, and in 1971 Wang allegedly helped break Lin Biao's plot against Mao. Now, believing that Hua Guofeng was Mao's true heir, Wang ordered the troops of Unit 8341 to arrest the Gang of Four on October 6 as they were assembling for a meeting. Although much about Wang's career remains obscure, the extent and nature of his power hints at the conspiratorial substructures that bonded military men and secret police at the very center of the CCP.

As more and more charges were brought against them in October and November, the phrase "Gang of Four" became known to everyone in China. Cumulatively they were accused of almost every possible crime in the political book: factional attacks on Zhou Enlai, forging Mao's statements, diluting the criticism of Lin Biao to save their own skin, organizing their own armed forces, tampering with education (and concocting the story of the blank examination paper), inciting the masses to fight each other, attacking worthy government cadres and schoolteachers, criticizing Dazhai and Daqing, disrupting industrial production, hindering the earthquake relief work, defaming Hua Guofeng, slandering army veterans, producing subversive films, sabotaging foreign trade, leading the young to oppose Marxism, and using the public-security apparatus for their own purposes. The members of the group that had proved so ingenious in fabricating a miasma of charges against prominent CCP leaders and intellectuals during the Cultural Revolution now found themselves on the receiving end of the same process.

Those who had been baffled by the fall of Lin Biao would now have further food for thought, but they would not be encouraged to show their doubts in public. On October 7, 1976, Hua Guofeng was named to succeed Mao as chairman of the Central Committee and of the Military Affairs Commission, positioning him at the apex of each section of that three-part structure of army, state, and party that constituted the government. At the end of October 1976, rallies of over 1 million people in both Shanghai and Beijing saluted the beginning of Chairman Hua's era. In November Hua laid the foundation stone for the new mausoleum in Tiananmen Square that would receive the remains of Mao Zedong. The mausoleum was to rise on the central axis radiating from the Forbidden City, an axis that in olden days had carried the eye southward through gate after gate, as in imagination the central force of imperial power spread through the city and beyond the outer wall to the people of the country. Now, though this had surely not been Hua's intended purpose, the shrine for Mao's embalmed corpse would form a permanent barrier to that vision.

CHAPTER 24

Redefining Revolution

THE FOUR MODERNIZATIONS

With Mao Zedong embalmed and at rest, the struggle for power in the CCP entered a new stage. After his ouster in April 1976, rumors circulated that Deng Xiaoping had fled to Guangzhou to live under the protection of Xu Shiyou, an old ally and a powerful regional military governor. But Deng had remained with his family in Beijing, with his location kept secret from his political enemies on Mao's orders. Allies in the provinces such as Xu later proved instrumental in paving the way for Deng's reinstatement. Meanwhile, senior officials in the Central Committee also began pressuring Hua Guofeng to rehabilitate Deng. Having ascended to the top as Mao's successor, Hua was understandably reluctant to permit the return of a formidable rival. But unable to counter the rising chorus of support for Deng, he acquiesced after Deng wrote a public letter acknowledging Hua's leadership. In July 1977, Deng was formally reappointed to all of his previous positions, placing him third in rank in the CCP hierarchy, behind Hua Guofeng and veteran general Ye Jianying.[1]

Not surprisingly, given the different political orientations of Deng and Hua, China's direction in both domestic and foreign policy remained ambiguous throughout 1977 and 1978. The communes continued to be the main form of rural social organization, and peasants were still criticized or penalized for engaging in excessive sideline production, while industry remained tied to inflexible government plans. At the same time, there were a number of signal achievements requiring high levels of technological skill: the dramatic expansion of domestic and international airline systems, the completion of an immense dry-dock facility at the Hebei port of Shanhaiguan, a seabed cable linking China to Japan, and the launch of the nation's first oil tanker in the

50,000-ton class. Scientists successfully conducted several hydrogen-bomb and other nuclear tests, continued the active satellite-launching program begun in 1975, and began work on the development of an ICBM warhead-delivery system. And although economic exchanges with the United States were slow to develop, the PRC negotiated a U.S.$10-billion industrial agreement with Japan. New agreements launched joint Sino-Japanese exploration for oil in the North China Sea and forged extensive new commercial ties with Great Britain and France.

Domestically, Chairman Hua was in command, still championing the radical programs of "learning from Dazhai and Daqing" in agriculture and industry. He claimed this was the true way to obtain the "Four Modernizations," as they were now regularly termed, in agriculture, industry, national defense, and the linked areas of science and technology. At the same time, Deng Xiaoping was maneuvering with growing success to bring back ever more of the party cadres ousted in the Cultural Revolution, and to move toward full implementation of a modernization plan that would incorporate foreign investment and technology. When Deng pushed for Chinese students to study abroad, and when he emphasized the promotion of science and education as top priorities, he had to contend with substantial resistance from those who viewed such policies as elitist and "bourgeois." Through persuasion and persistence, Deng maneuvered around political opposition and bureaucratic inertia to reinstitute the system of university entrance exams in the fall of 1977. It was a colossal task, accomplished in less than three months. As universities reopened in 1977 and 1978, class background was eliminated as a factor in admissions decisions.[2]

During a National Science Conference held in Beijing in March 1978, at which both Deng and Hua made speeches, the modernization plan gained further momentum. In the high-priority areas of energy sources, computers, laser and space technology, high-energy physics, and genetics, a crash training program for 800,000 scientific researchers was announced, along with the development of new research centers integrated into a national system. Over the following months, plans were drawn up for eighty-eight "key universities" and a number of technical colleges. Scientists sent to the countryside over the previous years were recalled and reassigned to professional jobs. During 1978 some 480 students, selected for academic excellence, were dispatched to twenty-eight countries to study.

In the latter part of 1978 the PRC government followed up these initiatives with an extraordinary range of important decisions in both foreign and domestic policy. The key foreign-policy events were the ratification of the Sino-Japanese Treaty of Peace and Friendship in October; Deng Xiaoping's denunciation of the new Soviet-Vietnamese Treaty of Friendship and

Cooperation in early November; the announcement in mid-December that the United States and China would establish full diplomatic relations on January 1, 1979; and the condemnation of Vietnam for backing a "Kampuchean national united front" to overthrow Pol Pot's regime, also in mid-December.

Domestically, there were announcements of important political reversals in mid-November. The April 1976 Tiananmen demonstrations in memory of Zhou Enlai, previously judged to be "counterrevolutionary," were reassessed as a "completely revolutionary action." Millions of people who had been condemned, going back to 1957 antirightist campaign, would be rehabilitated. In Beijing a long wall poster appeared, declaring that Mao Zedong had been a supporter of the Gang of Four and was responsible for the ouster of Deng Xiaoping after the Tiananmen Incident. At the same time, a host of new writings was given wide circulation through the state-controlled press and journals. Focusing on the horrors and tragedies experienced by many in the Cultural Revolution, this "scar literature," as it was called, stimulated debate and reflection about China's past and its future prospects. Other signs pointed to a cultural thaw, including the decisions to stage Wu Han's play *The Dismissal of Hai Rui from Office* and Bertolt Brecht's *Galileo*, both in Beijing. Another was the convening of a conference (in far-off Kunming in Yunnan, admittedly) to study the long-taboo subject of comparative religion, with papers delivered on Buddhism, Daoism, Islam, and Christianity.

But it was the events of December 1978, at the meetings formally known as the Third Plenum of the Eleventh Central Committee of the CCP, that were to mark the most dramatic change in overall party policy since the launch of the Cultural Revolution. And in their long-run effects, the decisions at the Third Plenum were to have greater impact than that earlier cataclysm. First, the plenum laid out the requirements of the Four Modernizations in relation to industrial production, stating that with the struggle against Lin Biao and the Gang of Four brought to a "successful conclusion," it was time to move "the emphasis of the Party's work and the attention of the people of the whole country to socialist modernization." The decision would not be a light one.

> Carrying out the Four Modernizations requires great growth in the productive forces, which in turn requires diverse changes in those aspects of the relations of production . . . not in harmony with the growth of the productive forces, and requires changes in all methods of management, actions and thinking which stand in the way of such growth. Socialist modernization is therefore a profound and extensive revolution.[3]

One problem facing this new revolution was familiar—the continuing presence of "a small handful of counter-revolutionary elements and criminals who hate our socialist modernization and try to undermine it." But although "class struggle" against such subversive forces must continue, "large-scale turbulent class struggles of a mass character have in the main come to an end." The focus would now be on "political stability and unity." In the crucial realm of economic management, the "over-concentration of authority" was a "serious shortcoming." In words that could be interpreted as hinting at critical changes to come, the plenum noted that authority should be shifted "from the leadership to lower levels" and emphasized that the party must not usurp government functions. "Managerial personnel" should have greater responsibilities in defining efficiency, and the number of meetings and the amount of paperwork should be reduced.

Second, referring to agricultural policy, the plenum added this important observation:

> The rapid development of the national economy as a whole and the steady improvement in the living standards of the people of the whole country depend on the vigorous restoration and speeding up of farm production, on resolutely and fully implementing the policy of simultaneous development of farming, forestry, animal husbandry, side-occupations and fisheries, the policy of taking grain as the key link and ensuring an all-round development, the policy of adaptation to local conditions and appropriate concentration of certain crops in certain areas, and gradual modernization of farm work.

The key phrase here was "side-occupations," those myriad local initiatives in growing and marketing grains, fruit, vegetables, livestock, and poultry that had so often been attacked as evidence of stubborn capitalist tendencies. Such "small plots of land for private use by commune members," the plenum declared, along with domestic side-occupations and village fairs, were "necessary adjuncts of the socialist economy and must not be interfered with." The plenum recommended that the price paid by the state for quota grain be raised by 20 percent following the summer 1979 harvest; that the price for grain harvested over and above the quota be raised by 50 percent; and that the prices of farm machinery, fertilizers, and insecticides made by state factories be cut by 10 to 15 percent. To protect urban workers from the effects of these reforms, food subsidies would be raised proportionally as a "guarantee against a fall in their living standards."[4]

Third, the plenum stressed the "dialectical relationship between democracy and centralism" as key to the success of modernization, and affirmed the importance of law in maintaining that success. References to the independence of judicial organizations, "the equality of all people before the people's laws," and the "imperative to strengthen the socialist legal system" signaled major shifts to come.[5] What exactly this meant, given the absence of an independent judiciary, was far from clear. Nonetheless this was an important acknowledgment that a new world of commercial initiatives and independent production, not to mention increased foreign contacts, was bound to bring demands for legal adjudication for which the government would have to offer new kinds of safeguards.

Sprinkled throughout the published report of the Third Plenum and underlined in its conclusion was the argument that the central recommendations were anchored in the "indelible" achievements of Mao Zedong Thought. But there was also an oblique admission that Mao had not been free of "all shortcomings and errors." Looking forward, it would be the "lofty task" of the Central Committee to lead the people of the whole country to "integrate the universal principles of Marxism–Leninism–Mao Zedong Thought with the concrete practice of socialist modernization and develop it under the new historical conditions."[6]

The Third Plenum adjourned on December 22, 1978. Three days before, on December 19, Boeing executives in Seattle, Washington, announced that the PRC had ordered three jumbo 747 jet airliners. On the same day, the chairman of Coca-Cola in Atlanta, Georgia, announced an agreement to sell the soda inside China and open a bottling plant in Shanghai.

Thereafter events continued their headlong pace. On Christmas Day, a large Vietnamese force invaded Cambodia to oust Pol Pot's regime. On January 1, 1979, as planned, the United States and the PRC announced the opening of full diplomatic relations, and Washington severed its formal ties with Taiwan. On January 28, the same day that the Central Committee ordered the ending of discrimination against the children of landlords or rich peasants, Deng Xiaoping flew to Washington, D.C. He was greeted by cheering crowds and an eager press, pictures of which were beamed back by satellite to Chinese television. In Washington, Deng visited President Carter and congressional leaders, and was given a gala reception at the Kennedy Center. He then traveled to Houston, where he observed the training facilities for American astronauts and attended a rodeo. In Atlanta and Seattle, Deng toured the production facilities of Coca-Cola and Boeing. On February 8, after a two-day visit to Tokyo to brief the Japanese prime minister, Deng was back in Beijing.

One might have thought that at this point China would have done everything possible to assure the world of its steady path toward the Four Modernizations so as to encourage foreign investment and international confidence. But at dawn on February 17, a large PLA force crossed the border into the northern part of Vietnam. The Chinese claimed that their invasion was a response to a series of border provocations, and a protest against both Vietnam's actions in Cambodia and the country's dramatic tilt toward the Soviet Union. One can also see another motive for the display of force. At a time when domestic economic expansion was being given so much prominence, Chinese leaders were determined to show that in their focus on agricultural reform, technical training, and industrial development, they were not neglecting the fourth modernization: national defense.

The Fifth Modernization

The Third Plenum and Deng's visit to the United States took place in what initially seemed to be a new atmosphere of intellectual freedom in the PRC. For over two decades almost no one had felt free to speak out against the state that constrained them; the Red Guards were no exception, since they spoke out against one orthodoxy in the name of another, and rationalized their critiques with the thought of Mao Zedong. But at the end of 1978, stimulated in part by the "reversal of verdicts" against the Tiananmen demonstrators of 1976 and in part by the new opening to the West, thousands of people began to put their thoughts into words, their words onto paper, and their papers onto walls to be read by passersby. The most famous focus for these displays was a stretch of blank wall just to the west of the former Forbidden City in Beijing, part of which was now a public museum and park, and part the cluster

Passerby reads dazibao ("big character" posters) at Democracy Wall, 1979.

of residences for the CCP's most senior leaders. Because of the frankness of some of these posters, including the message that democratic freedoms should be introduced in China, this area became known as Democracy Wall.

The main modes of expression in this movement were wall posters—composed of either essays or poems—and a wide range of small magazines run by groups of friends and printed or mimeographed in limited editions. Just as the flurry of publications in the May Fourth movement had done, so did the names of these magazines evoke the powerful aspirations they represented: *China's Human Rights*; *Exploration*; *Enlightenment*; *April 5 Forum*; *Harvest*; *Science, Democracy and Law*; and *Beijing Spring*. Some of the poems in these magazines were political paeans of Deng Xiaoping, with little or no aesthetic subtlety.

> *Deng Xiaoping*
>
> Wise and talented, like the Duke of Zhou,[*]
>   he's Hua's right hand.
> He'll chat and laugh easily, and by lifting a finger
>   make people and country happy and peaceful.
> Don't be surprised that he's fallen twice and risen
>   three times,
> There are always traitors on the road to revolution.[7]

Other poets reflected bitterly on Mao's reign and likened him to the tyrants of the past:

> Chairman's tomb and Emperor's palace
>   face each other across the square,
> One great leader in his wisdom
>   made our countless futures bare,
> Each and every marble staircase
>   covers heaps of bones beneath,
> From the eaves of such fine buildings
>   fresh red blood drops everywhere.[8]

But the moment also inspired some young poets to explore themselves and their world with a freedom that had not been permitted to appear in print since the founding of the PRC, in part because such emotions were oblique, ambivalent, beyond class analysis, and aloof from political programs. Here is

---

[*] The Duke of Zhou was a sage adviser to the founder of one of China's earliest dynasties, and a figure extolled by Confucius in his writings. The name had also been allegorically used to refer to Zhou Enlai in the anti-Confucius campaign of 1973–1974.

the poem "Let's Go," by one of the finest poets to emerge in the democracy movement, Bei Dao:

> Let's go—
> Fallen leaves blow into deep valleys
> But the song has no home to return to.
> Let's go—
> Moonlight on the ice
> Has spilled beyond the river bed.
> Let's go—
> Eyes gaze at the same patch of sky
> Hearts strike the twilight drum.
> Let's go—
> We have not lost our memories
> We shall search for life's pool.
> Let's go—
> The road, the road
> Is covered with a drift of scarlet poppies.[9]

Of the flood of words that appeared in this period, none had more impact than those of Wei Jingsheng. Wei's influence came partly through the force of his ideas and partly through the inspired title he chose for his poster of December 5, 1978: "The Fifth Modernization." This was obviously a gauntlet flung in the face of the CCP leadership—including Deng Xiaoping, who had declared the Four Modernizations a sufficient basis for transforming China. Wei insisted that without the fifth modernization—democracy—the other four would be "merely another promise." He defined democracy as the "holding of power by the laboring masses themselves," rather than by the corrupt representatives of the party-state who had imposed a new "autocracy" on the people. "What is true democracy?" he asked rhetorically in his poster. "It means the right of the people to choose their own representatives [who will] work according to their will and in their interests. Only this can be called democracy. Furthermore, the people must also have the power to replace their representatives any time so that these representatives cannot go on deceiving others in the name of the people."[10]

Articulate, courageous, and angry, Wei was very much the voice of a new China. Born in 1950, the son of a zealous revolutionary who held a good job in the party bureaucracy, Wei as a child had to learn a page of Mao's works each day before he could have dinner. During the Cultural Revolution he was a Red Guard in a prestigious Beijing unit composed largely of cadre children. But when that unit fell afoul of rival groups loyal to Jiang Qing, Wei was arrested and jailed for four months. After his release, he trained as an electrician and joined the PLA, serving for four years before returning to his electrician's job.

Deeply moved by the April 1976 demonstrations, he also fell in love with a young Tibetan woman living in Beijing whose father had been persecuted. Wei's 1978 writings were drawn from this emotionally charged background.

Wei wrote as an ardent socialist and as one who saw much good in the earliest phase of the Cultural Revolution, before it was co-opted by the "autocratic tyrant." He felt that in its first stage the Cultural Revolution had shown the strength of the Chinese people and the force of their struggle for democracy. Wei also wrote as one who had observed the terrible poverty all around him, but did not accept that such poverty was inevitable. In pursuit of his analysis, he challenged the basic assumptions of Lenin as well as Mao. Wei wrote that democracy was not solely the *result* of social development, as Lenin had claimed; it was also the *condition* for the development of higher productive forces. "Without this condition, the society will become stagnant and economic growth will encounter insurmountable obstacles."[11]

In two addenda to his opening poster, which were published in the December 1978 and January 1979 issues of the journal *Exploration*, Wei took these arguments further. Most of the justifications for China's austerity could be turned back on themselves, he wrote; one had only to look at the slums, the prevalence of prostitution (or its close copy—the sexual abuse of women by Communist cadres), and the omnipresence of grinding poverty to see that the CCP had not solved the country's problems. It was an awful fact that the great social novels of nineteenth-century Europe (was Wei thinking of Dickens? of Balzac? of Zola?), which were used in China to show the rottenness of Western civilization, "could perfectly well have drawn upon our present situation for their examples; it is almost as though history had stood still." The vaunted collectivism of the world's "socialist" countries—which by no coincidence also happened to be the poorest—was flawed because it allowed "no room for the independent existence of individualism." We must fight for the right "to live a meaningful life," concluded Wei. "We must never be enslaved again."[12]

The democracy movement was fought with more than words. On December 17, 1978, twenty-eight young people held a demonstration in Tiananmen Square to protest living and working conditions in the rural southwest. The small number of protesters claimed to speak for 50,000 sent-down youths, who had been holding a general strike since December 9 in opposition to local cadres who had "trampled on their human rights." (The date of December 9 had presumably been chosen to echo the courage of the December Ninthers of 1935, who had marched in Beijing to protest the Guomindang government.) In another incident, on January 8, 1979, several thousand people who had been sent to the countryside around Beijing held a demonstration in the city, carrying banners that read "We don't want hunger" and "We want human rights and democracy." In late January, an estimated 30,000 more sent-down workers and their children entered the capital, camping out around the railway station and in side streets, attempting to petition government leaders for help. Many wore only rags in the subzero weather; at least eight people died from exposure to the cold. In Shanghai, rusticated youth marched into the city and besieged the party headquarters for several hours. In Hangzhou, posters went up demanding "the right to live as human beings" and protesting the acute housing shortage, which made it difficult even for married couples to live in a single room of their own.

The government crackdown began in mid-January 1979, before Deng Xiaoping left for his U.S. visit. Deng had initially encouraged the Democracy Wall posters because their views on modernization supported his agenda, and because they criticized or mocked the attitudes of Hua Guofeng and other radical Maoists. But when they went too far, challenging the fundamental premises of CCP rule, he turned against them. Deng's actions thus ran parallel to Mao's in 1957, when Mao unleashed the antirightist campaign in order to smother the Hundred Flowers movement that he had just set in motion. Deng himself had also played a major part in enforcing the purge of intellectuals in 1957.

The first victim of the 1979 crackdown was a young woman, Fu Yuehua, charged with instigating and organizing the rusticated youth demonstrators in Beijing. Fu had had a tragic life, suffering a broken marriage and repeated rape attempts by her unit boss, who finally dismissed her from her job. Her appeals for an investigation of his behavior had gone unanswered, and it is probable that she had turned to helping the demonstrators out of her personal anger and sorrow. Fu Yuehua was sentenced to a two-year jail term.* Other arrests followed, many involving underground journal writers and editors, who were accused of "impairing the state system" and of doing so with the aid of foreigners, which edged their activities toward the category of treason. In late March 1979, Wei Jingsheng, who in the meantime had written several more provocative pieces, was arrested and brought to trial. Charged for his writing and with espionage for leaking information on the Sino-Vietnam war to a foreign journalist, he was convicted and sentenced to fifteen years in prison. Wei's appeals, based in part on his claim that he had no access to confidential information of this kind, were rejected.

The special irony of this charge was that China's war with Vietnam—designed as a short, sharp surgical strike to teach the Vietnamese a lesson for invading Cambodia, and to demonstrate the effectiveness of the modernizing PLA—had been extremely costly. After absorbing heavy casualties and expe-

*At the end of her jail term she was sent to a labor camp.

riencing paralyzing logistical difficulties, the PLA began their withdrawal on March 5, 1979, and completed it by March 16, almost two weeks before Wei's arrest. In subsequent developments, following a condemnation of the democracy movement's excesses by Deng Xiaoping himself, the remaining journals were closed one by one, and on April 1 the right to hang wall posters was withdrawn, except at a few specified locations under police supervision.

Some of the responses to the brief movement's passing were extraordinarily articulate, and gave warning to the government that the forces released here could not be suppressed indefinitely. One protester, arrested in May 1979, wrote that he had been trying to speak for the "second generation" that had grown up under Communist rule. He noted that there were two kinds of critics: those who believed the CCP had failed because it had not been true to Marxist-Leninist principles, and those who believed that the CCP *had* been properly Marxist-Leninist. In this second case, "it is precisely this Marxism-Leninism itself which is absurd and erroneous." The democracy movement might have done far more, he believed, if intellectuals en masse had joined in, but for the most part they had stayed aloof, unwilling to risk the pleasant "tidbits" that the ruling party casually flung to them. The moving spirits of the movement were young workers who had only a middle-school education. Nevertheless, the anonymous writer concluded, the movement had shown its potential strength, for despite the apparent omnipotence of the CCP and its massive bureaucracy and army, "a few little sheets of paper and a few lines of writing, a few shouts and they're frightened out of their wits."[13]

Others preferred to abandon political analysis and return to poetry. Just after the announcement of the crackdown, according to observers, a young man pushed through the onlookers at Democracy Wall and posted one final poem, now forbidden, before walking swiftly away without saying a word. He signed his poem with the pseudonym "Icicle" and entitled it "For You":

> My friend,
> Parting time is pending.
> Farewell—Democracy Wall.
> What can I briefly say to you?
> Should I speak of spring's frigidity?
> Should I say that you are like the withered wintersweet?
> No, I ought instead to talk of happiness,
> Tomorrow's happiness,
> Of pure orchid skies,
> Of golden wild flowers,
> Of a child's bright eyes.
> In sum we ought
> To part with dignity,
> Don't you agree?[14]

TAIWAN AND THE SPECIAL ECONOMIC ZONES

The opening up of China to the United States, and the challenge to government authority posed by the democracy movement activists, occurred as Taiwan was entering a new era of prosperity and struggling to define its own future. In their official statement on the establishment of diplomatic relations with the United States in 1979, the CCP had made this declaration:

> As is known to all, the Government of the PRC is the sole legal government of China and Taiwan is a part of China. The question of Taiwan was the crucial issue obstructing the normalization of relations between China and the USA. It has now been resolved between the two countries in the spirit of the Shanghai communiqué and through their joint efforts, thus enabling the normalization of relations so ardently desired by the people of the two countries. As for the way of bringing Taiwan back to the embrace of the motherland and reunifying the country, it is entirely China's internal affair.

The American statement had a different flavor, since it included additional sections concerning the termination of diplomatic relations with Taiwan, the cancellation of the mutual-defense treaty between Taiwan and the United States, and plans for the withdrawal of military personnel. On the question of Taiwan's future, the United States had acknowledged "the Government of the PRC as the sole legal government of China." But it elaborated what this meant for Taiwan in a separate passage:

> In the future, the American people and the people of Taiwan will maintain commercial, cultural, and other relations without official government representation and without diplomatic relations. . . .
>   The USA is confident that the people of Taiwan face a peaceful and prosperous future. The USA continues to have an interest in the peaceful resolution of the Taiwan issue and expects that the Taiwan issue will be settled peacefully by the Chinese themselves.[15]

The PRC statement that "bringing Taiwan back to the embrace of the motherland" was an "internal affair" made sense only if Taiwan was considered part of China, a province that had temporarily lost its home. In fact, although Taiwan still claimed that its own government represented the Chinese people, its course of development since 1949 had made it a fully independent society in important ways. Chiang Kai-shek, acting partly on advice from the United States and partly in the interests of his own survival, had in the 1950s and 1960s instituted thorough and successful reforms on the island. The government of Taiwan remained dominated by the 2 million supporters of the Guomindang who had fled from the mainland in 1948 and

1949; the earlier Taiwanese settlers were barred from independent political action, although they flourished economically under the reforms and could advance up through the ranks if they joined the Guomindang.

In 1979, Taiwan's population stood at 17.1 million, a tiny fraction of the PRC's estimated population of 950 million. Yet Taiwan's per capita GNP was around six times larger, having risen 416 percent since 1952. This growth had not been easy to achieve, and had initially been fostered by the United States, especially through the Joint Commission on Rural Reconstruction, which in the 1950s supervised rent-reduction and land-sale programs to help owner-cultivators. Essential to the success of these programs was control of the hyper-inflation that had afflicted the island along with the mainland in the 1940s. Currency reform in 1949 was carried through successfully (unlike the disastrous gold-yuan experiments in 1947 on the mainland), in large part because Taiwan's comparatively small size made it possible to check speculation and control gold sales. A 1949 inflation rate of around 3,400 percent was dramatically reduced: to 306 percent in 1950, 66 percent in 1951, and 3 percent by 1961.

The techniques used to battle inflation were initially similar to those used in the PRC. By instituting interest rates on savings of around 10 percent and controlling specie circulation, the government kept a grip on the new currency. Under a land-to-the-tiller program, shares in state enterprises were distributed to farmers, and tenant farmers were promised title to the land they worked if they contracted to provide the state quota payments of grain for a decade. Since Taiwan was also a one-party state—controlled by the Guomindang still dominated by Chiang Kai-shek—no democratic process was required to institute these reforms.

As agricultural production rose to meet domestic needs, the government made a determined effort to shift the economy from its base in exporting mainly rice and sugar, developed during the Japanese colonial period of 1895 to 1945, to a focus on advanced industrial production. The results were startling, especially in the export sector, where between 1953 and 1962 the share of industrial products increased from 7 to 51 percent of all exports. The economy's focus in the 1960s was largely on electronics and other technologically advanced industries, but there was also a dramatic increase in the production of textiles, rubber, chemicals, and plastics. The 1973–1974 world oil crisis brought serious disruptions to Taiwan's economy, with its overdependence on oil imports. Food-price subsidies during the emergency period, coupled with extremely severe monetary policies, kept the crisis from becoming a catastrophe.

In comparison to those in the PRC, Taiwan's growth rates were similar during the mainland's First Five-Year Plan, but broke away swiftly with the post–Great Leap Forward economic disruptions and held that lead during the

Growth Rates: Taiwan, PRC, and Japan, 1952–1972[16]

	1952–1960	1960–1965	1965–1972
Percentage rates of overall GNP growth			
Taiwan	7.2	9.6	10.1
PRC	6.0	4.7	5.7
Japan	8.3	9.8	10.8
Percentage rates of per capita GNP growth			
Taiwan	3.6	6.4	7.3
PRC	3.6	2.9	3.3
Japan	7.2	8.8	9.5

Cultural Revolution. Comparative figures show that Taiwan almost matched Japanese growth rates in this period (see the above table).

As much as it could, the government on Taiwan restricted imports of products that would worsen its balance-of-payments problems, especially luxury goods or those that competed directly with domestic manufactures. The state actively promoted exports by making cheap credit available to manufacturers of export goods and through the creation of export processing zones. The first of these was established in 1966 at the southern port of Kaohsiung; two more such zones were established in 1969. In these zones, a streamlined bureaucracy reduced government red tape, and there were tax incentives and exemptions from import duties on special machinery if all of the finished products were exported.

Although the Shanghai communiqué of 1972 did not decisively affect Taiwan's economic status, the absence of consultations with Chiang's government prior to its announcement was humiliating. And when the Taiwanese pondered this humiliation along with the loss of the UN seat, the sense of anger and rejection mounted. Anti-U.S. riots erupted in Taiwan during 1971–1972, fed as well by protests against the undemocratic nature of the Guomindang government, and the severe restrictions on individual freedom that were still a part of life in Taiwan. The majority of the population—those who had settled on the island before 1945—resented the political and economic dominance of post-1949 refugees from the mainland. Acute differences between these two constituencies spilled over into everything from marriage patterns to education, and there was a distinct possibility of serious violence. Chiang's government feared that the widespread protests might encourage the growth of the small but passionate independence movement, a potential threat to Guomindang power. But the Guomindang was able to suppress dissent through strict police and political control, backed by military force when necessary.

The 1979 normalization agreements were more threatening to Taiwan. Chiang Kai-shek had died in 1975, and though his son Chiang Ching-kuo soon took over the presidency, there was concern that he might not have the prestige to hold Taiwan together. The termination of official American diplomatic concourse with Taiwan meant that relations would be conducted through two "institutes," one in Taipei and one in Washington, D.C. Particularly threatening, in the eyes of Taiwan's supporters, were the U.S. plans to withdraw all its military personnel from the island, the abrogation of the mutual-security treaty, and the agreement reached with the PRC by which the United States would not supply new offensive arms to Taiwan and would gradually reduce overall military support.

Members of the U.S. Congress were aggravated over the Carter administration's secret negotiations with the PRC, which had been conducted without their input and the results presented as fait accompli. Critics issued a barrage of complaints: some emphasized the lack of consultation with congressional leaders; some contended that forsaking a loyal ally would damage American credibility; others underlined Carter's abandonment of his professed commitment to human rights. When the president sent a bill to Congress in January 1979, setting a future framework for "unofficial" relations with Taiwan, it took nearly three months of committee hearings and debates to produce legislation acceptable to the different constituencies. The Taiwan Relations Act, which passed with bipartisan support in April 1979, included a stronger affirmation of American commitment to Taiwan and more explicit security provisions than the draft bill. Most notable were the statements that the decision to establish diplomatic relations with the PRC "rests upon the expectation that the future of Taiwan will be determined by peaceful means," and that the United States would "consider any effort to determine the future of Taiwan by other than peaceful means, including by boycotts or embargoes, a threat to the peace and security of the Western Pacific area and of grave concern." Furthermore, the promise of providing "Taiwan with arms of a defensive character" was accompanied by the pledge to "resist any resort to force or other forms of coercion that would jeopardize the security, or the social or economic system, of the people on Taiwan."[17]

The provisions of the Taiwan Relations Act helped soften the loss of U.S. diplomatic recognition, and gloomy predictions of detrimental effects on the Taiwanese economy did not come to pass. On the contrary, 1979 proved to be an exceedingly strong year as Taiwan's GNP grew by 20.3 percent to an all-time peak. Although Taiwan cut back its reliance on U.S. trade to some extent—which was in any case a practical move—overall trade, conducted with 120 different countries, rose 31 percent the same year. Foreign investment in Taiwan also rose dramatically, by over 50 percent. The main problem continued to be dependence on oil imports, which at 380,000 barrels a day cost over U.S.$2 billion a year, but the expansion of the island's nuclear-power facilities promised to offset this problem to some extent.

The leaders of the PRC were aware of Taiwan's prosperity. They also realized that regardless of their strident rhetoric concerning "reunification," there was no realistic expectation for such reconciliation if the economic disparities between the two countries remained as broad as they were. The challenge for the PRC was to adopt some means for accelerating the Four Modernizations (the "fifth" was not in question here) and for gaining access to the world financial community. To spearhead this new initiative, Deng Xiaoping chose a former Shaanxi party leader, Xi Zhongxun, who had been close to Mao during the Yan'an years. Xi's previously rapid rise had been checked in 1962, when Mao accused him of sponsoring opposition views and demoted him. In late 1978 Deng promoted Xi to party secretary of Guangdong, with instructions to transform the coastal economy.[18] Deng Xiaoping pushed the idea at a work conference of the Central Committee in April 1979, and a work team was accordingly sent to Guangdong and Fujian. In July the Central Committee moved to establish four "special zones for export"; the following year the name was changed to "special economic zone" (SEZ) to suggest their broader range of economic activity.

The first four SEZs were chosen for their proximity to foreign-capital sources and their accessibility. Zhuhai is adjacent to Macao, Shenzhen just over the northern border of Hong Kong, Shantou and Xiamen are opposite Taiwan. In the nineteenth century, Shantou (Swatow) and Xiamen (Amoy) had been among the treaty ports forced on the Qing dynasty by the British. Those imperialist echoes might have bothered some, but China's leaders seemed confident they could avoid foreign dominance over these zones by vigorously maintaining control and supervision. Nevertheless, the facilities extended to foreigners and overseas Chinese in the four SEZs were considerable. The PRC offered to build plants to the specifications of investors, and to provide preferential tax rates and a well-trained (and presumably obedient and nonunionized) labor force at competitively low wages.

Investors did respond, but not as quickly or with the commitment of advanced technology as had been expected. The Chinese work force was often not as skilled as foreign investors had hoped, the bureaucracy remained cumbersome, and quality standards were low. The SEZs did take off—especially Shenzhen, which began to resemble the less affluent sectors of its high-rise neighbor, Hong Kong—but the boom was expensive to PRC planners, who had to invest more state funds in construction and other support systems than they had expected. The planners were surprised too when imports *into* Shenzhen grew at an alarming rate. At the same time, social problems emerged in the SEZs, from the use of Hong Kong currency, black markets, and corruption among officials to street crime and prostitution. Government leaders—some perhaps already wary of Deng Xiaoping's ambitious plans—grew anxious about the accelerated pace of change.

As early as July 1979 the National People's Congress had argued for readjusting the economy to pay more attention once again to agriculture. The following year, the veteran economic planner Chen Yun, raised to the Standing Committee of the Politburo, called for a period of retrenchment. One factor in this decision was the discovery that, exciting though the prospects for economic growth might be, and however potentially profitable the special economic zones, the foreign-trade deficit for the year 1979–1980 had turned out to be U.S.$3.9 billion, by far the largest in China's history. Integration into the global economy was going to be an expensive business.

At a different scale of activity but equally disturbing was the disclosure in April 1989 of the worst case of corruption yet uncovered in the PRC. A middle-level party cadre named Wang Shouxin, working in Heilongjiang province with a group of associates, many of whom also held party and bureaucratic positions, had embezzled state property worth at least 536,000 yuan in a series of scams and thefts spread over seven years. Wang Shouxin's case was a convoluted one, involving the manipulation of the coal company she supervised and the distribution system that went with it. The case attracted the attention of journalist Liu Binyan, who had suffered in the antirightist campaign and the Cultural Revolution for his outspokenness. The profession of "investigative reporter" was, in the late 1970s, being encouraged as one way of airing popular complaints against corrupt cadres, and Liu was a dramatic example of how effective such a role could be, even in the world of a state-controlled press. He traveled to Heilongjiang to interview people in Wang's unit and to try and unravel the details of the case. His remarkable exposé, a sixty-page essay that he entitled "People or Monsters?" was published in *People's Literature* in September 1979. Since this was an "official journal," the CCP cultural authorities obviously agreed with Liu's indictment of certain echelons within the party itself.

Wang Shouxin, the "coal queen" in Liu's sardonic portrayal, was "a warmly sentimental woman with clearly defined likes and dislikes. Her tens of thousands of tons of coal and her nine trucks were the brush and ink that she used every day to compose her lyric poems." These "poems" were designed to protect and promote her own family, and to ingratiate herself with party members and cadres at all levels through selective manipulation and corruption. Wang was not so special, Liu observed; only the scale of her operations was unusual. She was merely a symptom, a dishonest person whose behavior had for years been "covered up by the general decline in social morality, by the gradual legalization of criminal activity, and by the people's gradual acclimatization to the moral decay around them."[19] If Wang was indeed a symptom rather than an isolated case, then China's reform and opening was going to offer as many temptations as opportunities.

"TRUTH FROM FACTS"

The ups and downs in Chinese economic policy during the four years after Mao's death in 1976 reflected disagreements at the center of the government between Deng Xiaoping and Hua Guofeng. Considering the importance of the stakes, and the absence of mechanisms for peaceful transitions at the top of the power structure, either Deng or Hua was going to have to shunt aside his rival. In the event, it was Deng who succeeded in the power struggle.

Although Hua Guofeng held the more impressive formal positions—as chairman of the CCP, premier of the State Council, and chairman of the Military Affairs Commission—Deng had the more powerful connections in the party and in the army, as well as among leading intellectuals. Hua had based his ascent on his contention that he was Mao's chosen successor. After the arrest of the Gang of Four, however, as criticism of Mao began to be voiced publicly, Hua discovered that this was not a helpful legacy. Furthermore, Deng Xiaoping worked patiently in the late 1970s and in 1980 to discredit his rival. Hua's statement that all the Chinese needed to do to achieve a happy future was to "obey whatever Mao had said and to ensure the continuation of whatever he had decided" caused him and his associates to be dubbed believers in "the two whatevers." Deng, publicly espousing the Maoist slogan to "seek truth from facts," pushed the image of himself as a pragmatist, and broadened the interpretation of Mao's phrase by adding the crucial clause "and make practice the sole criterion of truth."

Deng consolidated his victory over Hua by grooming two protégés for power. Hu Yaobang, the elder of the two, was born in Hunan in 1915 (some sources say 1913) to a poor family, and had been recruited for Mao's ill-fated Autumn Harvest Uprisings of 1927. He joined the CCP in the Jiangxi Soviet in 1933, fought on the Long March, and rose steadily in the party ranks during the Yan'an and civil war periods, becoming director of the Communist Youth League. He was ousted from power in 1966 when the Red Guards targeted the league—by then some 30 million strong—as a potential rival in the Cultural Revolution's struggle for leadership. Returned to office in 1975 as party secretary of the prestigious Academy of Sciences, Hu swiftly developed a reputation as a defender of science, with a refreshingly outspoken style after decades of Maoist rhetoric. "The Academy of Sciences is the Academy of Sciences," as Hu put it once. "It is not an Academy of Production. It is a place where one studies, not a place where one plants cabbages. It is not a potato patch, it is a place where one does science, the natural sciences."[20] Disgraced along with Deng Xiaoping in 1976, Hu returned in 1977 as codirector of the Central Party School and as director of the Central Committee's organization department. In late December 1978 he was named to the Politburo and in 1980 elected to its Standing Committee. Later that year Deng arranged for Hu to be named general secretary of the party, a key move toward the eventual removal of Hua Guofeng from power, which was achieved successfully in 1981.

Deng's second protégé, Zhao Ziyang, was from a completely different background than Hu and experienced a different career pattern, but like Hu he was a fine administrator and a seasoned political operator. Born in 1919 to a landlord family in Henan, Zhao joined the Communist Youth League in 1932. At nineteen he entered the CCP and worked as a guerrilla-base organizer in central China during World War II and the civil war. After the Communist victory, Zhao was transferred to Guangdong and rose steadily in the provincial hierarchy there, becoming party secretary in 1961. Adaptable to the political winds, he had pushed land reform vigorously in the early 1950s, defended family-unit production after the Great Leap disasters, and rode out the first phase of the Cultural Revolution by posing as a leader of the Red Guards in Guangzhou, until he was ousted by a more radical faction in 1967. By the mid-1970s, after a brief spell of service in Inner Mongolia, Zhao was back in Guangzhou.

It was after his transfer to Sichuan in 1975 as party secretary and political commissar to the Chengdu region that Zhao's career really took wing. Sichuan, previously a prosperous province, with a population of 97 million in mid-1970, had suffered disastrous setbacks during the Cultural Revolution. The zeal with which radical cadres promoted extreme policies severely disrupted agriculture and industry, and for the first time in decades Sichuan ceased to be self-supporting in grain production. The complex politics of the province also allowed it to remain a bastion for Lin Biao supporters long after his death.

As party secretary, Zhao had to overcome this troubled legacy. In late 1976 he began to implement a series of policies designed to reverse the economic radicalism that had marked first the Great Leap period and then the decade of the Cultural Revolution. Realizing that local farmers were once again working hard on private plots and dramatically increasing production, Zhao authorized up to 15 percent of the land in communes to be farmed privately; the produce of those plots were permitted to be sold in private markets without price controls. He also authorized sideline industries by which individual families could supplement their incomes. The result was a spectacular leap in production as economic initiative found a new freedom in Sichuan, with grain production increasing 24 percent between 1976 and 1979.

Zhao was equally flexible with state industries. Plant managers were given financial autonomy, allowed to negotiate access to markets, and permitted to form joint industrial ventures. Workers received bonuses for hitting high production targets, and factory operations were tightened up. The result was an even more extraordinary jump of 80 percent in industrial production during the same three-year period of 1976–1979 in Sichuan. A folk saying punning on the similar pronunciation of the word "to look for" and Zhao's surname began to circulate at this time: "If you want to eat, go and look for Ziyang" (*"Yao chi liang, zhao Ziyang"*). When Deng Xiaoping, himself a Sichuanese, returned to power in 1977, he named Zhao an alternate member of the Politburo. Thereafter Zhao's rise was swift, culminating in 1980 with his appointment to the Standing Committee of the Politburo and replacing Hua Guofeng as premier. Reviewing this record of successful innovation, we can see how the example of what Zhao had achieved gave Deng confidence to draw up the guidelines for reform at the Third Plenum.

Deng Xiaoping, who in 1978 had assumed the post of chairman of the Military Affairs Commission, consolidated control over the top echelon of power by 1980. Hua Guofeng was not penalized but allowed to keep some rank and dignity as an ordinary member of the Central Committee. His chance of running the country as Mao's successor, however, had ended. To emphasize the break with the past, Deng led the party in the delicate task of evaluating Mao's legacy, an undertaking fraught with problems if the party was not to undermine its prestige or yield ideological ground to the discredited democracy movement. The CCP began by publicizing harrowing cases of those who had tried to criticize aspects of Mao's policies in the 1960s and 1970s, and had been persecuted or killed for their stubborn determination to right the record. Then the Central Committee conducted its own careful analysis, which it completed in the summer of 1981. Mao was blamed for certain "leftist" excesses in his later years, such as his beliefs that mass revolution against revisionism should be encouraged, and that there was need for "continuing the revolution under the dictatorship of the proletariat." The final summation was that Mao had been correct 70 percent of the time and incorrect 30 percent of the time, with most of those errors bunched near the end of his life. But it would be "entirely wrong to try to negate the scientific value of Mao Zedong Thought and to deny its guiding role in our revolution and our construction just because Comrade Mao Zedong made mistakes in his later years," the Central Committee concluded. "Mao Zedong Thought is the spiritual asset of our Party. It will be our guide to action for a long time to come."[21]

As this political struggle was slowly edging toward an open break, the state press began to issue reports emphasizing examples of local initiative and showing how small enterprise could flourish. The initial examples were modest, as in the story of an elderly couple who had for decades been running a small guesthouse in a former general store. The couple's "Heavenly Justice Guest House," used by people visiting Beijing who could not afford regular hotels, could sleep eight men at a time on a *kang* (the raised brick platform, heated from below and covered with bedding, that was the customary sleep-

Deng Xiaoping reviewing an honor guard on the thirty-fifth anniversary of the founding of the People's Republic, 1984

ing place in north China). Women guests had to sleep with the proprietress, while her husband moved in with the men. Across a span of thirty years, the couple had in this simple way cared for 46,000 guests, apparently oblivious to all the shifts in the political wind. Their venture was not to be considered "capitalist," the party press declared in 1980, since the couple always "relied on their own labor and did not exploit anyone."[22]

In another much-publicized story that same year, several families near Chengdu were awarded certificates for achieving "wealth through diligent labor." Such families used the new "responsibility system" to contract for the right to work a given plot of commune land. Surplus produced above the state quota could be sold on the free market. Sideline production included raising silk cocoons and pigs. Families engaged in these activities might make as much as 700 yuan a year. Since the per capita income in Sichuan's richest communes was 160 yuan a year and the provincial average was 55 yuan, this new system represented a startling opportunity. By the end of the year, such stories of commercial success in the countryside were becoming commonplace. The only minor villains in these vignettes were local cadres, who often dithered over bureaucratic procedures and took months to process the paperwork.

In this same atmosphere of excitement over independent enterprise, the once-disgraced party leader Liu Shaoqi was formally vindicated of all the charges leveled against him during the Cultural Revolution. Liu himself had died years before, in 1969, from the cruel withdrawal of medical care. But his widow, Wang Guangmei, who had been tortured and imprisoned in solitary confinement, was still alive and present to hear the speeches in her late husband's honor. The rehabilitation of Liu must have seemed as baffling to many young party members as the original charges had been to their parents. Since Liu's disgrace the CCP had more than doubled in size—from 18 million in 1966 to 38 million in 1980. Half the membership had grown up with the conviction (or at least the public appearance of belief) that Liu Shaoqi had been "a traitor, a scab, and a number one person in authority taking the capitalist road." As with the story in 1971 of Lin Biao's death, party credibility was stretched to the limits.

It was apt that during this transitional year of 1980 the Gang of Four should finally be brought to trial. There were ten defendants in all: the Gang of Four; five senior army officers accused of conspiring with Lin Biao; and Chen Boda, Mao's former secretary who had been a leading figure in the early years of the Cultural Revolution. National and international interest in the trial focused on the notorious four, who were accused of "persecuting to death" an estimated 34,800 people and of having "framed and persecuted" 729,511 others during their years in power. In concentrating on crimes committed during the later 1960s and early 1970s, the prosecutors moved away from charges of crimes dug up (or fabricated) that went far back into the past. At the time of her original arrest, for instance, Jiang Qing was accused of cooperating with the Guomindang and betraying members of the underground to Chiang Kaishek's police. Zhang Chunqiao allegedly joined the Guomindang Blueshirts in the mid-1930s, while Yao Wenyuan covered up the fact that his family had been landlords for five generations. Wang Hongwen, the youngest of the group, who had not even been alive in the early days of the revolution, was charged with having wrangled a change of assignment during the Korean War—from signalman to trumpet player in the band.

During the trial, Jiang Qing was defiant, shouting at witnesses and calling the judges "fascists"; she had to be removed from the courtroom at times. She clung to her defense that Mao had supported her activities in the Cultural Revolution and that she was obeying his will. Zhang Chunqiao took the opposite tack and remained silent, refusing to answer the prosecutor's questions. Most of the other defendants were more docile, apparently beaten down by years of harsh detention. But the trial did little to reassure observers that

Jiang Qing sits in the defendant's box during the trial of the Gang of Four, 1981.

the rule of law now mattered. In fact the proceedings were a bizarre public spectacle that many Chinese discounted, even though they were glad to see these particular former leaders brought low.

In the formal sentences, handed down on January 25, 1981, Jiang Qing and Zhang Chunqiao were condemned to death, but with a two-year reprieve during which time they might "repent" and avoid execution. Wang Hongwen was given life imprisonment, Yao Wenyuan a twenty-year sentence. Chen Boda and the five army officers received prison sentences of sixteen to eighteen years.

These verdicts and the political demise of Hua Guofeng brought the era of "leftism" to a close. This was underlined not only by the posthumous rehabilitation of Liu Shaoqi, but also by the favorable reassessment of such long-vilified leaders of the late 1920s and early 1930s as Qu Qiubai and Li Lisan. It seemed that the party leadership now realized that if they were to restructure the country's socialist economy, they were also going to have to restructure the CCP's didactic vision of its own past.

CHAPTER 25

Levels of Power

ONE BILLION PEOPLE

By the year 1981, despite the continuing disagreements among the CCP leadership over the pace of economic change, a consensus had emerged that without vigorous intervention, the population surge would eat up any material gains that might be achieved. There had been two previous censuses in the PRC, one in 1953 that counted a population of 582.6 million, and one in 1964 that yielded a figure of 694.6 million. But neither of these had been monitored with precision. To make intelligent plans for the future, the leadership realized, it was essential to know the precise size of the population and the rate of its growth. Accordingly, a target date for a full national census was set: July 1, 1982.

The results of the census confirmed what Chinese demographers and planners had expected: the total population was now more than 1 billion. Although foreign analysts questioned some aspects of the methodology employed, especially in areas where the stated totals matched projections too neatly, the figures were accepted as generally reliable. The census was carried through with advice from United Nations experts on population and had been carefully planned several months in advance. Over 5 million canvassers gathered the data, and twenty-nine colossal computers digested it. The final figure of 1,008,175,288 was therefore considered to be as accurate as possible, given the circumstances. Because political necessity required counting Taiwan as part of China, the full total released was 1,031,882,511, which included the estimated populations of Taiwan, Hong Kong, and Macao.

One fact emphasized by the 1982 census was the extraordinary youthfulness of the population. The data showed that around 60 million women were currently in their thirties, 80 million in their twenties, and 125 million

AGE COMPOSITION OF CHINA'S POPULATION, 1982[1]

Age group	Total	Male	Female	Sex ratio (female = 100)
Total	1,008,152,137*	519,406,895	488,745,242	106.27
0–4	94,704,361	48,983,813	45,720,548	107.14
5–9	110,735,871	57,026,296	53,709,575	106.18
10–14	131,810,957	67,837,932	63,973,025	106.04
15–19	125,997,658	64,420,607	61,577,051	104.62
20–24	76,848,044	40,300,907	36,547,137	110.27
25–29	93,142,891	48,310,132	44,832,759	107.76
30–34	73,187,245	38,153,148	35,034,097	108.90
35–39	54,327,790	28,669,005	25,658,785	111.73
40–44	48,490,741	25,878,901	22,611,840	114.45
45–49	47,454,949	25,123,395	22,331,554	112.50
50–54	40,856,112	21,568,644	19,287,468	111.83
55–59	33,932,129	17,530,819	16,401,310	106.89
60–64	27,387,702	13,733,702	13,653,367	100.59
65–69	21,260,370	10,171,973	11,088,397	91.74
70–74	14,348,045	6,434,731	7,913,314	81.32
75–79	8,617,043	3,496,703	5,120,340	68.29
80+	5,050,091	1,765,823	3,284,268	53.77

*In some cases the precise age was unclear; hence this figure is slightly lower than the total census figure.

between ten and twenty—already (or soon to be) of marriageable age (see the table above). At the same time, life expectancy was also rising dramatically. This enormous potential pool of childbearing women gave added urgency to the arguments of those seeking a stronger family-planning policy. Ever since the founding of the PRC there had been a tension in this policy debate between socialist optimism and the pessimism of the "Malthusian" laws of population limitation,* which implicitly contradicted the expectation that socialism would bring the most dramatic changes in human life. In the early 1950s, some of China's foremost economists had warned of trouble if close attention was not paid to the nation's overall population picture. A host of factors increased the chances of rapid growth: the marriage law of 1950 that allowed women as well as men the opportunity to leave uncongenial partners

* According to Thomas Malthus (1766–1834) in his *Essay on the Principle of Population* (1798), the population of a given country was doomed to be checked by famine, disease, war, or other catastrophes when it pushed too hard against the limits of available resources. At almost the same time, late in Qianlong's reign, the scholar Hong Liangji had also warned that rapidly rising population might harm China.

and find new ones; the drop in infant mortality because of improved health care; a rise in life expectancy because of better diet and health services for the elderly; and the persistence of cultural preferences for lineage continuity through large families, especially many sons.

These warnings had initially prompted the approval in 1953 of laws on birth control and abortion, and the formation in 1954 of birth-control study groups. In 1956 Premier Zhou Enlai urged limitations on childbirth. But the more influential economists holding such views were purged in the antirightist campaign of 1957 (Zhou survived in power), and during the politically extremist years of the Great Leap Forward and the Cultural Revolution little attempt was made to analyze or limit population growth. Throughout the 1960s and early 1970s many families had five or six children. Had it not been for the catastrophic famines of the post–Great Leap years, and the dismal health conditions afflicting the poorer parts of rural China, the rate of population growth would have been even higher.

But whereas in 1974 Chinese participants at international conferences still insisted that "population explosion" theories were a "fallacy peddled by the superpowers,"[2] the government had already begun to check population growth through mass propaganda and the spread of birth-control devices. The fertility rate of women, which stood at 4.2 percent in 1974, dropped to 3.2 percent in 1976 and 2.2 percent in 1980. In September 1980 Hua Guofeng, who still served as the government spokesperson on some important matters, told the National People's Congress that henceforth families must strive to have only one child, and that family planning must be built into China's long-term development strategy. Exceptions would be allowed only for the "minority peoples."

Following Hua's speech, a new marriage law was promulgated in 1980, setting the earliest marriage age permitted for men at twenty-two and for women at twenty. (It had been twenty and eighteen respectively in the 1950 legislation.) Because of government policies urging late marriage, actual marriage ages for men and women were already higher than these new levels. The law was intended to formalize the rules and prevent earlier marriages while encouraging "later marriage, later childbirth." The guidelines for women were first marriage at twenty-four, first (and only) childbirth at twenty-five.

Reinforcing Hua's statements, the State Family Planning Commission pointed out that studies showed almost 6 million babies had been born in 1981 to families who already had one child. In an alarming 1.7 million cases, the families had five or more children. Spurred by these trends, the government intensified the rigor of its birth-control programs, ordering compulsory IUD insertion for women who had borne one child, and compulsory sterilization of either husband or wife after the birth of a second child. Provincial sterilization quotas were passed down to the counties and municipalities for implementation, and in many cases women were coerced into having late-term abortions. Furthermore, party administrators handed out land contracts to peasant families on the condition that they sign a second contract promising not to have a child while they worked the land. Such families would be fined or even forced to forfeit the land if they violated the contractual terms. There were reports of couples fleeing as local sterilization teams entered their villages, and some birth-control cadres felt so threatened that they requested armed escorts. In all, between September 1981 and December 1982, 16.4 million women underwent sterilization by tubular ligation, and 4 million men received vasectomies.[3]

The one-child policy also posed new problems in the countryside. Since the household incentive system put a premium on family-based labor, for many rural families it was more important to have several children to work on the land and care for parents in old age than to follow the state's mandate to limit reproduction so drastically. And although family-planning aids were widely available in the cities, these were less easily obtainable in the countryside. Furthermore, the breakup of the hierarchically integrated agricultural production system of teams, brigades, and communes made the state's implementation of its population-control measures much harder to achieve.

To enforce the one-child limit, the state introduced severe penalties for families who violated it. Whereas couples with only one child received special economic, educational, and housing benefits, those with several children were fined and denied housing and education for the "extra" children. In many tragic instances, desperate families resorted to female infanticide. The state harshly condemned this practice, but the very harshness of the critique hinted at the scale of the problem, believed by some Western analysts of Chinese demographic data to be around 200,000 female babies a year. Some parents used the newly available technique of amniocentesis to detect the gender of the fetus early in pregnancy, and then obtained an abortion if the tests showed the baby to be female. In other cases, seriously ill girls were abandoned and left to die.

Another way out of the predicament of overpopulation, some analysts might have suggested, would have been to encourage more people not to marry at all. Some women had followed this route in the late nineteenth and early twentieth centuries, when they had formed "sisterhoods" whose members lived together and shared incomes and employment opportunities. But marriage had become a nearly universal expectation for women in the PRC: figures from the 1982 census showed that less than 1 percent above age thirty were single. Marriage rates were also high for men, at more than 90 percent for those above age thirty. But with a male-female ratio for those in their twenties and thirties that ranged between 102–107 men to 100 women, it continued to be difficult for some men to find wives.[4]

Among the many other factors that had to be taken into careful account by Chinese planners as they pieced together a new policy of population control, perhaps five were the most important: the availability of land suitable for agriculture, the overall age profile of the population, the balance of urban and rural growth, the characteristics of the labor force, and the levels of education attained by the population. In all these areas the 1982 census figures offered new and significant details.

First, in the amount of agricultural land per capita, China compared unfavorably with many other parts of the world and had little room for imaginative maneuver. China's land area was larger than the United States' (960 million hectares* compared with 930 million) but comprised only around half as much cultivated land (99 million hectares against 186 million in the late 1970s). When this smaller area of cultivated land was combined with a vastly larger population, the resulting per capita amount of cultivated land stood at only 0.25 acres for China, compared to 2.10 acres for the United States. Furthermore, China's available agricultural land had been slowly shrinking since it peaked in size just before the Great Leap Forward. This was the result in part of government decisions that had disastrous effects on the country's ecology and environment—such as uncontrolled deforestation, poorly planned hydroelectric dams, and massive industrial pollution—and in part of the ongoing construction of homes, factories, roads, and rail lines. New crop strains, more intensive and efficient land use, irrigation, and chemical fertilizer could offset this loss to some extent. The shrinkage of the land available for agriculture, however, was alarming and meant that new incentives would have to be successful in boosting productivity.

Second, the overall age profile of the population was rising rapidly with the eradication or effective control of infectious and parasitic diseases. By 1982, over 63 percent of the deaths in China's cities came from strokes, heart disease, or cancer, and the same three causes accounted for 53 percent of all deaths in the countryside. Partly because of these changes in disease patterns, by 1981 the life expectancy for men was sixty-nine in the cities and sixty-five and a half in the countryside; for women life expectancy was seventy-two and a half in the cities and sixty-eight and a half in the country. (The comparable figures for 1957 had been sixty-three and a half and fifty-nine and a quarter for men, and sixty-three and fifty-nine and three-quarters for women.)

In the third area, the urban/rural balance, it was clear that the population was gradually becoming more urban. The process had been slower than in

---

* A hectare is a unit of land measurement equivalent to 2.47 acres.

many other developing nations because of effective control over mobility through the hukou system, and the compulsory dispatching of millions of urban young (as well as "rightist" intellectuals and disgraced cadres) to the countryside. But considering the population size, the shift in urban/rural composition was still drastic. In 1949, 10.6 percent of the population had lived in cities. By 1983, that figure had increased to 23.5 percent.[5]

For many—perhaps the majority—of peasants, the dismantling of the communes and the establishment of a contract system operating at the household level brought new freedom and new profits. But the changes were not universally welcomed. Those who had thrived in the collective structure of the communes and production brigades, who believed the political rationalization for that form of social and economic organization to be convincing, and who considered the communes the main benefit brought by China's long and bloody revolution, now found that they had to go into contract farming with their families (or on their own if they had no families). With production brigades no longer guaranteeing a minimum grain allowance, those who could commute to nearby market towns often did so to earn a basic wage, leaving agricultural work to women, children, or the elderly. Within this overall picture, the 1982 census highlighted regional disparities. It showed, for example, that around six times more infants died before the age of four in certain poor areas than in the large cities, with their superior healthcare facilities.

In the fourth vital area, labor, there were also challenging circumstances to be confronted. Compared with workers in Japan or the United States, China's workers started young and retired early. According to the 1982 census, 18 percent of the workforce fell within the fifteen-to-nineteen-year-old age bracket. (By contrast, 3.25 percent of Japanese workers and 8 percent of American workers were in this category.) Within the 1982 Chinese workforce of 521.5 million, 56.3 percent were men and 43.7 percent were women. Men were heavily concentrated in such manual trades as construction (81.13 percent male) and in mining and lumber work (80.64 percent male). Despite the claims of gender equality, men held about 80 percent of the positions in government, party, and mass organizations; of those held by women, the majority were at the lower end of the spectrum. There was near gender parity in the catering trades, commerce, public-utilities work, and neighborhood services, as there was in agricultural work.

The census also documented low levels of education in the overall labor force, which came as a shock to many observers, especially to those who had believed the emphatic claims that illiteracy had been virtually eliminated in the PRC. Less than 1 percent of the workforce had college degrees,

10.54 percent a high school education, and 26 percent a junior-middle-school education; 34.38 percent had stopped their education after primary school, and 28.2 percent were classified as "illiterates or semi-illiterates." As the census computers teased out these various figures, making different types of analysis possible, China's leaders may have accepted with equanimity that nearly three-fourths of the nation's peasants had still not progressed beyond primary school. More unsettling, certainly, must have been the finding that 27 percent of bureaucratic and party cadres had never progressed past primary school, and about 43 percent had ended their education at the junior-middle-school level. That left only 22 percent who had received a high school education, and 6 percent with some kind of college degree. Such figures would have been irrelevant in the days of guerrilla warfare, or in the early stages of land reform, the Great Leap, and the Cultural Revolution. But in the context of new ambitions for achieving the Four Modernizations, the clear indicators of inadequate education could not but appear daunting.

GOVERNING CHINA IN THE 1980s

By the late 1980s, the government of the PRC faced the task of controlling 1 billion people, handling foreign contracts worth several billion yuan, completely restructuring its economy, and improving its schools and universities to make them places where intellectual and scientific research could flourish. But the governance system in place was a sprawling one, full of overlaps and inconsistencies, and not necessarily equipped to meet these challenges. Furthermore, the PRC government had been shaken to the core several times in its short life. The Great Leap Forward and the Cultural Revolution had been the most dramatic examples, but other events had also shown how deeply divided the leaders were over fundamental political, economic, and intellectual issues: the antirightist campaign of 1957, the arguments in the Socialist Education Campaign of 1964, Lin Biao's death in 1971, the purge of Deng Xiaoping and arrest of the Gang of Four in 1976, the dramatic policy turn-arounds of the Third Plenum in 1978. The bitterness of the arguments on these occasions, the dismissals, arrests, and deaths, emphasized the extent to which the PRC was a government above the law, a one-party state that allowed no public or impartial forum for the airing of grievances and no effective mechanisms for the peaceful transition of power. It is worth looking at the shape of this government during the early to mid-1980s to see how countervailing sources of power made it hard for any individual leader to implement particular reforms or projects in a timely fashion.

At its summit, China was run by a shifting group of between twenty-five and thirty-five people, of whom all but one were men.* This ruling group was not formally acknowledged as such, and its members could not necessarily be identified by office or titular rank. One had to be moderately familiar with Chinese politics to know who was in this circle.[6] Within this ruling group were four categories. One category consisted of four or five party elders with vaunted experience and prestige, such that even if they held no substantive office their advice was generally heeded.[†] Their contacts with other senior party and military comrades were essential to the implementation of most key decisions. The second category consisted of the figure identified as the preeminent leader, whose views could never be ignored even if they might not always be followed. From 1978 onward, this person was Deng Xiaoping. Even if Deng had twice been purged and publicly vilified (in 1966 and 1976), his revolutionary credentials were impeccable. Furthermore, his long years of service as secretary-general of the CCP, and subsequently as chairman of the Military Affairs Commission, had enabled him to develop an extensive network of friends and colleagues who were permanently in his debt.

The third category of the ruling group comprised specialists whose areas of expertise were essential to effective decision-making; the most important of these were the economy, the energy sector, the military, and propaganda and internal security. These leaders might be members of the Standing Committee of the Politburo, the premier or one of the vice premiers of the State Council, heads of the PLA or other armed services, or heads of important ministries or commissions. The same offices provided bases for those in the fourth category of the ruling group: the generalists, whose broad-based political experience made them adept at long-range policy planning that could cut across special-interest lines. Prominent in this group by the mid-1980s were Zhao Ziyang, Hu Yaobang, and a younger man—Li Peng—who was in charge of energy policy.

The immense range of problems that these leaders had to address meant that they could not handle them on their own, as had been more possible in the days of Yan'an or the civil war, and to some extent in the simpler economic and technical universe of the 1950s. Thus by the 1980s, the ruling group relied on networks of research institutes and experts, and on four institutions that

---

* The lone woman to be in or on the edge of this inner circle was Qian Zhengying, appointed minister of water resources and electric power in 1982. Born in 1922, Qian had studied engineering in college and served with the New Fourth Army in World War II. She subsequently rose swiftly in the energy bureaucracy.

† In the early 1980s this group included Li Xiannian, Peng Zhen, Chen Yun, and Ye Jianying.

worked closely with the leaders and their staffs to evaluate and coordinate national policy: the State Planning Commission, the State Economic Commission, the State Science and Technology Commission, and the Ministry of Finance. Plans approved by the leaders and their staffs, and deemed feasible by the commissions and fundable by the Ministry of Finance, would be passed to the thirty-eight regular-line ministries in Beijing for discussion and implementation. Each of these ministries had its special area of expertise, its own staff and budget. Since these ministries were considered equal in rank to the individual provinces, no ministry could simply impose its will on a given province. To carry out "national policy," a ministry had to negotiate carefully with the province that was affected by, or expected to contribute to, that policy decision.

The provincial governments had their own structures and their own priorities, which did not necessarily align with the structures and priorities of Beijing. Provincial political life was directed by three officials: the first party secretary, the governor, and the ranking PLA officer. The party secretary oversaw ideological work, mass campaigns, rural policies, and personnel assignments; the governor supervised education and economic development; the PLA officer controlled military affairs, many aspects of internal security, as well as various economic endeavors (factories, mines, communications) linked to the PLA.[7] The balance of power among the three top officials varied from province to province according to whether the party, government, or military leader was the predominant personality or had the strongest networks in the capital.

The three provincial leaders each had their own staff and bureaucracy, with descending levels of command from cities to counties and communes or townships. At the base of the structure every working person was registered in a work unit—the *danwei*—whether that be a factory, rural production brigade, hospital, school, or office. Danwei leaders had immense power over their members, since their approval was needed for job assignments, educational opportunities, travel at home or abroad, or permission to marry and to have a child. Students were registered by household and by school affiliation.

Demographic factors, personal interests, long-term relationships, and local contacts all played an important part in this complex pull of forces between central and provincial power. Some provinces were more populous than others— by the mid-1980s the leaders were Sichuan with 100 million people, Henan and Shandong each with 75 million, and Jiangsu and Guangdong each with just over 60 million—and had greater claims to central government attention. Some had crucial reserves of raw materials that brought entire sub-bureaus of the three national commissions or the ministries into their provincial capitals. Some members of the central ruling group had strong attachments to their native provinces and could be expected to edge favors their way.

What these arrangements meant in practice can be seen through three examples of the 1980s, in coal mining, dam building, and oil production, each important to the long-term growth of the national economy and of the region concerned. In Shanxi province, where Deng Xiaoping had personally expressed an interest in using foreign technology to develop open-pit mines, the central government could not simply enforce its will over coal production. Mines in the province fell into three administrative categories, each subdivided into further classifications, and all with their own bureaucracies, supervisors, and workers. The Ministry of Coal operated seven large mines, while the Shanxi Local Coal Management Bureau supervised 209 smaller operations, which were organized into five subgroups distinguished by their type of management. One subgroup was jointly managed by municipal or county governments and shipped all its coal out of the province. One subgroup was locally managed and kept most of its production for use in Shanxi. A third subgroup was jointly managed by the relevant communes and by the Shanxi Number Two Light Industry Department. A fourth group was comanaged by the Provincial Labor Reform Bureau using convict labor. The fifth subgroup was coadministered by the PLA, with its output allocated to military needs. Townships operated a further 3,000 small mines, with production coordinated by yet another agency, the Shanxi Township Enterprise Management Bureau. Cutting across all these divisions were the national, provincial, and municipal bureaus that supervised transportation of the coal and determined its allocation. A central decision to reallocate coal or open a new mine was thus not a simple act. Although Deng Xiaoping finally succeeded in getting the mines he wanted, it took years of bargaining and trade-offs.[8]

These tensions between the center and the provinces, and within the hierarchy of each province, could have a paralyzing effect on state planning. Navigating the planning process often meant running through a maze of channels before reaching the localities. Though first discussed in the mid-1950s, one of the greatest projects ever envisioned in China, the Three Gorges Dam on the upper Yangzi River, was still under process of evaluation through the decade of the 1980s (and construction only at last began in 1995). The dam was designed to end the flooding that had plagued China for millennia—the most recent catastrophe had been in 1870, with serious floods occurring in 1931, 1935, 1949, and 1954—and to increase national hydroelectric power by an annual 64.9 billion kwh. But the dam was controversial for its ecological and scenic impact, and because of the potential for disaster for cities lower down the river, should the dam be breached.

In the 1980s, as thirty years of inconclusive debate continued concerning the feasibility of the dam, its exact location and height, and the desired depth of the water level above the dam, the following actors were involved: the

Yangzi Valley Planning Office (with a staff of 12,000 as of 1985); numerous ministries (particularly Finance, Water Resources and Electric Power, Electronics, Communications, and Machine Building); members of the central ruling group, their staffs, and the key commissions in Beijing; the governments of all the affected provinces along the river, from Sichuan to Jiangsu, along with the independent municipality of Shanghai; Chongqing city; all the major towns between the potential dam sites and Chongqing that might either be flooded or chosen as sites for the relocation of people displaced from other areas; fifty-eight units and factories that specialized in relevant research, design, and construction; eleven research institutes and universities; and numerous consultants and entrepreneurs from the United States, Japan, and other countries.[9]

Only slightly less complicated were the bureaucratic structures responsible for developing China's offshore oil resources in the southeast, involving as they did the same central commissions, a range of key ministries, the Bank of China, and the China National Offshore Oil Corporation (founded in 1982 as an offshoot of the Ministry of Petroleum Industries). This corporation spawned a host of subsidiary organizations up and down the east coast to coordinate its work with foreign firms and with scores of local municipalities. Virtually anyone at any point in these intermeshing networks could stall or block plans considered crucial by someone else. For officials, frustration levels ran high, as did the possibilities for enormous profits and graft.

The rulers of the Qing dynasty had struggled for two centuries of their rule to streamline bureaucratic procedures, supervise officials, subordinate the provinces to the center, and defuse the social discontents caused by corrupt behavior. Under the Guomindang, the battle was even harder as the bureaucracy grew and the central government weakened, contributing to dishonesty, malaise, and inefficiencies. The PRC leadership, having tried to dissociate itself completely from such past abuses, now found that even the most advanced levels of technological planning were subject to the same tenacious tugs of localism and human frailty.

THE PROBLEMS OF PROSPERITY, 1983–1984

By 1982 the idea that it might be permissible to criticize Mao Zedong—first broached at the time of the Third Plenum—had become generally accepted. The consensus was that he had been a great leader during the formative years of the revolution, but that from the Great Leap onward his policies had been erratic and at times destructive. The stockpiles of Mao's works now languished in the corners of bookstores, largely unread, while slowly around the country his portrait came down from walls and public places. Many concrete statues of his coat-draped form, one arm raised in salute, that had dominated urban landscapes and public squares were removed. The spirit of Dazhai, publicly denigrated in 1980 by a *People's Daily* article that described the brigade's economic projects as "folly," was laid to rest when its leader Chen Yonggui lost the last of his posts and his Politburo seat in 1981. And the PLA's revolutionary model-hero, the selfless Lei Feng, after a brief and unconvincing resurrection in the early 1980s also passed once more from the scene.

With these once potent symbols of revolutionary dedication now deprived of their power, economic growth became the prime focus of attention, with only its speed and intensity subject to debate. Following the first boom of economic optimism in 1979 and the large trade deficit that resulted in 1980, the years 1981 and 1982 marked a period of cautious development, the course favored by the party elder Chen Yun. Investments were cut back, many costly foreign contracts canceled, the domestic budget trimmed, and the trade deficit overcome by vigorous export policies. The PRC announced a trade surplus of 6.2 billion yuan in 1982, and 5.2 billion yuan in 1983.

In culture and the arts, there was a political backlash against the burst of innovation and excitement that had been sparked in part by foreign movies and exhibitions of Western abstract painting, and in part by the kind of critical self-exploration that had appeared in the days of Democracy Wall. By 1982 the configurations of a new campaign were clear, which took the form of a blanket condemnation of "spiritual pollution," a term designed to suggest the extent of the damage wrought by decadent influences. The sentimental love songs of Deng Lijun, the Taiwanese pop star known as Teresa Deng, were singled out for censure and banned for being "pornographic." Popular sayings punning on the singer's name and indicative of her appeal were alarming to party leaders, such as "We want Little Deng [Deng Lijun] not Old Deng [Deng Xiaoping]" or "We listen to Old Deng during the day and listen to Little Deng at night." The campaign against spiritual pollution dismayed intellectuals and investors, both inside China and abroad, because it reinforced the view that the CCP intended to exercise control over the lives of its citizens in still significant ways. Coming at a time when thousands of Westerners were traveling to China and in many cases living there for long periods to conduct business, work in joint ventures, do research, or teach, the campaign dampened enthusiasm for China and optimism about its interactions with the world.

At the same time, overlapping the "anti–spiritual pollution" campaign was a new phase of reform that intended to implement more fully the range of ideas sketched out at the Third Plenum of 1978, to shake up the whole economy, and to dismantle the collective system that had dominated economic life for almost thirty years. A New Year's Day editorial published in *People's Daily* in 1983 set the tone with the promise that this would prove a significant year in the modernization program. The national priorities would be completing "structural reforms . . . to improve Party work style" at the provincial, prefectural, and city levels, and maintaining economic development at a level equal to 1981. While Premier Zhao Ziyang called for deeper economic change, other party leaders pushed for the rapid promotion of younger cadres, urging that those with college education or professional training be given leading provincial positions in both the CCP and the government. In doing so, they were following the wishes of Deng Xiaoping, who at the Twelfth Party Congress of 1982 had encouraged veteran cadres to retire and set a target of selecting fifty people younger than age fifty for the Central Committee. Deng was disappointed, as only fifteen appointees met his parameters.[10] But at the regional level, provinces such as Sichuan embraced the charge. Provincial leaders reported that they dropped the average age for incumbent officials from 60.6 to 52.5, and raised the proportion of government staff with college education from 16.8 percent to 32.2 percent. In local administration, the municipalities undercut the role of the communes. Each was now declared to be the "political, economic, financial, scientific, cultural, educational and medical center of its neighboring areas," with the important feature of exercising economic leadership. As townships took the place of communes, villages supplanted production brigades. There were reports that similar initiatives were launched in Liaoning, Jiangsu, and Guangdong.

Much attention was given to local successes in attaining the Third Plenum goals of speeding up and modernizing farm work through the new rural contract system, or the "agricultural production responsibility system," as it was officially titled. By 1983 at least three variants had emerged. One was a labor-contract system under which small groups of families, a household, or an individual contracted with their local village to do specific farm work (sowing, transplanting, harvesting) to fixed levels of performance in terms of quantity, quality, and cost. Their payoff was a higher work-point allocation—meaning more cash or food—if they were successful, a lower allocation if they failed in some way. In a second variation, there was an output-contract system in which households undertook to produce a given amount of crop on a specified area; they could keep the surplus if they achieved one but had to make up the shortfall if they failed. A third variant, that of a net-output delivery system, required contracted households to meet state quotas and provide a surplus for the collective. In return the contractors were granted complete freedom over production methods and what amounted to ownership over the farm implements and draft animals made available to them. By 1982, about 70 percent of production teams nationwide had adopted a version of the household responsibility system. The result was a dramatic increase in national agricultural production—from 320 million tons of grain in 1980 to 407 million tons in 1984. In combination with private markets and services, handicrafts and other sideline production, the rural economy was transformed.[11]

In industry, there were also important steps towards reforms. Enterprises now had to pay tax on revenues to the state, but they were allowed to keep half the profits that remained after deducting production costs, with the other half going to the state; previously they had passed on all profits to the state. This incentive system, it was hoped, would bolster industrial production as much as the rural incentive system had inspired peasant families. Tentative steps were taken to establish a contract system in some industries. A number of key areas were designated as experimentation centers in which factory managers alone would take responsibility for the operation of their plants. This change effectively abandoned the idea of collective leadership under party supervision that had been the basis of industrial organization since the mid-1950s. Because the experimentation centers contained most of the bases for heavy industrial production in the heartland—including Dalian and Shenyang, Beijing, Tianjin, and Shanghai—it was clear that these reforms were going to become standard. Other directives from the State Council gave managers some power to appoint factory heads, punish incompetent workers by dismissal, and reward outstanding contributors with promotions or bonuses.

When Liu Binyan in 1979 had electrified his readers by revealing the crooked ways of the "coal queen" Wang Shouxin, he had presented the scandal as emblematic of the Cultural Revolution's corrosive effects. But in the 1980s, with Wang Shouxin dead from a firing squad's bullets and the Gang of Four behind bars, the crimes continued and grew in scope and audacity. New patterns of corruption emerged, as administrative controls over the economy were loosened and the pursuit of profits was sanctioned, but auditing and legal mechanisms were not in place to restrain illegal behavior. Officials who controlled access to scarce resources or had the authority to approve new economic activities used their influence to enrich themselves, their families, and friends. This included those in charge of customs, tax collection, safety inspection, land use, housing, loans, and utilities. Corruption was a capacious category that could range from accepting gifts in exchange for favors to brazen acts of fraud. Moreover, with a sizeable gray zone of gifts and favors that were considered customary, it is difficult to gauge the extent of corrupt practices with any precision. But we know that in Guangdong province more than 1,000 people were executed in 1982–1983 for various kinds of economic crimes, and some 45,000 cases of bribery, smuggling, speculation, and embezzlement were reported nationwide in 1983 and 1984.

The most egregious case to come to light was the scheme perpetrated in 1984–1985 in Hainan, the SEZ linked to Guangdong province. Local officials, initially authorized to import vans for use on the island, quickly realized that they could make enormous profits by reselling the vehicles to work units not permitted to purchase foreign goods. The scheme soon proliferated and eventually tallied 89,000 motor vehicles, 2.9 million television sets, 252,000 video recorders, and 122,000 motorcycles. From January 1984 to March 1985, the fraudulent schemes involved sums in excess of U.S.$1.5 billion.

A hundred-person team sent from Beijing spent two months tracking down the purchases and the profiteering. The investigators concluded that Hainan officials found willing buyers all over the country, in twenty-seven out of twenty-nine provinces and metropolitan areas. But the misconduct was concentrated in Guangdong, where 872 companies and 88 departments in the regional government participated, including schools and kindergartens. At least U.S.$700 million of the money was unrecoverable, and hundreds of Japanese trucks and cars rusted in Hainan's sea air as the probe continued. There were indications of disagreements among the central leadership about how to handle this scandal, which had received national and international attention. In the end, the principal offenders were treated leniently, with demotions for "serious mistakes" but no further punishments. Many of the confiscated cars that remained in good condition were subsequently shipped to Beijing and sold by other officials.[12]

Among the CCP leadership, some saw dangerous signs here. The revelations of such widespread corruption gave strong ammunition to critics of the drive to open up the economy. But the secretary-general of the CCP, Hu Yaobang, was unruffled. As he succinctly put it in a briefing to party cadres during an inspection tour of Henan and Hubei, "Do not fear prosperity."[13] Against those who urged a slower pace or even retreat from the path of reform, Deng Xiaoping declared, "Our policy is to let some people and some regions get rich first." Deng believed that in time his new vision of socialism would eliminate poverty and bring prosperity to all. But in the short term the radical equality upon which the CCP had staked its revolutionary legitimacy would no longer be the moving force of social transformation.

REBUILDING THE LAW

The various shifts in the implementation of reform did not end with the bold decisions of 1984. The policies led to such overheating of the economy, combined with serious problems of unemployment, inflation, and renewed trade deficits, that the more cautious faction of leaders demanded a second period of retrenchment in 1985 (matching that of 1981–1983). This lull was brief, however, and in 1986 those seeking speedy change returned to the attack: price controls were dropped from a range of manufactured goods, experimentation with labor-incentive systems was again encouraged, more rural production came into the hands of family contracting units, the need to allow open markets for raw materials was debated, and some state or collective enterprises were leased to individual entrepreneurs or groups of workers. In some cases, these enterprises raised funds by floating stock issues and forming their own boards of directors, and in Shanghai a small stock exchange was established.

But whether the pace of change sped up or slowed down, one fact was inescapable: the Chinese government had now entered a world where law, in all its manifold complexities, would have to be studied, understood, and practiced. There were so many facets to this problem that it defied simple solution. By looking briefly at four areas—the training of lawyers, the nature of tax law, the enforcement of family law, and the study of international law—we can get a general sense of what this major adjustment entailed.

An essential preliminary step in developing and implementing a legal code was the training of lawyers. This offered special challenges, since the growth of legal expertise in the later years of Guomindang rule had effectively ceased after the Communist victory of 1949, when all private practice of law was banned and the application of legal expertise limited to those in certain government ministries and within the state-controlled judiciary. At the time of the Hundred Flowers movement there were some 800 "legal adviser's offices" with 2,500 full-time and 300 part-time lawyers. Most of these skilled practitioners were dismissed during the antirightist campaign of 1957, and in 1959 the Ministry of Justice was abolished altogether. Though some law schools remained open, they had few students and concentrated on political rather than professional legal training. In serious criminal cases the "law," such as it was, was handled by a system of state courts and state prosecutors. In national security matters the Ministry of Public Security was in control, and for party members who transgressed there was a separate system of review and punishment meted out by the provincial party committee structure. Most of what might be called civil cases were handled at the local city-ward or rural-brigade level by mediators. Early in the Cultural Revolution the few remaining law schools were closed, their libraries dispersed or destroyed, and their faculty sent to the countryside.

This situation lasted just over ten years, until 1979, when the government began to rebuild the legal system. Law schools were reopened, legal personnel were rehabilitated, the Ministry of Justice was reestablished, and the system of state courts was revamped. Regulations stipulating that "counterrevolutionaries and antisocialist reactionaries" could be sent to labor camps without trial, however, showed the continuing party control of this system. By 1982 there were 5,500 full-time and 1,300 part-time lawyers once again working. To bring more personnel into the legal profession, an ingenious linkage was made with the PLA, which the government was currently trying to cut back in size. The Ministry of Justice announced in 1982 that 57,000 "outstanding army officers" were being transferred to the civilian sector and given legal training, prior to being assigned to the court system or public security departments. And in emulation of the "barefoot doctors" charged with extending the range of the medical profession, 200,000 "judicial workers" with some government experience were assigned to the legal system.

By 1982, twenty universities and institutes were offering some form of four-year undergraduate legal training to 2,000 enrolled students. To become lawyers, these students had to complete their course work, prove that they "cherished the PRC and supported the socialist system," serve at least a two-year apprenticeship, and pass a bar examination. One hundred other colleges and the Ministry of Justice offered legal training by correspondence or on a part-time basis. Despite the politicization of the entrance exams, once admitted to law programs the students gained a good general grounding. Most of their teachers were survivors from a much older generation, many of them trained in Europe, Japan, the United States, or the Soviet Union, and they offered in each school a core curriculum of Chinese constitutional law, legal theory and jurisprudence, and civil and criminal law.

Special areas of the law rapidly assumed importance and reinforced the complexity of changes in the economy and in society. One was tax law, now crucial since under the reform guidelines bonuses and certain types of profits were to be taxed, as were profits from foreign joint ventures and wholly foreign-owned enterprises. The PRC's first income-tax laws, enacted in 1980, excluded most Chinese individuals by allowing a deduction of 800 yuan a month, when incomes rarely reached above 50 yuan for city workers and around 15 yuan in the countryside. The early tax laws were directed largely at foreign residents in China and perhaps specifically Americans, since the details of the code closely followed Internal Revenue Service regulations. In 1983, a corporate tax law was introduced, stipulating a graduated scale topping at 55 percent for businesses that made more than 200,000 yuan in profit. With more than 4.2 million domestic enterprises subject to taxation, the government had to create a new bureaucracy capable of collection and enforcement—and do so quickly. Tax collectors, never popular, received a hostile reception, while evasion and fraud were reportedly widespread.[14] There followed a roiling debate on the implementation of a national-enterprise bankruptcy law. Economic reformers were keen to develop a legal mechanism for shuttering hopelessly unprofitable state-owned enterprises—nearly

25 percent were reportedly losing money in 1985, many of them mired in debt. The reformers, however, could not easily overcome the objections of those apprehensive of the social turmoil that could result from laying off millions of workers, as well as the incongruity of "bankruptcy" in an allegedly socialist society. After six months of arguments, a provisional bankruptcy law was finally approved in December 1986.[15]

Another area of emerging complexity was that of marriage and inheritance law. The 1980 Marriage Law reiterated rights and protections for women, but in fact they were frequently violated. The sale of women and girls into marriage, and various forms of "bride price" and betrothal gifts, remained common practices in many areas of the country. Legal disputes frequently arose over broken marriage contracts, and the amounts concerned were large considering the current incomes. Betrothal gifts, for instance, could run from 1,000 up to 5,000 yuan, or include demands for coveted consumer items such as watches, appliances, and furniture. In one case a bride's family had demanded from the groom a 125-yuan watch, 19 *jin* (a *jin* being 1.3 pounds) of husked rice, 19 ducks, 109 *jin* each of pork, eggs, and oranges, and 1,900 yuan in cash. (The prevalence of the auspicious number 9 here seems to hark back to earlier geomantic ideas of good fortune as well as to the merely mercenary.) These changes in gift patterns showed how the reciprocal dowry structure of the once parentally dominated joint family had been replaced by the financial imperatives of the conjugal family unit.[16]

A major change introduced in the 1980 legislation involved the criteria for divorce and produced complex social consequences. The provision in the previous marriage law of 1950 had stipulated that either spouse could request marital dissolution. Mutual consent divorces were registered with the district people's government, while unilateral requests were subjected to several rounds of mediation. In practice, however, there had to be "legitimate reasons" to support divorce petitions, and these were usually political ones. In the 1960s and 1970s, divorces were granted primarily in cases where a husband or wife had been condemned as an "antirightist" or a "counterrevolutionary." The new legislation, implemented in 1981, inserted a clause stipulating the "breakdown of mutual affection" as grounds for divorce. In implying that the absence of love constituted an acceptable justification for ending a marriage, the law also signaled that the government's divorce policy would be more permissive.

The door thus opened to a flood of divorce cases, initially from those who felt long trapped in unhappy marriages, or former sent-down youths who had married in the countryside and now wished to leave those spouses and return to the cities of their origin. Within a few years of the new legislation's passage, animated public discussions in a burgeoning popular press indicated that extramarital affairs, domestic abuse, and the euphemistic category "failure to deliver marital goods" (referring to sexual impotence, infertility, or broken promises to provide household furnishings) were routinely cited as reasons for marital breakdown. Depending on particular circumstances, women benefitted from or were victimized by the changing landscape of divorce. For some, leaving a marriage meant escaping an abusive husband or gaining the freedom to seek love and companionship. For others, divorce meant losing custody of a child or children, or confronting significant social stigma as divorced women. (In the 1980s, the stigma was much more damaging for women than for men.)[17]

Overall, the incidence of divorce increased dramatically through the 1980s. By one count the number of divorce court cases nearly doubled in the first two years of the law's implementation, from 187,000 in 1981 to 370,000 in 1983. In addition to the verdicts issued by the courts—about 500,000 in 1985—the civil affairs department handled another 200,000 divorces a year.[18]

As during the first marriage law's implementation in the early 1950s, there was a discernible trend of women initiating divorce in the 1980s. The new legislation renewed protections for divorced women making legal claims for the joint property once shared in marriage. Divorcing couples who together had contracted out for farmland or orchards under the new economic system had to subdivide them in some way that would not affect their financial obligations to the state. The prosperity brought about by the economic reforms and the dismantling of the communes increased the stakes over property. Similarly, in families that adhered to the one-child policy, the fights over child custody became extraordinarily bitter. As they grew in numbers and intensity, divorce cases were handled in a variety of ways that included formal court judgments, the use of legal advisers or mediators, or the application of pressure by families and work units. To handle the increasing caseload, the government pledged to train more lawyers, with the state goal of 50,000 by 1990.

One other area of Chinese jurisprudence, international law, underwent significant changes in the 1980s once it was identified as a priority area of study. In September 1979 Beijing University admitted thirty students as undergraduate majors in international law—the first such program in the nation. Scholarly works proliferated swiftly. The publication of a definitive textbook of international law in 1981, with contributions from twenty Chinese jurists, gave direction to the development of the field as a whole.[19] Beijing officials also invited numerous foreign legal experts to visit China and help them analyze international procedures, as in the case of deliberations over the enterprise bankruptcy law. In the international arena, a significant symbol of the departure from Maoist ideological principles was the election of a Chinese delegate, Ni Zhengyu, to the International Court of Justice at The Hague.

Ni, a pre–World War II graduate of Stanford University Law School, was seventy-five at the time of his election; his acceptance of the honor—and the dedicated work he performed on the court—signaled China's return to the international world order. In the United Nations General Assembly, the PRC tended to vote with the Soviet Union and a majority of the Third World countries, despite Beijing's ongoing rhetoric of hostility toward Moscow.

Another striking example of China's new international status was the accord it reached with Great Britain over Hong Kong. During 1983 and 1984 the PRC government negotiated firmly and tenaciously to fix the future status of the British colony, that "barren and uninhabited rock," the seizure of which in 1840 had been reluctantly ratified by the Qing in the Treaty of Nanjing two years later. In 1898 the British had bolstered the colony's strength by "leasing" for ninety-nine years an area of the Chinese mainland adjacent to Hong Kong Island known as the New Territories. When early in the 1980s the British raised questions about the future status of the colony, the PRC government made it clear that the lease on the New Territories, set to expire in 1997, would not be renewed. Knowing Hong Kong was not defensible militarily, the British decided they had little choice but to also return Hong Kong Island by the same date.

The freewheeling economy of Hong Kong made it difficult to see exactly how it would fit into the PRC's evolving system. Both the British and the Chinese stalled on that question and the Hong Kong Chinese, who had only minimal electoral representation in the colony's government, were barely consulted. The agreement, signed in Beijing on September 26, 1984, stipulated that sovereignty over Hong Kong would revert to the PRC on July 1, 1997. For fifty years after that date the former colony would be a "special administrative region" with a capitalist economy under the formula "one country, two systems." Beijing would control foreign and defense policy, but the island would be largely autonomous economically, continuing as a free port and world financial center. Its residents would not pay taxes to the PRC, and English would remain the official language during that fifty-year period.

Two clauses in the agreement attempted to reassure Hong Kong's residents that their rights would be protected. Clause 3 stated that "the laws currently in force in Hong Kong will remain basically unchanged." Clause 5 was even more sweeping:

> The current social and economic systems in Hong Kong will remain unchanged, and so will the life-style. Rights and freedoms, including those of the person, of speech, of the press, of assembly, of association, of travel, of movement, of correspondence, of strike, of choice of occupation, of academic research and of religious belief will be ensured by law in the Hong Kong Special Administrative Region.[20]

These were the same "rights" that the PRC government had guaranteed to its own subjects in its various constitutions, and yet had consistently withheld. It remained to be seen if the CCP had now reconsidered the meaning of law so thoroughly that it might be willing to protect such freedoms, or whether it would continue, as it had done since 1949, to disregard laws when they did not suit its purposes.

CHAPTER 26

Testing the Limits

DEMOCRACY'S CHORUS

Initially almost forgotten in the race for new entrepreneurial arrangements in the countryside were the millions of urban youths sent to rural areas over the previous decades, who had not been permitted to return home. Some had been radical Maoists and had found meaning in the commune system; with the demise of collective agriculture, they were now simply exiles from their homes and families. In April 1985, hundreds of people who had gone as youngsters to Shaanxi to serve the revolution returned to Beijing illegally. Defying the ban on such activities, they staged a sit-in on the steps of the CCP headquarters and appealed to Deng Xiaoping to hear their case. They were not seriously harassed by police but received no clear answers to their request to be allowed to return to the capital. The petitioners claimed to speak for 20,000 such "urban exiles"; over 400,000 people had been sent to Shaanxi in all. The situation presented the government with a knotty problem, especially given that the waiting list for even minimal housing in Beijing was already several years long.

Other public protests in 1985 were fueled by economic frustrations and social problems. In May a soccer riot broke out in Beijing after the Hong Kong team defeated the PRC team in a World Cup qualifying match. Angry youths smashed up the stadium, burned cars and buses, and turned their ire on foreigners with glass bottles and bricks. Thirty police officers were injured, and more than a hundred people were arrested. Near year's end in 1985, when it appeared that other student groups were preparing protest demonstrations, the government announced its own rallies for December 9, apparently to pre-empt any flare-up of hostility similar to that staged by the December Ninthers against Chiang Kai-shek exactly fifty years before. But such games had to be

545

*In a small city in Xinjiang province, a
Uyghur woman reflects in front of an
educational mural, 1985.*

played with caution. The last thing
that Deng or the other veterans
of the Cultural Revolution purges
wanted was a new wave of youthful
violence that would pit one wing of
an uncontrollable mass movement
against another. They had already
seen where that could lead.

Although Deng calculated correctly on this occasion and there were
no large antigovernment demonstrations on December 9, a few days later
between 10,000 and 15,000 Uyghur
university students demonstrated in
downtown Urumchi, the provincial
capital of Xinjiang. Their long list of
grievances included inequalities in
educational opportunities for ethnic
minorities and coercive family planning policies; they demanded true
autonomy for Xinjiang, a stop to atmospheric nuclear testing, and measures to
protect the environment. The action spread to other cities, with several hundred
Uyghur students turning out in Beijing and Shanghai. In Urumchi, party officials met with student representatives but dismissed their demands. The students were told to stop making trouble and go back to school.[1]

The general malaise continued to grow. It was becoming clear that millions of people—students especially, but also many of their teachers and
growing numbers of unemployed youth—found it difficult to get their bear-
ings in the shifting landscape or to see where they were going. Many now
began to express their bafflement and discontent in stories, plays, rock lyrics,
poems, paintings, cartoons, and films, some of which were censored by party
officials but most of which circulated with greater freedom than had been
allowed at any time since 1949. Some, like the authors of the "Not-Not Manifesto," proclaimed in Chengdu, Sichuan, on May 4, 1986, saw current politics
as absurd, and responded with imagery and logic that seemed to be drawn
in part from Daoism and in part from the Western Dadaist movement of
the 1920s.

> Not-Not: a blanket term covering the object, form, contents, methodology, process, way
> and result of the principles of Pre-cultural Thought. It is also the description of the pri-
> mordial mien of the universe. Not-Not is not "no."

    After deconstructing the relationship between man and objects to their pre-cultural state, there is nothing in this universe that is not Not-Not.

    Not-Not is not the negation of anything. It is only an expression of itself. Not-Not is aware that liberation exists in the indefinite.[2]

Writing from Xi'an in Shaanxi, the poet Li Shan presented the country he called "Endland" as a sad place:

> Ants mawing hair and nails
> Bringing rotten news from below ground . . .[3]

A dark view of Chinese culture as a whole was provided by a provocative pamphlet that began circulating in 1986. This was *The Ugly Chinaman*, written in 1984 by a Taiwan-Chinese author using the pseudonym Bo Yang. That this sardonic work could circulate at all in the PRC was surprising, since Bo Yang attacked the Chinese for their failures and self-inflicted degradations with an energy and bitterness that recalled Zou Rong's *The Revolutionary Army* of the late Qing, or Lu Xun's biting essays of the 1930s. "What makes the Chinese people so cruel and base?" asked Bo Yang. "What makes the Chinese people so prone to self-inflation?" His answers were harsh:

> Narrowmindedness and a lack of altruism can produce an unbalanced personality which constantly wavers between two extremes: a chronic feeling of inferiority, and extreme arrogance. In his inferiority, a Chinese person is a slave; in his arrogance, he is a tyrant. Rarely does he or she have a healthy sense of self-respect. In the inferiority mode, everyone else is better than he is, and the closer he gets to people with influence, the wider his smile becomes. Similarly, in the arrogant mode, no other human being on earth is worth the time of day. The result of these extremes is a strange animal with a split personality.[4]

Yet the despair suggested by the writings of Bo Yang, the Not-Nots, and Li Shan was not shared by all their compatriots. Despite their sufferings, the Chinese were resilient and showed an irrepressible awareness of the paradoxes of life. In one exploration of this mood, two writers traversed the country, interviewing men and women from all walks of life and transcribing their interviews from tape recorders into printed form. Though some of those interviewed asked to be protected by anonymity, their trenchant stories and views were received with fascination by readers when they appeared in small-circulation literary journals in early 1985 and in book form in 1986. Now people from all backgrounds could see how their fellow citizens reacted to the circumstances of their lives. A hair stylist at a once-fashionable beauty salon in Chongqing, for instance, gave his own inimitable view of politics:

I tell you, nobody can beat a hairdresser when it comes to spotting political changes. Take the campaign against Hu Feng. All the educated people stopped coming to get their hair done right away. They were like rats, terrified of being noticed, remembered and dragged into the case. If you ask me, that campaign was what started educated people on the downward slope. Every time there was a movement our business fell off—the anti-rightist movement, class struggle in 1962, the "four clean-ups" in 1964, and so on till the beginning of the Cultural Revolution in 1966. By then the only women's style left was bobs.[5]

A former peasant, who had survived the Great Leap famine by begging in the streets, now sold polyvinyl moldings from his hometown factory and hustled on the side. This was his view of surviving the Four Modernizations:

Tricks of the trade? Plenty! I don't rely on a notebook. If you lose it you're sunk. I keep everything in my head—what everyone else's job is, what they like eating, what they want, what I can get from them. When I go to a new place I find out what's in short supply— it's scarcity makes things valuable. Isn't that what the national economy and the people's livelihood is all about? They look after the national economy with their state plans, and I sort out the people's livelihood—food, clothes, consumer goods, entertainment.[6]

And a quietly proud mother reflected on her daily commute of two hours by bicycle in Beijing to get to and from her factory job:

None of us riders know each other, we don't talk to each other, we all ride our different ways. I think all cyclists are the same, workers, students and ordinary cadres going to work or back. I once had the idea that someone should make a film of us and show it to our children and grandchildren in twenty or thirty years' time. They should see how we raised them, cycling like this, taking our licences, ration books, grain coupons and oil coupons with us. . . . From morning till night, for the sake of the country and our families, we weave in and out of the traffic on our bikes to help modernize China.[7]

The children interviewed also responded honestly and often humorously to questions, sharing their sense of the strains and joys within their families and trying to place their lives of incessant and competitive schoolwork in the broader context of an open future. "I think a lot about traveling to the moon and other planets," as one nine-year-old boy put it. "It would be fun to go there. On the moon the gravitational force is weak, so a person can jump very high and then come down slowly. That sounds like a lot of fun." "I want to be an athlete, a runner," said a girl of thirteen. "I want to run faster; I want to get better. Also I want to study medicine. I want to become a doctor." "When I am at home all by myself," said a boy of twelve, "I imagine I can invent things. I imagine these things, but I can't really build them." "I fantasize about everything," said a fifteen-year-old boy. "My ambition is to become a high official. You probably think it's funny, but I really mean it. I want to become a high official. . . . Sometimes I fantasize that I have conversations with foreigners. I want to know all about world affairs, about U.S. politics, for example. I am interested in their presidential election."[8]

Self-doubt, cynicism, pride, and hope—each here expressed by different voices from a range of generations—found a curious unity in the mind of Fang Lizhi. Born in 1936, a brilliant student who entered Beijing University at sixteen to study astrophysics, only to be disgraced and dismissed from the party in the antirightist campaign of 1957, Fang was rehabilitated in the late 1970s and became a well-known professor. Appointed vice president of the University of Science and Technology in Hefei, the capital city of Anhui province, Fang was instrumental in reshaping the school in a new, more open mold, one that reflected his views on the fundamental premises of democracy: power had to be shared in order to prevent abuses, decisions had to be made openly, and free speech had to be protected. Thus could the university's best contribute to the nation's life and advance the Four Modernizations. Addressing students in speeches around the country, Fang singled out "unethical behavior by Party leaders" as especially to blame for "the social malaise in our country today." He elaborated on this theme, saying,

> Another cause is that over the years our propaganda about communism has been seriously flawed. In my view this propaganda's greatest problem has been that it has had far too narrow an interpretation—not only too narrow but too shallow. I, too, am a member of the Communist Party, but my dreams are not so narrow. They are of a more open society, where differences are allowed. Room must be made for the great variety of excellence that has found expression in human civilization. Our narrow propaganda seems to imply that nothing that came before us has any merit whatsoever. This is the most worthless and destructive form of propaganda. Propaganda can be used to praise Communist heroes, but it should not be used to tear down other heroes.[9]

Fang Lizhi touched a major national chord with these words. When even children were intrigued by American elections, it was not surprising that college students would be too. Deng Xiaoping, Zhao Ziyang, and others had called for "reforms" in government, but no concrete measures had been enacted to open the political system to genuine mass participation. Electoral laws, established in 1953 and modified in 1979, had set up a four-tier system of allegedly representative government. At the base were congresses in each of the communes (by 1986 these had become administrative townships) elected every two years. Above these were county congresses elected for three-year periods, followed by the five-year congresses of the twenty-nine provinces, autonomous regions, and major metropolitan areas. At the top was the National People's Congress. The party defined this system as "democracy under the leadership of centralism,"[10] and made sure that all candidates followed the CCP line. Students trying to give real force to these elections had occasionally contested seats for the commune- and township-level congresses, waging vigorous campaigns in Beijing and Changsha in 1980. But even when elected, these students were prevented from taking their seats. The CCP had effectively clamped down on such disputed elections in 1982 and again in 1984 by insisting on their proposed slates.

Party leaders who assumed they had done so again in 1986, however, miscalculated. In Hefei on December 5 and again on December 9, at least 3,000 students rallied against the manipulated elections. Their slogans and wall posters echoed the past while addressing the present: "No democratization, no modernization," and "Almost every day the newspapers talk about democracy. But where can we actually find any?"[11] At least 5,000 more marched in Wuhan that same week. News of the disturbances soon reached Beijing, where posters demanding democracy also began to appear on campuses along with others complaining about poor living conditions and low pay for graduates. The posters were removed overnight by university authorities but were replaced with new ones—and in greater numbers—on successive days. Since demonstrations and the display of unauthorized posters were forbidden after the Democracy Wall movement of 1979, these student participants faced the prospects of suspension, ruined career chances, and even imprisonment.

Undeterred, thousands of students marched in Shanghai on December 19 and 20, parading through People's Square and the "Bund," where party and government offices were housed in the imposing stone buildings built in the nineteenth century by British firms. An estimated 30,000 to 40,000 city residents joined the students. Among the banners, the most common proclaimed "Long Live Freedom" and "Give Us Democracy." The demonstrations proceeded without harassment by police, but students attempting sit-ins at municipal buildings were forcibly removed. Other protests were reported at Kunming, Chongqing, and the Shenzhen economic zone. Some students in Shanghai had prepared a manifesto, recalling in tone and content the one put forward by the May Fourth demonstrators in 1919, which the students printed on slips of paper and handed out to the crowd.

> To our countrymen:
>   Our guiding principle is to propagate democratic ideas among the people. Our slogan is to oppose bureaucracy and authoritarianism, and strive for democracy and freedom. The time has come to awaken the democratic ideas that have long been suppressed.[12]

Other posters and slogans flung their messages with a directness that raised the debate to a confrontational level:

"When will the people be in charge?"
"If you want to know what freedom is, just go and ask Wei Jingsheng."
"To hell with Marxism–Leninism–Mao Zedong Thought."[13]

Government officials prevented media coverage of the students' views. Ingeniously, the students avoided the news blackout by mailing hundreds of letters and manifestoes to friends across the country. Other students ringed the railway stations asking departing passengers to spread the word; still others assembled outside the United States consulate, shouting that their views should be heard abroad. Finally, after three days of demonstrations, the Shanghai police issued a ban on all such assemblies. The government statement tried to discredit the protest movement by blaming it on a few troublemakers, describing them as "a tiny number of people" taking advantage of "the patriotic zeal of students and their longing for democracy."[14] Despite the bans and condemnations of the authorities, fresh demonstrations broke out in Tianjin and Nanjing. And in Beijing, although threatened with arrest, thousands of students from four universities continued to protest in the bitter winter cold and in the face of large forces of police.

The meaning of the call for "democracy" was hotly debated by the students. Some saw it as a meaningless slogan; others picked up the ideas of the Hefei students and invoked the term in conscious opposition to elections with CCP-vetted slates of candidates. Students argued that these elections were mockeries of a valid political idea. Yet others saw it as the crucial second component to the call for liberation through "science and democracy" that had been at the center of the May Fourth movement.

In a chilling follow-up to the demonstrations, a number of political leaders issued condemnations of the students' behavior and demanded greater discipline and political indoctrination on campuses. University students in Beijing took to the streets through the end of December; they defied attempts by administrators to lock down the campuses and ignored warnings that their big-character posters were "illegal instruments." On January 1, several thousand students marched to Tiananmen Square intending to hold a rally there, only to find the entrances blocked by a human chain of police. Government rhetoric denouncing the demonstrators characterized them as "socialist enemy elements" and their activities as "counter-revolutionary."[15]

Thereupon the party hardliners (who could be called "conservatives" or "radicals" according to one's interpretation of their actions) moved swiftly to quash the burgeoning movement, striking at those the students found most inspirational. One of these was Fang Lizhi. The announcement of Fang's dismissal, from the CCP and from all teaching duties, assailed his political doctrines:

Fang Lizhi advocated bourgeois liberalization, defamed the party's leadership and party officials, negated the achievements of the party over the past decades, and slandered the socialist system. He also sowed discord among the party and the intellectuals, especially the young intellectuals.[16]

The second prominent victim was the writer Liu Binyan, whose exposé of corruption in "People or Monsters?" had been so influential in 1979. Liu had followed that essay with other provocative writings, including criticisms of party conservatives for obstructing reforms and failing to see the value of a loyal opposition. Such opposition was essential to a healthy nation, he argued in an incisive story entitled "A Second Kind of Loyalty." Liu's dismissal from the party on grounds of excessive sympathy to capitalism and bourgeois ideas, and of "violating party principles and discipline," was particularly ironic.

The purges of these figures at first diverted attention from the fact that the secretary-general of the CCP, Hu Yaobang, had not been seen at any public functions in January 1987. When Deng Xiaoping, in mid-January, joined in the attacks on "bourgeois liberalization" it became apparent that Hu Yaobang would be made the scapegoat for the unrest, which had spread to more than 150 universities in twenty cities. Hu's outspoken support for rapid reform and his almost open contempt of Maoist excesses had made him a controversial leader in any case. In one well-known example, Hu had told the graduates of the party training school never again to espouse the "radical leftist nonsense" of preferring "socialist weeds" to "capitalist seedlings."[17] On January 16 it was announced that Hu had "resigned" as CCP secretary-general after making "a self-criticism of his mistakes on major issues of political principles." Although he was allowed to remain a member of the Standing Committee of the Politburo, Zhao Ziyang took over Hu's duties as secretary-general on an acting basis until a full-time successor was appointed.

A few days later the government announced the creation of a new state agency whose express role was to control all press publications and oversee distribution of supplies needed in printing, including ink, paper, and presses. A number of "troublemakers" in cities where the demonstrations had taken place were identified, arrested, and given long prison sentences for "counter-revolutionary activities." In early February, the head of the CCP's propaganda department—a former protégé of Hu Yaobang—was dismissed and replaced by the deputy editor of the hardline party journal, *Red Flag*. Bowing to the times, Zhao Ziyang attacked the "pernicious" influence of Western ideas and declared that the central tasks facing China were to "increase production and practice economy" and to "combat bourgeois liberalization."

In a gesture that showed its profound disinterest in the pro-democracy demonstrators' arguments, the party once again resurrected Lei Feng as a model.

The national campaign reminded the people of the PLA soldier's spirit of self-sacrifice and spotlighted his aspiration—"I will be a screw that never rusts and will glitter anywhere I am placed." In 1987 this metaphor again made the rounds.[18] As the head of the PLA Political Department proclaimed at the "Lei Feng Spirit Forum" in March,

> The Lei Feng spirit is the Communist spirit, the spirit of serving the people wholeheartedly, and the spirit of warmly loving the Party wholeheartedly, and the spirit of warmly loving the motherland and socialism, of studying painstakingly, of waging arduous struggle, of being selfless, and of taking pleasure in helping others. . . . It is representative of the advanced ideology of the young generation and has become a vital part of the great spirit of our times.[19]

There could hardly be a sharper way of saying that the democracy demonstrators were not only not "advanced" but were running contrary to the true needs of the nation.

BROADENING THE BASE

These power shifts and countershifts seemed to suggest that Deng Xiaoping had been checked in his moves for a sustained level of rapid change. Yet an alternative hypothesis is that Deng remained an ideological conservative where party organization was concerned, and saw his role as a mediating one between the cautious forces in the party leadership and the eager prophets of reform. To hold this balance, Deng was willing to sacrifice Hu Yaobang, if necessary, but that did not mean he would not also curb the hardliners if they threatened the policy of opening up to the West and developing substantial free enterprise within the socialist economy. It was along these latter lines that Deng worked through the summer and fall of 1987.

The forum for these critical decisions on the direction of PRC policy was the CCP's thirteenth congress, which convened in Beijing on October 25, 1987. The determination to keep lines open to the West was indicated by the decision to admit Western reporters to the congress for the first time. This was more than a mere gesture. Only three weeks earlier, scenes from an uprising in Lhasa by hundreds of Tibetans protesting China's presence there had been photographed by Western journalists and circulated abroad, including footage of protestors killed by police. The Chinese government had imposed martial law in Lhasa and ordered all Western journalists out of Tibet. Party officials subsequently imposed a news embargo on the region.

Addressing the 1,936 party delegates in the Great Hall of the People on October 25, 1987, Zhao Ziyang insisted on the need to maintain market pricing for all except a few staple items. He suggested further that the CCP should slowly separate itself from the administration of government and industry, leaving leadership there in the hands of professional civil servants and managers. At a press conference the next day, the director of the Rural Policy Research Bureau announced that the government was considering allowing the peasants to buy and sell rights to the land they had contracted to work, and also to pass on such land rights as inheritances to their children.

The presence of foreign journalists at the congress ended abruptly after only two days, when they were excluded from the proceedings, suggesting the seriousness of the deliberations that were now under way following Zhao's speech and the statement on the possible sale of land rights. Rumors swept Beijing that Deng Xiaoping, now eighty-three, was battling for his vision of reform and would agree to leave the Central Committee if he felt his policies were safely in place. The November 1 announcement of Deng's resignation from the Central Committee, along with the resignations of hardliners Chen Yun and Peng Zhen seemed to confirm these rumors. Four other senior Standing Committee members also resigned. The following day Zhao Ziyang was formally elected secretary-general of the CCP.

Four new members were elected to serve with Zhao Ziyang on the Politburo Standing Committee. They represented a substantially younger age group than the retiring old guard, for though one of them was seventy, the other three were in their late fifties or early sixties. Of the four, Li Peng had the best connections.[*] A Sichuanese, born in 1928, Li had been only seven when the Guomindang killed his father. Zhou Enlai, who did not have children of his own, befriended the boy in Chongqing during 1939 and later looked after him in Yan'an. After the war, Li received advanced training in energy-related engineering in Moscow. Upon his return to China and through the 1960s, powerful figures in the energy bureaucracy groomed him for leadership and promoted him until he was named minister of electrical power in 1979. (He had survived the Cultural Revolution without harm because he was in charge of Beijing's power supply at that time.)[20] Informed observers were not surprised when Zhao Ziyang named Li Peng acting premier in late November 1987.

But Deng Xiaoping remained the preeminent leader and continued to serve as the chairman of the Military Affairs Commission, which gave him ultimate control over the PLA. Deng also arranged for the eighty-four-year-old Yang Shangkun to be named China's president. Yang had powerful

---

[*] The other three were Yao Yilin, Qiao Shi, and Hu Qili.

connections throughout the party and the army, and like Deng he was a Sichuanese whose life embodied the country's revolutionary history. He had worked in Shanghai as a young labor organizer in 1927, had studied in Moscow and been one of the "returned Bolsheviks" of 1930, and had risen through the party ranks in Yan'an and during the civil war.

With such powerful backing, Zhao Ziyang and Li Peng had an excellent chance to forge ahead with economic reforms. There was urgency to this task, since the indicators in early 1988 were not encouraging. Prices continued to rise, and production of staple food crops was declining as peasants moved to work in factories or raised more lucrative cash crops. Highly unpopular rationing of such items as pork, sugar, and eggs had to be reintroduced.

After preliminary discussions of the most pressing issues in early 1988, the party leaders decided to use the March and April sessions of the seventh National People's Congress as the forum for cementing the desired changes. These congresses had generally acted as rubber stamps for predetermined decisions; in 1988, however, the meetings became the venue for real debate and discussion. Seventy-one percent of the 1,970 delegates were newly elected, and many of them expressed independent and assertive views. In a break with precedent, delegates began to cast negative votes. This trend was started by a lawyer from Hong Kong, attending as a member of the Guangdong delegation, who objected that she could not vote on a slate of committee candidates because she had no knowledge of how they had been selected. A former resident of Taiwan, now living and working as a scientist in China, also spoke out, urging delegates not to vote for an eighty-nine-year-old candidate for a committee chairmanship. "He is too old and should be given more time for a rest," said the delegate; after a startled pause, a burst of clapping came from his fellow delegates.[21] Encouraged by these examples, more delegates began to speak up and cast negative votes—as many as 200 in the case of the vice presidential candidate Wang Zhen, who had been a hardline critic of the student demonstrators the previous year. In another departure, segments of the congress were shown on national television, allowing viewers to see that genuine debate was indeed possible. Foreign journalists were permitted to attend the main sessions and press conferences.

The most important issues before the seventh congress were presented by Li Peng. Though he sometimes hedged his statements with qualifications and calls for caution, he conveyed a strong endorsement of the ideas guiding the accelerated pace of the Four Modernizations. Most radical in its implications was the decision that constitutional protection would be given to the freedom of people to buy and sell their land-use rights or their stakes in enterprises. (Since 1985 such rights could be inherited in the case of the contractor's death, but now transfers would be much more flexible.) Also of great potential importance was Li Peng's determination that housing should be a market commodity, to be bought and sold in free markets. Li suggested that housing be treated in this regard like "refrigerators or bicycles," but such a parallel understated the significance of what he was really proposing. In very short supply, housing was a key measure of power and status. If housing now came on the market, it would place great pressures on the system of party patronage and reinforce emerging economic inequalities in both city and countryside.

Of equal importance were plans for bureaucratic restructuring that were presented to the congress by another member of the Politburo. Building on ideas formulated by Zhao Ziyang, these plans called for a 20 percent reduction in personnel throughout the bureaucracy. Such cuts would remove millions of people from the contacts and perquisites they had enjoyed, in many cases for decades. The ministries of railways, petroleum, coal, and nuclear power would be abolished and replaced by corporations with independent management. The streamlined bureaucracy would then—in this visionary plan—become a true civil service, staffed by those chosen based on merit rather than party service.

In two of these ministries, institutional change was already under way. As we have seen, there were ongoing experiments with reorganizing coal production, and in the petroleum industries Chinese corporations were operating joint ventures with foreign companies. But the problem of how an independent civil agency might run China's fledgling nuclear industry, in a world just coming to grips with the implications of the accidents at Chernobyl and Three Mile Island, was an inordinately complex one. Similarly, the scale of the railway network, which had been expanded enormously since 1949, made the idea of corporate management problematic. The need for reform in the railway system was highlighted, however, by the news—released while the seventh congress was still meeting—that 290 people had been arrested in a train-ticket scalping operation in Shanghai. Buying up blocks of tickets, the scalpers then sold them to desperate passengers for up to six times their face value.

The PLA was undergoing institutional changes of its own. In the mid-1980s a demobilization plan targeted almost one quarter of the 4.2 million members of the armed forces. Forty-seven thousand senior officers were edged into retirement. The last traces of Lin Biao's egalitarianism vanished when full insignia for all ranks were restored. To encourage the army to take an innovative role in weapons and delivery-systems development, the government allowed the PLA to sell its weapons worldwide and to keep for its own use a large proportion of the foreign currency obtained through such deals. The fruits of this policy could be seen in early 1988 as both Iran and Iraq, ravaged by their almost decade-long war, began to bombard each other's cities with Chinese computer-guided, short-range "Silkworm" missiles, either sold directly to them by the PLA or filtered through intermediaries. In 1988 there were also discussions of selling a new 375-mile-range M-9 missile, capable of delivering chemical warheads, to Syria and Libya.

The commitment to develop independent zones of enterprise was reaffirmed by the final act of the seventh congress, taken after it had approved proposals on constitutional, economic, and institutional reform. This final vote approved the separation of Hainan from the jurisdiction of Guangdong and made the island a province. As such, Hainan would have wide autonomy in developing foreign investment, expanding tourism, and allowing a virtually free flow of goods and services. Foreign visitors to Hainan would not require visas. This decision—a bold one in view of the notorious import scandals revealed the year before—could be seen either as a trial balloon for learning how to handle Hong Kong, or as an experiment in developing separate administrative and economic structures that might in the long term heighten China's attractiveness to Taiwan. If successful, the model would also be adopted in major Chinese cities.

The issue of Taiwan had become all the more relevant after Chiang Ching-kuo, president of Taiwan since 1978, died in early 1988, changing the tenor of Taiwan-PRC relations. During the last years of his presidency, Chiang Ching-kuo had carried through democratic reforms of considerable significance. The Taiwanese themselves were now running much of their country. Lee Teng-hui, the vice president, who under Taiwan's constitution assumed the presidency, was a native Taiwanese. Born in 1923 to a rural family of rice and tea farmers, Lee grew up during the Japanese occupation and received his college education in Japan before returning to study agricultural economics in Taipei. He subsequently enrolled in graduate programs in the United States, receiving an M.A. from Iowa State University and a Ph.D. from Cornell.

On taking office, President Lee continued to invoke Chiang Ching-kuo's rhetoric about there being only one China, and made it clear he was not in sympathy with the Taiwan independence movement. Within a few months of his accession, travel restrictions were lifted on Taiwanese who wished to visit their relatives in the PRC. The result was a rush of visitors to the mainland that reached 10,000 people a month by May 1988. Taiwanese businesses that had for years surreptitiously routed their dealings with the PRC through Hong Kong agents or subsidiaries began openly to move production to China. These entrepreneurs were eager to take advantage of tax incentives in the SEZs and of wage rates that in some cases were one-tenth the pay scale on Taiwan.

These expanded contacts, however, emphasized the immense disparities between the two societies as much as their shared heritage, and there seemed little likelihood of speedy reunification, even on a variant of the Hong Kong model. In July 1988 President Lee was elected chairman of the Guomindang;

this greatly strengthened his power base and promised to bond the Taiwanese and the post-1949 Chinese refugees on the island into an even more prosperous union. Taiwan, which had seemed almost a pawn of American policy makers in 1972 and 1979, was now an independent and capable actor on the international scene. Before Taiwan cultivated any closer political ties with the mainland, the PRC would have to prove that it could indeed achieve a sustained level of economic growth and development.

SOCIAL STRAINS

While repression continued in China against those who spoke of democracy or who allegedly subscribed to "bourgeois-liberal" values, it nevertheless appeared that millions were benefiting from the reforms and becoming unabashedly materialistic. As a lighthearted popular joke put it, mocking the former inclination to list categories of political behavior by number, a man in contemporary society needed the "Three Highs" and the "Eight Bigs"; the "Four Musts" were no longer enough. The "Four Musts" had been a bicycle, a radio, a watch, and a sewing machine. In the new world of reform they were replaced by the "Eight Bigs": a color television, a refrigerator, a stereo, a camera,

A man in Suzhou peddles a bicycle rickshaw carrying a new washing machine, one of the "Eight Bigs."

a motorcycle, a suite of furniture, a washing machine, and an electric fan. As for the "Three Highs," those were prerequisites for marriage: a high salary, an advanced education, and a height of over five feet six inches.

The Chinese and foreign media in early 1988 emphasized this approach by extolling entrepreneurs who were making a success of the new flexibility, either by privatizing previously bankrupt state industries or by mechanizing agricultural production. But late in 1988 and early in 1989, it became clear that this entrepreneurialism was taking place in an economic and bureaucratic context of great tensions and problems. Taken cumulatively, these problems showed how difficult it was for Deng Xiaoping and his allies to contain the new forces that their decisions had set in motion. Among the difficulties discussed at the plenum of the Central Committee in late 1988 and in the National People's Congress of early 1989, and which were extensively covered in the press, seven were paramount: inflation, low grain production, labor unrest, graft, unregulated population movements, rapid population growth, and illiteracy.

The income now accruing to those benefiting from the Four Modernizations and economic liberalization had led to an insatiable demand for consumer goods and for new housing and capital construction. For a time, this level of demand generated more employment opportunities and greater options for workers and peasants, but at the same time it pushed inflation, which had been around 20 percent earlier in 1988 and rose up to 26 percent or more in urban areas by year's end. Living standards fell for many in the cities, and retrenchments in capital projects ordered by the government threw many out of work. Panic buying and hoarding affected a wide range of products, from grain and edible oils to toothpaste and soap.

Hoarding exacerbated the problems created by the decline in grain production in 1988. The reasons for the decline were many. State procurement prices for grain, though raised by the government in answer to peasant unrest, were still unrealistically low when compared to market prices and the profits that could be gained from cash crops like sugar and tobacco. Short of cash, the government began paying peasants with promissory notes for their procurement quotas. Yet the peasants were not allowed to use these IOUs in trade for food and fuel. The available amount of arable land continued to shrink in the face of alternative uses—80 percent of all new enterprises, for instance, were situated in rural areas. Peasants began to stockpile their own grain when they saw the surplus they sold to township governments resold at markups of two and a half times or more.

Labor unrest sprang in part from urban inflation and in part from the harsh work conditions imposed by the new breed of entrepreneurial managers. These managers worked closely with the local party bureaucracy in most cases, and continued to rely on local political leaders for lucrative contracts, access to raw materials, transportation of goods, and favorable tax rates that increased their profits. As wages lagged and workers were laid off, many began to strike. Though not on a scale familiar from the republican era, the extent of some strikes in 1988 was considerable: 1,500 workers at a Zhejiang textile mill, for instance, walked out for two days; 1,100 workers at a medical-appliance factory stayed out for three months.

Graft and corruption among CCP members—many of them the associates of local managers—continued to grow. Figures for 1987 released in 1988 showed that 150,000 CCP members—out of an unknown number investigated—had been punished for corruption or abuse of authority. Over 25,000 had been dismissed from the party. Half of all enterprises in the same year had dodged taxes in various ways, as had 80 percent of individual entrepreneurs. In rural areas, agricultural production further suffered from the authorized sale of substandard insecticides, chemical fertilizers, and seed. The government ordered that henceforth every CCP member would have to face an annual assessment of honesty and party loyalty.

Internal migrations of parttime workers and disaffected or unemployed rural and urban populations also emerged as an increasingly destabilizing problem. Government figures indicated that 8 million people a year were moving to urban areas, and that 400 million were now residing in the 365 largest cities, marking another decided increment in the shift away from rural residence shown in the 1982 census. Thirty thousand migrant workers were reported *daily* in Sichuan rail stations; the "floating population" of unemployed or laid-off workers was estimated to be 1.8 million in Shanghai and over 1.1 million in both Beijing and Guangzhou. Such migrations were only part of a larger looming problem. Changes in rural land use and production methods, coupled with government retrenchments and a freeze on new capital construction projects, had made 180 million farm workers "redundant"; 200 million more were expected to be in the same plight over the next decade.

The overall population-growth figures gave little solace to government planners. Taking into account the size and youthfulness of the childbearing population, the relevant state bureaus estimated that 20 million babies would be born each year for at least the next eight years. With a current urban birth rate per thousand of 14.3, and a rural birth rate of 25, the population was projected to reach 1.3 billion by the year 2000. The policy of one child per family was proving hard to enforce: 32 percent of all current births were second children and 15 percent were third children. Grain imports were contributing to the trade deficit of $3 billion, but per capita annual grain consumption was falling steadily: down 40 kilos (from 400 to 360) between 1984 and 1988. It was also likely that much of this rising population would be less well educated than the preceding generation. As many as 230 million people (95 percent of them rural and 70 percent of them female) were defined as "illiterate" by the State Statistical Bureau; the State Education Commission noted growing resistance even to primary education among parents and employers seeking child labor for their farms and enterprises. More than 7 million children dropped out of school in 1988, a figure that included almost 7 percent of junior-middle-school students and 3.3 percent of all those in primary school.[22]

All these domestic problems made planning for economic growth seem inextricably mired, and the foreign news was not much better. Although there was an overall foreign investment in the PRC of some $5.2 billion in 1988 and close to 6,000 joint-venture contracts, this was lower than expectations. Exports for 1988 were $47 billion, but imports totaled $54 billion. As a world exporter, China ranked sixteenth, whereas Hong Kong was eleventh, and Taiwan twelfth. In many cases, official figures of foreign investment turned out to be greatly inflated when scrutinized. Some of the most publicized joint ventures—such as that of American Motors and Beijing Jeep—had run into major crises, marked by low production levels, delays and evasions by Chinese managers (matched by American intransigence and unrealistic expectations), and hostility among workers on the shop floor. Oil drilling by joint-venture corporations off the southeast coast had not yielded the immense discoveries predicted a few years before. And the SEZs were often mismanaged and graft ridden. So many of the enterprises in the zones were run by the children or relatives of the most senior party officials that those outside this inner circle began to talk openly and bitterly of a "clique of heir apparents" and "the princes' clique." Contacts in patronage networks seemed to be the only way to advance in the society. For young, educated Chinese, the new "freedoms" to find their own employment were precarious, for securing lucrative jobs depended on connections. To compound the disillusion, persistent cost cutting had left the facilities of many colleges and universities badly dilapidated. Students and professors complained that it was impossible to do work effectively in them. The dream of reforming the economy and modernizing the nation seemed to be evaporating before people's eyes.

THE BREAKING POINT

Nineteen eighty-nine promised to be an anniversary year of special significance: the 200th anniversary of the French Revolution, the 70th anniversary of the May Fourth movement, the 40th birthday of the People's Republic, and the passage of 10 years since the establishment of diplomatic relations with the United States. A number of prominent intellectuals—including the dismissed party member Fang Lizhi and the poet Bei Dao—sent letters to Deng Xiaoping and other leaders asking them to seize this symbolic moment to take steps that would emphasize the new openness of Chinese politics. They advocated for the release of Wei Jingsheng, who had now served ten years in prison for his role in the 1978 Democracy Wall movement, along with others imprisoned for their dissident views. They also urged the government to invest more money into education, and to grant the rights of free expression that would allow the lively intellectual exchanges essential to scientific and economic progress. Delegates to the National People's Congress suggested that a "socialist democracy" promised a solution if it could combine "political, social and cultural democratization" with the economic reforms currently under discussion. Other intellectuals urged a return to the kind of pragmatism implied by Deng Xiaoping's famous remark from the late 1970s: "It does not matter whether a cat is black or white: as long as it catches mice it is a good cat." Others went further, like the former head of the Marxism-Leninism-Mao Zedong Thought Institute, Su Shaozhi, who suggested that the divorce between theory and practice was now a "chronic malady" in China. Echoing the disgraced party secretary-general Hu Yaobang, he pointed out that Marxism in China currently seemed frozen in the grip of "ossified dogmas." Surely genuine reform could invigorate Marxism while rejecting all "ideological prejudices and bureaucratism," all "cultural autocracy."[23]

Such voices were a reaffirmation of what the university students in Hefei had called for in 1986, and of what Wei Jingsheng had suggested in 1978 and 1979: without abandoning the spirit of Marxism itself, surely there was still room for creative growth and change. Neither Deng Xiaoping, Li Peng, nor Zhao Ziyang responded publicly to these overtures, leaving the task to their subordinates, whose response was harshly dismissive. Such critiques, they observed, were "incitements" to the public and an attempt to exert "pressure" on the government. Since there were no political prisoners in China, the request to "release" Wei Jingsheng and others was a meaningless one.

In this uneasy atmosphere, on April 15, 1989, Hu Yaobang died suddenly of a heart attack. Hu had been Deng Xiaoping's handpicked secretary-general of the CCP until he was made the scapegoat for the 1986–1987 student demonstrations. At the time of his dismissal, the Central Committee had made him issue a humiliating "self-criticism"; Deng's role in condoning the disgrace of his former protégé had left many feeling dismayed. As soon as the news of Hu's death was released, students in Beijing saw an opportunity to pressure the government to move more vigorously with economic and democratic reforms. After all, it was Deng Xiaoping who had "reversed the verdicts" on the 1976 Tiananmen demonstrations in homage to Zhou Enlai, thus openly acknowledging the legitimacy of such actions. By launching a pro–Hu Yaobang demonstration and demanding a reversal of the verdict against him, the students hoped to push the issues of the 1986–1987 pro-democracy protests once more to the forefront of the nation's attention.

This idea seems to have originated with students in the party-history department at Renmin University in Beijing. Many of these students were party members and the children of senior CCP cadres. They understood how to apply political pressure and how to maintain it. Thousands of students from the other campuses joined them in a rally in Tiananmen Square on April 17. Their purpose was to mourn Hu's passing and to call for an end to corruption and nepotism in government, for more democratic participation in decision making, and for better conditions in the universities. Wall posters—declared illegal by the party since 1980—appeared in many places, openly praising Hu and his support of political and economic reform. After class, and when the libraries closed, excited groups of young people joined together; from such gatherings sprang new student associations. Students in Shanghai and other cities caught the mood and took up the same cry. On April 18, students held a sit-in near the Great Hall of the People in Tiananmen Square; that night, with bravado unparalleled under the PRC, they staged sit-ins at the party headquarters and in front of the most senior party leaders' residence compound on the edge of the Forbidden City. The government declared April 22 to be the official day for Hu Yaobang's funeral ceremonies; demonstrations were forbidden and the whole of Tiananmen Square would be closed. But by clever preparation and inspired coordination, students entered the square before the police had taken up their positions and held a peaceful demonstration. In a ritualistic gesture, reminiscent of Qing practice, several students knelt on the steps of the Great Hall and begged Premier Li Peng to come out and talk to them. He declined to do so. On April 24, students began a mass boycott of classes in an attempt to pressure government leaders into hearing their requests.

Up to this point, compromise of many kinds appeared possible, even if the demonstrators had gone beyond anything attempted in 1976, 1978, or 1986. Students believed Zhao Ziyang and members of his senior staff to be receptive to dialogue; in his position as CCP secretary-general, Zhao could presumably urge the party in the same direction. For his part, Zhao may have seen the students' demonstrations as a potential force that could strengthen his own position. But in late April the students and their supporters were stunned by an editorial in *People's Daily* that referred to their movement as a "planned conspiracy," with the implication that all those following the current action might be subject to arrest and prosecution. Zhao was away on a state visit to North Korea at the time, and the *People's Daily* editorial obviously represented the views of the hardline faction.

Instead of being intimidated, the students reacted with anger and defiance. They were joined now by many of their teachers, by scores of journalists, and by citizens of Beijing. The rallies and marches grew larger, the calls for reforms and democratic freedoms bolder. The government leaders appeared paralyzed, reluctant to act in any manner on the anniversary of the May Fourth demonstrations that would trigger parallel reminders of the warlord era. May 4 came and went peaceably, though over 100,000 marched in Beijing, dwarfing the student demonstrations of 1919. Similar rallies and parades were held in cities throughout China, but Beijing remained the focus for world media attention. The reason was the imminent arrival of Soviet leader Mikhail Gorbachev in mid-May for a long-planned summit meeting with Deng Xiaoping. This summit was expected to mark the end of the rift between the Soviet Union and China that had lasted for thirty-three years, ever since Khrushchev had shocked Mao with his "secret speech" attacking Stalin's memory.

Gorbachev was enthusiastically welcomed by the demonstrators, not least because his attempts to introduce political and intellectual freedoms in the Soviet Union could be contrasted sharply with the Chinese leaders' resistance to such change. But the significance of Gorbachev's visit was overshadowed as the student demonstrators introduced a new tactic—the hunger strike—to emphasize their pleas for reform. Tiananmen Square became a vast camp with close to 3,000 hunger strikers laid out in makeshift tents, surrounded by tens of thousands of their classmates and curious onlookers. Planned ceremonies for Gorbachev had to be canceled or changed at the last minute. As television cameras broadcast the scene around the world, ambulances raced in and out of the square attending to those so dangerously weakened by their fast that there was a real chance they would die. "Democracy is the most noble meaning of life; freedom is a basic human right," declared hunger-strike students in an announcement. "It is with the spirit of death that we fight for life."[24]

Nothing like this had been seen in China before. Although crowds as large had assembled during the Cultural Revolution, those gatherings had been orchestrated to salute Mao Zedong as supreme leader. Now, even though Zhao Ziyang tried to mute the conflict and suggested that the *People's Daily*'s condemnation of the students had been too harsh, the demonstrators began openly calling on Deng Xiaoping and Li Peng to resign. Boisterous and angry, sometimes chanting and dancing, at other times deep in political discussion or sleeping in exhaustion, the students and their supporters were at once a potent political challenge to their government and an endlessly engrossing spectacle to the rest of China and the world. Li Peng did invite the hunger-strike leaders to one meeting, but it went badly. Li found the students rude and incoherent, while they found him arrogant and aloof. On May 17 and again the following day, the number of demonstrators in and around Tiananmen Square passed the 1 million mark. Muzzled until now by government controls, journalists and editors of newspapers and television news began to cover the protests as comprehensively as they could. On May 19, appearing close to tears, Zhao Ziyang visited the hunger strikers and pleaded with them to end their fasts. Li Peng also briefly talked with strikers, but he made no pleas and no promises. On May 20, Premier Li Peng and President Yang Shangkun declared martial law and ordered PLA units brought into Beijing to clear the square and return order to the city.

But for two weeks the soldiers could not clear the square, their efforts stymied by the courage and unity of the citizens of Beijing. Workers, initially sought out as allies by the students, now organized to join in the protests and to stem the soldiers' advance. With a kind of fierce yet loving solidarity, city residents took to the streets and erected makeshift barricades. They surrounded the army convoys, sometimes to let the air out of tires or stall engines but more often to argue with or cajole the troops, urging them not to enforce the martial-law orders and not to turn their guns on their fellow citizens. For their part the troops, some distressed by their assignment, practiced considerable restraint while the central leadership was clearly divided. Enraged by the students' intransigence and the mounting disorder in the streets, which surely reminded him of the Cultural Revolution, Deng Xiaoping lobbied for hardline support and ordered each of the regional PLA commanders to send a number of their seasoned troops to the capital. Zhao Ziyang found himself without a sufficient base of support among his colleagues and was unable to check the hardline approach from gaining ground.

The students who had emerged as leaders of the demonstrations over the previous month now found themselves in charge of a huge square crammed with their supporters but also awash with dirt and garbage that threatened the outbreak of serious disease. At May's end they began to urge their fellow students to end the hunger strikes and return to their campuses; the majority of the Beijing students did so. But new recruits arrived to take their place, often from other cities where major demonstrations were also occurring. Speakers espousing a combative stance insisted that retreat would mean a betrayal of their principles, and that they needed to maintain the pressures they were currently exerting through their numbers and tenacity. A group of art students provided the movement with a new symbol that drew all eyes—a thirty-foot-high white plaster and Styrofoam statue of their version of Liberty, fashioned as a young woman with head held proudly aloft, clasping in both her hands the torch of freedom.

Late at night on June 3, the army struck. These were not inexperienced soldiers like those deployed up to this time, but well-armed troops from

The Goddess of Democracy and Freedom   Modeled after the Statue of Liberty, this symbol was erected in Tiananmen Square during the spring 1989 protests by students of the Central Academy of Fine Arts.

An unarmed Chinese civilian halting a tank convoy heading for Tiananmen Square, June 5, 1989   After speaking to the crew of the lead tank, he was pulled away to safety. His fate is unknown.

veteran units with proven loyalty to Deng. Backed by heavy tanks and armored personnel carriers that smashed through the barricades, crushing those who tried to halt their progress, the troops converged on Tiananmen Square down the avenues to its east and west. Armed with automatic weapons, they fired on crowds along the streets, at anyone who moved in nearby buildings, and at those who approached their positions.

In the small hours of June 4, PLA forces blocked all the approaches to Tiananmen Square and turned off all the lights there. After protracted and anguished debates, the remaining demonstrators decided to leave. As they walked out in bedraggled but orderly formation, troops and tanks overran their encampments and crushed the liberty statue to pieces. There followed a period of terrifying chaos, as the army gunned down students and citizens both near the square and in other areas of the city. Screams echoed through the night, and flames rose from piles of debris and from army trucks or tanks hit by homemade explosives. Hospitals were overwhelmed by the numbers of dead and wounded, but in many cases were forbidden to treat the civilian casualties. PLA soldiers also died, some killed by enraged crowds who had just seen unarmed demonstrators mowed down. Rumors spread swiftly that the fires in Tiananmen Square were piles of corpses burned by the army to hide the evidence of their brutality. Whether that was true or not—and no

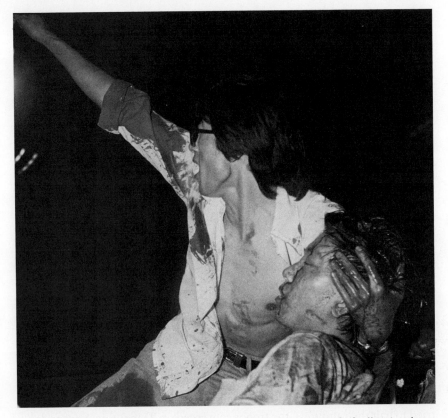

Tiananmen Square Massacre, Beijing, June 3–4, 1989 This picture of a fatally injured student being helped by a friend became a symbol of the bloodbath.

one could get past the troops to check—there were enough bodies in full view elsewhere, lying in the roads, in hospitals, or tangled up in their bicycles where they had fallen, to indicate the scale of the violence. Many hundreds were dead and thousands more wounded. The callousness of the killings evoked memories of the worst episodes of China's earlier civil wars and the Cultural Revolution.[25] Similar violence was meted out to civilian demonstrators by the armed police in Chengdu and perhaps other cities, but the thoroughness of the government's news blackout made it hard to gauge the scale. Foreign journalists were forbidden to take photographs or conduct interviews, and satellite links abroad were cut.

For a few days rumors swirled that other units of the PLA, shocked by the massacre, might start a civil war, or that the country's workers would unite in a national strike, or that sympathy riots in other major cities would bring down the government. None of those things happened. The hardliners had "won," if that is the right word. Zhao Ziyang was dismissed, the second of Deng's successors to meet that fate. Li Peng and Deng Xiaoping publicly thanked the PLA officers and soldiers for clearing the square and praised their courage. To replace Zhao, Deng turned to a comparatively unknown figure, the sixty-three-year-old party secretary of Shanghai, Jiang Zemin. A Russian-trained electrical engineer, Jiang's unspectacular but steady rise through the ranks began from student activist and factory director to ministerial positions in the industrial sector, and finally to Shanghai mayor in 1985 and party secretary in 1987. Jiang had been summoned to Beijing in the spring of 1989 to help control the demonstrations. His main claim to his new office was that he had at the same time successfully kept the situation in Shanghai from getting out of hand. Now Jiang joined in as the party launched a concerted campaign blaming the demonstrations on counterrevolutionaries and "hooligans," and mounted an extensive hunt for the student leaders and their main supporters. Many of the "most wanted" students eluded the police for weeks, and some managed to leave China secretly, suggesting the range of public support for their actions and the solidarity of their organizations. But thousands of other students were arrested and interrogated. The government also determined to avoid the formation of any autonomous unions of workers and showed special ferocity toward those who had joined in the protests. Many were arrested and executed.

Foreign governments were stunned by these events, though uncertain how to act. Many of them expressed outrage, evacuated their nationals, imposed economic sanctions, and talked of barring China from various international associations. But they did not break diplomatic relations with the PRC. The U.S. embassy gave sanctuary to Fang Lizhi and his wife when they requested it, an act blasted by the PRC government as interference in its internal affairs. But in a confidential letter, hand-delivered to Deng Xiaoping, the United States president George H. W. Bush appealed for calm and spoke of his belief that "good relations between the United States and China are in the fundamental interests of both countries."[26]

On June 9, Deng Xiaoping issued a harsh attack on the demonstrators in a speech that clearly represented the official interpretation of events and became the mandatory text for study sessions all over the country. What the government had suppressed, said Deng, was nothing less than a "counterrevolutionary rebellion." Moreover, it was a rebellion "determined by the international and domestic climate, it was bound to happen and was independent of man's will." Yet while offering this long-range, almost cosmic interpretation of events, Deng told the assembled party leaders and army officers, "We face a rebellious clique and a large number of the dregs of society, who want to topple our country and overthrow our party." Deng did not make clear who these dregs were, but they were to be distinguished from the "masses," the "young students," and the "onlookers." He praised the army's exemplary courage in suppressing the rebellion but made no attempt to explain why the students had been demonstrating with such tenacity, or why so many citizens supported them. Any effort to discredit CCP leadership and the paramountcy of "Marxism, Leninism, and Mao Zedong Thought" must be resolutely quashed, Deng insisted, along with any move to introduce "the American system of the separation of the three powers." Yet this did not mean China should again become a "closed country" or that the government leaders should go "back to the old days of trampling the economy to death." Deng's speech concluded with a ringing affirmation of national economic growth: more railways, more ships, more roads, more steel, more electric power. He called for a doubling of the gross national product in twelve years followed by fifty years of 2 percent annual growth, so that China would reach the level of a "moderately developed nation" by the year 2050.

In his assessment of the "crux of the current incident," as he referred to the crackdown of June 3 and 4, Deng did speak to wider ideological themes. The country was facing a great struggle, he said. It was between socialism on the one hand and the forces of "bourgeois liberalization and spiritual pollution" on the other. This was the battle that China under the leadership of the CCP would be fighting into the foreseeable future. Nostalgic for the austere yet exciting days of the Jiangxi Soviet, of Yan'an, and of the founding years of the PRC, Deng called for a return to simple values and standards, for "plain living" and the "enterprising spirit in hard struggle." Only so could China achieve its own vision of "reform and openness" without "importing evil influences from the West."[27]

It was not only that nothing had changed, Deng seemed to be telling the nation; it was as if nothing of any real significance had even occurred. The course that China must take had been set for a decade; now all the people had to do was follow it to its logical conclusion.

CHAPTER 27

Century's End

RETURNING TO GROWTH

Despite Deng Xiaoping's expressions of confidence, the crisis of 1989 showed that aspects of China's past were still much in evidence. To take one short-term parallel, the political maneuvering by Deng proved how far the CCP was from solving its leadership and succession problems. Deng's rejection of his two chosen heirs, Hu Yaobang and Zhao Ziyang, and his sudden benediction of the previously little-known Jiang Zemin as CCP secretary-general, were reminiscent of Mao's attempt to install Hua Guofeng after he had turned against Liu Shaoqi and Lin Biao. In a longer historical context, Deng's insistence that economic reforms should be kept separate from changes in the political structure and modes of public expression reawakened historical memories of the late Qing dream—that China could join the world on its own terms, without sacrificing its prevailing ideological purity. Some Chinese even noticed parallels between Deng's suppression of the democracy movement in 1989 and the Empress Dowager Cixi's counter-coup in the face of Emperor Guangxu's ambitious reform program of 1898.

The intellectuals and students who had joined together to vent their frustrations in the spring of 1989 themselves raised echoes of those who had taken great risks to emphasize that educated Chinese had a moral obligation to criticize the shortcomings of their rulers, even if it meant severe punishment. Wittingly or not, the protestors who marched and spoke out in 1976, 1978, 1986, and 1989 shared a great deal with the anti-Guomindang patriots of the 1930s, the May Fourth experimenters of the 1920s, the anti-Qing activists of the late nineteenth century, the "evidential research" scholars of the eighteenth century, and both the Donglin partisans and the Ming loyalists of the seventeenth century.

At a different level, the outbursts of vindictive rage on the part of some citizens, however much they had been provoked to such acts by the very soldiers they killed, pointed to a different kind of tradition. Again and again, ordinary people with little or no education and no particular guiding ideology had risen against those who oppressed or exploited them. Dreams for a better life, a sense of hopelessness, and bitterly impoverished living conditions—these had proven potent provocations to action against apparently unyielding and uncaring governments. And those with no weapons who wished to kill soldiers had to use their bare hands until they had seized their enemies' arsenals. Late-Ming peasant rebels; desperate followers of Wang Lun, Lin Qing, or the White Lotus sects; the Nian; the Boxers; peasants and urban workers in Hunan or Shanghai in the twentieth century—all showed that there were limits to the indignities they would endure.

Finally, one other set of echoes in mid-1989 had considerable historical resonance. Many of the student leaders on the government's "most wanted" list and some of the well-known intellectuals critical of the government managed to escape to sanctuaries overseas. It seemed that they might be able to establish a potent base in exile from which to continue their criticisms of the state. Such criticism might, in turn, bring down the current government, or at least lay the groundwork for reforms that would prepare the way for a successor regime more sympathetic to the aspirations for change. Constitutional reformers like Kang Youwei and Liang Qichao, Sun Yat-sen and the leaders of the Revolutionary Alliance, young Communists in the 1920s (including Zhou Enlai and Deng Xiaoping) had all found shelter and ideological freedom to develop their ideas in foreign countries, from Japan to Mexico, and from the United States to Great Britain and France.

But though various foreign countries initially gave considerable financial assistance and media attention to exiled groups of 1989 dissidents, enthusiasm and support waned as the dissidents quarreled among themselves and competed for attention. They lacked effective leaders with ideas and organizational structures to focus their energies. For a time they lobbied, with near success, to pressure individual corporations and foreign governments to cut back trade and investment in China unless flagrant human rights abuses were corrected. Through newsletters and other writings, they also awakened Western consciences to the continuing crackdown against all dissidents, to the horrors of Chinese forced labor systems, to the tens of thousands of political prisoners who were incarcerated in such camps on the flimsiest charges, and to the role that the products of prison labor played in the growing export trade. But in the long run, the economic incentives for continuing trade with China overwhelmed the moral arguments, and by 1991 foreign investment matched pre-1989 levels, and then began to rapidly exceed them.

Deng Xiaoping's position, however, had been seriously weakened by the events of 1989, and he was placed more on the defensive than he had been before. The second half of 1989 and much of 1990 were occupied with rounding up pro-democracy protesters and their supporters in the media and the bureaucracy. Many thousands were arrested and jailed or sent to labor camps, and several—mainly workers—were executed. Thousands of party cadres were purged from government research institutes, from academies teaching Marxist-Leninist and Maoist thought, and especially from "think-tanks" established by Zhao Ziyang—who, according to rumor, had refused to issue a self-criticism of his leniency toward the student demonstrators. Zhao was removed from his official posts and placed under house arrest in Beijing, where he would remain, unforgiven, until his death in 2005.[1]

Deng's critics within the party leadership pointed out that the headlong rush to embrace the West had led to an erosion of socialist values, produced severe imbalances within the economy, and caused serious inflation. Li Peng, the premier who presided over economic planning policy, urged hewing to an annual growth limit of 6 percent per year, to avoid the inflationary crises that had helped spark the disorders of 1989. As if current problems were not enough, the collapse of communist states across Eastern Europe, the sudden fall of Mikhail Gorbachev, and the subsequent swift fragmentation of the Soviet Union seemed ominous harbingers to many CCP leaders of China's own impending fate. Absolute suppression of domestic dissidents, tightened security in border areas with large "minority" populations such as Tibet and Xinjiang, and the reining in of economic change all became government priorities. A group of thirty-two senior party members even suggested that the SEZs be abolished altogether.

In the year or so following the bloody suppression of the 1989 democracy movement, there was much anxious speculation outside China about what the future might hold for the country. The scenarios ranged from internal political upheavals by students or workers leading to the ouster of Li Peng and the return of Zhao Ziyang, to a military coup, and even to the fragmentation of the country along regional lines and a return to something approaching the warlordism of the early Republic. What most people did not anticipate was that the CCP would be able to hold onto its power—and vastly increase its members' wealth—through a delicate balancing act of selectively stifling domestic criticism and dissent while at the same time allowing rapid economic growth for large sectors of the country.

Because no one could doubt his own long loyalty to the revolution, Deng was able to steer around people like Chen Yun who wanted to continue strong centralized planning, and some of the tougher-minded Maoists who wished to restore rigorous programs of ideological indoctrination. The hardliners knew too that Deng's Cultural Revolution experiences had soured him on youthful enthusiasms in the name of revolution. At the same time, Deng's public praise for the PLA for its steadfastness in the face of "hooligans," along with his approval of the military's international arms sales and domestic investments, assured him of the support of the armed services.

The forces inhibiting rapid economic growth showed surprising tenacity, however. The "gold-digging" attitudes of the young workers in Shenzhen came under harsh criticism, and the August 1991 coup against the Soviet leader Gorbachev by senior figures in his own party showed the vulnerability of even the most powerful leaders pushing for economic change.[2] In January 1992 Deng decided to take a bold initiative in which he would use his remaining prestige to reassert the validity and viability of China's greatest centers of economic dynamism and change: the SEZs in the southeast. In 1984 Deng had made a brief trip to Shenzhen to emphasize his faith in the new zone there, but the 1992 visit was more elaborate and took place in a more critical environment. Curiously, Deng described this venture as an "inspection visit to the South," using the same term Emperor Kangxi had used for the six tours that he made between 1684 and 1707. When Kangxi went to the "south" this meant the Yangzi valley economic centers of Yangzhou, Nanjing, Suzhou, and Hangzhou; the emperor never went farther south, into the subtropical region of Guangdong province. On his tour Deng Xiaoping included Shanghai and the inland industrial region of Wuhan, but he concentrated his main attention on Guangzhou, Zhuhai (near Macao), and Shenzhen, across the border from Hong Kong. Specifically referring to certain "conservative forces within the party," Deng noted that "ideology cannot supply rice." He praised the region of Guangdong for being a "leading force in economic development" and urged further acceleration to catch up with Hong Kong, Singapore, Taiwan, and South Korea—known as the "four little dragons" of East Asia.

The hostility to Deng among many Communist stalwarts—perhaps even the overt threat that he posed to several senior leaders—can be inferred from the silence with which the Chinese media initially greeted this tour. But later in the spring Deng succeeded in having the significance of the tour and information about the crucial economic role of the new regions widely disseminated in the press, and also formally incorporated in the proceedings of the National People's Congress and in Central Committee documents. The PLA played its part, too. During the spring of 1992 the chief commanders of all seven military regions and fifty-seven other generals dutifully visited the Shenzhen and Zhuhai SEZs. They allegedly returned from the visits "convinced of the success" of the zones and determined "to learn from the experience" there. Not to carry out "reform and opening," not to "develop the economy," could "only be the road to ruin," noted Deng. In addition, *rapid* development was essential to China: "Low-speed development is equal to stagnation or even retrogression."

It was overly "leftist," Deng also observed, to see such reforms as capitalist or as a corrosive form of "peaceful evolution" with dangerous consequences for the country. "Socialism's real nature is to liberate productive forces, and the ultimate goal of Socialism is to achieve common prosperity." In an only thinly veiled reference to the crises of 1989, Deng added his own promise that all Chinese studying overseas would be welcomed if they came home to contribute their skills to the economy. To underline this point, he added that Hu Yaobang and Zhao Ziyang had fallen from power not because they had pushed for rapid economic growth, but because they had "stumbled on the issue of opposing bourgeois liberalization."[3]

Z O N E S   A N D   G A M E S

On his southern tour, Deng Xiaoping had mused aloud that Shanghai should have been included in the list of the first designated SEZs. Once he had won the grudging acquiescence of his leading opponent within the CCP, the redoubtable Chen Yun (who had predicted that Deng's policies would lead to the collapse of the party along Soviet and East European lines), Deng moved to correct this lapse. He declared Shanghai to be the new "dragon head" of the Yangzi, the anchor for trade of five major river cities that were now to be opened to foreign investments.* At the same time, five other cities in Manchuria, the northwest, and the southwest were also to be developed as "open cities" for foreign trade and investment, along with various "border regions" in Xinjiang, Fujian, and Yunnan.† The geographical spread of the areas now opened to global trade replicated the range of treaty ports at the peak of their growth in the late nineteenth century, though Deng was confident that there would be no repeat of the exploitation that had marked that period of Western arrogance and declining Qing power.

Mao Zedong had consistently shown his suspicion of the disruptive potential of cities, especially Shanghai, although he had been willing to use the Shanghai-based radical faction of the early Cultural Revolution period for his own political goals. The city had remained into the 1980s a vast and lumbering metropolis, with its huge population living in dilapidated housing, served

---

* The five cities were Wuhu, Jiujiang, Wuhan (Hankou), Yueyang, and Chongqing.

† This second group of five cities consisted of Harbin, Hohhot, Urumchi, Kunming, and Nanning.

by antiquated transport and harbor facilities, and working for the most part in vast and inefficient collective factories. Nevertheless, experience in Shanghai administration had proved crucial to Jiang Zemin, who found himself plucked by Deng Xiaoping from the city's party secretaryship in the summer of 1989 to take over the entire CCP of 52 million members. Deng used Jiang in two capacities at once: first, to disarm the critics of rapid growth by launching a campaign against "mammonism, hedonism and ultraegoism" within the CCP—in a rather blunter moment Jiang dropped the euphemism and explained that he meant "exchanging money for power and indulging in lavish eating and illegal sex"—and by backing up the threats with arrests and executions;[4] and second, to have Jiang use his office to endorse the 1992 southern tour and issue a new definitive version of Deng's economic goals for the nation. As reward for his loyalty, Jiang received two new appointments in 1993 as chairman of the Military Affairs Commission and as president of the PRC. (The last person to hold these offices while also heading the party had been Hua Guofeng.)

In the summer of 1992 Deng reached out to another Shanghai official, Zhu Rongji—a Hunanese, born in 1928 and trained originally as an electrical engineer before becoming Shanghai's mayor in the 1980s—and made him one of the architects of economic growth. Zhu became, in rapid succession, a vice premier, a member of the Standing Committee of the Politburo, and governor of the Bank of China (which had assets of 1,107 billion yuan at the time, with annual profits of 9 billion yuan). In his policy statements, Zhu emphasized that to foster growth, enterprise managers must be able to fire workers and assume responsibility for profit and loss, just as directors must be able to make key decisions without constant outside interference. Enterprise wage increases should be "strictly in line with enterprise returns." To put such concepts in the context of population growth, reports in that same summer of 1992 noted that the fourth national census (based on the population count as of July 1, 1990) had been 1.13 billion people. There were 318 million women of childbearing age, and it seemed unlikely the State Family Planning Commission goal of holding the population under 1.3 billion by the year 2000 was feasible. Other figures suggested the current "floating population" of those away from their registered residence was about 70 million.

The economy was beginning to overheat. The growth of the gross domestic product (GDP)—which had risen from the cautious post-1989 6 percent to 12 percent in 1992—rose again in 1993, to 14 percent, and returned to 12 percent in 1994. One result of this growth was inflation, which reached 25 percent in 1993. Another was wild speculation in real estate in Beijing, Shanghai, and other cities, exacerbated by many banks' willingness to grant enormous loans for the flimsiest of reasons and with the weakest of collateral to those who had good party connections. Zhu Rongji sought to control these dangers by reducing GDP growth to 8 or 9 percent through different measures: cutting government spending, curbing luxury imports, checking speculation in stocks, firming up tax collection, boosting savings through forced purchase of government bonds, and raising interest rates.

Zhu's policies clashed with Deng Xiaoping's now apparently unstoppable optimism about growth. Although the two men avoided open conflict, Deng's new slogan that "Slow growth is not socialism" clearly militated against austerity, especially when coupled with a final visit by the now ninety-year-old Deng to Shanghai in 1994. National TV coverage made it clear that Deng was very frail and unable to speak clearly. His presence in Shanghai, however, was a strong political signal that stimulated economic growth again. For a brief time inflation rose to a dangerous 30 percent in major cities, and reached 22 percent for the country as a whole. At the same time, foreign investment continued to pour into China, the number of joint ventures and their geographic distribution increased rapidly, and countries like the United States without tariff barriers began to experience enormous trade deficits. Figures issued for the calendar year 1991 had already shown a trade surplus for China of U.S.$12 billion, listed 37,215 active foreign-funded enterprises, and showed that 33 million visitors from overseas had traveled to China in that year alone.

The government's success in curbing social unrest after the spectacular public demonstration and crackdown of 1989 undoubtedly boosted its self-confidence. In this ambiance of heightened foreign visibility and growing international interconnections, the PRC sought to have its newfound self-identity as an emerging great power ratified in a dramatic way. By mid-1993 the leadership had seized on the goal of hosting the 2000 Olympic Summer Games in Beijing—a symbolic and literal entry into the new millennium that would prove conclusively that China had arrived. To this end, the government conducted an energetic and at times flagrant lobbying program with all the major national delegations that would have the final say in the selection process. Chinese athletes were themselves becoming world-class competitors in many sports, especially diving, track and field, and gymnastics. Beijing and other cities, by late 1993, were awash with billboards and posters stating that China was the natural site for the Olympics, and the Olympic logo with Chinese characters was everywhere on display.

When foreign Olympic delegations were present, the government made special efforts to curb the noxious pollution from Beijing's factories by temporarily closing some of them; it banned the cheaper taxis and many private automobiles from the streets as well. Schoolchildren were assigned to clean the traffic signs, and shop assistants were given lessons on posture and friendliness. In similar vein, peddlers, poor migrant laborers, and beggars were kept out of sight, and the PLA and the police forces aimed to demonstrate their ability to maintain a high level of public security for visiting athletes and dignitaries.

To underline the general message of China's new openness, the prominent dissident Wei Jingsheng, author of "The Fifth Modernization," was suddenly released on September 14, 1993. Wei had been in prison since 1979 and had served fourteen years of a fifteen-year sentence. His release was well publicized to coincide with the Chinese representatives' final lobbying of the Olympic delegates while the voting began in Monaco on September 23. The votes were breathtakingly close, as the rival cities of Istanbul, Manchester, and Berlin were defeated one by one, leaving Beijing still in the running by the final ballot. Because China had invested so much emotional and real capital in a favorable outcome, the ultimate loss to Sydney in Australia, by a total of two votes (45 to 43, with 1 abstention), was a shattering disappointment.

One immediate scapegoat was Wei Jingsheng, who was re-arrested shortly after the negative vote and held secretly in detention, on the grounds that he had plotted against the state. Wei had met with several of the 1978 and 1989 dissidents after his release and had spoken to foreign journalists. Furthermore, once the Olympic vote was over Wei wrote a spirited essay on human rights issues. In this essay, entitled "The Wolf and the Lamb," he explained that China's rulers found it difficult to accept that other countries really cared about human rights; they also believed President Bill Clinton's remarks on the topic were "just an affectation." Washington's mistake, wrote Wei, lay in thinking that "the Communist Party resembles a bunch of slow-witted rulers of a backward culture and that China doesn't comprehend that violations of human rights are evil." In fact, China's leaders knew full well what they were doing, which was "to deprive the people of their freedom" deliberately. Wei noted that the Americans were acting like the lamb in Aesop's fable: "After the wolf accuses the lamb of fouling his drinking water, the lamb protests: 'I could not have fouled your water because I live downstream from you.' The wolf eats the lamb anyway."[5]

Wei's essay was published on the op-ed page of *The New York Times* in November 1993, and he also talked with the U.S. deputy assistant secretary in charge of human rights. It was clearly these two events within the context of the Olympic Games rejection that led to Wei's arrest and the severity of the charges. After a long period of secret incarceration, Wei was given a trial as manipulated as his first one in 1979, but this time none of his friends were able to smuggle a tape recorder into the courtroom. Wei was given little chance to speak in his own defense and was sentenced to fourteen more years in prison. The tensions between the party's nationalistic pride on the world stage and its continuing harshness at the level of the obdurate individual dissident had rarely been shown with such clarity. Only in 1997, after Deng Xiaoping's death, was Wei again released and allowed to settle in the United States.

LITTLE DRAGONS

Despite the government's inflexible stance toward those like Wei Jingsheng who tried to call openly for more democracy, there were signs within China that gradual change might be stirring. For example, when the controversial project for the Three Gorges Dam on the Yangzi River was brought before the National People's Congress of 1992, backed with the full authority of Premier Li Peng and other party elders, debate was extremely lively, with heated discussions of safety factors and environmental and social impact. When the final vote was tallied, although 1,767 delegates voted in favor, 177 had the courage openly to vote against it. In addition, 664 delegates abstained, and several others cast no vote at all. To have close to a third of the members of this normally acquiescent body register disapproval of such a major government-sponsored project was an extraordinary new development. Over the following years critics continued to express open opposition to many

Water rushes out of the completed Three Gorges Dam, 2006. A massive flood control and hydroelectric project under construction on the Upper Yangzi River above Yichang, the Three Gorges Dam required the forced relocation of 1.3 million residents along the river and the flooding of the beautiful, culturally significant gorges.

aspects of the dam, to interview those who might be adversely affected by its construction, and to circulate negative reports from engineers and bureaucrats who opposed the project. Similarly, in village "elections" where there had normally been automatic acceptance of candidates from the party's designated list, in several cases party nominees were rejected and more popular local candidates were substituted.

But such scenarios were still highly unusual and were dependent on the personal commitment of remarkable individuals. The most important models for shifts in a democratic direction from within Chinese communities came from two of those "four little dragons" that Deng Xiaoping had identified as economic models, namely Taiwan and Hong Kong.

Of the two, it was Taiwan that had been making the most dramatic changes. The crucial event here was the decision by President Chiang Ching-kuo to move toward full and open elections for the island's two chambers, the Legislature (where seats changed every three years) and the National Assembly (where many old Guomindang members still held their seats on the basis of elections held in Nanjing in 1947). Chiang determined to encourage the development of all aspects of full democracy: competitive political parties, clear and fair electoral rules and procedures, interparty coalitions, and an open, broad-based electorate of all adult citizens. He took the first key step in 1987 by ending martial law, legalizing opposition parties, and removing most press curbs and sedition laws. The death of Chiang Ching-kuo in 1988 ended the domination of the Guomindang by mainland-born party elders. In a crucial change of direction, the Taiwan-born Lee Teng-hui, whom Chiang had groomed for the role, succeeded to the presidency. A new stage was reached with the 1991 decision that the surviving members of the National Assembly elected in 1947 should retire that same year, opening up the institution to new candidates. This move was followed by the decision to hold open elections for the president and vice president by all Taiwanese citizens, as opposed to the past practice of ratifying those leaders by an Assembly vote. In a supplementary gesture designed to help heal old wounds, the Guomindang agreed to permit public study of the February 1947 massacre of Taiwanese people and expressed regret for the tragedy.[6]

The main rival to the Guomindang, the Democratic Progressive Party (DPP), which had been openly advocating independence, won 20 percent of the seats in the National Assembly elections of 1991 and 31 percent of those for the Legislature in 1992. In 1993 a third party split off from the former Guomindang, making the competition even more lively. In 1994 the DPP candidate won a significant victory in the contest for mayor of Taipei over the Guomindang candidate. The climax to this process came with the first full election for Taiwan's president in 1996, in which candidates from all the major parties ran for office. An impressive 76 percent of eligible voters went to the polls, and Lee Teng-hui won a majority with 54 percent of the vote. The PRC government attempted to intimidate potential supporters of Taiwan independence during these elections by holding missile tests and conducting fleet maneuvers in the waters around the island, which almost brought trade to a standstill. With this vote one could fairly say that the "tutelage system" envisioned by Sun Yat-sen as the crucial intermediary stage of development toward democracy had at last ended—at least for this society on China's periphery.

In socioeconomic terms, Taiwan seemed established as the kind of society that Deng Xiaoping hoped the mainland would become. In the mid-1990s the population of 21 million enjoyed a per capita average income of U.S.$10,556, ate an average of 3,000 calories per day, had life expectancies of seventy-one for men and seventy-seven for women, and an annual population increase below 1 percent. Fifty-seven percent of Taiwanese received some form of post-secondary-school education, and more of its bureaucrats and legislators had advanced degrees than the comparable group in any other society. Unemployment in the 9-million-strong labor force stood at 0.9 percent.

By contrast, Hong Kong's road toward democracy was slower and more limited, conducted as it was under the shadow of the impending reversion to PRC rule in 1997. In the summer of 1991, the British loosened their colonial grip by allowing the first open elections for eighteen of the seats on Hong Kong's sixty-member Legislative Council (Legco). Half of the other forty-two seats were filled with government-appointed members, and half from indirectly elected "constituency groups," such as doctors, lawyers, teachers, trade unionists, and businessmen. At least ninety-five candidates ran for office from a wide spectrum of pro-Beijing, pro-business, pro-democracy groups, and from those with individual agendas of their own. The elections gave a strong majority to the United Democrats of Hong Kong, led by the articulate lawyer Martin Lee, who was a vocal critic of PRC human rights abuses and of mainland interference in Hong Kong's affairs. The pro-China candidates were almost all defeated.

In October 1992 the newly appointed British governor, Christopher Patten, announced plans to open the constituency seats to elections, at the same time reducing to ten those appointed by the governor. He stated that this would be followed by an open election by all Hong Kong residents eighteen and older for the Legislative Council, scheduled for 1995. Patten claimed these changes did not violate the 1984 Sino-British agreement, but the PRC government disputed his contention and responded angrily with the announcement that it would abolish the Legislative Council on July 1, 1997. In preliminary elections in September 1994, the United Democrats gained twice as many seats as the pro-China parties. When the greatly anticipated Legco elections were held in 1995, they gave a strong victory yet again to the United Democrats and a near-rout to the pro-China groups. But this time, the election turnout was only a disappointing 35 percent of those eligible. The PRC government reiterated its vow to cancel the body after Hong Kong returned to Chinese control on July 1, 1997.

The PRC government's attitude thus closely reflected the ideas expressed by Deng Xiaoping: the economic achievements of the people of Hong Kong and Taiwan were clearly a source of pride to China and were even seen as worthy of emulation, in terms of trade and investment strategies and management practices. But if those moving to new levels of prosperity sought democratic reforms, they were to be deflected—whether by threat, by force, or by simple abrogation once the CCP was able to control the situation on its own terms. For China itself, the period of tutelage was unquestionably still in existence.

INTO THE SEA

It was not just the opposition to these ventures in democracy that gave China a hard-edged look in these last years of Deng Xiaoping's rule as "paramount leader." A whole slew of policies and pronouncements suggested that confrontation with Western powers—especially the United States—was now as much in the air as accommodation. In early 1994 China shifted the basis of its rhetoric by branding the United States as the new "hegemonist" power, an abusive label that from the 1960s to the 1980s had been used to describe the Soviet Union and its alleged attempts to sabotage the Chinese revolution. By some accounts, Deng Xiaoping tried to stop this application of the polemical terminology to the United States, but he was unsuccessful, indicating that his personal power was waning. The attacks on the United States were linked to insistent pressure from senior party leaders and generals—spurred on by what they had seen of the military technology used in the Gulf War—to give the PLA more money to modernize and adapt its forces to the demands of a confrontational world. The "blatant interference by the American hegemonists," as the PLA chief of general staff put it in May 1994, was offering "open support for the debilitating activities of hostile elements inside our country as well as opposing and subverting our socialist system." A member of the Politburo Standing Committee underlined the message, noting that the American goals were no less than "subverting the Chinese government and strangling China's development."[7]

Surely more was meant here than the United States' willingness to allow its officials to meet with Wei Jingsheng and discuss human rights, and more than injured dignity over the rejection of Beijing to host the 2000 Olympic

Games. Looming larger were the protracted debates in the United States over withdrawing the "most-favored-nation" trading status for China (restored in 1980) and offering support to the exiled Dalai Lama, and charges that the PRC was defying international agreements by selling nuclear technology to countries such as Iran and Pakistan. Chinese responses to these and other "hegemonic" threats ranged from shadowing American warships in the Yellow Sea region with nuclear-powered submarines, re-arresting many of the 1989 dissidents, purchasing large quantities of Russian fighters and transport planes, and building an early-warning radar net in the disputed area of the Spratly Islands (lying between Vietnam and Indonesia), to which China laid claim despite the islands' enormous distance from the mainland.

But in truth, significant though the perceived threats from the West may have been, if any forces were conducting "debilitating activities" and "subverting the socialist system," they were forces within China itself, and mostly without any overt or covert Western support. It was changes in the nature of party rule, a growing popular awareness of the party's past lies and inconsistencies, and the influx of new hopes and ambitions among the people that were putting the CCP on the defensive. Though adulation of Mao Zedong was still expressed, it now often took on the dimensions of a pop cult rather than of a deeply held and passionate belief. A new generation of filmmakers used aesthetic evocations of old China to underline its messages of the suffering in the People's Republic and to outline the inconsistencies and fallacies in current party attitudes toward ideas of justice and history. Swaggering novels and stories of street-smart youth, iconoclastic Chinese versions of rock and rap, sardonic cartoons, and witty graffiti all carried their own messages of decay and change. A wry joke caught these levels well: after shouting in the streets that Premier Li Peng was a "melonhead," a man was arrested and sentenced to twenty years in prison. The sentence combined two separate charges: one of five years for the expression of counterrevolutionary sentiments, and one of fifteen years for revealing state secrets.

At the same time, urban and rural landscapes were in constant change. Roads were rammed through city neighborhoods, and whole villages were demolished, without regard for historic preservation, local lifestyles, or aesthetic considerations. Without the benefit of either city planning or gracious architecture, forests of high-rise hotels and business towers began to ring Beijing and Shanghai and to change the skylines of small provincial towns. Corruption cases became almost routine: there were 140,000 "legal and disciplinary cases" involving party members in just the first six months of 1994. As urban unemployment spread and the outmoded collective industries struggled to survive in the newly competitive marketplace, agricultural lifestyles changed, too, sending millions of former farmers into the cities to find

By 1992 millions of people—children and adults—had illegally migrated across China, mainly
into the cities, in search of jobs.

work at the booming building sites and in sweatshops. Shanghai's migrant
labor force swelled to 2.8 million; 60,000 were entering Beijing in search of
work in a single day; Jilin province in Manchuria issued a call of alarm when
over 10 percent of its rural workers had migrated elsewhere. Thousands of
academics and civil servants found their slender pay inadequate in the world
of sharply rising prices and new consumer patterns. They added second or
even third jobs to their schedules, in the race to exploit the current moment
by "jumping into the sea," as the common phrase put it.

The temper of the times can also be gauged by another phenomenon:
the rising number of those who imbued the idea of "jumping into the sea"
with a new literalness. These were a new generation of Chinese migrants—
many from Fujian province—who tried to buy their way overseas. The
case of the *Golden Venture*, a vessel loaded with illegal immigrants that
ran ashore on Long Island near New York City in the summer of 1993,
revealed dramatically that thousands of Chinese were promising payments
of U.S.$20,000 or more to smugglers for a chance to get to the United
States. Each time one route was cut by American immigration authorities and the Coast Guard, others opened up: first through the Caribbean by
air, and then via complex trails through Southeast Asia. The scale of these
operations revealed the power of Chinese organized crime, often linked (at

least by name) to the old secret societies such as the Triads, which had been powerful in the late Qing.

Only individual life stories can give a sense of this mix of turmoil, disequilibrium, excitement, and opportunity, and a wide variety of interviews conducted in rural China highlighted the factors at work here. They showed how once-illiterate peasants, reared in the sufferings of the 1920s and 1930s—who had seen their families starve, the Japanese invade their land, and the Communists infiltrate their villages—gladly worked with the CCP after 1949 and lived for and by the voice of Chairman Mao. But under the new policies of the reform era, they were venturing out into the unknown as they witnessed the breaking up of their communes and the decollectivization of agriculture. A wide range of unofficial sources also showed that in the 1990s and the first years of the new century there were many more attempts at strikes, and far more serious industrial unrest, than the government had been willing to acknowledge. Many of the educated victims of the antirightist campaign and the Cultural Revolution also wrote their stories, but usually these focused on their experiences in the 1960s and 1970s rather than on their subsequent attempts at readjustment in the Deng Xiaoping years.

For the young and middle-aged urban professionals of the 1990s, tension was endemic. Many spoke of their lives as a constant flux: though to some extent anchored by parents and spouses, they also felt the need to cope as loners in an unsettled society. Young couples often hedged their bets, with one spouse entering the uncertain world of higher technology, marketing, or foreign trade, while the other stayed tight within what was left of the socialist net, to work for low pay in return for health and social benefits and access to adequate (if not spacious) housing. Most such couples had only one child in obedience to party dictates, but that single child was cherished, though paradoxically often raised by grandparents or sent to boarding school because of the insistent work pressures on the parents. These young professionals read widely, thought freely, and were sarcastic about the party, even while admiring many of its past achievements. They felt the CCP still had some role to play in stopping the country from sliding into anarchy. They saw the democracy movement, at least as manifested from 1986 to the mid-1990s, as having little to offer China at the current time. They were starting to think of personal appearance, of family vacations, of surrounding themselves with aesthetically beautiful objects, and they were both frugal and shrewd. Those who had been teenagers during the Cultural Revolution remembered the humiliations of their parents as strongly as they remembered their own, but they felt well steeled by those past deprivations to cope in the current world.

The parents, for their part, especially those who were born in the 1920s or 1930s and had joined the CCP during World War II or the civil war, were often nostalgic for the clarity of choice that the world had offered, for the promise of a better society that then seemed within reach. They vividly remembered the sharpness of the transition they had lived through, and their optimistic sense that they were in the mainstream of history. They were saddened in the 1990s by the tumult and the lack of vision; they watched with bemused affection or concern as their children floundered. The generational sequencing was stark: one generation in the republic having large landholdings, or perhaps studying overseas; the next joining the CCP, working underground, building the revolution, and living in comparative security during the 1950s; a third weathering the Cultural Revolution, studying with passion through college, and then plunging into a succession (or often an overlapping sequence) of jobs.

To take just one example drawn from interviews in the late 1990s, a child born in 1955 was left to fend for himself when his parents were arrested in 1966, and he subsequently worked in a steel mill and as an educational cadre. Acquiring a job in a state-run venture capital firm, he went from there to assembling real-estate packages for a Hong Kong conglomerate, before creating a business selling TV advertising time. The profits from these ventures then funded investments in the design and patent of car accessories, a social club for wealthy party cadres, a massage parlor, retail apparel, publishing, and information storage on the internet.[8] The lives of his contemporaries, who were drawn to the scholars' life, were equally filled—by the pursuit of knowledge (with homage duly paid to the past complexities of Chinese history and culture) and by deep respect for their own teachers, a tireless willingness to work, and strong ambitions to make a mark in the national and international world of letters.

If such men and women subverted the state and party, it was through their energy, independence, and integrity, not by deliberate opposition or in pursuit of nefarious ends. Their goal was to find an opening for their hopes inside a China that they knew was changing, under leaders they could no longer admire.

DENG'S PASSING

An intriguing book that appeared in China in late 1994 gave a strange kind of focus to the country's mood. Entitled *Looking at China through a Third Eye*, the book was allegedly authored by a German scholar, but this fabrication was soon exposed. The author was a close friend of party leader Chen Yun's son. The book boldly asserted that Deng's policies had led the country into the trap of revering rapid and uneven economic growth, with the result of leaving 800 million peasants "a living volcano" that could erupt at any time. This volatile force was already flooding the cities. The author sketched in vivid detail how Deng had laid the groundwork for a potential catastrophe even worse than the Great Leap famine, which had led to tens of millions of deaths. In this newly emerging context, the book warned, Deng's policies would lead to an apocalypse of uncontrollable lawlessness that would dwarf the disasters of the Mao era.[9]

The leadership scenario in China had indeed become increasingly bizarre to outside eyes, as had the setting in which the largely silent struggle was taking place. While individual thugs (with or without party backing) were taking over many industries and even whole rural communities,[10] China was now operating two major nuclear power plants, foreign exchange reserves were over U.S.$30 billion, and the United States' trade deficit with China was close to U.S.$20 billion. At the same time, the PLA was making large purchases of advanced tanks, air-defense missile systems, and inflight refueling aircraft from the assembled stockpiles of the now defunct Soviet Union.

It was in this world of change and turbulence that the last representatives of Mao's legacy passed from the scene, the roster of their names providing a cumulative summary of the revolution's tumultuous history. In 1992 Li Xiannian and Nie Rongzhen died, Li at the age of eighty-three and Nie at ninety-three. A carpenter from Hubei, Li Xiannian had joined the CCP as a teenager in 1927 and was a key leader of the anti-Japanese guerrilla forces in central China. He later became the Minister of Finance and finally president of the PRC from 1983 to 1988. Nie Rongzhen, from a Sichuan landlord family, had traveled to France in 1920 with the work-study group that included Deng Xiaoping and joined the party there in 1923. A brilliant military strategist, Nie played a leading part in the Long March, the Yan'an years, and the civil war before becoming a marshal of the PLA and director of the Special Technology Commission in charge of nuclear weapons and missile programs. The following year, 1993, the Hunan-born railroad worker Wang Zhen, who rose to be vice president and the hardest of hard-liners, died at eighty-five.

Perhaps most important, for Deng Xiaoping and his close allies, was the death of Chen Yun in 1995 at the age of eighty-nine. Chen had joined the party in 1924 and became a labor organizer. He helped to orchestrate the Shanghai strikes of 1927, became a member of the Central Committee in 1931, serving subsequently as Mao's most important economic adviser and as the architect of post-1949 socialist reconstruction. From the 1980s onward, he had emerged as the most important critic of decollectivization and unchecked growth, and of what he saw as the accompanying erosion of moral and spiritual values. His death removed the main pillar of support for those planners who still espoused what they considered the fundamental Marxist-Leninist values, and who looked to ideological discipline, fiscal egalitarianism, and restraint as the keys to an ordered future.

During the mid-1990s, Deng Xiaoping's exact role was an enigma to most political observers. After his 1992 southern tour, he made no more dramatic public gestures or statements. The blurred pictures from his 1994 Shanghai visit were the last ones publicly circulated. Deng's prestige was sustained in his old age by the government now headed by Jiang Zemin and Li Peng, who made sure that the "Collected Works of Deng Xiaoping" were widely disseminated, and who constantly referred to him as the "paramount leader" despite his relinquishment of all formal government posts. But if Deng was paramount leader, it was mainly as an offstage presence whose often enigmatic remarks were filtered through his daughters and a small group of senior generals. There were few references anymore even to the competitive bridge games with a circle of friends, which had long been his recreational passion—though to the end Deng retained his title as "Honorary Chairman of the China Bridge Association." Deng was said to be keeping up with events in a general way and enjoying the company of his grandchildren.

In the meantime, the leadership of the country seemed to be on hold, even as the frenzied and uncoordinated spate of economic growth continued. Premier Li Peng—whose own term of office was due to end in 1998—issued a statement in 1995 that a transition "from the second-generational central leading collective, with Deng Xiaoping at the core" was underway; the "third-generational leading collective, with Comrade Jiang Zemin at the core" was now in place. Behind these remarks were complicated political maneuverings. Almost immediately after Chen Yun's death, Jiang Zemin had forced the resignation of a key rival, the powerful Beijing party secretary Chen Xitong (whose deputy-mayor had just died by suicide in the midst of a major corruption scandal). In his position Chen Xitong could have called on the services of tens of thousands of police and security forces in the capital. With Chen's removal, Jiang brought to completion a series of preventive moves to ensure that he would not follow the fate of the Gang of Four after Mao's death. He had already appointed his own personal head bodyguard to be the commander of the Central Guards Regiment, also known as Unit 8341, which in 1976 had spearheaded the arrest of the Gang of Four.[11]

When the death of Deng Xiaoping on February 19, 1997, from a lung infection and complications of Parkinson's disease, was announced to the nation, there was a sense of uncertainty as much as loss. The government moved at once to make sure that demonstrators would not use the occasion to raise major criticisms of the regime, as they had done so conspicuously on two previous occasions: in April 1976, in the mourning for Zhou Enlai, and in April 1989, in the mourning for Hu Yaobang. The first case, that of 1976, grew into an open attack on Chairman Mao and his policies, and Deng Xiaoping was blamed for the upheaval by his political enemies. Once Deng regained power in 1979, he "reversed the verdicts" on the 1976 demonstrations, claiming that they had been justified as criticisms of the Gang of Four and the Cultural Revolution. But Deng never reversed the verdicts on the events of 1989, nor expressed any contrition for the deaths of students and civilians that occurred at that time. Police controls were tight in 1997, to make sure that his memory was neither excoriated nor overpraised in what might be seen as a slap to the current president and party secretary-general, Jiang Zemin. So muted, indeed, was the public response that the government had to encourage carefully controlled displays of emotion on the day of the state funeral, but only for specially invited delegations from state enterprises and work units. By Deng's own previous request, his ashes were scattered over the sea, as Zhou Enlai's had been in 1976.

The muted funeral also served to accentuate a more subtle political point, one that Jiang Zemin was anxious to establish: Deng Xiaoping had been on the sidelines for several years, and the de facto transfer of power had already been carried out. To emphasize this point, Jiang in his funeral oration expressed the hope that the remaining party elders—several of whom were at the ceremony—should now step aside. This would remove from influence such figures as Peng Zhen (ninety-five), Bo Yibo (eighty-nine), and Yang Shangkun (ninety), whose long revolutionary careers gave them a historical resonance that the younger Jiang Zemin—who was seventy-one—lacked. Such retirements would also mean that the senior military officers who controlled the PLA would also have to step down, thus giving Jiang Zemin a much stronger base on the all-important Military Affairs Commission.

The timing of Deng's death ensured Jiang Zemin the freedom to enjoy the limelight when, by the prior 1984 agreement with Great Britain, Hong Kong reverted to PRC control on July 1, 1997. At the stroke of midnight, the Union Jack and the former colonial Hong Kong flag were lowered, and the red flag with gold stars of the People's Republic was raised aloft next to the newly designed red bauhinia-blossom flag of the Hong Kong administrative region. Jiang Zemin sat next to Britain's Prince Charles on the stage of the vast new convention center, which was just being completed by a group of Hong Kong and Chinese real estate developers on a controversial landfill site at the edge of the main harbor.

The choice for the new chief executive of Hong Kong, to replace the departing British governor Christopher Patten, was the articulate, crew-cut businessman Chee-hua Tung. Known as C. H. Tung, he was born in 1937 to a wealthy Shanghai family that had built up a shipping business before and after World War II. After 1949 the family emigrated to Hong Kong and their business expanded rapidly both there and in Taiwan (where they received Guomindang support). C. H. Tung went to university in Britain and worked

On July 1, 1997, Hong Kong was returned to China after more than 150 years of British colonial rule. Members of the combined Chinese Armed Forces color guard raise the Chinese flag at the Hong Kong convention center, marking the moment Hong Kong reverted to PRC rule.

for a decade with corporations in the United States, before returning to Hong Kong to join his father. When the family business was threatened with collapse in the early 1980s, Tung staved off bankruptcy by negotiating a 120-million-yuan loan from Beijing. He owed his new position to his prominence among the elite group of Hong Kong's Chinese business leaders, and because his views coincided with what could loosely be called the "new authoritarianism" that now was fashionable. Tung publicly espoused law and order, denigrated any excessive race toward democracy, praised Singapore's government as a suitable model, and endorsed the stated Chinese decision to abolish the democratically elected Legislative Council. But at the same time, Tung reassured the people of Hong Kong that he would protect their distinctive way of life, faithfully enforce the laws on Hong Kong's future, and maintain the independence of the judiciary.

What all this said about the previous decades of Communist rule was of course not lost on satirists, who were once again ready to speak out with vigor and freshness. Wang Shuo, a veteran writer of irreverent Beijing street-life stories, caught the mood perfectly. As a little boy, Wang wrote in an essay published three days before the handover, he had been taught that "the Chinese people had all stood up, but Hong Kong people still served the British as their cows and horses." His boyish heart used to fill with pity as he heard that the Hong Kong people had no shoes and lived on fishbones. But now there was a bit of a mystery. Apparently Hong Kong people did wear shoes after all, and leather ones at that. They were also very rich, so rich that by their lascivious ways they had changed the "good old adultery" of the "pure and honest mainlanders" into prostitution. Some of his muddled friends, Wang Shuo continued, said Hong Kong's prosperity showed that China might have done better in the past to leave Qingdao in German hands and Dalian to the Japanese, and let them become wealthy "cash boxes" like Hong Kong. Nothing would have been lost: "The motherland would still be the great motherland." But perhaps at that point he had better stop, Wang wrote. "Poor dad still has a bad temper, and he'll beat his kid over any little thing." The best policy remained, as before: "Be like the Shanghainese: Work hard, then send your own people to Beijing to take over the Politburo."[12]

Looming behind the celebration of the end of foreign control over Hong Kong lay the question of Taiwan. Weeks before the Hong Kong transfer, as a giant clock in Tiananmen Square counted down the days, hours, and minutes, banners displayed in Beijing carried slogans stating that "China was eagerly welcoming the return to the motherland of Hong Kong, Macao, and Taiwan." Macao's return, after more than four and a half centuries of total or partial Portuguese control, was already set for 1999. But the case of Taiwan was infinitely more complex. Even as Chinese authorities were citing pro-independence rallies as the kind of demonstrations that would not be tolerated in Hong Kong, any more than those demanding independent rights for the people of Tibet or Xinjiang would, the government of Lee Teng-hui was working with a coalition of rival parties to end the "provincial government" of Taiwan. This was a vestigial legacy of the civil war and the early 1950s, when Taiwan claimed to be the temporary base for a Republic of China national government in exile. With the abolition of this provincial representation, Taiwan would become, in effect, an independent political unit, with no more formal governmental interdependence with the mainland. Thus the PRC attacked the decision as a dangerous provocation.

The facts were curious. On its path forward China could be propelled by twin legacies to which it had long been opposed: one, the very system built up in Hong Kong under British imperialism against which the Communist party had fulminated since its inception; the other, the Taiwan economic and political dynamo that had sprung out of Japanese colonialism by way of half a century of rule under the CCP's bitterest domestic enemy, the Guomindang. No one could doubt that Hong Kong and Taiwan had become flourishing and prosperous societies. But with 6.3 million and 21.6 million people respectively, the two societies were dwarfed by the People's Republic of close to 1.3 billion people. And the PRC itself was still facing the future on the basis of the state's dominance over key areas of the economy. In mid-1997, state-owned enterprises employed 67 percent of the urban workforce and contributed 60 percent of the state's revenues; in key industries, state control was even higher: 77 percent in chemicals, 79 percent in metallurgy, and over 90 percent in both electrical power and oil production. Deciding to confront this anomaly directly, in September 1997 China's leaders announced their decision to sell off at least 10,000 of the remaining 13,000 large and medium state-owned enterprises. Dodging the word "privatization," they argued that selling stock in those companies would constitute "public ownership." The decision was a bold one, for it would take the most imaginative and courageous planning to sell off these companies without raising unemployment to explosive levels and without producing further environmental imbalances in a country already suffering water shortages, dangerous levels of soil erosion and air pollution, and shrinking amounts of arable land.

In public, some CCP stalwarts continued to express belief in the socialist values with which they had been raised. As one acerbic party member noted in an anonymous special report, "the mentality of imitating Hong Kong and Taiwan culture, worshipping everything foreign, and yearning for the capitalist world has been passed from ignorant young people to some intellectuals and party and government cadres." The author conjured up a world of "speculation in stocks and real estate, trading of false invoices, pornography, production and selling of counterfeit goods, and even smuggling," within a society where 2 percent of all bank depositors contributed 80 percent of the total deposits. The report's author went on to paint a scenario of industrial strikes, violence, rural impoverishment, and weakened morale coexisting with the world of "nightclubs, golf courses, saunas, massage parlors, and brothels." In his view, "almost all ugly phenomena of the old society prior to the establishment of the Republic have been revived."[13]

Irresponsible leaders, a luxury-loving elite, a morally lax middle class, and an exploited rural and manufacturing sector living on the edge of dire poverty: this was also close to the social scene invoked not only by Ming patriots as they watched their dynasty fall to the upstart Qing, but also by Chinese revolutionaries at the Qing dynasty's end and by the Communists as they marshalled against the world of perceived republican decadence. From such a viewpoint, the negative forces now confronting the people of China were little different from what they had been in the bad old days. But there was something too tidy about such a pattern of argument and criticism. A book published by Qian Ning, a student recently returned from studying at the

University of Michigan, presented an alternative view. "Chinese students who went to America had simple but firm beliefs that their leaders should control the people," he commented. "We thought the values and standards in our society were only natural and absolute. It was only when we got into another society that we realized the limitation of our own ideology." The son of the foreign minister, Qian Ning was no ordinary student. He contrasted his first impressions of campus life in Ann Arbor (singing, laughter, and the smell of barbecue at parties) to what he had witnessed in Beijing just months earlier, in the spring of 1989. "This world in front of my eyes was so different" from Tiananmen Square, such that "it was impossible to connect them together in my mind." He continued, "But at that moment I understood a simple thing. We Chinese—at least the younger generation of Chinese—can have a different kind of life, free from the repetitive political movements in the past and life-and-death struggles."[14]

On an official visit to the United States in October 1997, President Jiang Zemin implicitly supported a more open stance, as he included both Independence Hall in Philadelphia and the New York Stock Exchange in his itinerary. A few weeks later, just after construction workers had completed their diversion of the Yangzi River so that work could begin on the second stage of the Three Gorges Dam project, the dissident Wei Jingsheng was released from prison and allowed to go abroad. A few months later, in his inaugural speech as the new premier, Zhu Rongji spoke at length of the economic challenges but never once mentioned the name of Mao Zedong. Such juxtapositions of a pragmatically developmental attitude with a more open ideological one offered a constructive road into the rapidly approaching new century. Perhaps, once again, the skills and the insights of China's people would be allowed full range to blossom, along a forward path that incorporated the lessons and legacies of the past while forging a new vision for the future.

CHAPTER 28

Breakthrough?

THE RANGE OF OPTIONS

The death of Deng Xiaoping and the end of British colonial rule over Hong Kong in 1997 served as vivid markers between the older China that still had not totally vanished and the new world that might lie ahead. But though both these events were poignant, they were not more important than a number of other economic, political, and cultural developments of this same time. Among them was the dramatic 2000 presidential election in Taiwan, won by Chen Shui-bian, the first leader of the opposition Democratic Progressive Party to assume office. Chen's ensuing talk about possible Taiwanese independence brought a new complexity to East Asian politics and compelled the leaders of the Nationalist Party—so long dominated by Chiang Kai-shek and his family—to reassess their own relationships with the People's Republic.*

In China the pressures on the older generations of revolutionaries and PLA veterans (many of whom were in their nineties) to face retirement became insuperable, opening routes of power and influence to younger party members. At the same time, the September 11, 2001, terrorist attacks on the World Trade Center in New York City and the Pentagon brought a whole new concept of war into the United States, along with a shifting of U.S. military preoccupations away from East Asia to Afghanistan, Iraq, and the Middle East.

Shortly before that tragedy, China had returned to the vexed arena of bidding for the Olympic Summer Games. This time the humiliations of the failed bid to host the 2000 Games were laid to rest with the international vote

---

* After finishing a second term as Taiwan's president in 2008, Chen was tried on charges of corruption and sentenced to nineteen years in jail.

to award the 2008 Games to Beijing. Though that date seemed far off, the Chinese moved into high gear by launching an immense plan for the construction of new facilities, housing, and transportation routes—including ambitious targets for curbing air pollution—involving architects and other specialists from all over the world. When the Games opened under tight security in August 2008, they were inaugurated by spectacular displays of Chinese arts, music, and history, showcasing a vibrant sense of cultural nationalism and saluting China's global greatness. The Games were also a triumph for Chinese athletes, who won 48 gold medals and 100 overall, the finest performance in the nation's Olympic history.

Even these few examples, crowded together at the beginning of the new century, can serve to remind us of the role of chance in human history and to underline the fact that there was no conceivable way that Chairman Mao and his fellow revolutionaries could have known exactly where they were heading in 1949, any more than Chinese patriots in 1912 could have grasped all the implications of the collapse of the Qing empire. Virtually every step of the Communists' march to the future had been contingent on myriad unforeseeable events, with their vast country the elaborate backdrop to their vaguely glimpsed vision of the future.

We can recall that, when Mao finally met Stalin face to face in late 1949, in what was Mao's first trip outside the country he was fighting to transform, the Soviet dictator asked Mao what he most needed or wanted for his country. Mao's response seemed reflective: what he would most like, he replied, was two or three years of peace, which would enable China to recover from the protracted agonies of the Japanese invasion and the subsequent civil war, and to lay out a workable framework for the future. Instead, what ensued was not a program of steady development but a bewildering succession of unforeseeable events. Among these were a protracted and costly war in Korea, revolution in the cities and the countryside, a murderous battle for control over culture, and a series of deliberately provocative misunderstandings that for a time in the 1960s brought China and the Soviet Union to the edge of war.

It had been Deng Xiaoping's inspiration to shift the direction of China's policies back into a manageable zone of planning, and to run with the opportunities as they presented themselves. But once Deng was gone, new leadership initiatives were required; the abandonment of extremist solutions was just one promising road that might be taken. We can guess that Deng deliberately chose a partial solution, but one that brought to the fore men—and a few women—who had strong records in both urban and rural governance. This cohort of leaders came to be called the "third generation" leadership, successors to Deng Xiaoping and Mao Zedong. It fell to Jiang Zemin to supervise the final Hong Kong takeover and to give full rein to the possibilities of foreign investment, and to the skillful financial specialist Zhu Rongji (as premier) to build the foundation for the long-term health of the banking system.

Zhu Rongji and Jiang Zemin were careful men, with strong links to senior party leaders. As their second five-year term neared completion, the secretive process of leadership selection generated swirling speculations about who would replace them. The sixteenth party congress in 2002 confirmed Hu Jintao as CCP secretary general and elevated Wen Jiabao to the Politburo Standing Committee—two men with solid records as administrators but little national stature or international visibility. Punning on Hu's name, foreign news outlets featured headlines such as "Who's Hu" and "Who/Hu's in charge?"[1] Born in 1942, Hu Jintao had been trained as a water conservancy engineer and was regarded as an experienced party theorist. In an apparently deliberate move to ensure power-sharing, Wen Jiabao, also born in 1942 and trained as a geologist, was named premier in the spring of 2003. Wen's promotion was surprising, since he was a protégé of Zhao Ziyang, held under house arrest ever since his tearful visit to Tiananmen Square during the demonstrations of 1989. Following recent precedent, this transition marked the emergence of the "fourth generation" of Chinese leadership. Past experience in retirement patterns indicated that both Hu and Wen could be expected to serve two five-year terms and then to retire, in their turn, in 2013.

Appointed to their new posts secretly, but apparently by consensus among the members of the Politburo Standing Committee, this new leadership group emerged at the head of a CCP membership of approximately 70 million people. The new leadership devoted much attention to recruiting more youthful and highly educated candidates for membership, along with business entrepreneurs and public media figures. In a sea change, the CCP expanded eligibility for membership to include capitalists and those who worked for foreign joint venture companies. This redefinition of the party's ideological foundation was intended to amplify its influence in society, but at the cost of jettisoning any remaining pretense of adhering to communism. At the same time, the immense size of China, and the announcement in 2005 that the population had surpassed 1.3 billion, confronted CCP leaders with a recurrent tangle of highly complex organizational problems—which included maintaining tight control over social organizations, patrolling the swiftly growing nationwide internet systems for evidence of possible dissidence or subversion, and keeping a watchful eye over economic growth and urban infrastructures.

At the very end of the twentieth century, a number of warning signs gave some advance notice of emerging problems that affected the thinking and behavior of the new leaders. One of these came in April 1999, when an estimated 10,000 members of a religious group called the Falun Gong assembled in Beijing and held a sit-in in front of the party leadership compound adjacent to the Forbidden City. Though the army and police had a fairly easy time breaking up the demonstration and arrested many of those present, the government was alarmed by the fact that so many people had been able to assemble at a fixed time and place without the state agencies being aware of the brewing storm. Besides banning Falun Gong as a "cult" and prosecuting its members, the government also intensified the focus on preventing similar attempts that might be made by other organized groups with petitions or criticisms to offer the Communist party.

Only one month later, in May 1999, as part of joint operations with NATO forces in former Yugoslavia, a U.S. airplane bombed the PRC embassy in the city of Belgrade, killing several Chinese nationals. The Clinton administration maintained that the incident was an accident, caused by faulty and outdated maps of the city and its major buildings. The Chinese at once rejected the explanation as inadequate, insisting that the Americans' usual pinpoint accuracy in such combat situations made an error of this magnitude unthinkable. Responses within China were furious and sustained, with mass rallies and anti-American demonstrations held in many cities and widespread threats of counteraction against U.S. property. Such manifestations of anti-American feeling had deep historical resonance, for reasons we have seen, and threatened

On May 8, 1999, Chinese students chant anti-U.S. and anti-NATO slogans outside the U.S. Embassy in Beijing during a protest against the bombing of the Chinese Embassy in Belgrade.

to sour relations that had for a time showed promise with prospects of mutually valuable Sino-American initiatives in space exploration, as members of the World Bank and the World Health Organization, and as supporters for a nuclear test ban treaty.

To many Chinese observers, the midair collision of an American "spy plane" and a patrolling Chinese fighter plane near Hainan Island in April 2001 was further proof—if any was needed—of how quickly moods could sour or skirmishes threaten to teeter out of control. In this shifting context, the 2001 attacks on the World Trade Center became a useful moment for the Chinese government to declare that dissident Muslim groups in Xinjiang province should be viewed as "terrorist" organizations. The attribution of previous acts of political violence to the "East Turkestan Islamic Movement," with allegedly close links to al Qaeda, was used to justify the harsh suppression that followed.[2]

THE HU/WEN YEARS

The "Hu/Wen years," if we may use a convenient, shorthand label for the decade from 2003 to 2013, were a period of astonishing economic growth, as can be seen from the 10.3 percent average gain in annual GDP. In per capita terms China still lagged behind countries such as South Korea and Brazil, but its rate of growth was the envy of the world.[3] As the country grew dramatically richer and assumed a larger role on the international stage, the paradoxes confronting ordinary people in their daily lives became more challenging. In what must surely have been the fastest and most comprehensive urban growth in the history of humankind, entire Chinese cities were reshaped, reconfigured, and rebuilt. It was not just metropolises like Shanghai and Beijing that were affected. Scores of provincial capitals and formerly sleepy rural townships were transformed, at a pace so swift and profound that the number of cities with populations of over 1 million soon moved well beyond the 100 mark. For those from overseas making regular visits to China during those years, the entire urban landscape could be transformed between visits: this was as true of towns in the hills of Shandong as it was of those in Anhui. These cities in turn were linked together by extensive networks of highways, new high-speed railway systems, provincial airports, and coastal and riverside harbors, so that one could see entire residential cities arising on farmland where only the choice of vegetables had defined land use in previous years.[4] Tens of millions of rural migrants contributed their labor to the construction of real estate development. Both Chinese and global technologies (including massive investment from domestic banks, along with those in Taiwan and Hong Kong) led to the growth of a new class of Chinese millionaires and then, by 2006 or so, of billionaires.

The scale of operations and the hunger for land to develop were so huge that new internal fault lines began to develop. Massive evictions from planned development sites became commonplace. Attempts at peaceful protest through the courts or by petitions to the local authorities were often condemned by the provincial or city branches of the Communist party, which had easy access to funds from state banks or could use the local police to block plaintiffs' access to legal redress. A new class of Chinese lawyers emerged to advise and represent those evicted, but even their principled procedures were branded by the state as excessive, or else they were themselves blamed for stimulating unrest or social dislocation.

Often the party bureaucrats echoed government demands—for example, in leveling hundreds of acres of prime land in the north of Beijing to build the "Bird's Nest" stadium and the national aquatic center for the Olympics. A parallel demand spread to Shanghai, where a colossal exposition center in the once decayed and fetid outlands of Pudong was constructed, to cater to the seventy million visitors who attended the World Expo in 2010. The immense scale of these projects also placed new demands on the power grid and on regulations then in place to stop water pollution, to protect the air from chemical wastes and acid rain, and to restrain the need to probe for ever deeper water tables. The immense Three Gorges Dam project to link the lower

Performers hit drums during the opening ceremony of the Olympic Games in Beijing on August 8, 2008.

Yangzi region to the inland megacity of Chongqing, completed in stages from 1994 to 2006, was at once part of the solution and part of the problem.

As one of their arguments for Beijing as a fitting Olympic host, China's leaders had implied that the anticipated "opening up" to the world that the Games and the Expo would entail could only help spread a broader sense of justice and a better understanding of international social and sporting norms. But during the event, the promised "open hot lines" installed by the authorities were mainly used to spot "troublemakers"; even minor complaints were concealed so as to keep any signs of the underlying problems from reaching foreign and domestic visitors. Ticket holders who peered down the leafy streets near the Olympic stadiums and venues could easily see police vehicles parked in the shade nearby. Because the armed police were largely out of sight did not mean that they were out of mind.

The nature of the complaints made by Chinese and foreign critics varied from year to year, but in the Olympic year of 2008, to take just one example, troubles were deep and difficult. One focus for protest sprang from the upheavals in Tibet, where political activists saw the route planned for the bearers of the Olympic flame as a recurring source of opportunities to underline the harsh policies of the Chinese government toward the Tibetans. The Olympic

flame, whether in Europe, the United States, or Tibet, served to reintroduce to public debate the concept of an independent Tibet separate from the burden of Han Chinese "improvements." Among the massive investments making inroads into Tibet in the name of progress, the most dramatic was the new railway line linking Lhasa with south and west China.

A second group of complaints sprang from the aftermath of the catastrophic earthquake near the city of Chengdu in Sichuan province, which occurred in May 2008, just before the Olympic Games were due

The World Expo in Shanghai, 2010 Tourists crowd the promenade on the renovated Bund. According to Chinese sources, the Expo was attended by over 70 million people.

to begin. An estimated 69,000 people died in the 7.9 Richter scale quake, and a further 374,000 were injured either then or in the hundreds of aftershocks that followed. In all, some 3 million homes in the region were destroyed. The complaints here were not that the government had failed to act—indeed Premier Wen Jiabao traveled to the disaster zone within a few hours of the eruption and served as director of the relief operations. The public anger came from two interlocking factors. First was the discovery that a large number of victims were children, who died when school buildings collapsed on top of them. Second was the revelation from further investigations showing that local school authorities had not only been guilty of shoddy or corrupt work, but also had tried to prevent many families from seeking redress through the courts for the fatal results of the shoddy construction. Lawyers seeking to represent the villagers were harassed or silenced, and thousands of grieving parents were forced to accept small offers of compensation without further redress.[5]

Equally depressing was the story of the government's attempt to deny the prevalence of the SARS (severe acute respiratory syndrome) virus in China during 2003, and to conceal its possibly fatal effect if not diagnosed and promptly treated. Here again, according to those familiar with the case, it was mainly tenacious watchers of the crisis—like the seventy-one-year-old surgeon Jiang Yanyong—who spread the word about SARS over the internet. Their efforts helped to break through the news blackout, which had lasted for several months and undoubtedly led to an increase in the number of deaths.[6]

Such ambiguities, or morally difficult stances, were commonplace at this time and can be seen as providing a running and often ironic commentary on the Hu/Wen years. One sees another example in the evasions and inconsistencies practiced by the regime, as it sought to prevent public mourning for the former party secretary Zhao Ziyang when he died at eighty-five in 2005. For a time the authorities blocked his children's cell phone calls about the funeral, and considered denying him a burial spot in Babaoshan, the cemetery for revolutionary heroes and high-ranking leaders, before grudgingly reversing their decision. The funeral came to constitute as complicated a political ballet as one can imagine.[7]

THE ECONOMIC CHALLENGES

Many other major problems confronted Hu Jintao and Wen Jiabao as they moved through 2008 and into a second five-year term. Although not so easily definable in impact, these problems often involved highly technical challenges that had become—or threatened to become—enmeshed in the life of the country. Several can be traced back to the priorities set by Mao Zedong during and after his ascent to power. To take just three areas of the many that preoccupied the Hu/Wen regime, we can consider the direction of the national economy, the central goals of foreign policy, and the problem of information management and censorship.

The extremist policies imposed on China's farmers from the Yan'an years until Mao's death in 1976—depicted now in numerous and vivid autobiographies and memoirs—had as their ultimate goal the implementation of a massive reorganization in agriculture. The revolutionary changes were intended to generate rural surpluses, which were to be used to feed the urban dwellers (both factory workers and party elites) and to sustain their productivity. When pushed to their ultimate conclusion such policies could lead—as had been the case in the famine that followed the Great Leap Forward—to the deaths of tens of millions of people.

Starting in the Deng Xiaoping years and accelerating through the 1990s, the emphasis of economic policy gradually shifted to closure of minimally productive or ineffective state-run collective industries, the reintroduction of local markets as a device for economic expansion, and the emergence of a class of independent factory managers. Support from local party leaders and an accommodating domestic banking structure made large capital investments highly profitable. The acceleration continued into the late 1990s at a startling pace, drawing large numbers of foreign investors to form "joint ventures" with Chinese capitalists. Some seeds of these new strategies had appeared in the late nineteenth century, when Chinese and foreigners had collaborated on translations of scientific textbooks, building arsenals for military production and training, and management of industrial projects. But the scale of the foreign joint ventures of the reform era was a new experience for all except those Chinese who had been entrepreneurs under the Guomindang's most productive period in the early 1930s, or who had grown up in Taiwan, Hong Kong, or Southeast Asia.

Chinese businesses, now released from many former constraints, quickly learned the necessary strategies for entering Western markets. The government proved adept at protecting the currency from the kinds of manipulation and near-collapse that had afflicted the economies of Japan, Thailand, and Indonesia. The loosening of the rural registration system and limits on labor mobility were a boon. These reforms generated a migrant population of tens of millions of workers, flowing between the poor areas of west China and the burgeoning cities in the central provinces and on the east coast. The development of coastal cities facilitated massive economic growth, especially after China reduced its tariffs as a response to the chance to enter the World Trade Organization in 2001.

China secured its own prosperity by the immense range of production in the subsequent Hu/Wen years, which soon moved beyond the low-cost manufacturing of such items as shoes, toys, and clothing, and came to include petrochemicals, polymers, machine tools, passenger aircraft, and the nurturing of a nascent automobile industry, backed by investments in roads, railways, and airfields.[8] Initial public offerings of Chinese banks and other companies became regular features of the stock exchanges in New York and Hong Kong, though China continued to face a stream of charges that it was deliberately keeping the value of its currency at artificially low levels to give its exports an unfair price advantage. Under such stimuli, in 2005 China replaced the United States as Japan's main trading partner. In the next few years China's GDP passed those of both Japan and Germany, and by 2006 total trade reached $1.4 trillion, of which $762 billion was with the United States. The favorable balance of trade with the United States continued to rise rapidly over the next several years, bolstered by holdings of American Treasury and other bonds that reached a level exceeding $3 trillion in 2008. By 2009 there was some clear evidence that China's economic focus was shifting, as worker wages steadily rose, and some businesses began in their turn to outsource to Vietnam, the Philippines, or India. Interestingly, tabulation of the percentage figures for CEO and senior management positions showed that in China 32 percent of such positions were held by women, as contrasted with 23 percent in the United States and 19 percent in the United Kingdom.[9]

GLOBAL PREOCCUPATIONS

Such global preoccupations and successes had not been a part of China's earlier strategic focus. Trade in the late Ming and early Qing did have international dimensions, and the presence of foreign traders in treaty ports and diplomats and missionaries in major cities was not unknown. But in general, China under the Qing dynasty and the early republican period was more victimized than transformed, until the major wars and revolutions of the mid-twentieth century irreparably challenged Western imperialist order. There was certainly no exact earlier precedent for the multiplicity of financial deals that China made between 2008 and 2011, as the country locked in its access to energy sources on a global scale, from Venezuela to Australia, from Nigeria and Somalia to Canada. Such agreements spanned a vast range: oil, natural gas, iron ore, coal, rare earth metals, forest products, and water sources.

But in scanning the daily newspapers, government publications, memoirs, and other information sources from China in the early twenty-first century, it is striking how similar many contemporary trouble spots were to the old

Qing preoccupations. Especially salient were the territories in the far western region of Xinjiang—occupied by Qing armies in the mid-eighteenth century but never fully assimilated. During the Hu/Wen years, government authorities treated any threats of political opposition and violence in Xinjiang with great severity. Despite (or perhaps because of) this strictness, cultural clashes were common, and intermittent violence continued to mar claims of "development" and "progress" for the whole region. On the northeast frontier of China, bordering on present-day North Korea, uneasy relations and interstate rivalries had sparked three wars between the 1620s and 1951, the last of which is still a living memory to elder Chinese. Taiwan, conquered by Kangxi's forces in the late seventeenth century and later ceded to Japan as a spoil of war, continued to be of uncertain status, though its commercial and cultural ties to the mainland became so close that it was hard to see how they could be separated. The uplands of Tibet, crucial for relations with Britain and Russia in the Qing, and now of great importance to relations with India, became strategically and ecologically linked to the prosperity and growth of Southeast Asia and the great rivers of China. Meanwhile, the exile of the Dalai Lama from his homeland for so many years continued to inflame relations between the PRC and India. In brief, China's past preoccupations clearly resonated with contemporary issues.

The third of these areas of preoccupation—that of information technology and censorship—loomed large. As of 2010, China had around 384 million internet users and 145 million bloggers, connected to over 1.5 million websites. The Ministry of Industry and Information Technology estimated in 2008 that more than 616 million people subscribed to mobile phones. But these imposing numbers did not translate into more robust press freedoms. The foreign nongovernmental organizations that monitor information flows often ranked China low in their listings of internet openness.[10]

With a colossal number of eager internet users, how news—especially political news—was assembled, cleared, and circulated became a critical issue of control. The Chinese government became an efficient censor and employed vast legions of employees to monitor the conversations on such sites as Twitter, Flickr, Wikipedia, Bing, Hotmail, and Facebook.[11] To give an example of the government's wariness in such matters, all such sites were closed for what was formally billed as "technical maintenance" during such potentially volatile periods as the twentieth anniversary of June Fourth in 2009 and the Xinjiang riots and deaths that occurred in July of the same year. As technology changed, the government developed ever more sophisticated means of censorship—though the sheer weight of numbers enabled protestors sometimes to spread their messages across systems as fast as the censors could delete them. Internet users also invented creative ways of evasion, using homophones and puns, or repurposing political slogans and quotations from Mao Zedong and Deng Xiaoping. To circumvent the ban on discussions about June 4th, for instance, the fictional date of May 35th was coined to refer to the government crackdown on the democracy movement in 1989. Others used the dynastic reference "celestial empire" to obliquely criticize the current regime and its imperial trappings.

In virtually every case mentioned here, and in countless other examples, some form of internet content was essential to allowing the public to get a sense of the pressing issues. In the case of massive chemical run-offs at a new plant being built in a heavily populated area of Xiamen, a large and vocal body of text messages circulated, eventually causing the project to be canceled. Similarly, as noted above, the rapid and initially unreported spread of SARS was communicated across the country through public sources. News from Xinjiang and Tibet would occasionally be picked up and passed around. Even small, local issues, such as the case of an elderly couple refusing to relinquish their home to urban development without adequate compensation, managed—though only by massive effort—to become known at a national level. News of a certain number (though by no means all) of the many fatal explosions and other catastrophes in coal mines also managed to get out to the public at large.

Occasionally, as with the case of the "Charter 08 manifesto," antigovernment criticism spread briefly on the internet before censors blocked all the sites. Charter 08 had been drafted by a small group of Chinese intellectuals, who circulated its powerful message in early December 2008. As the preamble stated, "The political reality, which is plain for anyone to see, is that China has many laws but no rule of law; it has a constitution but no constitutional government. The ruling elite clings to its authoritarian power and fights off any move toward political change." In a series of brief paragraphs, the manifesto listed nineteen major principles, including "legislative democracy," an independent judiciary, human rights, rural-urban equality, the freedom to assemble, the freedom of religion, and environmental protection. Many signers of the manifesto were tracked down by the police and arrested. Later one of them, the writer Liu Xiaobo, was awarded the Nobel Peace Prize. Liu had already been detained and charged with "incitement to subvert state power."[12] No one in his family was allowed to go and receive the award. The striking image of an empty chair at the Nobel awards ceremony in Oslo, where Liu received the prize in absentia, became a powerful visual symbol of dissent. Government censors soon blocked all photos of and references to empty chairs on the internet.

The deaths of thousands of children in the 2008 Sichuan earthquake also received wide coverage. The artist Ai Weiwei, who had designed the Bird's Nest Stadium for the Beijing Olympics, organized a "citizen investigation team" to gather information about the victims. After a year of phone calls and knocking on doors, they collected more than 5,000 names. Ai Weiwei created *Remembering*, an installation project to commemorate the young lives lost. Nine thousand children's backpacks spelled out the sentence "She lived happily in this world for seven years," invoking the words of a mother whose daughter died in the earthquake. (This work could not be displayed in China and was first featured in a show in Munich.) For his uncompromising artistic and online activism, Ai Weiwei was held in secret detention for eighty-one days in 2011.[13] At the time of his arrest, more than thirty years had passed since Wei Jingsheng wrote and circulated his own demands for democracy, but in that long span, little seemed to have changed in either the rhetoric of protest allowed to ordinary citizens or in signs of true flexibility by the government.

Cultural Parameters

While the struggles over information control continued forcefully during the Hu/Wen years, they constituted only one arena of conflict during the period. The world of publishing exploded in scale and focus, and Chinese cities and universities were filled with thriving bookshops that covered once taboo subjects such as the life of Chiang Kai-shek and the Soong family. Whereas in the past Chiang had been excoriated as "the enemy of the people," new works portrayed the Guomindang leader in a more sympathetic light, downplaying his anticommunism in favor of highlighting his commitment to a unified China. Other publications provided details of the extremism of the Mao years (including explosive accounts by former members of Mao's staff), examinations of the Nanjing massacre of World War II, and re-explorations of foreign imperialism, not neglecting comparisons with Stalinism. Books on foreign literary analysis and historiography were translated in vast numbers, with only limited scrutiny by state-appointed censors. The publishing enthusiasm spread to reprints of classical Chinese texts and translations of children's books in profusion—including many, like the stories of Roald Dahl, that might have previously been considered subversive. But in the Hu/Wen years it was mainly manifestoes directly summoning citizens to vigorous action on behalf of greater democracy and popular participation in government that remained deeply suspect. Such works were withdrawn from the shelves if their content was judged to be too provocative.

What could not be published as political commentary or history could be orchestrated as fiction, as had been the case with late-Ming and early-Qing novels such as *Outlaws of the Marsh* and *The Scholars*, which contained powerful social critiques. For instance, a grand sprawling novel like Mo Yan's *Life and Death Are Wearing Me Out* (2006, English translation 2008) presented the cruelties and random excesses of the Communist party during the Mao years and after. The author used the device of "reincarnation" by the gods of the underworld to show life through the skeptical gazes of a donkey, a pig, a dog, an ox, and other farm animals, so as to pinpoint absurdities and suggest avenues for reform and self-assertion. Short stories and novellas, such as *I Love Dollars* by Zhu Wen (2006, English translation 2007), explored the rootlessness of a new generation of mercenaries and showed how everything from hospital treatment of the seriously ill to the purchase of a melon or the repair of a bicycle could inflame entire communities. The parody of Maoist values, as presented in Yan Lianke's *Serve the People* (2005, English translation 2007), mockingly suggested that the truest way for a PLA soldier to follow Chairman Mao's call for service to the revolution was to wage a passionate affair with the lustful wife of his regimental commander. In the final scenes of this novel, the two coupling sinners consummate their passion among the shards of Mao's memorial statues and the shredded pages of his collected works. Such tales had an immediate relevance that separated them from works criticizing China or its government written by Chinese migrants, refugees, and fugitives in the United States or Europe, and published overseas in non-Chinese languages.

In the Hu/Wen years, poetry, opera, film, popular music, and other art forms also contained thinly disguised or even overt criticism of government practices and local abuses. Film had been especially prominent and original in the last years of the twentieth century and was given a further boost in 2002 when the government legalized productions outside the state studio system. Even though small-budget films faced fierce competition from lavishly funded Chinese language productions made in Hong Kong, they often responded successfully either by means of deliberately provocative and violent representations of Chinese youth and their music, or in blockbusters that flourished because the state enforced the quota that two-thirds of films shown in China must be domestic productions.[14]

Films also kept alive the audience for more traditional Chinese arts, and classical "Peking Opera" or "Kunqu" drawn from later Ming dynasty forms continued to have enthusiastic followings. Such a traditional operatic focus coexisted with the Western operatic tradition that took root in academies in Shenyang, Beijing, and Shanghai, producing singers of strength, subtlety, and range. History had a part to play here as well, as for instance with the release of a fifty-DVD set devoted to the life, adventures, and love affairs of Emperor Kangxi, and another colossal set dedicated to his son Yongzheng. Poetry, even when monitored carefully by the state censorship apparatus, continued to appeal as an art form to the generations of post-democracy-movement or post-Tiananmen exiles, many of whom were forbidden to return home to China.

Painting became a major cultural force and took off in Beijing, where abandoned factories left derelict by the post-Mao changes in the economy provided spaces for art studios. In the southwest and in Shanghai, Western connoisseurs and collectors gathered in lucrative numbers, helping to generate a small but vocal group of chic and expensive artists. Even in art, however, overt political commentary was discouraged by the state authorities. The strongest of the art works criticizing the massive social dislocations caused by the Three Gorges Dam project was conceived not in China but in the United States, where the painter Ji Yunfei completed his masterly scroll depicting families displaced from their homes. Ji drew his inspiration from visits and photo safaris to China rather than from protracted residence in the region served by the dam. Once the draft was completed, Ji worked with accomplished carvers in China to transform the draft painting into a series of woodblocks for the final printed work of art.[15] Such hybrid collaborative projects flourished for many who had both the initiative and the skill to cross cultures.

There is always a thin line between government censorship and the self-censorship people themselves exercise. As instruments of policy, literary and historical works can be used in many ways and for many purposes, and we can by no means be sure what was intended by a given pronouncement, or which cultural elements have been driven by coercion out of the public domain. In the Hu/Wen years this was especially true of China's legacy from its own deep past. Histories of early China adopted a nationalistic inclination—old records were scoured for evidence that this or that region had been "Chinese" since antiquity, reinforcing the government's current insistence on maintaining its grip on regions that had by no means always been "part of China." In such a political context, archaeology became a thriving academic and polemical skill, and each new discovery could find its niches in the hierarchies of the past. Confucius himself had been analyzed for well over two millennia by Chinese scholars and commentators, who utilized (or even distorted) his writings to form the basis for the state's ideology. A curious example that showed the ambiguities of the Confucian legacy occurred in January 2011, when a massive statue of the sage was prominently displayed in Tiananmen Square and shortly thereafter suddenly removed without explanation. A popular joke circulated that Confucius had been "evicted" from Beijing because he lacked the proper *hukou* registration to live in the capital city.

Certainly there are some historical resonances here. Sometimes denigrated and sometimes praised over the years, Confucius had been rejected with exceptional hostility by many scholars active in the cultural milieu of the May Fourth period, and later by the Marxist-inspired teachers and policymakers of the People's Republic. Now once again in the Hu/Wen years Confucius was taken seriously as an expert in governance and as the guide to moral and humane behavior. This renewed interest in Confucian studies was not restricted to the intellectual elite but had countrywide dimensions. A new generation of students organized academic conferences, to which both scholars from Taiwan and the West were often invited. Chinese scholars, some on their own and others working at government-sponsored institutions and academies, studied both the old texts of the classical canon and the ever growing number of newly discovered excavated texts, still readable on the strips of bamboo on which they were originally written around the third century B.C.E. (Such bamboo texts were discovered by archaeologists in burial sites or put up for sale by grave robbers.) The new findings were scrutinized and published with care. Both the state-sponsored scholars and the independents used the energy and knowledge so generated to examine the extent to which "Confucian values" should be considered a foundational part of the Chinese state, an exemplary model either for the enlightened individual or for the "Harmonious Society" central to Hu Jintao's vision.

As an offshoot of this burgeoning field, Confucian texts were ransacked for the guidance they could bring to business entrepreneurs and to party bureaucrats, as they tried to steer their way through the turbulent waters of China's original belief systems. A new generation of talented university students were induced to channel their energies into studies of the classics. Confucianism also became a hot topic on talk shows, and a way for academics to reach popular audiences or influence opinionmakers through weekend retreats. Around the world, Confucius Institutes funded by the PRC government were established, combining Chinese language training with historical analysis to give a sympathetic view of China's present achievements and intentions. Confucius went global again, for the first time since the French Enlightenment.

As the Hu/Wen years took on their own individualistic texture, certain traits pushed to the fore. Hu Jintao appeared formalistic, inflexible, and determined to prevent any shaking of the ship of state that might arise from demands for change from those Chinese dispossessed by legal chicanery, or pushed out to the edges of society by their more affluent contemporaries. For Hu, quiescence was stability, a view he may have ingested earlier in his career when working in three of the country's poorest regions, the provinces of Gansu and Guizhou and the Tibetan autonomous region.

It may have been the determination of Hu Jintao not to yield prematurely any of his prerogatives to the upcoming fifth generation of leaders that helped to trigger the bizarre political events of 2012. On February 6, Chongqing police chief Wang Lijun unexpectedly visited the U.S. consulate in Chengdu. He stayed the night, left the next day, and surfaced in Beijing, where he was swiftly detained. Rumors began to spread on the internet, alleging that Wang had sought asylum from the Americans because he feared for his life, and that he had brought evidence of a murder and coverup implicating his boss, the Chongqing party secretary Bo Xilai. A member of the Politburo, Bo was a charismatic figure and a prominent contender for promotion into the top CCP echelon in the leadership transition, scheduled to take place in late 2012 at the eighteenth party congress. He had built a national reputation through his signature campaigns in Chongqing, known as "singing red and smashing black," which combined populist celebration of Maoist values with a crackdown on organized crime and corruption.

Wang Lijun had served as the chief enforcer in the anticorruption drive. His attempted defection prompted a series of revelations and a cascade of events, culminating in the arrest of Bo Xilai and his wife Gu Kailai. According to Wang's account, Gu and her aide had conspired to murder Neil Heywood, a British businessman who was found dead in a Chongqing hotel in November 2011. Called to the scene, Wang used his power as police chief to hide evidence implicating Gu. Separately, charges against Bo accused him of multiple acts of bribery, corruption, and abuse of power. The cases against Wang Lijun and Gu Kailai were swiftly prosecuted in August and September 2012; both were found guilty and sentenced to lengthy jail terms. (The case against Bo Xilai did not go to trial until a year later.)

On the eve of the party congress, scandal shattered the regime's appearance of measured and unruffled self-confidence. In addition to salacious gossip about Heywood's relationship with the Bo family and the circumstances of his death, there was chatter about a car crash involving a Ferrari, two young women, and the son of Ling Jihua, Hu Jintao's top aide. Twenty-three-year-old Ling Gu had died in March, when his car slammed into a wall on Beijing's fourth ring road. The allegations of coverup emerged when Ling Jihua was unexpectedly demoted in August; the charges included a fake name on the death certificate and millions of dollars paid for the women's silence.

As speculations about power struggles within the top leadership spread, the downfall of Bo Xilai and the unsavory rumors undermined the image of consensus and unity, key to the moment of leadership transition. No one could know with any certainty the factional battles and negotiations occurring behind the scenes; observers scrutinized every announcement and gesture for clues about the forthcoming transfer of power. When the eighteenth party congress finally convened in November 2012, Hu Jintao stepped down as expected, adhering to the two-term limit that Deng Xiaoping had put into place. He handed all three of his positions to Xi Jinping—CCP general secretary, president of the PRC, and chairman of the Military Affairs Commission—empowering Xi to fortify his network and paving the way for a new era of political consolidation.[16]

Epilogue

From the vantage point of 2024, the messy transition that placed Xi Jinping at the apex of the government seems a distant memory. Firmly in control, President Xi has accrued and consolidated more political power than any other leader since Mao Zedong. At the time of his ascension in 2012, however, the political climate was fraught, with the scandals from Bo Xilai's downfall still reverberating. The new leader expressed soaring aspirations for the "great rejuvenation of the Chinese nation" and for the PRC to stake its claim as a global power. But as he provided few details about his intentions for economic and political reforms, foreign policy, or solutions to domestic problems, there was much anxious commentary about the future direction of the country. The son of a veteran revolutionary, Xi Jinping was born in 1953 in Beijing and spent his childhood as a "red princeling" in the privileged inner leadership circle of the CCP. His father, Xi Zhongxun, rose to the position of vice premier before being purged in the early 1960s and eventually spent more than eleven years in prison. During the Cultural Revolution the entire family was attacked and suffered for the father's political sins. As a teenager, Xi Jinping was sent to a poor village near Yan'an, where he lived in a cave, worked in the fields alongside peasants, and helped build a dam. He was one of millions of sent-down urban youths in the rustication campaign of the Cultural Revolution. As he later recalled, the years of hardship imprinted him with the value of frugal living, appreciation for the struggles of the common people, and a will of iron.

One of Xi's first acts as the top leader was to launch a broad anticorruption drive targeting "tigers and flies." The corrosive effects of corruption, Xi said bluntly in a speech in November 2012, were serious enough to doom the party and the state. The crackdown that followed lasted more than four years and investigated millions of party members and officials. The high-profile "tigers" caught in the dragnet included senior military generals and some of Xi's

Projections of power   Construction workers in Shanghai gather to watch the televised 2019 National Day festivities in Beijing. The parade to celebrate the seventieth anniversary of the PRC included over 100,000 performers and proud displays of military power.

political rivals, most notably Zhou Yongkang, the former minister of public security and a member of the Politburo Standing Committee. The "flies" were lower-ranking cadres and officials, prosecuted for acts of malfeasance ranging from graft to unspecified "disciplinary violations."

By cleaning house, Xi Jinping sent the unequivocal message that official misconduct would not be tolerated. In doing so he also neutralized potential challengers and replaced them with his allies and loyal lieutenants. In the process of consolidating power, he upended the principles of CCP governance in place since Mao's death. Rather than collective leadership and decision-making by consensus, a cult of personality identified Xi as the party's "core" (*hexin*), a concept enshrined in the party constitutions in 2017 and 2022. The collected works of "Xi Jinping Thought on Socialism with Chinese Characteristics for a New Era" became required reading, just as Mao Zedong Thought had once been obligatory. When the National People's Congress removed the two-term limit on the presidency from the state constitution, and when Xi did not retire from leadership of the party in 2022 according to precedent, the door opened for him to remain "leader for life."

As he exerted increasing personal control over the party-state and the military, Xi Jinping pushed a harder ideological line than his immediate predecessors and sought to amplify the Communist Party's role in all arenas of life. Tighter restrictions on the private business sector, foreign investment, education, and media reined in potential challengers to the CCP's monopoly on power and suppressed possible sources of dissent. Concurrently, intensified population surveillance and censorship reduced the already limited spaces for political advocacy and civil society. In the early twenty-first century, there had been a period of relative tolerance for grassroots associations to organize, with environmental, feminist, labor, peasant, and human rights activists pushing the boundaries of permissible action. Under Xi Jinping, such tolerance evaporated. A 2017 law targeting foreign NGOs effectively shuttered their operations, while domestic activists were arrested for inciting "disorder" or threatening the "national interest." Forceful controls over religion suppressed the resurgence of spiritual practices, with a program of Sinicization targeting Christianity, Islam, and Tibetan Buddhism.

In education, scrutiny of ideology and conduct intensified. Mandatory political education classes provided strong doses of indoctrination to university students. State funding for academic research rewarded projects corresponding to the CCP's stated priorities. Student informants reported on professors who espoused views critical of the party or made "politically incorrect" comments in class. At all levels, from kindergartens to universities, the Ministry of Education mandated that teachers must uphold Xi Jinping Thought. In 2018, students and recent graduates of elite Beijing universities were arrested when they joined in collective protest with workers seeking to form an independent union. The students, self-proclaimed Marxists carrying portraits of Chairman Mao, had traveled to a manufacturing hub in Guangdong to support striking workers. In the aftermath, "Marxist Research Associations" and other like-minded groups at universities were banned. History had come full circle, with the CCP suppressing the same type of reading group that its cofounder Li Dazhao had formed at Beida in 1918.

In domestic governance, the looming demographic crisis may be the one arena of Chinese life to elude Xi Jinping's will and the CCP's dictates. Ironically, the problems are the consequences of the one-child policy succeeding too well. In effect since the early 1980s, the government's draconian measures to reduce the rate of population growth resulted in total fertility rates far below the replacement level of 2.1 children per couple. Accounting for the declining number of births and a rapidly aging population, forecasts estimated that a labor force of 700 million in the year 2050 will have to support nearly 500 million seniors. In contrast, when the working-age population peaked in 2011 at 900 million, there were fewer than 200 million retirees. Grave concerns about the impending "demographic cliff" and its implications for the economy compelled the CCP to change course—by raising the one-child limit to two children in 2015 and three children in 2021, followed by a campaign (with cash incentives and tax and welfare benefits) to persuade families to have more children. When the fertility rate plummeted to 1.1 in 2021, and when China recorded the lowest birth rate in the history of the PRC in 2023, the alarm became palpable.[1] But after decades of harsh measures to ensure compliance with the government's family planning policies, and in a context of increasing incomes, urbanization, and educational opportunities for women, the efforts to reverse the tide have proved resoundingly ineffective.

For the CCP in the twenty-first century, agitations on the peripheries were cause for immediate alarm and decisive action. In the summer of 2014, the "Umbrella Movement" erupted when the Hong Kong Special Administrative Region Government (following orders from Beijing) refused to hold a free election with universal suffrage for the position of chief executive, as promised by the 1984 Sino-British agreement. When protestors occupying the central business district raised a sea of umbrellas—to block the pepper spray used by police to disperse the crowds—the image became a symbol of popular discontent and demands for change. The residents of Hong Kong were also moved to action by the tangible erosion of civil liberties, press freedoms, and judicial independence since the 1997 takeover, as well as economic frustrations such as income inequality and the high cost of living. At the height of the movement, an estimated 20 percent of the population (more than one million people) participated. The PRC government, however, refused to budge. After seventy-five days, the protest encampments were cleared by court order, and some of the most vocal student leaders and activists were arrested.

Four years later, in the spring of 2019, even more people turned out on the streets of Hong Kong. The initial protests were triggered by a proposed amendment to the extradition law permitting the transfer of fugitives or criminal suspects from Hong Kong to the mainland. Such arrangements had not been formalized in Hong Kong law after 1997 due to major differences between the Chinese legal system and the island's common law system. After a series of high-profile cases involving the rendition of wanted persons with ambiguous status under the existing law, the Hong Kong government proposed a bill to plug the loopholes. Opposition to the provision for extradition to the PRC was swift. From April to December 2019, the protests grew in intensity and scale: the siege of the legislative building, a general strike, student boycotts of classes, the occupation of the airport and university campuses, violent clashes between the protestors and police. Although the Hong Kong government suspended the legislative proceedings on the proposed bill, protestors demanded its complete withdrawal, an independent inquiry into allegations of police brutality, the release of those arrested during the demonstrations, the resignation of the chief executive, and universal suffrage for

COVID-19 lockdowns   The Chinese government responded to the global pandemic by implementing rigid "zero COVID" policies, though not without resistance. Here, a resident peeks from a boarded-up building in Shanghai, which was under total lockdown from April to May 2022.

all elections. In November, public anger found a channel for expression in the district council elections. In these local electoral contests, pro-Beijing parties were decisively defeated, retaining only 58 seats while the opposition won 389.

After the outbreak of the COVID-19 pandemic in the winter of 2020 attenuated the momentum of Hong Kong's anti-extradition law movement, the passage of the national security law in June gave the PRC government the final word. In response to the upheaval of the previous year and in the name of restoring stability, the legislation imposed severe penalties for acts of secession, subversion, terrorism, and foreign collusion. Under its capacious and vaguely defined provisions, prodemocracy activists were prosecuted and sentenced to lengthy jail terms. New election rules also reduced the proportion of Legislative Council and local council seats open to direct vote, in favor of appointed representatives. These developments made it abundantly clear that the promises of "a high degree of autonomy" for Hong Kong under "One Country, Two Systems" have largely been rescinded, well before the stipulated expiration date of 2047.

In Tibet and Xinjiang, stability was also the rationale for the imposition of tight control. With ethnic tensions occasionally erupting into violence, the CCP imposed policies to suppress the activities of alleged "terrorists, separatists, and religious extremists." In parallel, a program of Sinicization sought to prevent "radicalization" by diluting the strength of ethnic and religious identities. Aggressive measures targeted religious practice with restrictions on prayer, pilgrimage, monastic life, and the management of temples and mosques. In education, decisive shifts toward Chinese language education, at the expense of minority languages, reversed previous policies that had been more accommodating of multilingualism.

In Xinjiang, the government attributed the waves of unrest and violence to separatists from the East Turkestan Islamic Movement and their foreign allies. The "strike first" campaign, launched in 2014, became "the people's war on terrorism" and grew in sophistication, developing a comprehensive surveillance network to track the population's movements and communications. The incarceration of an estimated one million Uyghurs in detention camps with conditions of forced prison labor have drawn international condemnation, but to little effect. In the case of Tibet, the CCP accused the fourteenth Dalai Lama of masterminding sporadic episodes of self-immolation and protests, some of which turned violent. Born in 1935, the highest spiritual leader of Tibetan Buddhism fled Lhasa in 1959 and has remained in exile ever since. When he dies, the struggle over his reincarnation and successor will be waged between Beijing and the Tibetan government-in-exile based in Dharamsala, India.

Throughout his tenure, Xi Jinping has reiterated an uncompromising resolve to combat domestic and foreign forces posing threats to national unity and security, wherever they may be situated. Any attempts to "split China in any part of the country will end in crushed bones and shattered bodies," he declared in 2019, in comments directed at Hong Kong and indirectly to Xinjiang, Tibet, and Taiwan.[2] In addition to harsh suppression techniques and high-tech surveillance methods, strengthening patriotic education has been crucial to Xi's vision of stability. First implemented in the aftermath of the 1989 democracy movement, successive iterations of the campaign have defined love for the nation as synonymous with loyalty to the CCP. The latest version, in the form of a law passed in 2023, codifies patriotic education as upholding the leadership of the Communist Party, encouraging love for "the nation, the party, and socialism," and preserving "national and ethnic unity."

Another crucial component of Xi Jinping's ideological arsenal is imposition of tight controls over the content and interpretation of party history. School textbooks present the historical record of the CCP as a triumphant narrative of redemption from imperialism and a linear account of revolutionary progress without mistakes. Reassessments and alternative interpretations are prohibited as transgressions of "historical nihilism." According to the CCP, this pernicious "ideological trend" includes dangerous manifestations of "rejecting the revolution," questioning the "accepted conclusions" on historical events and figures, and vilifying party leaders.[3] Historical analyses that underline the failures or problems of CCP governance could be construed as criminal acts.

Reaching further back into history, Xi Jinping has stressed his authoritative interpretation of the Confucian tradition with invocations of the concept of "benevolent rule." During widely publicized visits to Qufu, the ancestral home-town of the sage, he quoted passages from the Analects and visited the research institute dedicated to Confucian studies. The president's recent pronouncement that the Chinese civilizational continuity of more than 5,000 years must not be broken has infused the field of archaeology with politicized attention and funding. A recent declaration that Marxism constitutes the "soul" and Con-fucianism the "root" of Chinese culture presents a new synthesis overturning a century of CCP revolutionary ideology.

In the aftermath of the global COVID-19 pandemic, the PRC confronts an economic slowdown after nearly four decades of spectacular growth. Domes-tic problems include a crisis of youth unemployment and a decade-long specu-lative bubble in real estate markets that burst with disastrous effects. Foreign capital investment has been slow to return to prepandemic levels, with inves-tors wary of increasing geopolitical tensions and regulatory strictures. Signs of trouble have come from the Belt and Road Initiative (BRI), launched in 2013 to implant the Chinese development model throughout Africa, Latin Amer-ica, and Southeast Asia. A decade later, some BRI infrastructure projects have been plagued by management and operational problems, while others face allegations of predatory lending, corruption, waste, and environmental deg-radation. Despite all these issues, the China model has many admirers and continues to have wide appeal around the world.

In pursuit of his vision of a new global order anchored by Chinese domi-nance, Xi Jinping seeks to disrupt what he calls the Western values embed-ded in international organizations and championed by the United States and its allies. The Sino-American schism is sharper today than at any time since Richard Nixon's 1972 visit to Beijing reversed the previous decades of antago-nism. Conversely, Xi Jinping has forged a "partnership without limits" with Russia—recalling the heyday of Sino-Soviet friendship in the early 1950s, but now with China in a position of power rather than subservience. As he navi-gates the perilous terrain of global ambitions, Xi Jinping is putting his personal imprint on the adage from George Orwell's prophetic novel *1984*: "Who con-trols the past controls the future; who controls the present controls the past."

Notes

CHAPTER 1 *(pages 1–17)*

1. Tang Xianzu, *The Peony Pavilion*, trans. Cyril Birch (Bloomington: Indiana University Press, 1980), 14 and 32.

2. G. William Skinner, ed., *The City in Late Imperial China* (Stanford: Stanford University Press, 1977), 351.

3. Tang Xianzu, 34.

4. Wang Yangming, *Instructions for Practical Living and Other Neo-Confucian Writings*, trans. Wing-tsit Chan (New York: Columbia University Press, 1963), 146 (modified).

5. L. Carrington Goodrich and Fang Chao-ying, eds., *Dictionary of Ming Biography* (New York: Columbia University Press, 1976), 708; F. W. Mote, *Imperial China, 900–1800* (Cambridge: Harvard University Press, 1999), 736.

6. Timothy Brook, *The Troubled Empire: China in the Yuan and Ming Dynasties* (Cambridge: The Belknap Press of Harvard University Press, 2010), 249–255; Richard Von Glahn, *An Economic History of China* (Cambridge, U.K.: Cambridge University Press, 2016), 311.

7. Helen Dunstan, "The Late Ming Epidemics: A Preliminary Survey," *Ch'ing-shih wen-t'i* 3, no. 3 (1975): 29–30.

8. Dunstan, 39–40. The basic premises of traditional Chinese medicine are presented in Nathan Sivin, *Traditional Medicine in Contemporary China* (Ann Arbor: University of Michigan Press, 1987).

9. Cao Shuji, *Zhongguo renkou shi*. Vol. 4: *Ming shiqi* (Shanghai: Fudan daxue chubanshe, 2000), 451–452.

CHAPTER 2 *(pages 18–35)*

1. Nicola Di Cosmo, "The Manchu Conquest in World-Historical Perspective: A Note on Trade and Silver," *Journal of Central Eurasian Studies* 1 (2009): 43–60.

2. Franz Michael, *The Origin of Manchu Rule in China* (New York: Octagon Books, 1965), 121.

3. Gertraude Roth, "The Manchu-Chinese Relationship, 1618–1636," in Jonathan Spence and John Wills, eds., *From Ming to Ch'ing* (New Haven: Yale University Press, 1979), 9.

4. Mårten Söderblom Saarela, *The Early Modern Travels of Manchu: A Script and Its Study* (Philadelphia, PA: University of Pennsylvania Press, 2020).

5. Mark C. Elliot, *The Manchu Way: The Eight Banners and Ethnic Identity in Late Imperial China* (Stanford: Stanford University Press, 2001), 71–72, 402 fn 116 and fn 118.

6. Frederic Wakeman, "Localism and Loyalism during the Qing Conquest of Jiangnan: The Tragedy of Jiangyin" in *Telling Chinese History: A Selection of Essays* (Berkeley: University of California Press, 2009), 174–213.

7. Frederic Wakeman, *The Great Enterprise* (Berkeley: University of California Press, 1985), 55–58; Lynn Struve, *The Southern Ming, 1644–1662* (New Haven: Yale University Press, 1984), 47 and 58–61.

8. On marriages, see Pär Kristoffer Cassel, *Grounds of Judgment: Extraterritoriality and Imperial Power in Nineteenth-Century China and Japan* (Oxford: Oxford University Press, 2012), 21–22.

9. Robert Oxnam, *Ruling from Horseback* (Chicago: University of Chicago Press, 1975), 52 and 56.

CHAPTER 3 *(pages 36–58)*

1. Jonathan Spence, *Emperor of China: Self-Portrait of K'ang-hsi* (New York: Vintage Books, 1974), 32.

2. Gang Zhao, *The Qing Opening to the Ocean: Chinese Maritime Policies, 1684–1757* (Honolulu: University of Hawai'i Press, 2013), 86–94, 120–121.

3. Willard Peterson, "The Life of Ku Yen-wu, 1613–1682," *Harvard Journal of Asiatic Studies* 28, no. 3–4 (1968): 142.

4. Kong Shangren (K'ung Shang-jen), *The Peach Blossom Fan*, trans. Chen Shih-hsiang and Harold Acton (Berkeley: University of California Press, 1976), 278.

5. Richard Strassberg, *The World of K'ung Shang-jen: A Man of Letters in Early Ch'ing China* (New York: Columbia University Press, 1983), 275.

6. Strassberg, 219.

7. Spence, 165.

8. An example is in Catherine Jami, "Imperial Control and Western Learning: The Kangxi Emperor's Performance," *Late Imperial China* 23, no. 1 (June 2002): 28–49.

9. On the military entrepreneurship issue, see Yingcong Dai, "Yingyun Shengxi: Military Entrepreneurship in the High Qing Period, 1700–1800," *Late Imperial China* 26, no. 2 (December 2005): 1–67.

10. Richard von Glahn, *Fountain of Fortune: Money and Monetary Policy in China* (Berkeley: University of California Press, 1996), 211–215.

11. Spence, 148–149.

CHAPTER 4 *(pages 59–78)*

1. These three macroregion case studies are drawn from Susan Naquin and Evelyn Rawski, *Chinese Society in the Eighteenth Century* (New Haven: Yale University Press, 1987), ch. 5. The basic works introducing and expanding the macroregion concept are the

essays by G. William Skinner in the volume he edited, *The City in Late Imperial China* (Stanford: Stanford University Press, 1977).

2. Cao Shuji, *Zhongguo renkou shi*. Vol. 4: *Ming shiqi* (Shanghai: Fudan daxue chubanshe, 2000), 451–452, and Vol. 5: *Qing shiqi* (Shanghai: Fudan daxue chubanshe, 2001), 703–704.

3. From James Lee and Robert Eng, "Population and Family History in Eighteenth Century Manchuria: Preliminary Results from Daoyi, 1774–1798," *Ch'ing-shih wen-t'i* 5, no. 1 (June 1984): 31. Also see James Lee and Cameron Campbell, *Fate and Fortune in Rural China: Social Organization and Population Behavior in Liaoning, 1774–1873* (Cambridge: Cambridge University Press, 1997), chs. 4 and 5; Sijie Hu, "Descendants over 300 Years: Marital Fertility in Five Lineages in Qing China," *Asia-Pacific Economic History Review* 63, no. 2 (July 2023), 200–224.

4. Taisu Zhang, *The Ideological Foundations of Qing Taxation: Belief Systems, Politics, and Institutions* (Cambridge, U.K.: Cambridge University Press, 2023).

5. Madeleine Zelin, *The Magistrate's Tael: Rationalizing Fiscal Reform in Eighteenth-Century Ch'ing China* (Berkeley: University of California Press, 1984), 80. For a richly detailed study of the realities and rhetoric of eighteenth-century government service, see especially William T. Rowe, *Saving the World: Chen Hongmou and Elite Consciousness in Eighteenth-Century China* (Stanford: Stanford University Press, 2001).

6. This paragraph and the rest of this section are based on the material in Beatrice S. Bartlett's *Monarchs and Ministers: The Rise of the Grand Council in Mid-Ch'ing China, 1723–1820* (Berkeley: University of California Press, 1990).

7. Cited (with slight modifications) from Beatrice S. Bartlett, "The Vermilion Brush: The Grand Council Communications Systems and Central Government Decision Making in Mid-Ch'ing China" (Ph.D. diss., Yale University, 1980), 57 and 61.

8. Yingcong Dai, "Yingyun Shengxi: Military Entrepreneurship in the High Qing Period, 1700–1800," *Late Imperial China* 26, no. 2 (December 2005): 1–67, especially 24–32.

9. A detailed analysis of the Zeng Jing and Lu Liuliang case, and of the trial and "repentance" of the central figures, and the emperor's ultimate solution, is given in Jonathan Spence, *Treason by the Book* (New York: Viking, 2001).

10. Fu Lo-shu, *A Documentary Chronicle of Sino-Western Relations, 1644–1820*, 2 vols. (Tucson: University of Arizona Press, 1966), vol. 1, 162–164.

CHAPTER 5 *(pages 79–98)*

1. Peter Perdue, *China Marches West: The Qing Conquest of Central Eurasia* (Cambridge: The Belknap Press of Harvard University Press, 2005), 270–289.

2. James Millward, *Eurasian Crossroads: A History of Xinjiang* (New York: Columbia University Press, 2022), 95–100.

3. On the details of these revenue-enhancing procedures, see Yincong Dai, "Yingyun Shengxi: Military Entrepreneurship in the High Qing Period, 1700–1800," *Late Imperial China* 26, no. 2 (December 2005): 1–67, especially 50–51.

4. See Matthew Mosca, "The Literati Rewriting of China in the Qianlong-Jiaqing Transition," *Late Imperial China* 32, no. 2 (December 2011): 89–132.

5. The *I-ching* or *Book of Changes*, trans. Richard Wilhelm and Cary Baynes (Princeton: Princeton University Press, 1950), 213 and 670. The key study of the *kaozheng*

movement, on which these paragraphs are based, is Benjamin Elman, *From Philosophy to Philology* (Cambridge: Harvard University Press, 1984).

6. The discussion of women's education draws from Susan Mann, *Precious Records: Women in China's Long Eighteenth Century* (Stanford: Stanford University Press, 1997), and Xiaorong Li, *Women's Poetry of Late Imperial China: Transforming the Inner Chambers* (Seattle: University of Washington Press, 2012).

7. Cao Xueqin, *The Story of the Stone [Dream of the Red Chamber]*, trans. David Hawkes, vol. 1 (New York, 1973), 51 and 55 (slightly modified).

8. Susan Naquin, *Shantung Rebellion: The Wang Lun Uprising of 1774* (New Haven: Yale University Press, 1981), 60.

9. Arthur Hummel, ed., *Eminent Chinese of the Ch'ing Period*, 2 vols. (Washington, D.C., 1943), vol. 1, 223. On the "penitence silver" case details, see Ting Zhang, "'Penitence Silver' and the Politics of Punishment in the Qianlong Reign (1736–1796)," *Late Imperial China* 31, no. 2 (December 2010): 34–68.

10. Harold Kahn, *Monarchy in the Emperor's Eyes* (Cambridge: Harvard University Press, 1971), 255; J. L. Cranmer-Byng, ed., *An Embassy to China: Lord Macartney's Journal, 1793–1794* (London, 1962), 120.

11. Cranmer-Byng, 281–283.

CHAPTER 6 *(pages 99–116)*

1. On geographical and ethnographic research about the frontiers of the Qing empire, see Matthew Mosca, *From Frontier Policy to Foreign Policy: The Question of India and the Transformation of Geopolitics in Qing China* (Stanford: Stanford University Press, 2013); Zhang Xue, "Imperial Maps of Xinjiang and Their Readers in Qing China, 1660–1860," *Journal of Chinese History* no. 4 (2020): 111–133; Laura Hostetler, *Qing Colonial Enterprise: Ethnography and Cartography in Early Modern China* (Chicago: University of Chicago Press, 2001).

2. Gang Zhao, *The Qing Opening to the Ocean: Chinese Maritime Policies, 1684–1757* (Honolulu: University of Hawai'i Press, 2013).

3. Stephen Platt, *Imperial Twilight: The Opium War and the End of China's Last Golden Age* (New York: Alfred A. Knopf, 2018), 3–9.

4. Henrietta Harrison, "The Qianlong Emperor's Letter to George III and the Early-Twentieth-Century Origins of Ideas about Traditional China's Foreign Relations," *The American Historical Review* 122, no. 3 (June 2017): 680–701, quote on 684.

5. J. L. Cranmer-Byng, ed., *An Embassy to China: Lord Macartney's Journal, 1793–1794* (London: Vernor and Hood, 1962), 340.

6. William Rowe, *China's Last Empire: The Great Qing* (Cambridge: The Belknap Press of Harvard University Press, 2009), 147–148.

7. Derk Bodde and Clarence Morris, eds., *Law in Imperial China* (Cambridge: Harvard University Press, 1967), 390. On the Qing code see Zheng Qin, "Pursuing Perfection: Formation of the Qing Code," *Modern China* 21, no. 3 (July 1995): 310–344.

8. The discussion of the *Lady Hughes* and the *Emily* cases is drawn from Li Chen, *Chinese Law in Imperial Eyes: Sovereignty, Justice, and Trans-cultural Politics* (New York: Columbia University Press, 2016), and Joseph Benjamin Askew, "Re-visiting New Territory: The Terranova Incident Re-examined," *Asian Studies Review* 28 no. 4 (December 2004), 351–371.

9. Paul A. Van Dyke, *Merchants of Canton and Macao: Politics and Strategies in Eighteenth-Century Chinese Trade* (Hong Kong: Hong Kong University Press, 2011), 13–17.

10. Figures drawn from H. B. Morse, *The International Relations of the Chinese Empire*, 3 vols. (Shanghai and London: Longmans, Green, 1910–1918), vol. 1, 173 and 209, and Hsin-pao Chang, *Commissioner Lin and the Opium War* (Cambridge: Harvard University Press, 1964), 223. On early Qing antitobacco policies see Carol Benedict, "Between State Power and Popular Desire: Tobacco in Pre-Conquest Manchuria, 1600–1644," *Late Imperial China* 32, no. 1 (June 2011): 13–48.

11. Yangwen Zheng, *The Social Life of Opium* (Cambridge: Cambridge University Press, 2005).

12. Jonathan Spence, "Opium Smoking in Ch'ing China," in Frederic Wakeman and Carolyn Grant, eds., *Conflict and Control in Late Imperial China* (Berkeley: University of California Press, 1975), 143–173 (slightly modified).

13. François Marie Arouet de Voltaire, *Essai sur les moeurs et l'esprit des nations* (Geneva, 1771), vol. 1, 36.

14. Adam Smith, *An Inquiry into the Nature and Causes of the Wealth of Nations*, ed. Edwin Cannan (Chicago: Chicago University Press, 1976).

15. Georg Wilhelm Friedrich Hegel, *The Philosophy of History*, trans. E. S. Haldane and Frances Simon (New York: Humanities Press, 1974).

Chapter 7 *(pages 117–136)*

1. William Rowe, *China's Last Empire: The Great Qing*, (Cambridge: The Belknap Press of Harvard University Press), 154–55.

2. Wolfgang Bauer, *China and the Search for Happiness*, trans. Michael Shaw (New York: Seabury Press, 1976), 257.

3. Shen Fu, *Six Records of a Floating Life*, trans. Leonard Pratt and Chiang Su-hui (New York: Penguin Books, 1983), 73; Lin Yu-tang's rendering in *T'ien Hsia Monthly* 1 (1935): 316.

4. On the Amherst mission, see Stephen Platt, *Imperial Twilight: The Opium War and the End of China's Last Golden Age* (New York: Alfred A. Knopf, 2018), 159–180.

5. Richard Von Glahn, *The Economic History of China: From Antiquity to the Nineteenth Century* (Cambridge: Cambridge University Press, 2016), 363–367.

6. Julie Lovell, *The Opium War: Drugs, Dreams, and the Making of China* (London: Picador, 2011), 5–8; Platt, 285–86, 300.

7. Hsin-pao Chang, *Commissioner Lin and the Opium War* (Cambridge: Harvard University Press, 1964), 134–135.

8. Arthur Waley, *The Opium War through Chinese Eyes* (London: Macmillan, 1958), 44, 46, 49.

9. Waley, 47, quote from Hsin-pao Chang, 160.

10. Morse, 622.

11. Hsin-pao Chang, 191; Morse, 253.

12. Hsin-pao Chang, 206–207.

13. Morse, 241.

14. Morse, 661–662.

15. Gerald Graham, *The China Station: War and Diplomacy, 1830–1860* (New York: Oxford University Press, 1978), 117–118, 183, 215–218; Tonio Andrade, *The Gunpowder Age: China, Military Innovation, and the Rise of the West in World History* (Princeton: Princeton University Press, 2016), 258–266.

16. The full text of the Treaty of Nanjing is from Godfrey Hertslet, *Treaties etc. between Great Britain and China and between China and Foreign Powers*, 2 vols. (London: Harrison & Sons, 1908), vol. 1, 7–12.

17. Morse, 330.

18. John K. Fairbank, *Trade and Diplomacy on the China Coast* (Cambridge: Harvard University Press, 1953), 113.

Chapter 8 *(pages 137–159)*

1. William Rowe, *Speaking of Profit: Bao Shichen and Reform in Nineteenth-Century China* (Cambridge: Harvard University Asia Center, 2018), 2–11.

2. Susan Naquin, *Millenarian Rebellion in China: The Eight Trigrams Uprising of 1813* (New Haven: Yale University Press, 1976), 83.

3. Naquin, 93.

4. Frederic Wakeman, *Strangers at the Gate* (Berkeley: University of California Press, 1966), 89.

5. Jen Yu-wen (Chien Yu-wen), *The Taiping Revolutionary Movement* (New Haven: Yale University Press, 1973), 93–94.

6. Franz Michael and Chung-li Chang, *The Taiping Rebellion: History and Documents*, 3 vols. (Seattle: University of Washington Press, 1966–1971), vol. 2, 314.

7. Michael and Chang, vol. 1, 168, 174.

8. Tobie Meyer-Fong, *What Remains: Coming to Terms with Civil War in 19th Century China* (Stanford: Stanford University Press, 2013); Stephen Platt, *Autumn in the Heavenly Kingdom: China, the West, and the Epic Story of the Taiping Civil War* (New York: Alfred A. Knopf, 2012). Meyer-Fong and Platt persuasively argue that the convention of referring to the Taiping as a "rebellion" reflects a political stance that adopts the dynastic perspective. "The term 'civil war' eliminates implicit value judgments and transcends the totalizing political and moral narratives that emphasize national priorities over individual and collective suffering" (Meyer-Fong, 11).

9. H. B. Morse, *The International Relations of the Chinese Empire*, vol. 1 (Shanghai: Longmans, Green, 1910), 579.

10. Ssu-yü Teng, *The Nien Army and Their Guerrilla Warfare, 1851–1868* (Paris: Mouton, 1961), 169.

11. David Atwill, *The Chinese Sultanate: Islam, Ethnicity, and the Panthay Rebellion in Southwest China, 1856–1873* (Stanford: Stanford University Press, 2006).

12. Atwill, 161–184, quote on 183.

13. Wen-djang Chu, *The Moslem Rebellion in Northwest China, 1862–1878: A Study of Government Minority Policy* (The Hague: Mouton, 1966), 91–92, citing Wang Boxin.

14. Hodong Kim, *Holy War in China: The Muslim Revolt and State in Chinese Central Asia, 1864–1877* (Stanford: Stanford University Press, 2004); James Millward, *Eurasian Crossroads: A History of Xinjiang* (New York: Columbia University Press, 2007), 126–129.

15. Millward, 128.

Chapter 9 *(pages 160–179)*

1. Cited from Andrew Cheng-kuang Hsieh, "Tseng Kuo-fan, a Nineteenth Century Confucian General" (Ph.D. diss., Yale University, 1975), 23.

2. Adapted from "Feng Guifen: On the Manufacture of Foreign Weapons," translated in *Sources of Chinese Civilization, Volume II: From 1600 through the Twentieth Century*, comp. Wm. Theodore de Bary and Richard Lufrano, second edition (New York: Columbia University Press, 2000), 235–237.

3. Ssu-yü Teng and John K. Fairbank, *China's Response to the West: A Documentary Survey, 1839–1923* (Cambridge: Harvard University Press, 1954), 62.

4. Mary Wright, *The Last Stand of Chinese Conservatism: The T'ung-chih Restoration, 1862–1874* (Stanford: Stanford University Press, 1957), 213.

5. Masataka Banno, *China and the West, 1858–1861: The Origins of the Tsungli Yamen* (Cambridge: Harvard University Press, 1964), 228.

6. H. B. Morse, *The International Relations of the Chinese Empire*, vol. 2 (Shanghai and London: Longmans, Green, 1910), 37.

7. Immanuel Hsü, *China's Entrance into the Family of Nations: The Diplomatic Phase, 1858–1880* (Cambridge: Harvard University Press, 1960), 132.

8. Hsü, 133–134.

9. Fred Drake, *China Charts the World* (Cambridge: Harvard University Press, 1975), 159, 164–165, refer to 187 and 245 for details on the Washington Monument.

10. Wright, 252.

11. Yung Wing, *My Life in China and America* (New York: H. Holt and Company, 1909), 3–4.

12. Katherine F. Bruner, John K. Fairbank, and Richard Smith, eds., *Entering China's Service: Robert Hart's Journals, 1854–1863* (Cambridge: Harvard University Press, 1986), 230–232.

13. Beth Lew-Williams, *The Chinese Must Go: Violence, Exclusion, and the Making of the Alien in America* (Cambridge: Harvard University Press, 2018).

14. Frederick Wells Williams, *Anson Burlingame and the First Chinese Mission to Foreign Powers* (New York: Scribner's, 1912), 136–139.

15. Michael Hunt, *The Making of a Special Relationship: The United States and China to 1914* (New York: Columbia University Press, 1983), 92.

16. Hunt, 93, citing James G. Blaine.

CHAPTER 10 (pages 180–204)

1. James Millward, *Eurasian Crossroads: A History of Xinjiang* (New York: Columbia University Press, 2007), 137–151 (quote on 140); Eric Schluessel, *Land of Strangers: The Civilizing Project in Qing Central Asia* (Cambridge: Columbia University Press, 2020).

2. H. B. Morse, *The International Relations of the Chinese Empire*, 3 vols. (Shanghai and London: Longmans, Green, 1910), vol. 3, 35.

3. Victor Purcell, *The Boxer Uprising, a Background Study* (New York: Cambridge University Press, 1963), 225 (modified).

4. Zou Rong (Tsou Jung), *The Revolutionary Army: A Chinese Nationalist Tract of 1903*, trans. John Lust (The Hague: Mouton, 1968), 122.

5. Zou, 126.

6. W. H. Brewer Papers, Yale University Archives, 1/6/185/18v.

7. Don Price, *Russia and the Roots of the Chinese Revolution, 1896–1911* (Cambridge: Harvard University Press, 1974), 215.

Chapter 11 *(pages 205–225)*

1. R. Douglas Reynolds, *China, 1898–1912: The Xinzheng Revolution and Japan* (Cambridge: Council on East Asian Studies, Harvard University, 1993), 13.

2. Henrietta Harrison, *The Man Awakened from Dreams: One Man's Life in a North China Village, 1857–1942* (Stanford: Stanford University Press, 2005).

3. Ryan Dunch, *Fuzhou Protestants and the Making of a Modern China, 1857–1927* (New Haven: Yale University Press, 2001).

4. Ralph Huenemann, *The Dragon and the Iron Horse: The Economics of Railroads in China, 1876–1937* (Cambridge: Harvard University Press, 1984), 79.

5. Don Price, *Russia and the Roots of the Chinese Revolution, 1896–1911* (Cambridge: Harvard University Press, 1974), 130.

6. Martin Bernal, *Chinese Socialism to 1907* (Ithaca: Cornell University Press, 1976), 37.

7. Bernal, 95.

8. Bernal, 117.

9. Edmund Fung, *The Military Dimension of the Chinese Revolution* (Vancouver: University of British Columbia Press, 1980), 138.

10. Li Chien-nung, *The Political History of China, 1840–1928*, trans. Teng Ssu-yü and Jeremy Ingalls (Princeton: D. Van Nostrand, 1956), 260.

Chapter 12 *(pages 226–243)*

1. Li Chien-nung, *The Political History of China, 1840–1928*, trans. Teng Ssu-yü and Jeremy Ingalls (Princeton: D. Van Nostrand, 1956), 268.

2. David Strand, *An Unfinished Republic: Leading by Word and Deed in Modern China* (Berkeley: University of California Press, 2011), 41–42, 117–120, quote on 120.

3. C. F. Remer, *Foreign Investments in China* (New York: The Macmillan Company, 1933), 76.

4. James Reed, *The Missionary Mind and American East Asia Policy, 1911–1914* (Cambridge: Harvard University Press, 1983), 36–37.

5. Cyril Pearl, *Morrison of Peking* (Sydney, Australia: Angus and Robertson, 1967), 289.

6. Lee-hsia Hsu Ting, *Government Control of the Press in Modern China, 1900–1949* (Cambridge: Harvard University Press, 1974), 13.

7. Donald Gillin, *Warlord: Yen Hsi-shan in Shansi Province, 1911–1949* (Princeton: Princeton University Press, 1967), 63.

8. Michael Summerskill, *China on the Western Front: Britain's Chinese Work Force in the First World War* (London: M. Summerskill, 1982), 69.

9. Summerskill, 166.

10. Summerskill, 102.

11. Chow Tse-tsung, *The May Fourth Movement: Intellectual Revolution in Modern China* (Cambridge: Harvard University Press, 1960), 86.

Chapter 13 *(pages 244–263)*

1. Benjamin Schwartz, *In Search of Wealth and Power* (Cambridge: Harvard University Press, 1964), 45–46.

2. James Pusey, *China and Charles Darwin* (Cambridge: Harvard University Press, 1983), 101–103.

3. Martin Bernal, *Chinese Socialism to 1907* (Ithaca: Cornell University Press, 1976), 100. On the "national essence movement" see Tang Xiaobing, *Global Space and the Nationalist Discourse of Modernity* (Stanford: Stanford University Press, 1996).

4. Pusey, 435.

5. Pusey, 439.

6. Lin Yü-sheng, *The Crisis of Chinese Consciousness: Radical Anti-traditionalism in the May Fourth Era* (Madison: University of Wisconsin Press, 1979), 59.

7. Mao Zedong, "A Study of Physical Education" (1917), translated in *Mao's Road to Power: Revolutionary Writings, 1912–1949*, ed. Stuart R. Schram (Armonk, NY: M. E. Sharpe, 1992), vol. 1, 113–127.

8. Mao Zedong, "The Great Union of the Popular Masses, Part I" (1919), translated in *Mao's Road to Power: Revolutionary Writings, 1912–1949*, ed. Stuart R. Schram (Armonk, NY: M. E. Sharpe, 1992), vol. 1, 380.

9. Stuart R. Schram, *The Political Thought of Mao Tse-tung* (New York: Praeger, 1972), 335–336; Roxane Witke, "Mao Tse-tung, Women and Suicide in the May Fourth Era," *China Quarterly* 31 (1967): 142.

10. Maurice Meisner, *Li Ta-chao and the Origins of Chinese Marxism* (Cambridge: Harvard University Press, 1967), 64–65.

11. Meisner, 144.

12. As listed in Chow Tse-tung, *The May Fourth Movement: Intellectual Revolution in Modern China* (Cambridge: Harvard University Press, 1960), 179.

13. Julia Lin, *Modern Chinese Poetry: An Introduction* (Seattle: University of Washington Press, 1972), 209.

14. Chen Pingyuan, *Touches of History: An Entry into "May Fourth" China*, trans. Michel Hockx (Leiden: Brill, 2011), 124–125.

15. Vera Schwarcz, *The Chinese Enlightenment: Intellectuals and the Legacy of the May Fourth Movement of 1919* (Berkeley: University of California Press, 1986), 44.

16. Schwarcz, 48.

17. Lin Yü-sheng, 76.

18. Jerome Grieder, *Hu Shih and the Chinese Renaissance: Liberalism in the Chinese Revolution, 1917–1937* (Cambridge: Harvard University Press, 1970), 124.

19. Jonathan Spence, *The Gate of Heavenly Peace* (New York: Viking Press, 1981), 217.

20. Lu Hsün (Lu Xun), *Selected Stories* (New York: Norton, 1977), 64 (modified).

21. Schwarcz, 7.

22. Robert North, *Moscow and Chinese Communists* (Stanford: Stanford University Press, 1963), 61.

23. North, 63.

CHAPTER 14 *(pages 264–287)*

1. Xenia Eudin and Robert North, *Soviet Russia and the East, 1920–1927: A Documentary Survey* (Stanford: Stanford University Press, 1957), 141.

2. John Fitzgerald, *Awakening China* (Stanford: Stanford University Press, 1996), 147–159.

3. Lee Feigon, *Chen Duxiu, Founder of the Chinese Communist Party* (Princeton: Princeton University Press 1983), 169; Maurice Meisner, *Li Ta-chao and the Origins of Chinese Marxism* (Cambridge: Harvard University Press, 1967), 191 and 222.

4. Fitzgerald, 180–185.

5. Philip Short, *Mao: A Life* (New York: Henry Holt, 2000), 147.

6. Jonathan Spence, *Gate of Heavenly Peace* (New York, 1980), 197.

7. Spence, 207.

8. Donald Jordan, *The Northern Expedition: China's National Revolution of 1926–1928* (Honolulu: University of Hawaii Press, 1976), 64 (modified).

9. Jordan, 63.

10. Jordan, 76.

11. Gavan McCormack, *Chang Tso-lin in Northeast China, 1911–1928: China, Japan and the Manchurian Idea* (Stanford: Stanford University Press, 1977), 210.

12. Eudin and North, 292–294.

13. Robert North, *Moscow and Chinese Communists* (Stanford: Stanford University Press, 1963), 98 (modified).

14. Mao Zedong, "Hunan nongmin yundong kaocha baogao," *Zhanshi* (Hunan), no. 35–36, 38, 39 (March 5–April 3, 1927), and *Zhongyang fukan* (Wuhan), no. 7 (March 28, 1927).

15. Mao Zedong, "Report on an Investigation of the Peasant Movement in Hunan," translated in *Selected Works of Mao Tse-Tung* (Beijing: Foreign Languages Press, 1975), vol. 1, 23–59.

16. Myron L. Cohen, "Cultural and Political Inventions in Modern China: The Case of the Chinese 'Peasant'," *Daedalus* 122 no. 2 (Spring 1993): 151–170; Charles Hayford, "The Storm over the Peasant: Orientalism and Rhetoric in Construing China," in *Contesting the Master Narrative: Essays in Social History*, eds. Jeffrey Cox and Shelton Stromquist (Iowa City: University of Iowa Press, 1998), 150–172.

17. North, 105–106.

18. Nie Rongzhen, *Inside the Red Star: The Memoirs of Marshal Nie Rongzhen* (Beijing: New World Press, 1988), 74–79.

CHAPTER 15 *(pages 288–311)*

1. Liping Wang, "Creating a National Symbol: The Sun Yatsen Memorial in Nanjing," *Republican China* 21, no. 2 (1996): 23–63.

2. "Treaty Regulating Tariff Relations Between the United States of America and the Republic of China" (July 25, 1928), in *Papers Relating to the Foreign Relations of the United States, 1928* (Washington: United States Government Printing Office, 1943), vol. 1, 475–477.

3. Philip Thai, *China's War on Smuggling: Law, Economic Life, and the Making of the Modern State, 1842–1965* (New York: Columbia University Press, 2018); Felix Boecking, *No Great Wall: Trade, Tariffs, and Nationalism in Republican China, 1927–1945* (Cambridge: Harvard University Asia Center, 2017).

4. Arthur N. Young, *China's Nation-Building Effort, 1927–1937: The Financial and Economic Record* (Stanford: Hoover Institution Press, 1971), 38, table 15:1.

5. George Kates, *The Years That Were Fat: The Last of Old China* (Cambridge: MIT Press, 1967 reprint).

6. Ding Ling, "Miss Sophie's Diary," in *Miss Sophie's Diary and Other Stories*, trans. W. J. F. Jenner (Beijing: Panda Books, 1985).

7. Jonathan D. Spence, *The Gate of Heavenly Peace: The Chinese and Their Revolution, 1895–1980* (New York: Viking Press, 1981), 215.

8. Chiang Kai-shek, *Outline of the New Life Movement*, translated by Madame Chiang Kai-shek (Nanchang: The Association for the Promotion of the New Life Movement, n.d., ca. 1934), 2.

9. Maggie Clinton, *Revolutionary Nativism: Fascism and Culture in China, 1925–1937* (Durham, NC: Duke University Press, 2017), Chapter 4; Federica Ferlanti, "The New Life Movement in Jiangxi Province, 1934–1938," *Modern Asian Studies* 44, no. 5 (2010): 961–1000; Chiang, 7.

10. Clinton, ch. 5; Eastman, *The Abortive Revolution: China under Nationalist Rule, 1927–1937* (Cambridge: Harvard University Press, 1974), 45–46.

11. Liu Jianqun 劉健羣, *Fuxing Zhongguo geming zhi lu* 復興中國革命之路 (Nanjing: Zhongguo wenhua xuehui, 1934), 14.

12. W. L. Tung, *The Chinese in America, 1820–1973: A Chronology and Fact Book* (Dobbs Ferry, NY: Oceana Publications, 1974), 18–31.

13. Okamoto Shumpei, "Japanese Response to Chinese Nationalism: Naitō Konan Torajirō's Image of China in the 1920s," in F. Gilbert Chan and Thomas Etzold, eds., *China in the 1920s: Nationalism and Revolution* (New York: New Viewpoints, 1976), 164, 167; Tam Yue-him, "An Intellectual's Response to Western Intrusion: Naitō Konan's View of Republican China," in Akira Iriye, ed., *The Chinese and the Japanese* (Princeton: Princeton University Press, 1980), 172, 175.

14. Tam, 178.

15. James Crowley, *Japan's Quest for Autonomy: National Security and Foreign Policy, 1930–1938* (Princeton: Princeton University Press, 1966), 155–156.

16. Crowley, 185–186.

CHAPTER 16 *(pages 312–337)*

1. Reworked from H. G. W. Woodhead, ed., *The China Year Book, 1936* (Shanghai: North-China Daily News & Herald, 1936), 322.

2. *The China Year Book, 1936*, 321.

3. Drawn from Augusta Wagner, *Labor Legislation in China* (Peking: Yenching University, 1938), 47; Sidney D. Gamble, *How Chinese Families Live in Peiping: A Study of the Income and Expenditure of 283 Chinese Families Receiving from $8 to $550 Silver per Month* (New York and London: Funk & Wagnalls Company, 1933), ch. 9.

4. Wagner, 50, quote on 99. On shantytowns, see Janet Y. Chen, *Guilty of Indigence: The Urban Poor in China, 1900–1953* (Princeton: Princeton University Press, 2012).

5. Chen, *Guilty of Indigence*, ch. 3.

6. Philip Huang, *The Peasant Economy and Social Change in North China* (Stanford: Stanford University Press, 1985), 189.

7. Adapted from Huang, 186, table 11:1, 188, table 11:2, extracting data on households 1, 5, 8, and 10.

8. Mao Zedong, "An Analysis of the Various Classes among the Chinese Peasantry and Their Attitudes toward the Revolution" (1926), translated in Stuart R. Schram, ed., *Mao's Road to Power: Revolutionary Writings, 1912–1949* (Armonk, NY: M. E. Sharpe, 1994), vol. 2, 303–309 (quote on 308).

9. Roger Thompson, trans. and ed., *Mao Zedong: Report from Xunwu* (Stanford: Stanford University Press, 1991), 181.

10. Mao Zedong, "A Single Spark Can Start a Prairie Fire" (1930), translated in *Selected Works of Mao Tse-tung* (Peking: Foreign Languages Press, 1975), vol. 1, 124.

11. Mao Zedong, "Report on an Investigation of the Peasant Movement in Hunan" (1927), translated in *Selected Works of Mao Tse-Tung* (Peking: Foreign Languages Press, 1975), vol. 1, 45–46.

12. Gail Hershatter, *Women and China's Revolutions* (Lanham: Rowman & Littlefield, 2019), 168–170.

13. William Kirby, ed., *The People's Republic of China at 60* (Cambridge: Harvard University Asia Center, 2011), 111–119.

14. Kirby, 117.

15. Helen Praeger Young, *Choosing Revolution: Chinese Women Soldiers on the Long March* (Urbana: University of Illinois Press, 2001).

16. Benjamin Yang, "The Zunyi Conference as One Step in Mao's Rise to Power: A Survey of Historical Studies of the Chinese Communist Party," *China Quarterly* 106 (1986): 263–264.

17. Mao Zedong, "On Tactics Against Japanese Imperialism" (1935), translated in *Selected Works of Mao Tse-Tung* (Peking: Foreign Languages Press, 1975), vol. 1, 160.

18. Lao She, *Cat Country*, trans. William Lyell (Columbus: Ohio State University Press, 1970), 169–173, 181, 268–269, 280–281.

19. Wu Tien-wei, *The Sian Incident: A Pivotal Point in Modern Chinese History* (Ann Arbor: Center for Chinese Studies, 1976), 25–26.

20. Wu, 92.

Chapter 17 *(pages 338–369)*

1. James Crowley, *Japan's Quest for Autonomy: National Security and Foreign Policy, 1930–1938* (Princeton: Princeton University Press, 1966), 316–317.

2. Crowley, 331, 335.

3. Crowley, 338–339.

4. Rana Mitter, *Forgotten Ally: China's World War II, 1937–1945* (New York: Houghton Mifflin Harcourt, 2013), 94–96; Hans Van de Ven, *China at War: Triumph and Tragedy in the Emergence of New China, 1937–1952* (Cambridge: Harvard University Press, 2018), 71–72.

5. Mitter, 100.

6. Stephen MacKinnon, *Wuhan, 1938: War, Refugees, and the Making of Modern China* (Berkeley: University of California Press, 2008).

7. Micah S. Muscolino, *The Ecology of War in China: Henan Province, the Yellow River, and Beyond, 1938–1950* (New York: Cambridge University Press, 2015).

8. MacKinnon, 47–51.

9. On living under Japanese occupation and the issue of collaboration, see Timothy Brook, *Collaboration: Japanese Agents and Local Elites in Wartime China* (Cambridge: Harvard University Press, 2007); Poshek Fu, *Passivity, Resistance, and Collaboration: Intellectual Choices in Occupied Shanghai, 1937–1945* (Stanford: Stanford University Press, 1993).

10. F. F. Liu, *A Military History of Modern China: 1924–1949* (Princeton: Princeton University Press, 1956), 133.

11. Lee McIsaac, "The City as Nation: Creating a Wartime Capital in Chongqing," in Joseph Esherick, ed., *Remaking the Chinese City: Modernity and National Identity, 1900–1950* (Honolulu: University of Hawaii Press, 1999), 174–191; Danke Li, *Echoes of Chongqing: Women in Wartime China* (Urbana: University of Illinois Press, 2010).

12. Lyman Van Slyke, *Enemies and Friends: The United Front in Chinese Communist History* (Stanford: Stanford University Press, 1967), 92–93.

13. Robert North, *Moscow and Chinese Communists* (Stanford: Stanford University Press, 1963), 185–187.

14. From Liu, 145.

15. Van Slyke, 141–144.

16. Mitter, 207–210, 215–220; Van de Ven, 121–122.

17. Arthur Young, *China and the Helping Hand, 1937–1945* (Cambridge: Harvard University Press, 1963), 435–437.

18. Young, 114.

19. Edna Tow, "The Great Bombing of Chongqing and the Anti-Japanese War, 1937–1945," in Mark Peattie, Edward Drea, and Hans Van de Ven, eds., *The Battle for China: Essays on the Military History of the Sino-Japanese War of 1937–1945* (Stanford: Stanford University Press, 2011), 256–282.

20. James Reardon-Anderson, *Yenan and the Great Powers: The Origins of Chinese Communist Foreign Policy, 1944–1946* (New York: Columbia University Press, 1980), 12.

21. Liu, 209.

22. Chen Yung-fa, "The Blooming Poppy under the Red Sun," in Anthony Saich and Hans Van de Ven, eds., *New Perspectives on the Chinese Communist Revolution* (Armonk, NY: M. E. Sharpe, 1995), 263–298.

23. Bonnie McDougall, *Mao Zedong's "Talks at the Yan'an Conference on Literature and Art": A Translation of the 1943 Text with Commentary* (Ann Arbor: University of Michigan Press, 1980), 69–70.

24. Hsü K'ai-yu, ed. and trans., *Twentieth Century Chinese Poetry: An Anthology* (Ithaca: Cornell University Press, 1970), 403. The poet is Yuan Shui-p'ai.

25. Theodore White and Annalee Jacoby, *Thunder out of China* (New York: William Sloane Associates, 1946, 1961), 169.

26. Chen Yung-fa, *Making Revolution: The Communist Movement in Eastern and Central China, 1937–1945* (Berkeley: University of California Press, 1986), 103–104.

27. Frederick Teiwes with Warren Sun, "From a Leninist to a Charismatic Party: The CCP's Changing Leadership," in Saich and Van de Ven, 339–387, especially 373–375.

CHAPTER 18 *(pages 370–394)*

1. "Generalissimo Chiang Kai-shek's Victory Message" (August 15, 1945), China News Service, in *United Nations Review* 5, no. 5 (September 15, 1945): 206–207.

2. Lin Huiyin, quoted in Diana Lary, *China's Civil War: A Social History, 1945–1949* (New York: Cambridge University Press, 2015), 36.

3. Lary, 90–91.

4. Quoted in Robert Shaffer, "A Rape in Beijing, December 1946: GIs, Nationalist Protests, and U.S. Foreign Policy," *Pacific Historical Review* 69, no. 1(February 2000): 37. See also James A. Cook, "Penetration and Neo-Colonialism: The Shen Chong Rape Case and

the Anti-American Student Movement of 1946–47," *Republican China* 22, no. 1 (November 1996): 65–97.

5. William Hinton, *Fanshen: A Documentary of Revolution in a Chinese Village* (New York: Vintage Books, 1966), 137–138 (modified).

6. Suzanne Pepper, *Civil War in China: The Political Struggle, 1945–1949* (Berkeley: University of California Press, 1978), 177.

7. This summary of events in Manchuria is drawn from Steven Levine, *Anvil of Victory: The Communist Revolution in Manchuria, 1945–1948* (New York: Columbia University Press, 1987). On the CCP's takeover of cities, see also James Z. Gao, *The Communist Takeover of Hangzhou: The Transformation of City and Cadre, 1949–1954* (Honolulu: University of Hawaii Press, 2004), and Joseph K. S. Yick, *Making Urban Revolution in China: The CCP-GMD Struggle for Beiping-Tianjin, 1945–1949* (Armonk, NY: M. E. Sharpe, 1995).

8. Lloyd Eastman, *Seeds of Destruction: Nationalist China in War and Revolution, 1937–1949* (Stanford: Stanford University Press, 1984), 174.

9. Chang Kia-ngau (Chia-ao), *The Inflationary Spiral: The Experience in China, 1939–1950* (Cambridge: MIT Press, 1958), 356.

10. Chang, 359.

11. Lionel Chassin, *The Communist Conquest of China: A History of the Civil War, 1945–1949*, Timothy Osato and Louis Gelas, trans. (Cambridge: Harvard University Press, 1965), 177.

12. Mao Zedong, "Report to the Second Plenary Session of the Seventh Central Committee of the Communist Party of China" (March 5, 1949), in *Mao's Road to Power*, vol. 10, 605.

CHAPTER 19 *(pages 395–415)*

1. Mao Zedong, "On the People's Democratic Dictatorship: In Commemoration of the Twenty-Eighth Anniversary of the Chinese Communist Party" (June 30, 1949), in *Mao's Road to Power*, vol. 10, 696.

2. Mao, "On the People's Democratic Dictatorship," 701, 703–4.

3. Mark Selden, *The People's Republic of China: A Documentary History of Revolutionary Change* (New York: Monthly Review Press, 1979), 187–193.

4. Felix Wemheuer, *A Social History of Maoist China: Conflict and Change, 1949–1976* (Cambridge: Cambridge University Press, 2019), 58–62.

5. Julia Strauss, "Rethinking Land Reform and Regime Consolidation in the People's Republic of China: The Case of Jiangnan, 1950–1952," in Mechthild Leutner, ed., *Rethinking China in the 1950s* (Berlin: Transaction Publishers, 2007), 24–34.

6. Du Runsheng, 杜润生, *Zhongguo di tudi gaige* 中國的土地改革 (Beijing: Dangdai Zhongguo chubanshe, 1996), 559–560; Wemheuer, 55.

7. Neil Diamant, *Revolutionizing the Family: Politics, Love, and Divorce in Urban and Rural China, 1949–1968* (Berkeley: University of California Press, 2000).

8. Elizabeth Perry, "Masters of the Country? Shanghai Workers in the Early People's Republic," in Jeremy Brown and Paul G. Pickowicz, eds., *Dilemmas of Victory: The Early Years of the People's Republic of China* (Cambridge: Harvard University Press, 2007), 59–79.

9. James Gao, *The Communist Takeover of Hangzhou: The Transformation of City and Cadre, 1949–1954* (Honolulu: University of Hawaii Press, 2004), 19–20; Frederick Wakeman, "'Cleanup': The New Order in Shanghai," in Jeremy Brown and Paul G. Pickowicz,

eds., *Dilemmas of Victory: The Early Years of the People's Republic of China* (Cambridge: Harvard University Press, 2007), 37–39.

10. Gao, 92–96; Wakeman, 46–47.

11. Ezra Vogel, *Canton under Communism: Programs and Politics in a Provincial Capital, 1949–1968* (Cambridge: Harvard University Press, 1969), 53.

12. Liu Shaoqi (Liu Shao-ch'i), *How to Be a Good Communist* (Peking: Foreign Languages Press, 1951), 8.

13. From Lionel Chassin, *The Communist Conquest of China: A History of the Civil War, 1945–1949*, Timothy Osato and Louis Gelas, trans. (Cambridge: Harvard University Press, 1965), 243.

14. Alexander V. Pantsov and Steven I. Levine, *Mao: The Real Story* (New York: Simon & Schuster, 2012), 368–371.

15. Shakabpa Tsepon, *Tibet, a Political History* (New Haven: Yale University Press, 1967), 299–305.

16. Allen Whiting, *China Crosses the Yalu: The Decision to Enter the Korean War* (New York: Macmillan, 1960), 21 (modified).

17. Whiting, 18.

18. U.S. Department of State, comp., *United States Relations with China, with Special Reference to the Period 1944–1949* (Washington, D.C., 1949; Stanford: Stanford University Press, 1967), xiv.

19. Howard Boorman, comp., *Biographical Dictionary of Republican China* (New York: Columbia University Press, 1967–1971), vol. 2, 173.

20. Quoted in Whiting, 84–85.

21. Chen Jian, *Mao's China and the Cold War* (Chapel Hill: The University of North Carolina Press, 2001); Shen Zhihua, *Mao, Stalin, and the Korean War: Trilateral Communist Relations in the 1950s*, Neil Silver, trans. (London: Routledge, 2012).

22. Quoted in Yang Kuisong, "Reconsidering the Campaign to Suppress Counterrevolutionaries," *The China Quarterly* 193 (March 2008): 108.

23. Yang, 120. According to Yang's analysis, the actual number of executions was likely much higher than the figure reported.

CHAPTER 20 *(pages 416–439)*

1. Koji Hirata, "Made in Manchuria: The Transnational Origins of Socialist Industrialization in Maoist China," *American Historical Review* 126, no. 3 (September 2021): 1072–1101; Morris Bian, *The Making of the State Enterprise System in Modern China: The Dynamics of Institutional Change* (Cambridge: Harvard University Press, 2005).

2. Thomas Rawski, *China's Transition to Industrialism: Producer Goods and Economic Development in the Twentieth Century* (Ann Arbor: University of Michigan Press, 1980), table, 39.

3. Alexander Eckstein, *China's Economic Revolution* (Cambridge: Cambridge University Press, 1977), table, 186.

4. Frederick C. Teiwes, *Politics at Mao's Court: Gao Gang and Party Factionalism in the Early 1950s* (London and New York: Routledge, 1990), 119–120.

5. Zhongguo minzu renkou ziliao 中国民族人口资料, ed. State Statistical Bureau and Economic Department of State Nationalities Affairs Commission (Beijing: Zhongguo tongji

chubanshe, 1994), 2–3; Thomas Mullaney, *Coming to Terms with the Nation: Ethnic Classification in Modern China* (Berkeley: University of California Press, 2011).

6. Gardner Bovingdon, "Heteronomy and Its Discontents: 'Minzu Regional Autonomy' in Xinjiang," in Morris Rossabi, ed., *Governing China's Multiethnic Frontiers* (Seattle: University of Washington Press, 2004), 117–154.

7. Quoted in Christopher J. Lee, *Making a World After Empire: The Bandung Moment and Its Political Afterlives* (Athens: Ohio University Press, 2010), 5.

8. John Gittings, *The Role of the Chinese Army* (New York: Oxford University Press, 1967), 126.

9. Gittings, 189.

10. Ellis Joffe, *Party and Army: Professionalism and Political Control in the Chinese Officer Corps, 1949–1964* (Cambridge: Harvard University Press, 1965), 57.

11. Jin Yuelin, "A Confession Document," reprinted in Robert Lifton, *Thought Reform and the Psychology of Totalism* (New York: Norton, 1961), 473–484 (Appendix).

12. Merle Goldman, *Literary Dissent in Communist China* (Cambridge: Harvard University Press, 1967), 109.

13. Goldman, 131, 145.

14. Roderick MacFarquhar, *The Origins of the Cultural Revolution*, vol. 1: *Contradictions among the People, 1956–1957* (New York: Columbia University Press, 1974), 48–52.

15. The transcript of the original version of this speech is in Roderick MacFarquhar, Timothy Cheek, and Eugene Wu, eds., *The Secret Speeches of Chairman Mao from the Hundred Flowers to the Great Leap Forward* (Cambridge: Harvard University Press, 1989), 131–189.

16. MacFarquhar, *Origins of the Cultural Revolution*, vol. 1, 185, 212.

17. Roderick MacFarquhar, ed., *The Hundred Flowers* (London: Stevens & Sons, 1960), 92, 94.

18. MacFarquhar, *The Hundred Flowers*, 98, 105, 109, 177, 238.

19. James McGough, *Fei Hsiao-t'ung: The Dilemma of a Chinese Intellectual* (White Plains, NY: M. E. Sharpe, 1979), 62.

20. MacFarquhar, *Origins of the Cultural Revolution*, vol. 1, 289–290.

21. McGough, 81.

Chapter 21 *(pages 440–460)*

1. Stuart Schram, *The Political Thought of Mao Tse-tung* (New York: Praeger, 1972), 408–409.

2. For Henan, this is vividly portrayed in Jean-Luc Domenach, *The Origins of the Great Leap Forward* (Boulder, CO: Westview, 1995), 128–129.

3. Jerome Ch'en, *Mao Papers: Anthology and Bibliography* (New York: Oxford University Press, 1970), 62–63.

4. Schram, 352; Maurice Meisner, *Mao's China: A History of the People's Republic*, third edition (New York: The Free Press, 1999), 199.

5. Meisner, 221.

6. Mark Selden, *The People's Republic of China: A Documentary History of Revolutionary Change* (New York: Monthly Review Press, 1979), 402.

7. Selden, 410.

8. Selden, 413.

9. Kenneth Lieberthal, "The Great Leap Forward and the Split in the Yenan Leadership," in *Cambridge History of China*, vol. 14 (Cambridge: Cambridge University Press, 1987), 313, 317; Nicholas Lardy, "The Chinese Economy under Stress, 1958–1965," *Cambridge History of China*, vol. 14 (Cambridge: Cambridge University Press, 1987), 379–382.

10. Schram, 139, 142, 146.

11. Daiyun Yue, with Carolyn Wakeman, *To the Storm: The Odyssey of a Revolutionary Woman* (Berkeley: University of California Press, 1985), 80, 82.

12. Felix Wemheuer provides a succinct discussion of the debates over the mortality figures from the Great Leap famine: *A Social History of Maoist China: Conflict and Change, 1949–1976* (Cambridge: Cambridge University Press, 2019), 147–152. A more thorough analysis with comparative figures can be found in Jisheng Yang, *Tombstone: The Great Chinese Famine, 1958–1962*, trans. Stacy Mosher and Guo Jian (New York: Farrar, Strauss and Giroux, 2012), chapter 11.

13. Yang, 395.

14. Yang, 3–7.

15. Zhihua Shen, "The Twentieth CPSU Congress and the Eighth CCP Congress, 1956," in Zhihua Shen, ed., *A Short History of Sino-Soviet Relations, 1917–1991*, trans. Yafeng Xia (Singapore: Palgrave MacMillan, 2020), 161–174.

16. G. F. Hudson, Richard Lowenthal, and Roderick MacFarquhar, *The Sino-Soviet Dispute* (New York: China Quarterly, 1961), 42–45.

17. Hudson et al., 58 and 62; Lorenz Luthi, *The Sino-Soviet Split: Cold War in the Communist World* (Princeton: Princeton University Press, 2008), 146–148.

18. Allen Whiting, "The Sino-Soviet Split," in *Cambridge History of China*, vol. 14, 513–514; Luthi, 149–150.

19. Hudson et al., 93–94, citing *Red Flag*.

20. John Wilson Lewis and Xue Litai, *China Builds the Bomb* (Stanford: Stanford University Press, 1988), 160.

21. Danhui Li, "The Collapse of Party-Relations and the Deterioration of State Relations, October 1961–July 1964" in Zhihua Shen, ed., *A Short History of Sino-Soviet Relations, 1917–1991*, trans. Yafeng Xia (Singapore: Palgrave MacMillan, 2020), 241–243.

22. Li, 248–52; Luthi, 205–7.

23. Nicholas Lardy and Kenneth Lieberthal, eds., *Chen Yun's Strategy for China's Development: A Non-Maoist Alternative* (Armonk, NY: M. E. Sharpe, 1983), 156.

24. Wemheuer, 178–79; Richard Baum and Frederic Teiwes, *Ssu-Ch'ing: The Socialist Education Movement of 1962–1966* (Berkeley: University of California Press, 1968), 55–56.

25. Richard Baum, *Prelude to Revolution: Mao, the Party, and the Peasant Question, 1962–66* (New York: Columbia University Press, 1975), 117–121 (quote on p. 119, modified).

26. Kenneth Lieberthal and Michel Oksenberg, *Policy Making in China: Leaders, Structures, and Processes* (Princeton: Princeton University Press, 1988), 175–183, on Daqing oilfield.

27. Baum, 124.

28. Baum, 126, quoting Liu Zihou.

CHAPTER 22 *(pages 461–480)*

1. For Mao's personal life see the provocative and intimate account by his personal physician Li Zhisui, *The Private Life of Chairman Mao* (New York: Random House, 1994).

2. Covell Meyskens, *Mao's Third Front: The Militarization of Cold War China* (Cambridge: Cambridge University Press, 2020).

3. Merle Goldman, *China's Intellectuals: Advise and Dissent* (Cambridge: Harvard University Press, 1981), 32–34.

4. Merle Goldman, "The Party and the Intellectuals, Phase Two," in *Cambridge History of China* (Cambridge: Cambridge University Press, 1987), vol. 14, 446.

5. Clive Ansley, *The Heresy of Wu Han: His Play "Hai Jui's Dismissal" and Its Role in China's Cultural Revolution* (Toronto: University of Toronto Press, 1971), 76. A careful evaluation of the exact nature of Wu Han's work is given by Tom Fisher, "'The Play's the Thing': Wu Han and Hai Rui Revisited," in Jonathan Unger, ed., *Using the Past to Serve the Present* (Armonk, NY: M. E. Sharpe, 1993), 9–45.

6. Ansley, 90.

7. Roderick MacFarquhar and Michael Schoenhals, *Mao's Last Revolution* (Cambridge: Belknap Press of Harvard University Press, 2006), 14–19.

8. *CCP Documents of the Great Proletarian Cultural Revolution, 1966–1967*, comp. Union Research Institute (Hong Kong: Union Research Institute, 1968), 8, 9, 11.

9. Lin Biao (Lin Piao), *Important Documents on the Great Proletarian Cultural Revolution in China* (Beijing: Foreign Languages Press, 1970), 199, 208–215, 221.

10. Jerome Ch'en, *Mao's Papers: Anthology and Bibliography* (London: Oxford University Press, 1970), 24–25.

11. "Bombard the Headquarters," translated in Timothy Cheek, ed., *Mao Zedong and China's Revolutions: A Brief History with Documents*, (Boston and New York: Bedford/St. Martins, 2002), 170–171; "Decision Concerning the Great Proletarian Cultural Revolution," in Michael Schoenhals, ed., *China's Cultural Revolution, 1966–1969: Not a Dinner Party* (Armonk, NY: M. E. Sharpe, 1996), 33–43.

12. Rae Yang, *Spider-Eaters: A Memoir* (Berkeley: University of California Press, 1997), 123; Fan Shen, *Gang of One: Memoirs of a Red Guard* (Lincoln, NE: University of Nebraska Press, 2004), 59–60.

13. MacFarquhar and Schoenhals, 119–120; Anne Thurston, *Enemies of the People* (New York: Knopf, 1987), 102–103.

14. Lee Hong-yung, *The Politics of the Chinese Cultural Revolution: A Case Study* (Berkeley: University of California Press, 1978), 154.

15. MacFarquhar and Schoenhals, 200–214.

16. The British office was not rebuilt until 1971. For a detailed insider account, see Ma Jisen, *The Cultural Revolution in the Foreign Ministry of China* (Hong Kong: Chinese University Press 2004).

17. Mao's instruction to educated youths: *Renmin ribao*, December 22, 1968. On the experiences of *zhiqing*, see Michel Bonnin, *The Lost Generation: The Rustication of China's Educated Youths, 1968–1980*, trans. Krystyna Horko (Hong Kong: The Chinese University Press, 2013); Yihong Pan, *Tempered in the Revolutionary Furnace: China's Youth in the Rustication Movement* (Lanham, MD: Lexington Books, 2003); Emily Honig and Xiaojian Zhao, *Across the Great Divide: The Sent-down Youth Movement in Mao's China, 1968–1980* (Cambridge: Cambridge University Press, 2019).

18. Yang Jiang, *Six Chapters from My Life "Down Under"* (Seattle: University of Washington Press, 1984), 50 (translation modified).

19. Anita Chan, Richard Madsen, and Jonathan Unger, *Chen Village: The Recent History of a Peasant Community in Mao's China* (Berkeley: University of California Press, 1984), 170.

20. Philip Bridgham, "The Fall of Lin Piao," *China Quarterly* 55 (1973): 435.

21. Lin Biao, 14; Bridgham, 441; Chan et al., 231. On the attempt to erase Lin Biao's closeness to Mao, see Jin Qiu, "From 'Number Two Deity' to 'Number One Demon,'" *The Chinese Historical Review* 18, no. 2 (Fall 2011): 151–182.

Chapter 23 *(pages 481–500)*

1. Henry Kissinger, *White House Years* (Boston: Little, Brown, 1979), 733.

2. Kissinger, 1060–1063; Richard Nixon, *RN: The Memoirs of Richard Nixon* (New York: Grosset & Dunlap, 1978), 560–564.

3. "Quarterly Documentation," *China Quarterly* 50 (April 1972): 402.

4. "Quarterly Documentation," *China Quarterly* 50 (April 1972): 392.

5. Lee Hong-yung, "The Changing Cadre System in the Socialist State of China" (unpublished ms., 1988), 246 (cited with permission).

6. "Quarterly Documentation," *China Quarterly* 53 (January 1973): 192–193.

7. "Quarterly Documentation," *China Quarterly* 54 (April 1973): 408–409.

8. "Quarterly Documentation," *China Quarterly* 57 (January 1974): 207–209.

9. "Quarterly Documentation," *China Quarterly* 57 (January 1974), citing *Peking Review* no. 5.

10. "Quarterly Documentation," *China Quarterly* 56 (October 1973): 809–810.

11. "Quarterly Documentation," *China Quarterly* 58 (April 1974): 414–415.

12. "Quarterly Documentation," *China Quarterly* 59 (July 1974): 644.

13. Shannon Brown, "China's Program of Technology Acquisition," in Richard Baum, ed., *China's Four Modernizations* (Boulder, CO: Westview Press, 1980), 159.

14. Brown, 161. On the work and identity of "Liang Xiao" see Yue Daiyun, with Carolyn Wakeman, *To the Storm: The Odyssey of a Revolutionary Woman* (Berkeley: University of California Press, 1985), 375–362.

15. "Quarterly Documentation," *China Quarterly* 65 (March 1976): 168–173.

16. Ezra F. Vogel, *Deng Xiaoping and the Transformation of China* (Cambridge: Harvard University Press, 2011), 159.

17. "Quarterly Documentation," *China Quarterly* 66 (June 1976): 423.

18. "Quarterly Documentation," *China Quarterly* 66 (June 1976): 432.

19. Vogel, 166–167.

20. "Quarterly Documentation," *China Quarterly* 67 (September 1976): 607; Vogel, 168.

21. These announcements, dated April 7, 1976, appeared on the front page of *People's Daily* on April 8.

22. "Quarterly Documentation," *China Quarterly* 67 (September 1976): 673.

23. Lucien Bianco and Yves Chevrier, *La Chine: Dictionnaire bibliographique du mouvement ouvrier international* (Paris: Les Editions Ouvrieres, 1985), 169.

Chapter 24 *(pages 501–523)*

1. Ezra Vogel, *Deng Xiaoping and the Transformation of China* (Cambridge: Harvard University Press, 2011), 192–198.

2. Vogel, 201–207.

3. "Communique of the Third Plenary Session of the 11th Central Committee of the Communist Party of China," *Beijing Review* 52 (December 29, 1978), 11.

4. "Communique of the Third Plenary Session," 12–13.

5. "Communique of the Third Plenary Session," 14.

6. "Communique of the Third Plenary Session," 6–7, 15.

7. David Goodman, *Beijing Street Voices: The Poetry and Politics of China's Democracy Movement* (London: M. Boyars, 1981), 79.

8. Goodman, 95.

9. Bei Dao, *The August Sleepwalker*, trans. Bonnie S. McDougall (London: Anvil Press, 1988), 34.

10. James Seymour, *The Fifth Modernization: China's Human Rights Movement, 1978–1979* (Stanfordville, NY: Human Rights Publishing Group, 1980), 52.

11. Seymour, 54.

12. Seymour, 63–64, 69.

13. Goodman, 142.

14. Goodman, 122.

15. "Establishment of Diplomatic Relations with the U.S.," *China Quarterly* 77 (March 1979): 215–216.

16. James C. Hsiung, ed., *The Taiwan Experience, 1950–1980: Contemporary Republic of China* (New York: American Association for Chinese Studies, 1981), 132.

17. "Taiwan Relations Act," April 10, 1979 (Public Law 96-8, 96th Congress): https://www.congress.gov/96/statute/STATUTE-93/STATUTE-93-Pg14.pdf. Martin B. Gold provides a detailed analysis in *A Legislative History of the Taiwan Relations Act: Bridging the Strait* (Lanham, MD: Lexington Books, 2017).

18. On Xi Zhongxun, father of current president Xi Jinping, see Vogel, 397–400 and 739–740; Wolfgang Bartke, *Who's Who in the People's Republic of China* (Armonk, NY: M. E. Sharpe, 1981), 416.

19. Liu Binyan, *"People or Monsters?" and Other Stories and Reportage from China after Mao*, trans. Perry Link et al. (Bloomington: Indiana University Press, 1983), 23 and 51.

20. Lucien Bianco and Yves Chevrier, *La Chine: Dictionnaire bibliographique du mouvement ouvrier international* (Paris: Les Editions Ouvrieres, 1985), 246 (translated).

21. "Resolution on Certain Questions in the History of Our Party since the Founding of the People's Republic of China," adopted by the Sixth Plenary Session of the Eleventh Central Committee of the Communist Party of China on June 27, 1981; Andrew Nathan, *Chinese Democracy* (New York: Knopf, 1985), 103.

22. *New York Times*, March 31, 1980.

CHAPTER 25 *(pages 524–544)*

1. *New China's Population* (New York: China Financial and Economic Publishing House and Macmillan Publishing Company, 1987), 117, table 8:14.

2. Colin Mackerras, *Modern China: A Chronology from 1842 to the Present* (San Francisco: W. H. Freeman & Co., 1982), 578 (August 21, 1974).

3. Judith Banister, *China's Changing Population* (Stanford: Stanford University Press, 1987), 215.

4. *New China's Population*, 132, table 9:2.

5. *New China's Population*, 102, table 7:6, amending 1983 rural percentage.

6. This method of describing Chinese leadership is indebted to Kenneth Lieberthal and Michel Oksenberg, *Policy Making in China: Leaders, Structures, and Processes* (Princeton: Princeton University Press, 1988), 35–42.

7. Lieberthal and Oksenberg, 339–344.

8. On coal and offshore-oil data, Lieberthal and Oksenberg, chs. 5 and 7.

9. On the Three Gorges, see Lieberthal and Oksenberg, especially 283 and 320; Dai Qing, comp., *The River Dragon Has Come! The Three Gorges Dam and the Fate of China's Yangtze River and Its People*, trans. Yi Ming (Armonk, NY: M. E. Sharpe, 1988).

10. Joseph Fewsmith, *Rethinking Chinese Politics* (Cambridge: Cambridge University Press, 2021), 40–41.

11. Y. Y. Kueh, "The Economics of the 'Second Land Reform' in China," *China Quarterly* 101 (March 1985): 123; Kenneth Lieberthal, *Governing China: From Revolution Through Reform* (New York: Norton, 2004), second edition, 252 (citing *China Statistical Yearbook 2002*, table 12.2).

12. The discussion of corruption and the Hainan car scandal draws from *Beijing Review* 28:32 (August 12, 1985), 8–9, and Ezra Vogel, *One Step Ahead: Guangdong under Reform* (Cambridge: Harvard University Press, 1989), 291–295, 410–413.

13. Stuart Schram, "'Economics in Command?' Ideology and Policy since the Third Plenum, 1978–1984," *China Quarterly* 99 (September 1984): 454.

14. Orville Schell, *To Get Rich is Glorious: China in the Eighties* (New York: Pantheon, 1984), 34–36.

15. Orville Schell, *Discos and Democracy: China in the Throes of Reform* (New York: Pantheon, 1988), 41–44.

16. On the shifts to conjugal giving, see Yan Yuxiang, *The Flow of Gifts: Reciprocity and Networks in a Chinese Village* (Stanford: Stanford University Press, 1996), 176–204.

17. Emily Honig and Gail Hershatter, *Personal Voices: Chinese Women in the 1980s* (Stanford: Stanford University Press, 1988), 207–226.

18. Wen-hui Tsai, "Mainland Chinese Marriage and Family under the Impact of the Four Modernizations," *Issues and Studies* 24, no. 3 (March 1988), 116; *Beijing Review*, February 4, 1985, 18–20. The data are difficult to correlate, as methods of counting the number of cases and calculating the divorce rate varied widely.

19. Samuel S. Kim, "The Development of International Law in Post-Mao China: Change and Continuity," *Journal of Chinese Law* 1, no. 2 (1987): 117–160.

20. Text in *China Quarterly* 100 (December 1984): 920–922.

CHAPTER 26 *(pages 545–570)*

1. Brian Spivey, "The December 12th Student Movement: Uyghur Student Protest in Reform-Era China," *Journal of Asian Studies* 81 no. 4 (2022): 727–746.

2. Geremie Barmé and John Minford, eds., *Seeds of Fire: Chinese Voices of Conscience* (New York: Hill and Wang, 1989), 405.

3. Barmé and Minford, 410.

4. Barmé and Minford, 174.

5. Zhang Xinxin and Sang Ye, *Chinese Lives: An Oral History of Contemporary China* (New York: Pantheon, 1987), 174.

6. Zhang and Sang, 313.

7. Zhang and Sang, 153.

8. Annping Chin, *Children of China: Voices from Recent Years* (New York: Knopf, 1988), 53, 103, 201.

9. Orville Schell, *Discos and Democracy: China in the Throes of Reform* (New York: Pantheon, 1988), 132.

10. Andrew Nathan, *Chinese Democracy* (New York: Knopf, 1985), 197.

11. Schell, 213–214.

12. Edward A. Gargan, "China Denounces Student Protests as 'Illegal Acts,'" *New York Times*, December 11, 1986.

13. Schell, 224–225.

14. Gargan, "China Denounces Student Protests as 'Illegal Acts.'"

15. Schell, 231–241.

16. Edward A. Gargan, "China Ousts University Scientist Who Advocated Broader Rights," *New York Times*, January 13, 1987.

17. John F. Burns, "China Promises Creative Freedom for Writers," *New York Times*, January 6, 1985; John F. Burns, "20 Years Wasted, Top Chinese Says," *New York Times*, February 21, 1985.

18. Schell, 134, 291.

19. Schell, 292.

20. Information on Li Peng drawn from Kenneth Lieberthal and Michel Oksenberg, *Policy Making in China: Leaders, Structures, and Processes* (Princeton: Princeton University Press, 1988), 51–58.

21. Edward A. Gargan, "Among the Multitude of Ayes, Nays in the Chinese Congress," *New York Times*, March 31, 1988; Associated Press, "2 Backers of Change Named to Top Posts by Chinese Congress," *New York Times*, April 9, 1988.

22. All figures from "Quarterly Documentation," *China Quarterly* 117 (March 1989): 180–195, and 118 (June 1989): 391–407. Trade figures following from *MOR China Letter* 3, no. 3 (April 1989): 7, and courtesy of James Stepanik. On American Motors and China see Jim Mann, *Beijing Jeep* (New York: Simon and Schuster, 1989).

23. The open letters to Deng Xiaoping from intellectuals are translated in *Beijing Spring, 1989 Confrontation and Conflict: The Basic Documents*, Michel Oksenberg, Lawrence R. Sullvan, and Marc Lambert, eds. (Armonk: NY: M. E. Sharpe, 1990), 166–168; Su Shaozhi, "Speech at the Theoretical Discussion Meeting Marking the Tenth Anniversary of the Third Plenary Session of the Eleventh CPC Central Committee," in *Beijing Spring, 1989 Confrontation and Conflict: The Basic Documents*, Michel Oksenberg, Lawrence R. Sullvan, and Marc Lambert, eds. (Armonk: NY: M. E. Sharpe, 1990), 155–163.

24. "Hunger Strike Announcement," translated in *Beijing Spring, 1989 Confrontation and Conflict: The Basic Documents*, Michel Oksenberg, Lawrence R. Sullvan, and Marc Lambert, eds. (Armonk: NY: M. E. Sharpe, 1990), 258-260.

25. A detailed narrative with accompanying documents is in "Quarterly Documentation," *China Quarterly* 119 (September 1989): 666–734. Dramatic photographs of the demonstrations and the victims are shown in David and Peter Turnley, *Beijing Spring* (New York: Stewart, Tabori & Chang, 1989).

26. Fang Lizhi spent more than one year in the U.S. Embassy in Beijing before an agreement with the Chinese government permitted him to leave for the United States. See Fang Lizhi, *The Most Wanted Man in China: My Journey from Scientist to Enemy of the State,*

Perry Link, trans. (New York: Henry Holt, 2016). The letter from President George Bush is quoted in Ezra Vogel, *Deng Xiaoping and the Transformation of China* (Cambridge: Harvard University Press, 2011), 649.

27. The full text of Deng Xiaoping's June 9th speech is translated in *Beijing Spring, 1989 Confrontation and Conflict: The Basic Documents*, Michel Oksenberg, Lawrence R. Sullvan, and Marc Lambert, eds. (Armonk: NY: M. E. Sharpe, 1990), 376–382.

CHAPTER 27 *(pages 571–593)*

1. Maurice Meisner, *The Deng Xiaoping Era: An Inquiry into the Fate of Chinese Socialism, 1978–1994* (New York: Hill and Wang, 1996), 474–475.

2. Luo Xu, "The 'Shekou Storm': Changes in the Mentality of Chinese Youth Prior to Tiananmen," *China Quarterly* 142 (June 1995): 541–572.

3. *China Quarterly* 130 (June 1992): 454–56, and *China Quarterly* 131 (September 1992): 860.

4. *China Quarterly* 136 (December 1993): 1040–1041.

5. Wei Jingsheng, "The Wolf and the Lamb," *New York Times*, November 18, 1993. On the Three Gorges see the vivid scroll paintings by Ji Yunfei, in *Art Journal* 69, no. 3 (Fall 2010): 80–87.

6. *China Quarterly* 148 (December 1996), special issue on Taiwan.

7. This and the following paragraph drawn from Richard Bernstein and Ross H. Munro, *The Coming Conflict with China* (New York: Knopf, 1997), 72–76.

8. For this particular case study see Jonathan Spence and Annping Chin, "Letter from Beijing: Deng's Heirs," *The New Yorker*, March 10, 1997, 68–77. Other cases based on the same authors' unpublished interviews and impressions.

9. Patrick E. Tyler, "Bold Book in China Faults Deng on Policies," *New York Times*, October 8, 1994; Richard Baum, "China after Deng: Ten Scenarios in Search of Reality," *China Quarterly* 145 (March 1996): 153–175.

10. A vivid example is the case of Wang Zhiqiang in Henan, as recorded by Sheryl Wu Dunn, *New York Times*, May 16, 1993.

11. Wei Li, "The Security Service for Chinese Central Leaders," *China Quarterly* 143 (September 1995): 814–827, at 823.

12. Wang Shuo, "Welcome, Cash Box," *Asian Wall Street Journal*, June 27, 1997.

13. Anonymous [?Deng Liqun], "Ten Thousand Character Statement," *China Quarterly* 148 (December 1996): 1426–1441.

14. Quoted in Patrick E. Tyler, "America the Beautiful (A Rare Rave)," *New York Times*, July 21, 1997.

CHAPTER 28 *(pages 594–610)*

1. John Wong and Lai Hongyi, *China into the Hu-Wen Era: Policy Initiatives and Challenges* (Hackensack, NJ: World Scientific, 2003), 3–4.

2. James Millward, *Eurasian Crossroads: A History of Xinjiang* (New York: Columbia University Press, 2007), 330–333.

3. James Miles, "Rising Power, Anxious State," *The Economist*, June 25, 2011, 4.

4. A good survey is given in Thomas J. Campanella, *The Concrete Dragon: China's Urban Revolution and What It Means for the World* (New York: Princeton Architectural Press, 2008).

5. On the Sichuan earthquake and the relief operations see Yong Chen and David C. Booth, *The Wenchuan Earthquake of 2008: Anatomy of a Disaster* (Berlin: Springer, 2011); Bin Xu, *The Politics of Compassion: The Sichuan Earthquake and Civic Engagement in China* (Stanford: Stanford University Press, 2017).

6. Philip P. Pan, *Out of Mao's Shadow: The Struggle for the Soul of a New China* (New York: Simon and Schuster, 2008), 198, 203–204.

7. For details on Zhao's funeral, see Pan, 15.

8. Laurence Sullivan, *Historical Dictionary of the People's Republic of China* (Lanham, MD: Rowman & Littlefield, 2007), 271.

9. "Going, Going…" *The Economist*, August 27, 2011, 58.

10. Susan L. Shirk, ed., *Changing Media, Changing China* (Oxford: Oxford University Press, 2011), 2–4.

11. Shirk, 203.

12. Andrew Jacobs, "Trial in China Signals New Limits on Dissent," *New York Times*, December 23, 2009. The full text of the charter is reprinted in *The Search for Modern China: A Documentary Collection*, eds. Janet Chen, Pei-Kai Cheng, and Michael Lestz with Jonathan Spence (New York: W. W. Norton, 2014), 605–611.

13. Ai Weiwei, *1000 Years of Joys and Sorrow: A Memoir*, trans. Allan Barr (New York: Crown Books, 2021), 252–256, 294–327.

14. Sullivan, 122–128.

15. On art, see Wu Hong, *Contemporary Chinese Art: Primary Documents* (New York: Museum of Modern Art, 2012); for the social costs of the dam, see Ji Yunfei "Three Gorges Dam Migration," *Art Journal* 69, no. 3 (Fall 2010).

16. On the Bo Xilai scandal and the implications for the leadership transition, see Cheng Li, *Chinese Politics in the Xi Jinping Era: Reassessing Collective Leadership* (Washington, D.C.: Brookings Institution Press, 2016), 1–5.

Epilogue *(pages 611–617)*

1. Zhenwu Zhai and Guangzhao Jin, "China's Family Planning Policy and Fertility Transition," *Chinese Journal of Sociology* 9, no. 4 (2023): 479–496; Michael O'Hanlon, "China's Shrinking Population and Constraints on Its Future Power," The Brookings Institution, April 24, 2023, https://www.brookings.edu/articles/chinas-shrinking-population-and-constraints-on-its-future-power/.

2. "China's Xi Warns Attempts to Divide China Will End in 'Shattered Bones,'" Reuters, October 13, 2019, https://www.reuters.com/article/idUSKBN1WS07W/.

3. On "historical nihilism," see "Document 9: A ChinaFile Translation," ChinaFile, November 8, 2013, https://www.chinafile.com/document-9-chinafile-translation.

Further Readings

CHAPTER 1

Ming Society: Timothy Brook, *The Troubled Empire: China in the Yuan and Ming Dynasties* (Cambridge: Belknap Press, 2013); Fei Si-yen, *Negotiating Urban Space: Urbanization and Late Ming Nanjing* (Cambridge: Harvard University Asia Center, 2009); Jonathan Spence, *Return to Dragon Mountain, Memories of a Late Ming Man* (New York: Viking, 2007); Timothy Brook, *The Confusions of Pleasure: Commerce and Culture in Ming China* (Berkeley: University of California Press, 1998); Dorothy Ko, *Teachers of the Inner Chambers: Women and Culture in Seventeenth-Century China* (Stanford: Stanford University Press, 1994); Craig Clunas, *Superfluous Things: Material Culture and Social Status in Early Modern China* (Urbana: University of Illinois Press, 1991).

Ming Elite Life and Culture: Giovanni Vitiello, *The Libertine's Friend: Homosexuality and Masculinity in Late Imperial China* (Chicago: The University of Chicago Press, 2011); Jonathan Spence, *The Memory Palace of Matteo Ricci* (New York: Viking Penguin, 1984); Joanna Handlin, *Action in Late Ming Thought* (Berkeley: University of California Press, 1983); Patrick Hanan, *The Chinese Vernacular Story* (Cambridge: Harvard University Press, 1981); Tang Xianzu, *The Peony Pavilion*, trans. Cyril Birch (Bloomington: Indiana University Press, 1980); Willard Peterson, *Bitter Gourd: Fang I-chih and the Impetus for Intellectual Change in the 1630s* (New Haven: Yale University Press, 1979); W. T. deBary, ed., *Self and Society in Ming Thought* (New York: Columbia University Press, 1970).

Ming Biographies: Huang Tsung-hsi (Huang Zongxi), *The Records of Ming Scholars*, ed. Julia Ching (Honolulu: Hawaii University Press, 1987); L. Carrington Goodrich and Fang Chao-ying, eds., *Dictionary of Ming Biography, 1368–1644*, 2 vols. (New York: Columbia University Press, 1976).

Ming Government: David M. Robinson, *Ming China and Its Allies: Imperial Rulership in Eurasia* (Cambridge: Cambridge University Press, 2020); Ray Huang, *1587, a Year of No Significance: The Ming Dynasty in Decline* (New Haven: Yale University Press, 1981);

Charles Hucker, ed., *Chinese Government in Ming Times* (New York: Columbia University Press, 1969).

Ming Social Problems and Rebellions: Kenneth Swope, *The Military Collapse of China's Ming Dynasty, 1618–1644* (London: Routledge, 2014); Roger V. Des Forges, *Cultural Centrality and Political Change in Chinese History: Northeast Henan in the Fall of the Ming* (Stanford: Stanford University Press, 2003); *The Cambridge History of China*, vol. 7: *The Ming Dynasty, 1368–1644, Part I*, ed. Frederick Mote and Denis Twitchett (New York: Cambridge University Press, 1988).

CHAPTER 2

Manchu Identity: William T. Rowe, *China's Last Empire: The Great Qing* (Cambridge: Harvard University Press, 2009); Lynn A. Struve, ed., *The Qing Formation in World-Historical Time* (Cambridge: Harvard University Asia Center, 2004); Mark C. Elliott, *The Manchu Way: The Eight Banners and Ethnic Identity in Late Imperial China* (Stanford: Stanford University Press, 2001); Pamela Kyle Crossley, *A Translucent Mirror: History and Identity in Qing Imperial Ideology* (Berkeley: University of California Press, 1999); Evelyn S. Rawski, *The Last Emperors: A Social History of Qing Imperial Institutions* (Berkeley: University of California Press, 1998).

The Manchu Conquest and Consolidation: Nicola di Cosmo, *The Diary of a Manchu Soldier in Seventeenth-Century China* (London: Routledge, 2006); Pamela Kyle Crossley, *The Manchus* (Oxford: Blackwell, 1997); Frederic Wakeman, *The Great Enterprise: The Manchu Reconstruction of Imperial Order in Seventeenth-Century China*, 2 vols. (Berkeley: University of California Press, 1985); Jonathan Spence and John Wills, eds., *From Ming to Ch'ing: Conquest, Region, and Continuity in Seventeenth-Century China* (New Haven: Yale University Press, 1979); Robert Oxnam, *Ruling from Horseback: Manchu Politics in the Oboi Regency, 1661–1669* (Chicago: The University of Chicago Press, 1975).

Ming Loyalism: Lynn A. Struve, *Voices from the Ming-Qing Cataclysm: China in Tigers' Jaws* (New Haven: Yale University Press, 1993); Kahisg-i Sun Chang, *The Late Ming Poet Ch'en Tzu-lung: Crises of Love and Loyalism* (New Haven: Yale University Press, 1990); Wang Fangyu, Richard Barnhart, and Judith Smith, eds., *Master of the Lotus Garden: The Life and Art of Bada Shanren (1626–1705)* (New Haven: Yale University Press, 1990); Lynn A. Struve, *The Southern Ming, 1644–1662* (New Haven: Yale University Press, 1984); Jerry Dennerline, *The Chia-ting Loyalists: Confucian Leadership and Social Change in Seventeenth-Century China* (New Haven: Yale University Press, 1981).

Qing Biographies: Arthur Hummel, ed., *Eminent Chinese of the Ch'ing Period (1644–1912)*, 2 vols. (Washington, D.C.: U.S. Government Printing Office, 1943).

Social and Economic Aspects: Antonia Finnane, *Speaking of Yangzhou: A Chinese City, 1550–1850* (Cambridge: Harvard University Asia Center, 2004); Tobie Meyer-Fong, *Building Culture in Early Qing Yangzhou* (Stanford: Stanford University Press, 2003); Susan Naquin, *Peking: Temples and City Life, 1400–1900* (Berkeley: University of California Press, 2000); Philip Huang, *The Peasant Economy and Social Change in North China* (Stanford: Stanford University Press, 1985); Hilary Beattie, *Land and Lineage in China: A Study of T'ung-ch'eng County, Anhwei, in the Ming and Ch'ing Dynasties* (New York: Cambridge University Press, 1979).

CHAPTER 3

Kangxi as Ruler: Catherine Jami, *The Emperor's New Mathematics: Western Learning and Imperial Authority during the Kangxi Reign* (New York: Oxford University Press, 2012); Jonathan Spence, *Ts'ao Yin and the K'ang-hsi Emperor, Bondservant and Master* (New Haven: Yale University Press, 1988); Silas Hsiu-liang Wu, *Passage to Power: K'ang-hsi and His Heir Apparent, 1661–1722* (Cambridge: Harvard University Press, 1979); Jonathan Spence, *Emperor of China: Self-Portrait of K'ang-hsi* (New York: Vintage Books, 1974).

Maritime China and Foreign Powers: Melissa Macauley, *Distant Shores: Colonial Encounters on China's Maritime Frontier* (Princeton: Princeton University Press, 2021); Tonio Andrade, *Lost Colony: The Untold Story of China's First Great Victory over the West* (Princeton: Princeton University Press, 2011); Tonio Andrade, *How Taiwan Became Chinese: Dutch, Spanish, and Han Colonization in the Seventeenth Century* (New York: Columbia University Press, 2007); John Robert Shepherd, *Statecraft and Political Economy in the Taiwan Frontier, 1600–1800* (Stanford: Stanford University Press, 1993); John Wills, *Embassies and Illusions: Dutch and Portuguese Envoys to K'ang-hsi, 1666–1687* (Cambridge: Harvard University Press, 1984); Johanna Meskill, *A Chinese Pioneer Family: The Lins of Wu-feng, Taiwan, 1729–1895* (Princeton: Princeton University Press, 1979); Ralph Croizier, *Koxinga and Chinese Nationalism: History, Myth and the Hero* (Cambridge: Harvard University Press, 1977).

Culture and the Arts: Benjamin A. Elman, *A Cultural History of Civil Examinations in Late Imperial China* (Berkeley: University of California Press, 2000); Judith T. Zeitlin, *Historian of the Strange: Pu Songling and the Chinese Classical Tale* (Stanford: Stanford University Press, 1993); Patrick Hanan, *The Invention of Li Yu* (Cambridge: Harvard University Press, 1988); Richard Strassberg, *The World of K'ung Shang-jen, a Man of Letters in Early Ch'ing China* (New York: Columbia University Press, 1983); James Cahill, *The Compelling Image: Nature and Style in Seventeenth-Century Chinese Painting* (Cambridge: Harvard University Press, 1982); Irving Lo and William Schultz, *Waiting for the Unicorn: Poems and Lyrics of China's Last Dynasty, 1644–1911* (Bloomington: Indiana University Press, 1980).

Catholic Missions: Florence C. Hsia, *Sojourners in a Strange Land: Jesuits and Their Scientific Missions in Late Imperial China* (Chicago: The University of Chicago Press, 2009); Eugenio Menegon, *Ancestors, Virgins, and Friars: Christianity as a Local Religion in Late Imperial China* (Cambridge: Harvard University Asia Center, 2009).

CHAPTER 4

Eighteenth-Century Social Structures: William T. Rowe, *China's Last Empire: The Great Qing* (Cambridge: Harvard University Press, 2009); Kenneth Pomeranz, *The Great Divergence: China, Europe, and the Making of the Modern World Economy* (Princeton: Princeton University Press, 2001); James Lee and Cameron Campbell, *Fate and Fortune in Rural China: Social Organization and Population Behavior in Liaoning, 1774–1873* (Cambridge: Cambridge University Press, 1997); Susan Naquin and Evelyn Rawski, *Chinese Society in the Eighteenth Century* (New Haven: Yale University Press, 1987); G. William Skinner, ed., *The City in Late Imperial China* (Stanford: Stanford University Press, 1977); Mark Elvin, *The Pattern of the Chinese Past* (Stanford: Stanford University Press, 1973); Ho Ping-ti, *Studies on the Population of China, 1368–1953* (Cambridge: Harvard University Press, 1959).

Yongzheng as Ruler: C. Patterson Giersch, *Asian Borderlands: The Transformation of Qing China's Yunnan Frontier* (Cambridge: Harvard University Press, 2006); Beatrice S. Bartlett,

Monarchs and Ministers: The Rise of the Grand Council in Mid-Ch'ing China, 1723–1820 (Berkeley: University of California Press, 1990); Madeleine Zelin, *The Magistrate's Tael: Rationalizing Fiscal Reform in Eighteenth-Century Ch'ing China* (Berkeley: University of California Press, 1984).

Rural China: David Faure, *Emperor and Ancestor: State and Lineages in South China* (Stanford: Stanford University Press, 2007); Bradly W. Reed, *Talons and Teeth: County Clerks and Runners in the Qing Dynasty* (Stanford: Stanford University Press, 2000); Peter Perdue, *Exhausting the Earth: State and Peasant in Hunan, 1500–1850* (Cambridge: Harvard University Press, 1987); Evelyn Rawski, *Agricultural Change and the Peasant Economy of South China* (Cambridge: Harvard University Press, 1972); Hsiao Kung-chuan, *Rural China: Imperial Control in the Nineteenth Century* (Seattle: University of Washington Press, 1960).

Elite and the Bureaucracy: R. Kent Guy, *Qing Governors and Their Provinces: The Evolution of Territorial Administration in China, 1644–1796* (Seattle: University of Washington Press, 2010); Helen Dunstan, *State or Merchant: Political Economy and Political Process in 1740s China* (Cambridge: Harvard University Asia Center, 2006); William T. Rowe, *Saving the World: Chen Hongmou and Elite Consciousness in Eighteenth-Century China* (Stanford: Stanford University Press, 2001); John Watt, *The District Magistrate in Late Imperial China* (New York: Columbia University Press, 1972); Ho Ping-ti, *The Ladder of Success in Imperial China: Aspects of Social Mobility, 1368–1911* (New York: Columbia University Press, 1962); Ch'ü T'ung-tsu, *Local Government in China under the Ch'ing* (Cambridge: Harvard University Press, 1962).

CHAPTER 5

Philosophy and History: Chow Kai-wing, *The Rise of Confucian Ritualism in Late Imperial China: Ethics, Classics, and Lineage Discourse* (Stanford: Stanford University Press, 1994); Annping Chin and Mansfield Freeman, *Beyond Reason and Proof: Tai Chen's Evidential Study of the Meaning of Terms in the Book of Mencius* (New Haven: Yale University Press, 1990); R. Kent Guy, *The Emperor's Four Treasuries: Scholars and the State in the Late Ch'ien-lung Era* (Cambridge: Harvard University Press, 1987); Benjamin Elman, *From Philosophy to Philology: Intellectual and Social Aspects of Change in Late Imperial China* (Cambridge: Harvard University Press, 1984); David Nivison, *The Life and Thought of Chang Hsüeh-ch'eng, 1738–1801* (Stanford: Stanford University Press, 1966).

Culture, Women, and the Arts: Susan Mann, *Precious Records: Women in China's Long Eighteenth Century* (Stanford: Stanford University Press, 1997); Ellen Widmer and Kang-i Sun Chang, eds., *Writing Women in Late Imperial China* (Stanford: Stanford University Press, 1997); Evelyn Rawski, *Education and Popular Literacy in Ch'ing China* (Ann Arbor: University of Michigan Press, 1979); Cao Xueqin, *The Story of the Stone [Dream of the Red Chamber]*, trans. David Hawkes and John Minford, 5 vols. (New York: Penguin Classics, 1973–1982); Colin Mackerras, *The Rise of the Peking Opera, 1770–1870: Social Aspects of the Theatre in Manchu China* (New York: Oxford University Press, 1972); Arthur Waley, *Yuan Mei, Eighteenth Century Chinese Poet* (London: G. Allen and Unwin, 1956).

Dissenting Voices: Wu Jingzi, *The Scholars*, trans. Yang Hsien-yi and Gladys Young (New York: Columbia University Press, 1992); Philip Kuhn, *Soulstealers: The Chinese Sorcery Scare of 1768* (Cambridge: Harvard University Press, 1990); Dian H. Murray, *Pirates* *of the South China Coast, 1790–1810* (Stanford: Stanford University Press, 1987); Paul Ropp, *Dissent in Early Modern China: Ju-lin wai-shih [The Scholars] and Ch'ing Social Criticism* (Ann Arbor: University of Michigan Press, 1981); Susan Naquin, *Shantung Rebellion: The Wang Lun Uprising of 1774* (New Haven: Yale University Press, 1981).

The Emperor's World: Nancy Berliner, ed., *The Emperor's Private Paradise: Treasures from the Forbidden City* (Salem: Peabody Essex Museum, 2010); Mark Elliot, *Emperor Qianlong: Son of Heaven, Man of the World* (New York: Longman, 2009); Evelyn Rawski and Jessica Rawson, eds., *China, the Three Emperors, 1662–1795* (London: Royal Academy of Arts, 2005); Preston Torbert, *The Ch'ing Imperial Household Department: A Study of Its Organization and Principal Functions, 1662–1796* (Cambridge: Harvard University Press, 1977).

CHAPTER 6

Borders and Foreign Relations: Paul A. Van Dyke, *Merchants of Canton and Macao: Politics and Strategies in Eighteenth-Century Chinese Trade* (Hong Kong: Hong Kong University Press, 2011); Jennifer Rudolph, *Negotiated Power in Late Imperial China: The Zongli Yamen and the Politics of Reform* (Ithaca: Cornell University, 2008); Peter C. Perdue, *China Marches West: The Qing Conquest of Central Eurasia* (Cambridge: University of Harvard Press, 2005); James Millward, *Beyond the Pass: Economy, Ethnicity, and Empire in Qing Central Asia, 1759–1864* (Stanford: Stanford University Press, 1998); Mui Hoh-cheong and Lorna Mui, *The Management of Monopoly: A Study of the English East India Company's Conduct of Its Tea Trade, 1784–1833* (Vancouver: University of British Columbia Press, 1984); John K. Fairbank, ed., *The Chinese World Order: Traditional China's Foreign Relations* (Cambridge: Harvard University Press, 1968).

Qing Law: Ting Zhang, *Circulating the Code: Print Media and Legal Knowledge in Qing China* (Seattle: University of Washington Press, 2020); Matthew Sommer, *Sex, Law, and Society in Late Imperial China* (Stanford: Stanford University Press, 2000); Melissa Macauley, *Social Power and Legal Culture: Litigation Masters in Late Imperial China* (Stanford: Stanford University Press, 1998); Philip C. C. Huang, *Civil Justice in China: Representation and Practice in the Qing* (Stanford: Stanford University Press, 1996); Kathryn Bernhardt and Philip C. C. Huang, eds., *Civil Law in Qing and Republican China* (Stanford: Stanford University Press, 1994); Jonathan Spence, *The Death of Woman Wang* (New York: Viking, 1978); Derk Bodde and Clarence Morris, *Law in Imperial China, Exemplified by 190 Ch'ing Dynasty Cases* (Cambridge: Harvard University Press, 1967).

Western Attitudes: Urs App, *The Birth of Orientalism* (Philadelphia: University of Pennsylvania Press, 2010); Jonathan Spence, *The Chan's Great Continent: China in Western Minds* (New York: W. W. Norton, 1998); Colin Mackerras, *Western Images of China* (New York: Oxford University Press, 1989); Jonathan Spence, *The Question of Hu* (New York: Knopf, 1988); David Mungello, *Curious Land: Jesuit Accommodation and the Origins of Sinology* (Stuttgart: Franz Steiner Verlag, 1985).

CHAPTER 7

Social Contexts in Early Nineteenth-Century China: Benjamin Elman, *Classicism, Politics and Kinship: The Ch'ang-chou School of New Text Confucianism in Late Imperial China* (Berkeley: University of California Press, 1990); Frederic Wakeman, *Strangers at the Gate: Social Disorder in South China, 1839–1861* (Berkeley: University of California Press,

1966); Li Ruzhen (Li Ju-chen), *Flowers in the Mirror*, trans. Lin Tai-yi (Berkeley: University of California Press, 1965).

Lin Zexu and Opium: David A. Bello, *Opium and the Limits of Empire: Drug Prohibition in the Chinese Interior, 1729–1850* (Cambridge: Harvard University Asia Center, 2005); Zheng Yangwen, *The Social Life of Opium in China* (Cambridge: Cambridge University Press, 2005); Joyce A. Madancy, *The Troublesome Legacy of Commissioner Lin: The Opium Trade and Opium Suppression in Fujian Province, 1820s to 1920s* (Cambridge: Harvard University Asia Center, 2003); Arthur Waley, *The Opium War through Chinese Eyes* (London: Allen & Unwin, 1958); Chang Hsin-pao, *Commissioner Lin and the Opium War* (Cambridge: Harvard University Press, 1964).

Military and Diplomatic Dimensions: Mao Haijian, *The Qing Empire and the Opium War: Collapse of the Heavenly Dynasty*, trans. Joseph Lawson, Craig Smith, and Peter Lavelle (Cambridge: Cambridge University Press, 2016); Julia Lovell, *The Opium War: Drugs, Dreams, and the Making of China* (New York: Overlook Press, 2014); Pär Kristoffer Cassel, *Grounds of Judgment: Extraterritoriality and Imperial Power in Nineteenth-Century China and Japan* (Oxford: Oxford University Press, 2012); Robert Bickers, *The Scramble for China: Foreign Devils in the Qing Empire, 1832–1914* (London: Allen Lane, 2011); John K. Fairbank, *Trade and Diplomacy on the China Coast* (Cambridge: Harvard University Press, 1953); Hosea Ballou Morse, *The International Relations of the Chinese Empire*, 3 vols. (Shanghai and London: Longmans, Green, and Co., 1910–1918).

CHAPTER 8

Sects and Secret Societies: Yingcong Dai, *The White Lotus War: Rebellion and Suppression in Late Imperial China* (Seattle: University of Washington Press, 2019); David Ownby, *Brotherhoods and Secret Societies in Early and Mid-Qing China: The Formation of a Tradition* (Stanford: Stanford University Press, 1996); Dian H. Murray and Qin Baoqi, *The Origins of the Tiandihui: The Chinese Triads in Legend and History* (Stanford: Stanford University Press, 1994); B. J. Ter Haar, *The White Lotus Teachings in Chinese Religious History* (Leiden: Brill, 1992); Daniel Overmyer, *Folk Buddhist Religion: Dissenting Sects in Late Traditional China* (Cambridge: Harvard University Press, 1976); Susan Naquin, *Millenarian Rebellion in China: The Eight Trigrams Uprising of 1813* (New Haven: Yale University Press, 1976).

The Taiping Civil War: Tobie Meyer-Fong, *What Remains: Coming to Terms with Civil War in 19th Century China* (Stanford: Stanford University Press, 2013); Stephen Platt, *Autumn in the Heavenly Kingdom: China, the West, and the Epic Story of the Taiping Civil War* (New York: Knopf, 2012); Jonathan Spence, *God's Chinese Son: The Taiping Heavenly Kingdom of Hong Xiuquan* (New York: W. W. Norton, 1996); Rudolf Wagner, *Reenacting the Heavenly Vision: The Role of Religion in the Taiping Rebellion* (Berkeley: University of California Press, 1982); C. A. Curwen, *Taiping Rebel: The Deposition of Li Hsiu-ch'eng* (New York: Cambridge University Press, 1977); Franz Michael and Chang Chung-li, *The Taiping Rebellion: History and Documents*, 3 vols. (Seattle: University of Washington Press, 1966–1971).

The Nian and Muslim Rebellions: David Atwill, *The Panthay Rebellion: Islam, Ethnicity, and the Dali Sultanate in Southwest China, 1856–1873* (New York: Verso, 2023); Hodong Kim, *Holy War in China: The Muslim Rebellion and the State in Chinese Central Asia, 1864–1877* (Stanford: Stanford University Press, 2004); Elizabeth Perry, *Rebels and Revolutionaries* *in North China, 1845–1945* (Stanford: Stanford University Press, 1980); Teng Ssu-yü, *The Nien Army and Their Guerrilla Warfare, 1851–1868* (Paris: Mouton, 1961).

CHAPTER 9

Confucian Resistance and Restoration: Paul Bailey, trans. *Strengthen the Country and Enrich the People: The Reform Writings of Ma Jianzhong* (New York: Curzon, 1998); J. Y. Wong, *Deadly Dreams: Opium and the Arrow War (1856–1860) in China* (Cambridge: Cambridge University Press, 1998); Jonathan Ocko, *Bureaucratic Reform in Provincial China: Ting Jih-ch'ang in Restoration Kiangsu, 1867–1870* (Cambridge: Harvard University Press, 1983); Philip Kuhn, *Rebellion and Its Enemies in Late Imperial China: Militarization and Social Structure, 1798–1864* (Cambridge: Harvard University Press, 1970); Stanley Spector, *Li Hung-chang and the Huai Army: A Study in Nineteenth-Century Chinese Regionalism* (Seattle: University of Washington Press, 1964); Mary Wright, *The Last Stand of Chinese Conservatism: The T'ung-chih Restoration, 1862–1874* (Stanford: Stanford University Press, 1957).

Knowledge of the World: Jenny Huangfu Day, *Qing Travelers to the Far West: Diplomacy and the Information Order in Late Imperial China* (Cambridge: Cambridge University Press, 2018); Matthew Mosca, *From Frontier Policy to Foreign Policy: The Question of India and the Transformation of Geopolitics in Qing China* (Stanford: Stanford University Press, 2013); Charles Desnoyers, *A Journey to the East: Li Gui's A New Account of a Trip around the Globe* (Ann Arbor: University of Michigan Press, 2004); Jane Kate Leonard, *Wei Yuan and China's Rediscovery of the Maritime World* (Cambridge: Harvard University Press, 1984); Paul Cohen, *Between Tradition and Modernity: Wang T'ao and Reform in Late Ch'ing China* (Cambridge: Harvard University Press, 1974); J. D. Frodsham, *The First Chinese Embassy to the West: The Journals of Kuo Sung-t'ao, Liu Hsi-hung, and Chang Te-yi* (New York: Oxford University Press, 1974); Teng Ssu-yü and John K. Fairbank, *China's Response to the West: A Documentary Survey, 1839–1923* (Cambridge: Harvard University Press, 1954).

The Missionary Impact: Norman J. Girardot, *The Victorian Translation of China: James Legge's Oriental Pilgrimage* (Berkeley: University of California Press, 2002); Daniel H. Bays, ed., *Christianity in China: From the Eighteenth Century to the Present* (Stanford: Stanford University Press, 1996); Jane Hunter, *The Gospel of Gentility: American Women Missionaries in Turn-of-the-Century China* (New Haven: Yale University Press, 1984); John K. Fairbank, ed., *The Missionary Enterprise in China and America* (Cambridge: Harvard University Press, 1974); Edward Gulik, *Peter Parker and the Opening of China* (Cambridge: Harvard University Press, 1973); Paul Cohen, *China and Christianity: The Missionary Movement and the Growth of Chinese Antiforeignism, 1860–1870* (Cambridge: Harvard University Press, 1963).

Robert Hart: Hans Van de Ven, *Breaking with the Past: The Maritime Customs Service and the Global Origins of Modernity in China* (Cambridge: Cambridge University Press, 2014); Katherine F. Bruner, John K. Fairbank, and Richard Smith, eds., *Entering China's Service: Robert Hart's Journals, 1854–1863* (Cambridge: Harvard University Press, 1986); John K. Fairbank, Katherine Bruner, and Elizabeth Matheson, eds., *The I. G. in Peking: Letters of Robert Hart, Chinese Maritime Customs, 1868–1907*, 2 vols. (Cambridge: Harvard University Press, 1975).

Chinese Overseas in the Nineteenth Century: Mae Ngai, *The Chinese Question: The Gold Rushes and Global Politics* (New York: W. W. Norton, 2021); Beth Lew-Williams,

The Chinese Must Go: Violence, Exclusion, and the Making of the Alien in America (Cambridge: Harvard University Press, 2018); Philip Kuhn, *Chinese among Others: Emigration in Modern Times* (Lanham: Rowman & Littlefield, 2008); Chan Sucheng, *This Bittersweet Soil: The Chinese in California Agriculture, 1860–1910* (Berkeley: University of California Press, 1986); Yen Ching-huang, *Coolies and Mandarins: China's Protection of Overseas Chinese during the Late Ch'ing Period, 1851–1911* (Singapore: Singapore University Press, 1985); James Loewen, *The Mississippi Chinese: Between Black and White* (Cambridge: Harvard University Press, 1971); Watt Stewart, *Chinese Bondage in Peru, 1849–1874* (reprint, Westport, CT: Praeger, 1970); Yung Wing, *My Life in China and America* (New York: H. Holt, 1909).

CHAPTER 10

Late Qing Self-Strengthening: Edward Rhoads, *Stepping Forth into the World: The Chinese Educational Mission to the United States, 1872–1881* (Hong Kong: Hong Kong University Press, 2011); Ruth Rogaski, *Hygienic Modernity: Meanings of Health and Disease in Treaty-Port China* (Berkeley: University of California Press, 2004); Samuel C. Chu and Kwang-ching Liu, eds., *Li Hung-chang and China's Early Modernization* (Armonk, NY: M. E. Sharpe, 1994); William Ayers, *Chang Chih-tung and Educational Reform in China* (Cambridge: Harvard University Press, 1971); Kwang-ching Liu, *Anglo-American Steamship Rivalry in China, 1862–1874* (Cambridge: Harvard University Press, 1962); Albert Feuerwerker, *China's Early Industrialization: Sheng Hsuan-huai (1844–1916) and Mandarin Enterprise* (Cambridge: Harvard University Press, 1958).

Urban Change: Richard Belsky, *Localities at the Center: Native Place, Space and Power in Late Imperial Beijing* (Cambridge: Harvard University Asia Center, 2005); Di Wang, *Street Culture in Chengdu: Public Space, Urban Commoners, and Local Politics, 1870–1930* (Stanford: Stanford University Press, 2003); Kristin Stapleton, *Civilizing Chengdu: Chinese Urban Reform, 1895–1937* (Cambridge: Harvard University Asian Center, 2000).

Economic Developments: Qin Shao, *Culturing Modernity: The Nantong Model, 1890–1930* (Stanford: Stanford University Press, 2004); William Rowe, *Hankow*, vol. 2: *Conflict and Community in a Chinese City, 1796–1895* (Stanford: Stanford University Press, 1989); Susan Mann, *Local Merchants and the Chinese Bureaucracy, 1750–1950* (Stanford: Stanford University Press, 1987); Hao Yen-p'ing, *The Commercial Revolution in Nineteenth-Century China: The Rise of Sino-Western Mercantile Capitalism* (Berkeley: University of California Press, 1986); Michael Godley, *The Mandarin-Capitalists from Nanyang: Overseas Chinese Enterprise in the Modernization of China, 1839–1911* (New York: Cambridge University Press, 1982); Hao Yen-p'ing, *The Comprador in Nineteenth Century China: Bridge between East and West* (Cambridge: Harvard University Press, 1970).

1898 Reforms: Peter J. Carroll, *Between Heaven and Modernity: Reconstructing Suzhou, 1895–1937* (Stanford: Stanford University Press, 2006); Rebecca E. Karl and Peter Zarrow, eds., *Rethinking the 1898 Reform Period: Political and Cultural Change in Late Qing China* (Cambridge: Harvard University Asia Center, 2002); Joan Judge, *Print and Politics: Shibao and the Culture of Reform in Late Qing China* (Stanford: Stanford University Press, 1996); Luke Kwong, *A Mosaic of the Hundred Days: Personalities, Politics and Ideas of 1898* (Cambridge: Harvard University Press, 1984).

Emergent Nationalism: Liang Qichao, *Thoughts from the Ice-Drinker's Studio: Essays on China and the World*, trans. Peter Zarrow (New York: Random House, 2023); Guanhua

Wang, *In Search of Justice: The 1905–1906 Chinese Anti-American Boycott* (Cambridge: Harvard University Asia Center, 2001); Tang Xiaobing, *Global Space and the Nationalist Discourse of Modernity: The Historical Thinking of Liang Qichao* (Stanford: Stanford University Press, 1996); John Schrecker, *Imperialism and Chinese Nationalism: Germany in Shantung* (Cambridge: Harvard University Press, 1971); Chang Hao, *Liang Ch'i-ch'ao and Intellectual Transition in China, 1890–1907* (Cambridge: Harvard University Press, 1971); Zou Rong (Tsou Jung), *The Revolutionary Army: A Chinese Revolutionary Tract of 1903*, trans. John Lust (The Hague: Mouton, 1968); Joseph Levenson, *Liang Ch'i-ch'ao and the Mind of Modern China* (Cambridge: Harvard University Press, 1953).

The Boxers: David J. Silbey, *The Boxer Rebellion and the Great Game in China* (New York: Hill and Wang, 2012); Paul A. Cohen, *History in Three Keys: The Boxers as Event, Experience, and Myth* (New York: Columbia University Press, 1997); David Buck, *Recent Chinese Studies of the Boxer Movement* (Armonk, NY: M. E. Sharpe, 1987); Joseph Esherick, *The Origins of the Boxer Uprising* (Berkeley: University of California Press, 1987).

Sun Yat-sen's Early Years: J. Y. Wong, *The Origins of a Heroic Image: Sun Yat-sen in London, 1896–1897* (New York: Oxford University Press, 1986); Yen Ching-hwang, *The Overseas Chinese and the 1911 Revolution, with Special Reference to Singapore and Malaya* (Kuala Lumpur and New York: Oxford University Press, 1976); Harold Schiffrin, *Sun Yat-sen and the Origins of the Chinese Revolution* (Berkeley: University of California Press, 1970).

CHAPTER 11

Central Forces in the Revolution: Harold Schiffrin and Eto Shinkichi, eds., *China's Republican Revolution* (Tokyo: University of Tokyo Press, 1994); Roger R. Thompson, *China's Local Councils in the Age of Constitutional Reform, 1898–1911* (Cambridge: Harvard University Asia Center, 1995); Ralph Huenemann, *The Dragon and the Iron Horse: The Economics of Railroads in China, 1876–1937* (Cambridge: Harvard University Press, 1984); Stephen MacKinnon, *Power and Politics in Late Imperial China: Yuan Shi-kai in Beijing and Tianjin, 1901–1908* (Berkeley: University of California Press, 1980); Edmund Fung, *The Military Dimension of the Chinese Revolution* (Vancouver: University of British Columbia Press, 1980); Mary C. Wright, ed., *China in Revolution, the First Phase* (New Haven: Yale University Press, 1968).

Regions and Elites in the Revolution: Xiaowei Zheng, *The Politics of Rights and the 1911 Revolution in China* (Stanford: Stanford University Press, 2018); Stephen R. Platt, *Provincial Patriots: The Hunanese and Modern China* (Cambridge: Harvard University Press, 2007); Michael Szonyi, *Practicing Kinship: Lineage and Descent in Late Imperial China* (Stanford: Stanford University Press, 2002); Mary Rankin, *Elite Activism and Political Transformation in China, Zhejiang Province, 1865–1911* (Stanford: Stanford University Press, 1986); Joseph Esherick, *Reform and Revolution: The 1911 Revolution in Hunan and Hubei* (Berkeley: University of California Press, 1976); Edward Rhoads, *China's Republican Revolution: The Case of Kwangtung, 1895–1913* (Cambridge: Harvard University Press, 1975); Roger Des Forges, *Hsi-liang and the Chinese National Revolution* (New Haven: Yale University Press, 1973).

Intellectual Shifts: Douglas R. Reynolds, *China, 1898–1912: The Xinzheng Revolution and Japan* (Cambridge: Harvard Council on East Asian Studies, 1993); Paula Harrell, *Sowing the Seeds of Change: Chinese Students and Japanese Teachers, 1895–1905* (Stanford: Stanford University Press, 1992); Frank Dikötter, *The Discourse of Race in Modern China*

(Stanford: Stanford University Press, 1992); Joseph Levenson, *Confucian China and Its Modern Fate*, 3 vols. (Berkeley: University of California Press, 1958–1964), reissued as *Modern China and Its Confucian Past*; Martin Bernal, *Chinese Socialism to 1907* (Ithaca: Cornell University Press, 1976); Don Price, *Russia and the Roots of the Chinese Revolution, 1896–1911* (Cambridge: Harvard University Press, 1974); Michael Gasster, *Chinese Intellectuals and the Revolution of 1911: The Birth of Modern Chinese Radicalism* (Seattle: University of Washington Press, 1969); Benjamin Schwartz, *In Search of Wealth and Power: Yen Fu and the West* (Cambridge: Harvard University Press, 1964).

CHAPTER 12

The Early Republic: Marie-Claude Bergère, *Sun Yat-sen*, trans. Janet Lloyd (Stanford: Stanford University, 1998); Ernest Young, *The Presidency of Yuan Shih-k'ai: Liberalism and Dictatorship in Early Republican China* (Ann Arbor: University of Michigan Press, 1977); C. Martin Wilbur, *Sun Yat-sen, Frustrated Patriot* (New York: Columbia University Press, 1976); Edward Friedman, *Backward toward Revolution: The Chinese Revolutionary Party* (Berkeley: University of California Press, 1974); K. S. Liew, *Struggle for Democracy: Sung Chiao-jen and the 1911 Chinese Revolution* (Berkeley: University of California Press, 1971).

Warlordism: Kate Merkel-Hess, *Women and Their Warlords: Domesticating Militarism in Modern China* (Chicago: The University of Chicago Press, 2024); Edward A. McCord, *The Power of the Gun: The Emergence of Modern Chinese Warlordism* (Berkeley: University of California Press, 1993); Diana Lary, *Warlord Soldiers: Chinese Common Soldiers, 1911–1937* (New York: Cambridge University Press, 1985); Donald Sutton, *Provincial Militarism and the Chinese Republic: The Yunnan Army, 1905–1925* (Ann Arbor: University of Michigan Press, 1980); Robert Kapp, *Szechwan and the Chinese Republic: Provincial Militarism and Central Power, 1911–1938* (New Haven: Yale University Press, 1973); Donald Gillin, *Warlord: Yen Hsi-shan in Shansi Province, 1911–1949* (Princeton: Princeton University Press, 1967); James Sheridan, *Chinese Warlord: The Career of Feng Yü-hsiang* (Stanford: Stanford University Press, 1966).

The Business World: Niv Horesh, *Shanghai's Bund and Beyond: British Banks, Bank Note Insurance, and Monetary Policy in China, 1842–1937* (New Haven: Yale University Press, 2009); Sherman Cochran, *Chinese Medicine Men: Consumer Culture in China and Southeast Asia* (Cambridge: Harvard University Press, 2006); Brett Sheehan, *Trust in Troubled Times: Money, Banks, and State-Society Relations in Republican Tianjin* (Cambridge: Harvard University Press, 2003); Elisabeth Köll, *From Cotton Mill to Business Empire: The Emergence of Regional Enterprises in Modern China* (Cambridge: Harvard University Asia Center, 2003); Sherman Cochran, *Big Business in China: Sino-Foreign Rivalry in the Cigarette Industry, 1890–1930* (Cambridge: Harvard University Press, 1980); Andrea Lee McElderry, *Shanghai Old-Style Banks (Ch'ien-chuang) 1800–1935* (Ann Arbor: University of Michigan, 1978).

Foreign Elements: Xu Guoqi, *China and the Great War: China's Pursuit of a New National Identity and Internationalization* (Cambridge: Cambridge University Press, 2005); James Reed, *The Missionary Mind and American East Asia Policy, 1911–1915* (Cambridge: Harvard University Press, 1983); Michael Summerskill, *China on the Western Front: Britain's Chinese Work Force in the First World War* (London: M. Summerskill, 1982); Hou Chiming, *Foreign Investment and Economic Development in China, 1840–1937* (Cambridge: Harvard University Press, 1965).

CHAPTER 13

General Analyses of the May Fourth Movement: Chen Pingyuan, *Touches of History: An Entry into 'May Fourth' China*, trans. Michel Hockx (Leiden: Brill, 2011); Erez Manela, *The Wilsonian Moment: Self-Determination and the International Origins of Anticolonial Nationalism* (Oxford: Oxford University Press, 2007); Andrew D. Morris, *Marrow of the Nation: A History of Sport and Physical Culture in Republican China* (Berkeley: University of California Press, 2004); Lydia H. Liu, *Translingual Practice: Literature, National Culture, and Translated Modernity, China, 1900–1937* (Stanford: Stanford University Press, 1995); Vera Schwarcz, *The Chinese Enlightenment: Intellectuals and the Legacy of the May Fourth Movement of 1919* (Berkeley: University of California Press, 1986); James Pusey, *China and Charles Darwin* (Cambridge: Harvard University Press, 1983); Lin Yü-sheng, *The Crisis of Chinese Consciousness: Radical Anti-traditionalism in the May Fourth Era* (Madison: University of Wisconsin Press, 1979); Merle Goldman, ed., *Modern Chinese Literature in the May Fourth Era* (Cambridge: Harvard University Press, 1977); Chow Tse-tsung, *The May Fourth Movement: Intellectual Revolution in Modern China* (Cambridge: Harvard University Press, 1960).

Founding the CCP: Ishikawa Yoshihiro, *The Formation of the Chinese Communist Party*, trans. Joshua Fogel (New York: Columbia University Press, 2013); Yang Kuisong, *Zhongjian didai de geming: Guoji da beijing xia kan Zhonggong chenggong zhi dao* [Revolution in the middle zone: The CCP's road to success in international context] (Taiyuan: Shanxi renmin, 2010); Yeh Wen-hsin, *Provincial Passages: Culture, Space, and the Origins of Chinese Communism* (Berkeley: University of California Press, 1996); Christina Gilmartin, *Engendering the Chinese Revolution: Radical Women, Communist Politics, and Mass Movements in the 1920s* (Berkeley: University of California Press, 1995); Marilyn Levine, *The Found Generation: The Chinese Communists in Europe during the Twenties* (Seattle: University of Washington Press, 1993); Anthony Saich, *The Origins of the First United Front in China: The Role of Sneevliet (Alias Maring)*, 2 vols. (Leiden: Brill, 1991); Arif Dirlik, *The Origins of Chinese Communism* (New York: Oxford University Press, 1989); Lee Feigon, *Chen Duxiu: Founder of the Chinese Communist Party* (Princeton: Princeton University Press, 1983); Maurice Meisner, *Li Ta-chao and the Origins of Chinese Marxism* (Cambridge: Harvard University Press, 1967); Robert North, *Moscow and Chinese Communists* (Stanford: Stanford University Press, 1963).

Influential May Fourth Figures: Leiluo Cai, ed., *Cai Yuanpei: Selected Writings on Education* (Leiden: Brill, 2024); Xiaoming Chen, *From the May Fourth Movement to the Communist Movement: Guo Moruo and the Chinese Path to Communism* (Albany: State University of New York Press, 2008); Danian Hu, *China and Albert Einstein: The Reception of the Physicist and His Theory in China, 1917–1979* (Cambridge: Harvard University Press, 2005); Leo Ou-fan Lee, *Voices from the Iron House: A Study of Lu Xun* (Bloomington: Indiana University Press, 1987); Leo Ou-fan Lee, *The Romantic Generation of Chinese Writers* (Cambridge: Harvard University Press, 1973); Laurence Schneider, *Ku Chieh-kang and China's New History: Nationalism and the Quest for Alternative Traditions* (Berkeley: University of California Press, 1971); Jerome Grieder, *Hu Shih and the Chinese Renaissance: Liberalism in the Chinese Revolution, 1917–1937* (Cambridge: Harvard University Press, 1970); Charlotte Furth, *Ting Wen-chiang, Science and China's New Culture* (Cambridge: Harvard University Press, 1970).

CHAPTER 14

Urban Life and the Labor Movement: Janet Y. Chen, *Guilty of Indigence: The Urban Poor in China, 1900–1953* (Princeton: Princeton University Press, 2012); S. A. Smith, *A Road Is Made: Communism in Shanghai, 1920–1927* (Richmond: Curzon Press, 2000); Elizabeth Perry, *Shanghai on Strike: The Politics of Chinese Labor* (Stanford: Stanford University Press, 1993); David Strand, *Rickshaw Beijing: City People and Politics in the 1920s* (Berkeley: University of California Press, 1989); E. Perry Link, *Mandarin Ducks and Butterflies: Popular Fiction in Early Twentieth Century Chinese Cities* (Berkeley: University of California Press, 1981); Nicholas R. Clifford, *Shanghai, 1925: Urban Nationalism and the Defense of Foreign Privilege* (Ann Arbor: University of Michigan, 1979); Colin Mackerras, *The Chinese Theatre in Modern Times, from 1840 to the Present Day* (Amherst: University of Massachusetts Press, 1975); Jean Chesneaux, *The Chinese Labor Movement, 1919–1927*, trans. H. M. Wright (Stanford: Stanford University Press, 1968).

Rural China and the Peasant Movement: William T. Rowe, *Crimson Rain: Seven Centuries of Violence in a Chinese County* (Stanford: Stanford University Press, 2007); R. Keith Schoppa, *Xiang Lake—Nine Centuries of Chinese Life* (New Haven: Yale University Press, 1989); Fernando Galbiati, *P'eng P'ai and the Hai-lu-feng Soviet* (Stanford: Stanford University Press, 1985); Robert Marks, *Rural Revolution in South China: Peasants and the Making of History in Haifeng County, 1570–1930* (Madison: University of Wisconsin Press, 1984); Roy Hofheinz, *The Broken Wave: The Chinese Communist Peasant Movement, 1922–1928* (Cambridge: Harvard University Press, 1977).

The United Front and the Northern Expedition: John Fitzgerald, *Awakening China: Politics, Culture, and Class in the Nationalist Revolution* (Stanford: Stanford University Press, 1996); Gavan McCormack, *Chang Tso-lin in Northeast China, 1911–1928: China, Japan and the Manchurian Idea* (Stanford: Stanford University Press, 1977); Donald Jordan, *The Northern Expedition: China's National Revolution of 1926–1928* (Honolulu: University of Hawaii Press, 1976); Harold Isaacs, *The Tragedy of the Chinese Revolution* (Stanford: Stanford University Press, 1961); Xenia Eudin and Robert North, *M. N. Roy's Mission to China: The Communist Kuomintang Split of 1927* (Berkeley: University of California Press, 1963).

CHAPTER 15

The Guomindang Government: Felix Boecking, *No Great Wall: Trade, Tariffs, and Nationalism in Republican China, 1927–1945* (Cambridge: Harvard University Asia Center, 2017); Frederic Wakeman Jr., *Spymaster: Dai Li and the Chinese Secret Service* (Berkeley: University of California Press, 2003); Julia Strauss, *Strong Institutions in Weak Polities: State Building in Republican China, 1927–1940* (Oxford: Oxford University Press, 1998); Parks Coble, *The Shanghai Capitalists and the Nationalist Government, 1927–1937* (Cambridge: Harvard University Press, 1986); Joseph Fewsmith, *Party, State and Local Elites in Republican China: Merchant Organizations and Politics in Shanghai, 1890–1930* (Honolulu: University of Hawaii Press, 1985); William Wei, *Counterrevolution in China: The Nationalists in Jiangxi during the Soviet Period* (Ann Arbor: University of Michigan Press, 1985); Lloyd Eastman, *The Abortive Revolution: China under Nationalist Rule, 1927–1937* (Cambridge: Harvard University Press, 1974).

Republican Shanghai: Leo Ou-fan Lee, *Shanghai Modern: The Flowering of a New Urban Culture in China, 1930–1945* (Cambridge: Harvard University Press, 1999); Xun

Liu, *Daoist Modern: Innovation, Lay Practice, and the Community of Lay Alchemy in Republican Shanghai* (Cambridge: Harvard University Asia Center, 2009); Hanchao Lu, *Beyond the Neon Lights: Everyday Shanghai in the Early Twentieth Century* (Berkeley: University of California Press, 1999); Gail Hershatter, *Dangerous Pleasures: Prostitution and Modernity in Twentieth-Century Shanghai* (Berkeley: University of California Press, 1997); Brian Martin, *The Shanghai Green Gang: Politics and Organized Crime, 1919–1937* (Berkeley: University of California Press, 1996); Frederic Wakeman Jr., *Policing Shanghai* (Berkeley: University of California Press, 1995); Bryna Goodman, *Native Place, City, and Nation: Regional Networks and Identities in Shanghai, 1853–1937* (Berkeley: University of California Press, 1995); Christian Henriot, *Shanghai, 1927–1937: Municipal Power, Locality, and Modernization* (Berkeley: University of California Press, 1993).

Cultural Life under the Guomindang: Maggie Clinton, *Revolutionary Nativism: Fascism and Culture in China, 1925–1937* (Durham: Duke University Press, 2017); Frank Dikötter, *Exotic Commodities: Modern Objects and Everyday Life in China* (New York: Columbia University Press, 2006); Frank Dikötter, *Sex, Culture, and Modernity in China* (Honolulu: University of Hawaii Press, 1995); Wilma Fairbank, *Liang and Lin: Partners in Exploring China's Architectural Past* (Philadelphia: University of Pennsylvania Press, 1994); Christoph Harbsmeier, *The Cartoonist Feng Zikai: Social Realism with a Buddhist Face* (Oslo: Universitetsforlaget, 1984); Holmes Welch, *The Buddhist Revival in China* (Cambridge: Harvard University Press, 1968).

The United States and China: Lian Xi, *The Conversion of Missionaries: Liberalism in American Protestant Missions in China, 1907–1932* (University Park: Pennsylvania State University Press, 1997); Randall Stross, *The Stubborn Earth: American Agriculturalists on Chinese Soil, 1898–1937* (Berkeley: University of California Press, 1986); Mary Bullock, *An American Transplant: The Rockefeller Foundation and the Peking Union Medical College* (Berkeley: University of California Press, 1980); Philip West, *Yenching University and Sino-Western Relations, 1916–1952* (Cambridge: Harvard University Press, 1976); John Bowers, *Western Medicine in a Chinese Palace: Peking Union Medical College, 1917–1951* (Philadelphia: Josiah Macy Foundation, 1972); Jessie Lutz, *China and the Christian Colleges, 1850–1950* (Ithaca: Cornell University Press, 1971); James Thomson, *While China Faced West: American Reformers in Nationalist China, 1928–1937* (Cambridge: Harvard University Press, 1969); John K. Fairbank, *The United States and China* (Cambridge: Harvard University Press, 1948, and later editions).

Japan and China: Parks M. Coble, *Facing Japan: Chinese Politics and Japanese Imperialism, 1931–1937* (Cambridge: Harvard Council on East Asian Studies, 1991); Ito Takeo, *Life along the South Manchurian Railway*, trans. Joshua Fogel (Armonk, NY: M. E. Sharpe, 1988); Akira Iriye, ed., *The Chinese and the Japanese: Essays in Political and Cultural Interactions* (Princeton: Princeton University Press, 1980); Joshua Fogel, *Politics and Sinology: The Case of Naitō Konan (1866–1934)* (Cambridge: Harvard University Press, 1984); James Crowley, *Japan's Quest for Autonomy: National Security and Foreign Policy, 1930–1938* (Princeton: Princeton University Press, 1966).

Germany and China: William Kirby, *Germany and Republican China* (Princeton: Princeton University Press, 1984); Liang Hsi-huey, *The Sino-German Connection: Alexander von Falkenhausen between China and Germany, 1900–1941* (Amsterdam: Van Gorcum, 1978); Bernd Martin, ed., *The German Advisory Group in China* (Düsseldorf: Droste, 1981).

The Late Manchus: Edward J. M. Rhoads, *Manchus and Han: Ethnic Relations and Political Power in Late Qing and Early Republican China, 1861–1928* (Seattle: University of Washington Press, 2000); Pamela Kyle Crossley, *Orphan Warriors: Three Manchu Generations and the End of the Qing World* (Princeton: Princeton University Press, 1989); Puyi Aisin-Gioro, *From Emperor to Citizen*, trans. W. J. F. Jenner (New York: Oxford University Press, 1987); Lee Chong-sik, *Revolutionary Struggle in Manchuria: Chinese Communism and Soviet Interest, 1922–1945* (Berkeley: University of California Press, 1983); Lao She, *Beneath the Red Banner (An Autobiographical Manchu Novel)*, trans. Don Cohn (Beijing: Panda Books, 1982).

CHAPTER 16

Rural China and CCP Survival: Roger Thompson, trans. and ed., *Mao Zedong: Report from Xunwu* (Stanford: Stanford University Press, 1990); Ilpyong Kim, *The Politics of Chinese Communism: Kiangsi under the Soviets* (Berkeley: University of California Press, 1973); Jerome Ch'en, *Mao and the Chinese Revolution* (New York: Oxford University Press, 1965); Benjamin Schwartz, *Chinese Communism and the Rise of Mao* (Cambridge: Harvard University Press, 1958).

Perspectives on the Long March and the Xi'an Incident: Helen Praeger Young, *Choosing Revolution: Chinese Women Soldiers on the Long March* (Urbana: University of Illinois Press, 2001); Tony Saich and Hans van de Ven, eds., *New Perspectives on the Chinese Communist Revolution* (Armonk, NY: M. E. Sharpe, 1995); Gregor Benton, *Mountain Fires: The Red Army's Three-Year War in South China, 1934–1938* (Berkeley: University of California Press, 1992); Otto Braun, *A Comintern Agent in China, 1932–1939*, trans. Jeanne Moore (Stanford: Stanford University Press, 1982); Helen Wu Tien-wei, *The Sian Incident: A Pivotal Point in Modern Chinese History* (Ann Arbor: University of Michigan Press, 1976); Chang Kuo-t'ao, *Autobiography: The Rise of the Chinese Communist Party, 1921–1938*, 2 vols. (Lawrence: University Press of Kansas, 1972); Lyman Van Slyke, *Enemies and Friends: The United Front in Chinese Communist History* (Stanford: Stanford University Press, 1967); John Israel, *Student Nationalism in China, 1927–1937* (Stanford: Stanford University Press, 1966); Agnes Smedley, *The Great Road: The Life and Times of Chu Teh* (New York: Monthly Review Press, 1956); Edgar Snow, *Red Star over China* (New York: Random House, 1938).

Maintaining Confucian Values: Chunmei Du, *Guo Hongming's Eccentric Chinese Odyssey* (Philadelphia: University of Pennsylvania Press, 2019); Jerry Dennerline, *Qian Mu and the World of Seven Mansions* (New Haven: Yale University Press, 1988); Susan Chan Egan, *A Latterday Confucian: Reminiscences of William Hung (1893–1980)* (Cambridge: Harvard University Press, 1987); Guy Alitto, *The Last Confucian: Liang Shu-ming and the Chinese Dilemma of Modernity* (Berkeley: University of California Press, 1979); Charlotte Furth, ed., *The Limits of Change: Essays on Conservative Alternatives in Republican China* (Cambridge: Harvard University Press, 1976).

Writers of the 1930s: Tani Barlow and Gary Bjorge, eds., *I Myself Am a Woman: Selected Writings of Ding Ling* (Boston: Beacon Press, 1989); Paul Pickowicz, *Marxist Literary Thought in China: The Influence of Ch'ü Ch'iu-pai [Qu Qiubai]* (Berkeley: University of California Press, 1981); Jeffrey Kinkley, *The Odyssey of Shen Congwen* (Stanford: Stanford University Press, 1987); Hung Chang-tai, *Going to the People: Chinese Intellectuals and Folk Literature, 1918–1937* (Cambridge: Harvard University Press, 1985); Yi-tsi Mei Feuerwerker, *Ding Ling's Fiction: Ideology and Narrative in Modern Chinese Literature* (Cambridge:

Harvard University Press, 1982); Lao She, *Rickshaw*, trans. Jean James (Honolulu: Hawaii University Press, 1979); Olga Lang, *Pa Chin and His Writings: Chinese Youth between Two Revolutions* (Cambridge: Harvard University Press, 1967); Mao Dun (Mao Tun), *Midnight*, trans. Hsu Meng-hsiung (Beijing: Foreign Language Press, 1957).

Rural Life and Economy: Kate Merkel-Hess, *Rural Modern: Reconstructing the Self and the State in Republican China* (Chicago: The University of Chicago Press, 2016); Kenneth Pomeranz, *The Making of a Hinterland: State, Society, and Economy in Inland North China, 1853–1937* (Berkeley: University of California Press, 1993); Daniel Little, *Understanding Peasant China: Case Studies in the Philosophy of Social Science* (New Haven: Yale University Press, 1989); David Faure, *The Rural Economy of Pre-Liberation China: Trade Expansion and Peasant Livelihood in Jiangsu and Guangdong, 1870–1937* (New York: Oxford University Press, 1989); Prasenjit Duara, *Culture, Power, and the State: Rural North China, 1900–1942* (Stanford: Stanford University Press, 1988); Philip Huang, *The Peasant Economy and Social Change in North China* (Stanford: Stanford University Press, 1985); Ramon Myers, *The Chinese Peasant Economy: Agricultural Development in Hopei and Shantung, 1890–1949* (Cambridge: Harvard University Press, 1970); Fei Hsiao-t'ung (Fei Xiaotong), *Peasant Life in China* (London: G. Routledge and Kegan Paul, 1939).

The Urban Labor Force: Angelina Chin, *Bound to Emancipate: Working Women and Urban Citizenship in Early Twentieth-Century China and Hong Kong* (Lanham: Rowman & Littlefield, 2012); Emily Honig, *Sisters and Strangers: Women in the Shanghai Cotton Mills, 1919–1949* (Stanford: Stanford University Press, 1986); Gail Hershatter, *The Workers of Tianjin, 1900–1949* (Stanford: Stanford University Press, 1986); S. Bernard Thomas, *Labor and the Chinese Revolution: Class Strategies and Contradictions of Chinese Communism, 1928–1948* (Ann Arbor: University of Michigan Press, 1983); David Buck, *Urban Change in China: Politics and Development in Tsinan, Shantung, 1890–1949* (Madison: University of Wisconsin Press, 1978).

CHAPTER 17

The Military History of the War in China: Hans Van de Ven, *China at War: Triumph and Tragedy in the Emergence of New China* (Cambridge: Harvard University Press, 2018); Rana Mitter, *Forgotten Ally: China's World War II, 1937–1945* (Boston: Houghton Mifflin Harcourt, 2013); Stephen R. MacKinnon, Diana Lary, and Ezra F. Vogel, eds., *China at War: Regions of China, 1937–45* (Stanford: Stanford University Press, 2007); Gregor Benton, *New Fourth Army: Communist Resistance along the Yangzi and the Huai, 1938–1941* (Berkeley: University of California Press, 1999); Maochun Yu, *OSS in China: Prelude to Cold War* (New Haven: Yale University Press, 1996); Barbara Tuchman, *Stilwell and the American Experience in China, 1911–1945* (London: Macmillan, 1970); Sheldon H. Harris, *Factories of Death: Japanese Biological Warfare, 1932–45, and the American Cover-up* (London: Routledge, 1994); Joseph Stilwell, *The Stilwell Papers*, ed. Theodore White (New York: Schocken Books, 1948).

Wartime Society and Politics: Danke Li, *Echoes of Chongqing: Women in Wartime China* (Urbana: University of Illinois Press, 2010); Joshua Howard, Workers at War: Labor in China's Arsenals, 1937–1953 (Stanford: Stanford University Press, 2004); Chang-tai Hung, *War and Popular Culture: Resistance in Modern China, 1937–1945* (Berkeley: University of California Press, 1994); James C. Hsiung and Steven I. Levine, eds., *China's Bitter Victory: The War with Japan, 1937–1945* (Armonk, NY: M. E. Sharpe,

1992); Lloyd E. Eastman, *Seeds of Destruction: Nationalist China in War and Revolution, 1937–1949* (Stanford: Stanford University Press, 1984); Ch'i Hsi-sheng, *Nationalist China at War: Military Defeats and Political Collapse, 1937–1945* (Ann Arbor: University of Michigan Press, 1982).

The Japanese Occupation of China: Timothy Brook, *Collaboration: Japanese Agents and Local Elites in Wartime China* (Cambridge: Harvard University Press, 2005); David P. Barrett and Larry N. Shyu, eds., *Chinese Collaboration with Japan, 1932–1945: The Limits of Accommodation* (Stanford: Stanford University Press, 2001); Marcia Reynders Ristaino, *Port of Last Resort: The Diaspora Communities of Shanghai* (Stanford: Stanford University Press, 2001); Martha Smalley, ed., *American Missionary Eyewitnesses to the Nanking Massacre, 1937–1938* (New Haven: Yale Divinity School, 1997); Frederic Wakeman, *The Shanghai Badlands: Urban Terrorism and Urban Crime, 1937–1941* (Cambridge: Cambridge University Press, 1996); Poshek Fu, *Passivity, Resistance, and Collaboration: Intellectual Choices in Occupied Shanghai, 1937–1945* (Stanford: Stanford University Press, 1993); Edward Gunn, *Unwelcome Muse: Chinese Literature in Shanghai and Peking, 1937–1945* (New York: Columbia University Press, 1980); Lincoln Li, *The Japanese Army in North China, 1937–1941: Problems of Political and Economic Control* (Tokyo: Oxford University Press, 1975); John Boyle, *China and Japan at War, 1937–1945: The Politics of Collaboration* (Stanford: Stanford University Press, 1972); Gerald Bunker, *The Peace Conspiracy: Wang Ching-wei and the China War, 1937–1941* (Cambridge: Harvard University Press, 1972).

Yan'an Government and Politics: Gao Hua, *How the Red Sun Rose: The Origins and Development of the Yan'an Rectification Movement, 1930–1945*, trans. Stacy Mosher and Guo Jian (Hong Kong: The Chinese University Press, 2018); Pauline Keating, *Two Revolutionaries: Village Reconstruction and the Cooperative Movement in Northern Shaanxi, 1934–1945* (Stanford: Stanford University Press, 1997); Chen Yung-fa, *Making Revolution: The Communist Movement in Eastern and Central China, 1937–1945* (Berkeley: University of California Press, 1986); Bonnie McDougall, *Mao Zedong's "Talks at the Yan'an Conference on Literature and Art": A Translation of the 1943 Text with Commentary* (Ann Arbor: University of Michigan Press, 1980); Mark Selden, *The Yenan Way in Revolutionary China* (Cambridge: Harvard University Press, 1971); David Barrett, *Dixie Mission: The United States Army Observer Group in Yenan, 1944* (Berkeley: University of California Press, 1970); Chalmers Johnson, *Peasant Nationalism and Communist Power: The Emergence of Revolutionary China, 1937–1945* (Stanford: Stanford University Press, 1962);

CHAPTER 18

The Civil War: Diana Lary, *China's Civil War: A Social History* (Cambridge: Cambridge University Press, 2015); Odd Arne Westad, *Decisive Encounters: The Chinese Civil War, 1946–1950* (Stanford: Stanford University Press, 2003); Donald Gillin and Ramon Myers, eds., *Last Chance in China: The Diary of Chang Kia-ngau* (Stanford: Hoover Institution Press, 1989); Steven Levine, *Anvil of Victory: The Communist Revolution in Manchuria, 1945–1948* (New York: Columbia University Press, 1987); Suzanne Pepper, *Civil War in China: The Political Struggle, 1945–1949* (Berkeley: University of California Press, 1978); William Hinton, *Fanshen: A Documentary of Revolution in a Chinese Village* (New York: Monthly Review Press, 1966); George Kerr, *Formosa Betrayed* (Boston: Houghton Mifflin, 1965).

U.S. Policies: Richard Bernstein, *China 1945: Mao's Revolution and America's Fateful Choice* (New York: Vintage Books, 2014); William Stueck, *The Wedemeyer Mission: American Politics and Foreign Policy during the Cold War* (Athens: University of Georgia Press, 1984); Nancy Tucker, *Patterns in the Dust: Chinese-American Relations and the Recognition Controversy, 1949–1950* (New York: Columbia University Press, 1983); Wilma Fairbank, *America's Cultural Experiment in China, 1942–1949* (Washington, D.C.: U.S. Department of State, 1976); U.S. Department of State, comp., *United States Relations with China, with Special Reference to the Period 1944–1949* (Washington, D.C., 1949; reprint, Stanford: Stanford University Press, 1967).

Border Regions: Justin Jacobs, *Xinjiang and the Modern Chinese State* (Seattle: University of Washington Press, 2017); James A. Millward, *Eurasian Crossroads: A History of Xinjiang* (New York: Columbia University Press, 2007); Melvyn Goldstein, *A History of Modern Tibet: The Demise of the Lamaist State* (Berkeley: University of California Press, 1989); Andrew Forbes, *Warlords and Muslims in Chinese Central Asia: A Political History of Republican Sinkiang 1911–1949* (New York: Cambridge University Press, 1986).

Foreign Observers of the Civil War: John Melby, *The Mandate of Heaven, Record of a Civil War: China 1945–1949* (Toronto: University of Toronto Press, 1968); A. Doak Barnett, *China on the Eve of Communist Takeover* (New York: Praeger, 1963); Henri Cartier-Bresson, *From One China to the Other* (New York: Universe Books, 1956); Derk Bodde, *Peking Diary, 1948–1949: A Year of Revolution* (New York: H. Schuman, 1950).

CHAPTER 19

Consolidating the People's Republic: Jeremy Brown and Paul Pickowicz, *Dilemmas of Victory: The Early Years of the People's Republic of China* (Cambridge: Harvard University Press, 2007); James Z. Gao, *The Communist Takeover of Hangzhou: The Transformation of City and Cadre, 1949–1954* (Honolulu: University of Hawai'i Press, 2004); Neil Diamant, *Revolutionizing the Family: Politics, Love, and Divorce in Urban and Rural China, 1949–1968* (Berkeley: University of California Press, 2000); Kenneth Lieberthal, *Revolution and Tradition in Tientsin, 1949–1952* (Stanford: Stanford University Press, 1980); Ezra Vogel, *Canton under Communism: Programs and Politics in a Provincial Capital, 1949–1968* (Cambridge: Harvard University Press, 1969).

Analyses of PRC Structure: Richard Kraus, *Class Conflict in Chinese Socialism* (New York: Columbia University Press, 1981); Richard Solomon, *Mao's Revolution and the Chinese Political Culture* (Berkeley: University of California Press, 1971); A. Doak Barnett, *Cadres, Bureaucracy and Political Power in Communist China* (New York: Columbia University Press, 1967); John Wilson Lewis, *Leadership in Communist China* (Ithaca: Cornell University Press, 1966).

The Korean War and the PLA: Shen Zhihua, *Mao, Stalin, and the Korean War: Trilateral Communist Relations in the 1950s*, trans. Neil Silver (London: Routledge, 2012); James G. Hershberg, "The Cold War in Asia," *Cold War International History Project Bulletin 6/7* (Woodrow Wilson International Center for Scholars, 1995–1996); Chen Jian, *China's Road to the Korean War: The Making of the Sino-American Confrontation* (New York: Columbia University Press, 1994); Harvey Nelson, *The Chinese Military System: An Organizational Study of the People's Liberation Army* (Boulder, CO: Westview, 1977); Allen Whiting, *China Crosses the Yalu: The Decision to Enter the Korean War* (New York: Macmillan, 1960).

CHAPTER 20

Rebuilding the Economy: Jason M. Kelly, *Market Maoists: The Communist Origins of China's Capitalist Ascent* (Cambridge, Massachusetts: Harvard University Press, 2021); Arunabh Ghosh, *Making It Count: Statistics and Statecraft in the Early People's Republic of China* (Princeton: Princeton University Press, 2020); Thomas Rawski, *China's Transition to Industrialism: Producer Goods and Economic Development in the Twentieth Century* (Ann Arbor: University of Michigan Press, 1980); Alexander Eckstein, *China's Economic Revolution* (New York: Cambridge University Press, 1977); Katharine Huang Hsiao. *Money and Monetary Policy in Communist China* (New York: Columbia University Press, 1971); Peter Schran, *The Development of Chinese Agriculture, 1950–1959* (Champaign: University of Illinois Press, 1969); Dwight Perkins, *Market Control and Planning in Communist China* (Cambridge: Harvard University Press, 1966).

Early PRC Foreign Policy: James Chieh Hsiung, *Law and Policy in China's Foreign Relations: A Study of Attitudes and Practice* (New York: Columbia University Press, 1972); Jerome Cohen and Hungdah Chiu, *People's China and International Law: A Documentary Study*, 2 vols. (Princeton: Princeton University Press, 1974); Michael H. Hunt, *The Genesis of Chinese Communist Foreign Policy* (New York: Columbia University Press, 1996).

Ethnic Minorities: Thomas Mullaney, *Coming to Terms with the Nation: Ethnic Classification in Modern China* (Berkeley: University of California Press, 2011); Gardner Bovingdon, *The Uyghurs: Strangers in Their Own Land* (Columbia: Columbia University Press, 2010); Morris Rossabi, ed., *Governing China's Multiethnic Frontiers* (Seattle: University of Washington Press, 2004); Dru Gladney, *Dislocating China: Reflections on Muslims, Minorities, and Other Subaltern Subjects* (Chicago: The University of Chicago Press, 2004); Donald McMillen, *Chinese Communist Power and Policy in Xinjiang, 1949–1977* (Boulder, CO: Westview, 1979); Chang Chih-i, *The Party and the National Question in China*, ed. and trans. George Moseley (Cambridge: MIT Press, 1966).

The Hundred Flowers: Nieh Hualing, ed., *Literature of the Hundred Flowers*, vol. 1: *Criticism and Polemics*, vol. 2: *Poetry and Fiction* (New York: Columbia University Press, 1981); Roderick MacFarquhar, *The Origins of the Cultural Revolution*, vol. 1: *Contradictions among the People, 1956–1957* (New York: Columbia University Press, 1974); Merle Goldman, *Literary Dissent in Communist China* (Cambridge: Harvard University Press, 1967).

CHAPTER 21

The Great Leap Forward and Famine: Yang Jisheng, *Tombstone: The Great Chinese Famine, 1958–1962*, trans. Stacy Mosher and Guo Jian (New York: Farrar, Straus and Giroux, 2012); Frank Dikötter, *Mao's Great Famine: The History of China's Most Devastating Catastrophe, 1958–62* (London: Bloomsbury, 2010); Frederick C. Teiwes with Warren Sun, *China's Road to Disaster: Mao, Central Politicians, and Provincial Leaders in the Unfolding of the Great Leap Forward, 1955–1959* (Armonk, NY: East Gate, 1999); Roderick MacFarquhar, *The Origins of the Cultural Revolution*, vol. 2: *The Great Leap Forward, 1958–1960* (New York: Columbia University Press, 1983); Franz Schurmann, *Ideology and Organization in Communist China* (Berkeley: University of California Press, 1966).

The Sino-Soviet Rift: Shen Zhihua, ed., *A Short History of Sino-Soviet Relations, 1917–1991*, trans. Xia Yafeng (Singapore: Palgrave MacMillan, 2020); Lorenz M. Lüthi, *The Sino-Soviet Split: Cold War in the Communist World* (Princeton: Princeton University

Press, 2008); John Wilson Lewis and Xue Litai, *China Builds the Bomb* (Stanford: Stanford University Press, 1988); Andrew Wedeman, *The East Wind Subsides: Chinese Foreign Policy and the Origins of the Cultural Revolution* (Washington, D.C.: Washington Institution Press, 1987).

Mao and the Intellectuals: Eddy U, *Creating the Intellectual: Chinese Communism and the Rise of a Classification* (Berkeley: University of California Press, 2019); Li Zhisui, *The Private Life of Chairman Mao* (New York: Random House, 1994); Merle Goldman, *China's Intellectuals: Advise and Dissent* (Cambridge: Harvard University Press, 1981); Stuart Schram, *Chairman Mao Talks to the People: Talks and Letters, 1956–1971* (New York: Pantheon, 1971); Clive Ansley, *The Heresy of Wu Han: His Play "Hai Rui's Dismissal" and Its Role in China's Cultural Revolution* (Toronto: University of Toronto Press, 1971).

CHAPTER 22

Party and Politics in the Early 1960s: Timothy Cheek, *Propaganda and Culture in Mao's China: Deng Tuo and the Intelligentsia* (Oxford: Clarendon Press, 1998); Nicholas Lardy and Kenneth Lieberthal, eds., *Chen Yun's Strategy for China's Development: A Non-Maoist Alternative* (Armonk, NY: M. E. Sharpe, 1983); Jonathan Unger, *Education under Mao: Class and Competition in Canton Schools 1960–1980* (New York: Columbia University Press, 1982); Roderick MacFarquhar, *The Origins of the Cultural Revolution*, vol. 3: *The Coming of the Cataclysm, 1961–1966* (New York: Columbia University Press, 1977); Richard Baum, *Prelude to Revolution: Mao, the Party, and the Peasant Question, 1962–66* (New York: Columbia University Press, 1975); Richard Baum and Frederick Teiwes, *Ssu-Ch'ing: The Socialist Education Movement of 1962–1966* (Berkeley: University of California Press, 1968).

The Cultural Revolution, Analyses and Documents: Yiching Wu, *The Cultural Revolution at the Margins* (Cambridge: Harvard University Press, 2014); Roderick MacFarquhar and Michael Schoenhals, *Mao's Last Revolution* (Cambridge: Harvard University Press, 2006); Elizabeth J. Perry and Li Xun, *Proletarian Power, Shanghai in the Cultural Revolution* (Boulder, CO: Westview, 1997); Michael Schoenhals, ed., *China's Cultural Revolution, 1966–1969: Not a Dinner Party* (Armonk, NY: M. E. Sharpe, 1996); Lynn White, *Policies of Chaos: The Organizational Causes of Violence in China's Cultural Revolution* (Princeton: Princeton University Press, 1989); Roxane Witke, *Comrade Chiang Ch'ing* [Jiang Qing] (Boston: Little Brown, 1977); Anne Thurston, *Enemies of the People: The Ordeal of the Intellectuals in China's Great Cultural Revolution* (New York: Knopf, 1987); Margie Sargent, Vivienne Shue, Thomas Matthews, and Deborah Davis, *The Cultural Revolution in the Provinces* (Cambridge: Harvard University Press, 1971); Anita Chan, *Children of Mao: Personality Development and Political Activism in the Red Guard Generation* (Seattle: University of Washington Press, 1985); Stanley Rosen, *Red Guard Factionalism and the Cultural Revolution in Guangzhou* (Boulder, CO: Westview, 1982); Lin Biao (Lin Piao), *Important Documents on the Great Proletarian Cultural Revolution in China* (Beijing: Foreign Languages Press, 1970).

The Cultural Revolution—Participants and Victims: Xi Jiainlin, *Cowshed: Memories of the Cultural Revolution*, trans. Chenxin Jiang (New York: New York Review of Books, 2016); Rae Yang, *Spider Eaters, A Memoir* (Berkeley: University of California Press, 1997); Jung Chang, *Wild Swans: Three Daughters of China* (New York: Simon & Schuster, 1991); Gao Yuan, *Born Red: A Chronicle of the Cultural Revolution* (Stanford: Stanford University Press, 1987); Bei Dao, *Waves: Stories*, trans. Bonnie McDougall and Susette Cook (London:

Heinemann, 1987); Yue Daiyun, with Carolyn Wakeman, *To the Storm: The Odyssey of a Revolutionary Chinese Woman* (Berkeley: University of California Press, 1985); Yang Jiang, *Six Chapters from My Life "Downunder"* (Seattle: University of Washington Press, 1984); *The Wounded: New Stories of the Cultural Revolution*, trans. Geremie Barmé and Bennett Lee (Hong Kong: Joint Publishing Company, 1979).

Labor Camps: Kang Zhengguo, *Confessions: An Innocent Life in Communist China*, trans. Susan Wilf (New York: W. W. Norton, 2007); James Seymour and Richard Anderson, *New Ghosts, Old Ghosts: Prisons and Labor Reform in China* (Armonk, NY: M. E. Sharpe, 1998); Harry Wu, *Lao-gai: The Chinese Gulag* (Boulder, CO: Westview, 1992); Harry Wu and Carolyn Wakeman, *Bitter Winds: A Memoir of My Years in China's Gulag* (New York: J. Wiley, 1994).

CHAPTER 23

Foreign Policy and the United States: Margaret MacMillan, *Nixon and Mao: The Week that Changed the World* (New York: Random House, 2007); Henry Kissinger, *White House Years* (Boston: Little, Brown, 1979); Richard Nixon, *RN: The Memoirs of Richard Nixon* (New York: Grosset & Dunlap, 1978); Bruce Larkin, *China and Africa, 1949–1970: The Foreign Policy of the People's Republic of China* (Berkeley: University of California Press, 1971).

Campaigns and Cadres: Michel Bonnin, *The Lost Generation: The Rustication of China's Educated Youths, 1968–1980*, trans. Krystyna Horko (Hong Kong: The Chinese University Press, 2013); James Palmer, *Heaven Cracks, Earth Shakes: The Tangshan Earthquake and the Death of Mao's China* (New York: Basic Books, 2012); B. Michael Frolic, *Mao's People: Sixteen Portraits of Life in Revolutionary China* (Cambridge: Harvard University Press, 1980); Susan Shirk, *Competitive Comrades: Career Incentives and Student Strategies in China* (Berkeley: University of California Press, 1981); Harry Harding, *Organizing China: The Problem of Bureaucracy, 1949–1976* (Stanford: Stanford University Press, 1981); Thomas Bernstein, *Up to the Mountains and Down to the Villages: The Transfer of Youth from Urban to Rural China* (New Haven: Yale University Press, 1977).

Rural Life: Yuxiang Yang, *Private Life under Socialism: Love, Intimacy, and Family Change in a Chinese Village, 1949–1999* (Stanford: Stanford University Press, 2003); Dali L. Yang, *Calamity and Reform in China: State, Rural Society, and Institutional Change since the Great Leap Forward* (Stanford: Stanford University Press, 1996); Edward Friedman, Paul G. Pickowicz, Mark Selden, and Kay Ann Johnson, *Chinese Village, Socialist State* (New Haven: Yale University Press, 1991); John Burns, *Political Participation in Rural China* (Berkeley: University of California Press, 1988); Richard Madsen, *Morality and Power in a Chinese Village* (Berkeley: University of California Press, 1984); Gordon Bennett, *Huadong: The Story of a Chinese People's Commune* (Boulder, CO: Westview, 1978).

Urban Life: Deborah Kaple, *Dream of a Red Factory: The Legacy of High Stalinism in China* (New York: Oxford University Press, 1994); Martin Whyte and William Parish, *Urban Life in Contemporary China* (Chicago: The University of Chicago Press, 1984); John Wilson Lewis, ed., *The City in Communist China* (Stanford: Stanford University Press, 1971).

PRC Culture: Denise Ho, *Curating Revolution: Politics on Display in Mao's China* (Cambridge: Cambridge University Press, 2017); Brian DeMare, *Mao's Cultural Army: Drama Troupes in China's Cultural Revolution* (Cambridge: Cambridge University Press, 2015); Barbara Mittler, *A Continuous Revolution: Making Sense of Cultural Revolution Culture*

(Cambridge: Harvard University East Asia Center, 2012); Richard Kraus, *Pianos and Politics in China: Class, Nationalism and the Controversy over Western Music* (New York: Oxford University Press, 1989); Ellen Johnston Laing, *The Winking Owl: Art in the People's Republic of China* (Berkeley: University of California Press, 1988); Bonnie McDougall, ed., *Popular Chinese Literature and Performing Arts in the People's Republic of China, 1949–1979* (Berkeley: University of California Press, 1984).

Women in the Revolution: Gail Hershatter, *Women and China's Revolutions* (Lanham: Rowman & Littlefield, 2019); Zheng Wang, *Finding Women in the State: A Socialist Feminist Movement in the People's Republic of China, 1949–1964* (Oakland: University of California Press, 2017); Xiaoping Cong, *Marriage, Law, and Gender in Revolutionary China, 1940–1960* (New York: Cambridge University Press, 2016); Gail Hershatter, *The Gender of Memory: Rural Women and China's Collective Past* (Berkeley: University of California Press, 2011); Kay Ann Johnson, *Women, the Family and Peasant Revolution in China* (Chicago: The University of Chicago Press, 1983); Elisabeth Croll, *The Politics of Marriage in Contemporary China* (New York: Cambridge University Press, 1981); Margery Wolf and Roxane Witke, eds., *Women in Chinese Society* (Stanford: Stanford University Press, 1975).

CHAPTER 24

The Four Modernizations: Helen Siu, *Agents and Victims in South China: Accomplices in Rural Revolution* (New Haven: Yale University Press, 1989); Andrew Walder, *Communist Neo-Traditionalism: Work and Authority in Chinese Industry* (New York: Columbia University Press, 1986); William Joseph, *The Critique of Ultra-Leftism in China, 1958–1981* (Stanford: Stanford University Press, 1984); David Lampton, *Paths to Power: Elite Mobility in Contemporary China* (Ann Arbor: University of Michigan, 1986); Richard Baum, ed., *China's Four Modernizations: The New Technological Revolution* (Boulder, CO: Westview, 1980).

The Democracy Movement and the "Fifth Modernization": Wei Jingsheng, *The Courage to Stand Alone: Letters from Prison and Other Writings* (New York: Viking, 1997); Bei Dao, *The August Sleepwalker*, trans. Bonnie McDougall (London: Anvil Press, 1988); Anita Chan, Stanley Rosen, and Jonathan Unger, *On Socialist Democracy and the Chinese Legal System: The Li Yizhe Debates* (Armonk, NY: M. E. Sharpe, 1985); Andrew Nathan, *Chinese Democracy* (New York: Knopf, 1985); Liu Binyan, *"People or Monsters?" and Other Stories and Reportage from China after Mao*, ed. Perry Link (Bloomington: Indiana University Press, 1983); Perry Link, ed., *Stubborn Weeds: Popular and Controversial Chinese Literature after the Cultural Revolution* (Bloomington: Indiana University Press, 1983); James Seymour, ed., *The Fifth Modernization: China's Human Rights Movement, 1978–1979* (Stanfordville, NY: Human Rights Publishing, 1980); H. Lyman Miller, *Science and Dissent in Post-Mao China: The Politics of Knowledge* (Seattle: University of Washington Press, 1996).

Taiwan: Hsiao-ting Lin, *Accidental State: Chiang Kai-shek, the United States, and the Making of Taiwan* (Cambridge: Harvard University Press, 2016); Linda Chao and Ramon H. Myers, *The First Chinese Democracy: Political Life in the Republic of China on Taiwan* (Baltimore: The Johns Hopkins University Press, 1998); John Cooper, *A Quiet Revolution: Political Development in the Republic of China* (Washington, D.C.: Ethics and Policy Center, 1988); Thomas Gold, *State and Society in the Taiwan Miracle* (Armonk, NY: M. E. Sharpe, 1986); James C. Hsiung, ed., *The Taiwan Experience, 1950–1980: Contemporary Republic of China* (New York: Praeger, 1981); John Fei, Gustav Ranis, and Shirley Kuo, *Growth with Equity: The Taiwan Case* (New York: Oxford University Press, 1979).

Special Economic Zones: Juan Du, *The Shenzhen Experiment: The Story of China's Instant City* (Cambridge: Harvard University Press, 2020); George T. Crane, *The Political Economy of China's Economic Zones* (Abingdon, Oxon: Routledge, 2016); Harry Harding, *China's Second Revolution: Reform after Mao* (Washington, D.C.: Brookings Institution, 1987); Samuel S. Kim, ed., *China and the World: Chinese Foreign Policy in the Post-Mao Era* (Boulder, CO: Westview, 1984).

CHAPTER 25

Population and Environment: Elizabeth Economy, *The River Runs Black: The Environmental Challenge to China's Future* (Ithaca: Cornell University Press, 2010); Vaclav Smil, *China's Environmental Crisis* (Armonk, NY: M. E. Sharpe, 1993); George B. Schaller, *The Last Panda* (Chicago: The University of Chicago Press, 1993); Dai Qing, *The River Dragon Has Come! The Three Gorges Dam and the Fate of China's Yangtze River and Its People* (Armonk, NY: M. E. Sharpe, 1998); Judith Banister, *China's Changing Population* (Stanford: Stanford University Press, 1987).

Governing China in the 1980s: Ezra Vogel, *Deng Xiaoping and the Transformation of China* (Cambridge: Harvard University Press, 2011); Kenneth Lieberthal and Michel Oksenberg, *Policy Making in China: Leaders, Structures, and Processes* (Princeton: Princeton University Press, 1988); David Goodman, ed., *Groups and Politics in the People's Republic of China* (Armonk, NY, 1985); Vivienne Shue, *The Reach of the State: Sketches of the Chinese Body Politic* (Stanford: Stanford University Press, 1988); Elizabeth Perry and Christine Wong, eds., *The Political Economy of Reform in Post-Mao China* (Cambridge: Harvard University Press, 1985).

Chinese Law in the PRC: Jennifer Altenhenger, *Legal Lessons: Popularizing Laws in the People's Republic of China, 1949–1989* (Cambridge: Harvard University Asia Center, 2018); Michael Moser and Winston Zee, *China Tax Guide* (New York: Oxford University Press, 1987); R. Randle Edwards, Louis Henkin, and Andrew Nathan, eds., *Human Rights in Contemporary China* (New York: Columbia University Press, 1986); David Buxbaum, ed., *Chinese Family Law and Social Change in Historical and Comparative Perspective* (Seattle: University of Washington Press, 1978); Jerome Cohen, ed., *Contemporary Chinese Law: Research Problems and Perspectives* (Cambridge: Harvard University Press, 1970).

Chinese Writers: Ken Liu, ed. and trans., *Broken Stars: Contemporary Chinese Science Fiction in Translation* (New York: Tor, 2019); Kay Schaffer and Xianlin Song, eds., *Women Writers in Postsocialist China* (New York: Routledge, 2014); Merle Goldman, with Timothy Cheek and Carol Hamrin, *China's Intellectuals and the State: In Search of a New Relationship* (Cambridge: Harvard University Press, 1987); Jeffrey Kinkley, ed., *After Mao: Chinese Literature and Society, 1978–1981* (Cambridge: Harvard University Press, 1985).

Hong Kong: John Wong, *Hong Kong Takes Flight: Commercial Aviation and the Making of a Global Hub, 1930s–1998* (Cambridge: Harvard University Asia Center, 2022); Peter Hamilton, *Made in Hong Kong: Transpacific Networks and a New History of Globalization* (New York: Columbia University Press, 2021); John Carroll, *Edges of Empire: Chinese Elites and British Colonials in Hong Kong* (Cambridge: Harvard University Press, 2005); Chiu Hungdah, Y. C. Jao, and Yuan-li Wu, eds., *The Future of Hong Kong: Toward 1997 and Beyond* (Westport, CT: Praeger, 1987).

Life and Health: David Palmer, *Qigong Fever: Body, Science, and Utopia in China* (New York: Columbia University Press, 2007); Yunxiang Yan, *The Flow of Gifts: Reciprocity and*

Social Networks in a Chinese Village (Stanford: Stanford University Press, 1996); Arthur Kleinman, *Social Origins of Distress and Disease: Depression, Neurasthenia, and Pain in Modern China* (New Haven: Yale University Press, 1986); Gail Henderson and Myron Cohen, *The Chinese Hospital: A Socialist Work Unit* (New Haven: Yale University Press, 1984); Deborah Davis-Friedmann, *Long Lives, Chinese Elderly and the Communist Revolution* (Cambridge: Harvard University Press, 1983).

CHAPTER 26

A Range of Voices: Joseph W. Esherick, *Ancestral Leaves: A Family Journey through Chinese History* (Berkeley: University of California Press, 2011); Ying Ruocheng and Claire Conceison, *Voices Carry: Behind Bars and Backstage during China's Revolution and Reform* (Lanham: Rowman & Littlefield, 2009); *Seeds of Fire: Chinese Voices of Conscience*, ed. Geremie Barmé and John Minford (New York: Bloodaxe Books, 1989); Perry Link, Richard Madsen, and Paul Pickowicz, eds., *Unofficial China: Popular Culture and Thought in the People's Republic* (Boulder, CO: Westview Press, 1989); Chin Annping, *Children of China: Voices from Recent Years* (New York: Knopf, 1988); Emily Honig and Gail Hershatter, *Personal Voices: Chinese Women in the 1980's* (Stanford: Stanford University Press, 1988); Zhang Xinxin and Sang Ye, *Chinese Lives: An Oral History of Contemporary China* (London: MacMillan, 1987).

Economics and Politics: Carol Hamrin, *China and the Challenge of the Future: Changing Political Patterns* (Boulder, CO: Westview, 1989); Bruce Reynolds, ed., *Chinese Economic Policy: Economic Reform at Midstream* (New York: Paragon House, 1989); Jim Mann, *Beijing Jeep: A Case Study of Western Business in China* (New York: Simon and Schuster, 1989); Orville Schell, *Discos and Democracy: China in the Throes of Reform* (New York: Pantheon, 1988).

The 1989 Democracy Movement and the June Fourth Massacre: Jeremy Brown, *June Fourth: The Tiananmen Protests and the Beijing Massacre of 1989* (Cambridge: Cambridge University Press, 2021); Dingxin Zhao, *The Power of Tiananmen: State-Society Relations and the 1989 Student Movement* (Chicago: The University of Chicago Press, 2001); Carma Hinton and Richard Gordon, dirs., *The Gate of Heavenly Peace* (Long Bow Group, 1995); Roger Des Forges, Luo Ning, and Wu Yen-fo, eds., *Chinese Democracy and the Crisis of 1989: Chinese and American Reflections* (Albany: State University of New York Press, 1993); Timothy Brook, *Quelling the People: The Military Suppression of the Beijing Democracy Movement* (Oxford: Oxford University Press, 1992); *Beijing Spring, 1989 Confrontation and Conflict: The Basic Documents*, ed. Michel Oksenberg, Lawrence R. Sullivan, and Marc Lambert (Armonk: NY: M. E. Sharpe, 1990); Han Minzhu, ed., *Cries for Democracy: Writings and Speeches from the 1989 Chinese Democracy Movement* (Princeton: Princeton University Press, 1990); The Photographers and Reporters of Min Pao News, *June Four: A Chronicle of the Chinese Democratic Uprising*, trans. Zi Jin and Qin Zhou (Fayetteville: University of Arkansas Press, 1989); David and Peter Turnley, *Beijing Spring* (New York: Stewart, Tabori & Chang, 1989).

CHAPTER 27

Central Government: Kenneth Lieberthal, *Governing China, from Revolution through Reform* (New York: W. W. Norton, 2004); Dorothy J. Solinger, *Contesting Citizenship in Urban China: Peasant Migrants, the State, and the Logic of the Market* (Berkeley: University of California Press, 1999); Bruce Gilley, *Tiger on the Brink: Jiang Zemin and China's*

New Elite (Berkeley: University of California Press, 1998); Maurice Meisner, *The Deng Xiaoping Era: An Inquiry into the Fate of Chinese Socialism, 1978–1994* (New York: Hill and Wang, 1996); Yan Sun, *The Chinese Reassessment of Socialism, 1976–1992* (Princeton: Princeton University Press, 1995).

Cultural Critiques: Geremie Barmé, *Shades of Mao: The Posthumous Cult of the Great Leader* (Armonk, NY: M. E. Sharpe, 1996); Jing Wang, *High Culture Fever: Politics, Aesthetics, and Ideology in Deng's China* (Berkeley: University of California Press, 1996); Howard Goldblatt, ed., *Chairman Mao Would Not Be Amused: Fiction from Today's China* (New York: Grove Press, 1995); Jianying Zha, *China Pop: How Soap Operas, Tabloids, and Bestsellers Are Transforming a Culture* (New York: The New Press, 1993); Geremie Barmé and Linda Jaivin, eds., *New Ghosts, Old Dreams: Chinese Rebel Voices* (New York: Times Books, 1992).

Military and Strategic: Andrew J. Nathan and Robert Ross, *The Great Wall and the Empty Fortress: China's Search for Security* (New York: W. W. Norton, 1997); Richard Bernstein and Ross H. Munro, *The Coming Conflict with China* (New York: Knopf, 1997); Michael Pillsbury, ed., *Chinese Views of Future Warfare* (Washington, D.C.: National Defense University Press, 1996).

Economic Prospects: Leslie T. Chang, *Factory Girls: From Village to City in a Changing China* (New York: Spiegel and Grau, 2008); Deborah Davis, Richard Kraus, Barry Naughton, and Elizabeth Perry, eds., *Urban Spaces in Contemporary China: The Potential for Autonomy and Community in Post-Mao China* (Washington, D.C.: Woodrow Wilson Center Press, 1995); Lester R. Brown, *Who Will Feed China?* (New York: W. W. Norton, 1995).

CHAPTER 28

Emerging Structures in the New Century: William Kirby, ed., *The People's Republic of China at 60: An International Assessment* (Cambridge: Harvard University Asia Center, 2011); Susan Shirk, ed., *Changing Media, Changing China* (Oxford: Oxford University Press, 2011); Joseph Fewsmith, ed., *China Today, China Tomorrow: Domestic Politics, Economy and Society* (Lanham: Rowman & Littlefield, 2010); Yoshiko Ashiwa and David L. Wank, eds., *Making Religion, Making the State* (Stanford: Stanford University Press, 2009); Robert G. Sutter, ed., *Chinese Foreign Relations: Power and Policy since the Cold War* (Lanham: Rowman & Littlefield, 2008).

Chinese Reflections: Ian Johnson, *Sparks: China's Underground Historians and Their Battle for the Future* (New York: Oxford University Press, 2023); Ai Weiwei, *1000 Years of Joys and Sorrows: A Memoir*, trans. Allan Barr (New York: Crown Books, 2021); Fang Lizhi, *The Most Wanted Man in China: My Journey from Scientist to Enemy of the State*, trans. Perry Link (New York: Henry Holt, 2016); Liu Xiaobo, *No Enemies, No Hatred: Selected Essays and Poems*, ed. Amy Link (Cambridge: Harvard University Press, 2012); Chen Guidi and Wu Chuntao, *Will the Boat Sink the Water? The Life of China's Peasants*, trans. Zhu Hong (New York: Public Affairs, 2006).

Glossary

Amherst, Lord William (1773–1857): Leader of the second British diplomatic and trade mission to China. In 1816 Amherst attempted to meet with the Jiaqing emperor, but due to misunderstandings in protocol, his mission was refused.

Anhui: Province in east-central China, over 50,000 square miles in area. Capital: Hefei.

Annam: The central region of present-day Vietnam.

anti-American boycott of 1905: Boycott of American goods organized in response to the mistreatment of Chinese in the United States. The first united economic expression of Chinese nationalism against a foreign power.

anti–Lin Biao, anti-Confucius campaign: Mass propaganda movement launched in late 1973 that linked the disgraced (and dead) Lin Biao to Confucius and called for criticism of the reactionary, feudal aspects of Chinese society that the two figures allegedly symbolized.

anti–spiritual pollution campaign: Movement launched in 1982 by the CCP under Deng Xiaoping to criticize what was seen as Western-influenced decadence in writing and other arts.

Autumn Harvest Uprisings (September 1927): A series of unsuccessful attacks by peasant forces on several small towns near Changsha, Hunan province, led by Mao Zedong.

Bandung conference (1955): Meeting of delegates of Asian and African countries held in Bandung, Indonesia, in which Zhou Enlai called for Asian-African solidarity and won international recognition of China's new diplomatic role.

banner system: Method of military organization applied by the Manchus whereby fighting men (and their families) were grouped in divisions identified by different colored banners. Eight banners were devised, using the colors red, blue, yellow, and white: four plain and four bordered. The system, begun by Nurhaci, was phased out in the early twentieth century with the development of the Qing New Army.

baojia: Method of household organization and control, based on a system described in ancient texts and employed with varying degrees of success from the Song dynasty through the Qing. One hundred households were organized into a *jia.* Ten *jia* made a *bao*. The leaders of the units, selected on a rotating basis, were charged with maintaining local order, supervising community works, and enforcing tax collection.

Bei Dao (b. 1949): Poet, coeditor of the underground literary journal *Today*.

Beijing convention (1860): Treaty between Britain and China, negotiated between Lord Elgin and Prince Gong after British troops entered Beijing, razed the summer palace, and forced the Qing court to flee. In addition to reconfirming the terms of the Treaty of Tianjin, the convention stipulated the ceding of the Kowloon peninsula to Hong Kong, the opening of Tianjin as a treaty port, and the payment of 8 million taels in indemnity to Britain.

Beijing massacre (June 4, 1989): On orders of CCP hard-liners, several hundreds of prodemocracy demonstrators and Beijing citizens were killed by PLA troops following six weeks of rallies in Tiananmen Square.

Blueshirts: Paramilitary organization formed in the 1930s that functioned as Chiang Kai-shek's secret police. Led by Dai Li and other Whampoa graduates loyal to Chiang, the Blueshirts gathered intelligence on "subversive" activities and orchestrated assassinations of those thought to oppose Chiang.

Bogue: British corruption of the Portuguese *Boca Tigre* ("Tiger's Mouth"), the name for the mouth of the Pearl River at Guangzhou.

bourgeois liberalization: General term used by the CCP to describe and criticize the demands made by those calling for democracy and human rights in the student protests of 1986 and 1989.

Boxer Protocol (1901): Demands of foreign powers agreed to by the Qing government after the suppression of the Boxer Uprising, which included the payment of an indemnity that amounted to almost half of the Qing annual budget. Indemnity payments were later used to fund scholarships for Chinese students to study in America.

Boxer Uprising (1900): Anti-Christian, antiforeign peasant uprising that originated in northern Shandong and ended with the siege of the foreign legation in Beijing. Participants were mostly poor peasants who practiced a type of martial art that gave the name "boxer" to the movement. The uprising ended when a combined Western military expedition forced the empress dowager Cixi and her court to flee to Xi'an.

Buddhism: Religion of compassion and salvation based to some extent on the teachings of the Indian prince Siddhartha ("the Buddha," 563–483 B.C.E.). Influential in Chinese society since its introduction during the Han dynasty (206 B.C.E.–220 C.E.), Buddhism at various times contested against and blended with the two indigenous schools of Chinese religious and philosophical thought, Confucianism and Daoism.

Burma Road: Overland passage running 715 miles from Lashio in Burma to Kunming in the southwestern province of Yunnan. Used by the Allies in the early part of World War II to send supplies to Chiang Kai-shek's government in Chongqing. Closed in 1942 when Britain lost Burma to Japan.

Cai Yuanpei (1868–1940): President of Beijing University from 1916 to 1926. Important supporter of the May Fourth movement.

Campaign to Purify Class Ranks: Movement launched during the Cultural Revolution to investigate the class background of all cadres suspected of having "bad" elements in their past. Cadres "studied" their faults in May Seventh Schools set up throughout the country.

Central Committee: Central coordinating organ of the CCP. The powerful Politburo and its Standing Committee are drawn from its members.

Chen Duxiu (1879–1942): Important figure in the May Fourth movement; founded the journal *New Youth* in 1915 upon his return from studies in Japan. One of the earliest Chinese Marxists and, with Li Dazhao, a founder of the CCP.

Chen Yonggui: Leader of a production team in Dazhai; became nationally famous in 1964 when he was praised by Mao for using elements of Mao Zedong Thought to achieve dramatic increases in agricultural production.

Chen Yun (1905–1995): Shanghai typesetter who joined the Communist party in 1924 and went on to become the CCP's foremost economic planner after 1949. Helped orchestrate economic recovery after the Great Leap Forward. Criticized during the Cultural Revolution, he returned to high-level government positions in the 1980s as a conservative opponent of rapid economic change.

Chiang Ching-kuo (1910–1988): Soviet-educated son of Chiang Kai-shek. Served under his father in various Guomindang positions, including commissioner in charge of Guomindang financial reforms in the 1940s. Became president of Taiwan from 1978 and spearheaded political liberalization after losing diplomatic recognition from the United States.

Chiang Kai-shek (1887–1975): Military and political leader of the Guomindang after the death of Sun Yat-sen. Joined the anti-Manchu Revolutionary Alliance as a military student in Japan. Sent by Sun Yat-sen to the Soviet Union for military training in 1923 and named leader of the Whampoa Academy upon his return. After leading the Northern Expedition, he set up the Nationalist government in 1928 and fought for the next twenty years against militarists, the Japanese, and the Communists for the control of China. President of the Republic of China on Taiwan from 1949 until his death twenty-six years later.

Chongqing: Port city on the Yangzi River in Sichuan province. Served as the location of the Nationalist government during World War II.

Cixi (1835–1908): Concubine to Emperor Xianfeng; mother of Emperor Tongzhi; known to Westerners as "the empress dowager." From the time she became regent to the boy-emperor Tongzhi in 1861 until her death forty-seven years later, she held de facto power over the Qing government, naming two successive emperors to the throne.

Cohong ("combined merchant companies"): Chinese merchant guild, formally established in 1720, with a monopoly over maritime trade with Western countries. From 1760, when trade was restricted to Guangzhou, the Cohong acted as agents of the Qing government, collecting duties and handling negotiations with foreigners. The system was abolished in 1842 with the Treaty of Nanjing.

Confucianism: System of ethics based on the teachings of Kongfuzi (tr. 551–479 B.C.E.), who held that humans would be in harmony with the universe if they behaved with righteousness and restraint and adhered properly to specific social roles. With its emphasis on the study of the Classics, the worship of ancestors, and the submission to authority, Confucianism formed the dominant ethic of Chinese social units from the imperial government to the peasant family.

Cultural Revolution: Complex social upheaval that began as a struggle between Mao Zedong and other top party leaders for dominance of the CCP and went on to affect all of China with its call for "continuing revolution." Dates for the movement are usually given as 1966 to 1976.

Dai Zhen (1724–1777): One of the most important and influential *kaozheng* scholars of the eighteenth century. Served as a compiler of the *Four Treasuries*.

Dalai Lama: Supreme spiritual leader of Tibetan Buddhism; also the political leader of Tibet from 1642 to 1959. In various periods through Tibetan history, Chinese policy has had considerable influence on determining the placement and the power of the Dalai Lama. The Dalai Lama fled Tibet in 1959 and now lives in exile in India.

danwei: "Work unit" in post-1949 China; a company or an organization that functions as an employer and provides housing and social services for its employees.

Daoguang (1782–1850): Reign name of the second son of Emperor Jiaqing who succeeded him in 1821. His reign saw the worsening of conflicts between foreign powers and Qing interests that culminated in the Opium War (1839–1842).

Daoism: School of philosophy based on the writings of Laozi (tr. 604–521 B.C.E.) and Zhuangzi (369–286 B.C.E.), which teaches that liberation is achieved when humans are in harmony with the empty, spontaneous, and natural essence of "the way."

Dazhai: Rural brigade in Shanxi province, led by Chen Yonggui. Used in the early 1960s and again in the mid-1970s as a model for socialist agricultural production achieved through the application of Mao Zedong Thought.

December Ninth movement (1935): Series of protests against Japanese aggression and Chiang Kai-shek's inability to check that aggression. It was touched off by student demonstrations held in Beijing on December 9, 1935, and helped generate a climate sympathetic to the second Communist-Guomindang united front.

Democracy Wall: Stretch of wall edging the Forbidden City in Beijing, where posters that called for democratic freedom were displayed in 1978–1979. The most famous of these posters, composed by Wei Jingsheng, proposed the adoption of democracy as the fifth modernization.

Deng Xiaoping (1904–1997): Son of a Sichuanese landlord family, he joined the Communist party while on a work-study program in France in the 1920s. A veteran of the Long March, Deng rose to high positions in the Central Committee during the 1950s and early 1960s, and returned to power after a period of persecution during the Cultural Revolution, replacing Hua Guofeng as premier in 1980. Heralded for his visionary leadership of the reform era, he was instrumental in implementing the Four Modernizations and for crushing the 1989 democracy protests.

Ding Ling (1904–1986): Feminist writer and Communist party member whose famous works include "The Diary of Miss Sophie" and *The Sun Shines over the Sanggan River*. She was criticized during the Rectification Campaign of 1942 and imprisoned in the antirightist campaign following the Hundred Flowers movement and again during the Cultural Revolution.

Donglin ("Eastern Grove") Society: Academy founded in the early seventeenth century in Wuxi, dedicated to the restoration of "orthodox" Confucian morality. As a political faction, society members struggled against the power of the eunuchs in the imperial court; many suffered torture and death in a purge ordered by the powerful eunuch Wei Zhongxian in 1625.

Dorgon (1612–1650): Manchu military leader, the fourteenth son of Nurhaci, and half brother of Hong Taiji. Led the first Manchu attacks on China inside the Great Wall, capturing Beijing in 1644. Dorgon exercised power over the first Qing court in his role as coregent to Hong Taiji's son, the boy emperor Shunzhi.

Dream of the Red Chamber, The (Hong Lou Meng): Novel, also known as *The Story of the Stone*, written by Cao Xueqin during the reign of Qianlong. This tragic love story of the hero Jia Baoyu and Lin Daiyu is set amid courtyards of a large wealthy family in the Yangzi delta region.

Duan Qirui (1865–1936): Premier of the Republic of China after the death of Yuan Shikai.

Du Yuesheng (1888–1951): Shanghai racketeer, banker, financier, leader of the Green Gang secret society; friend and important ally of Chiang Kai-shek.

Eighth Route Army: Name given to the Communist Red Army placed under nominal Guomindang command during the second Communist-Guomindang united front against Japan (1937–1945).

Elliot, Charles: Named in 1836 as second British superintendent of foreign trade after the death of Lord Napier. Dismissed during the Opium War for not extracting enough concessions from the Qing in initial treaty negotiations.

Ever-Victorious Army: Foreign-officered mercenary army that fought alongside Qing forces to repel Taiping attacks in the lower Yangzi delta.

fabi: Unit of currency issued by the Nationalist government beginning in 1935. Runaway inflation after World War II prompted the government to abandon *fabi* in 1948 and establish a new currency, the gold yuan, whose exchange rate was 1 yuan for 3 million *fabi*.

Fang Lizhi (1936–2012): Prominent astrophysicist and dissident, expelled from the Communist party for "bourgeois liberalism"—that is, he supported student demonstrations for democracy in 1986.

Fei Xiaotong (1910–2005): Sociologist whose pioneering field work in the 1930s and 1940s explored the patterns of social change in rural China.

Feng Yuxiang (1882–1948): Militarist whose power base in the 1920s ranged from the northwestern province of Shaanxi to Beijing. Influenced by the Soviet Union, he decided to join the Guomindang during the Northern Expedition.

Feng Zikai (1898–1975): Illustrator and cartoonist whose simple line drawings portrayed and sharply criticized Chinese society of the 1930s.

fifth modernization: Taken from the title of a wall poster written by Wei Jingsheng, which asserted that without democracy as the "fifth modernization," the Four Modernizations would not succeed.

Five Anti campaign: Struggle launched in 1952 by the Communist party against Chinese industrialists and businessmen who had stayed on in China after 1949. The movement ended the independent operation of capitalists and helped consolidate CCP power over the economy.

Five Classics: Five works (*The Book of Rites* [Li Ji], *The Spring and Autumn Annals* [Chun Qiu], *The Book of History* [Shujing], *The Book of Poetry* [Shijing], and the *Book of Changes* [Yijing]) said to have been edited by Confucius. Together with the Four Books, they formed the central canon of Confucian learning.

Flying Tigers: "Volunteer" force of U.S. Army–Air Force pilots who fought for China against Japan in World War II. Led by former U.S. Army pilot and adviser to Chiang Kai-shek, Claire Lee Chennault.

Four Books: *Analects* (sayings of Confucius *[Lun Yu]*), *Mencius [Mengzi]*, *The Doctrine of the Mean [Zhong Yong]*, and *The Great Learning [Da Xue]*, which with the Five Classics formed the core of Confucian education.

"four cleanups": Action to eradicate rural corruption in the areas of accounting, granary supplies, property accumulation, and work-point allocation. Part of the Socialist Education Campaign begun in 1963 by Mao and others in the CCP to reestablish socialist morality in the countryside.

Four Modernizations: Goal of Chinese domestic policy, announced in 1978, to develop the four areas of agriculture, industry, national defense, and science and technology. In pursuit of this goal, China under Deng Xiaoping implemented an open-door policy toward the West, developing special economic zones and sending students abroad.

Four Treasuries: Massive anthology, compiled under Qianlong, of China's most famous literary and historical works. One of the great achievements of Chinese bibliography.

Fu, prince of (d. 1646): Title of a grandson of the emperor Wanli and claimant to the Ming throne. Was proclaimed emperor in 1644 in the original Ming capital of Nanjing. Manchu armies captured him in 1645 and sent him back to Beijing, where he died the next year.

Fujian: Province on the southeastern coast of China, 46,300 square miles in area. Capital: Fuzhou.

Gang of Four: Group consisting of Yao Wenyuan, Zhang Chunqiao, Wang Hongwen, and Jiang Qing, who were officially blamed for creating and directing the Cultural Revolution. Arrested under Hua Guofeng's orders in October 1976, the four were tried and convicted in nationally televised proceedings in 1980.

Gansu: Province in north-central China, 174,000 square miles in area, much of it barren plain and desert. Capital: Lanzhou.

Gao Gang (1905–1954): CCP leader responsible for planning the economic recovery of Manchuria after World War II. Accused during a purge in 1954 of attempting to set up his own power base in the northeast. His death by suicide was announced the same year.

Golden Lotus *(Jin Ping Mei):* Considered one of the major works of Chinese fiction, first published in the late Ming. Narrates the hedonistic pursuits of businessman/official/scholar Qing Ximen.

Gong, Prince (1833–1898): Sixth son of Emperor Daoguang, important figure in the Qing dynasty's late attempts at revitalizing its power and regaining its sovereignty in the face of foreign aggression. Negotiated the Convention of Beijing with invading British forces on behalf of his exiled half brother, Emperor Xianfeng. In 1861 became adviser to the empress dowager Cixi and leader of the newly formed Zongli Yamen, a position he held until 1884 and then again from 1894 to 1898.

Grand Canal: System of waterways connecting Beijing to the Yangzi River delta, allowing for the shipment of rice and other products from the south to the imperial capital.

Grand Council: Small chamber of highly trusted advisers to the emperor. First formed by Emperor Yongzheng as a secret council to expedite military planning and established as a formal institution under Emperor Qianlong, with power that superseded the Grand Secretariat and the six ministries.

Grand Secretariat: Administrative body of the central imperial government, consisting of a small group of Manchus and Chinese whose function was primarily to handle routine memorials passed up from the six ministries.

Great Leap Forward (1958–1961): Campaign launched by Mao Zedong to heighten economic productivity dramatically through mass organization and the inspiration of revolutionary fervor among the people. Exaggerated reports of the success of policies such as the formation of "people's communes" and the decentralization of industrial production temporarily masked economic disaster and widespread famine.

Green Gang: Secret society that dominated organized crime in Shanghai before 1949. In the 1920s and 1930s, Green Gang ties were exploited by businesses and the Guomindang to control workers' strikes and suppress CCP activities.

Guangdong ("Broad East"): Province in southeastern China, 81,000 square miles in area. Capital: Guangzhou.

Guangxi ("Broad West"): Zhuang autonomous region in southwestern China, 89,000 square miles in area. Capital: Nanning.

Guangxu (1871–1908): Reign name of the ninth emperor of the Qing dynasty, chosen at the age of four by his aunt Cixi to succeed his cousin, Emperor Tongzhi. Sympathetic to the appeals of reformers such as Kang Youwei, Guangxu launched the Hundred Days' Reforms of 1898. Imprisoned by Cixi that same year for allegedly plotting against her.

Guangzhou: Major southern city in the Pearl River delta. Capital of Guangdong province.

Gui, prince of (1623–1662): Title of the last known surviving grandson of the emperor Wanli and last major claimant to the Ming throne. Assumed the title of Ming emperor in 1646 from his court-in-exile in Guangdong. Forced by pursuing Manchu troops into Burma, where he was finally captured and executed by Wu Sangui.

Guizhou: Mountainous province in southwest China, 65,000 square miles in area, with a significant population of Miao and Zhao ethnic minorities. Capital: Guiyang.

Gu Yanwu (1613–1682): *Kaozheng* scholar of the early Qing, revered by later scholars as a model of intellectual precision and integrity.

Hakkas *(Kejia)*: Ethnic minority people of south-central China. Famous Hakkas include Taiping leader Hong Xiuquan and the Soong family.

Hebei ("River North"): Province in northeastern China, 69,500 square miles in area. Capital: Shijiazhuang.

Heilongjiang ("Black Dragon River"): Northeastern-most province in China, 180,000 square miles in area. Capital: Harbin.

Henan ("River South"): Province in east-central China, 61,800 square miles in area. Capital: Zhengzhou.

Heshen (1750–1799): Powerful minister and imperial adviser, accused at Emperor Qianlong's death of corruption and contributing to the decline of the empire. In one year, he rose from imperial bodyguard to among the highest positions in the government, where he used his power to enrich himself and his followers. Arrested and forced to die by suicide by Qianlong's son and successor, Emperor Jiaqing.

He Zizhen (1909–1984): Second wife of Mao Zedong, his companion on the Long March and in Yan'an until he left her for his third wife, Jiang Qing.

Hong Taiji (1592–1643): Eighth son of Nurhaci, emperor of the Manchus for seventeen years after the death of his father in 1626. With the help of Chinese advisers and troops, he extended Manchu rule east over Korea and south to the Great Wall. He died in 1643, leaving the final conquest of Beijing to his younger half brother, Dorgon.

Hong Xiuquan (1813–1864): Leader of the Taiping, an aspiring scholar from a poor Hakka family. Believing himself to be the brother of Jesus Christ, entrusted by God to drive the demon Manchus out of China, he formed the Society of God Worshipers in Guangxi province, proclaimed himself emperor of the "Heavenly Kingdom of Great Peace" (Taiping Tianguo), and led an uprising against the Qing that almost ended the dynasty.

Hoppo: Derived from *Hubu*, or "Ministry of Revenue." Official head of Maritime Customs for the Qing government before the Opium War. The Hoppo did not deal directly with foreigners but received duties and all communiqués from foreigners through Cohong merchants.

Hua Guofeng (1921–2008): Former party secretary of Hunan province who rose to the position of premier and head of the CCP after the death of Mao in 1976. Ordered the arrest of the Gang of Four to consolidate his power but was in turn edged out of his central positions in 1980 by an ascendent Deng Xiaoping.

Huai River: One of the major waterways of China, approximately 625 miles long, flowing west to east through the central provinces of Jiangsu, Anhui, and Henan.

Hubei ("Lake North"): Province in central China, 69,500 square miles in area. Capital: Wuhan.

Hu Feng (1902–1985): Poet, friend of Lu Xun, and Communist party member. Object of a major rectification campaign in 1955 for his insistence on the freedom of artistic expression.

Hu Jintao (b. 1942): CCP secretary-general, president of the PRC, and chairman of the Military Affairs Commission from 2002–2012.

Hunan ("Lake South"): Province in south-central China, 81,000 square miles in area. Capital: Changsha.

Hundred Days' Reforms (Summer 1898): Three-month period during which Kang Youwei and his supporters influenced Emperor Guangxu to issue edicts on political and economic reform. Ended when Cixi imprisoned the emperor and executed six reformers, including Kang Youwei's younger brother.

Hundred Flowers movement: Brief period of liberalization begun in May 1957, when Mao encouraged the "blooming of a hundred flowers and the contending of a hundred schools of thought" and called for the nation's intellectuals to criticize the Communist party. The resultant outpouring of expression was swiftly cut off by the end of June, when an "antirightist campaign" punished those who had spoken out.

Hu Shi (1891–1962): Writer, philosopher, leading figure of the May Fourth movement. Later served as the Nationalist government's ambassador to the United States from 1938 to 1942.

Hu Yaobang (1915–1989): Protégé of Deng Xiaoping who rose from leader of the Communist Youth League in the 1950s to secretary-general of the CCP in 1981. Dismissed from this position for supporting the student democracy protests of December 1986. His death in April 1989 served as a rallying point for the renewed student democracy protests that culminated in the Beijing massacre of June 4, 1989.

Hu Yepin (1907–1931): Poet, member of the League of Left-Wing Writers, and companion of Ding Ling. Executed by Guomindang authorities in Shanghai.

imperial household: A self-contained bureaucracy within the imperial palace, staffed by bannermen and bondservants who managed the financial and personal affairs of the emperor and the imperial family.

Inner Mongolia *(Nei Menggu)*: Autonomous region of deserts and grassland in northern China, 463,000 square miles in area. Shares a long border with the Mongolian People's Republic to the north. Capital: Hohhot.

Inspectorate of Customs: Foreign-managed service that collected maritime customs fees for the Qing court. Established in 1854 during the Taiping uprising.

Jiang Qing (1914–1991): Third wife of Mao Zedong, a former Shanghai movie actress who became a major political figure of the Cultural Revolution. Arrested in 1976 on charges that as the leader of the Gang of Four she was responsible for directly persecuting hundreds of party members and indirectly causing the suffering of millions of Chinese. She died by suicide in 1991.

Jiangsu: Province on the eastern coast of China, 38,000 square miles in area. Capital: Nanjing.

Jiangxi ("River West"): Province in southeastern China, 61,800 square miles in area. Capital: Nanchang.

Jiangxi Soviet: Rural Communist base government led by Mao Zedong, centered in the town of Ruijin on the border between Jiangxi and Fujian provinces. Established in 1928, it lasted until a Guomindang blockade of the area forced the Communists to escape in 1934 on what became the Long March.

Jiang Zemin (b. 1926): Received training in the Soviet Union as an electrical engineer, before embarking on a political bureaucratic career. Appointed mayor of Shanghai in 1985 and promoted to head CCP in summer 1989 after the dismissal of Zhao Ziyang. In the 1990s appointed president of the PRC and head of Military Affairs Commission.

Jiaqing (1760–1820): Reign name of the fifth Qing emperor, who took the throne in 1796 but only assumed full power after his father Qianlong's death in 1799. During his rule China was plagued by pirates, internal rebellions, and natural disasters. Target of an assassination attempt in 1813, when followers of the Eight Trigrams leader Lin Qing broke into the Forbidden City.

Jingdezhen: City in Jiangxi province, famous since the Yuan dynasty for its imperial porcelain factories.

Jinggang Mountains: Isolated area on the Jiangxi-Hunan border where Mao Zedong, after the failed Autumn Harvest Uprisings of 1927, attempted to set up a rural soviet.

jinshi: Highest degree attainable through the imperial examination system. Candidates sat for the test in Beijing, where it was given once every three years throughout the Ming and Qing dynasties until the abolition of the examination system in 1905. *Jinshi* degree holders were appointed to high offices in the provinces and the imperial capital.

Journey to the West, The *(Xiyou Ji)*: Major work of Chinese fiction, based on the pilgrimage of the Tang dynasty monk Xuan Zang to India in search of Buddhist sutras. First published in novel form in the late Ming.

Kangxi (1654–1722): Reign name of the second emperor of the Qing dynasty, who came to the throne at the age of seven and ruled for sixty-one years. Consolidated Manchu rule over China, personally leading successful military campaigns to the northwest border areas while his generals subdued the rebellious Three Feudatories in the south and captured Taiwan. During his reign the Qing was the largest and one of the most prosperous unified empires on earth.

Kang Youwei (1858–1927): Confucian scholar, influential in late Qing reform movements, who held that economic and political modernization could take place within a Confucian political and moral framework. His plans for reform were supported by Emperor Guangxu in the Hundred Days' Reforms of 1898.

Koxinga (1624–1662): Naval commander, supporter of the Ming cause who fought the Manchus through the 1650s along the southeastern coast of China. Defeated by Manchu troops at Nanjing in 1659, Koxinga went on to establish a military and commercial base on Taiwan.

Lao She (1899–1966): Novelist and playwright whose works criticized the corruption and injustice of Chinese society of the 1920s and 1930s. His most famous works include *Cat Country* and *Rickshaw*.

League of Left-Wing Writers: Organization of poets, novelists, and essayists, many of whom were Communist party members, formed in Shanghai in the 1930s. Members included Ding Ling, Hu Yepin, Qu Qiubai, and Lu Xun.

Lee Teng-hui (1923–2020): Politician who succeeded Chiang Ching-kuo to the presidency of Taiwan in 1988, the first native Taiwanese to hold the highest political office. Lifted restrictions on travel to the mainland to allow family visits and trade.

Lei Feng: Young PLA soldier whose humble demeanor and selfless death in the service of Mao Zedong and the Communist party has been upheld as a role model in various propaganda campaigns of the past sixty years, the first of which was launched by Lin Biao in 1963 in a campaign to "learn from the army."

Liang Qichao (1873–1929): Student of Kang Youwei. Fled to Japan after the Hundred Days' Reforms in 1898. He used his writings to raise support for the reformers' cause among overseas Chinese and foreign governments. Initially a supporter of Kang Youwei's ideas of constitutional monarchy, he later split with his teacher and advocated a liberal republicanism.

Liaoning: Province in northeastern China, 54,000 square miles in area. Capital: Shenyang (Mukden).

Li Dazhao (1889–1927): Important figure in the May Fourth movement, early Chinese Marxist, and one of the founders of the CCP. Captured and executed in Beijing by the militarist Zhang Zuolin.

Lifan Yuan ("the Office of the Administration of Outer Provinces "): Established in 1638 by Hong Taiji to handle relations with Mongols and other non-Han peoples in the northwest.

Li Hongzhang (1823–1901): Qing general and official, a major figure in the self-strengthening movement of the late nineteenth century. Came to prominence in the 1860s under the tutelage of Zeng Guofan as leader of the provincial Huai army against the Taiping. In the 1870s and 1880s spearheaded projects to develop railways, telegraph lines, shipping companies, and arms manufacturers.

Li Lisan (1900–1967): Early Communist labor organizer, replaced Qu Qiubai as CCP leader in 1928. Li was criticized and removed from his leadership position in 1930 for insisting that the urban proletariat, not the peasantry, would be the dominant force of the Chinese revolution.

Lin Biao (1907–1971): Military leader who helped transform the PLA into a conventional modern army; succeeded Peng Dehuai in 1959 as minister of defense. An ardent supporter of Mao, Lin compiled *Quotations from Chairman Mao* and was named to be Mao's successor in 1969. Allegedly died two years later in an airplane crash after a failed coup against Mao.

Lin Qing (1770–1813): Leader of the Eight Trigrams millenary Buddhist cult who organized his followers to stage anti-Qing uprisings in Henan in the early 1800s. Some of his supporters broke into the Forbidden City in an attempt to assassinate Emperor Jiaqing.

Lin Zexu (1785–1850): Scholar-official from Fujian province, appointed in 1838 as imperial commissioner to end the opium trade. His confiscation and destruction in 1839 of 3 million pounds of opium from British warehouses in Guangzhou outraged British traders and helped trigger the Opium War (1839–1842).

Li Peng (1928–2019): A Soviet-trained engineer who became premier in 1988. Initially regarded as a supporter of Deng Xiaoping's policies of rapid economic change, he emerged as a major hard-liner in 1989.

Liu Binyan (1925–2005): Writer and journalist, famous for his exposé "People or Monsters?" Expelled from the Communist party in 1987 in the campaign against "bourgeois liberalization."

Liu Shaoqi (1898–1969): Soviet-educated Communist organizer and theorist, author of *How to Be a Good Communist*. Publicly recognized in the early 1960s as Mao's successor to party leadership, Liu was purged and imprisoned during the Cultural Revolution. Died from the withdrawal of medical care in 1969.

Li Zicheng (1606–1645): Post-station attendant and army deserter who in 1644, with his own rebel forces, overthrew the Ming dynasty. From his base in Shaanxi province, Li established his rule over much of north and central China. He marched unopposed into Beijing in 1644, ending a dynasty already weakened by threats from the Manchus and from other rebel armies.

Long March (1934–1935): Journey of 6,000 miles made by Communist forces escaping the suppression campaign of Chiang Kai-shek. Only 8,000 to 9,000 of the original 80,000 who escaped from the Jiangxi Soviet in 1934 lived to establish a new Communist base at Yan'an.

Lu Xun (1881–1936): An icon of modern Chinese literature. His works targeted, with sardonic wit, the traditional culture and mentality of his fellow Chinese. Among his most famous works are "True Story of Ah Q" and "My Old Home."

Macao: Port city in southern China, 50 miles southwest of Hong Kong, under Portuguese territorial rule from 1557 to 1999.

Macartney, Lord George (1737–1806): Leader of the first official British diplomatic mission to China. Sent in 1793 by the British East India Company with the cooperation of the court of George III to establish trade and diplomatic relations with the court of Qianlong. Macartney managed to meet with the emperor in the summer imperial palace in Jehol, but his demands were politely refused, and the mission returned a failure.

macroregion: Area consisting of a central "core" of heightened population density and trade, surrounded by a "periphery" of weaker economic development. Used to analyze economic structures of Chinese society.

magistrate: Head administrator of a county, the lowest appointed government official in imperial China. Responsible for the collection of taxes, public works, and the administration of justice in the towns and the countryside.

Manchukuo ("Land of the Manchus"): Name given by the Japanese to the collaborationist regime established in Manchuria in 1932, with the deposed Qing emperor Puyi as "chief executive."

Mao Dun (1896–1981): Leftist writer, author of the novel *Midnight*, depicting the corrupt capitalist society of Shanghai in the 1930s. Served as the minister of culture in the PRC government after 1949.

Mao Zedong (1893–1976): Born in Hunan; became an early member of the CCP. Rose to party leadership by the 1930s, advocating that China's Marxist revolution would be won by the peasants, not by an urban proletariat. Led the CCP on the Long March and then to establish the PRC in 1949. Until his death in 1976 he was the paramount political leader and theorist of Chinese communism.

Marco Polo Bridge Incident: The Japanese taking of the Marco Polo railway bridge near Beijing on the night of July 7, 1937. The fighting that followed this maneuver marked the beginning of open hostilities and can be considered the first battle of World War II.

May Fourth movement: Term used to describe student demonstrations that took place in Tiananmen Square on May 4, 1919, to protest the terms of the Treaty of Versailles. Also refers to the period of iconoclastic intellectual ferment that followed the protests, which included movements to adopt the use of vernacular Chinese in literature and the exploration of different forms of Western cultural and political models.

May Seventh Cadre Schools: Labor camps established during the Cultural Revolution, combining hard agricultural work with the study of Mao's writings, to "re-educate" cadres and intellectuals in proper socialist thought.

May Thirtieth Incident: Incident of 1925 in which the British-led police fired on unarmed student and worker protesters in the International Settlement in Shanghai. Many demonstrators died, setting off a wave of demonstrations and strikes that expressed solidarity with the antiforeign nationalistic cause of the "May Thirtieth Martyrs."

memorial: Form of communiqué written by imperial government officials conveying information to the emperor for his review. Usually mediated through the Grand Secretariat, the common memorial lacked speed and confidentiality. The "palace memorial" system, a form of confidential, direct communication between trusted ministers and the emperor, was established by Kangxi and used extensively by his son, Yongzheng.

mou: Measure of land; equals one-sixth of an acre.

Mukden: Manchu name for the city presently known as Shenyang, in the northeastern province of Liaoning. Made the capital of Nurhaci's empire in 1625.

Mukden Incident: An outbreak of fighting between Chinese and Japanese troops on September 18, 1931, instigated by Japanese officers alleging that Chinese troops attacked them. Following this incident, Japan quickly mobilized its troops to take control of all of Manchuria.

Nanjing Massacre: Period of seven weeks in December 1937–January 1938 during which Japanese troops plundered the Nationalist capital city, killing an estimated 200,000 to 300,000 people and raping tens of thousands of women.

New Army: Modern system of military organization, based on the Western-influenced provincial armies of Zeng Guofan and Li Hongzhang, launched by the Qing government in 1901 to replace the Eight Banners system. Eventually the New Army fragmented into splinter groups under control of their influential regional commanders, such as the Beiyang army of Yuan Shikai.

New Fourth Army: Communist guerrilla forces left behind in central China during the Long March, reorganized during the second united front. The tenuous nature of the alliance was demonstrated in 1941 when 3,000 troops of the New Fourth Army were killed by Guomindang forces in an ambush that became known as the New Fourth Army Incident.

New Life movement: Set of beliefs, part fascist, part Confucian, part Christian, formulated by Chiang Kai-shek during the 1930s to change the moral character of the Chinese and create a productive, "militarized" society.

Nian Rebellion (1851–1868): Led by Zhang Luoxing, a guerrilla war fought mostly by impoverished peasants against the Qing in the area north of the Huai River (including parts of Shandong, Henan, Jiangsu, and Anhui). Defeated by the local Huai Army under the leadership of Li Hongzhang.

Ningxia: Autonomous region in north-central China, 60,000 square miles in area, with a significant population of Chinese Muslims (Hui). Capital: Yinchuan.

Northern Expedition (1926–1928): Military campaign, undertaken by allied Guomindang-Communist forces (the National Revolutionary Army) under the leadership of Chiang Kai-shek, to unify the country under one government. Two years after the launching of the campaign from Guangzhou, China as far north as Mukden was under Chiang's nominal.

Oboi (d. 1669): Manchu general who struggled for and achieved considerable power in the imperial court after the death of Dorgon in 1650. In 1661 became coregent for the seven-year-old emperor Kangxi. During his regency, Oboi reversed the policies of Kangxi's father Shunzhi and vigorously pushed for clear reassertion of Manchu power over the Chinese.

Opium War (1839–1842): Fought between Britain and China; triggered by British outcry against Lin Zexu's confiscation of British opium, and by Chinese anger at the murder of a Chinese by the British. Hostilities were initially confined to Guangzhou and to the east China coast as far north as Tianjin. When British forces threatened the Yangzi delta city of Nanjing, the Qing sued for peace and signed the Treaty of Nanjing in 1842.

Peng Dehuai (1898–1974): Veteran of the Long March and civil war, leader of the PLA "volunteer" forces in the Korean War. Purged in 1959 for criticizing Mao's Great Leap Forward policies.

Peng Zhen (1902–1997): Mayor of Beijing from 1951 to 1966, demoted and criticized during the Cultural Revolution. Returned to Chinese politics as member of the Central Committee. Known as a hard-liner who opposed rapid change in China.

people's commune: Central unit of economic and political organization in the countryside, some consisting of tens of thousands of households, introduced in the Great Leap Forward. Communes were further divided into brigades and production teams that directed labor and divided work points.

People's Liberation Army (PLA): Name given to the armed forces of the PRC. Begun as the Red Army famous for its guerrilla fighting tactics in the 1930s, the PLA evolved into a modern military organization of approximately 3 million soldiers by the late 1980s.

picul: Unit of weight, equaling approximately 130 pounds, used as measure for grain and opium.

Pottinger, Sir Henry (1789–1856): Appointed in 1841 as superintendent of trade and plenipotentiary of Chinese affairs for the British government, replacing the dismissed Charles Elliot. Presided over the signing of the Treaty of Nanjing.

Puyi (1906–1967): The last emperor of the Qing dynasty. Ascended the throne in 1908 at the age of two and abdicated four years later. Installed by the Japanese as the figurehead of the Manchukuo regime from 1932 to 1945. After 1945 he underwent over ten years of "rehabilitation" in a CCP prison and ended his life quietly in Beijing.

Qianlong (1711–1799): Reign name of Hongli, the fourth son of Emperor Yongzheng, who assumed the throne in 1736. His sixty-three-year reign saw a large growth in the Chinese population, the military conquest and occupation of Xinjiang, and the compilation of the *Four Treasuries*.

Qinghai ("Green Sea"): Province in west-central China, 278,000 square miles in area. Capital: Xining.

Qiu Jin (1875–1907): Anti-Manchu feminist revolutionary. Fled an arranged marriage and went to Japan to study. Returned to native Zhejiang province and established a school for girls. After attempting an uprising against the Qing, she was captured and executed.

queue: Manchu men's hairstyle that consisted of a high shaved forehead and a long braid down the back; originally developed to keep hair out of the face in battle. By Dorgon's decree issued in 1645, all Chinese men had to adopt the hairstyle or face execution. Anti-Manchu activists would often cut the queue as an act of defiance against the Qing.

Qu Qiubai (1899–1935): Early Chinese Communist who lived in Moscow in the early 1920s. As head of the CCP from 1927 to 1928, he bore the blame for a year of disastrous worker and peasant uprisings. Too ill to join the Long March, he was captured and executed by Guomindang forces in 1935.

Rectification Campaign (1942): Political struggle launched by Mao Zedong to strengthen the dominant role of his ideology in the Communist party. Major targets of the criticism in Yan'an included rival party leader Wang Ming and the feminist writer Ding Ling.

Red Guards: Groups of university and middle-school students who claimed allegiance to Mao and acted as the executors of the Cultural Revolution directives to attack "feudal" and "reactionary" elements of society. Lack of organization and overzealous revolutionary fervor led to violence among Red Guard factions and between Red Guards and the PLA in the late 1960s.

Rehe (Jehol): Site of the summer palaces of the Qing emperors, 100 miles northeast of Beijing. Now the city of Chengde in Hebei province.

renminbi ("people's currency"): Official unit of exchange in China. Informally known as yuan.

Revolutionary Alliance (Tongmeng hui): Anti-Manchu group founded in 1905 in Tokyo by Sun Yat-sen and Chinese students studying in Japan. It sponsored propaganda, fund-raising, and insurrectionary activities that culminated in 1911 with the Wuhan uprising and led to the fall of the Qing dynasty.

revolutionary committees: Small groups created during the Cultural Revolution to lead local urban governments, rural communes, universities, and other institutions. Each group consisted of representatives from "the masses," the PLA, and select cadres.

rites controversy: Conflict between the Catholic church and Emperor Kangxi over the nature of Chinese rites of ancestor worship and homage to Confucius. Kangxi insisted that such rites were civil, not religious, and that missionaries should allow Chinese Christian converts to practice them. The Vatican disagreed and prohibited missionaries from following Kangxi's order. The controversy resulted in the expulsion of many Catholic missionaries from China.

Sacred Edict: Emperor Kangxi's list of Confucian maxims on morality and social relations compiled in 1670 and promulgated throughout the empire.

Shaanxi: Province in north-central China, 73,000 square miles in area. Capital: Xi'an.

Shandong ("Mountain East"): Province in eastern China, 58,000 square miles in area. Capital: Jinan.

Shanghai communiqué: Document issued on February 28, 1972, at the end of President Nixon's visit to China, stating the positions of the PRC and the United States on questions such as the status of Taiwan and calling for working toward the normalization of Sino-American relations.

Shanxi ("Mountain West"): Province in north-central China, 73,500 square miles in area. Capital: Taiyuan.

Shunzhi (1638–1661): Reign name of the first emperor of the Qing dynasty. Placed upon the throne at the age of six under the regency of his uncle Dorgon. Fond of Chinese literature and culture, Shunzhi adopted a benevolent policy toward his Chinese subjects after Dorgon's death.

Sichuan ("Four Rivers"): Province in southwestern China, 220,000-square-mile area including fertile river valleys farmed by Han Chinese and towering foothills of the Himalayas inhabited by ethnic minorities. Capital: Chengdu.

single whip reforms: Attempt made by the Ming government in the mid-sixteenth century to rationalize the collection of tax revenues, whereby all levies previously collected in kind were merged into one tax, payable in silver.

six ministries: The major units of central government in Beijing. Modeled on a system established in the Tang dynasty, they included the ministries of Civil Office, Revenue, Rituals, War, Public Works, and Punishments.

Socialist Education Campaign: 1963 movement launched by the CCP to revive socialist values, with emphasis on class struggle and collective economic activity. Urban cadres were sent to work in the countryside.

Song Jiaoren (1882–1913): Early leader of the Guomindang. An ardent critic of Yuan Shikai, Song was assassinated on his way to assuming his leadership role in the first nationally elected parliament.

Soong, T. V. (1894–1972): Harvard-educated brother of the Soong sisters. Helped his brother-in-law Chiang Kai-shek finance the Northern Expedition and later served as minister of finance in the Guomindang government.

Soong Ailing (1889–1973): Eldest of the three Soong sisters, wife of financier/industrialist H. H. Kong.

Soong Meiling [spelled Soong May-ling in English] (1898–2003): Youngest of the Soong sisters, wife of Guomindang leader Chiang Kai-shek. An American-educated Methodist, she played an active role in the Guomindang war effort in the 1930s and 1940s, sponsoring refugee relief efforts and women's organizations as well as acting as spokesperson for China's cause, especially to international audiences.

Soong Qingling [spelled Soong Ching-ling in English] (1893–1981): The second Soong sister, wife of Sun Yat-sen. After his death, she supported the alliance of the Guomindang left with the CCP. Remained in China after 1949 and was named to several honorific positions within the PRC government.

special economic zones (SEZs): Cities designated to accept direct foreign investment to increase Chinese exports and act as a bridge for the adoption of foreign technology.

The first four special economic zones—Shenzhen, Zhuhai, Shantou, and Xiamen—were established in 1979, followed by fourteen other cities plus the island of Hainan in 1986.

Stilwell, Joseph ("Vinegar Joe"): U.S. Army general; after Pearl Harbor was named commander in chief of U.S. forces in the China-Burma-India theater and acted as President Roosevelt's liaison with Chiang Kai-shek. Personal animosity between Chiang and Stilwell was a factor that led to Stilwell's being replaced by General Albert Wedemeyer in 1944.

Sun Yat-sen (1866–1925): Considered the father of the Chinese republican revolution. Educated in medicine in Hong Kong, he became an anti-Manchu activist and through his Revolutionary Alliance helped overthrow the Qing dynasty. As leader of the Guomindang, Sun struggled against militarist factions to unite China throughout the 1910s and early 1920s. Accepted the help of the Soviet Union and entered into a united-front alliance with the CCP in 1923. Died in 1925, passing leadership of the Guomindang to Chiang Kai-shek.

Suppression of Counterrevolutionaries campaign: Mass movement launched by the Communist party in 1951, aimed at rooting out Guomindang sympathizers, secret-society members, and religious-sect adherents. Thousands were arrested and executed during the year-long mobilization.

tael: One ounce of silver; unit of exchange and tax payment in imperial China.

Taiping Uprising (1850–1864): Led by Hong Xiuquan; a military and social movement that sought to overthrow the Qing and establish a "Heavenly Kingdom of Great Peace" (Taiping Tianguo). With a combination of quasi-Christian beliefs and communal vision, the Taiping armies spread northeast through the middle Yangzi valley from their base in Guangxi province, capturing Nanjing in 1853, where they made their capital for eleven years. They were finally defeated in Qing counterattacks spearheaded by the Xiang provincial army led by Zeng Guofan. An estimated 20 to 30 million people died in the thirteen years of the civil war.

Tang Xianzu (1550–1617): Playwright, author of the romantic late Ming masterpiece *The Peony Pavilion*.

Three Anti campaign: Mass movement launched in 1951, aimed at eliminating the three vices of "corruption, waste, and obstructionist bureaucracy" among CCP members, government administrators, and factory managers. Held in conjunction with the Five Anti campaign.

Three Feudatories: Refers to (1) the area of south and southeast China, stretching from Sichuan to the eastern coast, left by the Qing government to the control of the three generals (Shang Zhixin, Geng Jingzhong, and Wu Sangui) who had helped subdue the region during the Manchu conquest, and to (2) the generals themselves. Wu rebelled against the Qing, announcing the establishment of his own dynasty in 1673. The ensuing civil war ended with Manchu victory in 1681.

Three Principles of the People: "Nationalism, democracy, and socialism," formulated by Sun Yat-sen as the basis of Guomindang ideology.

Tiananmen Incident: Mass demonstrations that occurred on April 5, 1976, in Tiananmen Square expressing grief over the death of Zhou Enlai. Held on the Qingming holiday of paying respects to deceased ancestors. Interpreted as a criticism of Mao and the Cultural Revolution.

Tianjin massacre (1870): Incident sparked by conflict between Catholics and Chinese in Tianjin in which angry crowds killed the French consul Fontanier along with fifteen other French men and women.

Tibet (Xizang in Mandarin): Taken over by the Chinese in 1950 and named an "autonomous region," 1,200,000 square miles in area. Capital: Lhasa.

ti-yong: Formulation combining *ti* (essence) and *yong* (practical use), used to describe the method of self-strengthening envisioned by Confucian reformers of the late nineteenth century: Chinese learning for the underlying "essence" of society and Western learning for "practical application" in economic development. A similar concept informed China's opening to the West after 1978.

Tongzhi (1856–1875): Reign name of the eighth Qing emperor of the Qing dynasty, who ascended to the throne in 1862 at the age of six. His mother, Cixi, ruled for him as regent until he reached his seventeenth birthday, and continued to exercise power over his decisions until his death at the age of nineteen.

Tongzhi Restoration: Period from the late 1860s to the late 1870s named after the Tongzhi reign, during which the Qing attempted to revitalize the government and the nation through a combination of Confucian morality and Western technology.

Treaty of Nanjing (1842): Treaty settlement signed by the British and the Qing governments to end the Opium War. Its twelve articles included the opening of five treaty ports to unrestricted British trade and residence, the cession of Hong Kong, the payment of a 21 million tael indemnity, and the abolition of the Cohong monopoly. It was supplemented in the following year by the Treaty of the Bogue, which contained the most-favored-nation clause, automatically giving to Britain any privilege granted by the Qing to another nation in a treaty agreement.

Treaty of Nerchinsk (1689): Treaty negotiated between the Qing court of Kangxi and Russia, setting the north-south border between the two countries at the Gorbitsa and Argun rivers.

Treaty of Shimonoseki (1895): Ending the Sino-Japanese War (1894–1895), this treaty for the Qing dynasty ceded to Taiwan and the Pescadores to Japan, opened four additional treaty ports, and promised to pay 200 million taels in war indemnities. Under its terms Korea effectively became a Japanese protectorate.

Treaty of Tianjin (1858): Agreement between Britain and the Qing court after the British, angered by the Qing refusal to renegotiate the Treaty of Nanjing, sent forces to threaten the port city of Tianjin. The treaty forced the Qing to accept the establishment of a British ambassador in Beijing, the unrestricted preaching of Christianity, and the opening of ten new treaty ports both on the coast and inland.

Triads: Secret society, originating in Taiwan and Fujian during the late eighteenth century, also known as the Heaven and Earth Society. Activities combined organized crime and banditry with anti-Manchu sentiments. Its ties with local bureaucracy and militia made it an important force in Chinese society.

Tung Chee-hua (b. 1937): Known as C. H. Tung. Hong Kong financier who studied in England and United States. Conservative politically, effective entrepreneur, chosen by Beijing to be the first chief executive of the new Hong Kong administrative region in 1997.

Twenty-One Demands: Issued in January 1915, in which Japan demanded economic rights in Manchuria, the prerogative to station police and economic advisers in Manchuria, and major economic concessions in China proper. Demands accepted by the government of Yuan Shikai despite popular protests.

Umbrella Movement: A widespread protest movement in the summer of 2014 in Hong Kong, demanding universal suffrage and a free election for the position of chief executive. When protestors raised a sea of umbrellas to block the pepper spray used by police, the image became the symbol of popular discontent and gave the movement its name. An estimated 20 percent of the population in Hong Kong participated.

united front: A tenuous policy of cooperation between the CCP and the Guomindang, effected twice for the purpose of achieving national goals. The first united front (1923–1927) aimed at reclaiming China from militarist forces; the second united front (1937–1945) sought to resist Japan in World War II.

Unofficial History of the Scholars *(Rulin waishi)*: Published in 1768, one of the major literary works of the Qing dynasty. The novel describes the plight of the degree-holding elite, many unemployed, in the eighteenth century.

Wang Guangmei (1921–2006): Veteran Communist revolutionary, wife of Liu Shaoqi. In 1964 Wang led an investigation of rural cadre corruption as part of the Socialist Education Campaign. Persecuted along with her husband during the Cultural Revolution, which she managed to survive, although Liu did not.

Wang Hongwen (1935–1992): Former cadre from a textile mill in Shanghai who rose to become a close associate of Shanghai party secretary Zhang Chunqiao during the Cultural Revolution. Tried and convicted in 1980 as one of the Gang of Four.

Wang Jingwei (1883–1944): Early associate of Sun Yat-sen who helped found the Revolutionary Alliance in Japan in 1905. Held several top positions in the Guomindang during the first Communist-Guomindang alliance and in Chiang Kai-shek's Nanjing government. In 1940 Wang agreed to be the titular head of a collaborationist regime in Nanjing sponsored by Japan.

Wang Yangming (1472–1529): Early Ming philosopher-official who held that the cultivation of the intuitive knowledge inherent in everyone leads to the understanding of Confucian truths. Accused by later scholars of fostering eccentric individualism and initiating the breakdown of moral standards that contributed to the fall of the Ming.

Wanli: Reign name of Zhu Yijun (1563–1620), the thirteenth emperor of the Ming dynasty. The beginning of his forty-eight-year rule saw the height of Ming glory, but by the time of his death, internal disorder and court intrigue had set the stage for the demise of the dynasty.

Wei Jingsheng (b. 1950): Worker and former PLA member active in the Democracy Wall movement of 1978–1979. His writings on the "fifth modernization" and on party corruption led twice to arrest and imprisonment. Released in 1997 and has lived in exile in the United States since.

Wen Jiabao (b. 1942): A protégé of Zhao Ziyang, unexpectedly promoted to the Politburo Standing Committee of the CCP in 2002. Served as the premier of the PRC from 2003 to 2013.

Whampoa: Military academy near Guangzhou, established by Sun Yat-sen in 1924 to train officers for the Guomindang. Many of its graduates were personally loyal to the academy's first leader, Chiang Kai-shek, and immeasurably strengthened his political power base.

White Lotus rebellion: Sporadic uprisings in north-central China in the late eighteenth–early nineteenth centuries by followers of a millenarian folk-Buddhism cult that evoked the powers of the "Eternal Venerable Mother" to overthrow Qing rule and establish a new order on earth.

Wu Han (1909–1969): Writer and historian, deputy mayor of Beijing under Peng Zhen in the early 1960s when he wrote *The Dismissal of Hai Rui from Office*, an allegorical criticism of Mao's purge of Peng Dehuai. The attack against the play by Yao Wenyuan was one of the opening acts of the Cultural Revolution.

Wuhan Uprising (October 1911): Triggered when explosives kept by Revolutionary Alliance members accidentally went off in the city of Hankou, uncovering their activities and forcing them to launch their uprising. New Army troops joined the mutiny against the Qing, beginning the revolution that led to the fall of the dynasty in 1912.

Wu Peifu (1874–1939): Most powerful militarist in the east-central area of Hubei and Hunan in the 1920s. Ordered the violent suppression of the Beijing-Hankou railway strike in 1923. His control of central China ended when Chiang Kai-shek's National Revolutionary Army took the city of Wuhan in 1926 as part of the Northern Expedition.

Xi Jinping (b. 1953): Succeeding Hu Jintao, Xi Jinping has served as secretary-general of the CCP and president of the PRC since 2012.

xian: County, unit of government administration below the level of province.

Xianfeng (1831–1861): Reign name of the seventh Qing emperor, the fourth son of the emperor Daoguang. Ruled during a period of continuing Sino-British conflict over treaty concessions. Forced in 1860 by invading British troops to flee to Rehe, where he died the following year, leaving power over the throne to his consort, the empress Cixi.

xiang: Township, unit of local government below the *xian* (county) level.

Xi'an Incident (December 1936): The kidnapping of Chiang Kai-shek by Zhang Xueliang in Xi'an. Attempting to force Chiang to agree to a united Chinese effort against the Japanese, Zhang held Chiang until negotiations between the Guomindang and the CCP resulted in Chiang's release.

Xinjiang ("New Territories"): Autonomous region in northwestern China, 617,000 square miles in area, with a majority population of Uyghur ethnic minority. Capital: Urumqi.

yamen: The residence and office of Chinese provincial or county officials.

Yan'an: Mountain-region town in Shaanxi province; CCP headquarters from the end of the Long March (1936) to its seizure by Guomindang forces in 1947.

Yan Fu (1854–1921): Went to England in 1877 to study naval science; later translated influential works by Charles Darwin, Thomas Huxley, Herbert Spencer, and Adam Smith. Became the first president of the modernized Beijing University in 1912.

Yang Xiuqing (1822–1856): Orphaned illiterate charcoal maker who joined the Taiping and became chief military adviser to its leader, Hong Xiuquan. Later attempted to usurp power from Hong and was killed in a coup.

Yangzi (Chang Jiang, "Long River"): One of the major waterways of the world and the longest (3,430 miles) in Asia, flowing from Qinghai to the East China Sea at Shanghai. Often considered the dividing line between north and south China, the Yangzi cuts through treacherous gorges in its upper reaches, while its fertile eastern delta fosters one of the most prosperous and populous regions of China.

Yan Xishan (1883–1960): Tenacious militarist who controlled Shanxi province from 1912 to 1949. Cooperated with Chiang Kai-shek in opposing Communist activities, even employing Japanese soldiers against CCP forces as late as 1949.

Yao Wenyuan (1931–2005): Colleague of Jiang Qing, author of an article attacking Wu Han's *The Dismissal of Hai Rui from Office*, considered the "first shot" of the Cultural Revolution. Tried and convicted in 1980 as a member of the Gang of Four.

Yellow River (Huang He): The second longest waterway in China, flowing 2,900 miles from Qinghai north through Inner Mongolia and then bending south and east to the Gulf of Bohai at Shandong province. Heavy silting caused constant floods.

Yen, James (1890–1990): Leader of mass-education movements in China and among overseas Chinese. Graduated from Yale in 1918; went to France, where he established a newspaper for Chinese workers. Continued his work through a YMCA-sponsored literacy and rural reconstruction program in Ding County, Hebei.

Yongzheng (1678–1735): Reign name of the third Qing emperor (r. 1723–1735), the fourth son of Emperor Kangxi. Deeply committed to direct involvement in government affairs, Yongzheng launched a vigorous reform of the Qing tax structure. To manage his military campaigns in the northwest, he bypassed the regular bureaucracy and formed a group of his most trusted advisers, which became known as the Grand Council under his son, the emperor Qianlong.

yuan: (1) "Institution" in Mandarin; the five main ministries of the Nationalist government: Executive, Legislative, Control, Judicial, Examination. (2) A monetary unit; also known as Chinese dollars.

Yuan Shikai (1859–1916): Leader of the powerful Beiyang (North China) army, initially loyal to the empress dowager Cixi, later instrumental in negotiating the Qing abdication in 1912. Because of Yuan's military strength, Sun Yat-sen yielded to him the presidency of the new republic. Yuan abused the office, purging the Parliament and proclaiming himself emperor in 1915. He died six months later, in 1916.

Yung Wing (Rong Hong, 1828–1912): First Chinese to graduate from an American university (Yale, 1854). Served Qing self-strengthening efforts such as assisting Zeng Guofan in buying machine equipment and arms from the United States.

Yunnan ("South of the Clouds"): Province in southwestern China, 168,000 square miles in area. Capital: Kunming.

Zeng Guofan (1811–1872): Confucian statesman/general/scholar; leader of the Hunan provincial army (Xiang) that defeated the Taiping forces in Nanjing. Played an important role in Qing self-strengthening efforts, advocating the use of modern military technology and enlisting a group of talented men around him to serve the Qing cause. Adhered to strict Confucian standards of discipline, diligence, and loyalty to the emperor.

Zhang Chunqiao (1917–2005): Head of the Shanghai CCP and close ally of Jiang Qing in the Cultural Revolution. Tried and convicted in 1980 as a member of the Gang of Four.

Zhang Xianzhong (1605–1647): Shaanxi native and army deserter; leader of an anti-Ming rebel army that controlled parts of central and southwestern China. Established a self-proclaimed kingdom based in Chengdu in 1644. Three years later he and his kingdom were eliminated by Manchu armies.

Zhang Xueliang (1901–2001): Son of Zhang Zuolin, known as the Young Marshal. In 1928, after his father's assassination, he inherited his father's Manchurian forces.

Pledged allegiance to Chiang Kai-shek's Nanjing government in 1928. Kidnapped Chiang in 1936 to force a united Chinese front against the Japanese.

Zhang Xun (1854–1923): Chinese general who remained loyal to the Qing even after the fall of the dynasty in 1912. Led coup in 1917 to restore the boy-emperor Puyi to the throne. Restoration attempt failed when the troops of other generals attacked Beijing, driving Zhang into political retirement.

Zhang Zhidong (1837–1909): General/official in the Qing government who was appointed to the governorship of several provinces, including Shaanxi, Guangdong/Guangxi, and Hubei/Hunan. Active in late Qing self-strengthening *ti-yong* projects with textile factories, arsenals, and railroads.

Zhang Zuolin (1875–1928): Militarist who came to prominence during the presidency of Yuan Shikai and later went on to control Manchuria, eastern Mongolia, and finally Beijing with his armies. Staunchly anti-Communist, he ordered the execution of Li Dazhao in 1927. Defeated by Chiang Kai-shek's National Revolutionary Army in 1928. Killed by a bomb planted by Japanese army officers.

Zhao Ziyang (1919–2005): Protégé of Deng Xiaoping who rose from party secretary of Guangdong in the 1960s to premier and CCP secretary-general in the mid-1980s. Considered an advocate of economic change and expanded contacts with the West. Removed from his party posts in 1989 for supporting student demonstrations that followed the death of Hu Yaobang. Held under house arrest until his death.

Zhejiang: Province in eastern China, 38,600 square miles in area. Capital: Hangzhou.

Zhou Enlai (1898–1976): One of the most powerful and respected leaders of the CCP from the days of the Long March to his death. Served as premier from 1954 and was influential in foreign policy for three decades.

Zhu De (1886–1976): Mao Zedong's chief military adviser from the days of the Jiangxi Soviet. Zhu was commander in chief of the PLA and long-time member of the Standing Committee of the Communist party Politburo.

Zhu Rongji (b. 1928): Electrical engineer, denounced in 1957 antirightist campaign, rehabilitated 1978. Rose rapidly in the CCP bureaucracy. Mayor of Shanghai, 1987; named to Politburo Standing Committee, 1992; deputy prime minister, head of economic and trade office, director of Bank of China, 1993. Skillful and forceful economic planner, succeeded Li Peng as premier in 1998.

Zongli Yamen ("Office for the Management of the Business of All Foreign Countries"): Established by the Qing in 1861 to deal with the crises presented by Western foreign powers. Under the leadership of Prince Gong and Wenxiang, the Zongli Yamen was involved in treaty negotiations and in a range of self-strengthening projects.

Zou Rong (1885–1905): Anti-Manchu revolutionary educated in Japan; author of *The Revolutionary Army* (1905), which called for the overthrow of the Qing and the establishment of democracy. Died in prison at the age of nineteen.

Zuo Zongtang (1812–1885): Leader of the Qing armies that suppressed the Muslim revolts in the northwest (1862–1873). Zuo, who had also led local militia campaigns against the Taiping, was appointed to important government and military posts by the Qing despite never receiving the *jinshi* degree.

Image and Text Credits

CHAPTER 6

Page 105: Private Collection/Bridgeman Images; p. 115: © DeA Picture Library/Art Resource, NY.

CHAPTER 7

Page 122: © Bonhams, London, UK/Bridgeman Images; p. 124: Pictures from History/David Henley/Bridgeman Images.

CHAPTER 8

Page 142: Sovfoto/UIG/Bridgeman Images; p. 147: CPA Media Pte Ltd/Alamy Stock Photo; p. 150: Digital image courtesy of Getty Museum's Open Content Program; p. 152: © BnF, Dist. RMN-Grand Palais/Art Resource, NY.

CHAPTER 9

Page 162: The History Collection/Alamy Stock Photo; p. 174: Courtesy of the General Commission on Archives and History of The United Methodist Church, Madison, New Jersey; p. 177: Science History Images/Alamy Stock Photo.

CHAPTER 10

Page 182: Library of Congress; p. 190 both: CPA Media Pte Ltd/Alamy Stock Photo; p. 192: Granger; p. 198: History and Art Collection/Alamy Stock Photo.

CHAPTER 11

Page 215: Sueddeutsche Zeitung Photo/Alamy Stock Photo; p. 221: Courtesy of the General Commission on Archives and History of The United Methodist Church, Madison, New Jersey.

CHAPTER 12

Page 228: akg-images/ullstein bild; p. 229: Courtesy of the General Commission on Archives and History of The United Methodist Church, Madison, New Jersey; p. 240: Agence Roger Viollet/Granger.

CHAPTER 13

Page 246: Collection J. A. Fox/Magnum Photos; p. 252: akg-images/Pictures from History; p. 256: Library of Congress.

CHAPTER 14

Page 271: The Picture Art Collection/Alamy Stock Photo; p. 273: Photo by Hulton Archive/Getty Images; p. 275: Sueddeutsche Zeitung Photo/Alamy Stock Photo.

CHAPTER 15

Page 293: © SZ Photo/Bridgeman Images; p. 309: CPA Media Pte Ltd/Alamy Stock Photo.

CHAPTER 16

Page 336: UtCon Collection/Alamy Stock Photo.

CHAPTER 17

Page 351: Wu Yinxian/Magnum Photos; p. 352: Wu Yinxian/Magnum Photos; p. 358: Wu Yinxian/Magnum Photos.

CHAPTER 18

Page 372: ullstein bild/Granger; p. 382: © Henri Cartier-Bresson Foundation/Magnum Photos; p. 393: © New China Pictures/Magnum Photos.

CHAPTER 19

Page 410: Xinhua/eyevine/Redux.

CHAPTER 20

Page 426: Bettmann/Getty Images; p. 438: Historic Collection/Alamy Stock Photo.

CHAPTER 21

Page 445: Keystone-France/Gamma-Keystone via Getty Images; p. 446: Pictures from History/Bridgeman Images.

CHAPTER 22

Page 469: © The Chambers Gallery, London/Bridgeman Images; p. 470: Everett Collection Historical/Alamy Stock Photo.

CHAPTER 23

Page 495: Top Photo Corporation/Alamy Stock Photo.

CHAPTER 24

Page 506: Associated Press; p. 521: New China Pictures/Magnum Photos; p. 523: Associated Press.

CHAPTER 26

Page 546: Alain Le Garsmeur China Archive/Alamy Stock Photo; p. 558: © Owen Franken/Getty Images; p. 566: Associated Press; p. 567: Associated Press; p. 568: Torbjorn Andersson/Kontinent.

CHAPTER 27

Page 579: China Photos/Getty Images; p. 584: Associated Press; p. 590: Forrest Anderson/ Getty Images.

CHAPTER 28

Page 597: AP Photo/Greg Baker; p. 599: Olivier Morin/AFP/Getty Images; p. 600: © Imago/Bridgeman Images.

EPILOGUE

Page 612: Yong He; p. 615: Yong He.

TEXT PERMISSIONS

Ling Bing: Excerpts from "For You." *Beijing Street Voices: The Poetry and Politics of China's Democracy Movement*, edited by David S. G. Goodman, Marion Boyers, 1981, p. 122. Reused with permission from David S. G. Goodman.

Bei Dao: "Let's Go" by Bei Dao, translated by Bonnie S. McDougall, from *The August Sleepwalker*, copyright © 1988 by Bei Dao. Translation and introduction copyright © 1988, 1990 by Bonnie S. McDougall. Reprinted by permission of New Directions Publishing Corp. and Carcanet Press Ltd.

Kai-Yu Hsu: "Headline Music" from *Twentieth Century Chinese Poetry* translated by Kai-Yu Hsu, translation copyright © 1963 by Kai-Yu Hsu. Used by permission of Doubleday, an imprint of the Knopf Doubleday Publishing Group, a division of Penguin Random House LLC. All rights reserved.

Richard Wilhelm: Used with permission of Princeton University Press, from *The I Ching or Book of Changes*, Richard Wilhelm (trans.), 1967; permission conveyed through Copyright Clearance Center, Inc.

A Note on the Calligraphy

Jacket and title page
   The character *zheng*, "struggle," written in *cao shu* or "cursive" style.

ABOUT THE CALLIGRAPHER

Liang Minwei was born in Canton, People's Republic of China, in 1962, and studied painting at the Yuexiu Art Institute. He was head of design at a major Canton retail firm for several years before continuing his study of Chinese painting under Ke Hejun at the Canton Academy of Fine Arts. Since his arrival in the United States in 1987, Liang Minwei's calligraphy and abstract landscapes have been exhibited widely in and around the New York metropolitan area.

Index

Note: Maps, notes, and tables are indicated by italic *m*, *n*, and *t*, respectively, following the page locator.